OXFORD EARLY CHRISTIAN TEXTS

General Editors
Gillian Clark   Andrew Louth

OXFORD EARLY CHRISTIAN TEXTS

The series provides reliable working texts of important early Christian writers in both Greek and Latin. Each volume contains an introduction, text, and select critical apparatus, with English translations *en face*, and brief explanatory references.

Titles in the series include:

The Case Against Diodore and Theodore
John Behr

Jerome's Epitaph on Paula
A Commentary on the *Epitaphium Sanctae Paulae*
Edited by Andrew Cain

The Life of Saint Helia
Critical Edition, Translation, Introduction, and Commentary
Edited by Virginia Burrus and Marco Conti

Nonnus of Panopolis
Paraphrasis of the Gospel of John XI
Konstantinos Spanoudakis

Damasus of Rome
The Epigraphic Poetry
Edited by Dennis Trout

Greek and Latin Narratives about the Ancient Martyrs
Edited by Éric Rebillard

Faith in Formulae
A Collection of Early Christian Creeds and Creed-related Texts
Edited by Wolfram Kinzig

Leontius of Byzantium
Complete Works
Edited by Brian E. Daley, SJ

Adrian's *Introduction to the Divine Scriptures*

An Antiochene Handbook for Scriptural Interpretation

EDITED WITH A STUDY, TRANSLATION, AND COMMENTARY
ON THE TEXT BY

PETER W. MARTENS

OXFORD
UNIVERSITY PRESS

OXFORD
UNIVERSITY PRESS

Great Clarendon Street, Oxford, OX2 6DP,
United Kingdom

Oxford University Press is a department of the University of Oxford.
It furthers the University's objective of excellence in research, scholarship,
and education by publishing worldwide. Oxford is a registered trade mark of
Oxford University Press in the UK and in certain other countries

First Edition published in 2017
Impression: 2

Published in the United States of America by Oxford University Press
198 Madison Avenue, New York, NY 10016, United States of America

British Library Cataloguing in Publication Data
Data available

Library of Congress Control Number: 2016942578

ISBN 978-0-19-870362-4

Printed and bound by
CPI Group (UK) Ltd, Croydon, CRO 4YY

for Rachel and Peter Nathaniel

Acknowledgements

It is my privilege to thank the many scholars who lent me their expertise so generously on this book project. I am grateful for the various forms of assistance that I received from Robert Allison, Theodora Antonopoulou, Davide Baldi, John Behr, Matthieu Cassin, Nicholas Constas, Brian Daley, Anne Debary, Mark DelCogliano, Eleonor Dickey, Gilles Dorival, Valentina D'Urso, Albertus Horsting, Anne Leader, Santo Lucà, Karin Metzler, Clarence Miller, Geoffrey Miller, William O'Brien, Ryan Platte, Franz Xaver Risch, Julia Schneider, Panagiotis Sotiroudis, Kenneth Steinhauser, monk Theologos (the librarian at Iviron), Warren Treadgold, Christopher Wright, and Philip Zymaris. I am deeply grateful for all your assistance!

The Franklin Research Grant from the American Philosophical Society allowed me to inspect a number of manuscripts in person at the Biblioteca Medicea Laurenziana (Florence), Bibliotheca Apostolica (Vatican City), and Bibliothèque nationale de France (Paris). I am especially thankful for the hospitality and resources of the Institut de recherche et d'histoire des textes in Paris where I was able to spend a week examining their rich microfiche collection. It is a privilege to trace my own editorial work back, as many before me have, to the visionary founder of the Institute's Greek section, Marcel Richard.

Saint Louis University offered generous funding to help me complete this project, including a Mellon grant to study Greek paleography at Lincoln College (Oxford University). This project began as a one-year fellowship from the National Endowment for the Humanities while I was at Yale University. I am deeply appreciative of the generous financial assistance that I have received while researching and writing this book.

I am especially indebted to my graduate assistant, Andrew Chronister. He has worked tirelessly and with an exacting eye on this project, and on more than one occasion helped me unravel a stubborn knot. He ensured the timely completion of this book.

Contents

General Abbreviations xi
Abbreviations: Authors and Works xiii

Introduction 1

PART I: STUDY

1. Authorship 7
   A. Name 8
   B. First Biographical Remarks 9
   C. An Antiochene 15
2. Title and Topic 20
   A. Title 20
   B. Topic 22
      1. On style and its three components 23
      2. Peculiarities of Scripture 26
      3. The "Hebrew" literary style 28
      4. The *Introduction* and parallels in Greco-Roman
         literary criticism 31
3. Structure and Scholarly Conventions 34
   A. Structure 34
   B. Scholarly Conventions 36
      1. Divisions 36
      2. Catalogues 38
      3. Space-saving conventions 39
      4. Problems and solutions 40
4. Exegetical Guidelines and Classroom Setting 43
   A. Preparation for Textual Analysis 43
      1. The purpose and subject matter of Scripture 43
      2. Literary peculiarities, figures, and tropes 45
   B. Exegetical Aims 48
      1. Precision 48
      2. Fittingness 49
      3. Clarity 50
   C. Classroom Setting 52

PART II: EDITION AND ANNOTATED TRANSLATION

1. Overview: Recensions, Manuscripts, and Editions of
   Adrian's *Introduction to the Divine Scriptures* 59

2. Editions and Translations—Past and Present   61
  A. David Hoeschel's *Editio Princeps* and Its Reprints   61
  B. Friedrich Goessling's Edition   63
    1. Representation of variant readings   64
    2. Stemma for Recension 1   64
    3. Karl Friedrich Schlüren's emendations   65
    4. Lollin's Latin translation of two Greek mss   66
    5. Fragments from the exegetical catenae   68
    6. Additional problems   69
  C. Modern Translations   70
  D. The Present Edition and Translation   71
    1. Recension 1   71
    2. Recension 2   71
    3. Catena fragments   72
    4. Translation   73

3. The Manuscripts   75
  A. Recension 1   75
  B. Recension 2   86
  C. Exegetical Catenae   88

4. *Recensio Codicum*   89
  A. Stemma: Recension 1   89
  B. Stemma: Recension 2   96

5. The Relationship between the Recensions   100
  A. Overview of the Recensions   100
  B. The Relationship between the Recensions   101
    1. Shared material between R1 and R2   102
    2. Distinctive material   103
    3. Catenae fragments   104
  C. Reconstructing R_a 105

6. Conventions of the Present Edition and Translation   108
  A. Edition   108
    1. *Textus*   108
    2. *Apparatus fontium*   116
    3. *Apparatus criticus*   117
  B. Translation   120

7. List of Symbols and Abbreviations   121

Text of Recensions and Translation   124

Fragments of Adrian's *Introduction to the Divine Scriptures* in the Exegetical Catenae   286

Bibliography   319
Index of Scripture   339

General Abbreviations

ACO	*Acta conciliorum oecumenicorum*
ACT	Ancient Christian Texts
ACW	Ancient Christian Writers
AnnSE	*Annali di storia dell'esegesi*
ANRW	*Aufstieg und Niedergang der römischen Welt*
BAV	Biblioteca Apostolica Vaticana
BDAG	Bauer, Walter. *A Greek–English Lexicon of the New Testament and Other Early Christian Literature*. 3rd ed. Rev. Frederick W. Danker, W. F. Arndt, and F. W. Gingrich. Chicago: University of Chicago Press, 2001
BDF	Blass, Friedrich and Albert Debrunner. *A Greek Grammar of the New Testament and Other Early Christian Literature*. Trans. R. W. Funk. Chicago: University of Chicago Press, 1961
CCSG	Corpus Christianorum, Series Graeca
CCSL	Corpus Christianorum, Series Latina
CPG	*Clavis Patrum Graecorum*
CSCO	Corpus Scriptorum Christianorum Orientalium
CSEL	Corpus Scriptorum Ecclesiasticorum Latinorum
DBS	*Dictionnaire de la Bible. Supplément*
DHGE	*Dictionnaire d'histoire et de géographie ecclésiastiques*
DNP	*Der Neue Pauly: Enzyklopädie der Antike*
EBR	*Encyclopedia of the Bible and its Reception*
FOTC	Fathers of the Church
GCS	Die griechischen christlichen Schriftsteller der ersten drei Jahrhunderte
GELS	Muraoka, T., ed. *A Greek–English Lexicon of the Septuagint*. Leuven: Peeters, 2009
HTR	*Harvard Theological Review*
HWP	*Historisches Wörterbuch der Philosophie*
HWRh	*Historisches Wörterbuch der Rhetorik*
JTS	*Journal of Theological Studies*
KP	*Der Kleine Pauly*
LCL	Loeb Classical Library
LEC	Library of Early Christianity
LSJ	Liddell, Henry G., and Robert Scott. Ed. Henry S. Jones and Roderick McKenzie. *A Greek–English Lexicon*. Rev. and aug. Oxford: Clarendon Press, 1996
LXX	Septuagint
NT	New Testament
NPNF	Select Library of Nicene and Post-Nicene Fathers
OT	Old Testament
PG	Patrologiae Cursus Completus, Series Graeca
PGL	Lampe, Geoffrey, ed. *A Patristic Greek Lexicon*. Oxford: Clarendon Press, 1961

PL	Patrologiae Cursus Completus, Series Latina
PTS	Patristische Texte und Studien
PW	*Pauly–Wissova (Paulys Realencyclopädie der classischen Altertumswissenschaft)*
RAC	*Reallexikon für Antike und Christentum*
RB	*Revue Biblique*
RSR	*Revue des sciences religieuses*
SBAW	*Sitzungsberichte der philosophisch-philologischen und der historischen Classe der k. b. Akademie der Wissenschaften zu München*
SC	Sources Chrétiennes
Smyth	Smyth, Herbert W. *Greek Grammar*. Rev. Gordon M. Messing. Cambridge, Mass.: Harvard University Press, 1959
ST	Studi e Testi
StPatr	*Studia Patristica*
TEG	Traditio Exegetica Graeca
TLG	*Thesaurus Linguae Graecae: A Digital Library of Greek Literature*
TRE	*Theologische Realenenzyclopädie*
TTH	Translated Texts for Historians
VC	*Vigiliae Christianae*
WGRW	Writings from the Greco-Roman World

Abbreviations: Authors and Works

Adrian.	Adrianus	*cat. Ps.*	*catenae in Pss.*
		cat. Job	*catenae in Job*
		intro.	*introductio in sacras scripturas*
Anast. S.	Anastasius Sinaita	*hex.*	*anagogicarum contemplationum in hexaemeron liber duodecimus*
Anon. Seg.	Anonymus Seguerianus	*ars rhet.*	*ars rhetorica*
Aps.	Apsines	*ars rhet.*	*ars rhetorica*
Arist.	Aristoteles	*ars rhet.*	*ars rhetorica*
Aug.	Augustinus Hipponensis	*loc. in Hept.*	*locutionum in Hept. libri septem*
		ver. rel.	*de vera religione*
		doc. Chr.	*de doctrina Christiana*
		retr.	*retractationum libri II*
Bas.	Basilius Caesariensis	*leg. lib. gent.*	*ad adolescentes de legendis libris gentilium*
Cass.	Cassiodorus Senator	*Ps.*	*expositio in Ps.*
		inst.	*institutiones*
Chrys.	Chrysostomus, Joannes	*Job*	*commentarius in Job*
		exp. in Ps.	*expositiones in Psalmos quosdam*
		de proph. obsc. hom.	*de prophetiarum obscuritate homiliae*
		hom. in Mt.	*homiliae 1–90 in Mt.*
		hom. in Jo.	*homiliae 1–88 in Jo.*
		hom. in 2 Cor.	*homiliae 1–30 in 2 Cor.*
		comm. in Gal.	*commentarium in Gal.*
		hom. 1–10 in 2 Tim.	*homiliae in 2 Tim.*
		laud. Paul.	*de laudibus Pauli*
		Diod.	*laus Diodori*
Cosm. Ind.	Cosmas Indicopleustes	*top.*	*topographia christiana*
Cyr.	Cyrillus Alexandrinus	*Ps.*	*explanatio in Pss.*
		Lc.	*fragmenta commentarii in Lc.*
Demetr.	Demetrius	*eloc.*	*de elocutione*
Diod.	Diodorus Tarsensis	*fr. Gen.*	*fragmenta in Gen.*
		Ps.	*fragmenta in Pss.*
		Rom.	*fragmenta in Rom.*

Didym.	Didymus Alexandrinus	*Ps.*	*expositio in Pss.*
		Zach.	*commentarius in Zach.*
Diony. Halic.	Dionysius	*2 Amm.*	*epistula ad Ammaeum 2*
	Halicarnassensis	*comp.*	*de compositione verborum*
		Lys.	*de Lysia*
		Th.	*de Thucydide*
Diony. Thrax	Dionysius Thrax	*ars gramm.*	*ars grammatica*
Eus.	Eusebius Caesariensis	*Ps.*	*commentarius in Pss.*
Eus. Em.	Eusebius Emesenus	*arb.*	*de arbore fici*
		fr. Gen. [Arm.]	*fragmenta armenia in Gen.*
		fr. Gen. [cat.]	*fragmenta ex catenarum in Gen.*
		fr. Gen. [Proc. G.]	*fragmenta ex Procopii in Gen.*
Eust.	Eustathius Antiochenus	*engast.*	*de engastrimytho contra Origenem*
Gal.	Galenus Medicus	*plac.*	*de placitis Hippocratis et Platonis*
Gennad.	Gennadius I Constantinopolitanus	*fr. Gen.*	*fragmenta in Gen.*
Geo. Monach.	Georgius Monachos	*chron.*	*chronicon*
Heracl.	Heraclitus	*all.*	*allegoriae = quaestiones Homericae*
Hermog.	Hermogenes	*form.*	*de formis*
Hier.	Hieronymus	*epp.*	*epistulae*
		tract. Ps.	*tractatus in Pss.*
Hom.	Homerus	*Od.*	*Odyssea*
Ibas	Ibas Edessenus	*ep.*	*epistula*
Isid. Pel.	Isidorus Pelusiota	*epp.*	*epistularum libri quinque*
Jo. D.	Joannes Damascenus	*f. o.*	*de fidei orthodoxa libri quattuor*
Junil.	Junillus Africanus	*inst.*	*instituta regularia divinae legis*
Nemes.	Nemesius Emesenus	*nat. hom.*	*de natura hominis*
Nest.	Nestorius Constantinopolitanus	*hom.*	*homilia contra* θεοτόκος
Nil.	Nilus Ancyranus	*epp.*	*epistularum libri quattuor*
Olymp.	Olympiodorus Alexandrinus	*fr. Job*	*fragmenta ex commentariis in Job*
Or.	Origenes	*Cels.*	*contra Celsum*
		ep. 2	*epistula ad Gregorium*
Phot.	Photius Constantinopolitanus	*cod.*	*bibliothecae codices*
Polychr.	Polychronius Apameensis	*fr. Job*	*fragmenta in Job*

Ps.-Aristid.	Pseudo-Aristides	*ars rhet.*	*ars rhetorica*
Ps.-Ath.	Pseudo-Athanasius	*fr. Ps.*	*fragmenta in Pss.*
Ps.-Chrys.	Pseudo-Chrysostomus	*synops.*	*synopsis sacrae scripturae*
		hom. in Ps. 50	*homiliae in Ps. 50*
Ps.-Greg.	Pseudo-Gregorius	*trop.*	*de tropis*
	Corinthius		
Ps.-Longin.	Pseudo-Longinus	*sublim.*	*de sublimate*
Ps.-Plu.	Pseudo-Plutarchus	*vit. Hom.*	*vita Homeri*
Quint.	Quintilianus	*inst.*	*institution oratoria*
Ruf.	Rufinus	*Orig. Princ.*	*de principiis libri IV*
Socr.	Socrates Scholasticus	*h.e.*	*historia ecclesiastica*
Soz.	Sozomenus Salaminus	*h.e.*	*historia ecclesiastica*
Thdr. Mops.	Theodorus	*hom. catech.*	*homiliae catecheticae*
	Mopsuestenus		
		fr. Gen.	*fragmenta in Gen.*
		fr. Job	*fragmenta in Job*
		Ps.	*fragmenta commentarii in Pss.*
		fr. Cant.	*fragmenta in Cant.*
		Os.-Mal	*commentarii in xii prophetas*
		Jo. [Syr.]	*fragmenta syriaca in Jo.*
		Rom.-Philm.	*commentarii in Pauli epistulas*
		fr. Heb.	*fragmenta in Heb.*
Thdt.	Theodoretus Cyrrhensis	*qu. in Gen.*	*quaestiones in Gen.*
		qu. in Ex.	*quaestiones in Ex.*
		qu. in Jud.	*quaestiones in Jud.*
		Ps.	*commentarii in Pss.*
		Cant.	*commentarius in Cant.*
		Os.-Mal.	*commentarii in xii prophetas*
		Is.	*commentarius in Is.*
		Ezech.	*commentarius in Ezech.*
		Dan.	*commentarius in Dan.*
		Rom.–Philm.	*interpretationes in Pauli epistulas*
		provid.	*orationes de providential*
		h.e.	*historia ecclesiastica*
Tryph.	Tryphon	*trop.*	*de tropis*
Xen.	Xenophon	*cyn.*	*cynegeticus*

Introduction

...few "introductions" to scripture have been more sensible than this.[1]

Adrian's *Introduction to the Divine Scriptures* is an important, yet oft-overlooked, late antique treatise of literary analysis. It stood in a long tradition of Greek textual scholarship whose origins are customarily dated to the early third century BCE when the Museum, a research institute with a library, was founded in Alexandria. By Adrian's day, perhaps the fifth century CE, grammarians had developed an impressive array of procedures to help them elucidate and criticize ancient writings. They established texts, created glossaries and lexica, drafted grammatical and rhetorical treatises, wrote synopses of famous works, investigated their backgrounds, and devoted considerable energies to composing commentaries on canonical literary works. Early Christian biblical scholarship, Adrian's *Introduction* included, was an expression of this flourishing tradition now applied to a new classic, the Christian Scriptures.

We know very little of Adrian. Scholars customarily date him to the early fifth century and regard him as a representative of the so-called Antiochene approach to scriptural scholarship, since there are striking verbal and thematic affinities between his *Introduction* and the exegetical writings of Diodore of Tarsus (d. ca. 394), two of his pupils, John Chrysostom (ca. 349–407) and Theodore of Mopsuestia (ca. 350–428), the latter's brother, Polychronius of Apamea (d. ca. 430), and Theodoret of Cyrus (ca. 393–ca. 457). Adrian opens the *Introduction*, his sole-surviving work, with an announcement of its overarching theme and structure: "There are three kinds of peculiarities of the Hebrew literary style: one will find that the first of these pertains to its message, the second to its diction, and the third to its syntax" (1). While the reference to the "Hebrew" literary style might suggest our author's familiarity with the original language of the Old Testament, inspection of the treatise quickly confirms otherwise. Adrian's interest rests primarily with the Septuagint, the church's official Greek translation of the Old Testament.

The central topic of the *Introduction* is the Septuagint's recurring stylistic oddities, which Adrian subdivides into three categories: peculiarities of message, diction,

---

[1] Robert M. Grant and David Tracy, *A Short History of the Interpretation of the Bible*, rev. ed. (Philadelphia: Fortress, 1984), 77.

and word arrangement. This tripartite classification system of style informs the general structure of the treatise. In the first section Adrian catalogues the anthropomorphic ways in which God is portrayed in Scripture (the Psalms in particular) and then explains how such expressions ought to be understood. The second section on diction identifies peculiar word usages, offers lexicographical analyses of semantically rich terms, and discusses a handful of tropes. The third section on syntax contains an illustrated list of figures. The treatise concludes with a series of appendices: a catalogue of twenty-two tropes defined and illustrated from Scripture, a twofold classification of Scripture into prophetic and narratival literature, an extended excursus on guidelines for interpreting Scripture, and, finally, another classification of Scripture into prose and poetry.

As noted above, few scholars are aware of Adrian's *Introduction*.[2] The work has never been translated into English, the *TLG* does not contain a digitized version of the Greek text, and the previous critical edition is out of print and held by only a few libraries worldwide. Yet the *Introduction* is an important treatise and merits far closer attention than it has hitherto received. It expands our knowledge of Antiochene biblical scholarship, which is especially significant, since many of the exegetical writings of Diodore and Theodore have been lost due to the condemnations of their authors in late antiquity.[3] The *Introduction* occupies a unique place in Antiochene scholarship: it is the only surviving handbook on scriptural interpretation from the leading fourth and fifth century figures of this tradition. While these scholars produced abundant homilies and commentaries on individual biblical books, they did not produce a concise guide to scriptural interpretation, or at least one that survives.[4] The *Introduction* is particularly attractive, then, since it succinctly codifies many of the guiding principles of Antiochene scriptural exegesis. As I will also argue in my study and demonstrate more fully in the annotations that accompany my

---

[2] A "small, frequently overlooked writing," says Christoph Schäublin in *Untersuchungen zur Methode und Herkunft der Antiochenischen Exegese* (Cologne: Peter Hanstein, 1974), 138 fn. 222. "This exegetical treatise remains untapped" ("Antiquité Chrétienne Grecque et Bible," in *Dictionnaire Encyclopédique de la Bible*, 3rd ed. [Turnhout: Brepols, 2002], 72). Hill never mentions Adrian's *Introduction* in the only other major study of Antiochene biblical scholarship (Robert C. Hill, *Reading the Old Testament in Antioch* [Leiden: Brill, 2005]).

[3] John Behr, *The Case against Diodore and Theodore: Texts and Their Contexts* (Oxford: Oxford University Press, 2011).

[4] Two other programmatic treatises on scriptural interpretation were written by the Antiochenes, but neither is extant. According to the *Suda*, the late tenth-century Byzantine encyclopedia, Diodore of Tarsus wrote a work entitled, *What is the Difference between Theoria and Allegoria?* (s.v. Διόδωρος [Δ 1149]). Theodore of Mopsuestia wrote a treatise, *On Allegory and History* (CPG 3862), with one surviving Latin fragment in Facundus of Hermiane, *Ad Iustinianum* [= *Pro defensione trium capitulorum*] 3.6.13–14. This latter work is likely the same as the five books against the allegorists credited to Theodore in the fourteenth-century catalogue of his writings by the Nestorian bishop, Ebedjesus (Giuseppe Simone Assemani, *Bibliotheca Orientalis Clementino-Vaticana*, vol. 3, part 1, *De Scriptoribus Syris* [Rome: Typis Sacrae Congregationis de Propaganda Fide, 1725], 34). Note as well that this latter text is not to be confused with Theodore's prologue to his *Commentary on Psalm 118* (the Syriac translation gives this prologue the title, *Against the Allegorists*).

translation, Adrian's approach to biblical interpretation resonates most clearly with the approach of Theodore of Mopsuestia. Given Theodore's later sobriquet ("the Interpreter") as well as the lacunose state of his exegetical writings, it is especially beneficial to be able to put this new study, edition, and translation of the *Introduction* into readers' hands.

The *Introduction* also contributes to our larger picture of early Christian biblical interpretation. Scholars with an interest in the emerging traditions of Psalm commentary in the fourth and fifth centuries will find the treatise instructive, since more than half the scriptural references in the work are to the Psalms. Also, those with an interest in the handbooks on Scripture in early Christianity will find the *Introduction* important. It is one of only a few such works that survive from the patristic period. While book four of Origen's *On First Principles*, or treatises like Augustine's *On Christian Teaching* and Junillus Africanus' *Handbook of the Basic Principles of the Divine Law*, have been studied very closely, Adrian's work has suffered from comparative neglect. A fuller appreciation of his *Introduction* will undoubtedly impact how we collectively view these early Christian guides to Scripture.

Arguably the most important advance in our understanding of early Christian biblical interpretation over the last half-century has been the growing recognition that there was little distinctive about the interpretive practices of early Christians. A number of pioneering studies on seminal early Christian biblical scholars have established the ubiquity of late antique exegetical techniques and projects: they surfaced among "pagans" and Christians alike.[5] Nor should this surprise. Christian youths, boys invariably, were drawn to the same teachers as their non-Christian counterparts. It was from these grammarians and rhetoricians that pupils learned how to study the writings of poets and prose authors. Indeed, Christian authors not infrequently exhorted would-be students of Scripture to utilize the same principles of literary scholarship that were being applied to the great works of Greek and Roman antiquity.[6] Adrian's *Introduction* is particularly instructive in this regard. In his closing paragraphs (75–8) he outlines the steps that teachers ought to follow when instructing students in Scripture—the same steps, he contends, that contemporary *grammatici* took with Greek poetry. The *Introduction* opens a window onto how late antique grammarians interacted with texts and pupils in their classrooms. It is important to remember that early Christian scholarship on its Scriptures often remains our best representation of the late antique *grammaticus* at work.

[5] See Louis Mariès, *Études préliminaires a l'édition de Diodore de Tarse sur les Psaumes, la tradition manuscrite* (Paris: Belles Lettres, 1933); Robert Devreesse, *Essai sur Théodore de Mopsueste* (Vatican City: BAV, 1948); Schäublin, *Untersuchungen*; Bernhard Neuschäfer, *Origenes als Philologe*, 2 vols. (Basel: Friedrich Reinhardt, 1987); Frances Young, *Biblical Exegesis and the Formation of Christian Culture* (Cambridge: Cambridge University Press, 1997), 76–96.
[6] For example, see Or., *ep.* 2; Bas., *leg. lib. gent.*; Ruf., *Orig. Princ.* second pref.; Aug. *doc. Chr.* 3.40; Cass., *proem. Ps.* 15.

This book attempts to rescue the *Introduction* from the obscurity to which it has been largely consigned. It has three major sections: a study, a series of edited texts, and annotated translations. The *Introduction* was last edited in 1887 by Friedrich Goessling, who prefaced his text and facing German translation with the first modern examination of this treatise. In the intervening 130 years, only a handful of short articles have been published on this work, and it receives perfunctory mention in the occasional reference work. While Goessling's study is still helpful in some ways, it has been superseded in many others. Today we are far better informed, for instance, about the disciplines of grammar and rhetoric in late antiquity. We are also better equipped, thanks to the *TLG*, to identify parallels between the *Introduction* and other Greek literature. My study will examine a handful of issues, including the authorship, title, topic, and structure of the work, its scholarly conventions, likely roles in classroom instruction, and finally, the exegetical guidelines advocated by Adrian. The biggest challenge of the *Introduction* is that it often reads like a closed text—the prose is terse, the arguments routinely lack amplification, and points are not always clarified with illustrations. The goal of my study is to provide readers with sufficient orientation so that the treatise and its late antique contexts become more accessible.

There are two modern editions of the *Introduction* that precede mine: the *editio princeps* by David Hoeschel in 1602, and the aforementioned edition by Goessling. There are a number of deficiencies with Goessling's edition that I will detail below. The most important problem is that the manuscript tradition, both direct and indirect, testifies to a second recension of the *Introduction* that escaped Goessling's attention. This is a problem since this recension often transmits a more original version of the *Introduction* than the text that Goessling or Hoeschel edited.[7] I present readers with both recensions of the treatise, as well as all the known catenae fragments from the work.

Finally, I provide the first English translation of the *Introduction*. The annotations explain technical exegetical terminology, reconstruct the sense of difficult passages, identify important parallels with other Antiochene exegetical writings, and provide bibliographic aids that take readers to important discussions in the scholarship.

A note on citations: since this book cites so heavily from ancient sources, I have simplified my apparatus by not identifying the translator (where applicable) and edition for every quotation. The reader will find this information in the bibliography. I indicate small modifications of a translation with "mod."

---

[7] There is an "urgent need for a complete examination of the manuscript tradition, a critical edition and a more detailed analysis of this writing" (Natalio Fernández Marcos, *The Septuagint in Context: Introduction to the Greek Versions of the Bible*, trans. Wilfred G. E. Watson [Leiden: Brill, 2000], 340 fn. 13).

PART I

Study

1

Authorship

We know very little of Adrian or the circumstances surrounding the composition of his sole-surviving work, the *Introduction to the Divine Scriptures*. He does not speak explicitly about himself, nor does he refer to contemporary events that might help us identify him or his setting more precisely. Yet the treatise yields some valuable clues about its author. If Adrian was not a *grammaticus*, then he certainly knew how to act like one. The late antique "grammarian" was not simply a teacher of language but also an expert in literature. He would often comment on a text with pupils by instructing them in its figures and tropes, its unfamiliar vocabulary, and in general informing them about its main subject matter and any peripheral topics raised by the author.[1] All these explanatory duties are either performed or discussed in the *Introduction*. Adrian also makes a few passing (and positive) remarks about how Greek epic and lyric poetry were studied outside Christian circles. This was precisely the domain of the *grammaticus*. And in the closing paragraphs of the *Introduction* our author identifies teachers of Scripture as his main readers and invites them to train their students according to the conventions of late antique grammatical commentary. The treatise breathes the air of the *grammaticus* and his classroom.

Anything else that we wish to know about our author must be gathered from other sources: scribal notations in the manuscript tradition, the reports of a handful of ancient and early medieval witnesses, and the biblical commentary that we find in other patristic sources that dovetails with what we encounter in the *Introduction*.

---

[1] For more on the grammarian and his duties, see Stanley F. Bonner, *Education in Ancient Rome: From the Elder Cato to the Younger Pliny* (London: Methuen & Co., 1977), 189–249; Teresa Morgan, *Literate Education in the Hellenistic and Roman Worlds* (Cambridge: Cambridge University Press, 1998), 152–89; Raffaella Cribiore, *Gymnastics of the Mind: Greek Education in Hellenistic and Roman Egypt*, 2nd ed. (Princeton: Princeton University Press, 2005), 185–219, esp. 205–15; Lisa Maurice, *The Teacher in Ancient Rome: The Magister and His World* (Lanham: Lexington Books, 2013), 10–13, 65–76. For education in Antioch, see Peter Wolf, *Vom Schulwesen der Spätantike: Studien zu Libanius* (Baden-Baden: Kunst und Wissenschaft, 1952); Raffaella Cribiore, *The School of Libanius in Late Antique Antioch* (Princeton: Princeton University Press, 2007).

A. NAME

Adrian is often referred to as "Hadrian" in the scholarly literature. Yet in only one derivative catena manuscript (ms) is his name given with the rough breathing mark: ἅδρια (i.e., ἁδριανοῦ) (Milan *C 98 sup.*, f. 37r).[2] Giovanni Mercati claimed to find the rough breathing twice in *Coislin. 10* on ff. 51r and 52r, but my inspection of this codex *in situ* indicates a smooth breathing in both places.[3] Cassiodorus, Photius, and almost all the mss that transmit the *Introduction* identify our author as "Adrian" (ἀδριανοῦ), including the ancestor of all known copies of recension 1 (R1): **L**. Two heavily corrupted descendants of this ms offer different names: in **K₂** we find αὐδριανοῦ—the confusion of the Greek minuscule α with αυ is a common occurrence.[4] In **I** a second hand has changed ἀδριανοῦ to ἀφρικανοῦ by superimposing a φ on the δ, and inserting a κ between ια, presumably attributing the *Introduction* to Julius Sextus Africanus. Since **I** was one of the mss used by Aloysius Lollin for his Latin rendering of the *Introduction*, this explains why we find "Africani seu Adriani" in the title of his translation. One additional variant of Adrian's name occurs in the exegetical catenae. In a few places we find ἀνδρ^α (*Ottob. Gr. 398*, f. 160r and *Sinod. Gr. 194*, f. 125r).

Additionally, Adrian receives two epithets in the ms tradition. There is the curious reference to him as an Antiochene: ἀδριανοῦ ἀντιο^χ (i.e., ἀντιοχείας) (*Coislin. 10*, f. 51r). And in the unedited florilegium designated *Florilegium patristicum tit. XIV distributum* by Marcel Richard, there is an extract attributed to Adrian the monk, though the material does not appear to come from the *Introduction* and it is not clear if it belongs to our Adrian: ἀδριανοῦ μοναχοῦ (e.g., Athens, *Ἐθνικὴ Βιβλιοθήκη τῆς Ἑλλάδος* [EBE], 233, f. 15r).[5] More on both of these epithets below.

Finally, there is the curious reference to Adrian as "Andronicus." In a footnote to the revised edition of Fabricius' *Bibliotheca Graeca* we learn that Alphonsus Ciacconius (1530/40–99) confused Adrian with Andronicus Comnenos, a Byzantine emperor (1183–5). But as is correctly noted there, this identification is erroneous since already Photius in the ninth century mentions Adrian. Fabricius also notes that Francisco Turrianus (ca. 1509–84) wrongly calls Adrian "Andronicus." However, Fabricius was incorrect in claiming that this name was

---

[2] For the position of the ms in the catenae mss on the Psalms, see Gilles Dorival, *Les Chaînes Exégétiques Grecques sur les Psaumes: Contribution à l'Étude d'une Forme Littéraire*, 4 vols. (Louvain: Peeters, 1986–95), vol. 4, 418–21.

[3] Giovanni Mercati, "Pro Adriano," *RB* 11 (1914): 247 fn. 3.

[4] Martin L. West, *Textual Criticism and Editorial Technique Applicable to Greek and Latin Texts* (Stuttgart: Teubner, 1973), 25.

[5] Marcel Richard, "Floriléges Grecs," *Dictionnaire de Spiritualité*, vol. 5 (Paris: Beauchesne, 1962), 505–6.

also given to Adrian in the ms that was stored in the library of John of Hamburg. The ms Fabricius describes is our L_H and nowhere on ff. 1r–v is Adrian called that.[6] A more likely explanation for "Andronicus" is that a scholar's abbreviation (such as "Adr.") was misread.

B. FIRST BIOGRAPHICAL REMARKS

There are only three authors who comment about Adrian from the patristic and early medieval period. The first unambiguous reference to him occurs in book one of Cassiodorus' (ca. 485–ca. 585) *Institutions of Divine and Secular Learning*. This treatise underwent numerous revisions in the last decades of Cassiodorus' life after he retired to his monastery, the Vivarium, on his family estate in Squillace.[7] The two introductory books of the *Institutions* were intended to orient readers to divine and secular learning respectively. By cataloguing leading ecclesiastical writers of an earlier age, as well as sketching a compendium of the seven liberal arts, Cassiodorus sought to create a scholarly monastic culture characterized by the informed study of the divine Scriptures.[8] But he did not envision his handbook as the only useful guide for students of Scripture:

> After reading this work [i.e., *Institutions*], our first concern should be to consider introductory manuals to Divine Scripture that I previously found, i.e., Tyconius the Donatist, St. Augustine *On Christian Learning*, Adrian, Eucherius, and Junilius. I have acquired their works with great care, and have united and gathered them into one collection since they have a similar purpose. By arranging the rules of usage to elucidate the text, and by comparisons of various examples, they have clarified what was hitherto obscure.[9]

Augustine's treatise is the only work Cassiodorus identifies by name. The other titles he likely gathered into this single collection were Tyconius' *Book of Rules*, Eucherius' *Formulas of Spiritual Understanding*,[10] and Junillus' *Handbook of*

---

[6] Johann Albert Fabricius, *Bibliotheca Graeca*, rev. ed., vol. 9 (Hamburg: Bohm, 1804), 381–2.

[7] For a brief discussion of the complex issues surrounding the dating of this work, see Mark Vessey, "Introduction," in James W. Halporn, trans., *Cassiodorus: Institutions of Divine and Secular Learning and On the Soul*, TTH (Liverpool: Liverpool University Press, 2004), 39–42. For Cassiodorus' chronology I follow the dates proposed by James J. O'Donnell, *Cassiodorus* (Berkeley: University of California Press, 1979), xv–xvi.

[8] *Inst.* 1.preface; 1.10; 1.16; 1.27.1. On Cassiodorus' aims in the *Institutions*, see Pierre Courcelle, *Late Latin Writers and Their Greek Sources*, trans. H. E. Wedeck (Cambridge, Mass.: Harvard University Press, 1969), 354–5; O'Donnell, *Cassiodorus*, 212; Vessey, "Introduction," in *Cassiodorus: Institutions*, 24–37.

[9] *Inst.* 1.10.1. Cassiodorus refers again to these introductory books at 1.11.3, 1.24.1, and the conclusion of book 2.

[10] This is likely the work to which Cassiodorus here alludes, as it is the source of *inst.* 2.4.8 (see R. A. B. Mynors, ed., *Cassiodori Senatoris Institutiones* [Oxford: Oxford University Press, 1937], 189; O'Donnell, *Cassiodorus*, 247 fn. 36).

the Basic Principles of Divine Law. The treatise of Adrian to which Cassiodorus alludes is certainly the *Introduction*, since it matches Cassiodorus' description of these introductory manuals: it too discusses language usage, offers numerous examples of unusual expressions, and identifies clarity as one of the stated aims of scriptural interpretation (76). Cassiodorus' reference to gathering into a single collection "introductory manuals to Divine Scripture" also distinctly echoes the title of Adrian's treatise, since this was the only work in Cassiodorus' list that used the term "introduction" in its title. And most decisively, as Pierre Courcelle already noted, excerpts from Adrian's *Introduction* surface elsewhere in the *Institutions.*[11]

The *Introduction* was the only Greek treatise in Cassiodorus' collection of introductory manuals, and thus was likely translated into Latin either at the Vivarium or earlier.[12] We can only guess at how Cassiodorus acquired his copy of the *Introduction*, but he lists it in the above paragraph as a work he "previously found," which leads us to infer that he likely procured a copy prior to settling at the Vivarium. The libraries and scholarly community in Constantinople, where we can place Cassiodorus between 540 and 554 before his return to Squillace, would have given him direct access to many of the leading writers of the Greek exegetical tradition. As O'Donnell has argued, it was likely in Constantinople that Cassiodorus acquired the writings, especially those in Greek, that would become the basis for his future library in Italy.[13]

The above paragraph from the *Institutions*, then, provides us with important information about the date of the *Introduction*: it could not have been written later than the last few decades of Cassiodorus' life when he was composing the *Institutions* (560s).[14] A few scholars have suggested that Cassiodorus provides

---

[11] See *inst.* 1.15.4 and Courcelle, *Late Latin Writers*, 355 fn. 2.

[12] On the translation of Greek works into Latin under Cassiodorus' patronage, see *inst.* 1.5.4; 1.7.6; 1.8.3–6, 15; 1.9.1, 5; 1.11.2; 1.17.1, *passim*. Adrian's *Introduction* might have been translated into Latin before Cassiodorus learned of it, since we know that Latin translations of Theodore of Mopsuestia were already in circulation in north Africa by the mid-sixth century (see H. B. Swete, ed., *Theodori episcopi Mopsuesteni in epistolas b. Pauli commentarii*, 2 vols. [Cambridge: Cambridge University Press, 1880–2], vol. 1, xli). The affinities between Adrian's *Introduction* and Theodore's exegetical writings are palpable (more on this below). On the broader phenomenon of the translation of Greek writings into Latin, see Courcelle, *Late Latin Writers*.

[13] O'Donnell, *Cassiodorus*, 193, 215.

[14] Indeed it might even have predated the years 540–548 when Cassiodorus was writing his *Explanation of the Psalms* in Constantinople. Cassiodorus drew upon several Greek sources for his commentary, and interestingly had a strong interest in the *idiomata* or *propriae locutiones* of the Psalms (O'Donnell, *Cassiodorus*, 141–2, 160 fn. 31). This was an issue highlighted by Theodore in the preface (now lost) to his *Commentary on the Psalms*. But it was also the central topic of Adrian's *Introduction*. Closer comparison of the *Introduction* and Cassiodorus' *Explanation of the Psalms* is required, but note the following passages: Cass., *Ps.* 7:9 with Adrian, *intro.* 2.1; *Ps.* 26:12 and 67:34 with *intro.* 37; *Ps.* 58:10 with *intro.* 65; *Ps.* 88:27 with *intro.* 60; *Ps.* 85:1 with *intro.* 4.2. Cassiodorus' work is also replete with observations about Greek figures and tropes, many of which we find discussed by Adrian. If in fact Cassiodorus was already using Adrian in Constantinople, this would push the latest possible date of the *Introduction* two decades earlier, and also suggest that the treatise had already been translated into Latin by this time.

us an additional clue to the dating of the *Introduction* since he appears to arrange the aforementioned biblical scholars in chronological sequence. Each of the authors, except Adrian, can be dated with reasonable confidence: Tyconius (fl. 370–390; *Book of Rules* ca. 383), Augustine (354–430; *On Christian Learning* completed 426–427), Adrian (?), Eucherius (ca. 380–ca. 450, with exegetical works dated from his episcopate beginning in the mid-430s), and finally, Junillus, whom Cassiodorus likely met in Constantinople (*Handbook* composed 542–548/9).[15] If Cassiodorus organized his entire list according to a chronology, then Adrian could be dated more narrowly to the first part of the fifth century. Using this line of argument, F. Goessling posited that Adrian flourished ca. 425 and died ca. 440, that is, after Augustine's death, but before Eucherius'.[16] While most scholars have accepted this dating, and there is some evidence (more below) that corroborates it, we should still be cautious about assuming that Cassiodorus was working with a correct chronology.[17]

After Cassiodorus, our only other sure reference to Adrian occurs in the *Bibliotheca* of Photius, the scholar and patriarch of Constantinople (ca. 810–ca. 895). The *Bibliotheca* was an ambitious literary catalogue that consisted of 280 entries, each devoted to a different treatise or series of treatises that dated from antiquity to early Byzantium. It is unlikely that Photius owned all the books he reviewed; he would also have relied on local libraries in Constantinople.[18] That a copy of the *Introduction* existed in one of these libraries is not improbable, since Cassiodorus almost certainly secured a copy during his stay in Constantinople three centuries earlier. In the second entry of Photius' catalogue he refers to Adrian's treatise as follows: Ἀνεγνώσθη Ἀδριανοῦ εἰσαγωγὴ τῆς Γραφῆς. Χρήσιμος τοῖς εἰσαγομένοις ἡ βίβλος ("Read an *Introduction to Scripture* by Adrian. This book is useful for beginners").[19] Two observations can be made about this very brief notice. First, the title Photius provides does

---

[15] Michael Maas, *Exegesis and Empire in the Early Byzantine Mediterranean: Junillus Africanus and the Instituta Regularia Divinae Legis*, Studien und Texte zu Antike und Christentum 17 (Tübingen: Mohr Siebeck, 2003), 13–16.

[16] Friedrich Goessling, *Adrians ΕΙΣΑΓΩΓΗ ΕΙΣ ΤΑΣ ΘΕΙΑΣ ΓΡΑΦΑΣ aus neu aufgefundenen Handschriften* (Berlin: Reuther, 1887), 12–13, following the earlier proposal for interpreting Cassiodorus' list by Credner, *Einleitung*, 12.

[17] There are a few scholars who date Adrian to the early *sixth* century. In the mid-nineteenth century Remy Ceillier suggested 533 as a date for Adrian (*Histoire générale des auteurs sacrés et ecclésiastiques*, new ed., vol. 11 [Paris: Louis Vivès, 1862], 95). This is likely the source of the occasional reference still today to Adrian living in the first half of the sixth century (e.g., Claudio Moreschini and Claudio and Enrico Norelli, *Early Christian Greek and Latin Literature: A Literary History*, trans. Matthew J. O'Connell, vol. 2 [Peabody, Mass.: Hendrickson, 2005], 705). As Goessling noted, however, Ceillier misquoted the chronologist James Ussher who had Adrian flourishing ca. 433 (Goessling, *Adrians ΕΙΣΑΓΩΓΗ*, 12). While it is possible that Adrian lived in the first part of the sixth century, this proposed date rests upon a typographical error.

[18] Nigel G. Wilson, trans., *Photius: The Bibliotheca: A Selection* (London: Duckworth, 1994), 6.

[19] Phot. *cod.* 2. There does not appear to be any significance to the fact that Adrian's treatise is the second work catalogued by Photius. In his letter of dedication he indicates that the works were "arranged in the order in which our memory recalled each of them."

not correspond to the usual title in the manuscript tradition. But there is reason to be cautious about positing another title under which this treatise circulated. It is not unlikely that Photius published an abridged and inaccurate title since in the dedicatory letter to his brother Tarasius he acknowledges incomplete or inaccurate notices, attributing these to composing the *Bibliotheca* from memory.[20] Without corroborating evidence in the direct ms tradition of the *Introduction* it seems best to be cautious about Photius' notice.

Second, this entry, like many others in this treatise, contains an assessment of the work under review. The εἰσαγωγή is "useful for beginners [τοῖς εἰσαγομένοις]." This punning comment is not far off the mark: Adrian's *Introduction* was primarily addressed to teachers of those students who were beginning to learn how to read Scripture (75–6). By calling attention to what he regarded as the work's target audience, and providing such a concise entry on Adrian's *Introduction*, Photius was likely also acknowledging that his brother possessed an expertise in Scripture that made Adrian's treatise redundant for him.[21]

Our last ancient testimony about Adrian comes from the correspondence of Nilus, though here we are on less certain footing. From his authentic surviving writings, we glean that Nilus was a monk who lived in or around Ancyra and flourished ca. 390–ca. 430.[22] We also gather that he was an admirer of his older contemporary, John Chrysostom. Forty-seven of Nilus' surviving letters consist largely, and in some cases entirely, of citations from John's writings.[23] There

---

[20] Phot. *proem. cod.* See also Tomas Hägg, *Photios als Vermittler antiker Literatur: Untersuchungen zur Technik des Referierens und Exzerpierens in der Bibliotheke* (Uppsala: Almquist och Wiksell, 1975); Jacques Schamp, *Photios, historien des letters: La Bibliothèque et ses notices biographiques* (Paris: Les Belles Lettres, 1987); Warren T. Treadgold, *The Nature of the Bibliotheca of Photius* (Washington, D.C.: Dumbarton Oaks, 1980).

[21] Another reason for the conciseness of this entry emerges in Photius' prefatory letter, where he acknowledges that he deliberately did not treat in detail works that were in wide circulation and probably already known to his brother (*proem. cod.*). While it is difficult to determine the circulation of Adrian's *Introduction* in Photius' day and no ninth-century manuscripts of the *Introduction* are extant, it is also possible that the short entry simply reflected the fact that Photius and his brother were already acquainted with the work.

[22] The biography of Nilus of Ancyra has been deeply contested. For orientation to the problem, see Daniel Caner, *History and Hagiography from the Late Antique Sinai*, TTH (Liverpool: Liverpool University Press, 2009), 53–6, 73–5. Until a modern critical edition of Nilus' letters is produced, it will remain unclear to what extent the correspondence that circulates under his name can be attributed to him. While a few letters falsely attributed to Nilus have slipped into his corpus, on balance, most scholars consider the letters authentic. See: Karl Heussi, *Untersuchungen zu Nilus dem Asketen* (Leipzig: J. C. Hinrichs, 1917), 31–117; Jean Gribomont, "La tradition manuscrite de saint Nil: I. La correspondance," *Studia Monastica* 11 (1969): 231–67; Alan Cameron, "The Authenticity of the Letters of St Nilus of Ancyra," *Greek, Roman and Byzantine Studies* 17 (1976): 181–96; Georgios Fatouros, "Zu den Briefen des Hl. Neilos von Ankyra," in *L'épistolographie et la poésie épigrammatique: projects actuels et questions de méthodologie*, ed. Wolfram Hörandner and Michael Grünbart (Paris: Centre d'études byzantines, néo-helléniques et sud-est européennes, 2003), 21–30.

[23] For the list of pertinent letters, see Fatouros, "Zu den Briefen des Hl. Neilos von Ankyra," 22, fn. 10.

are several letters in which Nilus portrays such an enthusiastic relationship with John that some scholars have suggested that he might even have been his pupil.[24] Even if we cannot determine the extent to which these two were personally acquainted, Nilus' letters certainly indicate an awareness of and appreciation for John.

Nilus addressed three letters to a certain Adrian (*epp.* 2.60; 3.118; 3.266). Is this addressee our Adrian? There is a tantalizing clue in this correspondence that suggests that the Adrian of the *Introduction* might have been the same person as Nilus' addressee. In *ep.* 2.60, the longest of the three letters, Nilus exhorts his Adrian to be attentive to the counsels and exempla in Scripture that deal with God's care for those in need.[25] After citing Philippians 4:5–6 ("For the Lord is near. Be anxious for nothing...") and Sirach 2:10 ("Look to the generations of old. Has anyone once trusted in the Lord and been neglected?"), Nilus concludes, "For you have read all these things."[26] The addressee is known by Nilus to be learned in Scripture, like the author of the *Introduction*. Yet this hardly constitutes decisive proof that we are dealing with one and same Adrian.

But two additional factors strengthen the link between Nilus' Adrian and the author of the *Introduction*: first, the dates when Nilus flourished are attractive, since they predate Cassiodorus' *Institutions* and indeed put Adrian in the first third of the fifth century, thereby supporting the hypothesis discussed above that Cassiodorus was listing the authors of the scriptural introductions in chronological order. And second, Nilus' place in Chrysostom's social network is even more promising since, as I will indicate below, there are a number of striking verbal and thematic similarities between the *Introduction* and the exegetical work of leading Antiochene scriptural interpreters of the late fourth and early fifth centuries.

---

[24] See esp. the following letters: 1.184; 1.309; 2.183; 2.265; 2.294; 3.13; 3.199; 3.279. An eighth-century monk was the first to report on this relationship: "He [John] had as disciples bishops Proclus, Palladius, Brisson, and Theodoret and the ascetics Mark, Nilus, and Isidore of Pelusium" (Geo. Monach., *chron.* 9.9). For literature on Nilus' use of John, see Sebastian Haidacher, "Chrysostomus-Fragmente in der Briefsammlung des hl. Nilus," in Χρυσοστομικά: *Studi e ricerche intorno a S. Giovanni Crisostomo*, vol. 1 (Rome: Pustet, 1908), 226–34; Heussi, *Untersuchungen zu Nilus dem Asketen*, 54–5; Cameron, "The Authenticity of the Letters of St Nilus of Ancyra," 188; Manfred Kertsch, "Gregor von Nazianz und Johannes Chrysostomus bei Nilus dem Asketen," *Gräzer Beiträge* 18 (1992): 149–53; Fatouros, "Zu den Briefen des Hl. Neilos von Ankyra," 22.

[25] Several scholars consider *ep.* 2.60 as authentic since parts of it appear in Nilus' later work, the *Ascetic Discourse* (Gribomont, "La tradition manuscrite de saint Nil: I. La correspondence," 247; Cameron, "The Authenticity of the Letters of St Nilus of Ancyra," 191). Daniel Caner draws a similar conclusion about its authenticity, but for different reasons: the letter testifies to a larger theme in Nilus' writings, monastic dependence upon patronage (*Wandering, Begging Monks: Spiritual Authority and the Promotion of Monasticism in Late Antiquity* [Berkeley: University of California Press, 2002], 186–7).

[26] PG 79.228A–C.

What we gather from Nilus and his correspondence with Adrian is certainly consistent with what we know of the Adrian who wrote the *Introduction*. It seems plausible—though by no means definitive—that we are dealing with one and same person: a figure with a relatively uncommon Greek name, flourishing in the first third of the fifth century, knowledgeable in Scripture and familiar with the approaches to commentary that circulated in Antiochene circles. If we are to accept this identification, what more can we learn about our author from Nilus' letters? Adrian was likely a monk who lived in Asia minor. *Ep.* 2.60 contains some biographical information about its recipient. Nilus addresses himself "to Adrian the monk," a title that corresponds to the opening lines of the letter in which Nilus exhorts his addressee not to become anxious and lose trust in God.[27] He reminds Adrian that an otherwise unknown Heron "honors the monks [τοὺς μοναχοὺς σέβοντα]" as does a deacon, Theodoulus, who is "himself a lover of monks [αὐτὸν φιλομόναχον]."[28] There is nothing obvious in the *Introduction* that would suggest that our author is a monk, though perhaps the privileged place of the Psalms in this treatise points to a monastic setting where the training of young monks in Scripture, the Psalms in particular, became a pressing need.[29] At any rate, the view has crept into modern scholarship that Adrian was a monk: this goes back at least to Fabricius who made the link between the addressee of Nilus' *ep.* 2.60 and the author of the *Introduction*.[30]

[27] Recall as well the epithet μοναχός (monk) given to a certain Adrian in the *Florilegium patristicum tit. XIV distributum* mentioned above. Goessling mistakenly claims that Adrian received *three* titles in Nilus' correspondence: monk, presbyter, and priest (Goessling, *Adrians ΕΙΣΑΓΩΓΗ*, 11–12, esp. fn. 4). *Ep.* 3.118 is addressed "to Adrian the presbyter" (PG 79.437B), while *ep.* 3.226 provides no title for Adrian, nor any indication of a title in its body. The designation πρεσβύτερος is ambiguous, but by the early fifth century probably designated "priest" (s.v. πρεσβύτερος PGL II.5 and 7). In short, two titles, and not three, are attributed to Adrian in the Nilus correspondence. However, we should be more cautious with the designation πρεσβύτερος in *ep.* 3.118. While monks could be ordained, many of the titles attributed to the addressees of Nilus' correspondence are spurious (Cameron, "The Authenticity of the Letters," 182–6). *Ep.* 3.118 is very short and offers nothing that points for or against its designee being a priest. On the other hand, the reference to Adrian as a monk in *ep.* 2.60 appears more certain, since this title corresponds to what we gather of him from the contents of the letter itself where Heron and Theodoulus are both said to support monks like Adrian.
[28] PG 79.226C–D.
[29] Recall the opening words of Theodoret, *proem. Ps.* 1 about the prominence of the Psalms in the early fifth century: "It would have been a pleasure for me to do a commentary on the inspired composition of the mighty David prior to the other divine sayings, especially since the students of religion, both city dwellers and in the country, have all given their attention to this work in particular. Not least of these, however, are those, who embrace religious life, and recite it aloud at night and in the middle of the day; they thus sing praise to the God of all and allay the bodily passions... You can find most people making little or no reference to the other divine Scriptures, whereas the spiritual harmonies of the divinely inspired David many people frequently call to mind, whether at home, in public places or while traveling, gain serenity for themselves from the harmony of the poetry, and reap benefit for themselves through this enjoyment." See also Diod., *proem. Ps.*
[30] Fabricius, *Bibliotheca Graeca*, rev. ed., vol. 9, 381–2.

C. AN ANTIOCHENE

We can glean more information about our author from the *Introduction* itself. As noted above, Adrian does not speak explicitly about himself, and there are very few markers in the text that would help us plot our author more precisely on a late antique map. For instance, he endorses the *post partem* virginity of Mary (60), a position already widespread by the mid-fourth century.[31] In that same paragraph he rejects the view that Samuel saw Saul again after his death, that is, Adrian presumably denies that the medium actually raised Samuel from the dead at Saul's behest. This position on 1 Kingdoms 28 was already attested by Eustathius of Antioch ca. 320 in his treatise *On the "Belly-Myther" of Endor*.[32]

But the most striking information about our author comes from a comparative inquiry: that he approached Scripture in a manner palpably similar to authors whom we often designate as "Antiochenes" today. A number of scholars, following Schlüren and Goessling, have contended that Adrian needs to be seen as a representative of the "Antiochene exegetical school."[33] While these labels have become notoriously unstable, and some have even called their validity into question, I will use them in this study because I think they remain helpful. A few remarks are in order, then, about how I understand these terms, before turning to a comparison of Adrian with these Antiochenes.

A number of late antique figures either flourished in the diocese of Antioch, or were clearly indebted to these figures, all of whom shared a similar approach to Scripture. By this I mean that in these authors we often find the use of the same biblical text, the employment of the same technical terms that marked privileged exegetical procedures, the same sequencing of these exegetical procedures, the same resistance to allegorical exegesis, and the same announced goals for exegetical activity. Yet perhaps the most overlooked (though obvious) way in which these exegetes resembled one another was that they offered similar, and sometimes even identical, interpretations of scriptural passages.[34] At

---

[31] A. Ziegenaus, "Jungfräulichkeit, II.1.b: Die Jungfräulichkeit in und nach der Geburt," in *Marienlexikon*, ed. Remigius Bäumber and Leo Scheffczyk, vol. 3 (Erzabtei St. Ottilien: EOS Verlag, 1991), 471–5. Also Luigi Gambero, *Mary and the Fathers of the Church: The Blessed Virgin Mary in Patristic Thought* (San Francisco: Ignatius Press, 1999), primary sources listed under "perpetual virginity of Mary," 434.

[32] Rowan A. Greer and Margaret M. Mitchell, trans., *The "Belly-Myther" of Endor: Interpretations of 1 Kingdoms 28 in the Early Church*, WGRW 16 (Atlanta: Society of Biblical Literature, 2006), ix, lix–lxxii.

[33] Karl Friedrich Schlüren, "Zu Adrianos," *Jahrbücher für Protestantische Theologie* 13 (1887): 159; Goessling, *Adrians ΕΙΣΑΓΩΓΗ*, 44.

[34] R. B. Ter Haar Romeny, *A Syrian in Greek Dress: The Use of Greek, Hebrew, and Syriac Biblical Texts in Eusebius of Emesa's Commentary on Genesis* (Leuven: Peeters, 1997), 131–9.

times these resemblances are so strong that copying, directly or indirectly, is the only plausible way that we can account for them. In these authors ranging from the early fourth through sixth centuries (at least), authors who span the Greek, Latin, and Syriac linguistic worlds of late antiquity, we find what might perhaps best be coined an Antiochene exegetical culture. Thus when I call Adrian an Antiochene, I mean that his approach to Scripture was often strikingly similar to what we find in Eusebius of Emesa, Diodore of Tarsus, Theodore of Mopsuestia, his brother Polychronius of Apamea, and a few other later figures.

My contention that there were exegetical similarities shared by a number of late antique figures associated with Antioch (thereby justifying the construct "Antiochene exegesis"), and that Adrian's approach to Scripture bears a striking familial resemblance to these exegetical approaches (thereby meriting his designation as an "Antiochene"), will be advanced in the notes to my translation. While not comprehensive, I identify numerous excerpts from the biblical exegesis of the aforementioned authors that are patently similar to what we find in Adrian's *Introduction*.

A few qualifications are also in order. I am not suggesting that Adrian simply copied his predecessors. There are certainly differences between his *Introduction* and what we find in these authors.[35] In calling Adrian an "Antiochene," I also do not mean to insinuate that he had personal contacts with the aforementioned people or affiliation with the ascetical institution in Antioch over which Diodore presided, though both are possible.[36] This label also does not make a claim about Adrian's geographic provenance or where he flourished. As we have already seen, the biographical evidence is too thin to sustain firm conclusions on these matters.[37] Nor, finally, do I preclude his interaction with "Alexandrian" authors. There is at least one place in the *Introduction* where

---

[35] Here are a few examples of differences between the *Introduction* and what we find in other Antiochene exegetical writings with which I suspect Adrian was familiar. (1) In Recension 2 Adrian reads Micah 4:2–3 as a prophecy of the gospel proclamation (73.13), but Theodore rejects such a view, explicitly arguing against seeing this text as a figure (τύπος) of the time of Christ. Instead he takes it to refer to the return from the Babylonian exile (*Mich.* 4:2–3). (2) Diodore, *Ps.* 45:3, says the preposition ἐν is used in place of ἐπί, whereas Adrian thinks it stands in place of σύν (*intro.* 65). (3) Adrian says αἰών has three different senses and in *Ps.* 77:66 associates the noun with the "passing of time in general" (62.2). But in Theodore the noun in this verse is allocated to one of Adrian's other proposed senses for this term, "perpetuity and endlessness" (*Ps.* 77:66). A number of additional discrepancies can be found between the *Introduction* and other Antiochene exegetical writings.

[36] There are only a few ancient references to this otherwise elusive institution. Socr., *h.e.* 6.3.6; Soz., *h.e.* 8.2; Thdt., *h.e.* 5.40; Chrys., *Diod.* 1, 3–4. For more on this institution, see René Leconte, "L'asceterium de Diodore," in *Melanges bibliques redigés en l'honneur de André Robert*, ed. J. Trinquet (Paris: Bloud & Gay, 1957), 531–7; André-Jean Festugière, *Antioche païenne et chrétienne: Libanius, Chrysostome et les moines de Syrie* (Paris: Boccard, 1959), 181–92.

[37] Goessling hypothesizes that Adrian might have been a Greek-speaking Syrian based upon the similarities between the *Introduction* and the writings of Theodore and Theodoret, both of whom hailed from the eastern Roman empire (Goessling, *Adrians ΕΙΣΑΓΩΓΗ*, 10). This tentative proposal has been passed along as a fact ("Adrien était un Syrien") by Siméon Vailhé, "10. Adrien," in *DHGE*, vol. 1 (Paris: Letouzey et Ané, 1912), 611.

I suspect Didymean influence (see 73.13 of Recension 2 [R2]). I am simply pointing to notable similarities between Adrian's approach to Scripture and what we find in other figures who are routinely designated as "Antiochenes."

A final note about a curious scribal annotation in an exegetical catena on the Psalms: As mentioned above, an authorial lemma in a tenth-century ms reads, ἀδριανοῦ ἀντιο͎ (i.e., ἀντιοχείας) (*Coislin. 10*, f. 51r). It is unclear what this designation means. The epithet might signify geography—the ostensible place of Adrian's birth or the ecclesiastical diocese with which he was thought to be affiliated. But it might also signify his exegetical disposition. It is important to remember that Theodore of Mopsuestia was often called Theodore "of Antioch" in the exegetical catenae, including *Coislin. 10*.[38] The possibility cannot immediately be excluded that the catenist—like many modern scholars— observed strong parallels between the scriptural exegesis of Adrian and Theodore on the Psalms and marked this similarity with the identical epithet.

To learn more about our author we need to attend to the sorts of similarities we see between the *Introduction* and the exegetical writings of other Antiochenes. A few representative examples will help us flesh out our skeletal biography of Adrian.[39] In the discussion of antiphrasis in his trope list, Adrian's text comes very close to what we find in the commentaries on Job by Polychronius and Olympiodorus. Here is Adrian (73.7 of R1):

> Antiphrasis: whenever it signifies exactly the opposite of what is said. For example, "surely he will bless you to your face" (Job 2:5), instead of "he will blaspheme." And, "he blessed God and king" (3 Kgdms 20:10 [1 Kings 21:10]), instead of "he insulted," "he did evil."

Polychronius and Olympiodorus both provide the same gloss on Job 2:5 (the passage really means "he will blaspheme"). Moreover, in their commentaries on Job 1:11 (which also reads "he will bless you to your face" as in Job 2:5) both authors juxtapose this verse with 3 Kingdoms 20:10, as Adrian does. It is notable that three authors would link the same passages with one another and interpret them in very similar ways.

Toward the end of the *Introduction* Adrian remarks that prophecy can be of the past, present, and future, not simply future (74). In R2 he illustrates a prophecy about the past as Moses narrating the creation of the world; the present

---

[38] For Theodore "of Antioch" in the exegetical catenae on the Psalms, see Georg Karo and Hans Lietzmann, "Catenarum graecarum catalogus," *Nachrichten von der Königl. Gesellschaft der Wissenschaften zu Göttingen*, Philologisch-historische Klasse (1902): type XIII (40); type XV (43); type XVI (48); type XVIII (53); type XIX, i.e., *Coislin. 10* (54); type XXI (57). Sometimes Theodore of Antioch = Theodore of Mopsuestia in the exegetical catenae: Dorival, *Les Chaînes Exégétiques*, vol. 3, 184, 560; see Robert Devreesse, *Les anciens Commentateurs Grecs des Psaumes*, ST 264 (Vatican City: BAV, 1970), 313 fn. 5 where ἀντιοχ. alone = Theodore of Mopsuestia.

[39] With a touch of exaggeration Herbert Newell Bate claims that "every line of Adrian can be illustrated from Theodore of Mopseuestia or Theodoret" ("Some Technical Terms of Greek Exegesis," *JTS* 24 [1922]: 66).

as Elisha revealing Gehasi's receiving payment from Naaman; and the future as (among other things) Isaiah's prophecy of the virgin birth. In Junillus' *Handbook* we find the same insistence that prophecy has three temporal references. Moreover, he illustrates this point as Adrian does. Prophecies of the past include: "In the beginning God created heaven and earth" (Gen 1:1); of the present: the theft by Gehasi (cf. 4 Kgdms 5:20–27); and of the future: "Lo, a virgin will conceive in her womb and bear a son, and his name will be called Emmanuel" (Is 7:14)" (*inst.* 1.4).

Finally, we can turn to Theodore of Mopsuestia, the only author whom Adrian consistently and conspicuously mirrors throughout his treatise. In section 32 of R1 of the *Introduction* Adrian writes,

> In many places Scripture also uses the word "bosom" of the notion of inseparability. For example, "Pay back sevenfold into the 'bosom' of our neighbors" (Ps 78[79]:12)!, instead of "render your multiplied punishment inseparable from them!" And, "which you bore in my 'bosom' from many nations" (Ps 88:51[89:50])!; and, "my prayer will return to my 'bosom'" (Ps 34[35]:13); and, "from the midst of your 'bosom' forever" (Ps 73[74]:11); and, "the only-begotten Son, who is in the 'bosom' of the Father, who made [him] known" (John 1:18).

In Theodore's *Commentary on the Psalms* we find two striking similarities. First, the same gloss on the word "bosom" occurs. Theodore writes on Ps 34:13, "It is customary with the divine Scripture to mention the 'bosom' not when referring to the actual thing called 'bosom' by us, but when wanting to suggest something inseparable and indivisible" (mod.). Second, Theodore comments on the similar uses of "bosom" in Ps 78:12, Ps 88:51, and Jn 1:18—that is, four of the five verses mentioned by Adrian to illustrate this connotation of "bosom" also occur in Theodore. Numerous examples of Adrian's proximity to Theodore are found in the notes to the translation of both recensions.

Parallels like these are so striking that we can confidently place Adrian in a textual network in which Theodore's exegetical writings, as well as a number of other biblical interpreters' texts, circulated. Indeed the parallels are in some cases so close, such as in the examples above, that we must posit dependence. Because we cannot date Adrian with confidence, it is not inconceivable that he was a mid-fourth-century figure whose work influenced the author with whom he shares the most material, Theodore of Mopsuestia. However, the more likely scenario is the reverse: that Adrian was indebted to Theodore and other earlier, fourth-century Antiochene interpreters. If we accept this dating, a few additional observations can be made. First, Theodore's exegetical oeuvre would provide us with a *terminus post quem* for the *Introduction*. Theodore's *Commentary on the Psalms* and *Commentary on the Minor Prophets*, both of which surface extensively in the *Introduction*, were likely composed in the late 370s through the early 380s.[40] Second, the prevalence of fourth-century

---

[40] J.-M. Vosté, "La chronologie de l'activité littéraire de Théodore," *RB* 34 (1925): 70–2.

Antiochene commentary in Adrian's *Introduction* indicates that he must have been intimately familiar with this tradition and perhaps even had access to a well-equipped library that carried the treatises he utilized. Finally, what is especially attractive about dating Adrian after the late fourth century is that it allows us to see him as a scholar who silently extended the legacy of his predecessors, especially Theodore.[41] It was Theodore who eventually received the illustrious epithet, "the interpreter,"[42] and who was already regarded in his own day as an influential teacher.[43] Whether Adrian was a pupil or near contemporary of Theodore is impossible to know. But his slender *Introduction* can perhaps best be viewed as a largely sympathetic abridgement of Theodore's teeming exegetical project, a handbook designed to make his oeuvre accessible to the next generation of biblical readers.[44]

To summarize: we can say very little that is definitive about our author. He was a learned student of Scripture, perhaps a *grammaticus*, and perhaps also a teacher. His approach to biblical commentary strongly resembled the approaches we find in a number of Antiochene scholars from the fourth through sixth centuries. At the very least, he had direct access to some of their treatises. And his *Introduction* predated Cassiodorus' *Institutions* (560s). Beyond these few points we can make some tentative suggestions. It is likely that Adrian flourished after the early 380s, that is, after Theodore had completed his exegetical work on the Psalms and minor prophets. The strong ties between the *Introduction* and Theodore's exegetical oeuvre would signal Adrian's strong respect for Theodore's work and, indeed, the growing legacy of the latter in the Greek-speaking world. Finally, if we accept the identification of Nilus' addressee with the Adrian of the *Introduction*, we can add some more color to our biography: Adrian was an early fifth-century monk likely living in Asia Minor.

---

[41] It was common in antiquity not to announce the sources one used. On this phenomenon in Diodore, see Schäublin, *Untersuchungen*, 45–9.

[42] This title is already attested at a synod in 596 (see Jean Baptiste Chabot, *Synodicon Orientale, ou, Recueil de synodes nestoriens* [Paris: Imprimerie Nationale, 1902], 198/459).

[43] For the depiction of Theodore as an influential teacher (διδάσκαλος), see Thdt., *h.e.* 5.27.3 and Ibas, *ep.* (*ACO* 2.1.3 §138:33.28–32).

[44] And perhaps also an *expansion* of Theodore's now-lost prologue to his *Commentary on the Psalms* in which he addressed the issue of Scripture's "peculiarities" (Thdr. Mops., *Ps.* 15:4). It is possible that Adrian's treatise—which focused almost exclusively on these peculiarities—used Theodore's prologue as a starting point for a lengthier discussion of this issue.

2

Title and Topic

A. TITLE

The *Introduction* has been transmitted in two recensions, each opening with a different heading. The mss that carry R1 provide the following title: εἰσαγωγὴ εἰς τὰς θείας γραφάς (i.e., *Introduction to the Divine Scriptures*). However this title is missing from the three mss that transmit R2. Instead they read as follows: ἐκ τοῦ περὶ τῶν ἰδιωμάτων τῆς θείας γραφῆς· καὶ μάλιστα τοῦ Δαυὶδ εἰσὶ ταῦτα.[1] Since ancient titles often began with περί ("about"), this is an ambiguous sentence: it is not clear if these mss are providing us with an alternate title for the treatise or simply a description of its contents. This heading could thus read either, "From the treatise, *About the Peculiarities of Divine Scripture...*" or, "From the treatise about the peculiarities of Divine Scripture..."[2] Either way, the language in this heading is inspired by the opening sentence of the *Introduction* which announces the theme of scriptural peculiarities, and it includes the recognition that many of the particularities discussed in the work come from the Psalms (i.e., "David").

Adrian's *Introduction* exemplified a pedagogical exercise well-attested in antiquity: the composition of treatises that oriented beginning students to complex disciplines or the writings of well-known authors. These introductory treatises carried a variety of titles, including εἰσαγωγή ("introduction"), τέχνη ("treatise"), στοιχεῖα ("elementary principles"), ὅροι ("definitions"), ἀρχαί ("first principles"), and ἐγχειρίδιον ("handbook").[3] As others have noted, introductory

---

[1] Note as well that *cat. Job* 1:11 has the following heading: Ἀδριανοῦ ἐκ τοῦ περὶ τῶν ἰδιωμάτων τῆς θείας γραφῆς.

[2] Eleonor Dickey, *Ancient Greek Scholarship: A Guide to Finding, Reading, and Understanding Scholia, Commentaries, Lexica, and Grammatical Treatises, from Their Beginnings to the Byzantine Period* (Oxford: Oxford University Press, 2007), 129–30.

[3] For overviews of these kinds of works, see K. Schäfer, "Eisagoge," *RAC* 4 (1959): 862–904; Herwig Görgemanns, "Isagoge," *DNP* 5 (1998): 1111–14; André-Jean Festugière, *La révélation d'Hermès Trismégiste*, vol. 2, *Le Dieu cosmique* (Paris: Gabalda, 1949), 345–50; Markus Asper, "Zu Struktur und Funktion eisagogischer Texte," in *Gattungen wissenschaftlicher Literatur in der*

textbooks varied widely in the themes they broached, so that it is difficult to delineate an "introductory genre" if we mean by that expression a standardized list of topics consistently addressed by commentators.[4] Even the issues discussed in self-standing introductions to important literary works, or in the prologues to their commentaries, were numerous: they could include biographies of their authors, discussions of the authenticity of the work under consideration, its theme, structure, or purpose, its literary features, its place in the larger corpus of an author, its usefulness, and so forth.[5] Some commentators addressed only a handful of these topics, while others were more thorough. What allows us to gather introductory works on literary texts under a single heading is less a uniform set of topical concerns, but their common formal features. These works tended to be brief, aspired to clarity, used a representative selection of material to advance key points, sometimes relied on earlier authorities, and, in general, were aimed at a student readership—usually beginners.[6]

Among educated Christians in antiquity we see a similar interest in producing introductory handbooks on the Bible. These works were often strikingly different from one another. Unlike today, where introductions to the Old and New Testaments have become relatively formalized so that readers can expect discussions of a number of discrete topics, we find little consensus among early Christians about what topics constituted an introduction to the Bible. Recall Cassiodorus' gathering of early Christian introductions to Scripture into one volume. These works had "a similar purpose. By arranging the rules of usage to elucidate the text, and by comparisons of various examples, they have clarified what was hitherto obscure" (*inst.* 1.10.1). Even if we accept this assessment,

Antike, ed. Wolfgang Kullmann, Jochen Althoff, and Markus Asper (Tübingen: Gunter Narr, 1998), 309–40; idem, *Griechische Wissenschaftstexte: Formen, Funktionen, Differenzierungsgeschichten* (Stuttgart: Franz Steiner, 2007), 214–314. Prior to Adrian, the only Christian work with the word εἰσαγωγή in its title was the *General Elementary Introduction* (Ἡ τοῦ καθόλου στοιχειώδης εἰσαγωγή) by Eusebius, written ca. 310. This was originally a ten-book treatise, of which books six through nine survive under the title *Eclogae Propheticae* (ἐκλογαὶ προφετικαί). It too was written as a handbook for students of Scripture (*CPG* 3474).

[4] Aaron P. Johnson, "Eusebius the Educator: The Context of the General Elementary Introduction," in *Reconsidering Eusebius: Collected Papers on Literary, Historical and Theological Issues*, ed. Sabrina Inowlocki and Claudio Zamagni (Leiden: Brill, 2011), 114.

[5] For discussions of the sorts of topics addressed in prolegomena to commentaries, see Schäublin, *Untersuchungen*, 66–72; Ilsetraut Hadot, "Les introductions aux commentaires exégétiques chez les auteurs Néoplatoniciens et les auteurs Chrétiens," in *Les règles de l'interprétation*, ed. M. Tardieu (Paris: Cerf, 1987), 99–122; Jaap Mansfeld, *Prolegomena: Questions to be Settled before the Study of an Author or a Text* (Leiden: Brill, 1994).

[6] On these formal features of introductions, see Manfred Fuhrmann, *Das Systematische Lehrbuch: Ein Beitrag zur Geschichte der Wissenschaften in der Antike* (Göttingen: Vandenhoeck & Ruprecht, 1960); Hadot, "Les introductions aux commentaires exégétiques"; Mansfeld, *Prolegomena*; Ronald E. Heine, "The Introduction to Origen's *Commentary on John* Compared with the Introductions to the Ancient Philosophical Commentaries on Aristotle," in *Origeniana Sexta*, ed. Gilles Dorival and Alain Le Boulluec (Leuven: Leuven University Press, 1995), 3–12; Asper, "Zu Struktur und Funktion," 309–14; esp. Asper, *Griechische Wissenschaftstexte*, 238–44; Johnson, "Eusebius the Educator."

quick inspection of the works he collected into a single volume (to say nothing of those he did not include) indicates that there were also important differences among them. Collectively they addressed a range of topics, including: plot summaries of books, interpretations of difficult passages, lists of figures and tropes, overarching themes, discussions of authorship, delineation of literary forms, principles that guided interpretation, qualifications or credentials of ideal readers, lists of canonical books, theoretical discussions of Scripture's divine inspiration, and so on.[7] Some of these introductions ranged widely, and others, like Adrian's *Introduction*, were more narrowly delineated: in his case, his treatise focused on Scripture's literary style, and even more specifically, its stylistic peculiarities.[8]

Adrian's treatise was well-titled. It shared many of the same formal features as other Christian and non-Christian introductory handbooks: it was a brief work, relied (tacitly) on the authority of earlier exegetes like Theodore of Mopsuestia, and drew upon representative biblical texts to advance its arguments. It was also a work pitched to the teacher as an aid for instructing beginning students in Scripture. And finally, its central topic—Scripture's literary peculiarities—was an issue that repeatedly surfaced in late antique introductions or prologues to major literary works.

B. TOPIC

Adrian's *Introduction* was not a scriptural commentary designed to help students understand a particular biblical book or set of passages, but rather a short guide intended to help them interpret all of Scripture well. To achieve this end, Adrian sought to convey organized knowledge about what he evidently thought was a key obscuring feature of Scripture for his audience. He announces this topic in the opening line of the *Introduction*: "There are three kinds of peculiarities of the Hebrew literary style: one will find that the first of these pertains to its message, the second to its diction, and the third to its syntax" (1). The remainder of this chapter will examine the topic of style, its conspicuous threefold division into message, diction, and syntax, and finally, the issue of peculiarities. An analysis of the technical rhetorical terms in this first

---

[7] There is still no comparative study of early Christian introductions to Scripture (and their relationship to the prolegomena to commentaries and homilies), a significant lacuna in the research. For a brief discussion of introductions, past and present, to the OT and NT respectively, see Hans-Jürgen Zobel and Werner Georg Kümmel, "Einleitungswissenschaft," *TRE* 9 (1982): 460–82.

[8] Note that questions concerning the terminology, genre, or literary style of Plato's and Aristotle's writings repeatedly surfaced in the introductions to the commentaries on their philosophical writings (Hadot, "Les introductions aux commentaries exégétiques"; Mansfeld, *Prolegomena*, under index entry "*isagogical* questions," 241–3).

sentence will bring Adrian's work into clearer focus and position the *Introduction* more clearly within its disciplinary and broader intellectual contexts.

1. On style and its three components

The *Introduction* was an exercise in the literary scholarship practiced by the *grammatici*. We learn from the scholia on the *Τέχνη γραμματική* attributed to Dionysius Thrax (ca. 170–90 BCE) that late antique grammarians pursued a range of activities when they turned to the central work of textual explanation (ἐξεγητικόν): the clarification of meanings (γλωσσηματικόν), an analysis of important grammatical and rhetorical features (τεχνικόν), metrical evaluation (μετρικόν), and a discussion of the text's subject matter (ἱστορικόν), which required the literary critic to delve into others fields—astronomy, botany, mathematics, history, and so on—that informed the text's main themes.[9] We encounter each of these explanatory activities in the *Introduction*, organized around the central topic of the stylistic oddities in Scripture, as Adrian saw them.

By highlighting the topic of style, the opening sentence of the *Introduction* announced a disciplinary expertise required for scriptural analysis: rhetoric. Style was one of the constitutive elements of classroom instruction in rhetoric and accounts of it surface in the major handbooks on rhetoric, for example, the *Institutio Oratoria* by Quintilian, the *Art of Political Speech* attributed to Anonymous Seguerianus and the *Art of Rhetoric* by Apsines of Gadara. A number of specialized treatises on style were also written, notably, *On the Sublime* by Pseudo-Longinus, *On Political Discourse* and *On Simple Discourse* both by Pseudo-Aelius Aristides, and a treatise that would have a lasting impact on later antiquity and Byzantium, Hermogenes' *On the Types of Style*.[10]

While the rhetor's precepts concerning style were designed for oratory and written composition, they were no less relevant for those performing a literary

---

[9] Hermann Usener, "Ein altes Lehrgebäude der Philologie," *SBAW* (1892) 4: 582–648. See as well Schäublin, *Untersuchungen*, 34–5 and Neuschäfer, *Origenes als Philologe*, 35–6. For editions of the *Τέχνη γραμματική* and the numerous scholia on it, as well as a translation of the work, see the section on ancient sources in the bibliography.

[10] The precepts of rhetoric were customarily divided into five parts: invention (developing the content and argument of a speech), arrangement (coherent organization), style (word choice, figurative language), memory (techniques to keep the speech in mind), and delivery (pronunciation and gesture). For surveys of the whole field, see Richard Volkmann, *Die Rhetorik der Griechen und Römer in systematischer Übersicht dargestellt*, 2nd ed. (Leipzig: Teubner, 1885); Josef Martin, *Antike Rhetorik: Technik und Methode* (Munich: Beck, 1974); George A. Kennedy, *The Art of Persuasion in Greece* (Princeton: Princeton University Press, 1963); *The Art of Rhetoric in the Roman World: 300 BC–AD 300* (Princeton: Princeton University Press, 1972); *Greek Rhetoric under Christian Emperors* (Princeton: Princeton University Press, 1983); Laurent Pernot, *Rhetoric in Antiquity*, trans. W. E. Higgins (Washington, D.C.: Catholic University of America Press, 2005).

analysis of a stylistically inventive or difficult work.[11] Thus discussions of style surfaced widely in Greco-Roman literary scholarship, particularly in the early Christian centuries.[12] Alongside the aforementioned theoretical discussions, literary critics often reflected on the style of the individual authors upon whom they were commenting: scholia, essays, letters, and commentaries on figures like Homer, the classical orators, historians, and philosophers invariably harbored important observations on literary style.[13] It is from this rhetorical tradition that early Christian literary critics like Adrian drew when they turned their attention to the style of their Scriptures.

The penchant for "rhetorical criticism" has long been associated with Antiochene biblical scholars, Adrian included.[14] This observation is undoubtedly correct, but it should not be heard as implying that these figures were uniquely interested in this approach to Scripture within the Christian ambit. Rhetorical criticism surfaced widely within early Christian biblical scholarship, including among "Alexandrian" interpreters like Origen who have often been juxtaposed to the Antiochenes.[15] Yet among authors like Diodore, Theodore, and Adrian, all of whom wrestled extensively with the language and imagery of Scripture, rhetorical analysis was a prominent instrument in their exegetical toolkit.[16]

---

[11] Donald A. Russell, *Criticism in Antiquity*, 2nd ed. (London: Bristol Classical Press, 1995), 114–15; George A. Kennedy, "Historical Survey of Rhetoric," in *Handbook of Classical Rhetoric in the Hellenistic Period 330 B.C.–A.D. 400*, ed. Stanley E. Porter (Leiden: Brill, 1997), 5.

[12] Donald A. Russell, "Greek Criticism of the Empire," in *Cambridge History of Literary Criticism*, vol. 1, *Classical Criticism*, ed. George A. Kennedy (Cambridge: Cambridge University Press, 1989), 297; Kennedy, "Historical Survey of Rhetoric," 5.

[13] For overviews of stylistic theory in antiquity, see Russell, *Criticism in Antiquity*, 2nd ed., ch. 9; Galen O. Rowe, "Style," in *Handbook of Classical Rhetoric in the Hellenistic Period, 330 B.C.–A.D. 400*, ed. Stanley E. Porter (Leiden: Brill, 1997), 121–57; for a schematic overview of style, see Heinrich Lausberg, *Handbook of Literary Rhetoric: Foundation for Literary Study*, ed. David E. Orton and R. Dean Anderson, trans. Matthew T. Bliss, Annemiek Jansen, and David E. Orton (Leiden: Brill, 1998), §§453–1082. For patristic Greek and Byzantine theory of rhetoric, including the topic of style, see Herbert Hunger, *Die hochsprachliche profane Literatur der Byzantiner*, vol. 1 (Munich: Beck, 1978), 65–196 (with bibliography); George L. Kustas, *Studies in Byzantine Rhetoric* (Thessaloniki: Patriarchal Institute for Patristic Studies, 1973); Elizabeth Jeffreys, "Rhetoric," in *The Oxford Handbook of Byzantine Studies*, ed. Elizabeth Jeffreys with John Haldon and Robin Cormack (Oxford: Oxford University Press, 2008), 827–37.

[14] This association of rhetorical criticism with Adrian is at least as old as Schlüren, "Zu Adrianos," 159. More recently, see Frances M. Young, "The Rhetorical Schools and Their Influence on Patristic Exegesis," in *The Making of Orthodoxy: Essays in Honour of Henry Chadwick*, ed. Rowan Williams (Cambridge: Cambridge University Press, 1989), 182–99; Sten Hidal, "Exegesis of the Old Testament in the Antiochene School with Its Prevalent Literal and Historical Method," in *Hebrew Bible/Old Testament: The History of Its Interpretation*, vol. 1, *From the Beginnings to the Middle Ages (Until 1300)*, Part 1: Antiquity, ed. M. Sæbø (Göttingen: Vandenhoeck & Ruprecht, 1996), 543–68; Hill, *Reading the Old Testament in Antioch*, 9, 107–33.

[15] On Origen's rhetorical criticism, see Neuschäfer, *Origenes as Philologe*, 218–46.

[16] There is often a fuzziness around the concept of "rhetorical criticism." In the case of Adrian's *Introduction* it seems to me that it can at the very least include: his concern for the tropes, figures, or other stylistic conventions of Scripture; his repeated use of paraphrase—an exercise practiced in the rhetorical schoolroom—to bring out the sense of the text; and the way in which the

To get a better idea of what Adrian meant by the "style" of Scripture, we need to turn to its threefold partition into the categories of "message," "diction," and "syntax." A handful of scholars have unsuccessfully inquired into the origins of this schema. At the end of his textual study of the *Introduction*, Karl Friedrich Schlüren remarked that Adrian "apparently used as his basis a grammatical-rhetorical schema that was common in his day," though Schlüren failed to identify a parallel tripartite classification system in the Greek rhetorical tradition.[17] Later that year, Friedrich Goessling released his edition and translation of Adrian's *Introduction*, and while examining the problem in greater detail, concluded that the tripartite division was "eclectic" since it apparently did not appear anywhere in the Greek philosophical and rhetorical traditions.[18] More recently, Alexis Léonas has echoed Goessling's conclusion: "Adrian's tripartite division of the peculiarities of biblical diction...appears rather arbitrary."[19]

But careful scrutiny of Greco-Roman rhetorical theory of style demonstrates how Adrian's division of the scriptural style into its message, diction, and word arrangement was not idiosyncratic.[20] Many rhetorical theorists demarcated the subject matter of a treatise from its style,[21] analyzing the latter in terms of the categories of individual word use and the compositional arrangement of words.[22] However, another approach to style resisted this dichotomy between content and manner of expression—content was not treated as something distinct from, but rather constitutive of style.[23] This comes out with particular clarity in the treatise *On Style*, attributed to a certain Demetrius, and usually dated toward the end of the second or beginning of the first century BCE.[24] Demetrius categorized style into three basic components: message or subject matter

rhetorician's stylistic ideals decisively shaped Adrian's view of Scripture and the task of exegesis: to bring "clarity" out of an often obscure text.

[17] Schlüren, "Zu Adrianos," 159.   [18] Goessling, *Adrians ΕΙΣΑΓΩΓΗ*, 51–6, esp. 54.

[19] Alexis Léonas, "Patristic Evidence of Difficulties in Understanding the LXX: Hadrian's Philological Remarks in Isagoge," in *Tenth Congress of the International Organization of Septuagint and Cognate Studies*, ed. Bernard A. Taylor (Atlanta: Society of Biblical Literature, 2001), 402.

[20] For a more expanded treatment of what follows, see Peter W. Martens, "Adrian's *Introduction to the Divine Scriptures* and Greco-Roman Rhetorical Theory on Style," *Journal of Religion* 93 (2013): 197–217.

[21] See, for instance, Arist., *ars rhet.* 3.1; Quint., *inst.* 8.proem.20–21; Diony. Halic., *comp.* 1 and 4; idem, *Lys.* 4; idem, *Th.* 22; Ps.-Aristid., *ars rhet.* 2.2.

[22] On this twofold classification for style, also see Arist., *ars rhet.* 3.2–5; 3.6–12; Quint., *inst.* 8.3.15; Diony. Halic., *Th.* 22; 24.1–2; Anon. Seg., *ars rhet.* 85; 238; Aps., *ars rhet.* 10.48.

[23] Russell, *Criticism in Antiquity*, 129–30; Cecil W. Wooten, "Appendix I: Hermogenes and Ancient Critical Theories on Oratory," in *Hermogenes' On Types of Style*, trans. Cecil W. Wooten (Chapel Hill: University of North Carolina Press, 1987), 133.

[24] For discussions of date and authorship, see W. Rhys Roberts, *Demetrius on Style: The Greek Text of Demetrius De Elocutione Edited after the Paris Manuscript with Introduction, Translation, Facsimiles, etc.* (Cambridge: Cambridge University Press, 1902), 49–64; G. M. A. Grube, *A Greek Critic: Demetrius on Style* (Toronto: University of Toronto Press, 1961), 39–56.

(διάνοια, πρᾶγμα, or ὑπόθεσις), diction (λέξις), and finally, the arrangement of words or syntax (σύνθεσις).[25] A similar tripartite schema surfaced in the writings of Dionysius of Halicarnassus. While he tended to speak of style in a way that suggested content is not integral to it, he could also depart from this tendency. In his essay on the Attic orator Lysias, Dionysius praised him for the virtues of his style: "There are three departments or aspects in which this quality manifests itself: thought, language, and composition [διανοίας τε καὶ λέξεως καὶ τρίτης τῆς συνθέσεως], and I declare him to be successful in all three."[26] Dionysius' use of these three nouns (διάνοια, λέξις, and σύνθεσις) is the closest verbal parallel to Adrian's opening sentence in all of Greek literature. According to the *TLG* database, he is the only other author to use these three nouns in a single sentence that discusses literary style.

There are a number of later rhetorical theorists who also spoke of the components of style in ways that resembled Demetrius and Dionysius.[27] Thus it is clear that Adrian's tripartite division of this topic was of a piece with other Greco-Roman treatments of style. In his hands, the first element of style, its "message" (διάνοια), concerned the recurring theme of God's providential action. The first section of the *Introduction* contains an impressive inventory of the anthropomorphic ways in which God was portrayed in Scripture, and then explains how such expressions ought to be fittingly understood. In the second section on "diction" (λέξις), Adrian identifies peculiar word usages, offers lexicographical analyses of semantically rich terms, discusses a handful of tropes, and in a few sections informs readers about how to safely hear potentially dangerous theological language. The third section, also the shortest, deals with syntax or the arrangement of multiple words in composition (σύνθεσις). Here Adrian follows the preceding rhetorical tradition by providing an illustrated catalogue of figures (σχήματα), that is, places where words are subtracted, added, or rearranged.

2. Peculiarities of Scripture

Adrian's *Introduction* did not offer a wide-ranging discussion of the three aforementioned components of the literary style of Scripture. Instead, it focused on their "peculiarities" (ἰδιώματα). This interest in scriptural ἰδιώματα was especially prominent among Antiochene biblical commentators.[28] Theodore of Mop-

---

[25] Demetr., *eloc.*, 38, 115–17, *passim.*   [26] Diony. Halic., *Lys.* 8.

[27] See esp. Ps.-Longin. *sublim.* 8.1; Ps.-Aristid., *ars rhet.* 1.2; 2.2; Hermog., *form.* 1.1 and 1.3.

[28] On scriptural "peculiarities" in the Antiochenes, see Devreesse, *Essai*, 58–68; Schäublin, *Untersuchungen*, 127–38; Ter Haar Romeny, *Syrian in Greek Dress*, 134–9; Jean-Noël Guinot, *L'Exégèse de Théodoret de Cyr* (Paris: Beauchesne, 1995), 346–56. For the theme in Cassiodorus (who knew Adrian's *Introduction*), see Courcelle, *Late Latin Writers*, 355 fn. 2; O'Donnell, *Cassiodorus*, 160–1. A perusal of other late antique writers with similar interests in peculiarities reveals that Adrian's *Introduction* (in both recensions) was far from comprehensive. Note, for

suestia, for instance, tells us that he composed a list of ἰδιώματα (*proprietates*) in the prologue to his *Commentary on the Psalms*.[29] This prologue is now lost, which is especially lamentable since its inventory of peculiarities was probably the closest parallel in early Christian literature to Adrian's *Introduction*. For Adrian the Scriptures were often stylistically inventive and difficult, and so the task of his treatise was to catalogue challenging linguistic features—peculiarities of thought, diction, and composition—that, left unsolved, obscured the meaning of Scripture.

But what exactly is an ἰδίωμα? In my translation I render it as "peculiarity," thereby attempting to bring out two important facets of this noun.[30] First, an ἰδίωμα is a linguistic peculiarity since it marks an author's *unconventional* use of language. Some peculiarities concern a theme, such as depictions of God that are anthropomorphic and, thus, technically erroneous if they are read in an unimaginative way. Others are lexical: for instance, terms like σάρξ and πνεῦμα have unusually wide semantic ranges that reach far beyond their customary definitions, "flesh" and "spirit," respectively (57, 59). And some are syntactical: that is, the alteration of straightforward syntax by adding, subtracting, or rearranging words. Peculiarities such as these were considered variations of (and not necessarily deviations from) standard or ordinary ways in which language was used. Invariably, the standard for determining the unconventional use of language was the everyday Greek of the literary critic's day.[31]

The second aspect of an ἰδίωμα is that it signified a *frequently occurring* literary irregularity—thus it designates a "peculiarity" not simply in the sense of something unexpected in Scripture, but a *recurring* oddity that marked an author's habitual or customary way of writing. Theodore will say that "Scripture habitually speaks this way (Καὶ συνήθως δὲ οὕτω λέγει)," when it uses the word "until" in an unusual fashion.[32] Theodoret, in his *Commentary on the*

example, Diodore's observation of the semantic range of σοφός (Ps. 48:10), or Theodore's observations about the syntactical construction γίνομαι + εἰς (Ps. 30:3—s.v. BDF §145) and the imperative denoting the future (*Zach.* 11:4). These remarks do not occur in the *Introduction*.

[29] Ps. 15:4.   [30] S.v. ἰδίωμα, LSJ II.

[31] William G. Rutherford, *A Chapter in the History of Annotation being Scholia Aristophanica, III* (London: Macmillan, 1905), 209–10; Fuhrmann, *Systematische Lehrbuch*, 23. In Dionysius of Halicarnassus' literary essay on the ἰδιώματα of Thucydides (*Second Letter to Ammaeus*), his glosses of this term highlight the unconventional nature of peculiarities. He notes that they "distinguish him [i.e., Thucydides] from all previous orators and historians [διαφέρειν ... τῶν πρὸ αὐτοῦ ῥητόρων τε καὶ συγγραφέων]" (2 Amm. 1.1); his syntax is not "in conformity to ordinary usage [ἀκολούθως τῇ κοινῇ συνηθείᾳ]" (11.2); or, his constructions marked a "departure from established usage [ἡ ἐξαλλαγὴ τῆς συνήθους χρήσεως]" (3.2). Such peculiarities, in turn, had an obscuring effect on readers. For instance, Thucydides often used a "figurative, obscure, archaic and strange diction [ξένην λέξιν], in place of that which was in common use and familiar to people of his day [ἀντὶ τῆς κοινῆς καὶ συνήθους τοῖς καθ᾽ ἑαυτὸν ἀνθρώποις]" (2.2); terms were "archaic and difficult to comprehend for most people [ἀπηρχαιωμένα καὶ δυσείκαστα τοῖς πολλοῖς]" (3.1) (also see *Th.* 49.1; 51.1; 55.2).

[32] Ps. 56:1. See also Ps. 18:1 (συνήθεια); Os. 9:3 (συνήθως); Os. 12:9 (συνήθης), passim. Diodore: "Now, if David referred to heaven as 'heavens,' this too is not unusual or out of keeping with Scripture [οὐ ξένον τῆς γραφῆς οὐδὲ ἀλλότριον] it being usual for it to speak of a single thing in the plural as many. Stating singular things as plural is a Hebrew peculiarity [ἰδίωμα ... ἑβραϊκὸν],

Psalms remarks that it is a "custom of Scripture (Ἔθος γὰρ τῇ γραφῇ)" to alternate the singular and plural number for the noun "heaven."[33] Adrian also has this aspect of the term in view. He will note that a peculiarity occurs "continually" (συνεχῶς) (61), "everywhere" (πανταχοῦ) (67), "in many places" (πολλαχοῦ) (25, 26, *passim*), or "frequently" (πολλάκις) (21, 27, *passim*), and will usually cite multiple verses to illustrate an ἰδίωμα, thereby underscoring that this peculiarity is, in fact, a commonplace in Scripture.[34]

An ἰδίωμα for Adrian, then, signaled an obscuring stylistic feature that was both *customary* of Scripture and *unusual* with respect to ordinary, unadorned Greek usage. It is also worth highlighting that Adrian, as with other Antiochenes, rarely made an attempt to profile peculiarities specific to an individual scriptural author or book.[35] Adrian's list of figures in 65–71 is illustrated specifically from the Psalms of "blessed David," but throughout the rest of the *Introduction* he illustrates ἰδιώματα with verses drawn from all parts of Scripture. This approach to the scriptural style conveys a notion of homogeneity that appears to have been primarily grounded not in a notion of the single divine authorship of the scriptural books, nor their collection into a single canon, but, as we will next see, in a common language.

3. The "Hebrew" literary style

The final issue in the opening sentence of the *Introduction* is Adrian's announced interest in the peculiarities of the "Hebrew" literary style, an expression that frequently occurs in Antiochene biblical commentary.[36] At first glance this terminology seems to suggest Adrian's interest in the Hebrew language, but this is not the case. There is no indication in the *Introduction* that he knew Hebrew. He engages Old Testament writings exclusively as translated texts—that is, he is a student of the Septuagint with occasional references to Symmachus' translation in R2.[37] Nor is the "Hebrew" literary style an oblique

---

especially in the case of heavenly things, either on account of their importance or also by another custom [διὰ συνήθειαν ἄλλην]" (*Ps.* 18:1 [mod.]).

[33] *Ps.* 18:2. The use of ἔθος in conjunction with ἰδίωμα is frequent: Thdr. Mops., *Ps.* 32:6; 58:9; *Mal.* 1:2, etc. Note as well, Isid. Pel.: κατὰ τοὺς τῆς ἱερᾶς Γραφῆς νόμους καὶ τὰ ἰδιώματα (*ep.* 1398).

[34] On attending to the recurring features of a poet's writing in non-Christian literary scholarship, see René Nünlist, *The Ancient Critic at Work: Terms and Concepts of Literary Criticism in Greek Scholia* (Cambridge: Cambridge University Press, 2009), 11.

[35] Schäublin, *Untersuchungen*, 158–9.

[36] Diod., *Ps.* 18:2: ἰδίωμα ἑβραϊκὸν; *Ps.* 31:6: ἰδίωμά…ἑβραϊκόν; Thdr. Mops., *Ps.* 30:3: ἰδίωμα …ἑβραϊκόν; *Ps.* 32:7: Ἰδίωμα…ἑβραϊκὸν; *Ps.* 50:7: ἀπὸ τοῦ ἑβραϊκοῦ ἰδιώματος; *Os.* 12:9: ἐκ τοῦ ἰδιώματος…τοῦ ἑβραϊκοῦ; Thdt., *Dan.* 11:9–10: ἰδίωμα…τῆς Ἑβραίων διαλέκτου; *qu. in 4 Reg.* 6: κατὰ τὸ Ἑβραίων…ἰδίωμα.

[37] On the limited or nonexistent knowledge of Hebrew among the Antiochenes, see Schäublin, *Untersuchungen*, 123–4, esp. fn. 153 (on Diodore and Theodore); Guinot, *L'Exégèse de Théodoret de Cyr*, 190–7.

reference to the Jewish Scriptures, the law and prophets. This would be an attractive option were it not for the discussions of New Testament passages sprinkled throughout the *Introduction*.

Adrian does not explain what he means by the "Hebrew" literary style, but if we take a number of the Antiochene exegetes from the fourth and fifth centuries as our guides on this issue, the expression appears to signal a *source* of the peculiarities in the Greek Bible.[38] The Septuagint was often considered more obscure than the other Greek translations of the OT because it was thought to have remained closer to the wording of the original Hebrew.[39] As a result, it did not filter out the Hebrew ἰδιώματα, as Theodore states: "Now, it is Hebrew peculiarities (*proprietates hebraicae*) in particular that made this place difficult for us, since they can hardly be explained through the Greek translation."[40] We find similar assertions in other Antiochene texts.[41] The peculiarities readers encountered in the Septuagint were a result of its translators directly importing peculiarities from the underlying Hebrew text.[42]

And what about Adrian's willingness to consider the peculiarities in the NT as indicative of the "Hebrew" literary style? In R2 of the *Introduction* he often follows an illustration of a peculiarity from the OT with one from the NT, prefacing the latter with an introductory ὅθεν: "'for which reason' the apostle also uses this peculiarity..." In other words, the Hebrew peculiarities in the OT served as a source or basis for the peculiarities in the NT. We again find similar assertions about Hebrew peculiarities in the NT in Diodore, Theodore, and Theodoret.[43] Note especially the passage in Theodore's *Commentary on the Psalms* where he observes how the Hebrew peculiarity of an exchange of

[38] For a similar proposal regarding Theodore of Mopsuestia, see Schäublin, *Untersuchungen*, 129–30.

[39] On the proximity of the LXX to the underlying Hebrew, see esp. Thdr. Mops., *Ps.* 55:7; 67:34; *Soph.* 1:4–6; Thdt., *Cant.* 3:6. Another indication of this proximity occurs in Adrian's *Introduction* where he writes conspicuously about the ἰδίωμα where prepositions are improperly exchanged: "Blessed David uses the preposition ἐν instead of σύν" (65). No longer has the Greek translator of the LXX faithfully brought the Hebrew peculiarity into Greek—David himself is made to appear as a Greek writer who directly inserts this peculiarity into the Septuagint!

[40] *Ps.* 16:14 (mod.).

[41] Thdr. Mops., *Ps.* 48:16: "Everywhere in the psalms the word *but* [πλήν] occurs not to convey a particular meaning, but is inserted because of the Hebrew particularity." Also see Thdr. Mops., *Ps.* 37:13; Thdt., *Is.* 9:20.

[42] It is important to note, however, that sometimes Antiochenes attribute the peculiarities to the Greek translators. Diodore, for instance, remarks that the ἰδίωμα of a change of speakers in the Psalms was an "obscurity obviously consequent upon the translation" (*Ps.* 20:13). Thdr. Mops., *Ps.* 55:7: "Now, we found this distinguishing feature used by blessed David in many other places in the psalms as well [i.e., unnecessary insertion of "and"], either arising from a Hebrew peculiarity or occurring this way in the translation" (mod.). Note as well how, speaking of the same peculiarity (ἐναλλαγὴ χρόνου), Theodore will sometimes says it arises "from the translation [ἀπὸ τῆς ἑρμηνείας]" (*Ps.* 34:8; 39:12), while at other times it is an ἰδίωμα Ἑβραϊκόν or an instance of Davidic usage (*Os.* 9:3; *Joel* 2:18). Thdt., *Ps.* 42:3; *Is.* 9:20. On this issue, see Schäublin, *Untersuchungen*, 130–1; Guinot, *L'Exégèse de Théodoret*, 347.

[43] Diod., *Rom.* 9:11; Thdr. Mops., *Ps.* 50:6; *Rom.* 9:22–4; Thdt., *Ps.* 109:1.

persons also occurs in the NT: "even in the New Testament" the exchange of persons "is found imported from the Hebrew peculiarity [ἐκ τοῦ ἑβραϊκοῦ ἰδιώματος… μετακομισθέν] by the blessed apostles."[44] While it is not entirely clear how Antiochene scholars thought NT authors were informed by Hebrew peculiarities (were they bilingual, or limited to one language, either Greek or Hebrew?), they clearly thought the Greek of the NT had been shaped by Hebrew literary conventions.[45]

In sum, Adrian's interest in the peculiarities of the "Hebrew" literary style was more specifically an interest in the Greek language of his two testaments whose peculiarities were ultimately derived from the Hebrew language. Is an ἰδίωμα of the Hebrew language, then, a "Hebraism" as some scholars have rendered the term?[46] I have resisted such a translation since it can easily mislead. "Hebraisms" are customarily understood to be unusual Greek linguistic features that can *only* be explained by the influence of a Semitic text or mindset.[47] There are certainly cases where Adrian identifies Hebraisms of this sort: for example, the instrumental use of ἐν (65),[48] the superfluous use of ἰδού (71.1), the connotations of "washing one's hands" (35), and the range of meanings of σάρξ (57).[49] But there are a number of peculiarities discussed in the *Introduction* that do not map onto this definition of a Hebraism. For instance, Adrian notes that the Bible can make comparisons without the particle ὡς ("like" or "as") (38), depict God anthropomorphically, and use a range of figures

---

[44] Thdr. Mops., *Ps.* 35:7.

[45] On Hebrew peculiarities in Paul, see esp. Guinot, *L'Exégèse de Théodoret*, 353–6. Note as well that Theodoret claims Paul wrote the letter to the Hebrews in Hebrew, and that it was subsequently translated into Greek by Clement (Thdt., *Heb.* [PG 82.677]; also see Chrys., *hom. in 2 Tim. 4.3*).

[46] Schäublin, *Untersuchungen*, 127–9; Guinot, *L'Exégèse de Théodoret de Cyr*, 346; Natalio Fernández Marcos, "Theodoret's Philological Remarks on the Language of the Septuagint," in *Jerusalem, Alexandria, Rome: Studies in Ancient Cultural Interaction in Honour of A. Hilhorst*, ed. E. G. Martínez and G. P. Luttikheizen (Leiden: Brill, 2003), 108.

[47] For example, BDF §4; Natalio Fernández Marcos, *The Septuagint in Context: Introduction to the Greek Versions of the Bible*, trans. Wilfred G. E. Watson (Leiden: Brill, 2000), 366. While it is widely acknowledged that Semitisms have left their mark on these Greek collections, especially influencing the style and semantic range of individual words, the degree and kinds of influence is still debated. For Semitisms and the LXX, see Henry St. John Thackery, *A Grammar of the Old Testament in Greek*, vol. 1, *Introduction, Orthography and Accidence* (Cambridge: Cambridge University Press, 1909), 25–54; Peter Walters, *The Text of the Septuagint: Its Corruptions and their Emendation* (Cambridge: Cambridge University Press, 1973); Swete, *Introduction to the Old Testament in Greek*, esp. 305–9 and 323–30; Sidney Jellicoe, *The Septuagint and Modern Study* (Oxford: Clarendon, 1968), 314–37; Marcos, *Septuagint in Context*, 18–31. For Semitisms and the NT: K. Beyer, *Semitische Syntax im Neuen Testament* (Göttingen: Vandenhoeck & Ruprecht, 1962); C. F. D. Moule, *An Idiom Book of New Testament Greek*, 2nd ed. (Cambridge: Cambridge University Press, 1963), 1–4; James H. Moulton and Wilbert F. Howard, *A Grammar of New Testament Greek*, vol. 2, *Accidence and Word-Formation* (Edinburgh: T. & T. Clark, 1963), 411–86. For a good overview of the debates surrounding the nature of NT Greek, see James W. Voelz, "The Language of the New Testament," *ANRW* 2.25.2: 893–977.

[48] S.v. ἐν BDAG 5.

[49] S.v. σάρξ BDAG 3.a; Swete, *An Introduction to the Old Testament in Greek*, 307–8.

and tropes that, while departures from a plain way of writing, obviously surfaced in Greek literature with no appreciable Hebraic backdrop. Peculiarities such as these are not "Hebraisms" in the sense noted above since they also occurred in Greek literature without a Hebrew influence. As noted above, when Adrian spoke of a Hebrew ἰδίωμα, this primarily signified an *unusual* and *recurring* literary feature in his Greek Bible that had some Hebrew precedent. While there are times when these unusual expressions were also *unique* to the Hebrew language, more often than not, they were simply unconventional expressions shared by a wide variety of authors, including Greek writers with no knowledge of Hebrew.[50]

4. The *Introduction* and parallels in Greco-Roman literary criticism

The *Introduction*, then, was a treatise on the unusual literary characteristics of the Greek Bible. Goessling claimed that Adrian's approach to the biblical material was "entirely original" when compared with the other early Christian introductions to Scripture.[51] Yet as we have seen in the preceding discussion, his interests were not unique to him: Antiochene biblical scholars repeatedly drew attention to these ἰδιώματα and Theodore's preface to his *Commentary on the Psalms* offered an extended discussion of this issue. It is also important to observe that Adrian's interest was not restricted to his own exegetical tradition. Even if not with the same frequency, the wider Greek[52] and Latin[53] exegetical worlds also evinced an interest in Scripture's unusual literary features. There is also an important treatise that Goessling overlooked within Augustine's exegetical corpus that provides a striking Latin parallel to the *Introduction*: the *Sayings on the Heptateuch* (*locutionum in Heptateuchum libri septem*) written from 419 to 422/423, perhaps contemporaneously to Adrian's own *Introduction*.[54] Augustine opens the work as follows: "There are scriptural expressions which appear to conform to the special literary properties (*proprietates*) of the Hebrew and Greek language, which the Greeks call *idiomata* (*Locutiones scripturarum, quae videntur secundum proprietates, quae idiomata graece vocantur, linguae hebraicae vel graecae*)." After this sentence he begins to list, in canonical order, unusual expressions in his Latin scriptural text, glossing

---

[50] So also Aug., *retr.* 2.54(80); Cass., *inst.* 1.15.2.   [51] Goessling, *Adrians ΕΙΣΑΓΩΓΗ*, 43.

[52] Or., *Cels.* 6.17; Eus., *Ps.* 25:1; Didym. *Ps.* 24:7; Cyr. *Ps.* 3:8; Isid. Pelus., *ep.* 1398.

[53] Hier., *tract. Ps.* 15:7; idem, *epp.* 55.1; 57.5; 85.5; 106.3; 106.30; Aug., *ver. rel.* 50.99; Cass., *inst.* 1.15.2–8; *Ps.* 2:7; 7:9; 16:2; 21:22; 26:12, etc., and in particular, his reference to several figures in the preceding Latin tradition (he names Jerome, Ambrose, Hilary, and Augustine) who were all interested in unusual scriptural expressions (*proem. Ps.* 15). Cassiodorus even inserted into the margins of his *Ps.* a symbol that identified the presence of a peculiarity in the biblical text (*inst.* 1.26.2; O'Donnell, *Cassiodorus*, 159–61, esp. 160 fn. 31).

[54] For orientation to this work, see Dorothea Weber, "Locutiones," in *Augustinus-Lexikon*, ed. Cornelius Mayer et al., vol. 3.7/8 (Basel: Schwabe, 2010), 1048–54.

these lemmata with a more comprehensible Latin paraphrase. While there are notable differences between this treatise and Adrian's, the central topic remains the same.[55] This work—outside every scholarly construct for the "Antiochene exegetical school"—is in fact the closest surviving parallel to Adrian's *Introduction* in early Christian literature.[56]

Yet the closest parallel to Adrian's treatise arguably does not even come from within the Christian ambit. The short literary essay on Thucydides by the Roman historian and rhetorician Dionysius of Halicarnassus (first century BCE) bears a number of remarkable terminological, thematic, and structural resemblances to Adrian's own work. Dionysius opens his *Second Letter to Ammaeus* as follows, alluding to his earlier treatise, *On Thucydides*:

> I thought I had sufficiently indicated the literary style of Thucydides [τὸν Θουκυδίδου χαρακτῆρα] when describing the most important and remarkable of his peculiarities [τῶν ... ἰδιωμάτων] which seemed to me to distinguish him the most from previous orators and historians.[57]

Here is the first parallel between Dionysius' letter and Adrian's *Introduction*: both authors share the same topic and use the same vocabulary to announce it. Dionysius, like Adrian, is focused on the "peculiarities" of "literary style" (ἰδιώματα and χαρακτήρ, respectively). Dionysius continues, relaying Ammaeus' request that he expound in more detail on an earlier section of his *On Thucydides*:

> you [Ammaeus] think that my description of the peculiarities of his style [τὴν δήλωσιν τῶν ἰδιωμάτων τοῦ χαραχτῆρος] would become more precise if, side by side with each of my assertions, I would illustrate with examples drawn from the author, which those who author rhetorical handbooks or introductions to literary composition do [ὃ οἱ τὰς τέχνας καὶ τὰς εἰσαγωγὰς τῶν λόγων πραγματευόμενοι ποιοῦσιν].[58]

---

[55] In his *Retractations* Augustine describes the *Sayings on the Heptateuch*, and its importance, as follows: "I composed seven books on the seven Books of the Divine Scriptures, that is, on the five Books of Moses, on the one of Josue, and on the one of Judges, noting in each the modes of expressions which are less frequently used in our language (*feci notatis locutionibus singulorum quae minus usitatae sunt linguae nostrae*). Readers, by giving insufficient attention to these forms of expression when seeking the meaning of the Divine Scriptures, although this is a special mode of expression (*cum sit locutionis genus*), sometimes extract a meaning which, indeed, is not inconsistent with the truth, and yet is found not to be the meaning intended by the author; but it seems more credible that he expressed this by employing a special mode of expression (*genere locutionis*). Accordingly, many obscure passages in the Holy Scriptures become clear only when one understands the mode of expression" (*retr.* 2.54[80]).

[56] It is unclear why Cassiodorus did not include the *Sayings on the Heptateuch* in his collection of introductions when it was far closer to the concerns of Adrian's *Introduction* than the work of Augustine that he did include, *On Christian Learning*. Perhaps the comparative brevity of the latter work proved attractive to Cassiodorus, or was what qualified it as an introduction in his mind. Note that Cassiodorus did mention the *Sayings on the Heptateuch* later in the *Institutions* (1.15.2) when discussing *proprietates*. See also *proem. Ps.* 15 where Cassiodorus mentions both *On Christian Learning* and the *Sayings on the Heptateuch* in the context of deciphering scriptural expressions.

[57] *2 Amm.* 1.1 (mod.).   [58] *2 Amm.* 1.2 (mod.).

Here is a second parallel. The basic structure of Dionysius' letter (first identifying a peculiarity, and then illustrating it with concrete examples) corresponds to the format of much of Adrian's treatise where peculiarities are also catalogued and illustrated. Moreover, this format, Dionysius notes, is employed by those who write "introductions [τὰς εἰσαγωγὰς] to literary composition." Of course, εἰσαγωγή is the very term Adrian uses in the title of his treatise. Adrian's use of this term signaled more than a general orientation to Scripture, but as Dionysius here notes, also a catalogue-style approach to textbook writing that was reflective of the classroom experience.[59] The third major parallel concerns the classification of stylistic peculiarities. Dionysius notes that the "peculiarities" of Thucydides' style fall into two main categories: diction (ἐκλογή) and word arrangement (σύνθεσις).[60] Adrian lists these two categories as well—diction (λέξις) and word arrangement (σύνθεσις)—and adds a third category, thought or message (διάνοια). While Dionysius only speaks here of two components of style, as we have seen above, he can elsewhere speak of the same three components that Adrian does, and marks them with the same vocabulary as well.

Dionysius' *Second Letter to Ammaeus* offers one of the most striking parallels to Adrian's *Introduction* in ancient Greek literature. The resemblances are both precise and extensive. When we consider, moreover, the penchant for rhetorical criticism that has long been associated with Antiochene biblical scholars, it is not implausible to suggest that Adrian was directly familiar with several writings in this rhetorician's corpus.[61]

---

[59] Dionysius capitulates to Ammaeus' request, saying he will "adopt the role of a teacher [τὸ διδασκαλικὸν σχῆμα λαβών]" (*2 Amm.* 1.2 [mod.]).

[60] *Th.* 24.1–2. The former includes unusual word choices (*2 Amm.* 3.1), while the latter includes syntactical oddities like using verbs for nouns, and vice versa (4–5); interchanging passive and active forms of verbs (7–8), as well as a number of other interchanges: the singular and plural (9), genders (10), cases (11), tenses (12), treating persons as things and vice versa (14); insertion of parenthetical clauses that obscure meaning (15); use of affected figures (17). Several of these peculiarities will also surface in Adrian's *Introduction*.

[61] On possible additional sources for Adrian from the rhetorical tradition, see Martens, "Adrian's *Introduction to the Divine Scriptures* and Greco-Roman Rhetorical Theory on Style," 210–11.

3

Structure and Scholarly Conventions

A. STRUCTURE

The threefold division of style in the opening sentence of the *Introduction* also signals the tripartite structure of the treatise. I outline the work as follows:

> Treatise Proper: Peculiarities of the Hebrew Literary Style
>> Prologue: Topic and Tripartite Outline (1)
>> Part I: Peculiarities of Message (2–18)
>>> List and Catalogue of Anthropomorphisms (2–2.15) and Transition Sentence (3)
>>> Solutions to Anthropomorphisms (4.1–17) with Conclusion (18)
>> Part II: Peculiarities of Diction (19–65)
>> Part III: Peculiarities of Syntax (66–71.5)
>> Conclusion of Treatise Proper (72)
> Appendices (73–9)
>> List and Catalogue of Twenty-Two Tropes (73–73.22)
>> Genres of Scripture and Temporal References of Prophecy (74–74.3.3)
>> Guidelines for Interpreting Scripture (75–8)
>> Prophecy, Prose, and Meter (79)

As is clear from this outline, the *Introduction* contains a coherent and self-standing treatise on the peculiarities of the Hebrew literary style ("Treatise Proper"), followed by a series of short, concluding appendices that address central issues in scriptural interpretation. The division between these two parts of the treatise is indicated in section 72 where, after illustrating the last figure of section three, Adrian writes, "After acquiring resources from this treatise, diligent students will discover in their zeal for knowledge that a path and gate leads [them] toward the meaning of sacred Scripture."[1] This invitation to further inquiry into Scripture based upon what the reader has

---

[1] Here is how the corresponding section in R2 reads: "Nothing should prevent us from also attaining clarity about the most common [scriptural] tropes for the purpose of a more beneficial

successfully gathered from the *Introduction* reads as a conclusion to the fore-going material. Immediately after this sentence Adrian provides a list of twenty-two tropes and concludes with the observation that these tropes "clearly go along with Scripture's literary peculiarities" that were discussed in the preceding section of the treatise (73).[2] This discussion of tropes begins the first postscript.

By modern conventions, Adrian's *Introduction* might appear to lack coherence with its four concluding appendices.[3] An open structure such as this, however, was not uncommon in many Greco-Roman manuals, even those prefaced with clear outlines. We often find a loose arrangement, with excurses embedded into the main discussion, or concluding sections annexed to the main material. Many examples could be provided to illustrate this point, but two will suffice. Eusebius' introduction to the Bible, the *General Elementary Introduction*, was originally a ten-book treatise of which only books six through nine now survive. In the first five books Eusebius seems to have addressed a largely pagan audience with an orientation to the life and teaching of Christ. But books six through nine were sufficiently different in scope, and perhaps audience, from the preceding books that Eusebius gave them a distinct subtitle: the *Prophetic Eclogues* (ἐκλογαὶ προφετικαί). In this section of his treatise he took a different approach to Scripture, providing readers with a christological reading of large swathes of the OT.[4] Pseudo-Plutarch's *Essay on the Life and Poetry of Homer* provides another example of an even less-structured treatise. This introduction to Homer was, in the words of its translator Robert Lamberton, "a rambling, encyclopedic work."[5] It had two main sections on Homeric diction and discourse, but interspersed throughout the treatise were a number of additional observations about his poetry. Not unlike Adrian's *Introduction* this treatise too concluded with "varia" loosely connected to the preceding material.[6]

While Adrian's concluding appendices are distinct from his discussion of peculiarities, they are not so unrelated as to raise questions about their authenticity.[7] There are some important links. For instance, a number of the tropes

apprehension of the literary style of divine precepts, so that we might also indicate some path and gate that leads to the meaning of sacred Scripture for those individuals of the same community of faith who are equally diligent and eager for knowledge."

[2] For more on structure of work, and my correction of Goessling's proposal (*Adrians ΕΙΣΑΓΩΓΗ*, 31–7; 40), see Martens, "Adrian's *Introduction to the Divine Scriptures* and Greco-Roman Rhetorical Theory on Style," 210–16.

[3] Léonas characterizes the treatise as a "work-in-process" ("Hadrian's Philological Remarks," 400–1).

[4] Johnson, "Eusebius the Educator," 106–7.

[5] J. J. Keaney and Robert Lamberton, *Plutarch: Essay on the Life and Poetry of Homer* (Atlanta: Scholars Press, 1996), 10.

[6] See as well, Malcolm Heath, "Codifications of Rhetoric," in *The Cambridge Companion to Ancient Rhetoric*, ed. Erik Gunderson (Cambridge: Cambridge University Press, 2009), 62–3; Roberts, *Demetrius on Style*, 28–31; Donald A. Russell, ed., *"Longinus" on the Sublime* (Oxford: Clarendon, 1964), xiii–xiv, xx–xxii; the concluding appendices to Hermog., *form.*

[7] As Goessling entertained at *Adrians ΕΙΣΑΓΩΓΗ*, 31.

defined and illustrated in the catalogue at the end of the *Introduction* (73–73.22) are already discussed in the preceding sections of the treatise: note the prior mention of metaphor (27; 38; 44), synecdoche (2.15; 17), and representational language (2; 4.10). In Adrian's discussion of the sequence for proper biblical interpretation he likens interpretation to potentially perilous travel by land and sea—the same metaphors he uses to conclude the treatise in section 72 when he talks about students who, following the principles of the *Introduction*, will find "a path and gate" that "leads" them to Scripture's message. In section 78 he talks about the body, limbs, and joints of Scripture, an allusion to his tripartite division of the scriptural style into its message, wording, and syntax (1). There are other connections as well. Since these concluding sections do not function as a coherent fourth part, nor recapitulate the contents of the work, it seems best to view them as a series of appendices, attached for the reader's additional benefit.[8]

B. SCHOLARLY CONVENTIONS

Adrian's *Introduction* exemplifies a number of important conventions widely used in Greco-Roman scholarly writing. I will highlight the following formal characteristics: the division of material into smaller parts, the use of catalogues, a variety of space-saving conventions, and finally, the problems-and-solutions format for literary scholarship.[9] Viewed collectively, these scholarly characteristics reinforce the interpretation that the *Introduction* was closely tied to the schoolroom—it was not only intended for teachers and students, but perhaps also emerged out of the classroom setting.

1. Divisions

One of the main procedures employed in Greco-Roman textbook writing was the method of division ($\delta\iota\alpha\acute{\iota}\rho\epsilon\sigma\iota\varsigma$) in which a topic was classified into its smaller, constituent parts (typically designated by terms like $\mu\acute{\epsilon}\rho\sigma\varsigma$, $\gamma\acute{\epsilon}\nu\sigma\varsigma$, or $\epsilon\mathring{\iota}\delta\sigma\varsigma$). In his study of representative Greco-Roman textbooks, Manfred Fuhrmann demonstrated how common this pedagogical technique was: authors of treatises—on rhetoric, grammar, architecture, medicine, and so forth—often

---

[8] See the similar approach to Pseudo-Aristides, *On Political Discourse* by Patillon, *Pseudo-Aelius Aristides: Arts Rhétoriques*, 2 vols. (Paris: Les Belles Lettres, 2002), vol. 1, xi–xii.

[9] The main studies on Greco-Roman textbooks are Fuhrmann, *Das Systematische Lehrbuch*; Asper, *Griechische Wissenschaftstexte*; Marco Formisano, *Tecnica e scrittura: Le letterature tecnico-scientifiche nello spazio letterario tardolatino* (Rome: Carocci, 2001). On the conventions of scholarly Greek, see Dickey, *Ancient Greek Scholarship*, 107–23.

presented a discipline to their readers first by subdividing it into smaller, more accessible parts and then analyzing and distinguishing these from one another.[10] Markus Asper has recently made a more thorough examination of Greek scholarly writing and argues that this "dihaeretical" structure was one of the basic literary formats of "introductions" in antiquity.[11]

Adrian's treatise strongly resembles the dihaeretical introduction. He avails himself of this technique several times in his *Introduction*, beginning with the opening sentence of the work: "There are three kinds [εἴδη] of peculiarities of the Hebrew literary style..." (1).[12] Toward the end of the *Introduction* Adrian again practices division, parsing Scripture into two literary forms: "Now there are two kinds [εἴδη] of divine Scripture: prophetic and narratival" (74). He continues, further subdividing prophecy into three classes based upon its temporal reference: some prophecies refer to the past, others to the present, and many to the future (74.1–3). We also often encounter division in Adrian's lexicographical analyses. For instance, the term σάρξ can refer either to the organism, badness, mortality, or kinship (57.1–4). The term πνεῦμα can signify will, a gift, an angel, the soul, a voice, or the wind (59.1–6). The noun αἰών gets used in three ways (62.1–3), and so on. In most cases, Adrian subdivides topics dichotomously or trichotomously, with the resulting parts syntactically connected with μέν-δέ, καί or ἤτοι-ἤ.

Traces of this same approach are scattered throughout Antiochene biblical commentaries. Diodore's *Commentary on the Psalms*, a work with which Adrian was almost certainly familiar, serves as a representative example. In Diodore's preface he announces that the "overall theme of the psalms, then, is divided into these two parts [διῄρεται τὰ μέρη], the moral and the doctrinal" (*proem. Ps.*). He continues with further subdivisions:

> The moral part is itself divided: certain psalms correct individual behavior, some deal with the race of the Jews alone, others with people in general...Likewise...the doctrinal content is divided into two: some psalms are addressed to those who believe things came into being of themselves, other ones to those claiming these things do not fall under providence. (*proem. Ps.*)

There are several other instances of division in this preface, but perhaps the most interesting for our purposes is Diodore's comment that "every prophetic literary form is divided into three [ὅτι τὸ προφητικὸν ἅπαν εἶδος τριχῇ τέμνεται]—future, present, and past" (*proem. Ps.*).[13] This is the very same point that Adrian makes in section 74.

---

[10] Fuhrmann, *Das Systematische Lehrbuch*, 7–8, *passim*.

[11] Asper, *Griechische Wissenschaftstexte*, 274–82, including the identification of a number of εἰσαγωγαί from antiquity (by Cleonides, Galen, Porphyry, Alypius) that represent the dihaeretical structure.

[12] Note as well the use of the technical term διαίρεσις (division, category) in section 3 to refer to the fifteen subcategories created in the preceding paragraphs.

[13] See as well Thdt., *proem. Ps.* 5.

2. Catalogues

Another widespread phenomenon in Greco-Roman textbooks was the production of lists.[14] As Fuhrmann has shown, catalogues were a standard feature of
general textbook writing, but they were especially prominent in introductory
manuals. We find confirmation of this point in Dionysius of Halicarnassus'
aforementioned *Second Letter to Ammaeus* where he associates the term
εἰσαγωγή with an illustrated catalogue:

> …you [Ammaeus] think that my description of the peculiarities of his [Thucydi-
> des'] style would become more precise if, side by side with each of my assertions,
> I would illustrate with examples drawn from the author, which those who author
> rhetorical handbooks or introductions to literary composition do [ὃ οἱ τὰς τέχνας
> καὶ τὰς εἰσαγωγὰς τῶν λόγων πραγματευόμενοι ποιοῦσιν].[15]

As already noted, the term εἰσαγωγή was associated by Dionysius, and likely
Adrian too, with a specific format of textbook writing in which authors provided readers with illustrations of the items they were listing or cataloguing.

There are three illustrated catalogues in Adrian's manual. The first occurs at
the beginning where he provides a list of fifteen kinds of anthropomorphisms
that readers will find in Scripture (2). He then moves sequentially from one
anthropomorphism to the next, illustrating each peculiarity with a number of
scriptural verses (2–2.15).[16] Another catalogue with a similar format occurs
toward the end of the treatise. Adrian provides a list of the most common tropes
in Scripture (73) before proceeding to define and illustrate them (73–73.22).[17]
Finally, section three on peculiarities of syntax is entirely a catalogue of figures
(66–71.5). However, it is formatted differently than the other two catalogues since
it lacks an introductory sentence that lists the figures that will subsequently be
illustrated. Rather, Adrian moves immediately into a discussion of the first
figure and again provides biblical verses that illustrate the figure in question.

Not surprisingly, we find catalogues such as these in other Antiochene exegetical writings. As already noted, in his now-lost prologue to his *Commentary on
the Psalms*, Theodore of Mopsuestia assembled a list of peculiarities in Scripture
(*inter proprietatum collectiones*).[18] An extant catalogue occurs in Diodore's
Commentary on Psalm 118 where he insisted that the interpreter "must classify

[14] Fuhrmann, *Systematische Lehrbuch*, 27, 57, 77, 97, 120; Asper, *Griechische Wissenschaftstexte*, 57–96. Markus Asper, "Katalog," *HWRh* 4 (1998): 915–22.
[15] *2 Amm.* 1.2 (mod.).
[16] Note Adrian's use of the term ὑπόδειγμα ("illustration") in 3 to refer to the biblical passages
that exemplify each of his anthropomorphic categories.
[17] Definitions, of course, played a prominent role in textbooks and had the additional advantage of helping students articulate the differences (διαφοραί) between items grouped under the
same umbrella heading (Fuhrmann, *Systematische Lehrbuch*, 7–8, 22, 37–8). Note Adrian's
related counsel that instructors need to teach the "differentiation of tropes [τὴν τῶν τρόπων
διάκρισιν]" (76).
[18] Thdr. Mops., *Ps.* 15:4.

and clarify [φυλοκρινεῖν καὶ σαφηνίζειν] each trope," and proceeded to define and illustrate ἀλληγορία, θεωρία, τροπολογία, παραβολή, ἔλλειψις, and αἴνιγμα (*proem. Ps. 118*). Another important catalogue occurs in the preface to Polychronius' *Commentary on Job*, where he lists ten causes for the obscurity in Scripture.[19] Listing is a conspicuous exercise in Antiochene biblical exegesis.

3. Space-saving conventions

Readers of the *Introduction* will immediately notice a stylized prose that is also typical of Greek scholarly writing. Eleanor Dickey identifies key stylistic features of Greek scholarship, including the use of short sentences, straightforward syntax, technical terminology, and space-saving conventions.[20] With the exception of the winding prose in a few concluding paragraphs of the *Introduction* (75–6), this description aptly characterizes the style of Adrian's Greek. I draw attention here briefly to the last item on Dickey's list, the employment of space-saving conventions. Some are more innocuous than others. For example, Adrian usually does not supply "Scripture" as the grammatical subject of a sentence.[21] There are also a number of occasions where the main verb is missing, as in 4.2 where it simply reads, Τὸ δὲ ἐξιλεωτικὸν αὐτοῦ ὦτα καὶ ἀκοήν. This can be translated as: "His appeasable nature [Scripture calls] 'ears' and 'hearing.'"

The most prominent space-saving feature in the *Introduction* occurs throughout scholarly Greek, especially the scholia on classical literature: it is the basic formula where a lemma (a word or phrase to be clarified) is followed by an illustration, definition, or explanation. For instance, the entry at 2.1 reads, Ἀπὸ μὲν μελῶν· ὡς τό, **τά βλέφαρα αὐτοῦ ἐξετάζει τοὺς υἱοὺς τῶν ἀνθρώπων**. This can literally be translated as, "From bodily parts: for example, 'his eyelids examine the sons of men.'" It is often more helpful, however, to expand this space-saving convention to make the prose more accessible. Adrian has something like the following in mind: "[There are depictions of God in Scripture drawn] from bodily parts: for example..." Note that Adrian also uses a sequence of lemmas in the *Introduction*, as in 73.4 (R1) where the initial lemma is followed by a definition, then this definition, in turn, serves as the lemma for the biblical illustration that follows, and finally, this illustration serves as the lemma for the actual interpretation. We read: Κατὰ συνεκδοχήν· ὅταν ἀπὸ μέρους τὸ ὅλον δηλοῖ· ὡς τό, **τὴν ψυχήν μου ἐπέστρεψεν**, ἵνα εἴπῃ ἐμέ. This can be translated as: "Synecdoche: whenever

---

[19] Polychr., *fr. Job* prol. 2.
[20] Dickey, *Ancient Greek Scholarship*, 107. Also see Nünlist, *The Ancient Critic at Work*, 8–14 for a brief discussion of the characteristics of Greek scholia.
[21] Dickey, *Ancient Greek Scholarship*, 121–2.

[Scripture] indicates the whole by means of a part. For example, [it says] 'he restored my soul' (Ps 22[23]:3), in order to say '[he restored] me.' "

Probably the most serious source of confusion for readers of the *Introduction* is the generally elliptical nature of the treatise. For instance, at 20 Adrian writes, "[Saying] 'teach' instead of 'cause.' For example, 'and teach me that you are God, my Savior' (Ps 24[25]:5)!" Even with the hermeneutical principle in mind ("teach" = "cause"), it is hard to know how Adrian thinks his readers ought to hear this verse. Fortunately, the close thematic relationship between the *Introduction* and Theodore's *Commentary on the Psalms* often allows us to reconstruct what Adrian might have had in mind. Here is how Theodore glosses the above verse: the Psalmist says " 'Teach me'—that is, Cause me to arrive at the knowledge of your divinity by the actual outcome of events" (*Ps.* 24:5). Or again, at 42 Adrian announces the principle that Scripture often attributes responsibility for an action to agents who are not actually culpable. He then illustrates with a biblical phrase: "in order that your foot may be dipped in blood" (Ps 67:24 [68:23]), and glosses as follows: ἀντὶ τοῦ ἀνάγκη πᾶσα. The reader is left with very little to reconstruct the sense. In this case, however, we find more help in R2 where the words ἀνάγκη πᾶσα are embedded in a larger sentence which helps the reader reconstruct what Adrian probably had in mind. This latter example is instructive since it highlights that it is not always clear who is responsible for the compressed nature of the *Introduction*. In this case, the subsequent scribal tradition is almost certainly responsible for the highly abbreviated explanatory gloss in R1, whereas there are other cases where the conciseness likely goes back to Adrian himself.

4. Problems and solutions

A widespread format for textual exegesis in classical and post-classical antiquity centered on the identification of difficulties or problems in the treatise at hand.[22] This style of inquiry was closely associated with the critical reception of Homer's poems, whose puzzles—in their critics' eyes—could range widely from

[22] In what follows I rely on the following: Karl Lehrs, *De Aristarchi studiis Homericis*, 3rd ed. (Leipzig: Hirzelium, 1882), 197–221; A. Gudeman, "Λύσεις," *PW* 13.2 (1927): 2511–29; Gustave Bardy, "La littérature patristique des 'Quaestiones et Responsiones' sur l'Écriture Sainte," *RB* 41 (1932): 210–36, 341–69, 515–37; 42 (1933): 14–30, 211–29, 328–52; Heinrich Dörrie and Hermann Dörries, "Erotapokriseis," *RAC* 6 (1966): 342–70; O. Dreyer, "Lyseis," *KP* 3.16–17 (1968/69): 832–3; Schäublin, *Untersuchungen*, 49–51, 55–65; Adam Kamesar, *Jerome, Greek Scholarship, and the Hebrew Bible: A Study of the Quaestiones Hebraicae in Genesim* (Oxford: Oxford University Press, 1993), 82–96; Lorenzo Perrone, "Sulla preistoria delle *quaestiones* nella letteratura patristica: Presupposti e eviluppi del genere letterario fino al IV sec," *AnnSE* 8 (1991): 485–505; Ter Haar Romeny, *A Syrian in Greek Dress*, 12–19; Annelie Volgers and Claudio Zamagni, eds., *Erotapokriseis: Early Christian Question-and-Answer Literature in Context* (Leuven: Peeters, 2004); Mansfeld, *Prolegomena*, 2–3; H. Greg Snyder, *Teachers and Texts in the Ancient World: Philosophers, Jews and Christians* (London: Routledge, 2000), 115–18.

grammatical and stylistic problems, to difficulties in content, chiefly Homer's troublingly anthropomorphic portrayals of the gods. Commentators would raise a question, difficulty, or problem in the text (customary terms include ζήτημα, ἀπορία, πρόβλημα) and in turn propose a solution (λύσις). The chief advantage of this approach to textual study was that it catered to the targeted interpretation of particularly challenging passages, rather than tying interpreter (and student or reader) to a systematic exposition of the entire text. This format of textual inquiry frequently surfaced in introductory treatises and often reflected the dynamics of the classroom setting where teachers and students wrestled with perplexing passages in classical literature. Numerous question-and-answer commentaries were written between the third century BCE and third century CE.

Not surprisingly, this approach to commentary also appeared among early Christian biblical scholars, many of whom were trained in this tradition of Homeric exegesis and wrestled with analogous difficulties in their own Scriptures. This approach to Scripture was especially prominent in the Antiochene exegetical tradition: Eusebius of Emesa (on the Octateuch), Diodore of Tarsus (on the Octateuch), Theodoret of Cyrus (on the Octateuch, Kingdoms, and Chronicles), and Junillus (*Handbook*) each wrote treatises on Scripture that adopted this problems-and-solutions or questions-and-answers format. Even though Adrian's *Introduction* has been overlooked as a representative of this style of interpretation, his treatise belongs to this particular tradition of textual scholarship. Indeed it fits particularly well: like the aforementioned tradition of Homeric scholarship (with which he was familiar), Adrian's work was also an introductory manual, addressed troubling anthropomorphisms that called for a solution, and was designed for classroom use.

The first part of Adrian's treatise is structured as a problems-and-solutions commentary on Scripture. Three features merit attention. First, this commentary is not tied to a particular biblical book, but rather orients itself around a theme, the anthropomorphic depiction of God in Scripture.[23] Adrian does not use the term ἀνθρωπόμορφος, yet that is precisely the concern of the opening section of his treatise: it is a peculiarity of the scriptural message to portray an incorporeal God as bodily and subject to emotion. As noted above, a prominent concern in the reception history of Homer was his portrayal of the gods as undignified and immortal—a concern that also surfaced in the questions-and-answers literature on his poetry (such as Heraclitus' *Homeric Problems*).[24] The same concern for the worrisome anthropomorphic depictions of God occasionally surfaced in the Antiochene exegetical tradition.[25] It is unlikely, however, that Adrian had a well-defined theological opponent in view here. In keeping

---

[23] On the thematic focus in other early Christian writers, see Schäublin, *Untersuchungen*, 50–1 fn. 31.

[24] Nünlist, *Ancient Critic at Work*, 13, 270, 278–9.

[25] Diod., *fr. Gen.* 6:6; Thdt., *qu. in Gen.* 23.

with the tenor of a manual pitched to beginning readers of Scripture, it seems more likely that a pedagogical rather than an adversarial or apologetic intent was being expressed.[26] The *Introduction* was designed to help students not stumble over anthropomorphic depictions of God, just like the student approaching Homer for the first time required counsel on avoiding a crassly superficial assessment of his poetry.

The second feature of Adrian's problems-and-solutions commentary is its atypical format.[27] Customarily, ancient interpreters dealt with textual problems in an alternating manner: a problem was followed by its solution, which gave way to the next problem and its corresponding solution, and so on. Adrian organized his material differently. In the opening section of the *Introduction* he first provides a list of anthropomorphisms (2–2.15), before offering a corresponding catalogue of explanations (4–4.17). But this different organization should not raise serious doubts about whether Adrian was employing a problems-and-solutions format in the first section of his treatise: he uses the technical term ἐπίλυσις ("explanation"). In the sentence that transitions readers from his list of anthropomorphisms to his interpretations of them, Adrian writes, "An explanation (ἐπίλυσις) of the categories of the aforementioned peculiarities will now be indicated that aims for a more complete presentation of their rationale." What immediately follows are Adrian's clarifications of the preceding list of anthropomorphisms.

Finally, a notable feature of his "solutions" is his stated desire not simply to gloss troubling depictions of God, but also to provide the underlying reason or rationale (αἰτιολογία) that accounts for why these depictions were used in the first place.[28] Here, for instance, is how Adrian accounts for the attribution of "anger" and "wrath" to God in Scripture:

> It calls the opposition of God's will to evil his "anger" and "wrath," since enmity toward hostile forces occurs among us. For example, "from then is your wrath" (Ps 75:8 [76:7]), instead of "from the beginning, and always, you have been disposed to oppose evil" (5).

We express anger against hostile forces or whatever might oppose us; God is also opposed to things (i.e., evil), and to communicate this, biblical writers have taken what occurs literally in us—our anger and wrath—and applied it figuratively to God. For Adrian the human sphere accounts not only for the peculiar language used to depict God (e.g., "anger") but also for what that language must signify (God's "anger," stands for his opposition to evil, since our anger is expressed against hostile forces).

[26] On the various audiences and purposes for problems-and-solutions commentaries on Scripture, see Thdt., *proem. qu. in Oct.* On the aims of these commentaries, also see Schäublin, *Untersuchungen*, 57–8.

[27] On the multiple formatting options, see Dörrie and Dörries, "Erotapokriseis," 342–70.

[28] On the articulation of the fundamental principles of a topic in "introductions," see Asper, *Griechische Wissenschaftstexte*, 238–44.

4

Exegetical Guidelines and Classroom Setting

In the concluding paragraphs of the *Introduction* Adrian identifies his audience as "those who profess to teach." He mentions "exegetical exercises of classroom teaching" and prescribes a sequence of steps for scriptural exegesis that will be useful for "pupils" (75–6). It is usually easier to call to mind the approach to Scripture that Antiochene authors vociferously criticized—allegory—than it is to identify their own approach to the biblical text. The concluding paragraphs of the *Introduction* become particularly valuable for us because Adrian presents in them a series of exegetical activities that will successfully guide students toward the meaning of Scripture. Above all else it is this "meaning"— διάνοια is the term used in 77–8—that his exegetical project aspires to grasp.[1] In these final paragraphs of the *Introduction* the Antiochene exegetical culture of this treatise arguably finds its clearest expression, advanced through vivid analogies and numerous technical terms that merit close attention. These paragraphs offer readers one of the most coherent and sustained accounts of how a late antique, Christian *grammaticus* with Antiochene sympathies went about the task of studying Scripture.

A. PREPARATION FOR TEXTUAL ANALYSIS

1. The purpose and subject matter of Scripture

Adrian draws his treatise to a close by identifying a number of preliminary issues that must be resolved before would-be students turned to a detailed, verse-by-verse analysis of Scripture. This interpretive strategy was commonly employed by late antique textual scholars: the theme, aim, or purpose of a work, its place in an author's wider corpus, the meaning of its title, and a number of

---

[1] A peripheral and uncertain existence is granted to θεωρία: it is contrasted with διάνοια and merits only passing mention in the *Introduction*. See my notes on paragraph 78 in the translation, the only place where Adrian mentions θεωρία.

other related issues frequently prefaced their commentaries on classical Greek literature. Not surprisingly, we find a similar range of prefatory matters in the prefaces to commentaries on Christian Scripture.[2] Here in the *Introduction* Adrian highlights several such issues that, when successfully resolved, guide students in an orderly manner through the subsequent details of textual analysis.

He maintains that students must first orient themselves to the biblical book in question by attending to its purpose (διάνοια) which is expressed through its contents (ὑποθέσεις). Once this preliminary step has been taken, the commentary on the words (ἡ κατὰ λέξιν ἑρμηνεία) will naturally follow.[3] "It is fitting," he writes,

> that students first fix their attention on the purpose [of a scriptural book] by means of the contents of its individual passages. Then, in this manner, the book's purpose properly furnishes the word-for-word commentary to students, since the link between words would be lost if the purpose is not established in advance. (75)

The worry about a disoriented exegesis ("the link between words *would be lost*") transitions Adrian to a nautical analogy in which a ship's steersman is similarly threatened with getting lost at sea if he does not have his eyes fixed on some target:

> For just as with those who steer ships, if some defined target does not lie somewhere before them, toward which they intend to direct the whole weight of the rudders, they are driven through the whole sea, forced to entrust their expertise here and there to every wind as they search wanderingly for refuge in a harbor. This is what will also certainly happen in the exegetical exercises of classroom teaching, whenever it is offered without some diligent preparatory study. (75)

This nautical image reinforces the approach to Scripture that Adrian is advocating. The ship's steersman first needs to have a target in view if he is to safely bring his ship to harbor amidst stormy conditions. The exegete is like this steersman: his target is the biblical book's purpose, as expressed in its subject matter, which guides him safely to his destination, the explanation of the individual words. This analogy is delightfully strengthened by a pun. The "target" of the ship's steersman is literally "some defined place *of aim* [τις ... ὡρισμένος τοῦ σκοποῦ ... τόπος]." The term σκοπός ("aim" or "intent") was a technical exegetical term widely used in ancient literary criticism to refer to an author's purpose. It is a synonym for Scripture's διάνοια, the term Adrian uses in the immediately preceding lines, when he says that readers first need to establish a book's "purpose" before turning to textual exegesis.

Immediately following this nautical image Adrian offers another comparison for his audience: between the Christian interpretation of Scripture and the

---

[2] See Schäfer, "Eisagoge"; Fuhrmann, *Das Systematische Lehrbuch*; Schäublin, *Untersuchungen*, 66–72; Hadot, "Les introductions aux commentaires exégétiques"; Mansfeld, *Prolegomena*.

[3] Each of these technical terms can be taken differently than how I render them here and in my translation. For justification of my interpretations, see the notes in my translation.

non-Christian exegesis of Homeric poetry. Once again his aim is to motivate his readers to prioritize the discovery of the contents of a biblical book.[4] Adrian acknowledges the commitment of non-Christian scholars to take the subject matter of the epic poems seriously, even when they know that these poems occasionally narrate fictitious people, deeds, or events. But since the readers of epic poetry still take its subject matter seriously before turning to actual word usage, so too should Christians take the contents of their Scripture seriously— writings *not* replete with fictions—before attempting to decipher its language.

> For how would it not be incredibly absurd, if it is impossible for scholars to inter-
> pret the epic poems which contain fictions, namely untrue events, in any other
> way than by first learning the content of each of these poems [τὴν ... ὑπόθεσιν],
> so as to reasonably bring forth the usage of the words in regard to their topic
> [πρὸς ταύτην (i.e., ὑπόθεσιν) εἰκότως ... τὴν τῶν λόγων χρῆσιν ἐκφέροιεν]—
> and not the winds—but we were to subject the words of our divine counsel to
> some unfounded conjectures, not being ashamed to impose random and discon-
> nected explanations on them?! (75)

The nomenclature for preparatory exegetical work is similar to what Adrian used above: the student first needs to learn the content (ὑπόθεσις) of Scripture before turning to the usage of individual words (ἡ τῶν λόγων χρῆσις). Note also that the nautical image resurfaces: the words of Scripture must be oriented to the larger subject matter, and not to "the winds" that threaten to drive the exegete further out to sea.

2. Literary peculiarities, figures, and tropes

Adrian offers a second account of the issues that need to be raised before embark-
ing upon the interpretation of Scripture. He presents an image of the scriptural neophyte who, like a traveler in a strange land, is in need of expert guidance:

> Thus how necessary it is for those departing for a completely unknown land, that
> people who are to a greater degree acquainted with it point out, first of all, the
> return path by which these should travel and, moreover, make known to them the
> signs along this way which, if they follow these, they will certainly not be led
> astray of the straight path. (76)

Speaking especially to teachers of Scripture (the informed travel guides), Adrian reminds them that their first task is to provide their pupils (the travelers) with

---

[4] Neither here nor elsewhere in the *Introduction* does Adrian suggest that the exegetical techniques used to interpret non-Christian literature might be incompatible with, or even different
from, those techniques needed to interpret his Scriptures. In one place, he even adopts a philosophical interpretation of an anthropomorphism (2.10). Adrian's real concern appears to be that
Christians, when studying their Scriptures, will fail to utilize the interpretive practices of the
grammatici of his day.

requisite knowledge (signposts) for the study of Scripture (the unknown land). These signposts turn out to be the critical preparatory steps that need to be traversed before embarking upon an analysis of the scriptural text:

> In the same way, someone—especially among those who profess to teach—should resolve that it is necessary that they first render the content, full of events [τὴν τῶν πραγμάτων ... ὑπόθεσιν], familiar to their pupils, in regard to which they might be obliged to supply the weight of their own understanding. Then [they ought to supply] the knowledge of literary peculiarities [τῶν γραφικῶν ἰδιωμάτων], the distinction between figures [τῶν σχημάτων] and the differentiation of tropes [τῶν τρόπων], and, not least, the clear, word-for-word commentary [τὴν τῆς κατὰ τὴν λέξιν ἑρμηνείας σαφήνειαν]—just like they would point out any signs for the journey, by means of which travelers might have the sureness and steadfastness for what lies ahead. (76)

This sequencing of exegetical activity is very similar to what he provided above. Interpretation begins with the "subject matter" of a biblical book (ὑπόθεσις)—that might require some scholarly amplification on the teacher's part if there are allusions or references in the text that require explanation—before turning to the "word-for-word commentary [ἡ κατὰ λέξιν ἑρμηνεία]." But what is striking about this passage is that Adrian inserts a second preliminary issue for the teacher to address: to instruct students in literary peculiarities (τὰ γραφικὰ ἰδιώματα), including the different kinds of figures (σχήματα) and tropes (τρόποι) that they will encounter in Scripture. Adrian has neatly introduced his own treatise into an ideal classroom curriculum. It is not enough for teachers to sketch out the subject matter of individual biblical books. They also need to teach their pupils the unusual characteristics of biblical language with the help of a textbook like the *Introduction*. I will return to how this book might have been used in the classroom.

Adrian's counsel mirrored what we find practiced across a wide swath of late antique textual scholarship, Christian and non-Christian. Among the Antiochene biblical scholars who often provide the most immediate context for Adrian's *Introduction*, it was a standard practice to preface their line-by-line commentary of a biblical book with a brief overview of a number of introductory issues which, in turn, would guide their subsequent textual analysis. In many cases they offer clear parallels with Adrian's remarks.[5] For instance, the prioritizing of a book's purpose (σκοπός) occurs in Theodore's *Commentary on Haggai*. In the prologue he explains how the prophet intended to accuse the Israelites of indifference when it came to rebuilding the Temple. "This, then is the book's purpose [ὁ τοῦ βιβλίου σκοπός]," Theodore writes. "Let us then

---

[5] Among non-Christian literary scholars, Proclus' commentaries on Plato address preliminary issues that are often quite close to those enumerated in the *Introduction*: the purpose, subject matter, and literary style of Plato's dialogues can all be discussed before turning to the text of a dialogue (Mansfeld, *Prolegomena*, 31–3, 34–5).

attend to these verses in detail [κατὰ μέρος]" (*proem. Ag.*). Customarily among the Antiochenes, however, prefatory discussion of a biblical book's "content" (ὑπόθεσις) was highlighted more frequently than its "purpose." Diodore explains, for instance, how his research on the Psalms will first offer a "precise outline of its contents [σύντομον ἔκθεσιν ... τῶν ὑποθέσεων]" before it turns to a "commentary on the text [τῆς κατὰ λέξιν ἑρμηνείας]" (*proem. Ps.*). Or again, in a key methodological paragraph in Theodore's *Commentary on the Psalms* he outlines his approach to the entire Psalter: "Now, this practice we shall particularly observe both in the present psalm and in all the others, to make a summary of the overall meaning (*omnem intellectum in summam redigentes*) and thus unfold precisely what has to be said."[6] And finally, as for Adrian's insistence on knowing the literary peculiarities of a book prior to embarking upon its interpretation, we are safe in assuming that this is precisely what Theodore advocated in the now-lost prologue to his *Commentary on the Psalms*. He tells us that he catalogued there a number of the Psalms' literary peculiarities, and it is hard to imagine any other reason for him addressing this issue in his prologue if he did not think it would inform his subsequent commentary.

This insistence for Adrian on identifying a biblical book's purpose or basic subject matter was not an exercise without consequence for the commentary that followed. It was intended to govern this exegesis by providing readers with a basic framework that helped them not get lost in the minutiae of the text or wander away from the topic so that they foisted "random and disconnected explanations" onto Scripture. Similar counsel surfaces in paragraph 77 the *Introduction* where Adrian insists on the importance of grasping the "sequence" of wording (ἀκολουθία) while striving for the meaning of the text. The sort of sequence he has in mind here is a larger literary unit that encompassed and informed the particular words being examined by the interpreter. Thus while the purpose or subject matter of a biblical book established a broad thematic framework to guide the textual exegesis that followed, attending to the "sequence" while moving through a text created a linguistic context that informed how interpreters wrestled with its verbal details. In both cases, Adrian's strategy was the same: to help the reader find orientation for the particulars of textual analysis.[7]

---

[6] Thdr. Mops., *Ps. hypoth.* 1. See the excellent discussion in Frances M. Young, *Biblical Exegesis and the Formation of Christian Culture* (Cambridge: Cambridge University Press, 1997), 34–6, 81, 171–2.

[7] See also the regulatory role given the *hypothesis* at Diod., *Ps. hypoth.* 5; Thdr. Mops., *Ps. hypoth.* 71; Thdt., *proem. Is.* "Before everything else, we will discuss the *hypothesis* of this prophecy; in this manner, the commentary on individual sections will be easily seen at once [Πρὸ δὲ πάντων ἐροῦμεν τὴν τῆς προφητείας ὑπόθεσιν· οὕτω γὰρ εὐσύνοπτος ἡ κατὰ μέρος ἑρμηνεία γενήσεται]."

B. EXEGETICAL AIMS

The goal of exegetical inquiry for Adrian was to uncover the basic meaning of the scriptural text, a meaning that was precise, fitting, and above all else, clear.

1. Precision

Adrian announces the first two of these aims for the scriptural interpreter in the following paragraph:

> But it is especially necessary to cling faithfully and completely to the sequence [of words]. Someone who properly grasps this sequence...with a view to attaining the precise meaning [τῆς ἀκριβοῦς διανοίας], cannot miss the fitting sense [τοῦ πρέποντος]. (77)

It is not entirely clear what he has in mind with exegetical precision here, but two possibilities come into view. The first follows the dynamics of the exegetical sequence as he has presented it. Textual interpretation moves from the general to the specific: it is preceded by an assessment of a book's overall theme or purpose before turning to the detailed analysis of the individual words. So, for instance, Theodoret of Cyrus writes, "This, then, is the letter's subject matter; commentary on individual verses [ἡ κατὰ μέρος ἑρμηνεία] instructs us more precisely [ἀκριβέστερον]" (*proem. Rom.*). The goal is to produce a commentary that advances κατὰ μέρος ("part by part," "in detail"), "verse by verse" (κατὰ στίχον)[8] or, in Adrian's words, κατὰ τὴν λέξιν ("word for word"). Note also how precision surfaces in the lines that immediately follow those cited above from the *Introduction*. Adrian contrasts a passage's διάνοια, likened favorably to a body, with its θεωρία, likened to a cloak wrapped around a body:

> For it is possible to point out the cloak quickly, even from afar, but it is possible to describe the body more precisely [ἀκριβέστερον] by way of both its limbs and its joints, provided that people imagine nothing beyond the body. (78)

These lines too suggest that a precise meaning is one that parses the details of a text and is not satisfied with a quick, sweeping interpretation that ignores the particulars.

But a "precise meaning" might also indicate—like "clarity" below—that the scriptural style was sometimes deemed to lack precision, so that it fell to the interpreter to bring out, when necessary, the exactness of detail. Theodore of

---

[8] Diod., *Ps.* 6:1.

Mopsuestia makes an intriguing remark about how the trope of synecdoche (where the part is referenced in place of the whole) compromises precision. In such cases the scriptural author can consider "preciseness of detail superfluous [περιττὴν...τὴν κατὰ μέρος ἀκριβολογίαν]."⁹ Here exactness of expression would have demanded the explicit mention of the whole, but instead, the author mentioned only the part, which was technically an inexact expression. It is not implausible that Adrian also saw tropes, and perhaps other literary peculiarities, like Theodore: as inexact uses of language that required a more precise rewriting for the unsuspecting reader.¹⁰

2. Fittingness

The person who grasps the "sequence" of a passage "with a view to attaining the precise meaning, cannot miss the fitting sense [τοῦ πρέποντος]." The notion of fittingness had wide resonance among literary critics and rhetoricians. It could be invoked when a passage raised thematic problems, such as morally or theologically inappropriate messages, but also when it presented the reader with a range of verbal or stylistic incongruities.¹¹ The latter option is a possibility here, since Adrian is advocating the discovery of the "fitting sense" amidst a reminder that the exegete pay attention to the "sequence" of wording. A "fitting sense" would be a meaning that emerges from positioning words or expressions within their natural habitat, that is, their larger literary context.

My suspicion, however, is that Adrian also entertained a thematically problematic message: there are times when Scripture did not suggest a particularly apt message, and so the task of the exegete became to draw out suitable content. The most obvious candidate for an inappropriate meaning would be Scripture's anthropomorphic depictions of God, such as those listed in part I of the *Introduction*.¹² But other cases of inappropriateness would include the presentation of God as responsible for morally reprehensible events (42) or making exaggerated claims for human righteousness (25). It is also important to note that while

---

⁹ Thdr. Mops. *Zach.* 14:20; also *Zach.* 1:18. See also Schäublin, *Untersuchungen*, 112, esp. fn. 107.

¹⁰ For more on precision, see Hill, *The Old Testament in Antioch*, 37, 39, 63, 103, 115, 120, 122, 126–7, 183.

¹¹ Max Pohlenz, "*Tὸ πρέπον*. Ein Beitrag zur Geschichte des griechischen Geistes," in *Kleine Schriften*, vol. 1, ed. Heinrich Dörrie (Hildesheim: Olms, 1965), 100–39; Heinrich Lausberg, *Handbook of Literary Rhetoric: Foundation for Literary Study*, ed. David E. Orton and R. Dean Anderson, trans. Matthew T. Bliss, Annemiek Jansen, and David E. Orton (Leiden: Brill, 1998), §§1055–62; Bonner, *Education in Ancient Rome*, 245–8.

¹² See also Thdr. Mops., *Ps.* 32:6 on how an anthropomorphic depiction of the Holy Spirit is unsuitable: "nor is the Holy Spirit called 'breath of his mouth,'... such an expression not befitting the dignity of the Holy Spirit [Οὐδὲ γὰρ πρέπουσα ἡ τοιαύτη φωνὴ τῇ τοῦ ἁγίου Πνεύματος ἀξίᾳ]." For more on fittingness in Scripture according to Theodore, see Schäublin, *Untersuchungen*, 78–9.

Adrian presents no elaborate theory about Scripture, there are a few hints scattered throughout the *Introduction* that suggest this interpretation of a "fitting sense." He uses two synonyms for Scripture: he can refer to it as the "literary style of the divine precepts [τῆς τῶν θειῶν παιδευματῶν ἑρμηνείας]" (72, R2) and as the words "of our divine counsel [τῆς θείας ἡμῶν ὑπφθημοσύνης]" (75, R1). Similarly, Adrian discusses the final trope on his list, "exhortation," as follows: "anyone who is pious will agree that, taken together, all the passages of divinely inspired Scripture, whether through words or deeds, reasonably seem to promote this end" (73.22, R2).[13] Taken together, this evidence opens windows onto the kind of text Adrian thought Scripture was: it had an educative function, providing guidance, teaching, and principles for living. The posture that Adrian envisioned Scripture taking toward its audience would have reinforced the need for the interpreter to bring out Scripture's theologically and morally "fitting sense."[14] Since τὸ πρέπον does not surface elsewhere in the *Introduction*, both of these options (and perhaps there are others) remain viable.

3. Clarity

Arguably the main goal of textual interpretation was to establish "the clear, word-for-word, commentary [τὴν τῆς κατὰ τὴν λέξιν ἑρμηνείας σαφήνειαν]." What is noteworthy about this expression is Adrian's use of the term σαφήνεια ("clarity"), a word that, along with its antonym ἀσάφεια ("obscurity"), surfaced throughout Antiochene biblical scholarship.[15] In his *Commentary on Haggai* Theodore remarked that it now fell to him "to clarify [ποιεῖσθαι τὴν σαφήνειαν]" this prophetic book (*proem. Ag.*). Theodoret of Cyrus, in the preface to his *Commentary on the Psalms*, reminded his readers that the predictions of the twelve prophets were "shrouded in obscurity [τὰς τῇ ἀσαφείᾳ κεκρυμμένας προρρήσεις]" and that he had, thus, rendered these books "clear and obvious [σαφεῖς ... καὶ δήλας]" for them (*proem. Ps. 2*). He also described his approach to the Song of Songs as follows: "to bring obscurity to clarity as far as possible [χρὴ γὰρ ἀσαφὲς ὂν σαφὲς εἰς δύναμιν καταστῆσαι]."[16] "Clarity" marked the goal to which Adrian and these Antiochenes aspired.

But the sort of clarity that they had in mind only emerges from their notion of textual obscurity. Particularly instructive in this regard is a fragment from

[13] It might also be significant that this is the only place in the *Introduction* where he refers to Scripture as "divinely inspired."
[14] And thus here too a similarity emerges between Adrian and his non-Christian counterparts: the Greek classics were similarly imbued in the Homeric scholia with an educative function and perceived to be models worthy of imitation. See Nünlist, *Ancient Critic at Work*, 13.
[15] See Mariès, *Études*, 126–7; Marguerite Harl, "Origène et les interprétations patristiques grecques de 'l'obscurité' biblique," *VC* 36 (1982): 334–71; Hill, *Reading the Old Testament in Antioch*, 39–42. For the themes of obscurity and clarity in philosophical and medical commentaries in late antiquity, see Mansfeld, *Prolegomena*, 144–76.
[16] Thdt., *Cant.* 4:12; also *proem. Cant.*

Polychronius' prologue to his *Commentary on Job*, which opens as follows: "Obscurity in the divine Scriptures has many causes [Ἡ ἐν ταῖς θείαις γραφαῖς ἀσάφεια πολλὰς ἔχει τὰς αἰτίας]." Theodore of Mopsuestia's brother proceeds to enumerate ten sources for obscurity, including the loss of the original structure of the Hebrew language when it was translated into Greek, the fact that a number of Hebrew words could not be translated in the LXX, the unannounced alteration of persons or speakers, the frequent use of ellipsis, and so on.[17] From Polychronius' list it becomes evident that obscurity resided principally on the level of wording. A number of these obscurities also surfaced in Adrian's *Introduction* (as I indicate in the notes to my translation). While Adrian never used the term ἀσάφεια, it is arguably implied throughout the *Introduction*: what presented beginning readers with difficulty was the peculiarities of the scriptural *literary style*.[18]

This sort of textual obscurity called for a corresponding aim: for the interpreter to bring out the "clarity" of the wording in such a way that its strange verbal dress was made accessible to the reader. To do this Adrian employed what has come to be known as "grammatical" paraphrase. This form of paraphrase was one of the key exercises performed in the grammatical and rhetorical schoolrooms of late antiquity, and it was often exegetical in nature: the teacher or pupil rewrote a text in "straightforward prose of no stylistic pretensions."[19] In the telling language of later Byzantine rhetoricians, this exercise sought to transform what was "unclear" into something "clear."[20]

Paraphrase was a hallmark of the Antiochene exegetical culture and arguably the main way in which its authors sought to establish and present the clarity of the biblical style for their readers.[21] The *Introduction* is replete with the following format through which paraphrase came to expression: first a scriptural word or phrase was quoted; then it was followed by a marker such as ἵνα εἴπῃ ("as if to say"), τουτέστιν ("that is"), or ἀντί ("instead of"); and finally, Adrian provided his explanatory gloss of the wording in Scripture. Scripture "often takes the word 'morning' with reference to swiftness. For example,...

[17] Polychr., *fr. Job* prol. 2. For more on Polychronius' text, see Bardenhewer, *Polychronius*, 52–8. The other extended discussion about obscurity in Antiochene circles is by John Chrysostom, *Homilies on the Obscurity of Prophecy*.
[18] The link between literary peculiarities and obscurity is stated explicitly by Thdr. Mops. at *Ps.* 16:14 and 55:7.
[19] Michael Roberts, *Biblical Epic and Rhetorical Paraphrase in Late Antiquity* (Liverpool: Francis Cairns, 1985), 47. This paragraph is indebted to Roberts's fine study. For more on paraphrase, see Rutherford, *History of Annotation*, 336–46; Schäublin, *Untersuchungen*, 141–2; Nünlist, *Ancient Critic at Work*, 8.
[20] On the type of paraphrase called ἀπὸ τοῦ ἀσαφεστέρου ἐπὶ τὸ σαφέστερον, Roberts writes, "It is evident that the paraphrase could be a useful exegetical tool, whether as a stylistically simple rewriting of authors whose vocabulary was no longer understood...or as a work with literary pretension of its own" (*Biblical Epic and Rhetorical Paraphrase in Late Antiquity*, 27).
[21] Thdt., *Ezech.* 40:1: "Lest, however, by length of discourse we wear out the readers of this book by commenting on every detail, we intend to give in summary form a kind of paraphrase [ἐν κεφαλαίῳ παράφρασίν τινα] of what was revealed in spiritual fashion to the divinely inspired prophet."

'"morning after morning" he will give his judgment' (Zeph 3:5), that is [τοῦτέστιν] 'immediately' [he will give his judgment]" (52, R1). Adrian's commitment to paraphrase in the *Introduction* is especially pronounced when he uses Symmachus' translation to gloss an obscure phrase in the LXX. For instance, he takes the words, "They will be foreigners and hide" (Ps 55:7 [56:6]), and gives readers Symmachus' rendering as the interpretation: "They assembled themselves secretly and scrutinized my tracks" (Ps 55:7 [56:6]) (29, R2).[22] In cases like these, Adrian intervenes as lightly as possible, allowing the alternative phraseology of one translation to help interpret the other.

For Adrian, then, the central and recurring problem with the scriptural text was not its recalcitrant *content* that required the allegorist's symbolic transformation, but rather its perplexing *wording* that demanded the grammarian's rhetorical expertise. The scriptural message had been obscured by stylistic peculiarities, which included an array of figures, tropes, and unexpected lexical decisions. As a result, the task of the scholar was—equipped with a knowledge of these features—to remove this obscurity by rewriting the passage with a clear, straightforward, and unadorned prose.[23] Wherever interpreters deemed it as their main task to reshape the language of the Bible, so that it emerged in a new, plain voice for the late antique Greek ear, it was because they were conditioned to see stylistic obscurity as the pressing problem with the Bible and, correspondingly, clarity as its aspirational ideal. It was, of course, rhetoric that taught them to put Scripture in this light, since according to its conventions, "clarity" was one of the main features of the good literary style.[24]

C. CLASSROOM SETTING

The picture that has emerged in this study is that the *Introduction* was closely affiliated with the classroom: its title, structure, scholarly conventions, and readership all point to a scholastic context. But to whose classroom did this treatise belong, and how did it connect with the activities of this classroom? The first part of this question is easier to answer. The explanatory activities that Adrian outlined fell within the remit of the late antique *grammaticus* who taught boys the Greek language and its literature.[25] Before reading a text aloud

---

[22] See as well the important comparison between Symmachus' translation and the LXX at Thdr. Mops., *Ps.* 55:7.

[23] So too Schäublin, *Untersuchungen*, 41 and 110–11.

[24] The first of the rhetorical virtues, said Quintilian, was clarity (*inst.* 8.2.22; 8.2.12). For more on "clarity" in rhetoric, see Lausberg, *Handbook of Literary Rhetoric*, §§528–37; Roos Meijering, *Literary and Rhetorical Theories in Greek Scholia* (Groningen: Forsten, 1987), 224–5.

[25] Quintilian claimed that the *grammaticus* had two areas of expertise, "the principles of speech and the exegesis of the authors (*ratio loquendi et enarratio auctorum*); the first of these is called 'methodical' and the second 'historical'" (*inst.* 1.9.1). For more on the grammarian and his duties, see Bonner, *Education in Ancient Rome*, 189–249; Morgan, *Literate Education*, 152–89;

with pupils, the *grammaticus* would provide them with basic orientation: a short biography of the author and general information about the treatise, including its subject, title, genre, literary style, and purpose.[26] Here we recognize Adrian's emphasis on foregrounding exegetical work by attending to the purpose and subject matter of a biblical book. But the *grammaticus* also performed significant interpretive work on the details of the text. Quintilian provides us the best description of this work. It merits lengthier citation since it overlaps with many of Adrian's prescriptions:

> In expounding his text, the *grammaticus* must also deal with more elementary matters...He must point out Barbarisms, improper usages, and anything contrary to the laws of speech, not by way of censuring the poets for these...but to remind the pupil of technical rules and activate his memory of them.
>
> At this elementary stage, it is also useful to show in how many ways particular words may be understood. "Glosses" also, that is to say words not in common use, are not the least important area of grammatical scholarship. The *grammatici*, however, should take greater care in teaching all the Tropes, which are the main ornaments not only of poetry but also of oratory, and both kinds of Schemata—that is to say, Figures of Speech (*lexis*) and of Thought (*dianoia*) as they are called...Above all, he should impress upon their minds what is meant by excellence in organization, and in propriety of subject matter; what is appropriate to particular characters; what is praiseworthy in thought or word; and when abundance is acceptable, and when restraint.
>
> A further task will be the explanation of historical allusions; this must be scholarly, but not overloaded with superfluous labour. (*Inst.* 1.8.13–18)

We recognize several of Adrian's concerns here: the importance of training students in literary peculiarities, tropes, and figures, highlighting the fittingness of the subject matter, and having the ability to elaborate on a subject by explaining historical allusions. For Quintilian and Adrian, the *grammaticus* ultimately has the same aim: to help students understand their text.[27]

If the intended user of the *Introduction* was a Christian *grammaticus* who taught not only from the Greek classics, but also the Psalms, what role might this manual have had in his classroom? Here we are on less certain footing, since a wide number of pedagogical methods would have been available to this teacher, and not all would have been preferred in every situation. Any number

---

Cribiore, *Gymnastics of the Mind*, 185–219, esp. 205–15; Maurice, *Teacher in Ancient Rome*, 10–13, 65–76. On the teaching of figures and tropes in the Psalms as part of the duties of the Byzantine *grammaticus*, see Thomas Conley, "Byzantine Teaching on Figures and Tropes: An Introduction," *Rhetorica: A Journal of the History of Rhetoric* 4 (1986): 351.

[26] Bonner, *Education in Ancient Rome*, 219–20, and the literature in fn. 2 above.

[27] Quint, *inst.* 1.8.2. Here is another description of the *grammaticus* that strongly parallels what we find in Adrian's *Introduction*: "Similarly, if a *grammaticus* is lecturing on correct speech, or explaining problems, or giving the historical background, or paraphrasing poems, all who hear him will profit by the lesson" (1.2.15).

of factors impacted the dynamics of the classroom experience: the number of students enrolled, their varying levels of expertise and personalities, teachers' own abilities, the difficulty of the text being examined, and so on. Lectures, one-on-one tutorials, the give-and-take of questions and answers and examinations were all possible teaching strategies.[28]

As we saw above, Adrian makes an oblique remark about how his treatise finds its way into classroom instruction. He proposes a pedagogical sequence in which the teacher begins by outlining for students the purpose or subject matter of a particular biblical book, and then supplies them with "the knowledge of literary peculiarities, the distinction between figures and the differentiation of tropes and, not least, the clear, word-for-word commentary." With the exception of the trope of "exhortation" that points to the general purpose of Scripture (to exhort worthy conduct from its readers), the bulk of the *Introduction* concerns Scripture's literary peculiarities, figures, and tropes.

What is clear is that Adrian saw his treatise as a supplementary work to the central text being studied with students: Scripture.[29] What is not entirely clear is how his treatise would have functioned in the pedagogical sequence outlined above. But we can propose a few likely scenarios. Amidst a general introduction to the Psalms, the *grammaticus* might have followed a discussion of the biblical book's main topics with orientation to its key literary features. Here large sections of the *Introduction* would have surfaced in the classroom. For instance, the list of figures in section 3 is explicitly associated with the Psalms as are most of the tropes and anthropomorphisms that are catalogued. Each of these sections of the treatise might have been presented in the form of a lecture or tutorial with students taking notes. Even the specialized observations in the section on diction might have surfaced in an ad hoc manner in the classroom: the teacher could draw upon any lexical observation provided it was relevant to the Psalm being analyzed that day. Most of the *Introduction* would also have lent itself to a question-and-answer or testing format.[30] The teacher might present an anthropomorphism and expect a gloss; put forward a word and require a series of definitions with illustrations; identify a trope and receive a definition. We can also envision specialized tutorials on the varieties of prophecy or the differences between prose and poetry, topics addressed in the concluding appendices. There were undoubtedly other ways in which teachers

---

[28] For an overview, see Maurice, *Teacher in Ancient Rome*, 65–78, 89–101.

[29] For more on "introductions" as supplementary and not stand-alone texts, and secondary to the direct classroom instruction, see Asper, *Griechische Wissenschaftstexte*, 278.

[30] On the close relationship between problems-and-solutions literature and the dynamics of the classroom, see Dörrie and Dörries, "Erotapokriseis," 346; Snyder, *Texts and Teachers*, 112–14; Yannis Papadoyannakis, "Instruction by Question and Answer: The Case of Late Antique and Byzantine *Erotapokriseis*," in *Greek Literature in Late Antiquity: Dynamism, Didacticism, Classicism*, ed. Scott Fitzgerald Johnson (Aldershot: Ashgate, 2006), 91–105; Mansfeld, *Prolegomena*, 2–3.

used the *Introduction*. Yet regardless of how the treatise was utilized, the likely expectation was that students would commit large sections of it to memory.[31]

While Adrian mentions teachers as his addressees, we should be cautious about concluding that they were the exclusive audience of the *Introduction*. Theodore of Mopsuestia remarked that Bibles were often owned privately in his day: "All of us, having come to faith in Christ the Lord from the nations, received the Scriptures from them [i.e., the apostles] and now enjoy them, reading them aloud in the churches and keeping them at home" (*Soph.* 1:4–6). Even if he exaggerated the extent of the private ownership of Bibles, it is certainly possible that the *Introduction* found its home with a general audience outside the formal classroom.[32] Educated readers who owned a Bible (or part of it) might have procured a copy of the *Introduction* because they too found it a useful guide for their own study of Scripture.

---

[31] See Quint., *inst.* 11.2.36 on the use of division and artistic structure to help students memorize. As noted in the section on scholarly conventions in the previous chapter, division is a significant formal feature of the *Introduction*.

[32] On the wide interest in the Psalms, see esp. the opening lines of Thdt., *proem. Ps.* 1. On the extent to which Antiochene commentators enjoyed a literate readership, see Harry Y. Gamble, *Books and Readers in the Early Church: A History of Early Christian Texts* (New Haven: Yale University Press, 1995), 132–8; Elizabeth A. Clark, *Reading Renunciation: Asceticism and Scripture in Early Christianity* (Princeton: Princeton University Press, 1999), 49; Hill, *Reading the Old Testament in Antioch*, 12–13, 48–50.

PART II

Edition and Annotated Translation

1

Overview: Recensions, Manuscripts, and Editions of Adrian's *Introduction to the Divine Scriptures*

Adrian's *Introduction to the Divine Scriptures* survives in two different recensions, R1 and R2.

Thirteen manuscripts transmit all or part of R1, attributing this work to Adrian and titling it εἰσαγωγὴ εἰς τὰς θείας γραφάς. The oldest of these manuscripts, dating to the turn of the twelfth century, is *Conventi Soppressi 39* (**L**) which today resides in the Biblioteca Medicea Laurenziana in Florence. At the beginning of the seventeenth century **L** was vandalized by Friedrich Lindenbruch, who cut out a number of folios and brought them back with him to Hamburg where they now reside in the Staats- und Universitätsbibliothek as *221 in Scrinio* (**L$_H$**). Adrian's *Introduction* survives in **L** and the first folio of **L$_H$**. **L/L$_H$** proves to be the ancestor of the other twelve manuscripts, all of which date to the sixteenth century or later. The first print edition of the *Introduction* was published in 1602 by David Hoeschel, who utilized two of the twelve descendants of **L**. Hoeschel's edition was reprinted in John Pearson's *Critici Sacri* (1660) and this latter text was, in turn, reprinted in Jacques-Paul Migne's *Patrologia Graeca* (1860). Both reprints introduced minor orthographic corrections and errors. In 1887 the second edition of the *Introduction* was made by Friedrich Goessling. He drew eclectically upon eight manuscripts, including **L** (but not **L$_H$**). Goessling's edition was informed by the *editio princeps* and its reprints, Karl Friedrich Schlüren's textual emendations that appeared in the essay, "Zu Adrianos: Vorarbeiten" (1887) and, finally, Aloysius Lollin's Latin translation of the *Introduction* (1611/1630). Goessling did not discover the two Greek manuscripts utilized by Lollin, though they can now be identified as two heavily corrupted descendants of **L**.

Recently a number of scholars have contributed to the discovery of a second recension of Adrian's *Introduction*. Two extended sections of R2 are transmitted by three manuscripts (**XYZ**), each dating to the sixteenth century. This recension has never been edited. In these manuscripts R2 is handed down anonymously and is prefaced as follows: ἐκ τοῦ περὶ τῶν ἰδιωμάτων τῆς θείας γραφῆς· καὶ μάλιστα τοῦ Δαυὶδ εἰσὶ ταῦτα. ("From the treatise about the peculiarities of Divine Scripture—these belong especially to David.") This heading reflects the language in the opening sentence of Adrian's treatise and highlights its focus on the Psalms (i.e., "David").

In addition to the transmission of these two recensions in the direct manuscript tradition, fragments of Adrian's *Introduction* survive in the exegetical catenae. Sixteen of these fragments were edited by Jean-Baptiste-François Pitra in his *Analecta Sacra* (1884), though they were not mentioned in Goessling's edition that appeared three years thereafter. Since Pitra's publication, a number of additional catenae fragments excerpted from the *Introduction* have come to light. Some of these fragments witness to the text of R1, some to the text of R2 and a number to another recension(s) for which we have no evidence in the direct manuscript tradition. Collectively, none of these fragments has been utilized in editing or reconstructing the history of the text of Adrian's treatise.

I am presenting readers a new edition of Adrian's *Introduction* that is based upon a comprehensive examination of all known manuscripts that transmit the treatise in whole or in part. The two preceding editions and the reprints of Hoeschel have also been carefully consulted. The results of this more methodical inspection of the manuscript and editorial tradition are as follows: a better text and more useful apparatus of R1 than Hoeschel or Goessling published; the first edition of R2; a more complete picture of the transmission of the *Introduction* and the relationship of these two recensions to one another. Furthermore, readers are also presented an annotated English translation facing the Greek text. This is the first English translation of the *Introduction*.

Chapter 2 presents the history of the previous editions of Adrian's *Introduction*, their contributions and deficiencies, and the manuscript basis for this edition. Chapter 3 is a catalogue of the manuscripts that transmit the work. Chapter 4 clarifies the relationships between the manuscripts that transmit each recension. Chapter 5 examines the relationship between R1 and R2 and provides an overview of the complex history of the transmission of the *Introduction*. The sixth chapter presents the conventions of my edition and translation. A list of abbreviations immediately precedes the Greek text and translation.

2

Editions and Translations—Past and Present

A. DAVID HOESCHEL'S *EDITIO PRINCEPS* AND ITS REPRINTS

There are two modern editions of Adrian's *Introduction* that precede this edition. The *editio princeps* was published in 1602 by David Hoeschel (1556–1617).[1] A student of the famous German humanist, Hieronymus Wolf, Hoeschel was himself a noted philologist. He was first a teacher and then the rector of the Sankt Anna-Gymnasium in Augsburg. From 1593 to his death he simultaneously served as the director of the Augsburg city library. Hoeschel edited a large number of patristic Greek texts from the manuscripts (mss) that were housed in the Bibliotheca Augustana and is perhaps most famous for his production of the first printed edition of Photius' *Bibliotheca* (1601).[2]

The *Introduction* is the opening work in a volume of treatises that Hoeschel edited: its text is flanked in the exterior margins by identifications of the scriptural passages Adrian cites. The apparatus (*Notae*) appears at the end of the volume. This volume opens with a dedicatory letter addressed to Marquard Freher, a scholar and counselor to the Elector of the Palatinate, in which Hoeschel indicates that his edition of Adrian's *Introduction* was based upon two mss. One he received from Freher himself; the other had been sent to him by Hans Georg Herwart von Hohenburg from the Bavarian court library in Munich.[3] The two mss in question were correctly identified by Ignatio Hardt in his nineteenth-century catalogue of the Greek mss in the court library: *Codex Gr. 477* (**A**) and *107* (**B**), respectively.[4] Hoeschel received **A** directly from Freher in Augsburg.

---

[1] *Adriani Isagoge, Sacrarum Literarum et antiquissimorum graecorum in Prophetas fragmenta* (Augsburg: Typis Ioannis Praetorii, 1602), 1–27 (text) and 88–9 (notes). A digital copy is available at: http://www.zvdd.de.

[2] For more on Hoeschel, see Leonard Lenk, "David Höschel," *Neue Deutsche Biographie*, vol. 9, Hess—Hüttig (Berlin: Duncker & Humblot, 1972), 368–9.

[3] *Adriani Isagoge*, pref. "Your Adrian returns to you, great man, nor is he without interest, as we believe. We have compared your [ms that contains Adrian] not only with another ms which Georg Herwart von Hohenburg sent from the Bavarian library, but we sought that the scriptural passages be accurately expressed in the margin."

[4] Ignatio Hardt, *Catalogus codicum manuscriptorum Graecorum Bibliothecae Regiae Bavaricae*, vol. 2, *Cod. graec. 106–233* (Munich: Seidel, 1806), 2; vol. 5, *Cod. graec. 473–574[–583]* (Munich: Seidel, 1812), 20.

This manuscript remained in the Augsburg city library until 1806 when the city was annexed to Bavaria and most of its Greek mss were transferred to the court library in Munich.[5] **B** entered the court library of Munich in 1571, having been purchased by Albrecht V, Duke of Bavaria, from Johann Jakob Fugger's private collection in Augsburg. This was the ms that Hoeschel—who was an acquaintance of the Fugger family—received from Herwart.[6]

We get a sense for how Hoeschel worked by the annotations he made in the margins of **A** while preparing his edition of the *Introduction*.[7] Marginalia include: the identification of scriptural passages cited by Adrian (these would later surface in the margins of his edition); emendations (e.g., in the exterior margin of 1r he conjectures six additional words that he would supply in his edition); variants he found in **B** (e.g., in the bottom margin of 6v he writes "πράξεως C(odex) B(avaricus)," which is in fact a reading only found in **B**); lexical remarks (e.g., in the exterior margin of 20v he writes the more familiar καταλογάδην as a gloss on λογάδην); alternative readings from the edited biblical texts of his day (e.g., in the bottom margin of 11r he writes "libri editi δύσουσι" where Adrian's text reads, οὐ δώσουσι).

In 1660 Hoeschel's edition, including his notes, was reprinted with minor orthographic corrections and errors in the monumental anthology of scriptural commentaries edited by John Pearson, the *Critici Sacri*.[8] This slightly altered form of the *editio princeps* was, in turn, reprinted in the *Patrologia Graeca* in 1860 (vol. 98, 1273–1312) with a few additional corrections and errors. The Greek text was supplemented with a facing Latin translation. Most of Hoeschel's original notes were printed at the bottom of each page. Mention should also be made of Athos, Panteleimon, 693 (**P**) which produces a handwritten copy of Hoeschel's edition on ff. 249r–265v.

The chief strengths of Hoeschel's edition include: a number of successful conjectures which have subsequently been adopted by Goessling and me; the identification of most of the biblical passages cited throughout the *Introduction*; and a short list of notes at the end of his volume indicating some of the places where Adrian's biblical text differed from other witnesses to the scriptural text, a handful of minor emendations Hoeschel made to the manuscript tradition, and a few observations of other patristic passages that paralleled

---

[5] For more on the history of **A**, see the description in the catalogue below (with bibliography).

[6] For more on the history of **B** (including its listing in Herwart's catalogue), see Marina Molin Pradel, *Katalog der griechischen Handschriften der Bayerischen Staatsbibliothek München*, vol. 2, *Codices graeci Monacenses 56–109* (Wiesbaden: Harrassowitz, 2013), 314–20 (with bibliography). See also the description of **B** in the catalogue below.

[7] It was an editorial practice of Hoeschel to add readings from other mss in the margins of the particular ms that he was using to prepare an edition. See Victor Tiftixoglu, *Katalog der griechischen Handschriften der Bayerischen Staatsbibliothek München*, vol. 1, *Codices graeci Monacenses 1–55*, with Kerstin Hajdú and Gerhard Duursma (Wiesbaden: Harrassowitz, 2014), 188; Pradel, *Katalog München*, 12–13.

[8] *Critici Sacri, sive Doctissimorum Virorum in SS. Biblia Annotationes et Tractatus*, vol. 8, *Tractatuum Biblicorum* (London: Jacobus Flescher, 1660), 9–23; the notes appear on 47–50.

themes in Adrian's *Introduction*. Aside from a few typographical errors and the occasional misidentification of a biblical passage, the chief weakness of Hoeschel's edition is the lack of clarity surrounding its construction. He did not identify where or how his two mss diverged from one another and which ms he was following when their readings diverged. He also did not have access to **L**, the ancestor of **A** and **B**.

B. FRIEDRICH GOESSLING'S EDITION

In 1887 Friedrich Goessling published his edition of the *Introduction* with a facing German translation and prefatory study. For the production of his edition he relied upon Hoeschel's *editio princeps*, the slightly corrected versions in the *Critici Sacri* and *Patrologia Graeca*, and eight mss. In addition to the two mss used by Hoeschel (**AB**), he drew upon six additional mss that he discovered in the spring of 1886 on his journey to the leading libraries of Italy. Five were in the Biblioteca Apostolica Vaticana: *Ottob. Gr. 194* (**C**); *Ottob. Gr. 270* (**D**); *Ottob. Gr. 379* (**E**); *Vat. Gr. 659* (**G**); *Vat. Gr. 1269* (**H**). The other ms, dating to the turn of the twelfth century, was in the Biblioteca Medicea Laurenziana in Florence: *Conv. Soppr. 39* (**L**). Goessling was unsuccessful in locating the last folios of **L**, that is, $\mathbf{L}_H$, which were in Hamburg.[9] Two additional sources informed Goessling's edition. He utilized a seventeenth-century Latin translation of the *Introduction* by the bishop of Belluno, Aloysius Lollin (1557–1625). Lollin's translation relied upon two Greek mss that Goessling argued were not among the aforementioned eight mss and that testified to a better class of the ms tradition. It also turns out that Goessling used the emendations proposed in Karl Friedrich Schlüren's essay, "Pro Adrianos: Vorarbeiten." This essay appeared a few months before Goessling's edition was published (more on this issue below).

Goessling made only a few claims about the relationships between his mss. He argued that **A** and **B** were both descendants of a common ancestor (now lost) since they shared a large number of the same errors and omissions. This ancestor, along with **CDEGHL**, were all independently derived from another lost ancestor. Collectively, Goessling considered all eight manuscripts to be of equal worth, relegated them to a more corrupt class when compared to the two Greek mss utilized by Lollin, and claimed that no additional conclusions could be drawn about how these mss might be interrelated. He insisted that it would be difficult for anyone to establish a more accurate stemma than what he was

---

[9] "Auch der Codex der *Εἰσαγωγή*, welcher nach Fabricius in der Johannis-Bibliothek zu Hamburg aufbewahrt sein sollte, war nicht zu entdecken" (Friedrich Goessling, *Adrians ΕΙΣΑΓΩΓΗ ΕΙΣ ΤΑΣ ΘΕΙΑΣ ΓΡΑΦΑΣ aus neu aufgefundenen Handschriften* [Berlin: Reuther, 1887], 17).

proposing.[10] Even though Goessling privileged Lollin's Latin translation, its variant readings—usually omissions—were almost always relegated to the apparatus. In only a handful of cases were Lollin's readings used to help establish the text of the *Introduction*.[11] In practice, Goessling did not privilege any of his mss at his disposal (including the Latin translation), thereby producing an eclectic text.

Goessling's edition has an *apparatus fontium* and an *apparatus criticus* at the foot of the Greek pages and an index of scriptural passages at the end of the book. The critical apparatus contains an assortment of information: a selection of variant readings from the Greek mss, Lollin's translation, and Hoeschel's edition (including its subsequent reprints); alternate variants of the biblical texts cited by Adrian from Tischendorf's editions of the OT and NT, or other patristic sources; tentative emendations (e.g., p. 72 line 4); and occasional interpretive remarks (e.g., p. 86 line 10).

The strengths of Goessling's edition include: a more comprehensive (and Arabic) numbering system than Hoeschel's; a more complete identification of scriptural citations; several successful emendations and sporadic use of **L**, the ancestor of all the remaining Greek mss. There are, however, a number of significant deficiencies in the construction and presentation of Goessling's edition that my edition sets out to correct.

1. Representation of variant readings

One of the fundamental problems with Goessling's edition is that it misreports the variant readings in the ms tradition. For example, concerning **L**, the ancestor of all the surviving mss, Goessling does not report the marginal ἐστὶν at 246r (2.2); he claims **L** lacks a verse, when in fact it has it (καί, ὁ οἰκοδομῶν εἰς τὸν οὐρανὸν τὴν ἀνάβασιν αὐτοῦ [2.10]); he claims it omits the τῆς after ἄφυκτον (7.4), the ὡς preceding ἱμάτιον (14), and the τό before εὐλογήκαμεν (23), though all are present. He claims **L** reads περὶ αὖτου when in fact it reads περὶ αὐτοῦ (17) or that it reads δικαιοσύνην μου whereas it has δικαιοσύνης μου (25). He fails to report the marginal note at 250r, which also reads differently from the marginal note of the other mss that he prints in his *apparatus criticus* (42). There are numerous other misrepresentations of **L** as well as of the other mss Goessling consulted. The apparatus is pervasively unreliable.

2. Stemma for Recension 1

It is unclear whether Goessling simply misreported his collations in the apparatus, or whether the collations themselves were also done sloppily. Regardless,

---

[10] Goessling, *Adrians ΕΙΣΑΓΩΓΗ*, 20–3.   [11] Ibid., 6–7 fn. 1, 20–2.

there was sufficient evidence at Goessling's disposal to produce a better stemma than he proposed.[12] I present this evidence in Chapter 4 below. Goessling's only major decision regarding his Greek mss was to posit **A** and **B** as the sole descendants of a lost common ancestor. However, the evidence he supplied did not justify his conclusion. The shared errors he noted for **A** and **B** were *also* attested in his other mss (**CDEGL/L$_H$–H** is largely illegible today): Τὴν κατὰ τῆς τῶν ἐχθρῶν (8); λέγεται εἶναι (12); ὑποτίθεται ὑποτίθεται (73.18); προκαίοιτο (75); ἐν παντὶ (75).[13] The underdeveloped stemma required Goessling to produce an eclectic text, rather than one based solidly on the ancestor of these mss to which he already had access (**L**). Below I will remark on Goessling's other erroneous decision to privilege the two mss that undergirded Lollin's translation.

3. Karl Friedrich Schlüren's emendations

K. F. Schlüren published, "Zu Adrianos: Vorarbeiten," a few months before Goessling's edition was issued.[14] This essay turns out to be an important piece to the puzzle of the editorial history of Adrian's *Introduction*. Schlüren's essay was an exercise in conjectural textual criticism, in which he made a series of "independent improvements and changes" to the Greek text of Adrian that was printed in PG.[15] In a footnote Goessling reported that he only came across Schlüren's essay after he had finished his research and was going forward to press. The footnote gives a deprecatory assessment of Schlüren's work and distances it from Goessling's own edition: Schlüren was too eager to emend the text and many useful conjectures escaped his attention. Goessling insisted that he significantly departed from the textual decisions made by Schlüren (and provided a sampling of these differences). It was only "[e]inzelne kleinere Observationen" that he took up.[16] Yet upon inspecting Schlüren's essay it becomes clear how misleading Goessling's footnote is. Numerous conjectures made by Goessling are, in fact, derived directly from Schlüren's essay, and nowhere is the latter credited for any of them.[17] Credit is restored in my critical apparatus.

---

[12] Already in one of the first reviews of Goessling's edition, Pierre Batiffol criticized him for the sparse remarks he offered on the relationship between the mss ("Dr. Friedrich Goessling: L'Isagoge d'Hadrien," *Bulletin Critique de littérature, d'histoire et de théologie* 10 [1889]: 1–2).

[13] Goessling, *Adrians ΕΙΣΑΓΩΓΗ*, 20 fn. 1.

[14] *Jahrbücher für Protestantische Theologie* 13 (1887): 136–59.

[15] Ibid., 138. [16] Goessling, *Adrians ΕΙΣΑΓΩΓΗ*, 6–7 fn. 4.

[17] Here is a particularly striking instance of Goessling's dependence on Schlüren: the latter argues that a οὕτως needs to be emended to ταῦτα "because of the subsequent infinitive construction" ("Zu Adrianos," 147). In Goessling's apparatus, the entry for the word in question reads, "οὕτως] propter seq. inf. expectaveris ταῦτα (Goessling, *Adrians ΕΙΣΑΓΩΓΗ*, 89 line 15). There is no acknowledgement of dependence upon Schlüren.

4. Lollin's Latin translation of two Greek mss

Then there is the more complex matter of Aloysius Lollin's 1611 translation of the *Introduction* that was published posthumously in 1630.[18] In the preface addressed to Francesco Barbaro (1546–1616), patriarch of Aquileia, Lollin stated that he used two Greek mss to prepare his translation. One of these came from Barbaro's own collection and the other from his own. Lollin also said that these two mss "were carefully compared with one another. They indicated a marvelous agreement in the remaining parts, a distinction only in the name of the author."[19] The key difference between the two mss was that Barbaro's attributed the *Introduction* to "Adrianus," whereas Lollin's attributed it to "Africanus," whom he identified with Sextus Julius Africanus (ca. 160–240). Lollin's translation is noteworthy because it differs significantly from all the surviving Greek witnesses to R1. Notably, there are around 170 biblical citations missing from Lollin's translation that are attested in the Greek mss; there are also eleven biblical citations in Lollin's translation that are absent from most of the aforementioned manuscripts.[20] On the whole, this translation reads like an abbreviated version of R1.

Goessling ultimately concluded that Lollin's translation was a privileged resource for reconstructing the text of R1—the translation rested not only on two mss unknown to him, but also on two better mss.[21] The argument for this conclusion was unsatisfactory. First, Goessling straightforwardly assumed that Lollin had more or less accurately translated his two Greek mss, offering reliable access to mss rather different from those in Goessling's possession.[22] But of course this is precisely the assumption that cannot be made. It is entirely possible that Lollin had simply taken liberties as a translator, introducing the

---

[18] The translation is entitled, *Africani seu Adriani Introductio in Scripturas Sacras* and is found in the book, *Aloysii Lollini patritii veneti Bellunensium antistitis, Episcopalium curarum characteres*, ed. Donatus Bernardius (Belluno: Castilionis, 1630), 257–73. Lollin was a patrician of Venice and bishop of Belluno. He was born in Crete (1552) where he first studied classics. He took refuge in Venice with his parents before the Turk invasion (1571–2) and studied in Padua for six years before returning to Venice where he continued his studies. He was called to the bishopric of Belluno in 1596. He died March 28, 1625, bequeathing his sizeable collection of mss to the Bibliotheca Vaticana. See Pierre Batiffol, "Les manuscrits grecs de Lollino évêque de Bellune: Recherches pour server à l'histoire de la Vaticane," *Mélanges d'archéologie et d'histoire École Française de Rome* 9 (1889): 29–31; Luigi Alpago-Novello, "La vita e le opera di Luigi Lollino, vescovo di Belluno (1596–1625)," *Archivio Veneto* 14 (1933): 15–116; 15 (1934): 199–304; Giovanni Mercati, *Per la storia dei manoscritti greci di Genova, di varie badie Basiliane d'Italia e di Patmo*, ST 68 (Vatican City: BAV, 1935), 117–48.

[19] "Collati inter se … codices non indiligenter. Mirificam in reliquis consensionem, discrimen tantummodo in nomine Authoris indicarunt" (Lollin, *Africani seu Adriani Introductio*, 256).

[20] Goessling, *Adrians ΕΙΣΑΓΩΓΗ*, 6.   [21] Ibid., 6–8, 21–2.

[22] "Wenn wir diese merkwürdige Abweichung der Lollinischen Uebersetzung von der εἰσαγωγή Adrians ins Auge fassen, einmal das 'Fehlen' ganzer Abschnitte, zum andern das 'plus' jener 11 Citate … so haben wir Beweismittel genug in den Händen, dass die beiden von Lollin benutzten Codices sich nicht unter der Zahl der wiederentdeckten finden" (ibid., 6–8).

aforementioned discrepancies.[23] Nevertheless, Goessling extended his argument, claiming, second, that Lollin's two Greek mss were more than additional witnesses to the text of the *Introduction*: they belonged to a *better* class than all the other mss. Here Goessling's argument—if it can be called that—was odd, because he provided no justification for this conclusion. He simply asserted that Lollin was "der Vertretrer der besseren Klasse."[24] It is now clear that this conclusion was wrong.

Goessling's assessment of Lollin drew initial criticisms from Pierre Batiffol and Giovanni Mercati.[25] The debates that have emerged surrounding Lollin's two mss are complex and do not need to be discussed in detail here. It is my contention that we can identify with reasonable certainty that Lollin used *Vat. Gr. 1665* (**I**) and *Vat. Gr. 1908* (**J**), neither of which were known to Goessling. My argument, in brief, is this: **I** belonged to Daniele Barbaro (1514–70) patriarch elect of Aquileia, and it remained in the Barbaro family collection throughout Lollin's career.[26] **I** would have been the ms that came from Barbero's collection. **J**, in turn, was likely Lollin's own copy of Adrian. **J** is a highly miscellaneous collection of ten different mss from three different centuries. In the several inventories of Lollin's collection of mss from his own day, only two of the ten different mss that now make up **J** are mentioned as belonging to him.[27] These inventories, however, are not complete, and so while it would be rash to conclude that all ten mss came from Lollin's own collection, the possibility is very real that Adrian's treatise belonged to this collection.[28]

A collation of Lollin's translation with its suspected sources **I** and **J** confirms this conclusion. It is striking that *every time* **IJ** omit material in comparison with the other mss, so too does Lollin: ὑπομένειν ἀντὶ τοῦ προσδοκᾶν· ὡς τό, καὶ νῦν τίς ἡ (41); καί, ὅπως ἂν ἐνδείξωμαι ἐν σοὶ τὴν δύναμίν μου (42); διὰ τὸ μὴ εἶναι ποιμένας· καί, δεῦτε ὀπίσω μου (73.1). Moreover, there are three significant omissions by **J** against all the other mss: καί, εἶπε γὰρ ἐν καρδίᾳ αὐτοῦ, οὐκ ἔστι θεός (45); χθὲς καὶ τρίτην ἡμέραν· καί, ἀδελφοί

---

[23] This was an especially odd assumption on Goessling's part, since he himself pointed out that a large number of the biblical citations in Lollin's edition presented the Vulgate text for these verses, and thus were not a straightforward translation (ibid., 6).

[24] Ibid., 22.

[25] Batiffol, "Dr. Friedrich Goessling: L'Isagoge d'Hadrien," 1–2; Giovanni Mercati, "Pro Adriano," *RB* 11 (1914): 246–55.

[26] Cyrus Giannelli, *Codices Vaticani Graeci*, vol. 5, *Codices 1485–1683* (Vatican City: BAV, 1960), 406–8; Paul Canart, *Les Vaticani Graeci 1487–1962: Notes et Documents pour l'Histoire d'un fonds de manuscrits de la Bibliothèque Vaticane*, ST 248 (Vatican: BAV, 1979), 150–2, 200; Canart, "Reliures et Codicologie: Les Manuscrits grecs de la Famille Barbaro," in *Calames et Cahiers: Mélanges de codicologie et de paléographie offerts à Léon Gilissen*, ed. Jacques Lemaire and Émile van Balberghe (Brussels: Centre D'Étude des Manuscrits, 1985), 13–25.

[27] Canart, *Codices Vaticani Graeci*, vol. 7, *Codices 1745–1962*, part 1, *Codicum Enarrationes* (Vatican City: BAV, 1970), 639–45; Batiffol, "Dr. Friedrich Goessling: L'Isagoge d'Hadrien," 1; Mercati, *Per la storia*, 125 fn. 2; Canart, "Alivse Lollino et ses amis grecs," *Studi Veniziani* 12 (1970): 580; Canart, *Les Vaticani Graeci 1487–1962*, 240; 48 fn. 40; 53 fn. 62.

[28] Canart, *Les Vaticani Graeci 1487–1962*, 14.

μου ὑμεῖς· καί (57.4); *καὶ κριὸν τριετίζοντα, καὶ τρυγόνα καὶ περιστεράν*
(74.3.3). Here again Lollin conspicuously omits each of these passages. But the
decisive evidence that Lollin was using **J** is the transposition of two biblical
verses that occurs only in this ms: *καί, οὐ μὴ φάγω κρέα εἰς τὸν αἰῶνα· καί,*
οὐ μὴ νίψῃς τοὺς πόδας μου εἰς τὸν αἰῶνα (62.1)—Lollin's translation also
follows this transposition (at p. 268 lines 10–11). It is certain, then, that Lollin
was using **J**. It is also very likely that he was using **I**. Recall that Lollin claimed
that the two mss he used were very similar to one another. This fits well with the
stemmatic analysis of R1 below that demonstrates that **J** was likely a copy of **I**.

It turns out, then, that the major claim in Goessling's stemma was wrong: **IJ**
are certainly not representatives of a "better class" of ms. In fact, as my stemma
below will substantiate, the opposite is the case: they are *far more corrupt* than
the mss that were already at Goessling's disposal. Furthermore, Goessling's
reliance on Lollin's translation turns out to be especially problematic since this
translation was—contrary to his assumption—quite loose. **IJ** do *not* contain
the eleven additional biblical citations that surface in Lollin's translation, nor
do they omit most of the biblical passages that are missing from this translation.[29] Lollin (or those who published his translation after his death) evidently
produced a very free translation of **IJ**, so that we could conclude that this
translation constitutes *yet another recension* of the *Introduction*. By relying on
it, Goessling was invariably departing from, not approaching, the text of R1. It
is clear, then, that Goessling erred in utilizing Lollin's translation for reconstructing the text of R1.

I should also draw attention to another oddity surrounding Goessling's
treatment of Lollin. While there are a handful of places in Goessling's edition
where Lollin impacted textual decisions, Goessling did not systematically
privilege Lollin's translation in the editing of R1.[30] Thus, even though he
announced the superiority of Lollin's Latin translation, the differences between
this translation and the readings of Goessling's Greek mss are usually restricted
to notifications in the apparatus and appear to have had primarily an informa-
tional and not an editorial function. When Lollin did impact the text of
Goessling's edition, it is unclear what principles informed the decisions.[31]

5. Fragments from the exegetical catenae

In 1914, Giovanni Mercati published a review essay of Goessling's edition in
which he identified several deficiencies, criticizing especially Goessling's failure

[29] Mercati, "Pro Adriano," 249–50.
[30] My critical apparatus will indicate the few places where Goessling identifies Lollin as the
source of his emendations.
[31] Goessling, *Adrians ΕΙΣΑΓΩΓΗ*, 7 fn. 1.

to take into account the excerpts attributed to Adrian's *Introduction* in the exegetical catenae on the Psalms.[32] Mercati highlighted sixteen fragments that Jean-Baptiste-Francois Pitra had published several years prior to Goessling's edition and that had somehow escaped his attention.[33] Many of these fragments were transmitted in manuscripts that were older than the manuscripts Goessling had used to create his edition. Even more striking, however, was Pitra's recognition that the exegetical catenae witnessed to a different version of the *Introduction*: the fragments from this indirect tradition invariably presented a text that was more expansive than the corresponding paragraphs in the *textus receptus*, that is, Hoeschel's edition. While Mercati cast doubt on the authenticity of a handful of Pitra's fragments, he accepted most, and supplied a number of additional excerpts from the catenae that were unknown to Pitra.[34] Mercati agreed with Pitra's earlier assertion that the received text of the *Introduction* was a "libri potius epitome quam integrum opus" (a summary of the book rather than the entire work).[35] There are a handful of ways in which Goessling's edition would have been strengthened had he taken these fragments into account (more on this below).

6. Additional problems

Finally, there are a number of smaller problems with Goessling's edition: (a) the Greek text is replete with typographical errors, which I will silently correct; (b) the presentation of the text is cluttered by the liberal and often irregular use of quotation marks and ellipses; (c) editorial symbols are not always used consistently; (d) the formatting of the text (and translation) do not adequately reflect the structure of the treatise; (e) there are a number of places where R1 has suffered from corruptions that require emendation;[36] (f) there are occasional paleographical errors (e.g., Goessling printed Ὅπως ἀπὸ μελῶν as the

---

[32] Mercati, "Pro Adriano," 246–55.

[33] J.-B.-F. Pitra, ed., *Analecta Sacra: Spicilegio Solesmensi*, vol. 2, *Patres Antenicaeni* (Tusculanis, 1884), 130–6.

[34] Mercati, "Pro Adriano," 251–5.

[35] Mercati, "Pro Adriano," 251–3 (referring to Pitra, *Analecta Sacra*, vol. 2, 128, 131, 134). Mercati's judgment was followed by Robert Devreesse, "Chaines Exégétique Grecques," *DBS*, vol. 1 (Paris: Letouzey et Ané, 1928), col. 1134. The entry on Adrian's *Introduction* in the *Clavis Patrum Graecorum* (no. 6527) adopts the shared assessment by Pitra, Mercati, and Devreesse: "Textus receptus libri potius epitome esse uidetur. Fragmenta nonnulla recensionis locupletioris occurrunt in catenis" (catenae in Ps.: ed. J.-B.-F. Pitra, *Analecta Sacra* II [Tusculi, 1884], 130–6; catena in Iob: ed. G. Mercati, "Pro Adriano," *Opere Minore* III [Rome, 1937], 388).

[36] Goessling is attentive to some of these cases (cf. *Adrians ΕΙΣΑΓΩΓΗ*, 40–3), but also overlooks others. There are also putative corruptions that are not, in fact, so (e.g., I do not agree with his claim that the opening sentence of paragraph 25 is corrupt [ibid., 90, apparatus entry for lines 14–16]).

opening words of 2.1, whereas the ms tradition presents these words as the heading for that section); (g) there is the occasional misidentification of a biblical passage; (h) and finally, there are a number of problems with the apparatus: the aforementioned incorrect reporting of variants; a random presentation of variants and orthographic mistakes; selective use of biblical editions and church fathers for alternate readings of biblical texts; the presence of Lollin; the absence of Schlüren and unsystematic cross-referencing between interrelated sections of the *Introduction*.

C. MODERN TRANSLATIONS

As noted above, Adrian's *Introduction* was translated by Aloysius Lollin into Latin in 1611 using **I** and **J**. In his *Bibliotheca Graeca*, Johann Albert Fabricius (1668–1736) reported on two additional Latin translations. His friend Christoph Woltereck (Glückstadt) (1686–1718) produced a translation that Fabricius had himself inspected. Fabricius says he looked through the pages of this translation, which had been prepared for printing "many years ago," but which had not yet been published (the footnote also corrects misinformation that says it was being printed in Leipzig). Fabricius also referred to Conradus Rittershusius (1560–1613) who intended to publish a Latin translation of Adrian ("Hoc Adriani opusculum latina versione donatum edere voluit pridem Conradus Rittershusius").[37] However, this translation (if it was ever produced), as well as Woltereck's, does not appear to have been published.[38] In 1860 another Latin translation appeared in the *Patrologia Graeca* series (PG 98, 1274–1312)—it was a translation of Pearson's reprint of Hoeschel's edition. Several years thereafter, J.-B.-F. Pitra took responsibility for the presence of Adrian in PG: after he had discovered this "rare work," he "ordered it to be inserted, with a new Latin translation" into the series.[39] There are two additional translations of the *Introduction*: Goessling published a facing German translation with his Greek text, and Anne Debary produced a French translation that has never been published.[40]

---

[37] *Bibliotheca Graeca*, rev. ed., vol. 9, 381–2.

[38] Schlüren, "Vorarbeiten," 137, and Goessling, *Adrians ΕΙΣΑΓΩΓΗ*, 4–5, both report that they were unable to track down the aforementioned translations.

[39] *Analecta Sacra*, vol. 2, 128. For more on Pitra's contribution to Migne's *Patrologiae*, see Adalbert Hamman, "Les Principaux Collaborateurs des Deux Patrologies de Migne," in *Migne et le Renouveau des Études Patristiques: Actes du Colloque de Saint-Flour, 7–8 juillet 1975*, ed. A. Mandouze and J. Fouilheron (Paris: Beauchesne, 1985), 179–91.

[40] Anne Debary, "La terminologie rhetoric-grammaticale dans *l'Isagogè* d'Adrien" (Mémoire de DEA, 9 October 2001, University of Paris IV-Sorbonne).

D. THE PRESENT EDITION AND TRANSLATION

1. Recension 1

Since Goessling's edition was produced, six additional mss have come to light that transmit this recension of the *Introduction* in whole or in part: *O II 17b* (Basel, Universitätsbibliothek) = **F**; *Vat. Gr. 1665* and *Vat. Gr. 1908* (Vatican City, Biblioteca Apostolica Vaticana) = **I** and **J**, respectively; *F9 (78)* (Rome, Biblioteca Vallicelliana) = **K₁** and **K₂**; *221 in Scrinio* (Hamburg, Staats- und Universitätsbibliothek) = **L_H**; Athos, Panteleimon *693* (Lambros 6200) = **P**. I have collated each of these mss, in addition to those used by Goessling. On the basis of the evidence presented for the stemma below, **L/L_H** is the ancestor of all known mss that transmit R1 and thus will serve as the basis for my text. The sources of emendations to this ms include: the corrections proposed by the scribes of the other mss derived from **L/L_H**, previous editors (including those who influenced Goessling: Lollin, Pearson, Migne, and Schlüren), catenae fragments that occasionally transmit the same text as we find in R1, the text of R2, and my own conjectures.

2. Recension 2

In recent years, the most important development concerning the text of the *Introduction* has been the discovery of another recension of this treatise. A number of scholars have played a role in this discovery. In 1970 Robert Devreesse identified the text on ff. 1r–2r of *Vat. Gr. 1447* (**Y**) as a continuous extract of the *Introduction* corresponding to §§60–90 in Goessling's edition (26–55 in my edition) and that this material constituted an alternate recension ("Nous avons deux editions de l'εἰσαγωγὴ εἰς τὰς θείας γραφάς d'Adrien").[41] While working on her unpublished "Memoire" under the guidance of Monique Alexandre, Anne Debary recorded the further discovery that there was a second extract of Adrian on ff. 11v–3r of **Y** corresponding to §§106–30 of Goessling's edition (72–74.3.3 in mine).[42]

More recently, I have been able to identify two additional mss that transmit R2: *Vat. Gr. 1862* (**X**) and Athos, Iviron, *1333* (Lambros 5453) (**Z**). In 1970 Paul Canart, in his catalogue entry for **X**, noticed that this ms transmitted a lengthy extract of Adrian that corresponded to Goessling §§60–90 (26–55 in mine).

[41] Robert Devreesse, *Les Anciens Commentateurs Grecs des Psaumes*, ST 264 (Vatican City: BAV, 1970), 312 and fn. 2.
[42] Debary, "La terminologie rhetoric-grammaticale," 24.

Canart notified readers of a parallel passage in **Z**.[43] Upon examining **X** and **Z** I was able to confirm that these mss transmitted the same first extract that we find in **Y**. After a closer examination of **Z**, I began to suspect on both internal and external grounds that it was very closely related to **Y**. With the help of Iviron's librarian, I was able to discover that **Z** also carried the second extract of Adrian that we find in **Y**. Thus **XYZ** carry the first excerpt of R2 and **YZ** also transmit the second excerpt.

The mss that form the basis of R2 are **XYZ**. The sources of emendation for this recension are the catenae fragments, the text of R1, and my own conjectures. My policy for using one recension to correct the other is restrictive: I only emend when a recension corrects a passage that in the other recension is patently incoherent. Therefore, even in places where I strongly suspect that one recension reads better than the other, provided both are intelligible, I preserve the difference.

I present R1 and R2 in parallel columns where they transmit corresponding material. There are two main reasons why I have decided not to privilege one recension over the other, or to reconstruct a single ancestor out of both recensions. First, a variety of evidence indicates that neither recension is a descendant of the other, but that they were independently derived from a lost ancestor. Thus, we cannot straightforwardly prioritize one version over the other. Yet neither can we easily reconstruct this lost ancestor from which both were derived. R1 and R2 are themselves expressions of a culture of pervasive scribal modification when it came to the transmission of non-literary works like Adrian's *Introduction*. As I explain in more detail in Chapter 5, the reconstruction of the ancestor of R1 and R2 is a largely hypothetical exercise. Second, there is a benefit to printing both recensions in parallel columns. Such a presentation allows readers today to encounter the two dominant forms in which this treatise has been transmitted and known to many, if not most, of its readers since the early medieval period. Indeed, this presentation often makes for interesting reading since it allows us to see how scribes have created two different recensions out of what was once likely a single treatise. A variety of scribal concerns—ranging from syntax to theology—have informed the current shape of R1 and R2.

3. Catena fragments

Adrian's presence in the exegetical catenae was first noted in 1884 by J.-B.-F. Pitra. In the intervening years a number of additional fragments of the *Introduction* have been identified in the catenae, mostly on the Psalms. Collectively,

---

[43] Canart, *Codices Vaticani Graeci*, vol. 7, part 1, 378–9. See as well the entry on **Z**: Spyridon P. Lambros, *Catalogue of the Greek Manuscripts on Mount Athos*, vol. 2 (Cambridge: Cambridge University Press, 1900; reprint, Amsterdam: Adolf M. Hakkert, 1966), 271.

they provide us a fuller picture of the text of the *Introduction* and its history. I have identified approximately forty different fragments from the *Introduction*. This number is certainly not exhaustive, since many questions still remain surrounding the authorship and authenticity of the fragments in the exegetical catenae. And many catenae mss have never been systematically examined. The number of fragments will undoubtedly rise as scholarship on the catenae continues.

For the purposes of my edition of the *Introduction*, the catenae fragments fall into two categories. Some witness to the same text that we have in R1 and R2, and thus are valuable because they occasionally offer us a better reading of these recensions than the mss in the direct tradition. There are, however, a number of fragments that read differently from the text of either recension— sometimes only roughly corresponding to these texts, and sometimes not at all. As will be clear in Chapter 5, some of these fragments point to yet another recension (or perhaps recensions) for which we have no evidence in the direct ms tradition. While fragments from this second category do not help us establish the text of our two recensions, they provide us a better picture of the transmission history of the *Introduction*, informing our understanding of the relationship between R1 and R2, and providing us some sense as to the original scope of the work. The *Introduction* was at one time significantly longer than either of our surviving recensions. I gather all known catenae fragments of the *Introduction* in an appendix and, where applicable, cross-reference them to the sections of the treatise to which they correspond.

4. Translation

Much of the *Introduction* is written in a compact, scholarly Greek style. I aspire to provide a clear and reasonably expansive translation so that readers who do not have expertise in Greek will also benefit from this treatise. A significant feature of my translation is the accompanying notes. These notes serve a number of functions: (1) they justify translations of particularly challenging passages; (2) they explain the rationale behind some of the textual decisions I have made; (3) they assign the fragments from the exegetical catenae to those passages in R1 and R2 with which they most closely correspond, so that readers can compare the text of the catenae with the recensions; (4) they provide parallel passages from other Greco-Roman authors, often those labeled "Antiochene" in the scholarship, who interpreted the biblical text similarly to Adrian (Eusebius of Emesa, Diodore of Tarsus, Theodore of Mopsuestia, his brother Polychronius, Theodoret, Junillus Africanus, Olympiodorus, and Cosmas Indicopleustes). Sometimes I quote at length from these authors because they help us understand what Adrian might have had in mind. His prose, or at least that of the scribal editors of R1 and R2, is at times cryptically concise. The parallel passages I supply, while not exhaustive, will make clear how closely Adrian's exegesis resembled these authors, especially Theodore of Mopsuestia. Whatever reservations might attach to the label "Antiochene," my notes will demonstrate that there was an exegetical tradition in the fourth through sixth centuries that was deeply rooted in the work of Theodore. Authors often shared identical approaches, perspectives and interpretations of Scripture. Finally, (5) I provide short bibliographic references to relevant scholarly literature. The studies by C. Schäublin and R. Nünlist are particularly important, since they orient readers to the "pagan" world of Greco-Roman literary scholarship that frequently paralleled, and sometimes inspired, the concerns of Adrian.

3

The Manuscripts

In the direct ms tradition Adrian's *Introduction* survives in two different recensions, R1 and R2. Thirteen mss transmit all or part of R1. This recension was previously edited by David Hoeschel and Friedrich Goessling. R2 is transmitted by three mss that have never been edited. Fragments of Adrian's *Introduction* survive in a number of mss that transmit exegetical catenae. The following catalogue provides brief descriptions of these mss. Beneath the identification line for each ms, I provide: basic codicological information; foliation, and, if known, the scribe's name; a brief discussion of the ms; whether it was used in previous editions; and finally, how I have inspected it. The bibliography for each ms identifies my sources, beginning with the relevant catalogue information (where a catalogue exists).

A. RECENSION 1

FLORENCE, BIBLIOTECA MEDICEA LAURENZIANA, *CONVENTI SOPPRESSI 39* (**L**)[1]
Parchment, 270 × 200 mm [text layout: 195 × 132 mm], ff. 254, 1095 or 1105, 35 lines/folio, 00D1—Lake I, 1a
Ff. 246r–254r, *Λουκᾶς μοναχός*

---

[1] Franciscus de Furia, *Supplementum Alterum ad Catalogum Codicum Graecorum, Latinorum, Italicorum etc. Bibliothecae Mediceae Laurentianae*, vol. 1, tome B (Florence: Biblioteca Mediceo-Laurenziana, 1846), 575; Enrico Rostagno and Nicolas Festa, "Indice dei Codici Greci Laurenziani non compresi Nel Catalogo del Bandini," vol. 1, "Conventi soppressi," *Studi italiani di filologia classica* 1 (1893), 131–96 (142), published as a supplement in Angelo Maria Bandini, *Catalogus Codicum Manuscriptorum Bibliothecae Mediceae Laurentianae*, vol. 3 (reprint: Leipzig: Zentral-Antiquariat der DDR, 1961), 12*. On the *stile rossanese*: Santo Lucà, "Rossano, il Patir e lo stile rossanese. Note per uno studio codicologico-paleografico e storico-culturale," *Rivista di Studi Bizantini e Neoellenici* 22–3 (1985–6): 93–170, esp. 99 fn. 23, 100 fn. 26, 103 fn. 49, 114 fn. 107, 159. On the scribe: Marie Vogel and Viktor Gardthausen, *Die Griechischen Schreiber des Mittelalters und der Renaissance* (Leipzig: O. Harrassowitz, 1909; reprint, Hildesheim: Georg Olms, 1966), 268; Lucà, "Rossano," 103 fn. 49; on the ink: Lucà, "Rossano," 99 fn. 23 (as well as 99–100 [fn. 26] and 114 [fn. 107] for other codicological features). On the dating of the ms: Girolamo

L is the oldest ms that transmits Adrian's *Introduction*. Of southern Italian provenance, it is well preserved and written with a clear minuscule in the *stile rossanese*. Each line is marked with a pointed instrument and the letters are written in suspension from the line. The heading (ἀδριανοῦ εἰσαγωγὴ εἰς τὰς θείας γραφάς) and initial letters of fresh paragraphs are written in red dye. At the beginning of the seventeenth century **L** was vandalized by Friedrich Lindenbruch (1573–1648), who cut out a number of folios from the end of the codex and brought them back with him to Hamburg where they now reside in the Staats- und Universitätsbibliothek as *221 in Scrinio* (**L_H**). As a result, Adrian's treatise is incompletely transmitted in **L**: it ends abruptly with the words, περὶ τοῦ δοθέν– at 254r (74.2). The *subscriptio* of the copyist Luke the monk occurs at the end of Theodoret of Cyrus' *Interpretation of the Psalms* on f. 245v (the folio immediately preceding Adrian's treatise). The scribe states that he finished copying the treatise on June 17, 6613 (i.e., 1105). However, this year does not correspond to the indiction that he also provided (γ´ = third indiction) which would date the ms to 1095. Due to this inconsistency, Girolamo Vitelli proposed moving the date of the ms back from 1105 to 1095. Yet most others now date it to 1105, correcting the indiction to ιγ´ = the thirteenth indiction. There are a few other additional codicological remarks in the literature.

Previous editions: Goessling ("L")
Inspection: *in situ*

HAMBURG, STAATS- UND UNIVERSITÄTSBIBLIOTHEK, *221 IN SCRINIO* (**L_H**)[2]
Parchment, 261 × 179 mm, ff. 6 (unbound), 1095 or 1105
Ff. 1r–1v, Λουκᾶς μοναχός

These are the folios cut out from **L** (above), thereby completing the oldest witness to Adrian's *Introduction*. 1r picks up precisely where 254r leaves off: –τος αὐτῷ χρυσίου (74.2). According to a report in Fabricius' *Bibliotheca Graeca* (1717, tome X, 687), a ms that transmitted Adrian's *Introduction* existed in what was then called the Nova Bibliotheca S. Johannis in Hamburg. It is almost certainly **L_H**, which was bequeathed to this library in 1649 from Friedrich Lindenbruch's

---

Vitelli and Cesare Paoli, *Collezione Fiorentina di Facsimili Paleografici Greci e Latini*, vol. 1 (Florence: Successori le Monnier, 1884), table 3 (with a reproduction of a folio); Lucà, "Rossano," 103 (fn. 49) and 159; Lucà, "Scrittura e produzione libraria a Rossano tra la fine del sec. XI e l'inizio del sec. XII," in *Paleografia e Codicologia greca*, ed. D. Harlfinger and G. Prato (Alessandria: Edizioni dell'Orso, 1991), 117–30 (esp. 121); Perséphone Antoniou, "Notes sur le colophon du Parisinus Gr. 1477," *Scriptorium* 43 (1989): 104. For additional bibliography on the *Conventi Soppressi* collection, see the website of the Biblioteca Medicea Laurenziana.

[2] Marina Molin Pradel, *Katalog der griechischen Handschriften der Staats- und Universitätsbibliothek Hamburg*, Serta Graeca, vol. 14 (Wiesbaden: Ludwig Reichert, 2002), 54–7 (with bibliography). See also Pradel, "Note su alcuni manoscritti greci della Staats- und Universitätsbibliothek di Amburgo," *Codices manuscripti* 34/35 (2001): 15–27, esp. 19–21.

private collection. Goessling indicated that he was unsuccessful in locating this ms in Hamburg.[3] The contents of **L/L**$_H$ become especially important when we examine below a number of sixteenth-century mss that transmit Adrian's *Introduction*. Adrian's treatise is followed in **L**$_H$ by two dialogues attributed to Jerome of Jerusalem: *De effectu baptismi* (f. 1v: incipit Τοῦ μακαρίου Ἰερωνούμου· φιλοπονίαι παντὶ χριστιανῷ ὠφελοῦσαι)[4] and *Dialogus de s. trinitate inter Iudaeum et Christianum sancta trinitate* (f. 3r: incipit Ἐρώτησις ἰουδαίου πρὸς τὸν αὐτόν).[5] This sequence of three relatively rarely attested treatises in the ms tradition surfaces throughout most of the sixteenth-century mss that carry Adrian's *Introduction* and will inform the discussion of the stemma.

Previous editions: none
Inspection: color JPG

A Brief History of L

Since **L** is the ms from which all other copies of R1 of the *Introduction* descend, I will make a few remarks about its history. This southern Italian manuscript is first attested in the library of Santa Maria di Firenze—the Badia Fiorentina (Florentine Abbey) as it is more commonly known—roughly three hundred years after it was first produced by Luke the monk. We know little of the history of **L** in the intervening years.

The Badia Fiorentina was founded at the end of the tenth century under the Rule of Saint Benedict by Countess Willa, daughter of Bonifazio, Margrave of Tuscany.[6] Its foundation date is officially given as May 31, 978. As with many Benedictine monasteries in Italy, it fell into a state of decline in the fourteenth century. At the beginning of the fifteenth, however, it underwent a series of reforms under the leadership of a Portuguese monk, Gomes (Gomezio) Ferreira da Silva. Accompanied by sixteen Benedictine monks, Gomezio arrived in Florence in 1418 and became abbot shortly thereafter in 1419. He remained abbot through 1439. At the time of Gomezio's arrival, the Badia was in such a state of decline that, according to his biographer Tommaso Salvetti, its library lacked scholarly Latin and Greek books.[7] One of Gomezio's chief initiatives was to build up the library. His coup was convincing Antonio Corbinelli

---

[3] Goessling, *Adrians ΕΙΣΑΓΩΓΗ*, 17.

[4] *CPG* III and IIIA 7817: PG 40, 860–5 and now Georges-Matthieu de Durand, *Marc le Moine: Traités II*, SC 455 (Paris: Cerf, 2000), 338–48.

[5] *CPG* 7815: PG 40, 848–60.

[6] On the history of the library of the Badia Fiorentina, the foundational study is by Rudolf Blum, *La Biblioteca della Badia Fiorentina e I Codici Di Antonio Corbinelli*, ST 155 (Vatican City: BAV, 1951). See also Maurilio Adriani, "La Badia Fiorentina, appunti storico-religiosi," in *La Badia Fiorentina*, ed. Ernesto Sestan, Maurilio Adriani, and Alessandro Guidotti (Florence: Cassa di Risparmio di Firenze, 1982), 13–46.

[7] Blum, *Badia Fiorentina*, 17–18, 20. This state of decline of the Badia might have been exaggerated by Gomezio's biographer to emphasize the effectiveness of his reform. See Anne Leader, *The Badia of Florence: Art and Observance in a Renaissance Monastery* (Bloomington: Indiana University Press, 2012), 53.

(1370/1375–1425), a wealthy Florentine and collector of Latin and Greek mss, to donate his extensive library to the Badia after his death.[8] Based upon Rudolf Blum's research, however, L was not a part of Corbinelli's collection.[9]

L is attested for the first time at the Badia Fiorentina at the beginning of the sixteenth century. In 1504, under the direction of its abbot Ignazio Squarcial-upi, a dedicated space was constructed to house the growing library of the Badia. Within a few years of this event, an inventory of the library was drawn up. This catalogue is found at *Conv. Soppr. 151*, ff. 2r–67r, and has been edited by Blum.[10] The entry for L reads, "20. Tractatus in psalmos in membranis volumine magno corio rubeo Theodoreti episcopi Chirensis."[11] This is our first record of L and provides us with the latest possible date for its entry into the Badia. The earliest date is likely sometime after Gomezio's arrival in 1418, when he discovered that the monastery had few, if any, books. The ms must, then, have been purchased by the abbey or received as a donation at some point between Gomezio's arrival and when the catalogue of the Badia's hold-ings was produced in the first decade of the sixteenth century.[12]

There is additional evidence that sheds light on the circumstances through which the Badia came to possess L. *Magliabechiano X 144* (Florence, Biblioteca Nazionale Centrale di Firenze) is a catalogue compiled in 1737 that records some of the works purchased or copied by the Badia monks from the 1470s through the early 1490s. This catalogue demonstrates a strong interest in the Psalms in this period: the Badia monks came to possess commentaries on the Psalms by Turrecremata (Rome, 1476), Eusebius of Caesarea (1480), Gilbert of Holland (Florence, 1485), Cassiodorus (Basle, 1491), and Ludolph of Saxony (1491).[13] In his study of the libraries, teachers, and classroom texts used by

[8] This donation is recorded in Corbinelli's testament of 1421, later confirmed in his final tes-tament of 1424. According to Blum, the monks compiled an inventory of the books Corbinelli donated, but only one folio of this inventory survives (see *Badia Fiorentina*, ch. 7)—the other folios are gone, and no fifteenth-century inventory from the Badia survives. On Corbinelli's death in 1425, the mss first went to a friend, Iacopo di Niccolò de' Corbizzi, before going to the monks at his death. We cannot ascertain the date of his death (Blum, *Badia Fiorentina*, 18). For more on A. Corbinelli, see Antonio Rollo, "Sulle trace di Antonio Corbinelli," *Studi medievali e umanistici* 2 (2004): 25–95, esp. 26 fn. 1, 30–1.

[9] Corbinelli donated a library of roughly 200 Latin and 80 Greek mss to the Badia Fiorentina (Blum, *Badia Fiorentina*, 18, 51–5). However, L was not part of the library (ibid., 76, 88, 115).

[10] Blum, *Badia Fiorentina*, 14, 26–31 for a discussion of the catalogue (the catalogue is printed on 114–72).

[11] Blum, *Badia Fiorentina*, 115 and 185 (for the table that compares the old numbering system with the contemporary *Conv. Soppr.* designations).

[12] For Blum's discussion of how Gomezio and subsequent abbots grew the library, see *Badia Fiorentina*, 20–2 (with examples of purchases, donations, and copying).

[13] The scriptural works in the Badia are listed on pp. 3–7 of the ms: Adrian's *Introduction* is listed twice on this register, at the bottom of p. 4 ("Isagoge in Sacras Scripturas...") and the top of p. 7 ("Theodoreti Epi. Cyrensis Expositiones in Psalmos...Ibidem Adriani Isagoge in Sacras scripturas..." While some of the entries in this catalogue are dated, the two that refer to Adrian's *Introduction* are not (*in situ* inspection). See also Barry Collett, *Italian Benedictine Scholars and the Reforma-tion: The Congregation of Santa Giustina of Padua* (Oxford: Oxford University Press, 1986), 31.

the Benedictine monks in Italy at the turn of the sixteenth century, Barry Collett has argued that they were particularly interested in biblical and patristic studies, including the Psalms and the Greek fathers.[14] From this acquisitions list, we immediately recognize how **L** would have been particularly attractive to the monks of the Badia, since most of the codex transmits Theodoret's *Commentary on the Psalms* (ff. 1r–245v) and Adrian's *Introduction* is itself strongly oriented toward the language of the Psalms. It is not surprising, then, that **L** should have found its way into the Badia sometime in the fifteenth or early sixteenth centuries.

There are a few other noteworthy episodes in the history of **L**. As noted above, at the beginning of the seventeenth century the ms was inspected and several folios removed by the collector of mss, Friedrich Lindenbruch. The circumstances in which Lindenbruch acquired these folios are murky, and perhaps also dubious. Marina Molin Pradel has proposed that it was "likely during one of his trips to Italy" that he acquired them—we know that he was at least twice in Florence, in 1606 and 1608, and there are two other Greek mss in his collection that come from the Badia Fiorentina library.[15] Lindenbruch removed at least 6 folios from **L**—these are now *In Scrinio 221* in Hamburg (**L**$_\text{H}$).[16] The first of these folios transmits the concluding sections of Adrian's *Introduction*.

What remained of **L** was still in the Badia at the beginning of the eighteenth century. In the spring of 1700, the French Benedictine Bernard de Montfaucon (1655–1741) visited the monastery in Florence and produced the first print catalogue of the holdings of the Badia. **L** is described as follows: "Codex membr. optimae notae, *Theodoreti* in Psalmos scriptus a quodam Luca anno 6613. id est Christi 1105. Ibidem *Hadriani* introductio in sacras Scripturas."[17] On April 29, 1808, by decree of the French (Napoleonic) general Administrator of Tuscany, L. J. E. Dauchy, the library of the Badia (as well as those of other monasteries) was confiscated.[18] A number of its mss were sent to the Laurenziana, including **L**, where it remains to this day. The librarian Francesco Del Furia (1777–1856) signed for the receipt of the codices on August 29, 1809.[19] Del Furia was the cataloguer of the *Conventi Soppressi* collection (vol. 1 of his catalogue recorded the mss that came from the Badia Fiorentina). Enrico Rostagno and Nicolas Festa offer a more up-to-date entry.

[14] Collet, *Italian Benedictine Scholars*, 28–54.
[15] Pradel, *Katalog Hamburg*, 8–9, 57. On Lindenbruch, see Eva Horváth, *Friedrich Lindenbruch, Späthumanist und Handschriftensammler des 17. Jahrhunderts: Ein Beitrag zur Hamburger Bibliotheks- und Gelehrtergeschichte* (Diss. Dr. Phil. Hamburg, 1988). See also Davide Baldi, "Sulla Storia di alcuni Codici Italogreci della Biblioteca Laurenziana," *Nea Rhome* 4 (2007): 374–5.
[16] Pradel, "Note su alcuni manoscritti," 19–21; Pradel, *Katalog Hamburg*, 54–7.
[17] Bernardo de Montfoucon, *Diarium Italicum. Sive monumentorum veterum, bibliothecarum, musaeorum, &c. Notitiae singulares in itinerario Italico collectae. Additis schematibus ac figuris* (Paris: J. Anisson, 1702): 363, lines 28–30 for the listing of L.
[18] For the decree, Baldi, "Storia," 371 fn. 74.
[19] Baldi, "Storia," 371–2; Blum, *Badia Fiorentina*, 11 fn. 23.

Sixteenth-century manuscripts

MUNICH, BAYERISCHE STAATSBIBLIOTHEK, *CODEX GRAECUS 477* (**A**)[20]
Paper, ff. 32, XVI
Ff. 1r–20v

A well-preserved ms with titles and initial letters written in red ink. Note that Ignatio Hardt's catalogue entry provides the wrong foliation for Adrian's *Intro-duction*: this treatise concludes at the midpoint of 20v, not at the bottom of 30v. In the intervening space are the two aforementioned treatises that we find in L_H: *De effectu baptismi* (ff. 20v–24r) and *Dialogus de s. trinitate* (ff. 24r–30v). At 31r–v is a short work on the Greek translations of the OT (incipit Πόσαι παραδόσεις εἰσὶ τῆς θείας γραφῆς τῶν προφητικῶν...). The mss with sig-natures *Codd. Graec.* 348–574 came to the Hofbibliothek in Munich from the Augsburger Stadtbibliothek after the annexation of Augsburg to Bavaria in 1806. Ignatio Hardt, with Goessling following, correctly concluded that this ms provided the base text for Hoeschel's edition, which was produced and published in Augsburg. David Hoeschel introduced a number of marginalia while preparing his edition (the kinds of notations he made are listed in Chap-ter 2 of Part II).

Previous editions: Hoeschel; Goessling ("a")
Inspection: black-and-white JPG

MUNICH, BAYERISCHE STAATSBIBLIOTHEK, *CODEX GRAECUS 107* (**B**)[21]
Paper, 348 × 230 mm [220/230 × 125/130 mm], ff. 372, ca. 1550
Ff. 1r–14r, "C. Probatares"

The first of four parts of this codex begins with Adrian's *Introduction*, and is followed by *De effectu baptismi* (14r–16r) and *Dialogus de s. trinitate* (16r–20v).

---

[20] Ignatio Hardt, *Catalogus Codicum Manuscriptorum Graecorum*, vol. 5, *Cod. graec. 473–574[-583]* (Munich: Seidel, 1812), 20–1; Kerstin Hajdú, *Katalog der griechischen Handschriften der Bayerischen Staatsbibliothek München*, vol. 10, 1, *Die Sammlung griechischer Handschriften in der Münchener Hofbibliothek bis zum Jahr 1803. Ein Bestandsgeschichte der Codices graeci Mona-censes 1–323 mit Signaturenkonkordanzen und Beschreibung des Stephanus-Katalogs (Cbm Cat. 48)* (Wiesbaden: Harrassowitz, 2002), 34.

[21] Marina Molin Pradel, *Katalog der griechischen Handschriften der Bayerischen Staatsbiblio-thek München*, vol. 2, *Codices graeci Monacenses 56–109* (Wiesbaden: Harrassowitz, 2013), 7–24, 314–20 (with bibliography); Hajdú, *Katalog München*, 43–55, 99–103, 139–43. On Fugger: Hajdú, "Johann Jakob Fugger und seine Bibliothek," in *Kulturkosmos der Renaissance: Die Gründ-ung der Bayerischen Staatsbibliothek. Katalog zur Ausstellung zum 450-jährigen Jubiläum* (Wies-baden: Harrassowitz, 2008), 125–7; Brigitte Mondrain, "Copistes et collectionneurs de manuscrits grecs au milieu du XVIᵉ siècle: le cas de Johann Jakob Fugger d'Augsbourg," *Byzantinische Zeitschrift* 84/85 (1991–2): 354–90. On the scribe: Canart, "Les manuscrits copiés par Emmanuel Provataris (1546–1570 environ): Essai d'étude codicologique," in *Mélanges Eugène Tisserant*, vol. 6, *Bibliothèque Vaticane: premiere partie*, ST 236 (Vatican City: BAV, 1964), 203–4; also see Mond-rain, "Copistes et collectionneurs," 369, 377 fn. 30, and 385 addendum 4); Pradel, *Katalog München*, 309.

Note that the ms attributes the *Introduction* to Ἀδριανοῦ (smooth breathing mark), not as the catalogue prints it, Ἁδριανοῦ (rough breathing mark). The ms dates to ca. 1550 and was bound in Venice. It was produced for Johann Jakob Fugger (1516–75), and entered into his library in Augsburg no later than 1557. It was acquired from Fugger's library by Albrecht V, Duke of Bavaria, for the Hofbibliothek in Munich in 1571. The Fugger collection played a large role in the dissemination of classical, antique, and medieval literature in Germany during the Renaissance. Hoeschel, for instance, used a number of these mss, as is clear from the marginal notes he left behind in *Codd. graec. 64, 65,* and *87.* This is the other ms that he used in making his edition.

Previous edition: Hoeschel; Goessling ("b")
Inspection: black-and-white JPG

VATICAN CITY, BIBLIOTHECA APOSTOLICA, *OTTOBONIANUS GRAECUS 194* (**C**)[22]
Paper, 250 × 170 mm, ff. 275, XVI
Ff. 242r–263r

This codex contains an assortment of theological treatises. Adrian's *Introduction* is followed by *De effectu baptismi* (ff. 263v–267r) and *Dialogus de s. trinitate* (ff. 267r–275r). The codex ends here. The ms was once owned by Guglielmo Sirleto (1514–88) and thereafter by Giovanni Angelo, Duke of Altemps (d. 1620), who acquired it from Sirleto's collection in 1611. This ms (as well as **D** and **E** below) was later purchased by cardinal Pietro Ottoboni, and eventually donated by his grandnephew to the Bibliotheca Vaticana.

Previous Edition: Goessling ("o.¹")
Inspection: *in situ*

---

[22] Ernest Feron and Fabiano Battaglini, *Codices Manuscripti Graeci Ottoboniani Bibliothecae Vaticanae* (Rome: Vatican, 1893), 114–15; Franchi de' Cavalieri, *Catalogus Codicum Hagiographicorum Graecorum Bibliothecae Vaticanae* (Brussels: Apud Editores, 1899), 265; Giovanni Angelo Altemps, *Catalogue des livres et des manuscrits composant la bibliothèque des Ducs d'Altemps* (Rome: Rossi, 1908); Elisabeth Pellegrin et al., *Les manuscrits classiques latins de la Bibliothèque Vaticane*, vol. 1, *Fonds Archivio San Pietra à Ottoboni* (Paris: Éditions du Centre national de la recherche scientifique, 1975), 437–8. On the dating: the ms has been variously dated from the fifteenth through seventeenth centuries. The most thorough analysis dates it to the sixteenth century: Albert Ehrhard, *Überlieferung und Bestand der Hagiographischen und Homiletischen Literatur der Griechischen Kirche von den Anfängen bis zum Ende des 16. Jahrhunderts*, vol 3.2.1/2 (Berlin: Akademie Verlag, 1952), 897 fn. 3.
Sirleto's library: Léon Dorez, "Recherches et documents sur la bibliothèque du Cardinal Sirleto," *Mélanges d'archéologie et d'histoire* 11 (1891): 457–91; Georg Denzler, *Kardinal Guglielmo Sirleto (1514–1585): Leben und Werke. Ein Beitrag zur Nachtridentinischen Reform* (Munich: Max Hueber, 1964), 70–2; Irena Backus and Benoît Gain, "Cardinal Guglielmo Sirleto (1514–1585), sa Bibliothèque et ses Traductions de Saint Basile," in *Mélanges de L'Ecole française de Rome, Moyen-Age, Temps modernes* 98 (1986): 889–955; Francesco Russo, "La Biblioteca del Card. Sirleto," *Il Card. Guglielmo Sirleto (1514–1585): Atti del Convegno di Studio nel IV Centenario della morte*, ed. Leonardo Calabretta and Gregorio Sinatora (Cantanzaro-Squillace: Istituto di Scienze Religiose, 1989), 219–99.

VATICAN CITY, BIBLIOTHECA APOSTOLICA, *OTTOBONIANUS GRAECUS 270* (**D**)[23]
Paper, 240 × 160 mm [220 × 122 mm], ff. 24, XVI
Ff. 1r–15v, Ἰωάννης Μαυρομάτης

The catalogue dates the ms to the seventeenth century, though we now know that the scribe was John Mauromates, who flourished in the middle to third quarter of the sixteenth century. The catalogue also presents an incomplete list of treatises in the ms. My *in situ* inspection reveals that the contents of the ms after Adrian's treatise are as follows: *De effectu baptismi* (16r–18v); *Dialogus s. trinitate* (18v–23v); the work on the Greek translations of the OT (23v–24r) and scholia on Job 9:9 (incipit Ἔχει ὁ Ἰὼβ περὶ ἀστροθεσίας τάδε·; desinit ἄλλων δὲ τοπικῶν ὀνομάτων ἐπιγείων ὑπομνησθέντες ποιούμεθα τὴν διήγησιν) and Ps 148:9 (incipit Ὄρη μὲν εἰσὶ φυσικῶς ὑψώματα; desinit εἰς τὸ μέσον συναγόμενον σταχυοει-) (24r–v). The last few words are missing (-δῶς σχηματίζεται—cf. **FGIK**) because a binder trimmed the margins of the ms too closely, often obscuring words on its exterior or bottom margins. The ms was once owned by G. Sirleto, and thereafter by Giovanni Angelo, Duke of Altemps, who acquired it from Sirleto's collection in 1611.

Previous edition: Goessling ("o.²")
Inspection: *in situ*

VATICAN CITY, BIBLIOTHECA APOSTOLICA, *OTTOBONIANUS GRAECUS 379* (**E**)[24]
Paper, 240 × 170 mm [152 × 92 mm], ff. 293, XVI (middle to third quarter)
Ff. 51r–59v, Ἰωάννης Μαυρομάτης

The codex contains an assortment of hagiographical and theological treatises by different hands. Adrian's treatise is not completely transmitted: it is interrupted at 59v with the words Τὴν ὁμοιότητα λέγει πολλάκις ἀντὶ τοῦ πράγματος (36) and is followed by three blank and unnumbered folios in the codex. The *Introduction* is not followed by the treatises that usually accompany it. The ms was owned by G. Sirleto and thereafter by Giovanni Angelo, Duke of Altemps, who acquired this ms from Sirleto's collection in 1611.

---

[23] Feron and Battaglini, *Codices Manuscripti Graeci Ottoboniani*, 152. On the scribe: Ernst Gamillscheg, Dieter Harlfinger, and Herbert Hunger, eds., *Repertorium der Griechischen Kopisten 800–1600* (Vienna: Verlag der Österreichischen Akademie der Wissenschaften, 1981–), attributes D to John Mauromates (1A = no. 171; 2A = 229; 3A = no. 283) (3A, p. 108). For biography and bibliography on this copyist, see 1A, p. 98; Annaclara Cataldi Palau, "Il copista Ioannes Mauromates," in *I manoscritti greci tra riflessione e dibattito. Atti del V colloquio Internazionale di Paleografia Greca (Cremona 4–10 ott. 1998)*, ed. Giancarlo Prato, vol. 1 (Florence: Gonnelli, 2000), 398.
[24] Feron and Battaglini, *Codices Manuscripti Graeci Ottoboniani*, 193; R. Devreesse, "Les manuscrits grecs de Cervini," *Scriptorium* 22 (1968): 263. On the scribe: *Repertorium* attributes E, ff. 51–59v to Ἰωάννης Μαυρομάτης (1A = no. 171; 2A = no. 229; 3A = no. 283) (3A, p. 108). For biography and bibliography, see *Repertorium*, 1A, p. 98; Palau, "Il copista Ioannes Mauromates," 362, 369, 378, 399.

Previous edition: Goessling ("o.³")
Inspection: *in situ*

BASEL, UNIVERSITÄTSBIBLIOTHEK, *O II 17B* (**F**)²⁵
Paper, 373 × 240 mm [232 × 130 mm], ff. 23 (unbound), XVI
Ff. 1r–13r, perhaps "C. Probatares" (cf. **B**)

A well-preserved and carefully written ms. Adrian's *Introduction* is followed by
the two treatises attributed to Jerome of Jerusalem, *De effectu baptismi* (13r–15r)
and *Dialogus de s. trinitate* (15r–19r); the work on the Greek translations of the
OT (19v–20r); and the scholia on Job and Psalms (Desinit εἰς τὸ μέσον
συναγόμενον στοχιοειδῶς σχηματίζεται· τέλος) (20r–20v). This ms comes
from the collection of Remigius Faesch (1595–1667). Faesch traveled extensively, including France, Germany, and a long trip throughout Italy in 1620–1.
He taught law at the University of Basel and was its rector in 1637, 1649, and
1660. Faesch's collection of mss and works of art (the so-called *Faeschische
Kabinett* or *Museum*) was bequeathed to the University of Basel in 1823.

Previous editions: none
Inspection: black-and-white PDF

VATICAN CITY, BIBLIOTHECA APOSTOLICA, *VATICANUS GRAECUS 659* (**G**)²⁶
Paper, 162 × 115 mm, ff. 211 (order of folios restored: 1–62v, 65r–66v, 63r–64v,
67r ss.), XVI
Ff. 61r–82r, Φραγκίσκος Συρόπουλος (d. 1567)

In this codex Adrian's *Introduction* is followed by *De effectu baptismi* (ff. 82v–
86r); *Dialogus de s. trinitate* (ff. 86r–93v); the work on the Greek translations
of the OT (ff. 94r–95r); the scholia on Job and Psalms (95r–96r). The scribe
(Franciscus Syropulos) flourished from the middle to second half of the sixteenth century and was a scriptor at the Bibliotheca Vaticana (1552–66). The
ms was also once owned by G. Sirleto.

Previous editions: Goessling ("v.¹")
Inspection: *in situ*

---

²⁵ Henri Auguste Omont, *Catalogue des Manuscrits Grecs des Bibliothèques de Suisse* (Leipzig:
Otto Harrassowitz, 1886), 2–4, 34–5 (no. 86); Gustav Binz, unpublished catalogue of "O. II. 17b
(Graec. 86)" on July 13, 1938 (courtesy of the Universitätsbibliothek Basel). On Faesch and his
mss: Remigius Sebastian Faesch, *Das Museum Faesch: Eine Basler Kunst- und Raritätensammlung
aus dem 17. Jahrhundert* (Basel: Merian, 2005), 13–20; Fredy Gröbli, "Basler Büchersammler III:
Remigius Faesch (1595–1667)," *Librarium* 20 (1977): 42–9; Gustav Friedrich Hänel, *Catalogi
Librorum Manuscriptorum, qui in Bibliothecis Galliae, Helvetiae, Belgii, Britanniae maioris, Hispaniae, Lusitaniae asservantur* (Leipzig: J. C. Hinrichs, 1830), col. 655–9 (Adrian is the first entry
on 657).
²⁶ Robert Devreesse, *Codices Vaticani Graeci*, vol. 3, *Codices 604–866* (Vatican City: BAV,
1950), 93–5; R. Devreesse, *Le Fonds Grecs de la Bibliothèque Vaticane des Origines a Paul V*, ST
244 (Vatican City: BAV, 1965), 470 fn. 4. On the scribe, cf. *Repertorium*, 3A: no. 605 (bibliography
on p. 211).

84 *Adrian's* Introduction to the Divine Scriptures

VATICAN CITY, BIBLIOTHECA APOSTOLICA, *VATICANUS GRAECUS 1269* (**H**)[27]
Paper, 240 × 160 mm, ff. 62, XVI
Ff. 1–27r

In many places the ms is illegible due to water damage. The ink is diffused and has often bled through to the opposite side of the folio. The ms appears to have been legible for Goessling when he was visiting Italian libraries in the spring of 1886 since his apparatus lists a number of readings illegible to me during my summer 2014 *in situ* analysis of the ms. The list of treatises is as follows: after Adrian, f. 27v is blank; then follows Jerome of Jerusalem, *De effectu baptismi* (28r–32r); *Dialogus de s. trinitate* (32r–41r); the work on Greek translations of the OT (41r–43r); the scholia on Job and Psalms (43r–v); 44r–45v are blank. The ms once belonged to Antonio Carafa (1538–91) who was named Prefect of the Bibliotheca Vaticana after Sirleto's death in 1585. At Carafa's death, he bequeathed his ms collection to the library.

Previous edition: Goessling ("v.²")
Inspection: *in situ*

VATICAN, BIBLIOTHECA APOSTOLICA, *VATICANUS GRAECUS 1665* (**I**)[28]
Paper, 325 × 218 mm [218 × 122 mm], ff. 286, 1566–8
Ff. 261r–276r, Ἰωάννης Μαυρομάτης

The heading originally attributed the treatise to ἀδριανοῦ (red ink), but a later hand has changed it to ἀφρικανοῦ, reshaping the δ into a φ and inserting a κ (with black ink). The catalogue description of the table of contents of this codex is inaccurate: Adrian's treatise is followed by Jerome of Jerusalem: *De effectu baptismi* (276r–278v); *Dialogus de s. trinitate* (278v–283v); the work on the seven translations of the OT (ff. 284r–v); the scholia on Job and Psalms (284v–285v); f. 286 is blank. At one time the ms belonged to Daniele Barbaro, patriarch elect of Aquileia (1514–70), and later became part of the library of his nephew, Francesco III, patriarch of Aquileia (1646–1716). Aloysius Lollin likely used **I** for his translation of the *Introduction* into Latin (cf. discussion in Chapter 2 of Part II).

---

[27] Johannes Bollig and Paulus de Lagarde, *Iohannis Euchaitorum Metropolitae quae in codice Vaticano graeco 676 supersunt* (Göttingen: Aedibus Dieterichianis, 1882), viii–ix; Pierre Batiffol, *La Vaticane de Paul III à Paul V d'après des documents nouveaux* (Paris: Ernest Leroux, 1890), 69–70; Canart, "Les manuscrits copies par Emmanuel Provataris," 204.

[28] Cyrus Giannelli, *Codices Vaticani Graeci*, vol. 5, *Codices 1485–1683* (Vatican City: BAV, 1960), 406–8; Canart, *Les Vaticani Graeci 1487–1962: Notes et Documents pour l'Histoire d'un fonds de manuscrits de la Bibliothèque Vaticane*, ST 248 (Vatican City: BAV, 1979), 150–2, 200; Canart, "Reliures et Codicologie: Les Manuscrits grecs de la Famille Barbaro," in *Calames et Cahiers: Mélanges de codicologie et de paléographie offerts à Léon Gilissen*, ed. Jacques Lemaire and Émile van Balberghe (Brussels: Centre D'Étude des Manuscrits, 1985), 13–25. On the scribe: see *Repertorium* 3A, p. 107 and bibliography for **D** above.

Previous editions: none
Inspection: *in situ*

VATICAN, BIBLIOTHECA APOSTOLICA, *VATICANUS GRAECUS 1908* (**J**)[29]
Paper, ca. 315 × 220 mm, ff. 120, various centuries: XIV, XVI, XVI–XVII
Ff. 18r–25r

This codex consists of ten mss (with significant differences in folio sizes) from various centuries that transmit a wide assortment of treatises. Adrian's work occurs on ms 4:

Paper, 305 × 215 mm [225/230 × 158], ff. 12, XVI–XVII

Pierre Batiffol claimed that **J** was owned at one time by Aloysius Lollin and served as one of the mss that he used for his Latin translation of the treatise. The ownership of **J**, however, is not quite clear: only two parts of this codex (mss 7 and 9, not 4, where Adrian is found) explicitly surface in the inventories of Lollin's collection of Greek mss. Since Lollin's inventories were not entirely complete, Canart warns against assuming that each of its parts was owned by Lollin. Nevertheless, a collation of **J** with Lollin's translation indicates that Lollin at the very least made use of this ms for making his translation, since he follows one of its crucial distinguishing errors: the transposition of verses in paragraph 62.1 (cf. discussion of Lollin's translation in Chapter 2 of Part II).

Previous editions: none
Inspection: *in situ*

ROME, BIBLIOTHECA VALLICELLIANA, *F9 (78)* (**K**)[30]
Paper, 245 × 176 mm, ff. 310, XVI (middle to second half)
Ff. 133r–156v (ff. rearranged: 144r–137v), *Φραγκίσκος Συρόπουλος*

The *Introduction* is attributed to *Αὐδριανοῦ* (f. 149r). This codex consists of diverse mss. On ms 8 it contains two extended and incomplete copies of the treatise written by the same hand. These folios are out of sequence:

K₁: paragraphs 55 through 79 (ff. rearranged: 144r–145v, 143r–v, 148r–v, 146r–147v, 141r)

K₂: paragraphs 1 through 74.3.3 (ff. rearranged: 149r–156v, 142v, 133r–137v)

In K_1 after the *Introduction* ends at the bottom of f. 141r, *De effectu baptismi* begins at the top of 141v and ends incomplete at the bottom of 142r. In K_2 after the *Introduction* ends on f. 137v, we find the customary sequence of treatises:

[29] Canart, *Codices Vaticani Graeci*, vol. 7, part 1, 639–45; Batiffol, "Dr. Friedrich Goessling: L'Isagoge d'Hadrien," 1; Mercati, *Per la storia*, 125 fn. 2; Canart, "Alivse Lollino et ses amis grecs," *Studi Veniziani* 12 (1970): 580; Canart, *Les Vaticani Graeci 1487–1962*, 240, 48 fn. 40, 53 fn. 62.

[30] Emidio Martini, *Catalogo di Manoscritti Greci Esistenti Nelle Biblioteche Italiane*, vol. 2, *Catalogus Codicum Graecorum qui in Bibliotheca Vallicellana Romae Adservantur* (Milan: Ulrico Hoepli, 1902), 128–30. On the scribe: see Bibliography for **G**.

De effectu baptismi (f. 137v–139v); *Dialogus de s. trinitate* (btm, f. 139v); the work on the Greek translations of the OT (ff. 160v–161v); then the scholia on Job and the Psalms.

Previous editions: none
Inspection: black-and-white PDF

Eighteenth-century manuscript

MOUNT ATHOS, Μονή Αγίου Παντελεήμονος, 693 (LAMBROS 6200) (P)[31]
Paper, 220 × 142 mm, ff. 355, XVIII
Ff. 249r–265v

Lambros provides the wrong foliation for Adrian's *Introduction*: the treatise ends toward the bottom of 265v, not on 269r, as is claimed in the catalogue. A short, anonymous work, entitled ὑπόθεσις τῶν προφητῶν, begins on 266r and concludes on 269r: it is the *Proemium Expositionis Sanctorum Prophetarum* by Theophylact, archbishop of Ohrid (1055–1107) (PG 126, 565–76). According to Lambros' catalogue, Theophylact is not preserved elsewhere in this ms. The text of the *Introduction* is a copy of Hoeschel's edition (including his text critical sigla and his marginal identifications of scriptural verses).

Previous editions: none
Inspection: black-and-white TIF

B. RECENSION 2

VATICAN CITY, BIBLIOTHECA APOSTOLICA, *VATICANUS GRAECUS 1862* (X)[32]
Paper, 175 × 140 mm, ff. 159, various centuries: XV, XVI, ca. 17 lines/folio
Ff. 72r–79v, Guglielmus Sirletus (1514–85)

This codex consists of eighteen different mss. Adrian is in the ninth:

Paper, 170 × 120 mm [140 × 90 mm], ff. 72r–87v (83v–87v blank), XVI (third quarter), 15–18 lines/folio

The top of 72r has the same heading as **YZ** (ἐκ τοῦ περὶ τῶν ἰδιωμάτων τῆς θείας γραφῆς καὶ μάλιστα τοῦ Δαυιδ εἰσὶ ταῦτα) and transmits an extended

[31] Spyridon P. Lambros, *Catalogue of the Greek Manuscripts on Mount Athos*, vol. 2 (Cambridge: Cambridge University Press, 1900; reprint, Amsterdam: Adolf M. Hakkert, 1966), 415–16.
[32] Canart, *Codices Vaticani Graeci*, vol. 7, part 1, 375–84. On Sirleto, see biography and bibliography in *Repertorium*, 2A = no. 117; 3A = no. 154; on Sirleto's hand, see Canart, "Les Manuscrits Copiés par Emmanuel Provataris (1546–1570 environ)," 212 with plate 16 (*Vat. Gr. 1890*, f. 489v). On his library, see the bibliography for **C**.

section of the *Introduction* (incipit Τὸ ἀγαπᾶν λέγει πανταχοῦ ἐπὶ τοῦ θεοῦ [26]; desinit τὰ σώματα αὐτῶν ἐν αὐτοῖς [55]). Guglielmo Sirleto, the copyist of **X**, was a significant scholar and ecclesiastic of the sixteenth century. He was commissioned to create an inventory of the Greek mss of the Bibliotheca Vaticana in 1548, was custodian of the library from 1554, and finally, Prefect from 1570–85. Recall from the preceding catalogue that Sirleto owned several copies of R1. He also owned **Y**.

Previous edition: none
Inspection: *in situ*

VATICAN, BIBLIOTHECA APOSTOLICA, *VATICANUS GRAECUS 1447* (**Y**)[33]
Paper, 216 × 156 mm [158 × 94 mm], ff. 288, 1534, ca. 40 lines/folio
Ff. 1r–2r and 11v–13r, Παχώμιος (second quarter of sixteenth century)

A well-preserved ms with titles and initial letters at the start of new sections in red ink. This ms transmits two extended sections of the *Introduction*. Section one (1r–2r) opens with the same heading as **X** and transmits the same first fragment. Section two (11v–13r) has a one-word heading, τοῦ, which might be an error for τοῦ αὐτοῦ. This section runs from 72–74.3.3 (incipit Κωλύσειειν δᾶν οὐδέν; desinit τὸ πραττόμενον ἐπὶ τοῦ Ἀβραάμ). The ms contains excerpts from a number of different authors. Based on an *in situ* analysis, the table of contents for the works that open this codex are: Adrian *Introduction* (1r–2r); blank (2v–3v); Ἐρωτήσεις Σχολαστικοῦ τινὸς πρὸς Συμεὼν τὸν ἐν ἁγίοις θεολόγον (4r–v); Ὅροι τῶν ἁγίων πατέρων (5r–11r) (excerpts from Anastasius of Sinai); Adrian *Introduction* (11v–13r); Ἐκ τῆς βίβλου Ἰωάννου τοῦ Δαμασκηνοῦ· ἧς ἡ ἐπωνυμία Πηγὴ γνώσεως (13v–21r); Εὐθυμίου μοναχοῦ τοῦ Ζιγαβηνοῦ· Πρόγραμμα βίβλου τῆσδε τῶν δογμάτων (21r); Πίναξ, ἤτοι ἐπὶ τίτλωσις τοῦ παρόντος βιβλίου τῆς Δογματικῆς Πανοπλίας (21r–21v); and so forth. The scribe is Pachomius who describes himself as "the least of the solitaries" (ὁ ἐλάχιστος ἐν μονοτρόποις). The ms dates to 1534 and was owned by G. Sirleto.

Previous edition: none
Inspection: *in situ*

---

[33] Hans-Georg Opitz, *Untersuchungen zur Überlieferung der Schriften des Athanasius* (Berlin: Walter de Gruyter, 1935), 102 fn. 5; G. Mercati, *Codici latini Pico Grimani Pio e di altra biblioteca ignota del secolo XVI, esistenti nell'Ottoboniana e I codici greci Pio di Modena*, ST 75 (Vatican City: BAV, 1938), 116–22, esp. 119; Bonifatius Kotter, *Die Überlieferung der Pege Gnoseos des hl. Johannes von Damaskos* (Ettal: Buch-Kunstverlag, 1959), 72; R. Devreesse, "Pour l'Histoire des Manuscrits du Fonds Vatican Grec," *Collectanea Vaticana in honorem Anselmi M. Card. Albareda a Bibliotheca Apostolica edita*, ST 219 (Vatican City: BAV, 1962), 334; Canart, *Catalogue des Manuscrits grecs de L'Archivio di San Pietro*, ST 246 (Vatican City: BAV, 1966), 60; R. Devreesse, *Les Ancien Commentateurs Grecs des Psaumes*, ST 264 (Vatican City: BAV, 1970), 312 fn. 2; Karl-Heinz Uthemann, *Anastasii Sinaitae: Viae Dux*, CCSG 8 (Turnhout: Brepols, 1981), lx. On the scribe: *Repertorium*, 3A: no. 543, p. 194 (no bibliography)—a description of his writing style in vol. 3B, p. 198; see Tafel 295 (3C) for a facsimile of f. 225v.

Seventeenth-century manuscript

MOUNT ATHOS, Μονή Ἰβήρων, *1333* (LAMBROS 5453) (**Z**)[34]
Paper, 207 × 145 mm [150/160 × 85/110 mm], ff. 79; XVI–XVII, ca. 26 lines/folio
Ff. 1r–4r and 18v–22v

Titles and intial letters in red ink. **Z** is very closely related to **Y**. It opens with the same heading as does **Y**, and transmits the same two extended sections of the *Introduction*: section one (1r–4r), and then later in the ms, section two (18v–22v). **Z** has the exact same sequence of treatises as **Y** through the Πίναξ of the chapters of Euthymius Zigabenus' Δογματικὴ Πανοπλία. After this, the mss part ways, with **Z** transmitting a work by Georgios Coressius, who died in the early seventeenth century. It is not clear whether the entire ms dates to the seventeenth century or only this last section. Lambros did not identify the author and work from which the first or second sections of the *Introduction* came. In the case of the second section that lists scriptural tropes, he offered the following descriptive entry in his catalogue: Καὶ περί τινων σχημάτων τοῦ λόγου. Additional similarities: **Y** and **Z** have the same marginal correction (τοῖς ἀναιρουμένοις) at 54.1; both insert the noun ὑποθέσεως under the same word (οἰκονομίας) in the last line of the second fragment (74.3.3); and both nearly always indicate the same scriptural quotations with symbols in the margins of the second fragment (a comma-shaped symbol in **Y**; an s-shaped symbol in **Z**).

Previous editions: none
Inspection: color JPG

C. EXEGETICAL CATENAE

For the mss that transmit the exegetical catenae and their descriptions, see the section following the Greek texts and translations, "Fragments of Adrian's *Introduction to the Divine Scriptures* in the Exegetical Catenae."

---

[34] Lambros, *Catalogue*, vol. 2, 271; Canart, *Codices Vaticani Graeci*, vol. 7, part 1, 378–9.

4

Recensio Codicum

A. STEMMA: RECENSION 1

The analysis that follows is based upon a complete collation of all the mss that transmit R1. **H** has suffered water damage and is only sporadically legible, while **EK₁K₂** transmit partial copies of the *Introduction*. When these mss are not listed in the lines of evidence below, it is because they are unclear or do not transmit the whole treatise. The presentation progresses downwards, from the ancestor of the surviving mss (**L/L_H**) to its descendants. A diagram of the stemma follows this discussion.

An investigation of the text of the *Introduction* as transmitted in **L/L_H** indicates that all of its errors are taken over by the other mss. Only a handful of mistakes are corrected by subsequent scribes. Thus all of the mss that transmit the *Introduction* derive directly or indirectly from **L/L_H**. Some of the more significant errors include:

126.6–7   ἢ ἀπὸ κινήσεων σωματικῶν ἢ ἀπὸ παθῶν ψυχικῶν **Hoeschel Goessling**: om. L et **ABCDEFGIJK₂**

146.12   Τὴν τῆς κατὰ τῶν ἐχθρῶν **Hoeschel Goessling**: Τὴν κατὰ τῆς τῶν ἐχθρῶν L et **ABCDEFGIJK₂**

148.13   κάθισιν *cat. Ps. 9:8* **Hoeschel Goessling**: καθίστησιν L et **ABC DEFGIJK₂**

150.6   εἴη δ’ ἂν **Hoeschel Goessling**: εἶναι L et **ABCDEFGIJK₂**

180.10   γενηθήτω Δ ἂν **Goessling** (*ex Schlüren*): ἐγενήθη τῷ Ἀδὰμ L et **ABCDEFGIJK₂ Hoeschel**: ἐγενήθη τῷ Δ ἂν **Hoeschel** (*notae*)

186.5–6   ὅπως ἂν δικαιωθῇς ἐν τοῖς λόγοις σου **Martens**, cf. *cat. Ps. 50:6, sim.* **Schlüren**: om. L et **ABCDEFGIJK₂ Hoeschel Goessling**

192.14–15   ἀποστολὴν δι’ ἀγγέλων πονηρῶν **R2 Schlüren**, cf. *Ps. 77:49* om. L et **ABCDEFGIJK₂ Hoeschel Goessling**

218.5   αἰσχίστων *cat. Ps. 77:66* **A** *p. corr.* **Goessling** (*ex A*): αἰσχίστως L et **BCDEFGIJK₁K₂**: αἰσχίσων **Hoeschel**

264.10–11   ὑποτίθεται **IJK₁K₂ C** et **G** *p. corr.* **Hoeschel Goessling**: ὑποτίθεται ὑποτίθεται L et **ABDF**

Stemma of the Manuscripts of the Two Recensions of
Adrian's *Introduction to the Divine Scriptures*

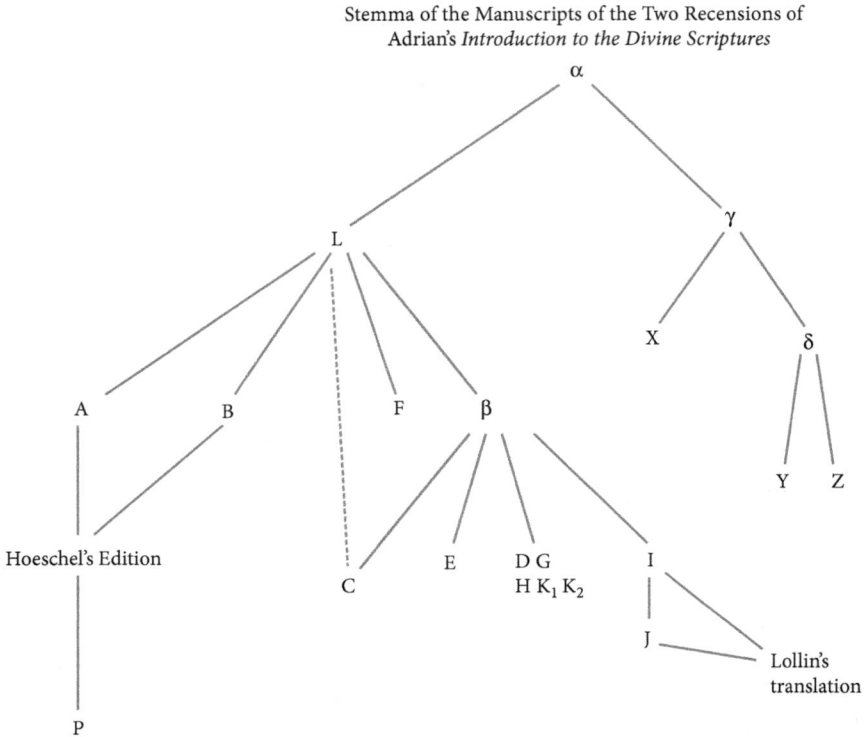

There are a number of additional shared errors in **CDEGHK₁K₂IJ** (=λ) that are avoided by **ABF**. Since these three mss each have errors of their own not found in λ, this family is not derived from any of these mss, but descends independently from **L**.

There are no significant errors—additional to those already contributed by **L**— that are held in common by any combination of **A**, **B**, or **F**. This suggests that these mss also descend independently from **L**. In **F** the main distinguishing error is:

194.15–17   καί, ἰδοὺ–πτώσεως [11 verba] **AB**: *om.* **F**

Significant omissions and transpositions in **A** include:

132.15   καί, ὁ οἰκοδομῶν–αὐτοῦ [9 verba] **BF**: *om.* **A**
136.4   προσώπου σου **BF**: *om.* **A**
198.11   σοῦ τοῦ **BF**: τοῦ σοῦ **A**
212.7–8   ἀντὶ προαιρέσεως–ἀντὶ προαίρεσιν [10 verba] **BF**: *om.* **A**
240.14   ἦν **BF**: *om.* **A**

Unlike the errors listed above in **A** and **F**, the mistakes in **B** below are less significant and could have been corrected individually by later scribal conjecture.

Yet **B** is likely not the ancestor of **A** and **F** (or **λ**) because none of its mistakes is transmitted to either of these two mss and it is doubtful that the scribes of **A** and **F** (and the ancestor of **λ**) corrected all these mistakes independently of one another. Distinguishing mistakes in **B** include:

146.14   οὐδὲ **AF**: οὐ οὐδὲ **B**
142.9   ῥοπὴν **AF**: ῥοπὴς **B**
152.4   ἐθῶν **AF**: ἐθνῶν **B**
172.7   ἀχωρίστου **AF**: χωρίστου **B**
184.4   ἔκρυψαν **AF**: ἔκρυψαι **B**
192.17   εἰρηνεύειν **AF**: εἰρηνεύει **B**
220.9   ἐπορεύθην **AF**: ἐπορεύθη **B**
222.1   ὡς τό **AF**: ὡς **B**
242.7   Ἰερουσαλὴμ Ἰερουσαλήμ **AF**: Ἰερουσαλήμ **B**
242.9   ἀγαλλιᾶσθε **AF**: ἀγαλλιᾶσθαι **B**

Thus, **A**, **B**, and **F** likely descended independently from **L**.

Three further issues—institutional, textual, and codicological—inform the shape of the stemma at this point. The lending and copying practices of the Badia Fiorentina, which housed **L** in the sixteenth century, are of obvious importance for proposing a stemma for the *Introduction*. Scholars have been able to reconstruct aspects of the Badia's policies about its manuscripts. The library allowed visitors to inspect mss *in situ* and there are several instances of lending.[1] As a general rule, in the fifteenth and sixteenth centuries, monasteries often loaned mss to important humanists and printers.[2] Unfortunately, no register exists for the Badia that recorded which manuscripts were loaned or inspected *in situ* during the sixteenth century when the *Introduction* was copied. Such registers were only introduced into Italian libraries toward the end of the late nineteenth century.[3] Another problem we face is that the scribes of **A**, **B**, and **F** remain unknown, and so it becomes much more difficult to track down their activities and whether they might have visited the Badia to copy **L** or received it on loan.[4] Noteworthy, however, is that **B** was produced in Venice for the German humanist, Johann Jakob Fugger (1516–75). Many of Fugger's Greek mss were made in Venice from exemplars in the

---

[1] For examples, see Blum, *Badia Fiorentina*, 22–4.
[2] Davide Baldi, "Il *Codex Florentinus* del Digesto e il 'Fondo Pandette' della Biblioteca Laurenziana (con un'appendice di documenti inediti)," *Segno e Testo* 8 (2010): 99–186.
[3] Davide Baldi, "Il catalogo dei codici greci della Biblioteca Riccardiana," in *La descrizione dei manoscritti: esperienze a confronto*, ed. Edoardo Crisci, Marilena Maniaci, and Pasquale Orsini (Cassino: Università degli Studi di Cassino—Dipartimento di Filologia e Storia, 2010), 139–75.
[4] The scribe for the Adrian material in **B** is unknown, though he has been dubbed "C. Probatares" by Paul Canart for the similarity of his hand to that of the prolific scribe, Emmanuel Probatares (Canart, "Les manuscrits copies par Emmanuel Provataris," 203–4; Mondrain, "Copistes et collectionneurs," 377 fn. 30 and 385, addendum 4). I also note that while the hand of the Adrian material in **F** has not been identified, it appears very close, if not identical, to the hand of **B**.

existing libraries of that city.[5] Nevertheless, some exemplars came from other libraries in Italy, and at least in some cases, we know that Fugger's scribes traveled to these other Italian libraries—including those in Florence—to make their copies.[6] The identity of the scribe of the Adrian material in **B** is unclear, but the strategies by which Fugger built his collection suggest that **B** might have been copied from **L** either at the Badia in Florence, or on loan from that library.

There is, next, some internal textual evidence that suggests that **A**, **B**, and **F** might have been direct descendants from **L**. For example: in the exterior margin of 246r the first hand of **L** writes ἐστὶν (to be inserted after χεὶρ κυρίου at 128.15), but the verb is missing from **ABF**, which would be an easy oversight; at 130.5 **L** abbreviates διασκορπισθήτωσαν as διασκορπισθήτω (under the ω there is a horizontal slash with an upturn at the end, signifying that the form given is an abbreviation), whereas **BF** transmit only the letters of the abbreviated word and **A** writes διασκορπισθήτων;[7] at 208.10 **L** abbreviates περί ambiguously (the superscript epsilon over the π is not decisively oriented to make the distinction between περί and παρά clear) and as such the preposition is expanded differently: περί (**A**); παρά (**BF**);[8] at 218.4 **L** offers another ambiguous abbreviation that is replicated by **A** and expanded differently by **B** and **F** (αὐ͡ **L** et **A**: αὐτῶν **B**: αὐτοῦ **F**). It is easy to see how these features of **L** would give rise to oversight or alternative interpretation in its direct descendants—precisely the issues which surface in **ABF**.

A final issue impacts the configuration of the stemma. There is a recurring pattern in the sequence of treatises that are transmitted by the mss that carry the *Introduction*, a pattern also overlooked by Goessling in his edition. The following works, which were not widely circulated in the ms tradition, follow a standard sequence:

1 = Adrian, *Isagoge in Sacras Scripturas*
2 = Jerome of Jerusalem, *De Effectu Baptismi*
3 = Jerome of Jerusalem, *Dialogus de s. Trinitate*
4 = 7 Greek versions of the OT
5 = Scholia on Job and Psalms

In **L**/**L**$_H$, we find the sequence: 1, 2, and 3. The sequence for the other mss is as follows:

> **A:** 1, 2, 3, 4
> **B:** 1, 2, 3
> **C:** 1, 2, 3

---

[5] Pradel, *Katalog München*, 7–8; Mondrain, "Copistes et collectionneurs," 382.
[6] Pradel, *Katalog München*, 10–11; Mondrain, "Copistes et collectionneurs," 374–5, 384–5.
[7] Note the same abbreviating symbol used one other time in **L**: αἰῶνα is abbreviated as αἰῶ at 216.19 (last word on line).
[8] See Pseudo-Gregorii Agrigentini seu Pseudo-Gregorii Nysseni, *Commentarius in Ecclesiasten*, ed. Gerard H. Ettlinger and Jacques Noret, CCSG 56 (Brepols: Turnhout, 2007), xxxii.

D: 1, 2, 3, 4, 5
E: 1 (*Introduction* not completely transmitted)
F: 1, 2, 3, 4, 5
G: 1, 2, 3, 4, 5
H: 1, 2, 3, 4, 5
I: 1, 2, 3, 4, 5
J: 1
K: 1, 2, 3, 4, 5

In **L/L$_H$** the *Introduction* is followed by works 2 and 3, and this same sequence is preserved in all the other mss with the exception of **E** and **J**. This recurring sequence throughout the ms tradition of the *Introduction* confirms the decision reached above that **L/L$_H$** is the common ancestor of the remaining mss. However, this evidence also raises an issue: since **L/L$_H$** in its current state only transmits works 2 and 3 after the *Introduction*, how do we account for the additional presence of 4 and 5 in the ms tradition? Unfortunately, the codicological evidence is indecisive. Lindenbruch mutilated **L** in the early seventeenth century, and an inspection of the ms indicates that its last quaternion has had its three final folios cut out.[9] These folios, along with three immediately following folios (unbound), are now in Hamburg (=**L$_H$**). But it is not clear whether there were additional folios, following the aforementioned six, on which treatises 4 and 5 might have been written.

There are then two basic options for constructing the stemma. If we assume that **L** did not originally have treatises 4 and 5, the stemma would require a lost intermediate that had treatises 2–5 after the *Introduction*, from which at least **A** (transmits 2–4), **F** (2–5), and **λ** (2–5) were dependent. The chief difficulty with this scenario is that it requires this intermediate to be an excellent copy of **L** since there are no significant shared errors by **A**, **F**, or **λ** that would indicate dependence on this hyparchetype. The second option is simpler and is supported by the fact that there are no shared errors between **AF λ** beyond those already supplied by **L**. This option would posit that **L** did, in fact, have treatises 4–5 at one point. This scenario accounts for the presence of treatises 2–5 throughout the ms tradition, which, as argued above, was dependent upon **L**. My diagram reflects this latter scenario.

The shared errors of family **λ** that are avoided by **ABF** include:

134.7	ὅσα ὅμοια **ABF C** *p. corr.*: τὰ ὅμοια **DEGK$_2$IJ**
146.14	ἵνα τί **ABCF**: ἵνα **DEGHK$_2$IJ**
158.4	εὐλογήκαμεν **ABCF**: εὐλογήσαμεν **DEGK$_2$IJ**
166.9	παρακεκλημένοι **ABF K$_2$** *p. corr.*: -μένη **CDEGIJ**
188.13–190.2	τῷ Δαυὶδ-ὀμνύει Κύριος [12 verba] **ABF C** *p. corr. in mg.*: *om.* **CDGK$_2$IJ**

---

[9] Based upon the *in situ* inspection by Davide Baldi (August 28, 2014).

192.6   οἴησιν **ABF C** *p. corr.*: οἴκησιν **CDG K₂IJ**

210.1   ὡς τὸ ὁ **AB**: ὡς ὁ **F**: ὡς τὸ **CDGK₁K₂IJ**

210.6   ὁσίων σου **ABF**: *om.* σου **CDGHK₁K₂IJ**

260.4   ὁ ὀφθλμὸς **ABF**: ὀφθλμὸς **CDGK₁K₂IJ**

Excluded as ancestors of λ are **DGHK₁K₂** (=μ) and **IJ** (=ν), which form two distinctive subfamilies, each characterized by their own additional distinguishing errors (more on these below).

There remains the possibility that **C** or **E** were ancestors of λ. It is unlikely that **C** was the ancestor. Its distinguishing errors include:

188.7   ἐκάθισα **DGK₂IJ**: ἐκάθεισα **C**

190.13   κληρονομήσωμεν **DGK₂IJ**: κληρωνομήσωμεν **C**

192.1   εὐθηνίᾳ **DGK₂IJ**: εὐθυνίᾳ **C**

212.7   προαιρέσεως **DGK₁K₂IJ**: προαιραίσεως **C**

228.4   γὰρ ἀλήθειαν **DGK₁K₂IJ**: γὰρ ἡ ἀλήθειαν **C**

242.5   προσκαλέσεται **DGK₁K₂IJ**: προσκαλέσαι **C**

258.3   ὑφηγήσεως **DGK₁K₂IJ**: ὑφυγήσεως **C**

280.3   προσυποδεικνύναι **DGIJ**: πρὸ ὑποδεικνύναι **K₁**: πρὸς ὑποδεικνύναι **C**

The conclusion that **C** is not the ancestor of λ is corroborated by its marginal and interlinear readings that often agree with the text of **L** against the other mss in λ. In the margin at f. 250v **C** reproduces a marginal note that is missing from **ABF** but is present in **L**. The scribe has written ὁ φίλιππος with a number of the mss in his family, including **GHIJ** (a book binder has removed the margin of **D** and **K₂** does not have the marginal note). But the scribe of **C** strikes out –ιππος and corrects with a supralinear: ος, a reading only attested in **L**. Other instances of correction in the direction of **L** include: at 130.5 **C** underlines αὐτοῦ, a reading in **BLF**; at 146.9 **C** corrects with a supralinear υ over an ε, thereby providing the reading ἄφυκτον in **ABLF**; at 170.9 **C** corrects φυλάσεις with an additional supralinear σ. There are a few cases where **C** simply agrees with **ABLF**: at 142.7 it reads πρακτικὸν instead of πρακτικῶν **DEGK₂IJ**; at 146.14 it reads ἵνα τί instead of ἵνα **DEGHK₂IJ**. Some of these examples could also be instances of conjectural correction and not dependence on readings found in **L**.[10] These emendations do not appear to come from another scribal hand and occasionally the ink is the same color as was used for rubrication, suggesting that at least some of these emendations were made at the time of the initial copying event (e.g., 76.16; 82.25; 108.14). If the auxiliary readings go back to this event, **C** is not the ancestor of λ since none of its scribal modifications is transmitted to the rest of the family.

---

[10] A few scribal emendations produce erroneous readings not dependent on L: at 162.2 **C** has φράζει with **DEGK₂IJ**, but writes ειν supralinearly; at 212.12 **C** has δεδεμένος with **GIJ**, but inserts a γ to read δεδεγμένος. Neither reading is attested in λ.

It is also unlikely that **E** was the ancestor of **λ**. In its current form, **E** transmits roughly the first third of the *Introduction*. For it to be the ancestor requires that two conditions be met: that it carried a complete version of the treatise before it was copied, and that in the part of the text now lost there were no significant distinguishing errors. In the part of the *Introduction* that **E** transmits, there are only a few, minor distinguishing errors that could have been corrected by later conjecture. However, it is unlikely that **C** and the ancestors of **μ** and **ν** all made the same corrections to **E** independently of one another:

128.10   προβάλλεται *CDGK₂IJ*: προβάλεται **E**
134.1   ἐφιλοσόφησαν *CDGK₂IJ*: ἐφιλοσόφισαν **E**
134.6–7 καί, πεσοῦνται *CDGK₂IJ*: *om.* καί **E**
146.2–3 καὶ ἐπισημοτέρους–περιβλεπτοτέρους [6 verba] *CDGK₂IJ*: *bis* **E**

My stemma will present the family **λ** as derived from hyparchetype **β**.

Within family **λ** there is a subfamily **DGHK₁K₂** (**μ**) that shares a number of additional errors. I was able to glean sufficient information from an *in situ* inspection of **H** to be able to confirm that this ms belongs to **μ**. In addition to shared spelling mistakes, the distinguishing errors of subfamily **μ** include:

128.18   ἦν *CE*: νῦν **DGK₂**
146.12   τε *CE*: *om.* **DGHK₂**
154.7   τὸ ἰδεῖν, ποτὲ δὲ *CE*: *om.* **DGK₂**
182.15–16 τὰς φωνάς–ἀντὶ τοῦ [8 verba] *C*: *om.* **DGHK₂**
210.10   ὡς τό, καὶ *C*: *om.* καὶ **DGK₁K₂**
222.1–2   ὡς τό,–εἰπών [10 verba] *C*: *om.* **DGHK₁K₂**
224.9–10 εἰς καταφυγήν–καί, κύριος [12 verba] *CK₂*: *bis* **DGHK₁**
260.18   εὖγε, εὖγε *C*: εὖγε **DGK₁K₂**
264.4–6   τίνος διώκεις–καὶ ὀπίσω [8 verba] *C p. corr. in mg.*: *om.* **DGK₁K₂**

It is difficult, however, to determine the inner structure of subfamily **μ**. We can make a few observations:

- **G** is not the ancestor:
  190.11–13 αὐτούς–κληρονομήσωμεν [5 verba] *DK₂*: *om.* **G**

- Nor is **K₂** the ancestor:
  210.20–1   ὅτι μιμνήσκη–ἄνθρωπος [9 verba] *DGK₁*: *om.* **K₂**

- And it is not likely that **K₁** is the ancestor:
  232.12   γενικώτατοι *DGK₂*: γενικώτοι **K₁**
  232.13   κατὰ παραβολήν *DGK₂*: κατὰ μεταπαραβολήν **K₁**
  278.7   ἔνεστιν *DG*: ἔστιν **K₁**
  282.3   μελῶν καὶ *DG*: μελῶν καὶ καὶ **K₁**

- K_2 also shares a series of errors with **D** (including a number of smaller spelling mistakes):

  140.8   Τὸ δὲ ἀποδεκτικὸν **G**: om. δὲ **DK**$_2$

  184.11   τινας εὕρῃ **G**: τις εὕρῃ **DK**$_2$

  188.3   παρανομούντων **G**: παρανούντων **DK**$_2$

- The only significant shared error in μ is between **G** and K_2:

  214.5   τῷ πνεύματι, προσεύξομαι **DK**$_1$: om. **GK**$_2$

Beyond these basic observations, however, the relationships within subfamily μ are difficult to determine since K_1 and K_2 do not transmit complete copies of the *Introduction*, **H** is pervasively illegible, and most of the errors that can be identified in μ are not significant, that is, they could have been corrected by subsequent scribes. For these reasons I leave the relationships within this family undetermined.

Within family λ there is another subfamily **IJ** (=ν) that shares a number of additional distinguishing errors. Key omissions include:

184.18–19   ὑπομένειν–τίς ἡ [10 verba] **CDEGK**$_2$: om. **IJ**

186.7–8   ἐνδείξομαι–ὅπως ἂν [9 verba] **CDEGK**$_2$: om. **IJ**

234.18–19   διὰ τὸ–ὀπίσω μου [9 verba] **CDEGK**$_1$**K**$_2$: om. **IJ**

I does not have significant distinguishing errors in ν, whereas J does, thus suggesting that J was copied from I. Examples of distinguishing errors in J include:

210.16–17   χθὲς–ὑμεῖς καί [9 verba] **I**: om. **J**

216.17–19   καί, οὐ μὴ νίψῃς τοὺς πόδας μου εἰς τὸν αἰῶνα· καί, οὐ μὴ φάγω κρέα εἰς τὸν αἰῶνα **I**: καί, οὐ μὴ φάγω κρέα εἰς τὸν αἰῶνα· καί, οὐ μὴ νίψῃς τοὺς πόδας μου εἰς τὸν αἰῶνα **J**

274.9–10   καὶ κριὸν–περιστεράν [7 verba] **I**: om. **J**

Finally, as already noted in Chapter 2 of Part II:

- **Hoeschel's** edition was made using **A** and **B**;
- **P** is a handwritten copy of **Hoeschel's** print edition;
- **Lollin's** Latin translation was made from **I** and **J**.

B. STEMMA: RECENSION 2

The analysis that follows is based upon a complete collation of all the mss that transmit R2. **XYZ** transmit fragment one; **YZ** transmit fragment two.

XYZ share a few errors, including:

162.2   φράζει **R1**: κράζει **XYZ**

176.1–2   ἐπὶ τοῦ < ἢ κοινωνῆσαι ἢ > μὴ κοινωνῆσαί **Martens**: ἐπὶ τοῦ μὴ κοινωνῆσαί **XYZ**

X is not the ancestor of **Y** or **Z** because it contains numerous errors, some of which are significant, that are not attested in these other two mss. These errors include:

166.2   παραβολὴν **YZ**: βαραβολὴν **X**
168.1   Σημαίνει **YZ**: Συνάγει **X**
172.8   συνῆφθαι **YZ**: συνῆφσθαι **X**
172.18 ὁ ἀχώριστος **YZ**: deest ὁ **X**
178.8   καὶ **YZ**: deest καὶ **X**
184.2   πράξεως **YZ**: πρᾶξιν **X**
184.3   οἱ ἄμωμοι **YZ**: deest οἱ **X**
192.20 μυρίων **YZ**: μυρίω **X**
198.15 κατέστρεψα **YZ**: -στραψα **X**
198.16 κατέστρεψεν **YZ**: -στραψεν **X**
204.12 τῇ **YZ**: τῷ **X**
204.28 τοῖς ἀναιρουμένοις in mg. ext. m. pr. **YZ**: τοὺς ἀναιρουμένους **XYZ**
206.3   ἔπεσε **YZ**: ἔχεσε **X**
206.11 σελήνη **YZ**: γῆ **X**
206.19 παρεκστάσει **YZ**: παρεστάστει **X**
206.21 αὐτῶν **YZ**: αὐτοὺς **X**

There are also a number of sections where **X** transmits less biblical text than **Y** or **Z**:

196.15–16 εἰς φέγγος–σου [5 verba] **YZ**: καὶ τὰ λοιπά **X**
204.19–20 ἐκ Σιὼν–Ἰερουσαλὴμ [6 verba] **YZ**: deest **X**
204.21–4   καὶ σεισθήσεται–Ἰσραήλ [19 verba] **YZ**: καὶ τὰ λοιπά **X**
206.12–17 καὶ τὰ ἄστρα–ἡ παρεμβολὴ αὐτοῦ [23 verba] **YZ**: καὶ τὰ λοιπά **X**
206.25–7   ἡμέρα νεφέλης–εὑρεθείη [11 verba] **YZ**: καὶ τὰ τοιαῦτα **X**
208.5–6   εἰς λόγους πονηρίας **YZ**: καὶ τὰ λοιπά **X**

These distinguishing errors and shorter readings ensure that **X** cannot be the ancestor of either **Y** or **Z**.

X has no significant errors in common with **Y** (against **Z**) or with **Z** (against **Y**). But **Y** and **Z** have binding errors that are avoided by **X**:

166.7   ὡς **X** p. corr. s. l.: deest **YZ**
168.7   πάντως **X**: πάντας **YZ**
184.21 προσδοκία **X**: ἡ προσδοκία **YZ**
186.13 τοιοῦτο **X**: τοιοῦτον **YZ**
186.18 γένωνται **X**: γενόνται **YZ**
200.7   πρωϊνὸν **X**: προϊνὸν **YZ**
200.9   εὑρίσκομεν **X**: εὑρίσομεν **YZ**
200.11 ἀθρόως **X**: ἀθρώως **YZ**
206.19 συννεφείας **X**: συνεφίας **YZ**

Y has generally minor errors from which Z is free:

168.4	κατακρύψουσιν Z: κατακρίψουσιν Y
170.3	κατακρύψεις Z: κατακρίψεις Y
178.10	Τὰ Z: Τὰς Y
186.9	ἐναντίων Z: ἐναντίον Y
188.1	κοινωνίας Z: κοινωνοίας Y
188.2	παρὰ τῷ Z: παρὰ τὸ Y
190.18	ἔνοχος Z: ἔνωχος Y
192.20	ἐργασία Z: ἐρσασία Y
194.17	οἰκείου Z: οἰκίου Y
198.3	ἤνεσά Z: ἤννεσά Y

Z has usually more serious errors from which Y is free:

172.12	καὶ Y: καὶ καὶ Z
172.17	εἰς τὸν κόλπον Y p. corr.: ἐν τοῖς Y a. corr.: ἐν τοῖς κόλποις Z
176.14	ματαιότης Y: ματαιότητος Z
186.6	τὸ aut τῷ Y: τὸν Z
186.17	βλέποντες² Y: βλέπωντες² Z
190.5	διάθεσιν Y: διάθησιν Z
190.7	φαυλότητος Y: φαυλοτοῦ Z
194.15	σου Y: συ Z
194.15	πίεσαι Y: πίεται Z
196.4	καὶ τὸ Y: καὶ τῷ Z
196.14	παρὰ τῷ Y: παρὰ τὸ Z
204.27	στερηθήσεσθαι Y: στερηθήσεται Z
206.2	τὸ Y: τῷ Z
244.14	ἐξελέξατο Y: ἐξελέξα Z
250.20	τὸ δὲ πᾶν Y: τὸ πᾶν Z
252.15	τόπους Y cat. Ps. 28:3(1): deest Z
254.10	κηρύγματος Y: κρύγματος Z
256.16	παιδίσκην Y: παιδίδισκην Z

The most straightforward account of the relationship between XYZ posits a lost ancestor γ from which these three mss are derived, thereby accounting for their shared errors. X and δ are independently derived from γ, while Y and Z are independently derived from δ. This stemma accounts for: the additional errors in X that are avoided by YZ; the shared errors in YZ not found in X and that must then be traced back to δ, and finally, the errors that distinguish Y and Z from one another. While the errors in Y are generally insignificant enough that they could have been corrected by the scribe of Z, such a scenario would also require that this scribe simultaneously introduced a whole series of careless mistakes into his copy. I think this is unlikely. Furthermore, the independent derivation of Y and Z from δ is suggested by the following at 172.17: in copying

Jn 1:18 (ὁ μονογενὴς γὰρ υἱὸς ὁ ὢν εἰς τὸν κόλπον τοῦ πατρός) the scribe of **Y** first wrote ἐν τοῖς and then corrected these words, reforming the letters to read εἰς τὸν. The unusual phrase ἐν τοῖς κόλποις (it is not attested in the *TLG* or Tischendorf's NT apparatus) occurs in **Z**, which would suggest that the scribes of **Y** and **Z** both found that reading in δ, and that **Y** was introducing a sensible correction. It would be hard to account for **Z** adopting such an idiosyncratic reading of the verse directly from **Y**. Nevertheless, generally considered, both **Y** and **Z** are strikingly similar mss (see catalogue description above).

Since **XYZ** usually diverge from one another in minor orthographic issues, it is invariably clear which reading to follow or conjecture. There are only two striking differences among these mss that require an editorial decision: the inconsistent use of titles by **Y** and **Z** in the trope list of fragment two (I discuss this topic in Chapter 6 of Part II), and several noticeably shorter readings of biblical verses in **X**. In a few places it is clear that several of these shorter readings are derivative of the corresponding material in **YZ**.

For example, at 208.4–6 **YZ** (and R1) read, μὴ ἐκκλίνῃς τὴν καρδίαν μου εἰς λόγους πονηριάς, which serves as an illustration of the tendency in the Bible to portray God as an agent of evil, whereas **X** omits εἰς λόγους πονηριάς and instead writes, καὶ τὰ λοιπά. But the prepositional phrase is crucial to the sense of the argument, which indicates that καὶ τὰ λοιπά is a corruption. Another example occurs in section 54.1 where **X** presents a much shorter reading of Joel 4:14–16 that is again a corruption of the text transmitted in **YZ**. In **X** the quotation begins with v. 14, but then instead of continuing with the next two verses (as in **YZ**), its material is altered in five ways: instead of οἱ ἀστέρες it has τὰ ἄστρα; instead of οὐ δώσουσι it has δύσουσι; instead of ὁ δὲ κύριος there is καὶ κύριος; it entirely skips ἐκ Σιὼν—ἐξ Ἰερουσαλὴμ; and instead of the last words of Joel 4:14–16, καὶ σεισθήσεται—Ἰσραήλ, **X** simply reads καὶ τὰ λοιπά. What has happened is the following: the text in **X** begins with the citation with Joel 4:14, but then presents a rewritten 4:15–16 in the aforementioned ways so that the citation reads like *Joel 2:10–11*. The mistake is understandable since these lines are similar to Joel 4:15–16.[11]

There are a few other places where **X** provides less biblical material than what we find in **YZ** (section 49 and the end of 54.2) and it is not entirely clear which reading to prefer. I will assign all shorter readings in **X** to the apparatus since I suspect that the catenist's instinct to abridge has also shaped this ms tradition. Nevertheless, the reader will benefit from attending to the readings in the apparatus, should they have been wrongly relegated there.

---

[11] Moreover, Adrian cites Joel 2:10–11 a few lines later (section 54.2) and here too **X** offers less text than we find in **YZ**: after a few words of citation we find, καὶ τὰ λοιπά. The biblical material has almost certainly been excised from the ms tradition of **X** so that the resulting, far shorter, biblical text repeats the fewest possible words of Joel 2:10–11 that were mistakenly inserted in 54.1 above.

5

The Relationship between the Recensions

The existence of multiple recensions of the *Introduction* confirms what we know about the transmission history of certain kinds of ancient texts. Some were more likely than others to be modified by subsequent scribes:

> Commentaries, lexica and other works of a grammatical nature were rightly regarded as collections of material to be pruned, adapted or added to, rather than as sacrosanct literary entities. When the rewritings become more than superficial, or when rearrangement is involved, one must speak of a new recension of the work, if not of a new work altogether.[1]

Adrian's *Introduction*—a treatise replete with catalogues, definitions, and illustrations—was precisely the sort of work open to later scribal modification. I now offer a brief comparison of the two main recensions and an analysis of their relationship to one another.[2]

A. OVERVIEW OF THE RECENSIONS

Three mss (**XYZ**) transmit two sections of R2 anonymously, introducing the treatise as follows: ἐκ τοῦ περὶ τῶν ἰδιωμάτων τῆς θείας γραφῆς· καὶ μάλιστα τοῦ Δαυὶδ εἰσὶ ταῦτα ("From the treatise about the peculiarities of Divine Scripture—these belong especially to David"). This heading is inspired by the opening sentence of the *Introduction* and highlights the prominence of the Psalms (i.e., David) in the treatise. There is no doubt that these three mss are transmitting another recension of Adrian's treatise since R2 shares significant sequences of very similar, and often the exact same, Greek text with R1.

---

[1] Martin L. West, *Textual Criticism and Editorial Technique Applicable to Greek and Latin Texts* (Stuttgart: Teubner, 1973), 16. Similar assessment in: Nigel G. Wilson and Leighton D. Reynolds, *Scribes and Scholars: A Guide to the Transmission of Greek and Latin Literature*, 3rd ed. (Oxford: Clarendon, 1991), 234.

[2] One could also argue that Lollin's Latin translation created a distinct recension—it is a significantly truncated version of the *Introduction* derived from R1. Similarly, there is noticeable variation within the ms tradition of R2: at several points **X** presents a text that is more abbreviated than what we find in **YZ** (it lacks parts of biblical verses, or whole verses).

Yet there are also a number of differences between these recensions:

- R1 often has material, usually biblical, that is missing from R2. For example, section 26 has three more verses from Psalms; 38 has thirteen additional biblical citations; 45 has six more verses, and so on. In a handful of cases, instead of this biblical material, R2 will have a phrase like καὶ τὰ ἐξῆς (e.g., at 234.20). Sometimes R1 cites more of the same verse found in R2: for example, Ps 118:1 in 40.

- On the other hand, R2 also has material that is missing from R1. R2 will often identify the biblical author before a citation: note references to the "apostle" (37), "Jeremiah" and "Moses" (43), "David" (73.17), and so on. R2 will repeatedly cite more text of a verse shared with R1: sections 26, 30, 55, and so on. R2 cites biblical verses not in R1: 37, 51, 52, 54, 73.21, and so on. Importantly, R2 offers longer discussions of Adrian's interpretive theses and frequently provides glosses of verses that are cited without comment in R1: 31, 32, 38, 42, 43, 45, and so on.

- Some other notable differences include: occasionally R1 and R2 illustrate the same point, but with different biblical verses: 36, 40, 41, 49. R2 cites from "Symmachus" (29, 33) whereas R1 never identifies this alternative translation, though still uses it (e.g., 27). R2 moves the trope of synecdoche up two places in the trope list. In terms of language, R2 sometimes uses infinitival constructions whereas R1 uses a finite verb (e.g., 38, 39, 40); R2 and R1 also introduce the tropes with different constructions (e.g., Τὰ δὲ κατὰ συνεκδοχήν and Κατὰ συνεκδοχήν, respectively).

B. THE RELATIONSHIP BETWEEN THE RECENSIONS

There are four basic possibilities for the relationship between R1 and R2: (1) both derive independently from a common lost ancestor; (2) R2 is derived from R1 which, in turn, derives from a lost ancestor; (3) vice versa, R1 is derived from R2 which, in turn, derives from a lost ancestor; (4) finally, Adrian (or perhaps Adrian and a student) are responsible for two versions, and R1 and R2 are each derived from these respective originals.[3] A variety of evidence considered below will indicate that both recensions are independently derived from the same lost ancestor (scenario 1).

---

[3] There is no obvious evidence for cross-contamination between the mss that transmit these recensions. Rarely does a variant reading in the ms tradition of one recension agree with the text of the other recension. But in those cases where this occurs, there are other explanations that more likely account for these agreements. For example, in section 28 we find ὡς τό, ὡς ἀγαθὸς in most mss of **R1** and **X** after the correction, whereas we find ὡς τό, ἀγαθὸς in **YZ** and **K₂** of **R1**. But there is no need to posit cross-contamination here: it is easy to see how the second ὡς inadvertently dropped out of **K₂** and how, since the particle was also part of a biblical citation, the scribe of **X** properly corrected his copy by inserting it.

1. Shared material between R1 and R2

Where both recensions transmit the same material, there are a handful of shared errors:

176.1-2   ἐπὶ τοῦ < ἢ κοινωνῆσαι ἢ > μὴ κοινωνῆσαί **Martens:** ἐπὶ τοῦ μὴ κοινωνῆσαί **R1 R2**

240.19-20   τῶν οἰκουμένων τοὺς οἰκοῦντας **Martens:** τῶν οἰκούντων τὰ οἰκούμενα **R1 R2**

These shared errors indicate that the recensions are probably not ultimately derived from their own ancestors. The "two originals" hypothesis above (scenario 4) is unlikely.

There are errors or omissions in R1 that are not in R2:

160.8   μετὰ τοῦ δικαίου **R2:** μετὰ τοῦ δικαιῶς **R1**

168.5-6   ἀπὸ τοῦ τὸν **R2:** ἀπὸ τούτων **R1**

192.16   ἀποστολὴν δι'ἀγγέλων πονηρῶν **R2 Schlüren,** *cf.* **cat. Ps. 77:49:** *om.* **R1**

200.14-15   ἀπὸ τοῦ τοὺς μὲν ἐν εὐθυμίᾳ **R2:** ἀπὸ τοὺς μὲν εὐθυμίᾳ **R1**

240.19   ἢ **R2:** καὶ **R1**

266.20-1   δὲ αἵρεσιν **R2:** διαίρεσιν **R1**

268.3-270.7   προφητικὸν μὲν οὖν ἐστι–ἀναιρετικόν [35 verba] **R2:** *om.* **R1**

272.4   προήγγειλεν **R2:** *om.* **R1**

R1 also offers definitions of three tropes—mockery, threat, and exhortation—that are not as satisfactory as those we find in R2:

260.16-20   Τὰ δὲ κατὰ ἐπιτωθασμόν· ὅταν ἐπὶ ταῖς τῶν ἐχθρῶν καταθυμίαις συμφοραῖς ἐπιγελαστικώτερον πρὸς αὐτοὺς διαλέγηται **R2:** Κατ' ἐπιτωθασμόν· ὅταν ἐπὶ ταῖς τῶν ἐχθρῶν αἰσχύναις λέγῃ **R1**

264.22-4   Τὰ δὲ κατὰ ἀπειλήν· ὅταν ἐπὶ κωλύσει τῶν ἀτόπων τὴν τιμωρίαν προβάλληται **R2:** Κατὰ ἀπειλήν· ὅταν ἀπειλῇ διὰ τοῦ θεοῦ **R1**

268.10-15   Τὰ δὲ κατὰ παραίνεσιν· πᾶς τις τῶν εὐσεβούντων ὁμολογήσειεν ὡς ἅπαντα ὁμοῦ τὰ τῆς θεοπνεύστου γραφῆς εἴτε διὰ λόγων εἴτε διὰ πραγμάτων εἰς ταύτην συντελεῖν ἔοικεν εἰκότως **R2:** Κατὰ παραίνεσιν· ὅταν πάντα ὁμοῦ τὰ τῆς θεοπνεύστου γραφῆς εἴτε διὰ λόγων εἴτε διὰ πραγμάτων, εἰς ταύτην συντελεῖν ἔοικεν εἰκότως **R1**

This evidence indicates that R2 is not derived from R1 (scenario 2).

There are also errors and omissions in R2 that are not in R1:

162.2   φράζει **R1:** κράζει **R2**

166.6   ὡς ἀγαθὸς **R1 et X** *p. corr. s. l.*: ἀγαθὸς **YZ et K**₂

179.2-3   ὡς τό, αἰνεῖτε τὸν κύριον ἐκ τῶν οὐρανῶν **R1:** *om.* **R2**

R2 also offers a definition of antiphrasis that is less satisfactory than what we find in R1. The definition in R1 follows more closely the definitions of the trope that circulated in late antique rhetorical treatises on tropes:

242.18–19   ὅταν δι' ἐναντίου τὸ ἐναντίον δηλοῖ **R1**: ὅταν ἕτερον ἀνθ' ἑτέρου λέγει **R2**

However, these errors, the missing verse, and the unsatisfactory definition could have been corrected by the scribe of R1 (scenario 3).

The aforementioned evidence suggests one of two remaining scenarios for the relationship between R1 and R2: either both recensions were independently derived from the same lost ancestor (scenario 1), or R1 was derived from R2 (scenario 3).

2. Distinctive material

This picture is corroborated by examining the material that is not shared by these recensions. R1 is missing material that occurs in R2 and that appears authentic: in section 42 R1 has an indecipherably short gloss on Ps 67:24, whereas R2 offers an expansive and more intelligent explanation of the verse; the whole discussion in 54 is much shorter than what we find in R2 and it is easier to explain how the shorter version emerged than the longer version; in the list of twenty-two tropes, R1 fails to define one (comparison), whereas R2 provides the expected definition (73.2); at 73.13 R2 provides a critique of allegorical exegesis in keeping with Diodore's and Theodore's assessment, a definition of the trope of allegory and a long discussion of this trope in Scripture—the critique, definition, and discussion are all missing from R1; in 73.14 R2 provides markers of subdivision that are absent from R1 though they are routinely present in that recension; at 74.3.1 R2 provides an illustration of a prophecy through words (διὰ λόγων) that points to Christ—this is missing from R1 even though a christological prophecy is promised in R1 at 74.3. This evidence strengthens the conclusion above that R1 is not the ancestor of R2 (scenario 2).

But there is also evidence that suggests—though not definitively—that R2 is not the ancestor of R1 (scenario 3). Generally, a number of the verses in R1 that are not in R2 come from the Psalms. But this use of Psalms is to be expected in a treatise on the "Hebrew literary style," especially one that draws attention to "blessed David" (65), and that has such a close relationship to Theodore's *Commentary on the Psalms*. There are also a few places where R2 is missing material that surfaces in R1 and that appears authentic: at 53.2 R1 provides a verse that illustrates Adrian's second hermeneutical point, but this (or some other similar) verse is missing in R2; at 73.6 R2 is missing markers of subdivision that are ordinarily present in the treatise. While these omissions from R2 are striking, it is also the case that they could have been subsequently supplied by R1.

3. Catenae fragments

It is only when we examine several catenae fragments excerpted from the *Introduction* that the relationship between the recensions comes into sharper focus. There are a number of fragments that transmit text of the *Introduction* where there is corresponding material in both R1 and R2. Some of these fragments transmit distinctive elements of both R1 and R2, that is, one part of the fragment has material attested only in R1 and a different part transmits material only in R2. For instance, *cat. Ps.* 77:49 contains a number of biblical verses only found in R1, but in its opening and final lines this fragment agrees nearly verbatim with the text of R2.

Τὸ κακὸν ἤτοι τὴν κακίαν ἀντὶ τιμωρίας λέγει, <u>ἀπὸ τῆς τῶν πασχόντων πρὸς</u> <u>αὐτὴν διαθέσεως</u>, ὥσπερ ἐνταῦθα· οὐ γὰρ τοὺς ἀποσταλέντας ἀγγέλους πονηροὺς βούλεται λέγειν, ἵνα τινὰς τῶν ἀποστατῶν νομίσῃς, ἐπεὶ μήτε πώποτε τοὺς τοιούτους ὑπὸ τοῦ θεοῦ προσταγέντας ἐπὶ τῆς θείας γραφῆς ἐγνώκαμεν, ἀλλ᾽ ὡς πρὸς τὴν τῶν κολαζομένων ᾗ καὶ πρόσθεν ἔφην διάθεσιν· <ὡς> καὶ τὸ παρὰ τῷ Ἡσαΐᾳ, **ἐγὼ κύριος** <u>**ποιῶν εἰρήνην καὶ κτίζων κακά**</u>, *ἵνα* <u>*εἴπῃ* ὅτι καὶ *εἰρηνεύειν ἐῶν καὶ πολεμεῖσθαι συγχωρῶν*· εἶτ᾽ αὖθις, **πρόσθες**</u> <u>**κακά, κύριε**, πρόσθες κακὰ τοῖς ἐνδόξοις τῆς γῆς</u>, ἀντὶ τοῦ δαψιλέστερον αὐτοὺς τιμωρεῖ τὴν οἰκείαν αὐτοῖς ἐπιτείνων· καὶ τὸ παρὰ τῷ Μιχαίᾳ, <u>ὅτι</u> <u>**κατέβη κακὰ παρὰ κυρίου** ἐπὶ πύλας Ἰερουσαλήμ· καὶ μὴν καὶ τὸ παρὰ τῷ</u> Μωυσῇ, **ἐκάκωσεν δὲ Σαρρὰ τὴν παιδίσκην αὐτῆς**, ἀντὶ τοῦ κάκιστα αὐτὴν αἰκισαμένη διέθηκεν· καί, **πρὸς Ἀβραὰμ** γινώσκων γνώσῃ ὅτι πάροικον ἔσται τὸ σπέρμα σου ἐν γῇ οὐκ ἰδίᾳ καὶ δουλώσουσιν αὐτὸ καὶ κακώσουσιν ἔτη τετρακόσια, <u>ἀντὶ τοῦ</u> κακῶς <u>παρασκευάσουσι· καὶ παρὰ τῷ Ἀμώς· **εἰ ἔστι**</u> <u>**κακία ἐν πόλει** ἣν κύριος οὐκ ἐποίησε· καὶ ὅσα τοιαῦτα· διὸ καὶ ὁ κύριος ἐν τοῖς</u> <u>**εὐαγγελίοις, ἀρκετόν**, φησί, **τῇ ἡμέρᾳ ἡ κακία αὐτῆς**, ἵνα εἴπῃ ὅτι ἡ αὐτῆς</u> ἐργασία μυρίων κόπων καὶ πόνων τοῖς ἀνθρώποις ὑπάρχει πρόξενος.

R1   **46**(81[κη΄]). *Τὸ κακὸν ἤτοι τὴν κακίαν πολλαχοῦ ἀντὶ τιμωρίας λέγει·* ὡς τό, **ἐξαπέστειλεν εἰς αὐτοὺς ὀργὴν θυμοῦ αὐτοῦ**, < ἀποστολὴν δι᾽ἀγγέλων πονηρῶν >· καί, **ἐγὼ** <u>**ποιῶν εἰρήνην καὶ κτίζων κακά**, *ἵνα*</u> <u>*εἴπῃ εἰρηνεύειν ἐῶν καὶ πολεμεῖσθαι συγχωρῶν*· καί, **πρόσθες** αὐτοῖς</u> **κακά, κύριε**· καί, <u>**κατέβη κακὰ παρὰ κυρίου**</u>· καί, <u>**ἐκάκωσε δὲ Σάρρα**</u> Ἄγαρ, <u>**τὴν παιδίσκην αὐτῆς**</u>· καί, **κακώσουσιν αὐτό**, <u>ἀντὶ τοῦ</u> κακοπαθῆσαι <u>παρασκευάσουσι·</u> καί, **τὴν κληρονομίαν σου ἐκάκωσαν**· καί, **μετανοῶν** ἐπὶ ταῖς κακίαις, ἀντὶ τοῦ ταῖς ὑπὲρ τῶν πλημμελημάτων τιμωρίαις· καί, **οὐκ ἔστι κακία ἐν πόλεσι**· καί, **ἀρκετὸν τῇ ἡμέρᾳ ἡ κακία αὐτῆς**, ἀντὶ τοῦ εἰπεῖν ὅτι ἡ ἐπ᾽αὐτῆς ἐργασία μυρίων κόπων καὶ πόνων τοῖς ἀνθρώποις ὑπάρχει πρόξενος.

R2   **46.** *Τὸ πολλαχοῦ τὸ κακὸν ἤτοι τὴν κακίαν ἀντὶ τιμωρίας λέγειν,* <u>ἀπὸ τῆς</u> <u>τῶν πασχόντων πρὸς αὐτὴν διαθέσεως·</u> ὡς τό, **ἐξαπέστειλεν εἰς αὐτοὺς** **ὀργὴν θυμοῦ αὐτοῦ** ἀποστολὴν δι᾽ἀγγέλων πονηρῶν· <u>διὸ καὶ ὁ κύριος ἐν</u> <u>εὐαγγελίοις, **ἀρκετόν** φησι **τῇ ἡμέρᾳ ἡ κακία αὐτῆς**, ἵνα εἴπῃ ἡ ἐπ᾽αὐτῆς</u> ἐργασία μυρίων κόπων καὶ πόνων τοῖς ἀνθρώποις ὑπάρχει πρόξενος.

The most plausible interpretation of this catena fragment is that it witnesses to an ancestor recension (R_a) that accounts for the distinctive material that we find in R1 and R2 today. These recensions would have been derived independently from this common lost ancestor, usually abridging but perhaps also expanding this ancestor (scenario 1). There are a handful of other catenae fragments which transmit material that survives partly in R1 and R2: *cat. Ps.* 31:4(2); 78:12(1); 78:12(2); 101:7–8; *cat. Job* 1:11.

C. RECONSTRUCTING R_a

There are a number of obstacles that make it impossible to ascertain the precise, original configuration of R_a. When they transmit the same material, it is likely that R1 and R2 witness to the text of R_a. But beyond these cases it becomes much more difficult to establish the text of the ancestor recension.

Where R1 and R2 transmit unique text, it is useful to distinguish between two kinds of material in the *Introduction*: the hermeneutical theses and scriptural glosses on the one hand, and the biblical passages on the other. Each block of material would have been susceptible to different kinds of editorial modification. Regarding the hermeneutical theses and glosses, it would seem odd if the longer versions of these (often in R2) did not usually approximate R_a more closely than the shorter versions (often in R1). Otherwise, we would need to posit a particularly ingenious scribe who consistently expanded upon these theses in a way that followed the contours of Adrian's style, syntax, and argument.[4] Moreover, such an unlikely scribe would also have had to have Theodore of Mopsuestia's *Commentary on the Psalms* in hand in order to make some of these expansions.[5] It is far more likely that this longer material approximates R_a more closely than the corresponding shorter material, and that instead we posit a scribe who excised, here and there, explanatory material that he thought was unnecessary. Such a scenario also reflects what we know about the ways in which the catenists operated: they were far more likely to abridge their sources than they were expand upon them.[6]

---

[4] The most glaring discrepancy between the recensions is the far longer discussion of allegory in R2. Even without comparing the discussion in R1 to its analog in R2, the reader's suspicions are raised because this trope is not defined in R1, which runs counter to Adrian's practice of defining the other tropes in his list. It seems far more plausible that a scribe severely truncated Adrian's discussion of allegory because it transmitted a Diodoran-Theodoran critique of allegory, than that a later scribe came upon a short discussion of this trope and added this critique, a lengthy catalogue of illustrations, and an open acknowledgement of the apostle Paul's limited education.

[5] See, for example, the lengthier gloss on Ps 67:23–4 in section 42 of R2 that is closely related to what we find in Thdr. Mops., *Ps.* 67:23–4.

[6] Scribes abbreviated by leaving out material or summarizing material more concisely (Carmelo Curti and Maria Antonietta Barbara, "Greek Exegetical Catenae," in *Patrology: The Eastern Fathers from the Council of Chalcedon (451) to John of Damascus († 750)*, ed. Angelo Di Berardino, trans. Adrian Walford [Cambridge: James Clarke & Co, 2006], 611).

But it is difficult to treat the distinctive biblical citations in the *Introduction* in a similarly straightforward manner. From the perspective of scribal activity, these citations would have been far easier to modify in a *number* of different ways: verses might be expanded or new ones added, truncated, or deleted, or replaced with alternatives, depending on the needs of the scribe, who was likely reproducing the *Introduction* for his own pedagogical ends. Two extreme, hypothetical scenarios illustrate the predicament the editor faces with the biblical material: the "minimalist" scenario would accept as authentic only the shared biblical verses between the recensions, rejecting all other verses and sections of verses unique to R1 and R2 as subsequent scribal additions to R_a. The "maximalist" scenario would accept all verses (and where verses are of differing length, the longer of the two citations) in R1 and R2 as authentic, on the grounds that R1 and R2 differ from R_a because their scribes only deleted biblical material. Of course, neither scenario captures how these recensions were composed—the scribes responsible for R1 and R2 were not only adding ("minimalist") or only deleting ("maximalist") material. Nor is it likely that one scribe was entirely faithful in the transmission of biblical material while the other was responsible for all additions or deletions. It is most likely the case that R1 and R2 were each the result of scribes who sometimes added, sometimes subtracted, and sometimes replaced verses. Provided that the unique verses we find in each recension illustrate the hermeneutical point in question, it is difficult, if not impossible, to know how to adjudicate the originality of the biblical material.[7]

The most I would venture for the unique biblical material in these recensions is that it will more often conform to the "maximalist" than the "minimalist" scenario sketched above, since this is in keeping with the catenists' tendency to abridge by suppressing material deemed inessential to the meaning of the passage. This conclusion is also confirmed by Lollin's translation, which can reasonably be considered another recension. In his case we are fortunate to possess the mss of the recension (R1) from which his translation was made: his approach, as noted above, was to remove far more verses (ca. 180) from **IJ** than he introduced (less than a dozen). It is also my suspicion that this abridging tendency explains why, within the ms tradition of R2, **X** has fewer verses than **YZ**.

The catenae fragments are also of limited help for reconstructing the text of R_a. There are, for example, a few cases where catenae fragments correspond with material transmitted in R1 but not R2 (these are the situations where R2 fails to transmit the material parallel to R1). In some of these cases fragments *expand* upon what we find in R1, by adding or lengthening a gloss to a verse (*cat. Ps.* 9:35; 16:1; 20:13; 24:5; 29:7; 43:24; 49:23; 61:12; 73:11(2); 76:18; 78:2

---

[7] Only one verse in R1 is suspicious to me: in section 55 we find Ps 26:9 cited, but it does not illustrate the point being made and so I delete it.

abridges and expands). However, these fragments do not necessarily come from R$_a$—they might come from the corresponding lost sections of R2 or some other, fuller recension.[8] Or again, there are a number of fragments that correspond to material transmitted by both R1 and R2, but in details they approximate the text of R1, not R2 (*cat. Ps.* 30:20–1; 50:6; 50:8; 67:31(1)). Noteworthy is that in each of these cases the fragments *expand* upon the text we find in R1 in the form of lengthier glosses on verses.[9] Unless we posit the unlikely scenario of a catenist who introduced glosses into the ms tradition, these fragments point more obviously to a now-lost direct ancestor of R1, and not R$_a$ itself. Most promising for the reconstruction of R$_a$ are those fragments that transmit distinctive elements of both R1 and R2. Especially auspicious are the fragments that transmit more material than is found in either of the corresponding sections of R1 or R2 (e.g., *cat. Ps.* 77:49, 78:12(1), and *cat. Job* 1:11).

In many of the above cases it is likely that the longer material in the catenae fragments—especially when it concerns a hermeneutical thesis or biblical gloss—approximates R$_a$ more closely than the corresponding shorter material in R1 and/or R2. But it is also important to remember that this longer material might still be an abbreviation of its source, and thus of restricted value for reconstructing the text of R$_a$. The catenists routinely abridged their sources, including the *Introduction*: a number of fragments fail to transmit seemingly authentic material that surfaces in the corresponding sections of R1 and R2 (see *cat. Ps.* 31:4(2); 77:49; 78:12(2); *cat. Job* 1:11).

Thus while I regard the reconstruction of R$_a$ to be a largely speculative exercise, those cases where a recension or catena fragment transmits a longer exegetical principle or scriptural gloss than what we find elsewhere in the ms tradition merit close attention, since they might gesture toward a more original version of the *Introduction*. Of this we can be certain: the *Introduction* was at one time a longer treatise, and perhaps even substantially longer, than our surviving recensions. Each of these are distinctive epitomes of this more expansive work.[10]

---

[8] While it is impossible to know with certainty, I hold it for likely that there once was a complete version of R2, and that some of these catenae fragments that expand upon what we find in R1—where there is no corresponding text transmitted by R2—were in fact drawn from the sections of R2 that are now missing in the direct ms tradition.

[9] In every case but *cat. Ps.* 67:31(1), the fragments *also abridge* what we find in R1 (in the form of fewer or shorter biblical citations).

[10] Earlier scholars asserted that the catenae fragments pointed to a longer, more original recension from which R1 was derived (Pitra, *Analecta Sacra*, vol. 2, 128, 131, 134; Mercati, "Pro Adriano," 251–3; R. Devreesse, "Chaines Exégétique Grecques," *DBS*, vol. 1, col. 1134; Natalio Fernández Marcos, *The Septuagint in Context: Introduction to the Greek Version of the Bible*, trans. Wilfred G. E. Watson [Leiden: Brill, 2000], 283 and 340). In light of a more thorough investigation of the catenae fragments and the recent discovery of R2, this assessment needs to be qualified: some fragments point to R1, others to R2 (a recension from which R1 was not derived), and still others to a longer, more original recension from which both R1 and R2 were derived.

6

Conventions of the Present Edition
and Translation

A. EDITION

1. *Textus*

A. *Sigla and text in bold*

Proposed additions to, or deletions from, the mss that underlie R1 (**L**) and R2 (**XYZ**) are signified with <> and [], respectively in the text. I maintain these sigla whether or not I (or previous editors) am responsible for the conjectures. When an emendation requires the addition of biblical text, I utilize the current critical editions.[1] The obeli ([†] [†]) mark a corruption. I use ˹ ˺ to indicate text that I think is genuine, but likely misplaced, and it remains unclear clear where it should be reassigned. The apparatus will sometimes suggest where this text might belong. I have reassigned a few sections of the treatise, and here the apparatus will also explain where the material originally stood in the mss and previous editions. Both the [†] and ˹ ˺ also appear in my translation.

 L (R1) as well as **XYZ** (R2) usually indicate a scriptural quotation by immediately prefacing it with a τὸ or καὶ: in both cases I change the accent to an acute, insert a comma after the article, and highlight the biblical text that follows in bold.

B. *Divisions and titles*

The treatise (as transmitted in R1) falls into three major sections as announced in the opening sentence of the work. The first and third of these sections receive the following titles in **L**: Ἀρχὴ τῶν ἐπὶ τῆς διανοίας and Ἀρχὴ τῶν

---

[1] For the Septuagint, I use the Goettingen edition if it is available for the biblical book in question, otherwise I cite from Rahlf's edition; for the New Testament, I print the text from Nestle–Aland's 28th edition. The texts of these modern editions will not always have corresponded verbatim with Adrian's biblical texts.

ἐπὶ τῆς συνθέσεως, respectively. The second section also receives a title, but in a different format: not the expected, Ἀρχὴ τῶν ἐπὶ τῆς λέξεως, but rather, *Τὰ δὲ ἐπὶ τῆς λέξεως οὕτως.* The third section draws to a close with paragraph 72, and is followed by what can be regarded as a series of appendices.[2]

The treatise is further subdivided into paragraphs in the ms tradition. In **L** the end of a paragraph is customarily marked off by the punctuation symbol [:–] and this symbol is usually followed by an initial rubric, signaling the beginning of the next paragraph. Some of these paragraph divisions are also indicated in the margins of **L** with Greek numerals, supplied there by Lukas the scribe. However, his numbering system is incomplete in two ways. Sometimes the punctuation within the treatise indicates a paragraph break (i.e., :– followed by initial rubric), but there is no corresponding marginal numeral (e.g., I supply 61.2 where the scribe at 252r provides :– and an initial rubric, but no marginal number). More noticeably, the marginal numbers begin at 2.1(3[α′]) and conclude abruptly at 62(97[μδ′]). Hoeschel followed the paragraph numbers of **B**, which are exactly those of **L**. The only difference is that **B** supplied α′, β′, and γ′ at 4.1(19[αβ′]) and 4.2(20[γ′])—those three numbers are missing from the interior margin of 247r in **L**. Pearson and Migne followed Hoeschel's numbering. Goessling gave a more comprehensive, Arabic numbering system that largely followed his predecessors, while retaining Hoeschel's system in brackets (e.g., §38[ιθ′]). My numbering system adapts Goessling's in an attempt to better capture the flow of thought in the treatise. For greater ease in the use of previous scholarship and editions I have retained the two preceding numbering systems in a smaller font. I generally follow the paragraph divisions in **L**, though occasionally group paragraphs together, and sometimes introduce new subdivisions. These departures are clear if the reader notes the Greek numerals. I indicate a handful of important departures from **L**'s paragraph divisions in the apparatus.

The corresponding material in R2 will be presented in a parallel column. In **Y** and **Z** paragraph divisions are usually signaled with a [:] and then followed by an initial rubric, signaling the beginning of the next paragraph. In **X** the scribe indicates some divisions with a low point and by beginning the next paragraph on a fresh line. A number of divisions are missing in **X**. In the second extended excerpt from the *Introduction* (**YZ**), titles are additionally indicated before the discussion of a trope—sporadically in **Y**, for most tropes in **Z**. The titles occur in the following form: ὅπως κατὰ + trope. These titles are rubricated and appear to have been written by the first hand.

It is notoriously difficult to determine whether the titles in the ms tradition go back to our author. While it is a possibility, it is also a distinct likelihood that they were introduced into the body of text, or more likely its margins, by

[2] Peter W. Martens, "Adrian's *Introduction to the Divine Scriptures* and Greco-Roman Rhetorical Theory on Style," *Journal of Religion* 93 (2013): 197–217.

later scribes as aids for readers, especially in a treatise such as the *Introduction* that provides extended lists. It is also the case that subsequent scribes often confused these marginalia with the author's original text and moved the titles from the margins into the body of the text. These titles, in turn, were again relocated to the margins by later scribes (as I suspect happened in a few cases in R1). Compounding the difficulty is that considerable inconsistency reigns in the use of titles of the ms traditions of R1 and R2. L, for instance, does not provide any titles for the individual tropes, whereas **Y** and **Z** do, though even here these two mss, which are otherwise very similar, diverge noticeably over which titles they record: **Y** provides far fewer titles than **Z**. Moreover, the titles are placed in different places on the page—sometimes they occur in the outer margins, but more commonly in the empty space at the end of the line where the previous trope was discussed. In one case, a title is centered and occupies its own line (ὅπως κατὰ μεταφοράν **Z**, f. 18v). Similar discrepanacies occur in the opening list of fifteen anthropomorphic categories. Only the first and last categories receive titles in **L**. Moreover, while this ms locates the titles in the body of the text (marking them off with punctuation), two descendant mss (**EG**) relocate these titles to the exterior margin. Finally, no mss in R1 provide titles for the different figures listed in section three—here we might expect titles, though none, in fact, occurs.

Given these inconsistencies, as well as the tendency of **L** not to proliferate titles, I have decided to be circumspect: I consider only the titles marking the first and third main subdivisions of the work to be original, and hesitatingly supply the title, Ἀρχὴ τῶν ἐπὶ τῆς λέξεως to mark the second section, so that three uniform titles begin the main sections of the work. Perhaps this title fell out because it was considered redundant with the immediately following text that, in turn, became punctuated as a title: Τὰ δὲ ἐπὶ τῆς λέξεως οὕτως. But it is also possible that I have supplied the aforementioned title erroneously and that what I regard as a derivative title was, in fact, original, but simply inconsistent with the titles for sections one and three. All other titles in **L** or **YZ** (for the anthropomorphic list and list of tropes) I consider subsequent scribal additions since they are employed incompletely and variably.

The facing English translation will sometimes introduce headings designed to aid comprehension. As this is a facing translation, it will be easy to determine when headings have been supplied by me, and when they occur in the ms tradition.

C. Punctuation

I have taken the punctuation of **L** into account. Lukas uses three punctuation marks with considerable consistency as follows:

1. [.] low point: this is the weakest indicated break and is almost always represented as a comma in this edition. The scribe often uses the low point more extensively than we do our comma, and in those cases it is not reported (e.g., it can mark off subject from predicate, predicate from object, set off a prepositional phrase, distinguish between the direct and indirect objects of a verb or demarcate disjunctive clauses). There are only a handful of places where the scribe uses a comma [,], which seems to correspond to his low point (e.g., line 28 on 248r = comma at 150.3).
2. [·] high point: a stronger break, which is usually represented as such in this edition (thus functioning as our colon, semi-colon, and sometimes full stop). When the high point marks the end of a question I repunctuate it as a question mark (i.e., [;]). Occasionally the high point is weak enough or strong enough that it is replaced in the edition by a comma or full stop, respectively. Sometimes a punctuation mark midway between the low and high point occurs, but it is difficult to discern different levels of strength. There are times when the high point distinguishes disjunctive clauses from one another, in which case it is not reported.
3. [:-] strongest punctuation: this symbol invariably signals the end of a paragraph, and thus it is represented in our edition by a full stop (or by a [;] if the paragraph ends with a question). When this symbol marks the end of a lemma, it is repunctuated with the high stop [·], thereby functioning like our colon.

While I generally follow the punctuation in **L**, the scribe is not always consistent in his use of these marks. In these cases I introduce consistency silently. However, in a few cases the scribe punctuates erroneously (e.g., introducing a false heading or false paragraph division). In the latter cases I note his alternate punctuation in my apparatus and repunctuate accordingly.

The punctuation in R2 will be adapted to what has been established for R1 as there is no value in introducing a significantly different punctuation style. Where the texts do not overlap, I extend the principles of punctuation already established, though I keep an eye on the punctuation of **YZ**. The only major discrepancy is that **YZ** utilize a weak punctuation mark (the low stop) more frequently than I use the comma. **X** punctuates very infrequently.

D. Orthography

Concerning R1

1. I standardize the following spellings in **L** (usually silently):

134.5	σκόλοψι] σκώλωψι	**L**
136.5	ἀπέρριμμαι] -ρ-	**L**
148.11	κῆδος] κῦδος	**L**

182.13 ἐρραδιούργησε] -ρ- **L**
192.3   ῥακὰ] -κκ- **L**
198.1   ὑπήρεισε] ὑπείρεισε **L**
260.7   κεκράξονται] -ωνται **L**
260.20 ῥέμβευσον] ῥεύβευσον **L**
266.1   στιλβώσει] στιλφώσει **L**
278.1   προκέοιτο] προκαίοιτο **L**
278.10 ὑποθημοσύνης] ὑποθυμοσύνης **L**

2. There are a few cases of misleading assimilation that I silently correct. I report only semantically interesting assimilations in the apparatus:

140.3   διὰ στόματος] διαστόματος **L**
156.2   ἀντὶ πράξεις] ἀντιπράξεις **L**
180.10   ἐφ᾽ ὁδοῦ] ἐφόδου **L**
220.13   Κατ᾽ ἔλλειψιν] κατέλλειψιν **L**
240.5   ἐπ᾽ ἐλπίδι] ἐπελπίδι **L**
240.6–7 πρὸ ἑωσφόρου] προεωσφόρου **L**

3. I draw the reader's attention to a few features of word division where I establish conformity around the scribe's usual practice: he writes οὐκ ἔτι and not οὐκέτι (260.21; 266.15); ὡσανεὶ occurs as one word (170.11 and 190.7) as does δηλονότι (234.8); ὥσπερ is written as one word (148.8; 150.4; 198.6) but two words in 262.18 (ὡς περ), and so I change the latter to one word; finally, ἐξ ἀρχῆς is written as two words (144.5; 162.11–12), ἐξ ἀνάγκης as two words (278.4–5), but ἀπαρχῆς is written as one word (218.23), so I write it as two: ἀπ᾽ ἀρχῆς.

4. The scribe invariably presents the iota subscript as an adscript (i.e., after the vowel and slightly smaller than a standard iota). In this edition the adscript will be represented as a subscript. Lukas frequently notes these subscripts, though he is not exhaustive. He tends to note it when it occurs with articles and pronouns, and on noun endings or verbal augments; he tends to omit it when it occurs on verbal endings; and he only occasionally notes it when it belongs to the root of a word. I restore all subscripts and correct those placed erroneously.

5. When it concerns biblical names, I follow the spelling, accents, and breathing marks of **L**. Note the following characteristics, which, unless otherwise noted, are also attested in other patristic Greek texts (confirmed with the *TLG*):

Ἀβραάμ always has rough breathing (e.g., 274.7); Ἐλισσαῖος (270.20) has a double sigma; Ἡσαΐας (284.2) is given a rough breathing; Ἱερεμίας (184.21; 284.2) is also given a rough breathing; "Jerusalem" is always spelled as Ἱερουσαλήμ (s.v. Ἱεροσόλυμα BDAG); Ἰούδα (180.9) is an unusual form and the dative is given as Ἰούδᾳ (272.10), which is declined from Ἰούδας (BDF §55.1.a; s.v. Ἰούδας BDAG); Ἰουδαῖα (218.9), with a circumflex, instead of an acute, is sporadically found in patristic Greek; Moses is given as Μωσῆς (nom. 244.26), Μωσέως (gen. 270.13), and Μωσεῖ (dat. 284.4); Πιλάτος (176.10) is spelled with the acute and not the more common circumflex (s.v. Πιλᾶτος BDAG); Ὡσηέ has smooth breathing (136.13).

6. Other matters: I print the coronis with the scribe: τοὐπίσω (136.8); τἀναντία (144.4); κἀνταῦθα (162.10); τοὐναντίον (202.10); κἀκεῖνο (284.1) (but not over προυπαρχούσης at 276.4 where it is missing from **L**). I print the diaeresis with the scribe: for example, πρωΐ (200.1). The scribe is consistent in the use of final *nu* and *sigma* (οὕτω/*s* and ἐκ/ἐξ), as well as in the alternation between οὐ, οὐκ, and οὐχ. I follow the elisions made in **L**. I silently expand abbreviations and shortened forms. Finally, I capitalize names for persons, peoples, places, titles of biblical books, and the designation "Christ."

Concerning R2

There are significant discrepancies in orthography between **XYZ**. Where decisions about spelling need to be made (such as with word division or the spellings of proper names) I take into account the conventions of **Y** since it offers consistently better readings for this recension.

1. **XYZ** are replete with non-standard spellings. These are silently modified if they involve the straightforward exchange of vowels (e.g., confusing -ι- for -υ- ; -ω- for -ο- and -ο- for -ω-; -οι- for -ι-; -οι- for -υ-; -η- for -ε-; -ι- for -ει- and -ει- for -ι-; -α- for -ε-; -ει- for -οι-; -η- for -οι-; -η- for -ει-) or the doubling of consonants (e.g., -νν- for -ν- and -ν- for -νν-; -λ- for -λλ-). Where the Greek language allows for widely attested alternative spellings (e.g., γιγν- or γιγ-), I follow the conventions of **Y**. A very partial list of these variant spellings is provided in the discussion of the stemma for R2.
2. There are a few cases of misleading assimilation that are usually corrected silently:

172.12	διὰ παντός **XZ**] διαπαντός **Y**
190.20	δῆλον ὅτι **YZ**] δηλονότι **X**
198.11	κατ' εἰκόνα **XZ**] κατεικόνα **Y**
238.11	παρ' ἐλπίδα **Martens**] παρελπίδα **YZ**
238.15	ὑπὸ νόμον **Z**] ὑπονόμον **Y**
242.11	ἀπὸ μέρους **Z**] ἀπομέρους **Y**
242.14–15	πρὸ ἑωσφόρου **Martens**] προεωσφόρου **YZ**
250.20	δῆλον ὅτι **Martens**] δηλονότι **YZ**
252.11	διὰ τὸ **Martens**] διατὸ **YZ**

3. An instance of misleading division:

188.7	εἰσέλθοι **XZ**] εἰς ἔλθοι **Y**

4. Word division is sometimes handled inconsistently among the mss. For instance: ἀναμέσον (**YZ**: 172.3; 256.8), but ἀνὰ μέσον (**X**: 172.3); or ἐξαρχῆς

(YZ: 162.6), but ἐξ ἀρχῆς (X: 162.6); or ὡς ἂν εἰ (YZ: 190.9), but ὡσανεὶ
(X: 190.9). In these cases my practice is to follow Y, accepting even its inconsistencies when no clear scribal preference can be discerned: note both ὡς
ἂν εἰ (Y: 190.9) and ὡσὰν (Y: 244.26); both γ' οὖν (Y: 172.12) and γοῦν
(Y: 194.16; 206.22); ἤτ' οὖν (Y: 196.18; 232.17) as well as ἤτουν (Y: 244.22).

5. The iota subscript is almost never used in YZ, and only sporadically in X.
I restore it.

6. As for biblical names, I follow the spelling, accents and breathing marks
of Y, introducing consistency only when the scribe reveals a clear tendency:

Ἀββακούμ with smooth breathing (196.14); Ἀβραάμ with rough breathing (266.20;
274.7; 274.15); Γιεζή (270.21) with acute instead of the more common circumflex;
Γόμορα (51) (s.v. Γόμορρα BDAG); Ἐλισσαῖος (270.20) has a double sigma;
Ἡσαΐας (182.9; 190.11; 196.5 [supplying missing diaeresis]; 240.11) is given a rough
breathing; "Ezekiel" is twice given with smooth breathing (Ἰεζεκιήλ: 194.14; 272.18)
and twice with rough breathing (Ἱεζεκιήλ: 234.19; 250.2); Ἱερεμίας (184.19; 188.2)
is given a rough breathing; "Jerusalem" is always spelled as Ἱερουσαλήμ (s.v.
Ἱεροσόλυμα BDAG); Ἰούδα is treated as indeclinable (180.3; 244.15, 17; 272.10)
(s.v. Ἰούδας BDAG); the genitive of "Moses" is given as Μωυσέως (270.13) and the
dative as Μωυσεῖ (188.6; 198.9—I bring Μωσῇ [180.2] into conformity with this
form); Πιλᾶτος (176.9) is spelled with the circumflex (s.v. Πιλᾶτος BDAG);
"Hosea" has smooth breathing: Ὠσηέ (200.7; 208.9) (s.v. Ὠσηέ BDAG).

7. I change a number of breathing marks if they are unattested in the TLG:
I print ἱματισμῷ (248.23) instead of the smooth breathing (YZ); ἔαρ (254.15;
256.1, 3) with the smooth breathing (Z) not rough (Y); ἅλωνα (264.19) instead
of the smooth breathing (YZ); ἔοικεν (268.15) with the smooth breathing (Z)
not rough (Y).

8. Other matters: I ignore the often inconsistent use of the tremma in YZ
(e.g., Ἰούδα appears twice in 73.8, once with the tremma over the initial *iota*
and once without it)—the tremma appears less frequently in X; I print the
coronis over τοὐναντίον as it occurs at 262.12 and 264.2 (YZ). The scribes of
XYZ are consistent in the use of the final *sigma* (οὕτω/ς and ἐκ/ἐξ), as well as
in the alternation between οὐ, οὐκ, and οὐχ. There is far less consistency in the
use of final *nu* among the mss, so here I follow the practice of Y. I print the
diaeresis with Y and follow its elisions. As with R1, I silently expand abbreviations and shortened forms, as well as capitalize names for persons, peoples,
places, titles of biblical books, and the designation "Christ."

E. Accents

Accentuation of R1 usually follows the conventions of L, unless there is a
noticeable internal discrepancy. There are three recurring situations where
the handling of enclitics in L differs from those taught in contemporary
grammars—I preserve these differences. First, some words that we class as

enclitics do not always have to be treated as such by Byzantine scribes.[3] There are two cases where **L** regards τίς/τί as indefinite but not as an enclitic (126.2: εὗροι τίς; 220.15: ἢ τί); there are two instances where εἰμί is not treated as an enclitic (216.16: καὶ εἰμί; 262.9: ποῦ ἐστὶ);[4] two instances where φημί is not regarded as an enclitic (212.18: πολλαχοῦ φησίν; 244.26–7: ὁ Μωσῆς φησίν); finally, πῶς is regarded as indefinite (200.16). Second, in cases where two or more enclitics follow one another, the scribe of **L** does not allow two syllables marked with acute accents to follow one another as sometimes happens in Byzantine mss (e.g., 132.8: πρωτότοκός μου ἐστίν; 276.5: μή που τίς).[5] And third, if a word in **L** preceding the enclitic receives a circumflex on its penult, it does not always receive an additional acute accent on the ultima (e.g., 128.6: χεῖρας σου, and not χεῖράς σου).[6] There are many such instances in the treatise, and only one place where the scribe inserts the acute (176.3: κοινωνῆσαί τινος).

Beyond enclitics, there are a few recurring features of accentuation that merit attention. In **L**, an oxytone often does not change its accent to a grave when it is followed by αὐτός in the genitive case (sg. or pl.). However, the scribe is quite inconsistent in this matter (e.g., ὁδὸν αὐτῆς at 134.5, but ὁδόν αὐτῆς at 134.6). Since the scribe seems to grant equal footing to both options, I have decided to bring uniformity to the text by reverting the acute to a grave as the modern reader would expect.[7] A number of other Byzantine features are preserved in the edition: Lukas writes μὴδέ and not μηδέ (130.3; 192.9; 200.18) as well as μὴδαμῶς and not μηδαμῶς (278.16);[8] we always find τοὐτέστι(ν) (158.6; 198.11; 200.5, 7; 202.10; 212.9); occasionally a vowel receives an acute accent instead of the expected circumflex (e.g., 148.2: μίσος; 202.11: θλίψιν).[9] I also retain those instances where we encounter a word with a less-attested accentuation: for example, 186.10: κρῖμα (instead of acute); 210.16: ὀστά (instead of circumflex); 236.1 ἴδε (instead of ἰδέ); 280.3

---

[3]   *Commentarius in Ecclesiasten*, ed. Ettlinger and Noret, xlvi.
[4]   Note also that the verb expresses existence when accented as ἔστι(ν), even if it is not at the beginning of a sentence (126.1: Τοῦ Ἑβραϊκοῦ χαρακτῆρος ἰδιωμάτων ἔστιν εἴδη τρία), but that this sense can also be conveyed by the enclitic form (268.16–17: Εἴδη μέντοι τῆς θείας γραφῆς ἐστι δύο). For more on this issue, see Philomen Probert, *A New Short Guide to the Accentuation of Ancient Greek* (Bristol: Bristol Classical Press, 2003), §282, with lit.
[5]   *Commentarius in Ecclesiasten*, ed. Ettlinger and Noret, xlvi.
[6]   See *Leonis VI Sapientis Imperatoris Byzantini: Homiliae*, ed. Theodora Antonopoulou, CCSG 63 (Turnhout: Brepols, 2008), ccxxiv.
[7]   The instances where we find the acute on the ultima are: 134.6: ὁδόν αὐτῆς; 138.5: οἱ ὀφθαλμοί αὐτοῦ; 140.1: ἐξιλεωτικόν αὐτοῦ; 146.8: κραυγήν αὐτῶν; 150.3: δημιουργικήν αὐτοῦ; 180.6 and 224.8: λειτουργούς αὐτοῦ (with correction from grave to acute visible at first usage); 188.9: βουλήν αὐτῶν; 204.9: παρεμβολή αὐτοῦ; 210.13: σαρκός αὐτοῦ. Instances where the scribe puts the grave on the ultima are: 132.7: ἀνὴρ αὐτῆς; 134.5 ὁδὸν αὐτῆς; 152.9: περὶ αὐτοῦ (2×); 174.9: ἀσφαλὲς αὐτῶν; 240.13–14: καιρὸν αὐτῆς.
[8]   See *Michaelis Pselli Chronographia*, vol. 2, *Textkritischer Kommentar und Indices*, ed. Diether Roderich Reinsch (Berlin: Walter de Gruyter, 2014), 499.
[9]   *Commentarius in Ecclesiasten*, ed. Ettlinger and Noret, xlii–xliii.

προσυποδεικνύναι (instead of acute). I do not print the occasional double accent on δέ and μέν.

In addition to these issues, there are a few inconsistencies or errors that I silently correct. Sometimes the scribe puts a grave accent on the ultima of a word that immediately precedes his punctuation, but usually not—I repunctuate to an acute, as this is his more common practice. I supply accents in the few cases where they are missing (e.g., 214.11: ἔμελλεν; 278.20: γραφικων).

Accentuation in R2 follows **Y** with only minor modifications. Regarding enclitics: I preserve the practice whereby the scribe treats some words as both enclitics and non-enclitics. For instance, with one exception εἰμί is consistently regarded as an enclitic (186.19: συνεχέστερον ἐστὶν). Regarding φημί, it is also usually regarded as an enclitic in **Y**, except in two cases (166.11: ἐθεασάμεθα φησὶ; 168.11: συνήγοντο φησὶ). The verb is often abbreviated, yet when fully written takes the final *nu* when a vowel follows, and lacks the final *nu* when a consonant follows. This is also in keeping with the scribe's practice for ἐστί(ν), and so I expand the abbreviated forms accordingly. The accented form τίς can be indefinite (274.14), as is the form πῶς (200.16). When περ is joined to the preceding word, it might form a double-accented compound if followed by εἰμί (196.2: ὅπέρ ἐστιν) or it might not (172.8–9: οὗπερ ἐστίν·).[10] Unlike **L**, when two or more enclitics follow one another, the scribe of **Y** can allow two syllables marked with acute accents to follow one another (232.8: ὁδόν τέ τινα). When a word preceding the enclitic receives a circumflex on its penult, it sometimes does not receive an additional acute accent—I preserve this variability (176.5: χεῖρας μου; 242.21: χεῖρα σου). Note the double accent on ὅταν when followed by an enclitic (248.4: ὅτάν τισι). Finally, I change λύπήν μου (200.23–4) to λύπην μου, and ὁδού σου (208.9) to ὁδοῦ σου, in keeping with the scribe's general practice.

Beyond enclitics, note the following features of accentuation: I preserve the circumflex instead of the expected acute, e.g., παρεμβολῆ (206.16); preserve alternate accentuations (ὁμοίων at 238.3 and 240.10; ἴδε in 234.26); change Ἰάκὼβ to Ἰακὼβ (234.17); and supply an accent on πληθυς (206.18).

2. *Apparatus fontium*

In this apparatus I identify biblical passages that Adrian quotes, paraphrases, or to which he alludes.[11] Biblical passages are identified according to chapter and verse markings in the NRSV. Where these differ from the LXX, I follow the

---

[10] *Homiliae*, ed. Antonopoulou, ccxxiv.

[11] For this section I am indebted to the discussion by John F. Petruccione in *Theodoret of Cyrus: The Questions on the Octateuch*, vol. 1, *On Genesis and Exodus*, John F. Petruccione and Robert C. Hill, Library of Early Christianity 1 (Washington, D.C.: Catholic University of America Press, 2007), lii–lv.

divisions of the latter, putting the NRSV in []. It is usually clear which biblical passage Adrian is quoting. There are only a handful of places where his citation is so brief, or different, from the texts of our biblical editions that more than one verse could be in mind. In those cases I supply references to the possible verses.

I consider a quotation to be a precise verbal correspondence with the Greek texts of our critical editions of the LXX and NT. As noted above, I place text in bold to signify a quotation. Where there are minor variations from our critical editions (altered word order, the addition or deletion of a brief word or phrase, etc.), a number of possibilities arise, including: Adrian is citing a biblical text verbatim that differs from the text printed in our biblical editions; he is mis-quoting his biblical text or paraphrasing it (this text may, or may not, have had the same reading as our editions); or the ms tradition of the *Introduction* has altered his original wording in some way. It is not always easy to resolve this issue, in part because we do not have sufficient data for the variant readings of the LXX and NT that were in circulation in antiquity. Thus, *also* where there is a strong verbal correspondence between Adrian's biblical text and our edi-tions, I place text in bold, but write "var." after the scriptural identification to signify that Adrian's Greek text differs from our editions in some way. Readers are encouraged to consult the critical apparatuses for the LXX and NT to see what biblical mss or patristic texts (if any) carry the variants Adrian cites. Where there are no variants that agree with Adrian's text, there is the possibil-ity that what I have identified as a quotation is, in fact, a misquote or para-phrase. Finally, where Adrian alludes to a biblical passage, no Greek text will be highlighted in bold and I will preface the scriptural indication with "cf."

A recurring phenomenon in the *Introduction* is Adrian citing noticeably less biblical text than what is printed in our editions. There are cases where Adri-an's biblical text is plausibly shorter, or he has deliberately abridged his biblical citation, trusting that his readers could supply what was missing or that what was missing was ultimately not important for his purposes. There are a num-ber of cases, however, where it appears that biblical material has fallen out of the ms tradition of the *Introduction*. Where material that seems crucial for the sense is missing, I emend accordingly by placing biblical text from our critical editions in <>. Otherwise I have left Adrian's text stand as transmitted. My translation inserts an ellipsis when I wish to signal to the reader that biblical text appears to have been intentionally abridged by Adrian. If I think the reader would benefit from the elided material, I supply it in my translation within [].

3. *Apparatus criticus*

R1 is based upon the text of **L**. The apparatus will not reproduce in any system-atic way the readings of the other mss, since these have been demonstrated to be ultimately dependent upon L. Readings from these mss are recorded only if they offer a successful conjecture to a corruption in L, or, on a few occasions, produce an interesting variant. There are four additional sources for emendations. First, there are the catenae fragments from Adrian's *Introduction* that usually do not help with editing R1 (or R2). However, in a few places they transmit a text that converges with the recensions and offers a better reading. Second, I occasionally draw upon R2. My basic principle is to resist homogenization of these two recensions, even in cases where I suspect that one offers a better reading than the other. However, there are places where R1 is in my judgment scarcely legible, or not at all, and here the text of R2 becomes valuable. The same principle holds for using R1 to edit R2. Third, a number of emendations are dependent upon the conjectures of Hoeschel, Schlüren, and Goessling. Finally, I am responsible for conjectures where no source is identified in the apparatus.

Another feature of my apparatus is that it records all the differences between my text and those of the two previous editions (less most cases of alternate punctuation, alternate orthography, and orthographic errors). It will be useful for readers to have my text as well as the texts of Hoeschel and Goessling before them—especially the latter, which is held by very few libraries around the world. But the potential for confusion arises if editors' names in the apparatus sometimes signify disagreement with my adopted reading and sometimes agreement (as noted above where a conjecture is accepted). The confusion runs deeper when the apparatus entry concerns an emendation to L: silence about an editor could signify his agreement with my adopted reading (e.g., when the editor conjectured correctly, but mss that have subsequently come to light and upon which I rely confirm that reading), or silence could signify disagreement (e.g., when my emendation is dependent upon one editor who is identified in the apparatus, but not the other, who goes unannounced).

Thus the policy on listing the two previous editions in the apparatus is as follows. Whenever I am not emending L, the apparatus straightforwardly records places where Hoeschel or Goessling *disagree* with my reading. If the departure of only one editor is listed, it will be understood that the other is in agreement with my text. When I am emending L, however, I record *all agreements* between the editors' texts and mine. I draw special attention to the three ways I signify this agreement:

1. In cases where the editor is following the same mss I am using to emend L, these mss precede his name and the source of his decision is acknowledged after his name: e.g., CDG *Goessling* (ex codd.);
2. There are a number of occasions where editors made successful conjectures that have been confirmed by mss that have subsequently come to light. Since it seems appropriate to honor these cases of philological acu-

men, I acknowledge the editor's name immediately after the mss that testify to his proposal: e.g., CDE *Hoeschel Goessling* (ex codd.) signifies that Hoeschel conjectured the reading in CDE whereas Goessling had this ms evidence to support it;

3. Finally, if the editor has made a successful conjecture not attested by any known ms, his name alone stands in the apparatus.

As a general rule, then, if an editor is not mentioned when I am emending **L** it is because he adopts the original reading in the ms tradition. If the editor has proposed an alternative emendation with which I disagree, that reading is provided for the sake of clarity. For important notifications on punctuation, I provide full information on how previous editors punctuated their texts. This policy should allow the reader to reconstruct the texts of Hoeschel and Goessling.

I also note that in the case of Goessling's edition, I track down the sources that informed his readings, which include the translation by Lollin (where I usually rely on Goessling's self-reporting), the revisions of Hoeschel's text by Pearson and Migne, and finally, Schlüren's essay. I do not offer a comprehensive report of Schlüren's emendations in my apparatus, as I find a number of suggestions overly invasive, involving extensive reordering of material, the addition of new sentences and, in general, an insistence upon a level of consistency that Adrian would not necessarily have had. But Schlüren does surface in three important ways: (1) as noted above, where he is the source of Goessling's emendations or has inspired them; (2) where he is the source of one of my emendations (or approximates it); (3) where his emendations anticipate what we find in other mss that transmit R1, R2 or the catenae. This policy reflects my attempt to restore credit to Schlüren's editorial work, which was suppressed in Goessling's edition.

R2 is based upon **XYZ** (fragment one) and **YZ** (fragment two). **Y** and **Z** are very closely related and where they diverge, it is usually clear which of the two offers the more satisfactory reading. The most striking differences between these mss concern the discrepant use of headings in **YZ** and the tendency in **X** to produce abridged or altered biblical citations (both issues have been discussed previously). The apparatus records all variants less minor orthographic issues. Emendations to this text come from the catenae fragments, R1, and my own conjectures. This text has not been previously edited.

Abbreviations in the apparatus should be clear, but I note here: *om.* indicates that material was likely omitted by a scribe or editor in error; *deest* again signifies that something is missing, but it is difficult to assign error to the scribe or more usually the editor who was following ms(s) that also leave out the material; the symbol—(or *del.*) indicates that the editor has bracketed text that he thought ought to be deleted; *susp.* indicates that an editor has raised doubts about the authenticity of the passage.

B. TRANSLATION

I am providing the first English translation of Adrian's *Introduction*. The translation aspires to readability, or as much as a work of technical, late antique Greek scholarship permits. Above I explained the presence of the †, ⌐ ¬, and the ellipsis in my translation. For ease of reference, I also supply scriptural identifications after quotes, paraphrases, and allusions.

As noted in the earlier section entitled "The Present Edition and Translation," the annotations to the translation address a number of issues: (1) they discuss particularly challenging words or passages; (2) examine important textual problems; (3) assign the fragments from the exegetical catenae to those passages in R1 and R2 with which they most closely correspond; (4) identify some parallel passages from other "Antiochene" biblical scholars; and (5) provide short bibliographic references to relevant scholarly literature.

7

List of Symbols and Abbreviations

CODICES

Recension 1 (R1)

A   Munich, Bayer. Staatsbibliothek, *Codex Graecus 477* (XVI)
B   Munich, Bayer. Staatsbibliothek, *Codex Graecus 107* (ca. 1550)
C   Vatican City, Bibl. Apost. Vaticana, *Ottobonianus Graecus 194* (XVI)
D   Vatican City, Bibl. Apost. Vaticana, *Ottobonianus Graecus 270* (XVI)
E   Vatican City, Bibl. Apost. Vaticana, *Ottobonianus Graecus 379* (XVI)
F   Basel, Universitätsbibliothek, *O II 17b* (XVI)
G   Vatican City, Bibl. Apost. Vaticana, *Vaticanus Graecus 659* (XVI)
H   Vatican City, Bibl. Apost. Vaticana, *Vaticanus Graecus 1269* (XVI)
I   Vatican City, Bibl. Apost. Vaticana, *Vaticanus Graecus 1665* (1566–8)
J   Vatican City, Bibl. Apost. Vaticana, *Vaticanus Graecus 1908* (XVI/XVII)
K   Rome, Bibl. Vallicelliana, *F9 (78)* (XVI)
L   Florence, Bibl. Medicea Laurenziana, *Conventi Soppressi 39* (1095/1105)
L$_H$ Hamburg, Staats- und Universitätsbibliothek, *221 in Scrinio* (1095/1105)
P   Mount Athos, Μονή Αγίου Παντελεήμονος, *693* (Lambros 6200) (XVIII)

Recension 2 (R2)

X   Vatican City, Bibl. Apost. Vaticana, *Vaticanus Graecus 1862* (XVI)
Y   Vatican City, Bibl. Apost. Vaticana, *Vaticanus Graecus 1447* (1534)
Z   Mount Athos, Μονή Ιβήρων, *1333* (Lambros 5453) (XVI–XVII)

EDITORES

Goessling   Friedrich Goessling, *Adrians ΕΙΣΑΓΩΓΗ ΕΙΣ ΤΑΣ ΘΕΙΑΣ ΓΡΑΦΑΣ aus neu aufgefundenen Handschriften* (Berlin: Reuther, 1887).

Hoeschel   David Hoeschel, *Adriani Isagoge, Sacrarum Literarum et antiquissimorum graecorum in Prophetas fragmenta* (Augsburg: Typis Ioannis Praetorii, 1602), 1–27 (text) and 88–9 (notes).

Lollin   Aloysius Lollin, *Aloysii Lollini patritii veneti Bellunensium antistitis, Episcopalium curarum characteres*, ed. Donatus Bernardius (Belluno: Castilionis, 1630), 257–73.

Migne   PG 98, 1274–1312.

Pearson   John Pearson, ed., *Critici Sacri, sive Doctissimorum Virorum in SS. Biblia Annotationes et Tractatus*, vol. 8, *Tractatuum Biblicorum* (London: Jacobus Flescher, 1660), 9–23 (text) and 47–50 (notes).

Schlüren   Karl Friedrich Schlüren, "Zu Adrianos: Vorarbeiten," *Jahrbücher für Protestantische Theologie* 13 (1887): 136–59.

CETERA

< >	addenda
[ ]	delenda
††	corrupta
⌐ ⌐	fortasse ponenda
–	delevit, deleverunt
+	addidit, addiderunt
a. corr.	ante correctionem
a. ras.	ante rasuram
app. cr.	apparatus criticus
ca.	circa
cat.	catena(e)
cf.	confer
cod(d).	codex, codices
del.	delevit
ed. pr.	editio princeps
edd.	editiones
ext.	exterior

fort.	fortasse
i.e.	id est
indic.	indicavit
in mg.	in margine
inf.	inferior
inf. l.	infra lineam
interpun.	interpunxit, interpunctio
lac.	lacuna
m. pr.	manus prima
m. sec.	manus secunda
om.	omisit, omiserunt
p. corr.	post correctionem
postscr.	postscriptum
propos.	proposuit
sim.	similia, similiter
s. l.	supra lineam
susp.	suspectus est (falsum esse)
titul.	titulus
transp.	transposuit, transposui

Ἀδριανοῦ
Εἰσαγωγὴ εἰς τὰς θείας γραφάς

1 Ἀδριανοῦ] ἀφρικανοῦ I p. corr. m. sec., Africani seu Adriani *Lollin*, αὐδριανοῦ K₂

2 Εἰσαγωγὴ εἰς τὰς θείας γραφάς] εἰσαγωγὴ τῆς γραφῆς Phot. cod. 2

Introduction to the Divine Scriptures
by Adrian

RECENSION 1

1(1). Τοῦ Ἑβραϊκοῦ χαρακτῆρος ἰδιωμάτων ἔστιν εἴδη τρία, ὧν τὸ μὲν ἐπὶ τῆς διανοίας εὕροι τίς ἄν, τὸ δὲ ἐπὶ τῆς λέξεως, τὸ δὲ ἐπὶ τῆς συνθέσεως.

Ἀρχὴ τῶν ἐπὶ τῆς διανοίας

2(2). Τὸ μὲν οὖν ἐπὶ τῆς διανοίας ἐστὶ τὸ ἀπὸ τῶν ἡμῖν προσόντων τοῦ θεοῦ
5 σχηματίζειν τὰς ἐνεργείας ἤτοι ἐπὶ καλῷ ἢ ἐπὶ κακῷ γινομένας· φημὶ δὴ ἢ
ἀπὸ μελῶν ἢ ἀπὸ αἰσθήσεων ἢ ἀπὸ κινήσεων ψυχικῶν < ἢ ἀπὸ κινήσεων
σωματικῶν ἢ ἀπὸ παθῶν ψυχικῶν > ἢ ἀπὸ παθῶν σωματικῶν ἢ ἀπὸ
διαθέσεων ἢ ἀπὸ κοινῶν δοξῶν ἢ ἀπὸ ἀξιωμάτων ἢ ἀπὸ ἐπιτηδευμάτων ἢ
ἀπὸ τόπων ἢ ἀπὸ στολισμῶν ἢ ἀπὸ ἐθῶν ἢ ἀπὸ σχημάτων ἢ ἀπὸ ὅλου τοῦ
10 ζῴου·

---

3 Ἀρχὴ τῶν ἐπὶ τῆς διανοίας] titul. L, in app. cr. transp. *Goessling*
7 ἢ–ψυχικῶν] + *Hoeschel Goessling*
9 ἐθῶν] CDG J p. corr. *Hoeschel Goessling* (ex codd.), ἐθνῶν L

1. There are three kinds of peculiarities of the Hebrew literary style:[1] one will find that the first of these pertains to its message, the second to its diction, and the third to its syntax.[2]

PART I: PECULIARITIES OF MESSAGE

2. It is a peculiarity of message to depict God's actions—whether they transpire for benefit or for harm—from human characteristics.[3] I mean, for example, [depictions of God] from bodily parts, or from senses, from self-induced movements of the soul or body, from movements of the soul or body induced from without, or from attitudes, or from familial distinctions, or from civil rank, or from occupations, or from places, or from dress, or from customary behaviors, or from gestures, or from the whole living being.

---

[1] For other extended discussions of "peculiarities" (ἰδιώματα) see Diony. Halic., 2. Amm. (on the style of Thucydides); Thdr. Mops., Ps. 15:4; Aug., loc. in Hept.; Cass., proem. Ps. 15.2. On the particular interest in ἰδιώματα among Antiochenes, see Devreesse, Essai, 58–68; Schäublin, Untersuchungen, 127–38; Ter Haar Romeny, Syrian in Greek Dress, 134–9; Guinot, L'Exégèse de Théodoret, 346–56.

[2] Adrian proposes a tripartite division of the literary style of Scripture into its "message" or meaning (which for him includes God's providential action in the world); Scripture's "diction" (which usually stands for singular word use); and finally its "syntax" or word arrangement, which entails the subtraction, repetition, inversion, transposition, and superfluous use of words. In section 76 Adrian calls these syntactical features "figures" (σχήματα). Note as well that the tripartite structure of the treatise follows this threefold distinction of style. For more on this distinction and the threefold arrangement of the treatise, see Martens, "Adrian's Introduction to the Divine Scriptures and Greco-Roman Rhetorical Theory on Style."

[3] The topic of the first section of the Introduction is the anthropomorphic portrayal of God's providence in Scripture. On divine providence as a major scriptural theme, see Diod., proem. Ps.; Junil., inst. 1.11, 12, 19. What makes the theme of God's providence a peculiarity (ἰδίωμα) is that it is depicted anthropomorphically. Note the verb σχηματίζειν ("to depict"), which for Adrian has the sense of using pictorial or imagistic language to portray an incorporeal reality. Also see his discussion of the trope σχηματισμός in 73.12 below, as well as the discussions of this term by Devreesse, Essai, 67–8 and Schäublin, Untersuchungen, 140 fn. 226. For other programmatic statements from the Antiochenes about Scripture's anthropomorphic language, see esp. Diod., fr. Gen. 6:6 [Deconinck no. 21]; Thdr. Mops., Ps. 5:2; 32:6 (Schäublin, Untersuchungen, 114); Thdt., Ps. 5:2; 10:3–5. Note also Adrian's claim that God's providential activities occur ἐπὶ καλῷ and ἐπὶ κακῷ, prepositional phrases also found at intro. 4.1; 4.6; 4.7. These phrases are rarely attributed to God's actions in Greek early Christian literature, though they tellingly surface in Diodore and Theodore: Diod., Ps. 118 (Mariès, Études, 126–7, and the related phrases ἐπ᾽ ἀγαθῷ/ἐπὶ φαυλῷ discussed at 124); Thdr. Mops., Ps. 73:3, etc. Elsewhere in the Introduction Adrian uses another set of related prepositional phrases: ἐπὶ σωτηρίᾳ ("for deliverance") and ἐπὶ τιμωρίᾳ ("for punishment") (2.1; note also 46 where Adrian claims that Scripture uses κακία but sometimes means τιμωρία). These phrases inform the translation I have adopted: God's actions do not transpire "for good" and "evil," but "for benefit" and "harm," corresponding to the treatment of the righteous and unrighteous respectively. S.vv. καλός, ή, όν BDAG 2.d.α; κακός, ή, όν BDAG 2, LSJ B, PGL B.3.a.

RECENSION 1

[Ὅπως ἀπὸ μελῶν]

2.1(3[α′]). ἀπὸ μὲν μελῶν· ὡς τό, **τὰ βλέφαρα αὐτοῦ ἐξετάζει τοὺς υἱοὺς τῶν ἀνθρώπων**· καὶ τό, **ὀφθαλμοὶ κυρίου ἐπὶ δικαίους**· καί, **στόμα κυρίου ἐλάλησε ταῦτα**· καὶ τό, **ἀγαθός μοι ὁ νόμος τοῦ στόματός σου**· καὶ τό, **ἦ**
5 **μὴν ἐξελεύσεται ἐκ τοῦ στόματός μου δικαιοσύνη**· καί, **πρόσωπον κυρίου ἐπὶ ποιοῦντας κακά**· καί, **ἔπαρον τὰς χεῖρας σου ἐπὶ τὰς ὑπερηφανίας αὐτῶν**· ⌜τὴν δεξιὰν ἐπὶ τῶν κρειττόνων οἶδεν ὀνομάζειν ὡς τιμιωτέραν, οἷον τό, **δεξιὰ κυρίου ἐποίησε δύναμιν**⌝· καὶ τό, **προσκυνήσωμεν εἰς τὸν τόπον οὗ ἔστησαν οἱ πόδες αὐτοῦ**· καὶ ὅσα τούτοις παραπλήσια· τούτων δὲ τὰ μὲν
10 ἐπὶ σωτηρίᾳ, τὰ δὲ ἐπὶ τιμωρίᾳ προβάλλεται·

2.2(4[β′]). [ὅπως] ἀπὸ αἰσθήσεων· ὡς τό, **ἐπέβλεψεν ἐξ οὐρανοῦ ὁ κύριος, εἶδε πάντας τοὺς υἱοὺς τῶν ἀνθρώπων**· καὶ τό, **φωνῇ μου πρὸς κύριον ἐκέκραξα καὶ ἐπήκουσέ μου**· καί, **κύριος εἰσακούσεταί μου**· καί, **ὠσφράνθη κύριος ὀσμὴν εὐωδίας**· καί, **ἐξαπόστειλον τὴν χεῖρα σου καὶ ἅψαι τῶν**
15 **ὀστέων αὐτοῦ**· καί, **χεὶρ κυρίου ἐστὶν ἡ ἁψαμένη μου**· καί, **ὁ ἁπτόμενος τῶν ὀρέων καὶ καπνίζονται**· καί, **ψηλαφήσω πᾶσαν τὴν ἀδικίαν τῆς γῆς ἐκείνης**· καὶ τό, **μὴ φάγωμαι κρέα ταύρων;** καὶ ὁ σωτήρ· **ἐγὼ βρῶσιν ἔχω φαγεῖν, ἣν ὑμεῖς οὐκ οἴδατε**· καί, **ἐμὸν βρῶμά ἐστιν ἵνα ποιῶ τὸ θέλημα τοῦ πατρός μου**· ⌜καὶ τὸ ὀξὺ τῆς αὐτοῦ παρουσίας ὑπερβολικῶς,
20 πτῆσιν ὀνομάζει· ὡς τό, **ἐπέβη ἐπὶ Χερουβὶμ καὶ ἐπετάσθη**⌝·

---

3 Ps 10[11]:4   3 Ps 33:16 [34:15]   4 Isa 1:20   4 Ps 118[119]:72 var.
5 Isa 45:23   6 Ps 33:17 [34:16] var.   7 Ps 73[74]:3   8 Ps 117[118]:16
9 Ps 131[132]:7 var.   12 Ps 32[33]:13 var.   13 Ps 3:5[4]   13 Ps 4:4[3]
14 Gen 8:21 var.   15 Job 2:5 var.   15 Job 19:21 var.
13 Ps 103[104]:32   17 Zech 3:9   17 Ps 49[50]:13 var.
18 John 4:32   19 John 4:34 var.   20 Ps 17:11 [18:10]

---

1 Ὅπως ἀπὸ μελῶν] titul. L, in mg. ext. EG, initium 2.1 (sed non titul.) *Hoeschel*, – *Goessling* (ex *Lollin*)
4 ἦ] ἢ *Hoeschel Goessling* (ex A)
8 τὴν δεξιὰν–δύναμιν] cf. 4.7, susp. *Schlüren*   11 Ὅπως] – *Goessling*
15 ἐστὶν] in mg. ext. m. pr. L, deest *Hoeschel* (ex AB) *Goessling* (ex codd.)
20 καὶ τὸ ὀξὺ–ἐπετάσθη] cf. 2.9 vel 6 vel 73.14, susp. *Schlüren*

Catalogue of Problems[1]

Bodily Parts

2.1. [Depictions of God] from bodily parts: for example, "his eyelids examine the sons of men" (Ps 10[11]:4); and, "the eyes of the Lord are on the righteous" (Ps 33:16 [34:15]); and, "the mouth of the Lord said these things" (Isa 1:20); and, "The law from your mouth is good for me" (Ps 118[119]:72); and, "surely righteousness will go forth from my mouth" (Isa 45:23); and, "the Lord's face is against evil doers" (Ps 33:17 [34:16]); and, "lift up your hands against their arrogance" (Ps 73[74]:3). 'Scripture can designate the right hand as more honorable on the basis of its mightier acts:[2] for example, "the right hand of the Lord acted powerfully" (Ps 117[118]:16).'[3] And, "Let us worship at the place where his feet stood" (Ps 131[132]:7). And all passages that resemble these. Some of them refer to deliverance, others to punishment.

Senses

2.2. [Depictions of God] from senses: for example, "The Lord looked down from heaven; he saw all the sons of men" (Ps 32[33]:13); and, "I cried out with my voice to the Lord and he heard me" (Ps 3:5[4]); and, "the Lord will listen to me" (Ps 4:4[3]); and, "the Lord smelled a pleasing odor" (Gen 8:21); and, "stretch out your hand and touch his bones" (Job 2:5); and, "the Lord's hand that has touched me" (Job 19:21); and, "the one who touches the mountains and they are black with smoke" (Ps 103[104]:32); and, "I will touch all the unrighteousness of that land" (Zech 3:9); and, "Surely I would not eat the flesh of bulls" (Ps 49[50]:13)?; and the Savior says, "I have food to eat which you do not know" (Jn 4:32); and, "it is my food that I do the will of my Father" (Jn 4:34). 'And the speed of God's coming Scripture hyperbolically calls "flight": for example, "he mounted upon the Cherubim and flew" (Ps 17:11 [18:10]).'[4]

---

[1] There are two subsections in the first part of the *Introduction*: the first provides a catalogue (2.1–2.15) of anthropomorphisms, and the second offers interpretations (4–17) of this language.
[2] Thdr. Mops., *Ps.* 15:8: "referring to help by 'right hand,' being the mightier one [ἀπὸ τοῦ δεξιοῦ καὶ τοῦ κρείττονος]" (mod.). See also Thdr. Mops., *Ps.* 44:5.
[3] Possibly a misplaced sentence. It belongs more obviously at 4.7 where a very similar explanation of the "right hand" of God occurs.
[4] A misplaced passage since the biblical verse does not portray God as having senses, but rather as having a body and mounting on the winged Cherubim. The passage might belong to 2.9 where God is likened to a king sitting on the Cherubim (see Thdr. Mops., *Ps.* 17:11; *fr. Gen.* 3:24 [Devreesse, *Essai*, 23–4 fn. 4d]); or 6 where Adrian discusses God's body-in-movement; or perhaps 73.14 where he examines hyperbole. This passage is likely genuine since we find similar glosses on the verse in Diod., *Ps.* 17:11: "'He rode on cherubs and flew,' indicating the rapidity of his coming [Τὸ τάχος λέγει τῆς παρουσίας αὐτοῦ] and the assistance"; and also in Thdt., *Ps.* 17:11: "the rapidity of his appearance [τὸ τῆς ἐπιφανείας ὀξύ]."

RECENSION 1

2.3(5[γ′]). ἀπὸ κινήσεων ψυχικῶν· ὡς τό, **κατεπάτησα αὐτοὺς ἐν τῷ θυμῷ μου, καὶ κατέθλασα αὐτοὺς ἐν τῇ ὀργῇ μου**· καὶ τό, **κύριε μὴ τῷ θυμῷ σου ἐλέγξῃς με, μηδὲ τῇ ὀργῇ σου παιδεύσῃς με**·

2.4(6[δ′]). ἀπὸ κινήσεων σωματικῶν· ὡς τό, **ἀναστήτω ὁ θεός, καὶ**
5 **διασκορπισθήτωσαν οἱ ἐχθροὶ < αὐτοῦ >**· καί, **ἐξεγέρθητι κύριε ὁ θεός μου ἐν προστάγματι ᾧ ἐνετείλω**· καί, **ὑπόμεινόν με εἰς ἡμέραν ἀναστάσεώς μου**· καί, **ἤκουσεν Ἀδὰμ τοῦ θεοῦ περιπατοῦντος**·

2.5(7[ε′]). ἀπὸ παθῶν ψυχικῶν· ὡς τό, **μετεμελήθην** φησὶν ὁ θεὸς **ὅτι ἐποίησα τὸν ἄνθρωπον**· καί, **ἐπείραζεν ὁ θεὸς τὸν Ἀβραάμ**· καί, **ἐπελάθου νόμων**
10 **θεοῦ σου, κἀγὼ ἐπιλήσομαι τέκνων σου**· καί, **νῦν ἔγνων ὅτι φοβῇ σὺ τὸν θεόν**· καί, **ἐξερευνήσω τὴν Ἰερουσαλὴμ μετὰ λύχνου**· καί, **Ἀδὰμ ποῦ εἶ;** καί, **μὴ λυπῆτε τὸ πνεῦμα τὸ ἅγιον**· καὶ τὰ ὅμοια·

2.6(8[ϛ′]). ἀπὸ παθῶν σωματικῶν· ὡς τό, **ἐξεγέρθητι, ἵνα τί ὑπνοῖς κύριε;** καί, **ἐξεγέρθη ὡς ὁ ὑπνῶν κύριος**· καί, **οὐ μὴ ὑπνώσῃ οὐδὲ νυστάξῃ ὁ**
15 **φυλάσσων τὸν Ἰσραήλ**· καὶ τὰ ὅμοια·

2 Isa 63:3 var.　　　3 Ps 6:2[1]　　　5 Ps 67:2 [68:1] var.　　　6 Ps 7:7[6]
6 Zeph 3:8 var.　　　7 Gen 3:8 var.　　　9 Gen 6:6 var.　　　9 Gen 22:1 var.
10 Hos 4:6 var.　　　11 Gen 22:12 var.　　　11 Zeph 1:12
12 Gen 3:9　　　12 Eph 4:30 var.　　　13 Ps 43:24 [44:23]
14 Ps 77[78]:65 var.　　　15 Ps 120[121]:4 var.

5 αὐτοῦ] ADEGHIJK₂ *Hoeschel* (ex A) *Goessling* (ex codd.), deest L

Self-Induced Movements of the Soul[1]

2.3. [Depictions of God] from self-induced movements of the soul: for example, "I trampled them in my wrath, and crushed them in my anger" (Isa 63:3); and, "O Lord, do not rebuke me in your wrath nor discipline me in your anger" (Ps 6:2[1]).

Self-Induced Movements of the Body

2.4. [Depictions of God] from self-induced movements of the body: for example, "Let God rise up and let his foes be scattered" (Ps 67:2 [68:1]); and, "Awake, O Lord my God, with the instruction which you commanded" (Ps 7:7[6]); and, "Expect me... on the day of my arising" (Zeph 3:8); and, "Adam heard God walking around" (Gen 3:8).

Movements of the Soul Induced from Without

2.5. [Depictions of God] from movements of the soul induced from without: for example, "I have regretted," God says, "that I made man" (Gen 6:6); and, "God tested Abraham" (Gen 22:1); and, "You forgot the laws of your God; I also will forget your children" (Hos 4:6); and, "now I know that you fear God" (Gen 22:12); and, "I will search out Jerusalem with a lamp" (Zeph 1:12); and, "Where are you Adam" (Gen 3:9)?; and, "Do not grieve the Holy Spirit" (Eph 4:30).[2] And similar passages.

Movements of the Body Induced from Without

2.6. [Depictions of God] from movements of the body induced from without: for example, "Wake up! Why do you sleep, O Lord" (Ps 43:24 [44:23])?; and, "Like one

---

[1] Adrian's distinction between the κίνησις and πάθος of the soul and body in these next four sections is not entirely clear. The latter term has a notoriously wide semantic range in antiquity (e.g., "The term πάθος is used equivocally" [Nemes., *nat. hom.* 16]). In 2.3–2.6 and 5–8 Adrian provides several illustrations of the κινήσεις and πάθη of soul and body. The distinction appears to be as follows: κίνησις indicates a self-initiated movement, like the soul directing anger against its enemies, or the body scattering foes, whereas πάθος marks a movement induced from outside. The examples Adrian provides of the soul's πάθη in 2.5 and 7.1–7.4 include movements—regret, grief, learning, forgetting, punishing—that have transpired because of, on the occasion of, or in response to other circumstances. Similarly for the body's πάθη in 2.6 and 8 which include being awoken by someone else. Thus I render κίνησις and πάθος as "self-induced movement" and "movement induced from without" respectively. See esp. Nemes., *nat. hom.* 16: "Generally they define an affection (*pathos*) as follows: an affection is a movement in one thing received from another [πάθος ἐστὶ κίνησις ἐν ἑτέρῳ ἐξ ἑτέρου]. An activity is a movement involving action. 'Involving action' means 'self-initiated' [ἐνέργεια δέ ἐστι κίνησις δραστική· δραστικὸν δὲ λέγεται τὸ ἐξ ἑαυτοῦ κινούμενον]." On the relationship between Nemesius and the Antiochenes, see Jaeger, *Nemesios von Emesa*, 5 fn. 2. See also Gal., *plac.* 6.1.5–17; Jo. D., *f. o.* 2.22.

[2] The topic of this first section of the *Introduction* is the anthropomorphic ways in which God is portrayed in Scripture (2). Most references in this opening section are to God the Father. Here there is a reference to the Holy Spirit and in 2.2 there is a reference to the Savior.

RECENSION 1

2.7(9[ζ′]). ἀπὸ διαθέσεων· ὡς τό, οὐκ ἀδελφὸς ἦν Ἠσαῦ τοῦ Ἰακώβ; καὶ ἠγάπησα τὸν Ἰακώβ, τὸν δὲ Ἠσαῦ ἐμίσησα· καί, ἀγαπᾷ κύριος τὰς πύλας Σιὼν ὑπὲρ πάντα τὰ σκηνώματα Ἰακώβ· καί, ἐζήλωκα τὴν Ἰερουσαλήμ, καὶ τὴν Σιὼν ζῆλον μέγαν·

5 **2.8**(10[η′]). ἀπὸ κοινῶν δοξῶν· ὡς τό, μνηστεύσομαί σε ἐμαυτῷ εἰς τὸν αἰῶνα, καὶ μνηστεύσομαί σε ἐν κρίσει καὶ ἐν δικαιοσύνῃ· καί, αὐτὴ οὐ γυνή μου, καὶ ἐγὼ οὐκ ἀνὴρ αὐτῆς· καὶ τό, καὶ ἔδωκα αὐτῇ βιβλίον ἀποστασίου· καί, ἐγενόμην τῷ Ἰσραὴλ εἰς πατέρα, καὶ Ἐφραὶμ πρωτότοκός μου ἐστίν· καί, αὐτὸς ἐπικαλέσεταί με πατήρ μου εἶ σύ, κἀγὼ πρωτότοκον θήσομαι
10 αὐτόν· καί, υἱὸς πρωτότοκός μου Ἰσραήλ· καὶ τὰ ὅμοια·

2.9(11[θ′]). ἀπό ἀξιωμάτων· ὡς τό, ὁ κύριος ἐβασίλευσεν, ἀγαλλιάσθω ἡ γῆ· καὶ τό, ὁ καθήμενος ἐπὶ τῶν Χερουβὶμ ἐμφάνηθι· καί, ἐκάθισας ἐπὶ θρόνου ὁ κρίνων δικαιοσύνην·

2.10(12[ι′]). ἀπὸ ἐπιτηδευμάτων· ὡς τό, ὁ στεγάζων ἐν ὕδασι τὰ ὑπερῷα
15 αὐτοῦ· καί, ὁ οἰκοδομῶν εἰς τὸν οὐρανὸν τὴν ἀνάβασιν αὐτοῦ· καὶ τό, ἔπλασε τὸν ἄνθρωπον ʿκαὶ ἐνεφύσησεν εἰς τὸ πρόσωπον αὐτοῦ πνοὴν ζωῆς· καὶ τό, ἀνέβη ἐμφυσῶν εἰς πρόσωπόν σου, ἀντὶ τοῦ φυσήματι διασκεδάζων ὑπʼ ὄψιν σου τοὺς ὑπεναντίους, ἵνα εἴπῃ οὕτω ῥᾳδίως καὶ ἀθρόως· τὸ γὰρ

2 Mal 1:2–3 var.   3 Ps 86[87]:2   4 Zech 8:2   6 Hos 2:21[19] var.
7 Hos 2:4[2]   7 Jer 3:8   8 Jer 38[31]:9   10 Ps 88:27, 28 [89:26, 27]
10 Ex 4:22   12 Ps 96[97]:1   12 Ps 79:2 [80:1]   13 Ps 9:5[4]
15 Ps 103[104]:3   15 Amos 9:6 var.   16 Gen 2:7 var.   17 Nah 2:2[1]

15 ὁ οἰκοδομῶν–αὐτοῦ] – Hoeschel (ex A)

who sleeps the Lord awoke" (Ps 77[78]:65); and, "The one who watches over Israel will never sleep nor slumber" (Ps 120[121]:4). And similar passages.

Attitudes

2.7. [Depictions of God] from attitudes: for example, "Was not Esau Jacob's brother? . . . and Jacob I loved, but Esau I hated" (Mal 1:2–3); and, "The Lord loves the gates of Zion more than all the dwellings of Jacob" (Ps 86[87]:2); and, "I am jealous for Jerusalem and Zion with great jealousy" (Zech 8:2).

Familial Distinctions[1]

2.8. [Depictions of God] from familial distinctions: for example, "I will betroth you to myself forever, and I will betroth you in integrity and in righteousness" (Hos 2:21[19]); and, "She is not my wife, and I am not her husband" (Hos 2:4[2]); and, "and I gave her a bill of divorce" (Jer 3:8); and, "I became a father to Israel, and Ephraem is my firstborn" (Jer 38[31]:9); and, "He will call upon me, 'You are my father' . . . , and I will appoint him a firstborn" (Ps 88:27, 28 [89:26, 27]); and, "Israel is my firstborn son" (Ex 4:22). And similar passages.

Civil Rank[2]

2.9. [Depictions of God] from civil rank: for example, "The Lord became king, let the earth rejoice" (Ps 96[97]:1)!; and, "You who sit upon the Cherubim, appear" (Ps 79:2 [80:1])!;[3] and, "You sat on a throne, you who judge with righteousness" (Ps 9:5[4]).

Occupations

2.10. [Depictions of God] from occupations: for example, "He who roofs his upper stories with waters" (Ps 103[104]:3); and, "who builds his passage up to heaven" (Amos 9:6); and, "He . . . molded man" ⸢"and blew into his face the breath of life" (Gen 2:7). And, "he rose up, blowing into your face" (Nah 2:2[1]), instead of "dispersing enemies with breaths before your sight," as if to say "so easily and suddenly"[4] – for

---

[1] The expression ἀπὸ κοινῶν δοξῶν is not entirely clear. My translation takes it cues from the next paragraph (ἀπὸ ἀξιωμάτων), which is about the high status that comes from civil rank. This paragraph seems to be about the distinction or honor that comes through familial relationships: God is portrayed as having a spouse and children (s.v. κοινός LSJ IV: "connected by common origin," "kindred").

[2] S.v. ἀξίωμα PGL 4.b.i.

[3] See Thdr. Mops., *fr. Gen.* 3:24 [Devreesse, *Essai*, 23–4 fn. 4d] on the royal imagery of Cherubim.

[4] On God's breathing or blowing as an anthropomorphic expression signifying the ease with which the divine action is accomplished, see Thdt., *qu. in Gen.* 23: "Holy Scripture uses this expression [i.e., God's "breath"] to bring out the ease of the creation [τῆς γὰρ δημιουργίας τὴν εὐκολίαν] . . . You should also understand that this idea would require us first to imagine lungs, muscles to squeeze and contract them, a windpipe attached to the lungs, a palate, and last of all a mouth to breathe in air. But, if the divinity is incorporeal, surely his breath should also be thought of in a manner befitting God."

RECENSION 1

ἐμφυσῶν σκορπίζων οἱ ἔξω ἐφιλοσόφησαν·` καί, ἰδοὺ ἐν τῇ χειρί μου
ἐζωγράφησα τὰ τείχη σου, πρὸς τὴν Ἰερουσαλήμ· καί, φραγμὸν περιέθηκα
καὶ ἐχαράκωσα καὶ ἐφύτευσά σε ἄμπελον Σωρήχ, καὶ ᾠκοδόμησα πύργον
ἐν μέσῳ αὐτῆς, καὶ προλήνιον ὤρυξα ἐν αὐτῇ· καί, ἰδοὺ ἐγὼ φράσσω
5 τὴν ὁδὸν αὐτῆς ἐν σκόλοψι, καὶ ἀνοικοδομήσω τὰς τρίβους αὐτῆς, καὶ οὐ μὴ
εὕρῃ τὴν ὁδὸν αὐτῆς· καί, ἐκπετάσω τὸ δίκτυόν μου ἐπ᾿ αὐτόν· καί,
πεσοῦνται ἐν ἀμφιβλήστρῳ αὐτοῦ οἱ ἁμαρτωλοί· καὶ ὅσα ὅμοια·

2.11(13[ιαʹ]). ἀπὸ τόπων· ὡς τό, ὑψώθητι ἐπὶ τοὺς οὐρανοὺς ὁ θεός· καί,
ἀνέβης εἰς ὕψος ᾐχμαλώτευσας αἰχμαλωσίαν· καί, ἔκλινεν οὐρανοὺς καὶ
10 κατέβη· καί, ἐγγὺς κύριος τοῖς ἐπικαλουμένοις αὐτόν· καί, ἵνα τί κύριε
ἀφέστηκας μακρόθεν; καί, ἰδοὺ κύριος κάθηται ἐπὶ νεφέλης κούφης·
καί, ἰδοὺ κύριος ἐκπορεύεται ἐκ τοῦ τόπου αὐτοῦ καὶ ἐπιβήσεται ἐπὶ τὰ
ὑψηλὰ τῆς γῆς·

2.12(14[ιβʹ]). ἀπὸ στολισμῶν· ὡς τό, ἐνεδύσατο κύριος δύναμιν, καὶ
15 περιεζώσατο· καί, περίζωσαι τὴν ῥομφαίαν σου ἐπὶ τὸν μηρόν σου· καί,
περιεζωσμένος ἐν δυναστείᾳ· καί, περιβαλλόμενος φῶς ὡς ἱμάτιον· καί,
τίς οὗτος ὁ παραγενόμενος ἐξ Ἐδώμ, ἐρύθημα ἱματίων αὐτοῦ ἐκ Βοσώρ;
οὗτος ὡραῖος ἐν στολῇ αὐτοῦ;

2 Isa 49:16 var.   4 Isa 5:2 var.   6 Hos 2:8[6] var.   6 Ezek 12:13
7 Ps 140[141]:10 var.   8 Ps 56:12 [57:11]   9 Ps 67:19 [68:18]
10 Ps 17:10 [18:9] var.   10 Ps 144[145]:18 var.   11 Ps 9:22 [10:1]
11 Isa 19:1   13 Mic 1:3 var.   15 Ps 92[93]:1   15 Ps 44:4 [45:3]
16 Ps 64:7 [65:6]   16 Ps 103[104]:2 var.   18 Isa 63:1 var.

1 καὶ ἐνεφύσησεν–ἐφιλοσόφησαν] cf. 6   4 αὐτῆς] αὐτοῦ Goessling
4 αὐτῇ] αὐτῷ Goessling

non-Christian philosophers have taken "blowing" as "dispersing."[1, 2] And concerning Jerusalem: "See, on my hand I have painted your walls" (Isa 49:16); and, "I have built a fence and fortified and planted you a vine of Sorech and built a tower in the middle of it and dug out a wine-vat in it" (Isa 5:2); and, "See, I am building a hedge of thorns on either side of her way and will wall up her paths, and in no way will she find her way" (Hos 2:8[6]); and, "I will cast my net over him" (Ezek 12:13); and, "sinners will fall into his net" (Ps 140[141]:10). And all similar passages.

Places

2.11. [Depictions of God] from places: for example, "Be exalted to the heavens, O God" (Ps 56:12 [57:11]); and, "you ascended on high, taking captivity captive" (Ps 67:19 [68:18]); and, "he sloped the heavens and came down" (Ps 17:10 [18:9]); and, "Near is the Lord to those who call upon him" (Ps 144[145]:18); and, "Why, O Lord, do you stand far away" (Ps 9:22 [10:1])?; and, "See, the Lord is sitting on a light cloud" (Isa 19:1); and, "See, the Lord is leaving his place and will tread upon the high places of the earth" (Mic 1:3).

Dress

2.12. [Depictions of God] from dress: for example, "the Lord was robed in power and girded himself" (Ps 92[93]:1); and, "gird your sword on your thigh" (Ps 44:4 [45:3])!; and, "girded with power" (Ps 64:7 [65:6]); and, "clothing yourself in light as in a garment" (Ps 103[104]:2); and, "Who is this one who comes out of Edom, his red garments from Bazra? This one is beautiful in his robe" (Isa 63:1)?

---

[1] The allusion is uncertain. There are a number of philosophical treatises on Homer from late antiquity that share Adrian's concern to reinterpret the poetic portrayal of the divine in a more favorable light—e.g., Heracl., *all.* and Ps.-Plu., *vit. Hom.* The latter work bears a number of striking affinities with Adrian's treatise. See as well the discussion of φιλοσοφέω in 18 below.

[2] I suspect that this block of material is genuine, but misplaced. The notion of God blowing does not obviously suggest a craft or trade. Also, the supplied interpretation of this expression does not belong in this section of the treatise, which catalogues anthropomorphisms, but normally does not explain them. This material fits more obviously in 6 where a bodily movement (which breathing more evidently suggests) is tied simultaneously to divine help and judgment. When discussing the divine breath Theodore and Theodoret also juxtapose divine liberation and punishment. Thdr. Mops., *Nah.* 2:2 glosses as follows: "a divine wrath resembling a blast completely snuffed out the one inflamed against you with the result that you will now not suspect any trouble from that direction." Thdt. on *Nah.* 2:2 is more striking: "God is the cause of this for you by his decision as though by some kind of blowing, destroying them but freeing you from their power: just as by blowing a breath of life into Adam he made him a living being." This passage is important because Theodoret, like Adrian, links the life-giving character of the divine breath in Nah 2:2 with Gen 2:7, suggesting that this material forms a coherent block of text. Perhaps it has been moved to this section of the *Introduction* because the first part of Gen 2:7 is cited as an illustration of God as a craftsman ("He...molded man").

RECENSION 1

2.13(15[ιγ´]). ἀπὸ ἐθῶν· ὡς τό, **ἀπέστρεψας τὸ πρόσωπόν σου καὶ ἐγενήθην τεταραγμένος**· καί, **ἵνα τί κύριε ἀπωθεῖς τὴν ψυχήν μου, ἀποστρέφεις τὸ πρόσωπόν σου;** καί, **μὴ ἐκκλίνῃς ἐν ὀργῇ ἀπὸ τοῦ δούλου σου**· καί, **μὴ ἀπορρίψῃς με ἀπὸ τοῦ προσώπου σου**· καί, **ἐγὼ δὲ εἶπα ἐν τῇ ἐκστάσει**
5 **μου**· **ἀπέρριμμαι ἀπὸ προσώπου τῶν ὀφθαλμῶν σου**· ⸀ἅπερ οἱ ὀργιζόμενοι καὶ λυπούμενοι πρὸς οὓς διαφέρονται καὶ ἐπιδείκνυνται·⸀

2.14(16[ιδ´]). ἀπὸ σχημάτων· ὡς τό, **ἵνα τί ἀποστρέφεις τὴν χεῖρα σου καὶ τὴν δεξιάν σου;** ⸀ἐκ μεταφορᾶς τῶν παρακαλουμένων καὶ εἰς τοὐπίσω τὰς χεῖρας ἀποστρεφόντων·⸀ καί, **ὅτι ἀρῶ εἰς τὸν οὐρανὸν τὴν χεῖρα μου καὶ ὀμοῦμαι**
10 **τῇ δεξιᾷ μου**· καὶ τὰ ὅμοια·

[ἀπὸ δὲ ὅλου τοῦ ζῴου]

2.15(17[ιε´]). ἀπὸ ὅλου τοῦ ζῴου κατὰ διαίρεσιν, νῦν μὲν ἀπὸ τῆς ψυχῆς, νῦν δὲ ἀπὸ τῆς σαρκός· ὡς τό, **σάρξ μου ἐξ αὐτῶν** παρὰ τῷ Ὠσηέ· ἀπὸ δὲ ψυχῆς· ὡς, **τὰς νεομηνίας καὶ τὰ σάββατα ὑμῶν μισεῖ ἡ ψυχή μου.**

---

2 Ps 29:8 [30:7] var.   3 Ps 87:15 [88:14]   3 Ps 26[27]:9
4 Ps 50:13 [51:11]   5 Ps 30:23 [31:22] var.   8 Ps 73[74]:11
10 Deut 32:40 var.   13 Hos 9:12   14 Isa 1:14 var.

---

6 ἅπερ–ἐπιδείκνυνται] cf. 15   9 ἐκ μεταφορᾶς–ἀποστρεφόντων] cf. 16
11 Ἀπὸ δὲ ὅλου τοῦ ζῴου] titul. L, in mg. ext. EG, initium 2.15 (sed non titul.) *Hoeschel, – Goessling* (ex *Lollin*)

Customary Behaviors

2.13. [Depictions of God] from customary behaviors: for example, "You turned your face away and I became troubled" (Ps 29:8[30:7]); and, "Why, O Lord, do you reject my soul, do you turn your face away" (Ps 87:15[88:14])?; and, "do not turn away in wrath from your servant" (Ps 26[27]:9)!; and, "do not throw me out from your presence" (Ps 50:13[51:11])!; and, "I spoke in my disorientation: 'I have been cast forth from before your eyes'" (Ps 30:23[31:22])! ⸢These are the behaviors that people who are angered and grieved also display to those with whom they quarrel.⸣[1]

Gestures

2.14. [Depictions of God] from gestures: for example, "Why do you turn your hand away, even your right hand" (Ps 73[74]:11)? ⸢—from an analogy with those to whom appeals are made, and yet who withdraw their hands behind their backs.⸣[2] And, "for I will lift up my hand to heaven and I will swear by my right hand" (Deut 32:40). And similar passages.

Whole Living Being

2.15. [Depictions of God] from the whole living being on the basis of a distinct part: sometimes its soul, and other times its flesh. For example, in Hosea: "My flesh among them" (Hos 9:12). An example with soul: "My soul despises your new moons and Sabbaths" (Isa 1:14).[3]

---

[1] A genuine passage, but perhaps misplaced. This sentence belongs more obviously in 15 below where the rationale behind the language of God turning away from people is supposed to be given. Note also that the expected explanation is missing in 15. See Thdr. Mops., *Ps.* 13:1 for the reason behind the language of God turning his face away from people: "This is expressed by a bodily metaphor in our fashion, since when we are angry with people, we turn our face from them to another object or direction." Also *Ps.* 43:25: "'Why did you turn your face away?': bring your anger against us to an end (a metaphor from people in anger turning their faces away)."

[2] A genuine passage, but possibly misplaced. It would fit more naturally at 16 where we expect this gesture to be explained, but is not. See Adrian., *cat. Ps.* 73:11(2) where a related, though longer, explanation of this hand gesture is offered: "by an analogy: those being summoned do not accept an appeal; previously holding their hands in their bosom, they put them behind their back when those making an appeal somehow wish to lay hold of them." See also Thdr. Mops., *Ps.* 73:11: "Now he says this by analogy with people holding something good in their hand and putting it behind their back when they are unwilling to give it."

[3] See the discussion of synecdoche in 73.4 below.

RECENSION 1

3(18). Καὶ ταῦτα μὲν ὑποδείγματος χάριν· πρὸς ἐντελεστέραν τῶν
ἰδιωμάτων αἰτιολογίας παράστασιν λελέξεται ἐπίλυσις τῶν ῥηθέντων
διαιρέσεων.

4.1(19[α′β′]). Τὸ τοίνυν ἀλάθητον τῆς τοῦ θεοῦ γνώσεως, ὀφθαλμοὺς οἶδε καὶ
5 βλέφαρα καὶ ὅρασιν καλεῖν· ἐπὶ μὲν καλῷ· ὡς τό, **ὀφθαλμοὶ κυρίου ἐπὶ
δικαίους**· ἐπὶ δὲ κακῷ· **οἱ ὀφθαλμοὶ αὐτοῦ ἐπὶ τὰ ἔθνη ἐπιβλέπουσιν**·

6 Ps 33:16 [34:15]   6 Ps 65[66]:7

---

1 post χάριν] interpun. *Goessling*, non interpun. L *Hoeschel* (ex AB)
1 post ἐντελεστέραν] τῆς + *Goessling* (ex *Schlüren*)
2 λελέξεται] λέξεται K₂ *Goessling* (ex *Schlüren*)
2 ῥηθέντων] ῥηθεισῶν *Goessling* (ex *Migne Schlüren*)
3 ἐπίλυσις–διαιρέσεων] titul. L *Hoeschel* (ex AB) *Goessling* (ex codd.)

3. [I have listed] these peculiarities for the sake of illustration. An explanation of the categories of the aforementioned peculiarities will now be indicated[1] that aims for a more complete presentation of their rationale.[2]

Catalogue of Explanations

Bodily Parts and Senses

Eyes and Seeing

4.1. Now Scripture can call the fact that nothing escapes the detection of God's knowledge, his "eyes" and "eyelids" and "vision."[3] [Sometimes this happens] for benefit: for example, "The eyes of the Lord are on the righteous" (Ps 33:16 [34:15]).[4] [At other times it happens] for harm: "His eyes gaze intently upon the nations" (Ps 65[66]:7).

---

[1] Reading the future perfect λελέξεται, with most mss (Smyth §1956).

[2] The term "explanation" (ἐπίλυσις) points to a style of biblical commentary that characterizes the first section of the *Introduction*: "problems and solutions" (προβλήματα καὶ λύσεις). The problems are the aforementioned anthropomorphisms, while the explanations that now follow are Adrian's interpretations of this puzzling language. Note as well that he wishes to uncover the "rationale" (αἰτιολογία) for the anthropomorphisms in Scripture. His recurring thesis is that the significance of this language lies in the human conduct that it mirrors: for instance, since we communicate with our mouths, talk of God's "mouth" in Scripture signifies his revelatory character (4.3). While there was considerable variety in the approach and format of commentary labeled "problems and solutions," this style of exegesis surfaced frequently among Antiochenes, especially in their commentaries on the Octateuch. For orientation, see Bardy, "La littérature patristique des 'quaestiones et responsiones' sur l'Écriture sainte"; Dörrie and Dörries, "Erotapokriseis"; Schäublin, *Untersuchungen*, 43–65; R. B. Ter Haar Romeny, *Syrian in Greek Dress*, 12–19; Volgers and Zamagni, eds., *Erotapokriseis*.

Note also that the mss punctuate this paragraph differently: no stop follows "for the sake of illustration" (ὑποδείγματος χάριν) and the expression ἐπίλυσις τῶν ῥηθέντων διαιρέσεων is marked off as the title of the subsequent section. The scribes, then, read the text as follows: "These things [that follow] will now be indicated for the sake of illustration that aims for..." But the problem with this punctuation is that the participle in the title does not agree with its proximate noun: τῶν ῥηθέντων διαιρέσεων. This disagreement led Schlüren and Goessling to emend the participle into its feminine form so that it agrees with the gender of διαίρεσις: ῥηθεισῶν. However, if we ignore the scribal punctuation and integrate ἐπίλυσις τῶν ῥηθέντων διαιρέσεων into the sentence as its subject, this allows the participle to modify τῶν ἰδιωμάτων so that an emendation is not required. The initial ταῦτα, then, is not treated as the subject of λελέξεται but as part of it own sentence, looking backwards at what has just been catalogued: "[I have listed] these things [i.e., peculiarities of thought] for the sake of illustration."

[3] Note Adrian's tendency in this section to interpret Scripture's metaphorical depictions of God as abstract divine attributes marked by the neuter adjective. For a brief discussion of this tendency in Theodore and the Homeric scholia, see Schäublin, *Untersuchungen*, 118–19; also Dickey, *Ancient Greek Scholarship*, 117.

[4] Thdr. Mops., *Ps.* 33:16: "by 'eyes' referring not simply to sight but also to what is done by God in beneficence and providence [τὸ ἐπὶ εὐεργεσίᾳ καὶ προνοίᾳ παρὰ τοῦ Θεοῦ γινόμενον]."

RECENSION 1

4.2(20[γ′]). τὸ δὲ ἐξιλεωτικὸν αὐτοῦ, ὦτα καὶ ἀκοήν·

4.3(21). τὸ δὲ ἐνδεικτικὸν τῆς βουλήσεως αὐτοῦ, λαλιὰν καὶ στόμα, ἀπὸ δὲ τοῦ παρ' ἡμῖν διὰ στόματος καὶ λόγων γνωρίζεσθαι τὰ κατὰ γνώμην φρονήματα·

5   **4.4**(22). ἐντεῦθεν καὶ βρῶσιν αὐτοῦ τὴν ἡμετέραν καλεῖ πρὸς ὅ βούλεται συνδρομήν, ἐκ τοῦ παρ' ἡμῖν διὰ τῆς γευστικῆς αἰσθήσεως τὸν τῆς φυσικῆς ἐνδείας ἐγγίνεσθαι κόρον·

4.5(23[δ′]). τὸ δὲ ἀποδεκτικὸν τῆς εἰς αὐτὸν ἡμῶν εὐνοίας, ὄσφρησιν·

4.6(24[ε′]). τὴν δὲ ἐπὶ πραγμάτων ἔνδειξιν αὐτοῦ, πρόσωπον καλεῖ, ὡς ἀπὸ 10 τοῦ παρ' ἡμῖν διὰ τούτου γίνεσθαι τὴν ἐμφάνειαν· εἴτε ἐπὶ καλῷ εἴτε ἐπὶ κακῷ· ὡς τό, **πρόσωπον δὲ κυρίου ἐπὶ ποιοῦντας κακά**·

---

10 E.g., Ps 4:7[6]   11 Ps 33:17 [34:16]

---

2 δὲ] – *Goessling* (ex *Schlüren*)   9 ὡς] – *Goessling* (ex *Schlüren*)
10 post τὴν] lac. indic. *Goessling*   11 τό] om. *Hoeschel*

Ears and Hearing

4.2. His appeasable nature Scripture calls "ears" and "hearing."[1]

Mouth and Speech

4.3. The revelatory character of God's will Scripture calls his "speech" and "mouth," since the thoughts of our mind are made known with a mouth and words.[2]

Taste and Food

4.4. From this [association of God's will with his "mouth"] Scripture also calls our collaboration with what is willed by God his "food," since among us satiety from physical hunger occurs through the sense of taste.[3]

Smell

4.5. Scripture links God's acceptance of our good will toward him with his sense of smell.[4]

Face

4.6. Scripture calls God's self-disclosure in response to [our] deeds, his "face," apparently because among us communication takes place through the face. [This happens] either for benefit (e.g., Ps 4:7[6]), or for harm, as in the passage, "the Lord's face is against evil doers" (Ps 33:17 [34:16]).[5]

---

[1] Thdr. Mops., *Ps.* 33:16: " 'And his ears open to their appeal': he also accepts their requests." Thdt., *Ps.* 5:2: " 'Give ear' ... stands for this, 'Let the words of my prayer reach your ears, listen kindly to my supplication, and carefully attend to the words of my appeal, since I know you are God and king." On our "ears," Thdr. Mops., *Ps.* 39:7: "By 'ears' he refers to obedience." Also Cass., *Ps.* 85:1.

[2] Thdr. Mops., *Ps.* 32:6: "You see, when it says 'mouth' in these cases, it intends to indicate an operation affecting visible creation, as when it also says 'hand' and 'feet' and the like. Elsewhere, too, Scripture says, 'The mouth of the Lord said this,' in the sense, God revealed what had been determined in our regard.' "

[3] Adrian clusters God's "mouth," "speech," and here in 4.4., "food" around the concept of the divine will. While we find nourishment through food, God finds satisfaction through his "food," i.e., our obedience to his will. The interpretation of food here is linked to Jn 4:32–4 (cited above in 2.2) where Jesus announces that his "food" is to do the "will of my Father." Also see Thdr. Mops., *Ps.* 49:12–15; *Jo.* 4:34 [Syr.].

[4] The verse listed in 2.2 above was "the Lord smelled a pleasing odor" (Gen 8:21). See Thdt., *qu. in Gen.* 53 on this verse: "This indicates God's kindliness toward Noah [Ὑπεδέξατο τοῦ Νῶε τὸ εὔγνωμον]—not that he was pleased with the smell. Nothing smells worse than burning bones, but God commended the attitude of the offerer."

[5] Thdr. Mops., *Ps.* 33:17: God "also watches over the wicked, but not in the same way as the good" (mod.).

RECENSION 1

4.7(25[s′]). τὸ ἀνυστικὸν τῆς ἐνεργείας αὐτοῦ, χεῖρας ὀνομάζει, ὡς < ἀπὸ > τοῦ παρ' ἡμῖν τὰ μάλιστα χρειώδη διὰ τῆς τῶν χειρῶν ἐνεργείας κατορθοῦσθαι· εἴτε ἐπὶ καλῷ εἴτε ἐπὶ κακῷ· ὡς τό, **ἐξαπόστειλον τὴν χεῖρα σου ἐξ ὕψους**· καί, **ἔπαρον τὰς χεῖρας σου ἐπὶ τὰς ὑπερηφανίας αὐτῶν εἰς**
5 **τέλος**· (25a[ζ′]). τὴν μέντοι δεξιὰν ἐπὶ μόνων τῶν αἰσίων ὡς ἀπὸ τιμιωτέρου τοῦ μέρους ἐκφωνεῖν ἔοικεν·

4.8(26[η′]). καὶ τὸ δι' ἀκριβείας αὐτοῦ εἰς πρακτικὸν ἐπιτατικώτερον, ψηλάφησιν καλεῖ·

4.9(27). τὴν δὲ πρὸς ἐπικουρίαν τῶν δεομένων ῥοπὴν, πόδας καὶ βάδισιν
10 ὀνομάζει· ὡς τό, **καὶ ἔκλινεν οὐρανοὺς καὶ κατέβη**· καί, **ἤκουσεν Ἀδὰμ τοῦ θεοῦ περιπατοῦντος ἐν τῷ παραδείσῳ**·

4.10(28[θ′]). μέντοιγε καὶ σῴζει πολλάκις τοῦ σχηματισμοῦ δι' ὅλου τὴν ἀκολουθίαν· ὡς ἐν τῷ ψαλμῷ διαγράφει τὸν θεὸν ὡς καταβάντα εἶτα κράξαντα εἶτα πέμψαντα βέλη· τὸ αὐτὸ δὲ ποιεῖν οἶδε καὶ ἐπὶ ἀνθρώπων·

---

4 Ps 143[144]:7   5 Ps 73[74]:3   10 Ps 17:10 [18:9] var.
11 Gen 3:8 var.   14 Cf. Ps 17:10, 14, 15 [18:9, 13, 14]

---

1 ὡς ἀπὸ] ἀπὸ Goessling (ex Schlüren)

Hands

4.7. Scripture designates the effectiveness of God's action, "hands," apparently since by the action of our hands pressing difficulties are successfully resolved.[1] [This happens] either for benefit, or for harm. An example [of the former]: "Send out your hand from on high" (Ps 143[144]:7). And [an example of the latter]: "Raise your hands against their arrogant acts completely" (Ps 73[74]:3).[2] However, Scripture seems to mention his "right hand" on auspicious occasions alone since it is the more honorable of the two hands.[3]

Touch

4.8. And it calls his heightened ability to act with precision, "touching."[4]

Feet and Walking

4.9. It designates God's propensity to come to the aid of those who are in need, "feet" and "walking." For example, "and he sloped the heavens and came down" (Ps 17:10 [18:9]);[5] and, "Adam heard God walking around in paradise" (Gen 3:8).[6]

4.10. To be sure, Scripture often also preserves the sequence of a particular image throughout a whole passage. For example, in a Psalm it describes God as descending, then shouting, and finally sending arrows (cf. Ps 17:10, 14, 15 [18:9, 13,

---

[1] For a similar passage, see Adrian., *cat. Ps.* 73:11(1): "through which [hands] things particularly important are achieved [δι᾿ ὧν μάλιστα τὰ σπουδαῖα τῶν πραγμάτων κατορθοῦσθαι]." Thdr. Mops., *Ps.* 44:5: "Your right hand will provide you with guidance, as if to say, You will not need the help of anyone else; instead, with your own strength you will utterly rout the adversaries, and you will use your own power as guide in achieving your goals [πρὸς τὴν τῶν σπουδαζομένων κατόρθωσιν]."

[2] Thdr. Mops., *Ps* 73:3 glosses this verse as follows: "punish them for being arrogant in our regard and glorying in all their awful hostility to us (by analogy with people who strike with their hands those they choose, and by 'hand of God' referring everywhere to his action transpiring either for benefit or for harm [καὶ γὰρ ἀπανταχοῦ χεῖρα Θεοῦ τὴν ἐνέργειαν αὐτοῦ καλεῖ εἴτε ἐπὶ καλῷ εἴτε ἐπὶ κακῷ γιγνομένην])" (mod.). See also Thdt., *Ps.* 137:7: "From this it is clear that he calls his operation 'hand' and his kind operation [τὴν ἀγαθὴν ἐνέργειαν] 'right hand': he involved his hand in the punishment of the foes, but his right hand in beneficence towards [τῇ ... εὐεργεσίᾳ τὴν δεξιάν] [the psalmist]."

[3] See 2.1 above where a similar point is made. The association between God's "right hand" and divine help is often made by Theodore (see *Ps.* 16:7; 43:4; 62:9; 73:11) and Theodoret (*Ps.* 117:15–16; 137:7).

[4] See Eus. Em., *fr. Gen.* 22:12 [Proc. G.] where he comments on the phrase "that I may know" (Gen 18:21): "it signifies the precision of judgment [σημαίνει δὲ δίκης ἀκρίβειαν]." See the cognates of ἀκρίβεια in 77 and 78 below, where the terms are associated with precision in scriptural exegesis.

[5] Diod., *Ps.* 17:10 glosses as follows: "all this was done by him [i.e., God] invisibly, whereas in tangible fashion I was the beneficiary of the assistance."

[6] See Diod., *fr. Gen.* 6:6 [Deconinck no. 24] for a shorter catalogue of body parts attributed to God, and how one ought to interpret them.

RECENSION 1

ὡς τό, **ἐρρύσω τὴν ψυχήν μου ἐκ μέσου σκύμνων**, καὶ τὰ ἑξῆς· εἴη δ᾽ ἂν
ταῦτα ἀπό τε τῶν μελῶν καὶ τῶν αἰσθήσεων.

5(29[ι´]). *Τὴν* πρὸς τὴν κακίαν ἐναντιότητα τῆς τοῦ θεοῦ βουλῆς, θυμὸν καὶ
ὀργὴν ὀνομάζει, ἀπὸ τοῦ παρ᾽ ἡμῖν τὴν ἀπέχθειαν πρὸς τἀναντία συμβαίνειν·
5 ὡς τό, **ἀπὸ τότε ἡ ὀργή σου**, ἀντὶ ἐξ ἀρχῆς καὶ ἀεὶ ἐναντίως πέφυκας ἔχειν
πρὸς τὸ κακόν· καί, **ἔκχεον τὴν ὀργήν σου ἐπὶ τὰ ἔθνη τὰ μὴ γινώσκοντά
σε·** εἴη δ᾽ ἂν ταῦτα ἀπὸ κινήσεων ψυχικῶν.

6(30[ια´]). *Τὴν* ἐπὶ μὲν τῇ τῶν οἰκείων βοηθείᾳ, τιμωρίᾳ δὲ τῶν ἐχθρῶν αἵρεσιν,
ἀνάστασίν τε τοῦ θεοῦ καὶ ἔγερσιν καλεῖ· ὡς τό, **ἀνάστα, κύριε, βοήθησον**
10 **ἡμῖν·** εἴη δ᾽ ἂν ταῦτα ἀπὸ κινήσεων σωματικῶν.

---

1 Ps 56:5 [57:4] var.   5 Ps 75:8 [76:7]   7 Ps 78[79]:6 var.   10 Ps 43:27 [44:26]

---

2 in mg. ext. L (f. 247v): αὗται αἱ θ´ διαιρέσεις ἀπό τε τῶν μελῶν καὶ τῶν αἰσθήσεων (i.e., 4.1–4.10)

14]).[1] Scripture can do the same even in the case of people. For instance, "you rescued my soul from the midst of young lions" (Ps 56:5 [57:4]), and what follows.[2]

These are depictions of God's actions from bodily parts and senses.[3]

Self-Induced Movements of the Soul

5. It calls the opposition of God's will to evil his "anger" and "wrath," since enmity toward hostile forces occurs among us.[4] For example, "from then is your wrath" (Ps 75:8 [76:7]), instead of "from the beginning, and always, you have been disposed to oppose evil."[5] And, "pour out your wrath upon the nations that do not know you" (Ps 78[79]:6)! These are depictions of God's actions from self-induced movements of the soul.

Self-Induced Movements of the Body

6. It calls God's decision to assist his own and punish his enemies, "standing up" and "awaking."[6] For example, "Stand up, O Lord; help us" (Ps 43:27[44:26])! These are depictions of God's actions from self-induced movements of the body.

---

[1] The point here is that while Scripture can portray God with a variety of anthropomorphic expressions, as has been catalogued in the preceding paragraphs, it can also use one image and extend it for several verses. In Psalm 17 God is presented as a military general (Diod., *Ps.* 17:15) or perhaps king (Thdr. Mops., *Ps.* 17:11). Note esp. Theodore's discussion of this passage at *Ps.* 17:10–12 where he remarks how the image in question (also $\sigma\chi\eta\mu\alpha\tau\iota\sigma\mu\acute{o}s$) is sometimes broken up with an insertion ($\pi\alpha\rho\acute{e}\nu\theta\epsilon\sigma\iota s$) before the Psalmist returns to the original image "picking up the sequence [$\tau\hat{\eta}s$ $\acute{a}\kappa\omega\lambda o\nu\theta\acute{\iota}\alpha s \lambda\alpha\beta\acute{o}\mu\epsilon\nu os$]." Also note the later discussion at *intro.* 77 of the importance of observing the sequence ($\acute{a}\kappa\omega\lambda o\nu\theta\acute{\iota}\alpha$) of wording in biblical texts.

[2] In the lines that follow the Psalmist's enemies are depicted with teeth and tongues, extending the image of a lion. Note that Thdr. Mops. also picks up on the continuous sequence of this image at *Ps.* 56:5: "You see, since he [the Psalmist] referred to them as lions, he was right to make mention of teeth and here speak of a tongue, since they have no difficulty in using warlike instruments against the enemy like lions using teeth and tongue."

[3] The referent of $\tau\alpha\hat{\nu}\tau\alpha$ in the recurring phrase $\epsilon\H{\iota}\eta$ $\delta'\H{\alpha}\nu$ $\tau\alpha\hat{\nu}\tau\alpha$ $\kappa\tau\lambda.$ is the $\acute{\iota}\delta\iota\acute{\omega}\mu\alpha\tau\alpha$ of thought, and in particular, the anthropomorphic portrayals of God's actions.

[4] The same text occurs in Adrian., *cat. Ps.* 75:8.

[5] Thdr. Mops., *Ps.* 75:8 glosses the verse nearly identically: "it is not at this time that you began in your wrath to punish those you wish; from the beginning and long beforehand [$\H{\alpha}\nu\omega\theta\epsilon\nu$ $\kappa\alpha\grave{\iota}$ $\acute{\epsilon}\kappa$ $\mu\alpha\kappa\rho o\hat{\nu}$ $\tau o\hat{\nu}$ $\chi\rho\acute{o}\nu o\nu$] you were able and have been doing it."

[6] See the discussion in 2.10 above about the juxtaposition of Gen 2:7 and Nah 2:2.
Note esp. Thdr. Mops., *Ps.* 67:2 (a passage cited by Adrian in 2.4 above): "There is evidence elsewhere as well that by 'God's rising' he refers to his taking steps to help his own and punish the adversaries [$\tau\grave{\eta}\nu$ $\acute{\epsilon}\pi\grave{\iota}$ $\beta o\eta\theta\epsilon\acute{\iota}\alpha$ $\tau\hat{\omega}\nu$ $o\acute{\iota}\kappa\epsilon\acute{\iota}\omega\nu$ $\kappa\alpha\grave{\iota}$ $\tau\iota\mu\omega\rho\acute{\iota}\alpha$ $\tau\hat{\omega}\nu$ $\acute{\epsilon}\nu\alpha\nu\tau\acute{\iota}\omega\nu$ $\kappa\acute{\iota}\nu\eta\sigma\iota\nu$], from the custom prevalent among us by which, when we intend to do something of this kind, we first sit down and pause and then rise to take action." Also Thdr. Mops., *Ps.* 7:7 (a verse also cited by Adrian in 2.4): "It is not that God is sometimes seated that he [i.e., the Psalmist] asks him to 'rise up'; rather, it is because we, when bent on vengeance, suggest by such a bodily movement [*tali motu corporis*] that we are ready to take punitive action. Thus, we apply words from our normal procedure to present petitions to God, as if to say, 'Take action to avenge me really and truly.'"

7(31[ιβ′]). Πεῖραν τοῦ θεοῦ καλεῖ, τὴν εἰς ἔργον τῆς τῶν οἰκείων αὐτοῦ εὐνοίας ἔκκλησιν, πρὸς τὸ λαμπροτέρους καὶ ἐπισημοτέρους αὐτοὺς καταστῆσαι καὶ περιβλεπτοτέρους· ὡς τό, **ὁ θεὸς ἐπείραζε τὸν Ἀβραάμ·** (32[ιγ′]) τὴν τῆς συνήθους αὐτοῦ προστασίας ἀναβολήν, λήθην ὀνομάζει· ὡς τό, **ἐπιλανθάνῃ**
5 **τῆς πτωχείας ἡμῶν;** (33[ιδ′]) τὴν τῆς προθέσεως εἰς ἔργον ἔκβασιν, πληροφορίαν τῆς τοῦ θεοῦ γνώσεως ἀποκαλεῖ, ὡς [τὸ] παρ' ἡμῖν ἀξιοπιστότερα τῶν λόγων τὰ πράγματα· ὡς τό, **καταβὰς οὖν ὄψομαι, εἰ κατὰ τὴν κραυγὴν αὐτῶν τὴν ἐρχομένην πρός με συντελοῦνται· εἰ δὲ μή, ἵνα γνῶ· καὶ τό, νῦν ἔγνων ὅτι φοβῇ σὺ τὸν θεόν·** (34[ιε′]) τὸ ἄφυκτον τῆς τοῦ
10 θεοῦ δίκης ἔρευναν καλεῖ· ὡς τό, **καὶ ἔσται ἐν τῇ ἡμέρᾳ ἐκείνῃ, ἐξερευνήσω τὴν Ἱερουσαλὴμ μετὰ λύχνου·** εἴη δ' ἂν ταῦτα ἀπὸ παθῶν ψυχικῶν.

8(35[ιϛ′]). Τὴν τῆς κατὰ τῶν ἐχθρῶν αὐτοῦ ἀμύνης ὑπέρθεσιν τήν τε πρὸς τοὺς οἰκείους ἐπίκουρον βραδυτῆτα, νυσταγμὸν καὶ ὕπνον καὶ καρηβαρίαν ἀποκαλεῖ· ὡς τό, **ἐξεγέρθητι, ἵνα τί ὑπνοῖς κύριε;** καί, **οὐ μὴ νυστάξῃ οὐδὲ**
15 **ὑπνώσῃ ὁ φυλάσσων τὸν Ἰσραήλ·** εἴη δ' ἂν ταῦτα ἀπὸ παθῶν σωματικῶν.

---

3 Gen 22:1   5 Ps 43:25 [44:24]   9 Gen 18:21   9 Gen 22:12 var.
11 Zeph 1:12   14 Ps 43:24 [44:23]   15 Ps 120[121]:4 var.

---

5 τὴν] – Goessling (ex Schlüren)   6 τὸ] – Hoeschel Goessling   9 τῆς] – Hoeschel (ex A)
11 in mg. inf. L (f. 247v): τὸ ιβ′ιγ′ιδ′ιε′ιϛ′ ιζ′ιη′ιθ′ ἀπὸ παθῶν ψυχικῶν (i.e., 7.1–9 (sic))
12 τῆς κατὰ] Hoeschel Goessling, κατὰ τῆς L

Movements of the Soul Induced from Without

7. The challenging of his people to an act of love, in order to make them more radiant and distinguished and admired, it calls "God testing." For example, "God tested Abraham" (Gen 22:1).[1] It names the delaying of his customary protection, "forgetting." For example, "do you forget our poverty" (Ps 43:25 [44:24])?[2] It calls[3] the realization of his purpose in an action [of ours], the "complete certainty of God's knowledge," since for us actions are more trustworthy than words.[4] For example, "So when I go down, I will see if they are acting in accordance with the outcry against them that is reaching me, but if not—that I may know" (Gen 18:21); and, "Now I have known that you fear God" (Gen 22:12).[5] It calls the unerring quality of God's judgment, "search." For example, "and it will be on that day, I will search out Jerusalem with a lamp" (Zeph 1:12).[6] These are depictions of God's actions from movements of soul induced from without.

Movements of the Body Induced from Without

8. It calls the postponement of vengeance against his enemies and the sluggishness with which he protects his own people, "drowsiness" and "sleep" and "heavy-headedness."[7] For example, "Wake up! Why do you sleep, O Lord" (Ps 43:24 [44:23])?;[8] and, "The one who watches over Israel will never slumber nor sleep"

---

[1] Eus. Em., *fr. Gen.* 22:12 [cat. 1267] where the testing of Abraham is designed to demonstrate Abraham's "love for God [τὴν εἰς θεὸν ἀγάπην]." Diod., *fr. Gen.* 22:1–14 [Deconinck no. 36] glosses as follows: God "did not really demand [that Abraham sacrifice his son], but was demonstrating that his faith was reliable [ἀλλὰ δόκιμον δεικνὺς αὐτοῦ τὴν πίστιν]." Thdt., *qu. in Gen.* 74 (on 22:1–14): "If God knows everything in advance, why did he put Abraham to the test? Not to learn what he already knew, but to teach the ignorant that he had good reason to love the patriarch. That was why he tested his love of God for three days and nights. The patriarch, torn between nature and faith and pulled both ways, decided in favor of faith. Having brought out his devotion, God stopped the sacrifice."

[2] Diod., *Ps.* 43:25 glosses as follows: "not even the excessive distress and lack of necessities make you turn toward us." Thdr. Mops., *Ps.* 43:25 paraphrases similarly: "stop ignoring us in our misfortunes and tribulations."

[3] Adrian uses the verb ἀποκαλέω three times: here, in 8, and in 10 (usually he uses καλέω or ὀνομάζω). Here and in 8 the term does not seem to have a negative connotation, but in 10 I have translated it as such (s.v. ἀποκαλέω LSJ II: "stigmatize").

[4] When God's will is fulfilled in some human action (e.g., Abraham's love for God on Mount Moriah), God is appropriately said to gain certainty of knowledge—not because God is ignorant of a person's character, but because this is how we talk: we derive more certitude from the actions than the words of people.

[5] Note also the juxtaposition of Gen 18:21 and 22:12 in Eus. Em., *fr. Gen.* 22:12 [Arm./cat. 1267/ Proc. G.] and Diod., *fr. Gen.* 22:12 [Petit, *coisliniana Gen. no.* 204 lines 1–14].

[6] Thdr. Mops., *Soph.* 1:12: "his meaning is, all the contents of Jerusalem will be searched for with great precision [μετὰ πολλῆς τῆς ἀκριβείας] so that nothing will escape the notice of the marauding enemy" (mod.).

[7] See Adrian., *cat. Ps.* 43:24 where an explanation is given of this language: "from the fact that we, after falling asleep, do not give any thought to our servants or family."

[8] Thdr. Mops., *Ps.* 43:24: "Speaking in rather human fashion, he means, 'Be moved to help us; how long will you be patient?'" Thdt., *Ps.* 43:24: "He calls long-suffering 'sleep': just as the sleeping person is unaware of what is happening, so the one practicing long-suffering puts up with being belabored and abused."

9(36[ιϛ′]). Τὴν καταθύμιον τῷ θεῷ πολιτείαν ἡμῶν, ἀγάπην αὐτοῦ μάλα γε εἰκότως ὀνομάζει· (37[ιη′]) μίσος δὲ, τὸ τὴν ἐναντίαν τῆς αὐτοῦ βαδίζειν βουλήσεως· (38[ιθ′]) καὶ ζῆλον, τὸ τοὺς οἰκείους τιμωρεῖν· ὡς τό, **ἐζήλωσε κύριος τὴν γῆν αὐτοῦ**· εἴη δ' ἂν ταῦτα ἀπὸ διαθέσεων.

5 **10**(39[κ′]). Τὴν τῆς Ἱερουσαλὴμ καὶ τὴν τῆς Σαμαρείας πρὸς τὸν θεὸν οἰκείωσιν, μνηστείαν τοῦ θεοῦ καλεῖ, διὰ τὸ θηλυκῶς κατὰ μετωνυμίαν ἀπὸ τῶν πόλεων τοὺς οἰκήτορας ὀνομάζειν· ἐκ μεταφορᾶς τῶν γυναικῶν· ὡς τό, **μνηστεύσομαί σε ἐμαυτῷ εἰς τὸν αἰῶνα**· (40[κα′]) ὥσπερ καὶ τὴν πρὸς τὰ εἴδωλα οἰκείωσιν, μοιχείαν ἀποκαλεῖ, δι' ἣν καὶ βιβλίον ἀποστασίου εἰς τὰς
10 χεῖρας λαμβάνει Ἱερουσαλήμ· (41[κβ′]) οὐδὲν ἧττον καὶ τῇ τοῦ πατρὸς προσηγορίᾳ, τὸ πρὸς αὐτοὺς τοῦ θεοῦ κῆδος ἐμφαίνει καὶ τῇ τοῦ πρωτοτόκου· εἴη δ' ἂν ταῦτα ἀπὸ κοινῶν δοξῶν.

11(42[κγ′]). Τὸ κράτος καὶ τὴν δίκην τοῦ θεοῦ, κάθισιν αὐτοῦ καὶ θρόνον ὀνομάζει, ἀπὸ τοῦ παρ' ἡμῖν τοὺς τὴν τοῦ κρίνειν τε καὶ κολάζειν ἔχοντας
15 ἐξουσίαν, ἐπὶ θρόνων καθημένους ποιεῖσθαι τὴν ἐξέτασιν· ὡς τό, **ἐκάθισας ἐπὶ θρόνου ὁ κρίνων δικαιοσύνην**· καί, **ὁ θεὸς κάθηται ἐπὶ θρόνου ἁγίου αὐτοῦ**·

4 Joel 2:18   8 Hos 2:21[19]   10 Cf. Jer 3:8   16 Ps 9:5[4]   16 Ps 46:9 [47:8]

7 *Τὴν τῆς Ἱερουσαλὴμ–γυναικῶν*] Τὴν τῆς Ἱερουσαλὴμ καὶ τὴν τῆς Σαμαρείας πρὸς τὸν θεὸν οἰκείωσιν μνηστείαν τοῦ θεοῦ καλεῖ, διὰ τὸ θηλυκῶς ἐκ μεταφορᾶς τῶν γυναικῶν ἀπὸ τῶν πόλεων τοὺς οἰκήτορας ὀνομάζειν κατὰ μετωνυμίαν Goessling Τὴν τῆς Ἱερουσαλὴν καὶ τὴν τῆς Σαμαρείας πρὸς τὸν θεὸν οἰκείωσιν, μνηστείαν τοῦ θεοῦ καλεῖ, διὰ τὸ κατὰ μετωνυμίαν ἀπὸ τῶν πόλεων τοὺς οἰκήτορας ὀνομάζειν—< τὰς δὲ πόλεις > θηλυκῶς ἐκ μεταφορᾶς τῶν γυναικῶν Schlüren
10 in mg. ext. L (f. 248r): τὸ κα′κβ′ (sic) ἀπὸ κοινῶν δοξῶν
11 κῆδος] Goessling (ex Schlüren), κῦδος L
13 κάθισιν] cat. Ps. 9:8 Hoeschel Goessling, καθίστησιν L

(Ps 120[121]:4). These are depictions of God's actions from movements of the body induced from without.

Attitudes

9. Scripture quite reasonably calls our way of life, when it is pleasing to God, his "love." But it calls going in the opposite direction of his will, his "hatred."[1] And Scripture calls the avenging of his own people, "jealousy." For example, "the Lord became jealous for his land" (Joel 2:18).[2] These are depictions of God's actions from attitudes.

Familial Distinctions

10. Using the metaphor of women, Scripture calls the affection of Jerusalem and Samaria for God their "betrothal" to God, because it refers to the inhabitants metonymously by means of their cities, and as feminine. For example, "I will betroth you to myself forever" (Hos 2:21[19]).[3] Just as Scripture also disparages the affection for idols as "adultery," on account of which even Jerusalem receives a bill of divorce in its hands (cf. Jer 3:8). No less does Scripture also indicate God's regard for his people with the designations of "father" and "firstborn." These are depictions of God's actions from familial distinctions.

Civil Rank

11. It calls God's power and judgment his "sitting" and "throne," since among us those who sit on thrones scrutinize closely, possessing the authority both to judge and to punish.[4] For example, "You sat on a throne, you who judge with righteousness" (Ps 9:5[4]);[5] and, "God sits upon his holy throne" (Ps 46:9 [47:8]); and, "Your

---

[1] These glosses on God's love and hatred refer specifically to Mal 1:2–3 and Ps 86:2 (both cited in 2.7 above). Thdt., *Mal.* 1:2–3: "yet not even commonality of nature or the one time of birth for both [i.e., Jacob and Esau] had the effect of giving them the same regard [ἴσην... διάθεσιν]... 'I hated' him [i.e., Esau] on account of his evil ways, but 'loved Jacob' as a devotee of virtue."

[2] Thdr. Mops., *Joel* 2:18: "he will be jealous and spare you if he sees you repentant and doing what was prescribed." Note also Thdr. Mops., *Zach.* 8:2 ("I am jealous for Jerusalem," a verse also cited by Adrian in 2.7) where God's jealousy is portrayed positively and linked to the language of "attitude" as Adrian also does. Theodore glosses as follows: "I have changed my attitude to it [i.e., Jerusalem] [μεταβέβληκά μου τὴν περὶ αὐτὴν σχέσιν] so as even to be very angry for what it suffered at the hands of those who wronged it." A few lines later, Theodore remarks about God's "favorable disposition to Mount Zion" (τὴν περὶ τὸ ὄρος Σιὼν διάθεσιν). Thdt., *qu. in Ex.* 39 (on Ex 20:5): "God calls himself 'a jealous God,' using a human expression... Jealousy is indicative of love."

[3] See Thdr. Mops., *Os.* 2:21 and Schäublin, *Untersuchungen*, 117–18.

[4] Very similar text in Adrian., *cat. Ps.* 9:8.

[5] Thdr. Mops., *Ps.* 9:5 glosses as follows: "in your capacity as judge you were quite rigid and demanding in doing what was appropriate to the fairest of observers—that is to say, You subjected what was done by them to examination so that the verdict of your severity should be delivered against them for the sins they committed against us. This is expressed, therefore, as a metaphor from earthly judges, who preside over a tribunal and normally wield the sword of vengeance on the guilty... when he is said to 'sit on his throne,' the judge's severity is implied."

RECENSION 1

καί, ὁ θρόνος σου ὁ θεὸς εἰς τὸν αἰῶνα τοῦ αἰῶνος· καί, ὁ καθήμενος ἐπὶ τῶν Χερουβίμ· εἴη δ' ἂν ταῦτα ἀπὸ ἀξιωμάτων.

12(43[κδ′]). Τὴν δημιουργικὴν αὐτοῦ ἐνέργειαν, ποτὲ μὲν διὰ προστάγματος ὡς ἐπὶ τῶν λοιπῶν, ποτὲ δὲ δι' αὐτουργίας ὥσπερ ἐφ' ἡμῶν παρίστησι·
5 καὶ ζωγραφεῖν τὴν Ἱερουσαλήμ καὶ φράττειν τὴν ὁδόν καὶ δίκτυον καὶ ἀμφίβληστρον πρὸς τὴν τῶν φαύλων σύλληψιν τίθεσθαι λέγεται· εἴη δ' ἂν ταῦτα ἀπὸ ἐπιτηδευμάτων.

13(44[κε′]). Τὴν ἐπὶ νίκῃ καὶ τροπαίων συστάσει συμμαχίαν αὐτοῦ, ἐγγύτητά τε καὶ ἀνάληψιν καὶ ὕψωσιν καλεῖ· ὡς τό, **ἐγγὺς κύριος τοῖς συντετριμμένοις**
10 **τῇ καρδίᾳ** (45) μακρότητα δέ, τὴν τῆς συμμαχίας ἀναβολήν· ὡς τό, **ἵνα τί κύριε ἀφέστηκας μακρόθεν;** εἴη δ' ἂν ταῦτα ἀπὸ τόπων.

14(46[κϛ′]). Τὴν ἐν ᾧπερ ἂν φαίνοιτο βοηθῶν τρόπῳ διάπειραν, ἐσθῆτα αὐτοῦ ὀνομάζει, ἐκ τοῦ παρ' ἡμῖν < τοὺς φαινομένους ἔμπροσθεν τῶν ἄλλων ἐν ἱματίοις περιβάλλεσθαι >· ὡς τό, **ὁ κύριος ἐβασίλευσεν εὐπρέπειαν**
15 **ἐνεδύσατο·** καὶ τό, **περιβαλλόμενος φῶς ὡς ἱμάτιον·** εἴη δ' ἂν ταῦτα ἀπὸ στολισμῶν.

---

1 Ps 44:7 [45:6]   2 Ps 79:2 [80:1]   4 Cf. Gen 1:3–25
4 Cf. Gen 2:7, 21–2   5 Cf. Isa 49:16   5 Cf. Hos 2:8[6]
6 Cf. Ezek 12:13; Ps 140[141]:10   10 Ps 33:19 [34:18] var.
11 Ps 9:22 [10:1]   15 Ps 92[93]:1   15 Ps 103[104]:2 var.

---

6 λέγεται· εἴη δ' ἂν] Hoeschel Goessling, λέγεται εἶναι· L
9 συντετριμμένοις] φοβουμένοις G   13 post ἡμῖν lac. indic. Goessling (ex Schlüren)
14 τοὺς–περιβάλλεσθαι] vel sim., διὰ τῶν στολισμῶν γνωρίζεσθαι τὰ κατὰ γνώμην φρονήματα Schlüren
15 ὡς] om. Hoeschel

throne, O God, is forever and ever" (Ps 44:7 [45:6]); and, "You who sit upon the Cherubim" (Ps 79:2 [80:1]).[1] These are depictions of God's actions from civil rank.

Occupations

12. It sometimes presents his activity as a craftsman [taking place] through a command when it concerns the rest of creation (cf. Gen 1:3–25), while at other times [it presents this activity taking place] through his own firsthand involvement, when it concerns us (cf. Gen 2:7, 21–2).[2] And God is said to paint Jerusalem (cf. Isa 49:16) and build a hedge along the way (cf. Hos 2:8[6]) and set up a net and a snare for apprehending the worthless (cf. Ezek 12:13; Ps 140[141]:10). These are depictions of God's actions from occupations.

Places

13. Scripture calls God's assistance in victory and the establishment of monuments of defeat, "nearness," and "taking up," and "raising high." For example, "The Lord is near the brokenhearted" (Ps 33:19 [34:18]).[3] But Scripture calls the delaying of his aid "remoteness." For example, "Why, O Lord, do you stand far away" (Ps 9:22 [10:1])?[4] These are depictions of God's actions from places.

Dress

14. It calls our experience[5] of the manner in which God is revealed as coming to our aid, his "clothes," since among us people are revealed before others clothed in garments.[6] For example, "The Lord reigned, he was robed in splendor" (Ps 92[93]:1); and, "clothing yourself in light as in a garment" (Ps 103[104]:2). These are depictions of God's actions from dress.

---

[1] Thdr. Mops., *Ps.* 79:2: "It is always in reference to power that he mentions the Cherubim"; "as if to say, 'he who rules powerfully'" (Thdr. Mops., *fr. Gen.* 3:24 [Devreesse, *Essai*, 23–4 fn. 4d]).

[2] Adrian is distinguishing between creating by command ("Let there be…") and creating the male and female with hands (e.g., forming man from the dust). Junillus distinguishes three ways in which God creates the world: by will alone; by will and utterance; by will, utterance, and command (*inst.* 2.2).

[3] Thdr. Mops., *Ps.* 33:19: "God will take extraordinary care of all the lowly, being anxious to make them his own (by 'near' referring to his disposition and attitude [τὴν διάθεσιν … καὶ τὴν σχέσιν])."

[4] Thdr. Mops., *Ps.* 9:22: "Now God is said to move away or come close in terms of disposition, not place [*Affectionaliter autem, non localiter*], he by nature being everywhere and present to everyone."

[5] No satisfactory definition of διάπειρα in the lexica. S.v. πεῖρα LSJ 1; BDAG 2.

[6] Thdr. Mops., *Ps.* 72:6: "they wrapped themselves in iniquity and impiety, always guilty of it, always giving an impression of it [ἐν τούτοις φαινόμενοι] (by analogy with people putting on clothes and appearing in them to bystanders [ἐκ μεταφορᾶς τῶν τὰ ἱμάτια περιβαλλομένων καὶ ἐν αὐτοῖς φαινομένων ἐν τοῖς ὄρεσιν])."

RECENSION 1

15(47[κη′]). Τὸ μὴ τὰς τῆς ψυχῆς ἱκεσίας προσίεσθαι τὸν θεόν, εἰκότως ἀπόρριψιν ὀνομάζει, διὰ τὸ τοῖς κακοῖς αὐτὴν ἐνστρέφεσθαι, ἥτις πάλιν ἀπαλλάττεσθαι παρακαλεῖ· ὡς τό, **ἵνα τί ἀπωθεῖς τὴν ψυχήν μου;** εἴη δ᾽ ἂν ταῦτα ἀπὸ ἐθῶν.

5   **16**(48[κθ′]). Τὴν ἀναβολὴν τῆς εὐμενείας αὐτοῦ, χειρῶν ἀποστροφὴν λέγει· ὡς τό, **ἵνα τί ἀποστρέφεις τὴν χεῖρα σου καὶ τὴν δεξιάν σου;** εἴη δ᾽ ἂν ταῦτα ἀπὸ σχημάτων.

17(49[λ′]). Ψυχὴν μέντοι καὶ σάρκα τοῦ θεοῦ λέγει, ὅταν μὴ ἀπὸ σχέσεως ἢ ἀπὸ ἐνεργείας τὸν περὶ αὐτοῦ ποιεῖται λόγον, ἀλλὰ περὶ αὐτοῦ ἰδικώτερον·
10   < ὡς τό, **σάρξ μου ἐξ αὐτῶν·** καί, **τὰς νεομηνίας καὶ τὰ σάββατα ὑμῶν μισεῖ ἡ ψυχή μου·** > < οὕτω καὶ παρ᾽ ἡμῖν· > ὡς τό, **ἴασαι τὴν ψυχήν μου,** ἀντὶ τοῦ ἐμέ· καί, **ἡ σάρξ μου κατασκηνώσει ἐπ᾽ ἐλπίδι,** ἀντὶ τοῦ ἐγώ.

---

3 Ps 87:15 [88:14] var.   6 Ps 73[74]:11   10 Hos 9:12
11 Isa 1:14 var.   11 Ps 40:5 [41:4]   12 Ps 15[16]:9

---

2 ἥτις] ὅθεν Goessling (ex Schlüren)   4 ἐθῶν] ἐθνῶν Hoeschel (ex B)
11 ὡς τό–ἡ ψυχή μου] sim. Schlüren (cf. 2.15)   11 οὕτω καὶ παρ᾽ἡμῖν] sim. Schlüren
12 ὡς τό, ἴασαι–ἀντὶ τοῦ ἐγώ] – Goessling (ex Lollin)

Customary Behaviors

15. It reasonably calls God not accepting the supplications of the soul, a "casting off," because continually engaging[1] in evils it[2] implores once more to be freed. For example, "Why... do you reject my soul" (Ps 87:15 [88:14])? These are depictions of God's actions from customary behaviors.[3]

Gestures

16. Scripture calls the delaying of his goodwill "a turning away of hands."[4] For example, "Why do you turn your hand away, even your right hand" (Ps 73[74]:11)?[5] These are depictions of God's actions from gestures.

Whole Living Being

17. Scripture mentions God's "soul," indeed even "flesh," whenever it gives an account of his intrinsic nature and not of a relationship or activity of his.[6] For example, "My flesh among them" (Hos 9:12); and, "My soul despises your new moons and Sabbaths" (Isa 1:14). So also among us: for example, "Heal my soul" (Ps 40:5 [41:4]), instead of "me." And, "My flesh will dwell in hope" (Ps 15[16]:9), instead of "I."[7]

---

[1] S.v. στρέφω LSJ B.III.

[2] Taking ἥτις as equivalent of ἥ and perhaps also ἥπερ (BDF §293; s.v. ὅστις, ἥτις, ὅ τι BDAG 3).

[3] See in 2.13 the fuller dossier of biblical texts that illustrate God's customary behaviors, including an explanation of this anthropomorphic language.

[4] For a similar text, see Adrian., *cat. Ps.* 73:11(1).

[5] See the discussion in 2.14 where this verse is also explained. Note the parallel passage in Thdr. Mops., *Ps.* 73:11.

[6] A more literal rendering: "whenever it gives an account of him based not on a relationship or activity, but a more proper [account] of him." "More proper" in the sense of what is the distinctive property or inherent nature of God (s.v. ἴδιος PGL C). That is, when the Bible talks about God's "soul" and "flesh," it is utilizing the trope of synecdoche (73.4 below) to highlight more fundamentally God's nature, and not a divine relationship or activity. For the distinctions between σχέσις (relationship) and ἐνέργεια (activity) on the one hand, and οὐσία (essence) or φύσις (nature) on the other, see the respective entries on these terms in *PGL*. Note as well Junillus' distinction between the four ways Scripture refers to God: it speaks of his "essence," his "persons," his "work," or by a "comparison" of him to his creatures (*inst.* 1.12).

[7] Thdr. Mops., *Ps.* 15:9: "By 'my flesh' he means 'I myself,' naming the whole from the part, the divine Scripture normally referring to the whole person by flesh and likewise by soul—by flesh in saying, 'All flesh had corrupted its way' [Gen 6:12] and by soul in saying, 'Jacob went down into Egypt with seventy-five souls [Gen 46:27].'" It is tempting to consider as a corruption the missing refrain that otherwise concludes the foregoing paragraphs, so that the editor should insert: εἴη δ'ἂν ταῦτα ἀπὸ ὅλου τοῦ ζῴου (so Schlüren, "Zu Adrianos," 146–7). However, the referent of ταῦτα is the portrayal of God's *actions* in Scripture (see 2), and this paragraph breaks the mold: it is not about divine action per se, but the divine nature.

18(52). Καὶ δὴ ταῦτα, καθὼς ἦν περὶ θεοῦ φιλοσοφεῖν, ὑπεστησάμεθα, μηδέν τι περαιτέρω φρονεῖν ἢ λέγειν ἔχοντες καὶ περὶ μὲν τῶν ἐπὶ τῆς διανοίας ἐπιτηδευμάτων ἐν τούτοις.

< Ἀρχὴ τῶν ἐπὶ τῆς λέξεως >

5   Τὰ δὲ ἐπὶ τῆς λέξεως οὕτως·

19(53[α′]). Τὸ ἀντὶ τῆς πράξεως ἤτοι τῆς ἀπολαύσεως τοῦ πράγματος λέγειν, ποτὲ μὲν τὸ ἀκοῦσαι, ποτὲ δὲ τὸ ἰδεῖν, ποτὲ δὲ τὸ γνῶναι·

1 ante Καὶ] Τὸ βέβαιον-ἡ γῆ in 64.1–2 infra transp.
2 ἢ λέγειν] om. *Hoeschel*   5 Τὰ-οὕτως] titul. L *Hoeschel* (ex AB) *Goessling* (ex codd.)

18. And so, to the degree that it was possible to philosophize about God,[1] we began with these things, having nothing further to think or say about the conventions[2] of [Scripture's] message in these preceding paragraphs.

PART II: PECULIARITIES OF DICTION

Peculiarities of diction are as follows:[3]

19. Speaking sometimes of "hearing," at other times of "looking," and at other times of "making known," instead of the performance of an action or the enjoyment of some thing.

---

[1] The expression περὶ θεοῦ φιλοσοφεῖν likely encompasses two distinct moves that Adrian has made in the preceding analysis. First, it points to his interpretations of anthropomorphisms, in which he explains the proper sense of this representational language for God. But this expression also signifies, second, Adrian's justifications of his interpretations, which occasionally surface in the preceding section. Note in 3 above where Adrian highlights his desire to analyze the logic behind the anthropomorphisms: "An explanation of the categories of the aforementioned peculiarities will now be indicated that aims for a more complete presentation of their rationale." This rationale (αἰτιολογία) is his thesis that the true sense of the anthropomorphic portrayals of God in Scripture is derived from the human conduct upon which God's actions are modeled. Here is a paragraph that illustrates both of these moves: "The revelatory character of God's will Scripture calls his 'speech' and 'mouth' [the interpretation of the anthropomorphism], since the thoughts of our mind are made known with a mouth and words [the justification of this interpretation]" (4.3). The expression περὶ θεοῦ φιλοσοφεῖν is appropriate, since both moves surface in late antique philosophical commentary on the Greek myths, including Homer's depictions of the gods. See Russell and Konstan, *Heraclitus: Homeric Problems*, xvii–xix.
[2] Note that ἐπιτήδευμα is functioning as a synonym for ἰδίωμα, though it underscores more strongly the recurring or habitual character of these literary peculiarities.
[3] In this section on diction Adrian lists unconventional uses of words or phrases. A handful of the tropes and figures he discusses later in the *Introduction* surface already here: e.g., metaphor (27, 38, and 49); ellipsis or omission (38); superfluous use of words (48). In a few cases he informs readers about how to safely hear potentially dangerous theological language: e.g., people who claim to be "righteous" in Scripture are not actually so (25); bald claims that God perpetrates evil have a benign explanation (55). However, most of the paragraphs in this section fall into two categories. Repeatedly Adrian claims that scriptural authors use a word or phrase in place of another word or phrase. Such shifts, alterations, or exchanges in scriptural language are usually signaled by Adrian with the marker ἀντί: one thing is said "instead of" another. For instance, Scripture uses the word "teach" instead of "cause" (20), or "way" instead of "conduct" (40). Adrian highlights a wide range of such changes in scriptural language: it uses the plural instead of the singular (37); one tense for another (61); exchanges one speaker for another (51); uses one mood instead of another (63); one preposition for another (65). In the next section of the treatise he also highlights how words have been inverted (68) or transposed (69) to create irregularities in syntax. Grammatical and rhetorical treatises referred to such a shifts or exchanges as ἐναλλαγαί or ἀλλοιώσεις (Lausberg, *Literary Rhetoric* §509). For an excellent late antique parallel to Adrian, see the catalogue of changes identified in Homer by Ps.-Plu., *vit. Hom.* §§41–64. Note the discussion of the figure of ἀλλοίωσις in Rutherford, *History of Annotation*, 310–12, as well as his list of the kinds of shifts identified in the scholia (331–3). For a catalogue of changes identified by Diodore, see Mariès, *Études*, 113–15.

19.1. τὸ μὲν οὖν ἀκοῦσαι· ὡς τό, **ἀκουτιεῖς μοι ἀγαλλίασιν καὶ εὐφροσύνην,** ἀντὶ πράξεις μοι·

19.2. τὸ δὲ ἰδεῖν· ὡς τό, **τοῦ ἰδεῖν ἐν τῇ χρηστότητι τῶν ἐκλεκτῶν σου,** ἀντὶ τοῦ ἀπολαῦσαι τῆς ἐσομένης περὶ ἡμᾶς σου χρηστότητος·

5 **19.3.** τὸ δὲ γνῶναι· ὡς τό, **ἐγνώρισάς μοι ὁδοὺς < ζωῆς >,** ἀντὶ τοῦ ἀπολαῦσαι με τῆς ζωῆς πεποίηκας.

20(54[β′]). Τὸ δίδαξον, ἀντὶ τοῦ παράσχου· ὡς τό, **καὶ δίδαξόν με ὅτι σὺ εἶ ὁ θεὸς ὁ σωτήρ μου.**

21(55[γ′]). Τὸ ἐλάλησεν ἐπὶ τοῦ θεοῦ πολλάκις, ἀντὶ τοῦ ἀπεφήνατο· ὡς τό, **ὁ** 10 **θεὸς ἐλάλησεν ἐν τῷ ἁγίῳ αὐτοῦ.**

22(56[δ′]). Τὸ ἅπαξ ἐπὶ τοῦ ἀμεταβλήτου· ὡς τό, **ἅπαξ ἐλάλησεν ὁ θεός·** καί, **ἅπαξ ὤμοσα.**

---

1 Ps 50:10 [51:8] var.   3 Ps 105[106]:5
5 Ps 15[16]:11   8 Ps 24[25]:5
10 Ps 59:8 [60:6]   11 Ps 61:12 [62:11]   12 Ps 88:36 [89:35]

---

2 ἀντὶ πράξεις] Goessling, τουτέστι πράξεις cat. Ps. 50:10, ἀντιπράξεις L
4 ἐσομένης] ἐπομένης Hoeschel Goessling   5 ζωῆς] + Goessling (ex *Lollin Schlüren*)

19.1. "Hearing": for example, "You will let me hear great joy and merriment" (Ps 50:10 [51:8]), instead of "You will bring about in me [great joy and merriment]."[1]

19.2. "Looking": for example, "looking at the goodness of your chosen ones" (Ps 105[106]:5), instead of "enjoying your goodness which will surround us."[2]

19.3. "Making known": for example, "You made known to me ways of life" (Ps 15[16]:11), instead of "You have made me enjoy life."[3]

20. [Saying] "teach" instead of "cause." For example, "and teach me that you are God, my Savior" (Ps 24[25]:5)![4]

21. Often [saying] "he spoke" with reference to God, instead of "he pronounced." For example, "God spoke in his holy place" (Ps 59:8 [60:6]).[5]

22. [Using] "once" in regard to unchangeableness. For example, "'Once' God spoke" (Ps 61:12 [62:11]); and, "'Once' I swore" (Ps 88:36 [89:35]).[6]

The other recurring observation in this section concerns the connotations of words or phrases. Adrian will usually note that a word is used "in regard to" ($\dot{\epsilon}\pi\dot{\iota}$ + genitive) something else, highlighting an auxiliary sense beyond the word's standard denotation. For example, "cup" can also be used with reference to punishment (47); "washing one's hands" can refer to participating or not participating in some thing (35); "morning" is also used with reference to swiftness (52); "flesh" (57) and "spirit" (59) each have a range of connotations beyond their denotative senses. In my translation of these terms I use scare quotes (' ') to signify that Adrian has an auxiliary, nonstandard sense in mind.

We should not exclude the possibility that in this section on diction Adrian is drawing anonymously on lexica. Schäublin raises the possibility that Theodore had access to a biblical glossary and some sort of larger Greek lexicon (*Untersuchungen*, 96–105, with numerous examples). For orientation to the Greek lexica, their interrelationships, studies, and editions, see Dickey, *Ancient Greek Scholarship*, 87–103.

[1] See Adrian., *cat. Ps.* 50:10 for a corrupted abridgement of 19–19.1. Thdr. Mops., *Ps.* 50:10: "by 'You will let me hear' meaning, You will make me hear [$\dot{\alpha}\nu\tau\dot{\iota}\ \tau o\hat{\upsilon}\ \dot{\alpha}\kappa o\hat{\upsilon}\sigma\alpha\iota\ \pi o\iota\dot{\eta}\sigma\epsilon\iota\varsigma$]".

[2] Similarly, Thdr., *Ps.* 105:5 where the verse is glossed as follows: "We beg … to share in the joy of your new people, and be made sharers in the goodness provided them."

[3] Thdr. Mops., *Ps.* 15:11: "you set me on the paths of life—that is, you made me live [*id est vivere me fecisti*]." For the observation in Diodore, see Mariès, *Études*, 125.

[4] Thdr. Mops., *Ps.* 24:5 paraphrases this verse as follows: "as if to say, Save me, he says, 'Teach me'— that is, Cause me [*fac me*] to arrive at the knowledge of your divinity by the actual outcome of events." See Adrian., *cat. Ps.* 24:5 where he illustrates this hermeneutical principle with another verse: "Teach me to do your will" (Ps 142:10). He glosses: "For they were not ignorant of the law, but rather called [upon God], because they were not allowed to practice the law in their captivity."

[5] Thdr. Mops., *Ps.* 59:8: "By 'God spoke' he means, He uttered and pronounced [$\dot{\alpha}\nu\tau\dot{\iota}\ \tau o\hat{\upsilon}\ \dot{\epsilon}\phi\theta\dot{\epsilon}\gamma\xi\alpha\tau o$ $\kappa\alpha\dot{\iota}\ \dot{\alpha}\pi\epsilon\phi\dot{\eta}\nu\alpha\tau o$]. In many places, in fact, when he refers to God being about to act, he uses 'he spoke' or 'he will speak' as if God, like a king, is pronouncing, and things happened in the way he ordered, as, for example, in Psalm 84, 'I shall listen to what the Lord God will say' (Ps 84:9)—that is, I shall learn what he pronounces will happen in our case; likewise in Psalm 61, 'Once God has spoken' (Ps 61:12)— that is 'He has pronounced, and I know that in consequence it definitely will happen.'"

[6] See Adrian., *cat. Ps.* 61:12 for a similar interpretation: "'once' [in Ps 61:12] is posited in regard to unshakeableness, instead of 'he pronounced firmly and unchangeably.' For example, 'Once I swore in my holy place' (Ps 88:36)." We find a similar lexicography, with the same two verses, in Thdr. Mops., *Ps.* 61:12: "'Once' means 'firmly' [$T\grave{o}\ \ddot{\alpha}\pi\alpha\xi\ \dot{\alpha}\nu\tau\grave{\iota}\ \tau o\hat{\upsilon}\ \beta\epsilon\beta\alpha\dot{\iota}\omega\varsigma$]: He does not revoke his statement, he is saying, and he does not repeat his pronouncement; instead, he made one pronouncement [$\ddot{\alpha}\pi\alpha\xi$ $\dot{\alpha}\pi\epsilon\phi\dot{\eta}\nu\alpha\tau o$], and of necessity it took effect. Similarly in Psalm 88, 'Once I swore by my holy place' (Ps 88:36)" (mod.).

RECENSION 1

23(57[ε΄]). Τὸ κατὰ ἀνταπόκρισιν περὶ τοῦ παντὸς λαοῦ τὴν κοινὴν εὐπραγίαν σημαίνει<ν>· ὡς τό, **ὦ κύριε σῶσον δή, ὦ κύριε εὐόδωσον δή· εὐλογημένος ὁ ἐρχόμενος ἐν ὀνόματι κυρίου,** ὡς ἑκάστου τῶν ἐκ τοῦ λαοῦ λέγοντος· ᾧ ἐπισυνάπτει καὶ τό, **εὐλογήκαμεν ὑμᾶς ἐξ οἴκου κυρίου.**

5 **24**(58[ϛ΄]). Τὸ μὴ ἐπὶ τόπου μόνον τὸ ἐκεῖ λέγειν, ἀλλὰ καὶ ἐπὶ πραξέως· ὡς τό, **ἐκεῖ ὁδός, ἣν δείξω αὐτῷ, τὸ σωτήριόν μου,** τουτέστιν εἰς τὴν θυσίαν· ἐπὶ τιμωρίας δέ, ὡς τό, **ἐκεῖ ἔπεσον πάντες οἱ ἐργαζόμενοι τὴν ἀνομίαν.**

25(59[ζ΄]). Πολλαχοῦ δικαιοσύνην τὸ εἴτε ἐφ' ἑαυτοῦ λέγει<ν> τοῦ ἀνθρώπου, μὴ τὴν ἐκ τοῦ βίου ἀρετὴν ἑαυτοῦ μαρτυροῦντα, εἴτε δὴ καὶ τὴν 10 ἐφ' ἑτέρων ὁμοίως· ὡς τό, **εἰσάκουσον κύριε δικαιοσύνης μου·** καὶ ὅσα τοιαῦτα· ὡς ἀπολαύοντος δικαίως τῆς παρὰ τοῦ θεοῦ βοηθείας ἢ καὶ τοῦ θεοῦ ὡς δικαίως παρέχοντος.

---

3 Ps 117[118]:25–26   4 Ps 117[118]:26
6 Ps 49[50]:23 var.   7 Ps 35:13 [36:12] var.   10 Ps 16[17]:1 var.

---

2 σημαίνειν] Goessling (ex *Schlüren*), σημαίνει L
5 πραξέως] πράξεων Hoeschel Goessling (ex A)
8 λέγειν] cat. Ps. 16:1 Goessling, λέγει L
10 Πολλαχοῦ–ὁμοίως] susp. Goessling (ex *Schlüren*)
10 δικαιοσύνης] δικαιοσύνην Hoeschel

23. Signifying the collective welfare by means of a verbal reply on behalf of the whole people.[1] For example, "Save, O Lord! Give success, O Lord! Blessed is the one who comes in the name of the Lord" (Ps 117[118]:25–6), as if each individual among the people is speaking. To these words Scripture adds the reply: "We blessed you from the house of the Lord" (Ps 117[118]:26).[2]

24. Using the term[3] ἐκεῖ not only with respect to place ("there"), but also conduct.[4] For example, "the way is 'there' which I will show to him, my salvation" (Ps 49[50]:23), that is "[the way is] in sacrificing."[5] And concerning punishment, for example: "'there' all those fell who were practicing lawlessness" (Ps 35:13 [36:12]).[6]

25. In many places using "righteousness" either with respect to the speaker himself, who is *not* attesting that this virtue is derived from his own life, or indeed, similarly [using] this term with respect to other people. For example, "Listen, O Lord, to my righteousness" (Ps 16[17]:1), and all passages such as this. [Scripture speaks of "righteousness" in this way] because the person is enjoying God's help righteously, or also because God is supplying [this help] righteously.[7]

---

[1] Taking περί as "on behalf of" (BDF §229(1)).
[2] The point seems to be this: that the whole people unites to say something in unison ("We blessed you from the house of the Lord"), which is expressive of a common sentiment, and not just each person expressing the same sentiment individually on his or her own. See the related discussion in Thdr. Mops., *Ps*. 74:3.
[3] S.v. λέγω LSJ III.9.b.
[4] Thdr. Mops., *Ps*. 49:23: "The word ἐκεῖ refers often not to place but to deed [οὐκ ἐπὶ τόπου λέγει, ἀλλ' ἐπὶ πράγματος]." Theodore lists several verses with this usage: Ps 49:23; Ps 35:12–13; Ps 132:3. The first two are those Adrian here cites. See as well Diod., *Ps*. 35:13, where he cites the same two verses as Adrian, though he interprets ἐκεῖ as suggestive of action *or* person (Mariès, *Études*, 121).
[5] See Adrian., *cat. Ps.* 49:23 which offers a fuller gloss on the verse: "instead of 'I will show a way of salvation to those who do these things and who are eager to send up a sacrifice of praise [θυσίαν αἰνέσεως ἀναπέμπειν]'." Diod., *Ps.* 49:23 paraphrases this verse as follows: "ἐκεῖ taking the place of an action, in the sense, This is the way and the behavior of people for them to be saved." So also, Thdr. Mops., *Ps*. 49:23: "This, then, is the meaning of ἐκεῖ in this case as well, namely, To such a person who offers me this sacrifice and is zealous in living thankfully I show the way of my salvation—as if to say, I save such people; I confer blessings on such people."
[6] No gloss survives, but the intended sense is something like this: "*by an act of divine punishment* all those fell who were practicing lawlessness." Thdr. Mops. glosses this verse as follows: "May sinners not gain control of me, since falling victim to such punishment is the fate of sinners" (*Ps*. 49:23).
[7] See Adrian., *cat. Ps.* 16:1 where there is a longer explanation of this use of "righteousness" in Scripture. It surfaces because "the person who is wronged by some deed... will certainly enjoy God's just help by the punishment of his enemies—and this is what Scripture calls 'righteousness,' either because this person is righteously enjoying the help, or because God is supplying [it] righteously." See as well, Diodore, Theodore, and Theodoret on this verse, where all disavow that David was testifying to his own righteousness, but rather referring more restrictively to his righteous request to be protected from Saul.

RECENSION 1	RECENSION 2

ἐκ τοῦ περὶ τῶν ἰδιωμάτων τῆς
θείας γραφῆς· καὶ μάλιστα τοῦ
Δαυὶδ εἰσὶ ταῦτα·

26(60[η′]). Τὸ ἀγαπᾶν λέγει πολλαχοῦ
5 ἐπὶ τοῦ θεοῦ κατ᾽ ἐπίτασιν· ὡς τό,
ἀγαπᾷ ἐλεημοσύνην καὶ κρίσιν ὁ
κύριος· καί, **ὅτι κύριος ἀγαπᾷ**
κρίσιν· καί, **δικαιοσύνην**
ἠγάπησεν, ἀντὶ μετὰ τοῦ δικαίου
10 κρίνειν ἐσπούδακεν· καὶ τό, **ἰδοὺ γὰρ**
ἀλήθειαν ἠγάπησας.

26. Τὸ ἀγαπᾶν λέγει πανταχοῦ ἐπὶ
τοῦ θεοῦ κατ᾽ ἐπίτασιν τῆς περὶ τὸ
πρᾶγμα σπουδῆς· ὡς τό, **ὅτι δίκαιος**
κύριος καὶ δικαιοσύνας ἠγάπησεν,
ἀντὶ μετὰ τοῦ δικαίου κρίνειν
ἐσπούδακεν.

---

7   Ps 32[33]:5 var.   7   Ps 10[11]:7
8   Ps 36[37]:28
9   Ps 10[11]:7 var.
11   Ps 50:8 [51:6]

---

9 ἀντὶ μετὰ τοῦ δικαίου] R2, ἀντὶ μετὰ τοῦ   2 post γραφῆς] non interpun. X
δικαίως L, ἀντὶ τοῦ μετὰ τοῦ δικαίως H   8 ἀντὶ μετὰ] ἀντὶ τοῦ μετὰ X
Hoeschel, ἀντὶ τοῦ δικαίως Goessling

From the treatise about the peculiarities of Divine Scripture—these belong especially to David:[4]

26. In many places Scripture speaks emphatically of God "loving." For example, "The Lord loves mercy and justice" (Ps 32[33]:5);[1] and, "because the Lord loves justice" (Ps 36[37]:28).[2] And, "he loved righteousness" (Ps 10[11]:7), instead of "he is eager to rule righteously." And, "For, look, you loved truth" (Ps 50:8 [51:6]).[3]

26. Scripture everywhere speaks of God "loving" to emphasize his zeal for some thing. For example, "because the Lord is just and loved righteous deeds" (Ps 10[11]:7), instead of "he is eager to rule righteously."

---

[1] Thdr. Mops., *Ps.* 32:5 glosses as follows: "In other words, he said that loving is characteristic of him, speaking perhaps excessively [ἐκ πολλοῦ τοῦ περιόντος ἴσως λέγων]."

[2] Thdr. Mops., *Ps.* 36:28: "by 'loves' meaning 'takes care of [ἐπιμελεῖται],' since we normally take care of what we love, as it says in Psalm 32, 'The Lord loves mercy and justice' [Ps 32:15]" (mod.).

[3] See Adrian., *cat. Ps.* 50:8 for a gloss on this verse: "as if to say, 'speaking the truth because of [your] great zeal for us'." On the emphasis, exaggeration or intensity (ἐπίτασις) associated with God's love in Scripture, see Thdr. Mops., *Ps.* 67:12–13; Thdt., *Rom.* 12:8–9; *1 Cor.* 13:2–3; *Heb.* 13:1.

[4] Or: From the treatise, *About the Peculiarities of Divine Scripture*....

162   Adrian's *Introduction to the Divine Scriptures*

RECENSION 1

RECENSION 2

27(61[θ′]). Πολλάκις τὰς παραβολὰς μεταφορικῶς φράζει, ἐπὶ τὸ μείζονα τοῦ λεγομένου παραστῆσαι τὴν ἔμφασιν· ὡς τό, **τῷ ἐπιβεβηκότι ἐπὶ**
5 **τὸν οὐρανὸν τοῦ οὐρανοῦ κατὰ ἀνατολάς**, ἐκ πρώτης τε καὶ ἐξ ἀρχῆς εἰπὼν ἐκ μεταφορᾶς τοῦ τὴν ἀνατολὴν εἶναι ἀρχὴν τῆς ἡμέρας· καὶ τό, **ἀπὸ ὕψους ἡμερῶν οὐ**
10 **φοβηθήσομαι**, κἀνταῦθα γὰρ τό, **ἀπὸ ὕψους**, ἀντὶ τοῦ ἄνωθεν καὶ ἐξ ἀρχῆς· καί, **ἡ συναγωγὴ τῶν ταύρων**, ἀντὶ τοῦ παμμεγεθῶν.

27. Πολλάκις τὰς παραβολὰς μεταφορικῶς φράζει, ἐπὶ τὸ μείζονα τοῦ λεγομένου παραστῆσαι τὴν ἔμφασιν· ὡς τό, **ἀπὸ ὕψους ἡμερῶν οὐ φοβηθήσομαι**, ἀντὶ τοῦ ἄνωθεν καὶ ἐξαρχῆς, ἐπειδὴ τὸ ἀνώτερον πάντως καὶ ὑψηλότερον.

6 Ps 67:34 [68:33]
10 Ps 55:3–4 [56:2–3] var.
13 Ps 67:31 [68:30]

5 Ps 55:3–4 [56:2–3] var.

2 φράζει] R1, κράζει XYZ

27. Scripture often expresses comparisons metaphorically, in order to produce an effect that is more striking than what is meant.[1] For example, "to the one [i.e., Lord] who rides on the heaven of heaven at sunrise" (Ps 67:34 [68:33]), thereby indicating "at first" and "from the beginning" in a metaphorical manner, since the sunrise is the beginning

27. Scripture often expresses comparisons metaphorically, in order to produce an effect that is more striking than what is meant. For example, "from the height of days I shall not fear" (Ps 55:3–4 [56:2–3]), instead of "from the beginning and from the outset," since what is older is certainly also higher.[2]

---

[1] See the important discussion in Thdr. Mops., *Ps.* 55:7 where he compares the LXX with Symmachus' translation. The LXX—which Theodore thinks follows the Hebrew original more closely—pays greater attention to effect or impact (ἔμφασις) than does Symmachus who is more interested in clarity (σαφήνεια). The idea is that the LXX possesses its vividness because it makes comparisons metaphorically, i.e., they lack the particle ὡς ("like" or "as"). But these comparisons come at the cost of clarity, since they are liable to be missed by the untutored reader who presumes them to be speaking facts. Symmachus achieves clarity by avoiding metaphors. In this passage Theodore mentions two of Adrian's three verses to illustrate the vividness of the septuagintal style:

> Let one or two cases be cited by way of support of this claim. In Psalm 67, "The assembly of the bulls in the calves" [Ps 67:31]: Symmachus says, "In a gathering of immense things," and while others went along with the Hebrew meaning, he put it more clearly. Likewise also in the verse "To the one who rides on the heaven of heavens at sunrise" [Ps 67:34], Symmachus says "at first," expressing the content more clearly. Now, the reason for this is that the Hebrew, in its wish to say many things with greater effect [ἐμφατικῶς], has this practice of speaking in similes and comparisons [καὶ τοῦτο ἔχων ἰδίωμα δι' ὁμοιωμάτων καὶ παραβολῶν]. But this hardly suffices for clarity of presentation: it mentions them by citing them not as similes but as facts, as in the above verse it said "bulls" for "immense things," not saying "like bulls" but simply "bulls" (mod.).

The parallels between Theodore and Adrian are striking, as both use the same two verses to illustrate the emphatic or vivid character of scriptural language when it makes comparison metaphorically. See 38 and 49 below where Adrian again speaks about comparisons made without "like" or "as"; see the discussion of metaphor and comparison in 73.1 and 73.2, respectively. Also noteworthy is that Adrian's glosses of these two verses are derived from Symmachus' translation, though this dependence is not announced. While R1 of the *Introduction* does not call attention to the alternate Greek translations of the OT, Symmachus is occasionally mentioned in R2 (29, 33). The use of alternate translations to explain difficulties in the LXX was a common feature among Antiochene biblical scholars: see Mariès, *Études*, 105–6; Ter Haar Romeny, *Syrian in Greek Dress*, 100–106. On Theodore's assessment of the quality of the Septuagint as a translation, see Schäublin, *Untersuchungen*, 123–7.

[2] The gloss on this verse is longer in R2 than R1 and its final clause appears to be drawn from Thdr. Mops., *Ps.* 55:4: "he is saying 'from the height of the days' to mean from the beginning, from the outset, from earlier days—since what is older than us is certainly also higher than us [Ἐπειδὴ γὰρ τὸ ἀνώτερον ἡμῶν πάντως καὶ ὑψηλότερον], he used 'height of our days' instead of 'former days'" (mod.). The basic point is that a spatial concept is used in place of a temporal one—a lofty thing is an earlier thing (s.v. ἄνω [B] LSJ II.i).

RECENSION 1

of the day.[1] And, "from the height of
days I shall not fear" (Ps 55:3–4 [56:2–3]),
for also here "from the height" means
"from the beginning and from the outset."[2] And, "The assembly of the bulls"
(Ps 67:31 [68:30]), instead of "[The
assembly] of immense things."[3]

---

[1] Thdr. Mops., *Ps.* 67:34: "by 'at sunrise' he refers to what is from the beginning and at first [ἐξ ἀρχῆς καὶ τὸ ἐκ πρώτης], since the rising of the sun is the beginning of the day and no day can appear before its rising, the implication being that it is impossible to imagine anything prior to God" (mod.).

[2] Note the parallel with Thdr. Mops., *Ps.* 55:4 (the similarity is more striking in R2): "he is saying 'from the height of the days' to mean from the beginning, from the outset, from earlier days [ἀντὶ τοῦ ἄνωθεν, καὶ ἐξ ἀρχῆς, ἀπὸ τῶν ἄνω ἡμερῶν]."

[3] See Adrian., *cat. Ps.* 67:31(1) where the explanation for this turn of phrase runs as follows: "instead of 'immense things,' from the fact that bulls appear to be larger in herds of cattle." This explanation is very close to what we find in Thdr. Mops., *Ps.* 55:7.

166   Adrian's *Introduction to the Divine Scriptures*

RECENSION 1	**RECENSION 2**

28(62[ιʹ]). *Τὴν ως συλλαβὴν διχῶς λέγει ἤτοι κατὰ παραβολὴν ἢ κατὰ βεβαίωσιν· κατὰ μὲν παραβολήν· ὡς τό,* **θοῦ αὐτοὺς ὡς τροχόν, ὡς**
5 **καλάμην**· *κατὰ δὲ βεβαίωσιν· ὡς τό,* **ὡς ἀγαθὸς ὁ θεὸς τῷ Ἰσραήλ,** *ἀντὶ τοῦ εἰπεῖν σφόδρα ἀγαθός· καὶ τό,* **ἐγενήθημεν ὡσεὶ παρακεκλημένοι**· *καί,* **ἐθεασάμεθα**
10 **τὴν δόξαν αὐτοῦ, δόξαν ὡς μονογενοῦς παρὰ πατρός,** *ἀντὶ τοῦ ἀληθοῦς.*

28. *Τὸ τὴν ως συλλαβὴν διχῶς λέγειν ἤτοι κατὰ παραβολὴν ἢ κατὰ βεβαίωσιν· κατὰ μὲν παραβολήν· ὡς τό,* **ὁ θεός μου θοῦ αὐτοὺς ὡς τροχόν, ὡς καλάμην κατὰ πρόσωπον ἀνέμου**· *καὶ ὅσα τοιαῦτα· κατὰ δὲ βεβαίωσιν· ὡς τό,* **ὡς ἀγαθὸς ὁ θεὸς τῷ Ἰσραήλ,** *ἀντὶ τοῦ εἰπεῖν σφόδρα ἀγαθός· ὅθεν καὶ ὁ εὐαγγελιστὴς τῷδε χρησάμενος τῷ ἰδιώματι,* **καὶ ἐθεασάμεθα** *φησὶ* **τὴν δόξαν αὐτοῦ, δόξαν ὡς μονογενοῦς παρὰ πατρός,** *ἵνα εἴπῃ ἅτε ὁλοτελῶς μονογενοῦς.*

5 Ps 82:14 [83:13]
6 Ps 72[73]:1 var.
9 Ps 125[126]:1 var.
11 John 1:14

5 Ps 82:14 [83:13]
8 Ps 72[73]:1 var.
12 John 1:14

7 ὡς²] X p. corr. s. l., deest YZ et K₂

TRANSLATION: R1	TRANSLATION: R2

28. It uses the syllable ως in two ways, either for comparison or for strengthening.[1] For comparison: an example, "make them like (ὡς) a wheel, like (ὡς) straw" (Ps 82:14 [83:13])! For strengthening:[2] for instance, "So (ὡς) good is God to Israel" (Ps 72[73]:1)!, instead of saying "Exceedingly good."[3] And, "we became people very (ὡσεί) comforted" (Ps 125[126]:1).[4] And, "we beheld his glory, glory of the very (ὡς) only begotten One from the Father" (John 1:14), instead of "[glory] of the true [only begotten One]."[5]

28. Using the syllable ως in two ways, either for comparison or for strengthening. For comparison: an example, "My God, make them like (ὡς) a wheel, like (ὡς) straw before the wind" (Ps 82:14 [83:13])!, and all examples such as this. For strengthening: for instance, "So (ὡς) good is God to Israel" (Ps 72[73]:1)!, instead of saying "Exceedingly good." Therefore[6] also the evangelist, making use of this literary peculiarity, says: "and we beheld his glory, glory of the very (ὡς) only begotten One from the Father" (John 1:14), as if to say "since [this glory was] of a perfectly only begotten One."

---

[1] This paragraph is connected to the previous: there the absence of the particle ὡς is discussed, here its presence (ὡς and ὡσεί) is analyzed. On this twofold use of ὡς in Diodore, see Mariès, *Études*, 117.

[2] On ὡς serving as a strengthener, s.v. ὡς *Etymologicum Gudianum*: ὡς ἐπίρρημα θαυμαστικὸν ἀντὶ τοῦ λίαν· ἢ ἐπίρρημα βεβαιώσεως ("ὡς is an adverb expressing astonishment, used in place of λίαν; or it is an adverb of strengthening") [Sturz, *Etymologicum Graecae Linguae Gudianum*, 582.1–2]. On the use of lexica by Theodore, as well as the utilization of his commentary on the Psalms by later lexica, see Schäublin, *Untersuchungen*, 95–108.

[3] Thdr. Mops., *Ps.* 72:1: "meaning 'How good [ὢ πῶς ἀγαθὸς] is God in regard to Israel.' " Thdt., *Ps.* 72:1: "He uses ὡς not in a comparative sense [οὐ παραβολικῶς] but to show the high degree of goodness [τῆς ἀγαθότητος.... τὴν ὑπερβολήν]."

[4] Thdt., *Ps.* 125:1: "The word ὡς here conveys intensity [ἐπιτάσεως]: we enjoyed great satisfaction when God put an end to punishment and granted freedom to the captives."

[5] Thdr. Mops., *Jo.* 1:14 [Syr.], who paraphrases the clause as follows: "the true Only Begotten Son." A few lines later: "It is the height of madness that some have dared to press the fact that the Evangelist most certainly said, 'as of an only Son' and not just 'of an only Son.' Who can ignore that the particle *as*, if used in a comparison, refers one thing to another but, if used as in our case, gives abundance and soundness to an expressed concept? This use is certainly frequent in Scripture." See also Chrys., *hom. in Jo.* 12.1 (on John 1:14).

[6] When Adrian provides an illustration from the NT in R2 he often introduces his sentence with ὅθεν (as here) sometimes with διό (e.g., 38, 46) and once with ἔνθεντοι (45), marking the source or basis for the NT illustration ("for which reason," "therefore"). His idea appears to be that NT authors were also using these Hebrew peculiarities because they were deriving them from what they found in the OT.

RECENSION 1 | RECENSION 2

29(63[ια']). Σημαίνει τινὰ ὧν βούλεται καὶ ἀπὸ τῶν προσόντων· οἷον (64) ὡς τό, **παροικήσουσι καὶ κατακρύψουσιν**, ἵνα εἴπῃ
5 συνάγονται καὶ ἐνεδρεύουσιν, ἀπὸ τοῦ τὸν εἰς ἕτερον ἀπιόντα τόπον ἐκεῖσε πάντως παροικεῖν, τῶν οἰκείων ἐκδημοῦντα.

10

29. Σημαίνει τινὰ ὧν βούλεται καὶ ἀπὸ τῶν προσόντων· καὶ τοῦτο πολλάκις· οἷον τό, **παροικήσουσι καὶ κατακρύψουσιν**, ἵνα εἴπῃ συνάγονται καὶ ἐνεδρεύουσιν, ἀπὸ τοῦ τὸν μὲν εἰς ἕτερον συνιόντα τόπον ἐκεῖσε πάντως παροικεῖν τῶν οἰκείων ἐκδημοῦντα τόπων, τὸν δὲ ἐνεδρεύοντα ἀναγκαίως κατακρύπτεσθαι· οὕτω καὶ Σύμμαχος, **συνήγοντο** φησὶ **λάθρα καὶ τὰ ἴχνη μου παρετήρουν προσδοκῶντες τὴν ψυχήν μου·** καὶ ὅσα τοιαῦτα.

---

4 Ps 55:7 [56:6]

4 Ps 55:7 [56:6]
13 Ps 55:7 [56:6] Symm.

---

1 post τινὰ] ἀφ' + Goessling
3 post οἷον] ὡς τό + Goessling et postea lac. indic., sim. *Schlüren*
6 τοῦ τὸν] R2, τούτων L
7 πάντως] πάντων A

1 Σημαίνει] Συνάγει X
1 ὧν] τῷ X
7 πάντως] πάντας YZ

29. It signifies some of the things it means also with multiple attributes.[1] For example, "They will be foreigners and hide" (Ps 55:7 [56:6]), in order to say "they assemble themselves and lay ambushes," from the fact that the person who goes away to a different place is surely a foreigner there, because he is living in exile from his homeland.[2]

29. It signifies some of the things it means also with multiple attributes. And it does this often. For example, "They will be foreigners and hide" (Ps 55:7 [56:6]), in order to say "they assemble themselves and lay ambushes," from the fact that the person who assembles in a different place is surely a foreigner there because he is living in exile from his homeland; and this person, laying ambushes, necessarily hides. So also Symmachus says: "They assembled themselves secretly and scrutinized my tracks, expecting to have my life" (Ps 55:7 [56:6]), and all passages such as this.[3]

[1] My translation reflects the following wording: Σημαίνει τινὰ τουτῶν ἃ βούλεται... In the transmitted text the relative pronoun has been attracted from the accusative case to the case of its antecedent (genitive), and the demonstrative pronoun to which it is attracted has been omitted (Smyth §2522).

[2] This is an elliptical paragraph, but some clarification can be found at Thdr. Mops., *Ps.* 55:7: "Now we found this peculiarity used by blessed David in many other places in the Psalms as well... namely, the frequent apparent contradiction where it seems that he is saying two different things, as when it says, 'They will utter and they will speak injustice' (Ps 93:4)... It seems that he is saying two things, especially with 'and' coming in between... whereas what he is saying is one thing, 'They give voice to injustice when they speak.' Similarly, in Psalm 49, 'The Lord God of gods spoke and summoned the earth' (Ps 49:1); in our commentary we indicated that he means one thing, but there seem to be two [ὅτι ἕν ἐστιν ὃ βούλεται εἰπεῖν, δύο εἶναι δοκοῦντα]" (mod). Theodore is drawing attention to hendiadys, i.e., the expression of a single idea by two words connected with "and." This appears to be Adrian's point as well, that multiple designations can be given in Scripture, though only one thing is in view: in this case, "they will be foreigners *and* hide" refers to the same phenomenon (Mariès, *Études*, 119; Devreesse, *Essai*, 61; Schäublin, *Untersuchungen*, 133–4). Here is how Theodore glosses Ps 55:7 (the verse Adrian is discussing): the clause "they will be foreigners and hide" is not actually attributing two different things to the people in question, but the same thing: "So he is saying, 'They came together in hiding.' " Some of Theodore's explanation of "they will be foreigners" occurs in Adrian above: "By 'they are foreigners' he means 'gather together,' since it is typical of those residing as foreigners to assemble there, to live and do everything where they live—hence his reference to their gathering as 'living as foreigners,' to bring out their enthusiasm in assembling for that purpose, because from staying in that place they formed assemblies as a necessary result of dwelling and living there, and so they plotted against me" (mod.). Note that in R2 Symmachus' rendering of Ps 55:7 is provided: it turns out that at least part of this translation informs Adrian's gloss of the verse here in R1.

[3] Symmachus' rendering of the verse (supplied here in R2 but not in R1) partly informs Adrian's gloss of the verse in the LXX. For orientation to Symmachus' translation, see Marcos, *Septuagint in Context*, 123–41.

RECENSION 1	RECENSION 2

30(65[ιβ′]). Λέγει τὸ κρύψαι καὶ ἐπὶ τοῦ θεοῦ αὐτὸν φυλάξαι· ὡς τό, **κατακρύψεις αὐτοὺς ἐν ἀποκρύφῳ τοῦ προσώπου σου**, ἀντὶ τοῦ
5 φυλάξεις· καὶ τό, **ἔκρυψέ με ἐν σκηνῇ αὐτοῦ·** καὶ τό, **ὡς πολὺ τὸ πλῆθος τῆς χρηστότητός σου, κύριε**, ἧς ἔκρυψας **τοῖς φοβουμένοις σε**, ἵνα εἴπῃ ἣν φυλάσσεις τοῖς
10 φοβουμένοις σε· καί, **τῶν κεκρυμμένων σου**, ὡσανεὶ τῶν παρὰ σοῦ φυλαττομένων· καὶ ἐφ' ἡμῶν· ὡς τό, **ἐν τῇ καρδίᾳ μου ἔκρυψα τὰ λόγιά σου.**

30. Λέγει καὶ τὸ κρύψαι καὶ ἐπὶ τοῦ θεοῦ, ἀντὶ τοῦ φυλάξαι· ὡς τό, **κατακρύψεις αὐτοὺς ἐν ἀποκρύφῳ τοῦ προσώπου σου ἀπὸ ταραχῆς ἀνθρώπων**, ἀντὶ τοῦ φυλάξεις· οὐδὲν δὲ ἧττον καὶ τό, **τῶν κεκρυμμένων σου ἐπλήσθη ἡ γαστὴρ αὐτῶν**, ἵνα εἴπῃ τῶν παρὰ σοῦ φυλαττομένων εἰς ἐκδικίαν κολάσεων· ἐνίοτε δὲ καὶ ἐφ' ἡμῶν· ὡς τό, **ἐν τῇ καρδίᾳ μου ἔκρυψα τὰ λόγιά σου ὅπως ἂν μὴ ἁμάρτω σοι.**

4 Ps 30:21 [31:20]
6 Ps 26[27]:5 var.
8 Ps 30:20 [31:19]
11 Ps 16[17]:14
14 Ps 118[119]:11

5 Ps 30:21[31:20]
8 Ps 16[17]:14
12 Ps 118[119]:11

1 τὸ κρύψαι καὶ] καὶ κρύψαι τὸ Goessling (ex *Schlüren*)
2 αὐτὸν] τινὰ Goessling (ex *Schlüren*)
9 ἣν] ἧς Goessling

9 σοῦ] R1, σοὶ XYZ

30. It also calls God guarding, "hiding."[1] For example, "You will hide them in a secret place of your presence" (Ps 30:21 [31:20]), instead of "you will guard." And, "he hid me in his tent" (Ps 26[27]:5).[2] And, "how great is the magnitude of your kindness, O Lord, which you hid for those who fear you" (Ps 30:20 [31:19])!," as if to say "which you guard for those who fear you."[3] And, "with your hidden things" (Ps 16[17]:14), as if "with those things guarded by you."[4] Also with respect to us [does Scripture call guarding "hiding"]: for example, "in my heart I hid your words" (Ps 118[119]:11).[5]

30. And it speaks even of God "hiding" instead of guarding. For example, "You will hide them in a secret place of your presence away from human tumult" (Ps 30:21 [31:20]), instead of "you will guard." No less also, "their belly was filled with your hidden things" (Ps 16[17]:14), as if to say "with those things guarded by you for the purpose of inflicting punishments." Sometimes also with regard to us [does Scripture call guarding, "hiding"]: for example, "in my heart I hid your words that I might not sin against you" (Ps 118[119]:11).

---

[1] Taking αὐτόν to refer to God, and thus functioning as the subject of φυλάξαι. This is closer to the wording of R2 and Adrian., *cat. Ps.* 30:20–1: Τὸ κρύψαι ἐπὶ θεοῦ ἀντὶ τοῦ φυλάξαι εἴρηται ("hiding is said with regard to God, instead of guarding"). Schlüren and Goessling emended αὐτόν to τινά, and made it the object of the infinitive, so that the sentence reads: "It also calls guarding someone, God 'hiding'."

[2] Thdr. Mops., *Ps.* 26:5: "and 'hid' meaning 'guarded' [ἀντὶ τοῦ ἐφύλαξεν], from the invariable practice of concealment by those wishing to guard something."

[3] See Adrian., *cat. Ps.* 30:20–1 where the additional explanation for this gloss on the verse is given: "from the fact that the person, who wishes to carefully guard something, attempts to hide it."

[4] Thdr. Mops., *Ps.* 16:14: "It is, in fact, the habit of the divine Scripture to speak of God as though he were some king in whose storehouses is kept a collection of winds, snow, sanctions, and other punishments of this kind... Likewise, at this point he said 'what is hidden' in reference to their sufferings, using 'what is hidden' of the punishments on account of their being inflicted on them not at all times but when needed, from the metaphor of the contents of storehouses... This applies also to God's goodness in its being hidden and as it were kept under guard in a certain place, not always being obvious as it deserves, and displayed by God at the opportune moment, as he says also in Psalm 30, 'How great the abundance of your goodness, Lord, which you hide from those who fear you' [Ps 30:20]." See also Diod., *Ps.* 9:1.

[5] Thdt., *Ps.* 118:11: "Whoever possesses gold or silver or precious stones does not display them; instead, he conceals them inside within storerooms and chambers so as to escape the hands of burglars. Likewise, the one in possession of the wealth of virtue hides it in the soul lest by idle display the thieves of souls carry it off."

RECENSION 1	RECENSION 2

31(66[ιγ']). Λέγει καὶ κοιμᾶσθαι ἐφ᾽ ἡμῶν τὸ καταπαύεσθαι· ὡς τό, **ἐὰν κοιμηθῆτε ἀνὰ μέσον τῶν κλήρων·** καί, **ἐν εἰρήνῃ ἐπὶ τὸ αὐτὸ** 5 **κοιμηθήσομαι καὶ ὑπνώσω.**

32(67[ιδ']). Τὸν κόλπον πολλαχοῦ καὶ ἐπὶ τοῦ ἀχωρίστου λέγει· ὡς τό, **ἀπόδος τοῖς γείτοσιν ἡμῶν ἑπταπλασίονα εἰς τὸν κόλπον** 10 **αὐτῶν,** ἀντὶ τοῦ ἀχώριστον αὐτοῖς παράσχου τὴν πολυπλασίονά σου τιμωρίαν· καί, **οὗ ὑπέσχου ἐν τῷ κόλπῳ μου πολλῶν ἐθνῶν·** καί, **ἡ προσευχή μου εἰς κόλπον μου** 15 **ἀποστραφήσεται·** καί, **ἐκ μέσου τοῦ κόλπου σου εἰς τέλος·** καί, **ὁ μονογενὴς υἱός, ὁ ὢν εἰς τὸν κόλπον τοῦ πατρός, ἐκεῖνος ἐξηγήσατο.**

31. Λέγει καὶ κοιμᾶσθαι ἐφ᾽ἡμῶν τὸ καταπαύεσθαι· ὡς τό, **ἐὰν κοιμηθῆτε ἀναμέσον τῶν κλήρων,** ἀπὸ τοῦ τὸν κοιμώμενον ἀναπαύσεως ἀπολαύειν.

32. Τὸν κόλπον πολλαχοῦ καὶ ἐπὶ τοῦ ἀχωρίστου λέγει, ἀπὸ τοῦ συνῆφθαι τὸν κόλπον τοῦ οὗπερ ἐστίν· ὡς τό, **ἡ προσευχή μου εἰς κόλπον μου ἀποστραφήσεται,** ἀντὶ τοῦ ἀχώριστός μου ἔσται διὰ παντός· ταύτῃ γ᾽οὖν καὶ ὁ εὐαγγελιστὴς τὸ πρὸς τὸν πατέρα τοῦ μονογενοῦς ἀχώριστον παραστῆσαι βουλόμενος, ἐχρήσατο τῷδε τῷ ἰδιώματι, **ὁ μονογενὴς γάρ** φησιν **υἱὸς ὁ ὢν εἰς τὸν κόλπον τοῦ πατρός,** ἵνα εἴπῃ ὁ ἀχώριστος αὐτοῦ καὶ ἀδιαίρετος.

3 Ps 67:14 [68:13]
5 Ps 4:9[8]
10 Ps 78[79]:12
13 Ps 88:51 [89:50] var.
15 Ps 34[35]:13
16 Ps 73[74]:11
18 John 1:18 var.

3 Ps 67:14 [68:13]
10 Ps 34[35]:13
18 John 1:18 var.

12 σου τιμωρίαν] τιμωρίαν σου *Goessling* (ex *Schlüren*)

8 συνῆφθαι] συνῆφσθαι X
12 καί] καὶ καὶ Z
17 εἰς τὸν κόλπον] Y p. corr., ἐν τοῖς Y a. corr., ἐν τοῖς κόλποις Z
18 ὁ] deest X

31. Scripture also calls our resting "lying down." For example, "If you lie down among the lots" (Ps 67:14 [68:13]);[1] and, "peacefully I will lie down and at that moment fall asleep (Ps 4:9[8])."[2]

32. In many places Scripture also uses the word "bosom" of the notion of inseparability. For example, "Pay back sevenfold into the 'bosom' of our neighbors" (Ps 78[79]:12)!, instead of "render your multiplied punishment inseparable from them!"[3] And, "which you bore in my 'bosom' from many nations" (Ps 88:51 [89:50])!; and, "my prayer will return to my 'bosom'" (Ps 34[35]:13); and, "from the midst of your 'bosom' forever" (Ps 73[74]:11); and, "the only begotten Son, who is in the 'bosom' of the Father, who made [him] known" (John 1:18).[4]

31. Scripture also calls our resting "lying down." For example, "If you lie down among the lots" (Ps 67:14 [68:13]), from the fact that the one lying down enjoys rest.

32. In many places Scripture also uses the word "bosom" of the notion of inseparability, since the bosom is joined to the one to whom it belongs. For example, "my prayer will return to my 'bosom'" (Ps 34[35]:13), instead of "it will always be inseparable from me."[5] Thus also the evangelist uses this peculiarity, wishing to represent the inseparability of the only begotten One with regard to his Father: "for the only begotten Son," he says, "who is in the 'bosom' of the Father" (John 1:18), as if to say "the One who is inseparable and indivisible from Him."

---

[1] Thdr. Mops., *Ps.* 67:14 renders this verse similarly: "you will enjoy repose [ἀναπαύσησθε] in the land."

[2] Diod., *Ps.* 4:9: "so let it be my good fortune to enjoy peace, respite, and rest [εἰρηνεύειν καὶ ἀναπαύεσθαι καὶ ἐφησυχάζειν] in these righteous thoughts."

[3] See Adrian., *cat. Ps.* 78:12(2) for a similar text.

[4] Four of the five verses mentioned by Adrian in this paragraph occur at Thdr. Mops., *Ps.* 34:13: "It is customary with the divine Scripture to mention the 'bosom' not when referring to the actual thing called 'bosom' by us, but when wanting to suggest something inseparable and indivisible [τὸ ἀχώριστον καὶ ἡνωμένον σημαίνειν βουλομένη]" (mod.). Theodore continues, illustrating with the first verse mentioned by Adrian in this paragraph, glossing its use of bosom as follows: "Repay them the taunting, attaching it to them and making it inseparable so that taunting of them may never be abolished in return for their taunting of you." Theodore then comments on the similar uses of "bosom" in Ps 88:51 and Jn 1:18. Theodore does not mention Ps 73:11 here, nor elaborate on the term when he interprets this verse later in his commentary. See as well, Thdr. Mops., *Jo.* 1:18 [Syr.]: "According to the custom of the Holy Scriptures, our term 'bosom' indicates what is united with us because what we keep in our bosom is intimately connected with us." Illustrations from Ps 78:12 and Ps 88:51 again follow.

[5] Thdr. Mops., *Ps.* 34:13 glosses as follows: "My petition was not kept apart; it did not go ahead of me, but remained within me unseparated from me, not going ahead, not accepted."

RECENSION 1	RECENSION 2

33(68[κε′]). Ψεῦδος καλεῖ τὸ ἀβέβαιον ἢ καὶ ψεύστην· ὡς τό, **πᾶς ἄνθρωπος ψεύστης**.

33. Ψεῦδος καλεῖ τὸ ἀβέβαιον ἢ καὶ ψεύστην· ὡς τό, **ἐγὼ εἶπα ἐν τῇ ἐκστάσει μου πᾶς ἄνθρωπος ψεύστης**· οὕτω γὰρ λέγει καὶ Σύμμαχος, **πᾶς ἄνθρωπος διάψευσμα**.

34(69[κς′]). Τὸ τῷ ἐλέῳ τοῦ θεοῦ τὴν ἀλήθειαν ἐπισυνάπτειν, διὰ τὸ ἀσφαλὲς αὐτῶν καὶ ἀδιάπτωτον τοῦτο ποιεῖ<ν>· ὡς τό, **ἔλεος καὶ ἀλήθεια συνήντησαν·** καί, **τὸ ἔλεός σου καὶ ἡ ἀλήθειά σου διὰ παντὸς ἀντιλάβοιντό μου·** καί, **δυνατὸς εἶ, κύριε, καὶ ἡ ἀλήθειά σου κύκλῳ σου,** < **ἔλεος καὶ ἀλήθεια προπορεύσεται πρὸ προσώπου σου** >· καί, **ἔλεος καὶ ἀλήθειαν αὐτοῦ τίς ἐκζητήσει;**

34. Πανταχοῦ τῷ τοῦ θεοῦ ἐλέῳ ἤτοι βοηθείᾳ τὴν ἀλήθειαν ἐπισυνάπτει, διά τε τὸ ἀσφαλὲς αὐτῶν καὶ ἀδιάπτωτον· ὡς τό, **ἔλεος καὶ ἀλήθεια συνήντησαν.**

---

3 Ps 115:2 [116:11]
11 Ps 84:11 [85:10]
13 Ps 39:12 [40:11] var.
16 Ps 88:9, 15 [89:8, 14]
17 Ps 60:8 [61:7]

4 Ps 115:2 [116:11]
6 Ps 115:2 [116:11] Symm.
11 Ps 84:11 [85:10]

---

10 ποιεῖν] K₂, ποιεῖ L

33. It designates unreliability as a "lie" or even "liar." For example, "Every person is a liar" (Ps 115:2 [116:11]).[1]

33. It designates unreliability as a "lie" or even "liar." For example, "I said in my alarm, 'Every person is a liar'" (Ps 115:2 [116:11]). For so also Symmachus says: "Every person is a lie" (Ps 115:2 [116:11]).[4]

34. Linking God's "truth" to his "mercy," because this establishes their unfailing and infallible nature. For example, "Mercy and truth met" (Ps 84:11 [85:10]); and, "May your mercy and your truth support me always" (Ps 39:12 [40:11]);[2] "You are powerful, O Lord, and your truth encircles you … mercy and truth will go in front of you" (Ps 88:9, 15 [89:8, 14]); and, "Who will search out his mercy and truth" (Ps 60:8 [61:7])?[3]

34. Everywhere Scripture links God's "truth" to his "mercy" or "help" because of their unfailing and infallible nature. For example, "Mercy and truth met" (Ps 84:11 [85:10]).

---

[1] Thdt., *Ps.* 115:2: the Psalmist "calls human prosperity a lie, disappearing as quickly as possible, and lacking anything permanent."

[2] Diod., *Ps.* 39:12: "Again 'Your mercy and your truth' means, Your true loving-kindness." Thdr. Mops., *Ps.* 39:12: "provide me constantly with that true and steadfast [ἐκείνην τὴν ἀληθῆ καὶ βεβαίαν] lovingkindness of yours."

[3] Thdr. Mops., *Ps.* 60:8: "by 'mercy' and 'truth' as usual referring to the firm and true [τὴν βεβαίαν καὶ ἀληθῆ] lovingkindness of God."

[4] Theodoret attributes this translation of the verse to Aquila: *Ps.* 115:2. See also Chrys., *exp. in Ps.* 115:2. On Aquila's translation, see Marcos, *Septuagint in Context*, 109–22. On Symmachus' version of the Psalms: Busto Saiz, *La traducción de Símaco*.

RECENSION 1	RECENSION 2

35(70[ιζ´]). Τὸ νίψασθαι τὰς χεῖρας ἐπὶ τοῦ < ἢ κοινωνῆσαι ἢ > μὴ κοινωνῆσαί τινος πράγματος, ἐπειδὴ τοῦτο νενομοθέτηται τοῖς παλαιοῖς·

5 ὡς τό, **νίψομαι ἐν ἀθῴοις τὰς χεῖρας μου**· καί, **τὰς χεῖρας αὐτοῦ νίψεται ἐν τῷ αἵματι τοῦ ἁμαρτωλοῦ**, ἀντὶ τοῦ ἀθῷον ἑαυτὸν τῆς ἐκείνου τιμωρίας ἀποδείξει· οὕτω καὶ

10 Πιλᾶτος ἐποίησεν.

35. Τὸ νίψασθαι τὰς χεῖρας ἐπὶ τοῦ < ἢ κοινωνῆσαι ἢ > μὴ κοινωνῆσαί τινος πράγματος, ἐπειδὴ νενόμιστο τοῦτο τοῖς παλαιοῖς· ὡς τό, **νίψομαι ἐν ἀθῴοις τὰς χεῖρας μου**· καὶ τό, **τὰς χεῖρας αὐτοῦ νίψεται ἐν τῷ αἵματι τοῦ ἁμαρτωλοῦ**, ἀντὶ τοῦ ἀθῷον ἑαυτὸν τῆς ἐκείνου τιμωρίας ἀποδείξει· τοῦτο δὲ καὶ Πιλᾶτος φαίνεται πεποιηκὼς ἐπὶ τοῦ κυρίου.

36(71[ιη´]). Τὴν ὁμοιότητα λέγει πολλάκις, ἀντὶ τοῦ πράγματος· ὡς τό, **καὶ ὁμοιωθήσομαι τοῖς καταβαίνουσιν εἰς λάκκον**, ἀντὶ

15 τοῦ καταβήσομαι.

36. Λέγει πολλάκις τὴν πρός τι ὁμοιότητα, αὐτὸ λέγων τὸ πρᾶγμα· ὡς τό, **ἄνθρωπος ματαιότητι ὡμοιώθη**, ἀντὶ τοῦ ματαιότης ἐστί.

6 Ps 25[26]:6
7 Ps 57:11 [58:10]
10 Cf. Matt 27:24
14 Ps 27[28]:1

5 Ps 25[26]:6
7 Ps 57:11 [58:10]
10 Cf. Matt 27:24
14 Ps 143[144]:4

---

2 ἢ κοινωνῆσαι ἢ] cf. Thdr. Mops. Ps 57:11

2 ἢ κοινωνῆσαι ἢ] cf. Thdr. Mops. Ps 57:11
14 ματαιότης] ματαιότητος Z

35. [Scripture speaks of] "washing one's hands" with reference to partaking or not partaking in some matter, since this has been legislated by the ancients.[1] For example, "I shall 'wash my hands' among innocent people" (Ps 25[26]:6).[2] And, "he will 'wash his hands' in the blood of the sinner" (Ps 57:11 [58:10]), instead of "he will demonstrate that he himself is innocent of that person's punishment."[3] Pilate also acted in this way (cf. Matt 27:24).[4]

36. Scripture often says "resemblance," instead of the thing [itself]. For example, "And I will resemble those who descend into a pit" (Ps 27[28]:1), instead of "I will descend."

35. [Scripture speaks of] "washing ones hands" with reference to partaking or not partaking in some matter, since this had been practiced by the ancients. For example, "I shall 'wash my hands' among innocent people" (Ps 25[26]:6). And, "he will 'wash his hands' in the blood of the sinner" (Ps 57:11 [58:10]), instead of "he will demonstrate that he himself is innocent of that person's punishment." Pilate is also seen to have done this with regard to the Lord (cf. Matt 27:24).

36. Scripture often says "resemblance" to something, instead of mentioning the thing itself. For example, "Man resembled a vanity" (Ps 143[144]:4), instead of "he is a vanity."

---

[1] Thdr. Mops., *Ps.* 25:6: "It was a custom with the ancients, when they wanted to remove themselves from association with people of some type or other, to wash their hands [see Deut 21:1–9]." But later in his commentary he modifies his interpretation of washing the hands: "The divine Scripture usually applies 'wash' in the case of sharing or not sharing, it being the custom of the ancients to indicate whichever they intended by 'washing hands'" (*Ps.* 57:11). On this double sense of "washing," see also Diod., *Ps.* 25:6 (Mariès, *Études*, 126).

[2] Diod., *Ps.* 25:6: "'I shall wash my hands,' in fact, means sharing with the innocent [κοινωνεῖν τοῖς ἀθῴοις]: washing hands is taken in both senses in the divine Scripture, either sharing in a thing or not sharing." Thdr. Mops., *Ps.* 25:6: "shunning the others, I took care to associate with those who have a concern to avoid sin."

[3] Thdr. Mops., *Ps.* 57:11: "So here he means, 'The righteous person will be shown to have no share with them in the slaughter and death of the sinner." Thdt., *Ps.* 57:11: "Now, he 'washes his hands' . . . to show he is innocent and has no association with the other's wickedness; he is not, in fact, washing them in blood, as some suggested, but washing them of blood, for the reason of having nothing in common with him."

[4] Diod., *Ps.* 25:6; Thdr. Mops., *Ps.* 57:11; Thdt., *Ps.* 25:6.

RECENSION 1	RECENSION 2

37(72[ιθ΄]). Τὸν οὐρανὸν πολλάκις
οὐρανοὺς καλεῖ· ὡς τό, **αἰνεῖτε τὸν
κύριον ἐκ τῶν οὐρανῶν.**

37. Τὸν οὐρανὸν πληθυντικῶς
οὐρανοὺς καλεῖ· < ὡς τό, **αἰνεῖτε τὸν
κύριον ἐκ τῶν οὐρανῶν·** > ὅθεν
ἀμέλει καὶ ὁ ἀπόστολος τῷ ἰδιώματι
τούτῳ χρησάμενος ἐπὶ τοῦ, **ἡμῶν δὲ
τὸ πολίτευμα ἐν οὐρανοῖς ὑπάρχει,**
πρὸς τὸ ἑνικὸν πάλιν ἀναστρέψας, **ἐξ
οὗ** φησι **καὶ σωτῆρα ἀπεκδεχόμεθα
κύριον Ἰησοῦν.**

Τὰ δὲ καὶ πρὸς τοὺς λοιποὺς
προφήτας ἔχοντα κοινωνίαν εἴη ἂν
ταῦτα·

5

10

3 Ps 148:1

3 Ps 148:1
9 Phil 3:20

3 ὡς τό–οὐρανῶν] R1
8 καὶ] deest X
10 Τὰ] Τὰς Y

37. It often designates heaven as "heavens." For example, "Praise the Lord from the heavens" (Ps 148:1)![1]

37. It designates heaven as plural: "heavens." For example, "Praise the Lord from the heavens" (Ps 148:1)![2] Therefore, for instance, the apostle also makes use of this peculiarity in the verse, "our citizenship is in the heavens," but reverting back to the singular, says, "from which [sg.] also we eagerly await a savior, the Lord Jesus" (Phil 3:20).

The following peculiarities are also shared with the other prophets:[3]

---

[1] An example of a change of number (ἐναλλαγὴ ἀριθμοῦ), where the plural is used instead of the more appropriate singular. Diod., *Ps.* 18:2: "Now, if David referred to heaven as 'heavens,' this too is not unusual or out of keeping with Scripture, it being usual for it to speak of a single thing in the plural as many. Stating singular things as plural is a Hebrew peculiarity, especially in the case of heavenly things, either on account of their importance or also by another custom" (mod.). The same observation can be found in Thdr. Mops., *Ps.* 32:6; Polychr., *fr. Job* prol. 2 (as the sixth cause of obscurity in Scripture); Thdt., *Ps.* 18:1 and 148:4. For additional texts, see Mariès, *Études*, 114–15; Devreesse, *Essai*, 59–60, 66; Schäublin, *Untersuchungen*, 132.

[2] An illustration from an OT book, such as the one I have supplied, has almost certainly been excised in the ms tradition. Customarily in R2 when Adrian introduces an illustration from the NT with a word like ὅθεν (marking the source or basis for the NT peculiarity), the illustration has been preceded by an OT citation. I provide the example that occurs in R1.

[3] The Psalms is the only prophetic OT book cited in the preceding paragraphs. From this point on, Adrian draws upon a wider array of prophetic books, including Jeremiah and Isaiah.

RECENSION 1	RECENSION 2

38(73[κ′]). Τὰς παραβολὰς ἄνευ τοῦ ὡς λέγει πολλάκις· ὡς τό, **καὶ ἀνήγαγέ με ἐκ λάκκου ταλαιπωρίας·** καί, **ὁ ποιῶν τοὺς**
5 **ἀγγέλους αὐτοῦ πνεύματα, καὶ τοὺς λειτουργοὺς αὐτοῦ πῦρ φλέγον·** καί, **διήλθομεν διὰ πυρὸς καὶ ὕδατος·** καί, **ἀναβαίνουσιν ὄρη·** καί, **σκύμνος λέοντος Ἰούδα·** καί,
10 **γενηθήτω Δὰν ὄφις ἐφ' ὁδοῦ·** καί, **συμβοσκηθήσεται λύκος μετὰ ἀρνός·** καί, **ἐξελεύσεται ῥάβδος ἐκ τῆς ῥίζης Ἰεσσαί·** καί, **ἰδοὺ ἐγὼ ἑτοιμάζω τὸν λίθον σου ἄνθρακα·**
15 καί, **ἵπποι θηλυμανεῖς < ἐγενήθησαν >·** καί, **ὅτι πῦρ ἀνάλωσε τὰ ὡραῖα τῆς ἐρήμου·** καί, **ξύλον ζωῆς ἐστι·** καί, **ἄκανθαι φύονται ἐν χειρὶ μεθύσου·**
20 καί, **ἐστράφην εἰς ταλαιπωρίαν ἐν**

38. Τὸ τὰς παραβολὰς ἄνευ τοῦ ὡς λέγειν· ὡς τὸ παρὰ τῷ Μωυσεῖ, **σκύμνος λέοντος Ἰούδα· ἐκ βλαστοῦ, υἱέ μου, ἀνέβης,** ἀντὶ τοῦ ὡς σκύμνος λέοντος καὶ ὡς ἐκ βλαστοῦ ἀνέθηλας· διὸ καὶ ὁ θεῖος ἀπόστολος τῷδε τῷ ἰδιώματι παρακολουθήσας, **ἔπινον δέ,** ἔφη, **ἐκ πνευματικῆς ἀκολουθούσης πέτρας, ἡ δὲ πέτρα ἦν ὁ Χριστός,** ἵνα εἴπῃ ὅπερ ἡμῖν ἐν ἀπορίᾳ σωτηρίας οὖσιν ἐκ παραδόξου Χριστὸς ἐνυπῆρξεν, τοῦτο δὴ ἐκείνοις ἐν ἀμηχανίᾳ ποτὲ τυγχάνουσι παρὰ πᾶσαν προσδοκίαν ἡ κατὰ τὴν ἔρημον πέτρα· ἔτι τε αὐτὸς ὁ κύριος περὶ τῶν δωρεῶν τοῦ πνευματὸς λέγει, **ὁ πιστεύων εἰς ἐμέ, καθὼς εἶπεν ἡ γραφή, ποταμοὶ ἐκ τῆς κοιλίας αὐτοῦ ῥεύσουσιν ὕδατος ζῶντος ἀλλομένου εἰς ζωὴν**

4 Ps 39:3 [40:2]
6 Ps 103[104]:4
8 Ps 65[66]:12
8 Ps 103[104]:8
9 Gen 49:9
10 Gen 49:17
12 Isa 11:6
13 Isa 11:1
14 Isa 54:11 var.
16 Jer 5:8
17 Joel 1:19 var.
18 Prov 3:18
19 Prov 26:9 var.

4 Gen 49:9
10 1 Cor 10:4 var.

---

10 γενηθήτω Δὰν] Goessling (ex *Schlüren*), ἐγενήθη τῷ Ἀδὰμ L Hoeschel (ex AB), ἐγενήθη τῷ Δὰν Hoeschel (notae)
10 ἐφ' ὁδοῦ] Goessling, ἐφόδου L

15 τε] δὲ X a. corr.
17 λέγει] cat. Ps. 31:4(2), λέγων XYZ
19 αὐτοῦ] deest X

38. It often makes comparisons without "like" or "as" (ὡς).[1] For example, "And he lifted me up from a pit of misery" (Ps 39:3 [40:2]);[2] and, "He who makes winds his messengers, and flaming fire his ministers" (Ps 103[104]:4); and, "we passed through fire and water" (Ps 65[66]:12);[3] and, "mountains ascend" (Ps 103[104]:8); and, "Judah is a lion's cub" (Gen 49:9);[4] and, "let Dan become a serpent on the path" (Gen 49:17);[5] and, "the wolf will graze with the lamb" (Isa 11:6); and, "a rod will go out from the root of Jesse" (Isa 11:1); and, "Look, I am preparing ruby to be your stone" (Isa 54:11); and, "they became lusty stallions" (Jer 5:8); and, "because fire has consumed the beautiful things of the wilderness" (Joel 1:19);[6] and, "it is a

38. Making comparisons without "like" or "as" (ὡς). For example, the verse in Moses, "Judah is a lion's cub; from a shoot, my son, you went up" (Gen 49:9), instead of "like a lion's cub" and "like from a shoot you sprouted." Thus even the divine apostle, conforming to this peculiarity, said, "they drank from the spiritual rock that followed [them], and the rock was Christ" (1 Cor 10:4), as if to say "what Christ unexpectedly took the initiative in doing[7] for us who are in need of salvation, this the rock in the wilderness [did] beyond all expectation for those who were once in a state of helplessness."[8] And again, the Lord himself says about the gifts of the Spirit: "The one who believes in me, as the Scripture said, rivers of living

---

[1] See the related discussion in 27 and 49 (as well as the discussion of ellipsis in 66). The observation that comparisons are made by eliding ὡς is often expressed by Antiochene exegetes: see Diod., *Ps. hypoth.* 118; Thdr. Mops., *Ps.* 32:7, 54:21 and esp. the long discussion in *Ps. hypoth.* 118 where he analyzes this feature of Scripture in the context of his larger polemic against allegorists. According to Theodore, they seize upon passages that lack ὡς ("like," "as") and, reading them as expressive of facts, argue that there is no meaningful sense in them, thereby justifying an allegorical interpretation. One of the passages discussed by Theodore surfaces in Adrian below (Isa 11:6). Note also that the ninth cause of obscurity in Scripture, according to Polychronius, is that Scripture often leaves out pertinent material, like the particle ὡς. He illustrates with Ps 103:8 which is also discussed by Adrian below (Polychr., *fr. Job* prol. 2).

[2] Thdr. Mops., *Ps.* 39:3: "as though in a very deep pit."

[3] Thdr. Mops., *Ps.* 65:12: "through many and varied troubles capable of burning us up and drowning us."

[4] Diod., *fr. Gen.* 49:9 [Petit, *coisliniana Gen.* no. 299]: "He compares [παραβάλλει] [Judah's] strength with a lion." Similar observation in Gennad., *fr. Gen.* 49:9.

[5] Eus. Em., *fr. Gen.* 49:16–17 [Arm.] and *fr. Gen.* 49:16 [cat./Proc. G.]; Gennad., *fr. Gen.* 49:17.

[6] Thdr. Mops., *Joel* 1:19: "because like fire all the place is devastated."

[7] S.v. ὑπάρχω LSJ A.4.

[8] See 73.3 below where 1 Cor 10:1–4 illustrates the trope of correspondence and not metaphor, as here.

RECENSION 1	RECENSION 2

τῷ ἐμπαγῆναί μοι ἄκανθαν· καί,   αἰώνιον, ἀντὶ τοῦ ὡς ποταμοὶ
ἔπινον ἐκ πνευματικῆς   ὕδατος ζῶντος.
ἀκολουθούσης πέτρας, ἡ δὲ πέτρα ἦν
ὁ Χριστός· καί, ποταμοὶ ἐκ τῆς
5 κοιλίας αὐτοῦ ῥεύσουσιν ὕδατος
ζῶντος.

39(74[κα′]). Ἀπὸ μέλους τὴν πρᾶξιν   **39.** Τὸ ἀπὸ μέλους τὴν πρᾶξιν
ἐμφαίνει· οἷον, ἡ ἀνομία τῆς πτέρνης   ἐμφαίνειν· οἷόν ἐστι τὸ παρὰ τῷ
μου κυκλώσει με, ἀντὶ τῆς   Ἡσαΐᾳ, προσέθηκέ μοι ὠτίον,
10 πράξεώς μου· καί, αὐτοὶ τὴν   ἀντὶ τοῦ ὑπακοήν· καὶ τό, ἡ γλώσσα
πτέρναν μου φυλάξουσι· καί,   τῶν κυνῶν σου, ἀντὶ τοῦ ἡ λάψις·
ἐπτέρνισέ με ἤδη, ἀντὶ τοῦ   καὶ ὅσα τοιαῦτα.
ἐρραδιούργησε· καὶ τό, συγχέωμεν
αὐτῶν τὰς γλώσσας, ἀντὶ τοῦ
15 τὰς φωνάς· καί, προσέθηκέ μοι
ὠτίον, ἀντὶ τοῦ ὑπακοήν· καί, ἡ
γλῶσσα τῶν κυνῶν σου, ἀντὶ τοῦ
ἡ λάψις· καὶ τό, γλῶσσαν, ἣν οὐκ
ἔγνω, ἤκουσεν.

1 Ps 31[32]:4   1 John 7:38 var.
4 1 Cor 10:4 var.   9 Isa 50:4
6 John 7:38   11 Ps 67:24 [68:23]
9 Ps 48:6 [49:5]
11 Ps 55:7 [56:6]
12 Gen 27:36 var.
14 Gen 11:7 var.
16 Isa 50:4
17 Ps 67:24 [68:23]
19 Ps 80:6 [81:5]

tree of life" (Prov 3:18); and, "thorns grow in a drunkard's hand" (Prov 26:9); and, "I was turned to wretchedness when a thorn was stuck in me" (Ps 31[32]:4);[1] and, "they drank from the spiritual rock that followed [them], and the rock was Christ" (1 Cor 10:4);[2] and, "rivers of living water will flow from his heart" (John 7:38).[3]

water will flow from his heart gushing up to eternal life" (John 7:38; 4:14), instead of "like rivers of living water."[8]

39. Scripture indicates conduct by means of a body part. For instance, "the lawlessness of my heel will encircle me" (Ps 48:6 [49:5]), instead of "the lawlessness of my behavior."[4] And, "my heel they will watch" (Ps 55:7 [56:6]).[5] And, "he kicked me now" (Gen 27:36), instead of "he acted recklessly." And, "Let us confound their tongues" (Gen 11:7), instead of "[Let us confound] their bragging." And, "he gave me an ear" (Isa 50:4), instead of "[he gave me] obedience." And, "the tongue of your dogs" (Ps 67:24 [68:23]), instead of "the lapping [of your dogs]."[6] And, "A tongue he heard, which he did not know" (Ps 80:6 [81:5]).[7]

39. Indicating conduct by means of a body part. For instance, there is the passage in Isaiah, "he gave me an ear" (Isa 50:4), instead of "[he gave me] obedience." And, "the tongue of your dogs" (Ps 67:24 [68:23]), instead of "the lapping [of your dogs]." And all passages such as this.

---

[1] See Adrian., *cat. Ps.* 31:4(2) where this verse is glossed as "like a thorn." Thdr. Mops., *Ps.* 31:4: "by 'thorn' referring to the illness because of the sudden onset of pain."

[2] Note 73.3 below where 1 Cor 10:1–4 illustrates the trope of correspondence (and not metaphor, as this paragraph suggests).

[3] Adrian., *cat. Ps.* 31:4(2) glosses this verse as follows: "like rivers of living water." See also Thdr. Mops., *Jo.* 7:38 [Syr.].

[4] Thdr. Mops., *Ps.* 48:6: " 'Heel' means 'way,' since we tread ways with our heel—in other words, 'conduct,' because he everywhere refers by 'way' to conduct [ὁδὸν γὰρ πανταχοῦ καλεῖ τὴν πρᾶξιν]" (mod.).

[5] Thdr. Mops., *Ps.* 55:7: "by 'heel' he means 'way' in the sense of 'conduct [τὴν ὁδόν, ἀντὶ τοῦ τὴν πρᾶξιν], as also in Psalm 48, 'The iniquity of my heel will encircle me' [Ps 48:6]" (*Ps.* 55:7)" (mod.).

[6] This gloss is likely derived from Symmachus' translation: Theodore notes that Symmachus renders this verse as follows: "Your dogs' tongue will lap [λάψει ἡ γλῶσσα]" (*Ps.* 67:24).

[7] Theodore and Theodoret both gloss "tongue" as the divine voice (*Ps.* 80:6).

[8] Text nearly identical to most of this paragraph occurs at Adrian., *cat. Ps.* 31:4(2).

RECENSION 1   RECENSION 2

40(75[κβ′]). Τὴν ὁδὸν πολλάκις ἀντὶ
πράξεως λέγει· ὡς τό, **μακάριοι οἱ**
ἄμωμοι ἐν ὁδῷ, οἱ πορευόμενοι < **ἐν**
νόμῳ κυρίου >· καί, **ἔκρυψαν ἱερεῖς**
5 **ὁδόν,** ἵνα εἴπῃ τὴν ἑαυτῶν πρᾶξιν·
καί, **τάξατε τὰς καρδίας ὑμῶν εἰς**
τὰς ὁδοὺς ὑμῶν· καί, **ἵνα τί**
ἐπλάνησας ἡμᾶς ἀπὸ τῆς ὁδοῦ
σου· καί, **αἱ ὁδοί σου καὶ τὰ**
10 **ἐπιτηδεύματά σου ἐποίησάν σοι**
ταῦτα· καί, **ὅπως ἐάν τινας εὕρῃ**
τῆς ὁδοῦ ὄντας· καί, **ὡς ταύτην**
τὴν ὁδὸν ἐδίωξα· καί, **κατὰ τὴν**
ὁδόν, ἣν λέγουσιν αἵρεσιν, οὕτω
15 **λατρεύω.**

40. Τὸ καὶ τὴν ὁδὸν πολλάκις ἀντὶ
πράξεως λέγειν· ὡς τό, **μακάριοι**
οἱ ἄμωμοι ἐν ὁδῷ· ὅθεν καὶ ἐν
τῇ τῶν Πράξεων βίβλῳ ὁδὸν
εἰρῆσθαι τὴν κατὰ Χριστὸν
πολιτείαν εὕροι ἄν τις· ὡς τό,
ἐγένετο δὲ κατὰ τὸν καιρὸν ἐκεῖνον
τάραχος οὐκ ὀλίγος περὶ τῆς ὁδοῦ.

41(76[κγ′]). Τὴν ὑπομονὴν πολλάκις
ἀντὶ τῆς προσδοκίας λέγει ἢ καὶ τὸ
ὑπομένειν ἀντὶ τοῦ προσδοκᾶν· ὡς
τό, **καὶ νῦν τίς ἡ ὑπομονή μου, οὐχὶ**
20 **κύριος;** ἵνα εἴπῃ ἡ προσδοκία μου
καὶ ἡ ἐλπίς· καὶ τὸ παρὰ Ἰερεμίᾳ,
ὑπομονὴ Ἰσραὴλ κύριε· καί,
ὑπέμεινα συλλυπούμενον· καί,
ὑπόμεινον τὸν κύριον· καί,
25 **ὑπόμεινόν με λέγει κύριος**· καί,
ὑπομεινάντων αὐτῶν φῶς.

41. Τὸ πολλάκις τὴν ὑπομονὴν ἀντὶ
τῆς προσδοκίας λέγειν ἢ καὶ τὸ
ὑπομένειν ἀντὶ τοῦ προσδοκᾶν· ὡς
τὸ παρὰ τῷ Ἰερεμίᾳ, **ὑπομονὴ**
Ἰσραὴλ κύριε, ἀντὶ τοῦ
προσδοκία ἡμῶν· καὶ τό, **ὑπομένων**
ὑπέμεινα τὸν κύριον καὶ προσέσχε
μοι, ἀντὶ τοῦ προσεδόκησα καὶ
τῶν κατ'ἐλπίδα ἔτυχον ἀγαθῶν· καὶ
ὅσα τοιαῦτα παρ'ἑκάστῳ αὐτῶν
εὑρεθείη.

4   Ps 118[119]:1
5   Hos 6:9
7   Hag 1:5 var.
9   Isa 63:17 var.
11 Jer 4:18 var.
12 Acts 9:2
13 Acts 22:4 var.
15 Acts 24:14
20 Ps 38:8 [39:7] var.
22 Jer 14:8
23 Ps 68:21 [69:20]
24 Ps 26[27]:14; Ps 36[37]:34
25 Zeph 3:8
26 Isa 59:9

3   Ps 118[119]:1
8   Acts 19:23
20 Jer 14:8
23 Ps 39:2 [40:1]

1   καί] δὲ X
2   πράξεως] πρᾶξιν X
3   οἱ] deest X
20 post τοῦ] ἡ + YZ

40. It often uses the term "way" instead of "conduct."[1] For example, "Blessed are those who are blameless in the way, who walk in the law of the Lord" (Ps 118[119]:1).[2] And, "priests have concealed the way" (Hos 6:9), as if to say "their own conduct."[3] And, "set your hearts on your ways" (Hag 1:5)!;[4] and, "why have you led us astray from your way" (Isa 63:17)?; and, "your ways and your customs did these things to you" (Jer 4:18); and, "that if he might find any who were of the way" (Acts 9:2); and, "since I persecuted this way" (Acts 22:4); and, "according to the way, which they call a sect, so I worship" (Acts 24:14).

40. Often using the term "way" instead of "conduct." For example, "Blessed are those who are blameless in the way" (Ps 118[119]:1). Therefore also in the book of Acts one will find that conduct conforming to Christ is called a "way": for example, "at that time there occurred no small disturbance concerning the way" (Acts 19:23).

41. It often uses the term "endurance" instead of "expectation," or also "enduring" instead of "expecting." For example, "And now, who is my endurance, if not the Lord" (Ps 38:8 [39:7])?, as if to say "my expectation and hope."[5] And the verse in Jeremiah, "O Lord, you are Israel's endurance" (Jer 14:8); and, "I endured for one who sympathizes" (Ps 68:21 [69:20]); and, "endure the Lord!" (Ps 26[27]:14; 36[37]:34);[6] and, "endure me, says the Lord" (Zeph 3:8);[7] and, "they having endured light" (Isa 59:9).

41. Often using the term "endurance" instead of "expectation," or also "enduring" instead of "expecting." For example, the verse in Jeremiah, "O Lord, you are Israel's endurance," (Jer 14:8) instead of "our expectation." And, "enduring, I endured for the Lord and he inclined to me" (Ps 39:2 [40:1]), instead of "I expected and obtained good things because of hope." Examples such as these can be found in each of the biblical books.

---

[1] Thdr. Mops., *Ps.* 48:6: "because he everywhere refers by 'way' to conduct [ὁδὸν γὰρ πανταχοῦ καλεῖ τὴν πρᾶξιν]" (mod.).

[2] Diod., *Ps.* 1:1: "by 'way' referring to behavior ["Ὁδὸν γὰρ τὴν πρᾶξιν καλεῖ], like the verse, 'Blessed are the blameless in the way (Ps 118:1)' that is, in behavior." The association of "way" with πρᾶξις is ubiquitous in Diodore (Mariès, *Études*, 123); Thdr. Mops., *Ps.* 35:5; 36:18; 48:6, etc.; Thdt., *Ps.* 48:14; 138:3; *1 Cor.* 4:17.

[3] Thdr. Mops., *Os.* 6:9 takes this expression to refer to Levi and Simeon who "took the opportunity to slay them all [Shechemites, on the occasion of the rape of Dinah] at the one time for the crime committed."

[4] See Thdr. Mops., *Ag.* 1:5.

[5] Thdr. Mops., *Ps.* 38:8: "Since things of this life are of no value and so vile, he is saying, I saw fit to place all my expectation in you [εἰς σε πᾶσαν ... τὴν προσδοκίαν]" (mod.).

[6] Thdr. Mops., *Ps.* 35:34: "expect help from God."

[7] Thdr. Mops., *Soph.* 3:8: "continue looking to me, expecting from me the help I shall provide you with in good time."

RECENSION 1	RECENSION 2

42(77[κδ′]). Τὰ ἀναίτια πολλάκις ὡς
αἴτια λέγει· ὡς τό, **ὅπως ἂν βαφῇ ὁ
πούς σου ἐν αἵματι,** ἀντὶ τοῦ
ἀνάγκῃ πᾶσα· καὶ τό, **σοὶ μόνῳ**
5 **ἥμαρτον** < **ὅπως ἂν δικαιωθῇς ἐν
τοῖς λόγοις σου** >· καί, **ὅπως ἂν
ἐνδείξωμαι ἐν σοὶ τὴν δύναμίν
μου·** καί, **ὅπως ἂν γνωσθῇ ἡ
δικαιοσύνη τοῦ κυρίου·** καί, **ἐγὼ
10 εἰς κρῖμα εἰς τὸν κόσμον ἦλθον, ἵνα
οἱ μὴ βλέποντες βλέπωσι·** καὶ τό,
**νόμος δὲ παρεισῆλθεν, ἵνα πλεονάσῃ
τὸ παράπτωμα·** καί, **ἵνα πᾶν
στόμα φραγῇ·** καί, **ἵνα μὴ ἃ ἂν
15 θέλητε ταῦτα ποιῆτε.**

20

42. Τὸ τὰ ἀναίτια πολλάκις ὡς αἴτια
λέγειν· οἷόν ἐστι τό, **εἶπε κύριος ἐκ
Βασὰν ἐπιστρέψω, ἐπιστρέψω ἐν
βυθοῖς θαλάσσης, ὅπως ἂν βαφῇ ὁ
πούς σου ἐν αἵματι·** οὐ γὰρ τοὺς
Ἰσραηλίτας ἐπὶ τὸ φόνον
ἐργάσασθαι πολὺν παρήγαγεν ἐκεῖθεν
ὁ θεός, οὔτε τοῦτο ἦν ἐκείνου τὸ
αἴτιον· ἐκ δὲ τῶν ἐναντίων δι' ἐκεῖνο
τοῦτο ἐγίνετο, ἐπειδὴ γὰρ τοὺς
Ἰσραηλίτας παρήγαγεν ἀνάγκῃ πᾶσα
τῶν ἀνθισταμένων φόνον ἱκανὸν
παρακολουθήσειν· τοιοῦτο δ' ἂν
εἴη καὶ τὸ παρὰ τοῖς εὐαγγελισταῖς
ὑπὸ τοῦ κυρίου, **ἐγὼ εἰς κρίμα
ἐλήλυθα εἰς τὸν κόσμον, ἵνα οἱ μὴ
βλέποντες βλέπωσι, καὶ οἱ βλέποντες
τυφλοὶ γένωνται·** ὅθεν καὶ παρὰ
τῷ ἀποστόλῳ συνεχέστερον ἐστὶν
εὑρεῖν τὸ τοιοῦτο ἰδίωμα.

---

3 Ps 67:24 [68:23]
6 Ps 50:6 [51:4]
8 Ex 9:16 var.; Rom 9:17 var.
9 Mic 6:5 var.
11 John 9:39 var.
13 Rom 5:20
14 Rom 3:19
15 Gal 5:17 var.

5 Ps 67:23–4 [68:22–3]
13 Cf. Num 21:33–5; Deut 3:1–7
18 John 9:39 var.

---

6 ὅπως ἂν δικαιωθῇς–σου] cf. cat. Ps. 50:6, sim.
Schlüren
15 in mg. ext. L (f. 250r): Τὰ ἐκβατικῶς
ὀφείλονται λέγεσθαι, αἰτιολογικῶς λέγει, ὡς
ὁ φίλος παραγέγονεν ἵνα μὴ δὲ σήμερον
ἐργάσωμαι, deest Hoeschel (ex AB), in app. cr.
Goessling (ex CGHIJ): τὰ] ἃ, φίλος] Φίλιππος
(ex CGH), ἐργάσωμαι] -ομαι

6 τὸ] τὸ aut τῷ Y, τὸν Z
10 ἐγίνετο] ἐγένετο X cat. Ps. 67:23–4
10 γὰρ] πάντας Z, post γὰρ] πᾶσα (?) Y a. ras.
13 τοιοῦτο] τοιοῦτον YZ

42. It often speaks about things that are not responsible as if they are responsible.[1] For example, "in order that your foot may be dipped in blood" (Ps 67:24 [68:23]), instead of "acute pressure" [was responsible for your foot being dipped in blood].[2] And, "Against you alone I sinned... in order that you may be justified in your words" (Ps 50:6 [51:4]);[3] and, "in order that I might exhibit my power in you" (Ex 9:16; Rom 9:17); and, "in order that the righteousness of the Lord might be known" (Mic 6:5); and, "I came into the world for judgment, in order that the blind might see" (John 9:39);[4] and, "the law was introduced in order that sin might

42. Often speaking about things that are not responsible as if they are responsible. For example, there is the passage, "the Lord said, 'I will bring [them] back from Bashan, I will bring [them] back in the depths of the sea, in order that your foot may be dipped in blood" (Ps 67:23-4 [68:22-3]). For God did not guide the Israelites from that place in order that they might perpetrate a mass killing, nor was this [entry into the promised land] responsible for that [killing]. Exactly the opposite: this [entry into the promised land] happened *because* of that [killing], since acute pressure by their resistors guided the Israelites, so that a measured killing

---

[1] In this paragraph Adrian argues that ἵνα and ὅπως, which usually convey purpose ("in order that"), sometimes indicate result or outcome ("so that," "with the result that"). There is a moral concern expressed in this lexicography: there are cases when, if the ἵνα or ὅπως clause is read as a customary purpose clause, a problematic responsibility or causality will be attributed to the main subject.

[2] This highly abbreviated gloss comes into clearer focus with the parallel text in R2 and Adrian., *cat. Ps.* 67:23-4. The point is that God did not redeem the Israelites in order that they might slaughter their enemies; rather, the killing of enemies was caused by their own resistance to the Israelites. It was the "acute pressure" of those who resisted the Israelites during their attempted entry into the promised land that was responsible for their killing. Thdr. Mops., *Ps.* 67:24 comments similarly: "He used the term ὅπως in a peculiar manner to express result instead of responsibility [τὸ αἰτιατὸν ἀντὶ αἰτίας]: it is not that he [i.e., God] frees them so as to slay the others; on the contrary, for the sake of their [i.e., Israelites'] freedom he even slays the others when they resist" (mod.).

[3] The point here is that Israel did not sin in order that God would be shown just, but rather that God appeared as a just judge because his people sinned. See Adrian., *cat. Ps.* 50:6, where the verse is glossed: "God is justified" because "those who have had kindnesses done to them acted ungratefully." See Diod., *Ps.* 50:6: "the people did not sin against God so that God might be proven righteous in giving judgment; rather, since the people were ungrateful, as the object of their ingratitude he consequently had good reason to level a charge against the ingrates. So the conjunction ὅπως occurs here not with reference to responsibility [ἐπὶ αἰτίας]...; instead, it explains the actual consequence [ἀλλ' αὐτὴν τὴν ἀκολουθίαν], namely, that after the people sinned, God was shown to be righteous in giving judgment against them" (mod.). Thdr. Mops., *Ps.* 50:6 follows Diodore closely, but also adds that the language of causality or responsibility is introduced when Scripture wishes to underscore that "something inevitably follows what happened [τι ἀναγκαίως ἔπηται πάντως τῷ γεγενημένῳ]" (on this passage in Theodore, see Schäublin, *Untersuchungen*, 152-5).

[4] Thdr. Mops., *Jo.* 9:38 [Syr.]: "And here he indicates the consequences of these events."

RECENSION 1	RECENSION 2

43(78[κε′]). Τὴν πρᾶξιν ἀπὸ κοινωνίας σημαίνει· ὡς τό, **καὶ μετὰ παρανομούντων οὐ μὴ εἰσέλθω,** ἀντὶ τοῦ οὐ μὴ παρανομήσω· καί, 5 **μακάριος ἀνὴρ ὃς οὐκ ἐπορεύθη ἐν βουλῇ ἀσεβῶν,** ἀντὶ τοῦ οὐκ ἠσέβησε· καί, **οὐκ ἐκάθισα ἐν συνεδρίῳ παιζόντων·** καί, **εἰς βουλὴν αὐτῶν μὴ εἰσέλθοι ἡ ψυχή** 10 **μου.**

43. Τὸ ἀπὸ κοινωνίας τὴν πρᾶξιν σημαίνειν· ὡς τὸ παρὰ τῷ Ἰερεμίᾳ, **κύριε παντοκράτορ· οὐκ ἐκάθισα ἐν συνεδρίῳ αὐτῶν παιζόντων,** ἀντὶ τοῦ οὐκ ἔπαιξα· καὶ τὸ παρὰ τῷ Μωυσεῖ ὑπὸ τοῦ Ἰακώβ, **εἰς βουλὴν αὐτῶν μὴ εἰσέλθοι ἡ ψυχή μου,** ἀντὶ τοῦ μὴ τοιαῦτα βουλευσαίμην.

44(79[κϛ′]). Τὸν ὅρκον ἐπὶ τοῦ βεβαίου λέγει· ὡς τό, **ὤμοσα Δαυὶδ τῷ δούλῳ μου·** καί, **ὤμοσε κύριος τῷ Δαυὶδ ἀλήθειαν·** καί, κατ'

44. Τὸ τὸν ὅρκον τοῦ θεοῦ ἐπὶ βεβαίου λέγειν· ὡς τό, **ὤμοσα Δαυὶδ τῷ δούλῳ μου.**

---

3 Ps 25[26]:4
6 Ps 1:1
8 Jer 15:17 var.
10 Gen 49:6 var.
13 Ps 88:4 [89:3]
14 Ps 131[132]:11

4 Jer 15:16–17
7 Gen 49:6 var.
13 Ps 88:4 [89:3]

---

3 παντοκράτορ]-τωρ X
7 μὴ εἰσέλθοι] οὐκ εἰσέλθῃ X

increase" (Rom 5:20);[1] and, "in order that every mouth might be shut" (Rom 3:19);[2] and, "in order that you do not do what you want" (Gal 5:17).[3]

43. It signifies conduct by means of an association. For example, "and I will never visit with lawbreakers" (Ps 25[26]:4), instead of "I will never break the law." And, "blessed is the man who did not walk in the counsel of the impious" (Ps 1:1), instead of "blessed is the man who did not behave impiously."[4] And, "I did not sit in the assembly of mockers" (Jer 15:17); and, "may my soul not enter into their counsel" (Gen 49:6).

44. It uses "oath" with reference to reliability.[5] For example, "I confirmed by an 'oath' with my servant David" (Ps 88:4 [89:3]); and, "the Lord confirmed

would be the natural consequence[6] (cf. Num 21:33–5; Deut 3:1–7).[7] Such a peculiarity is also [spoken] by the Lord in the evangelists: "I came into the world for judgment, in order that the blind might see and those with sight might become blind" (John 9:39). Whence it is also possible to find such a peculiarity frequently in the apostle.

43. Signifying conduct by means of an association. For example, in Jeremiah: "O Lord, ruler over all! I did not sit in the assembly of mockers" (Jer 15:16–17), instead of "I did not mock." And in Moses [the words] by Jacob: "may my soul not enter into their council" (Gen 49:6), instead of "may I not deliberate such things."

44. Using an "oath" by God with reference to his reliability. For example, "I confirmed by an 'oath' with my servant David" (Ps 88:4 [89:3]).

---

[1] Thdt., *Rom.* 5:20: "Now, he employed the word ἵνα, not to touch on causes, but in a peculiar sense [Τὸ δὲ ἵνα οὐκ ἐπὶ αἰτίας τέθεικεν, ἀλλὰ κατὰ τὸ οἰκεῖον ἰδίωμα]."

[2] Thdt., *Rom.* 3:19: "He employed ἵνα in a particular sense [Τὸ ἵνα πάλιν κατὰ τὸ οἰκεῖον ἰδίωμα τέθεικεν]: it is not that the God of all gives laws and offers human beings exhortations for the purpose of rendering them liable to punishment; rather, he does it in his care for their salvation, whereas they take the opposite path and bring punishment on themselves."

[3] Thdr. Mops., *Gal.* 5:17: "For he said ἵνα not to mean cause but to indicate result [τὸ γὰρ ἵνα οὐκ ἐπὶ αἰτίας εἶπεν, ἀλλ᾽ὡς ἀκόλουθον], according to his own peculiar style" (mod.).

[4] Diod., *Ps.* 1:1: "that is, the one who was not involved [ἀμέτοχος] in ungodly purposes." Thdr. Mops., *Ps.* 1:1: "In speaking of 'counsels of the godless,' he referred likewise to the deeds of sinners."

[5] Thdt., *Ps.* 88:35: "he used 'swore an oath' for reliability [ἐπὶ τοῦ βεβαίου], since those who make promises confirm them with an oath" (mod.). Thdt., *Ps.* 118:106: "He called the firm decision of the soul [Τὴν βεβαίαν τῆς ψυχῆς κρίσιν] an 'oath' since most [human] affairs are confirmed by an oath [ὅρκῳ βεβαιοῦται]."

[6] S.v. παρακολουθέω PGL 3.

[7] See similar text at Adrian., *cat. Ps.* 67:23–4.

RECENSION 1	RECENSION 2

ἐμαυτοῦ ὤμοσα, λέγει κύριος·
καί, ὀμνύει κύριος κατὰ τῆς
ὑπερηφανίας Ἰακώβ.

45(80[κζ′]). Τὴν διάθεσιν πολλάκις
5 ἀπὸ ῥημάτων δεικνύει· ὡς τό,
εἶπον τίς ὄψεται αὐτούς; ἀντὶ τοῦ
οὕτως ἔπραττον ἅπαντα ὡσανεὶ οὐκ
ὄντος τινὸς τοῦ ἐφορῶντος· καί, **εἶπε**
γὰρ ἐν καρδίᾳ αὐτοῦ, οὐκ ἔστι
10 **θεός·** καί, **εἶπον δεῦτε καὶ**
ἐξολοθρεύσωμεν αὐτοὺς ἐξ
ἔθνους· καί, < **εἶπαν** >
κληρονομήσωμεν ἑαυτοῖς τὸ
ἁγιαστήριον τοῦ θεοῦ· καί, **εἶπον**
15 **ἐν τῇ καρδίᾳ αὐτῶν αἱ συγγένειαι**
αὐτῶν ἐπὶ τὸ αὐτό, < **δεῦτε καὶ**
κατακαύσωμεν πάσας τὰς ἑορτὰς
τοῦ θεοῦ ἀπὸ τῆς γῆς >· καί,
εἴπατε ἐν τίνι ἐφαυλίσαμεν· καί,
20 **σὺ δὲ εἶπας ἐγώ εἰμι, καὶ οὐκ ἔστιν**
ἑτέρα· καί, **σὺ δὲ εἶπας ἐν τῇ**
καρδίᾳ σου, < **εἰς τὸν οὐρανὸν**
ἀναβήσομαι, ἐπάνω τῶν ἄστρων τοῦ
οὐρανοῦ θήσω τὸν θρόνον μου >·

45. Τὸ πολλάκις ἀπὸ ῥημάτων τὴν
διάθεσιν πειρᾶσθαι δεικνῦναι εἰς
παράστασιν μᾶλλον τῆς τοῦ τρόπου
φαυλότητος· ὡς τό, **εἶπον τίς**
ὄψεται αὐτούς; ἀντὶ τοῦ οὕτως
ἔπραττον ἅπαντα ὡς ἂν εἰ οὐκ ὄντος
τινὸς τοῦ ἐφορῶντος· καὶ τὸ παρὰ
τῷ Ἡσαΐᾳ περὶ τῆς Βαβυλῶνος, **σὺ**
δὲ εἶπας ἐγώ εἰμι, καὶ οὐκ ἔστιν
ἑτέρα, ἀντὶ τοῦ οὐδεμιᾷ τῶν
πόλεων σαυτὴν παραβαλεῖν
ἠξίωσας· ἔνθεντοι καὶ ὁ κύριος
τῷδε κεχρημένος τῷ ἰδιώματι·
ὁ λέγων φησὶ **τῷ ἀδελφῷ αὐτοῦ ῥακὰ**
ἢ μωρέ, ἔνοχος ἔσται τῷ συνεδρίῳ
καὶ τῇ γεέννῃ τοῦ πυρός· τὴν οἴησιν
τῆς κατὰ ψυχὴν δῆλον ὅτι κολάζων
κρίσεως, ἀντὶ τοῦ ὁ τοσαύτῃ τῇ κατὰ
τοῦ πέλας ὑπεροψίᾳ κεχρημένος, ὡς
μήτε τοῦ τυχόντος αὐτὸν ἄξιον
ἡγεῖσθαι λόγου.

---

1 Gen 22:16
3 Amos 8:7 var.
6 Ps 63:6 [64:5] var.
10 Ps 13[14]:1 var.; Ps 52:2 [53:1] var.
12 Ps 82:5 [83:4] var.
14 Ps 82:13 [83:12]
18 Ps 73[74]:8 var.
19 Mal 1:6
21 Isa 47:10 var.
24 Isa 14:13 var.

8 Ps 63:6 [64:5] var.
13 Isa 47:10 var.
19 Matt 5:22 var.

---

5 ἀπὸ] ὑπὸ DGIJ
9 ἐν] ἐκ Hoeschel
12 εἶπαν] εἶπον + Goessling

7 φαυλότητος] φαυλοτοῦ Ζ
8 ὄψεται] ὄψονται Υ
15 ἔνθεντοι] ἔνθεν δὴ Χ
20 δῆλον ὅτι] δηλονότι Χ

the truth for David with an 'oath'" (Ps 131[132]:11); and, "by myself I confirmed an 'oath,' says the Lord" (Gen 22:16); and, "the Lord confirms an 'oath' by the pride of Jacob" (Amos 8:7).

45. It often displays a disposition through a speech. For example, "They said, 'Who will see them?'" (Ps 63:6 [64:5]), instead of "they were doing everything in this manner, as if no one was monitoring."[1] And, "for he said in his heart, 'there is no God'" (Ps 13[14]:1; Ps 52:2 [53:1]); and, "they said, 'Come and let us destroy them from being a nation'" (Ps 82:5 [83:4]); and, "they said, 'Let us seize for our own possession the sanctuary of God'" (Ps 82:13 [83:12]); and, "they said in their heart, their families together, 'Come, and let us burn all the feasts of God from off the land'" (Ps 73[74]:8); and, "you said, 'how did we despise…?'" (Mal 1:6); and, "you said, 'I am, and there is no other'" (Isa 47:10); and, "you said in your heart, 'I will ascend to heaven, I will set my throne above the stars of heaven'" (Isa 14:13); and,

45. Often attempting to display a disposition through a speech, especially to represent the wickedness of a way of life. For example, "They said, 'Who will see them?'" (Ps 63:6 [64:5]), instead of "they were doing everything in this manner, as if no one was monitoring." And the passage in Isaiah concerning Babylon: "you said, 'I am, and there is no other'" (Isa 47:10), instead of "you thought you had the privilege not to compare yourself with any of the cities." Whence also the Lord, making use of this peculiarity, says: "the one who says to his brother, 'empty-head' or 'fool,' will be liable to the council and to the hell of fire" (Matt 5:22); it is clear that Jesus is chastising the self-conceit of a soul that passes judgment, [saying the above] instead of "the one who acts with such arrogance against his neighbor, so as not to regard him as worthy of a trivial word."

---

[1] Thdr. Mops., *Mal.* 1:2: "It is normal for the divine Scripture, remember, to use the word for the event, and to indicate by a word the disposition of those doing something [τὴν φωνὴν ἐπὶ πράγματος λέγειν καὶ τὴν τῶν τι ποιούντων διάθεσιν φωνῇ σημαίνειν], as for example, They said, 'Who will see them [Ps 63:6]?', meaning 'Their attitude was that no one was observing [οὐδενὸς ἐφορῶντος] what was happening.'" See also Thdr. Mops., *Ps.* 2:3.

RECENSION 1   RECENSION 2

καί, ἐγὼ δὲ εἶπα ἐν τῇ εὐθηνίᾳ μου,
οὐ μὴ σαλευθῶ εἰς τὸν αἰῶνα·
καί, ὁ λέγων τῷ ἀδελφῷ αὐτοῦ ῥακὰ
ἢ μωρέ, ἔνοχος ἔσται τῷ συνεδρίῳ
5 καὶ τῇ γεέννῃ τοῦ πυρός· τὴν
οἴησιν τὴν κατὰ ψυχὴν δηλοῖ
κολάζων, ἀντὶ τοῦ τοσαύτῃ κατὰ τοῦ
πέλας ὑπεροψίᾳ κεχρημένος, ὡς
μηδὲ τοῦ τυχόντος αὐτὸν ἄξιον
10 ἡγεῖσθαι λόγου.

46(81[κη′]). Τὸ κακὸν ἤτοι τὴν κακίαν   **46.** Τὸ πολλαχοῦ τὸ κακὸν ἤτοι τὴν
πολλαχοῦ ἀντὶ τιμωρίας λέγει· ὡς   κακίαν ἀντὶ τιμωρίας λέγειν, ἀπὸ
τό, **ἐξαπέστειλεν εἰς αὐτοὺς ὀργὴν**   τῆς τῶν πασχόντων πρὸς αὐτὴν
θυμοῦ αὐτοῦ, < **ἀποστολὴν**   διαθέσεως· ὡς τό, **ἐξαπέστειλεν εἰς**
15 **δι᾽ ἀγγέλων πονηρῶν** >· **καί,**   **αὐτοὺς ὀργὴν θυμοῦ αὐτοῦ**
ἐγὼ ποιῶν εἰρήνην καὶ κτίζων   **ἀποστολὴν δι᾽ ἀγγέλων πονηρῶν**·
κακά, ἵνα εἴπῃ εἰρηνεύειν ἐῶν   διὸ καὶ ὁ κύριος ἐν εὐαγγελίοις,
καὶ πολεμεῖσθαι συγχωρῶν· καί,   **ἀρκετόν** φησι **τῇ ἡμέρᾳ ἡ κακία**
πρόσθες αὐτοῖς κακά, κύριε· καί,   **αὐτῆς,** ἵνα εἴπῃ ἡ ἐπ᾽ αὐτῆς
20 **κατέβη κακὰ παρὰ κυρίου·** καί,   ἐργασία μυρίων κόπων καὶ
ἐκάκωσε δὲ Σάρρα Ἅγαρ, τὴν   πόνων τοῖς ἀνθρώποις ὑπάρχει
παιδίσκην αὐτῆς· καί,   πρόξενος.

2 Ps 29:7 [30:6]   16 Ps 77[78]:49 var.
5 Matt 5:22 var.   19 Matt 6:34
15 Ps 77[78]:49
17 Isa 45:7 var.
19 Isa 26:15
20 Mic 1:12
22 Gen 16:6 var.

6 οἴησιν] οἴκησιν DGK₂IJ C a. corr.   20 ἐργασία] ἐρσασία Y
6 δηλοῖ] δῆλος Goessling (ex Schlüren)   20 μυρίων] μυρίω X
15 ἀποστολὴν–πονηρῶν] R2 Schlüren, cf. cat.
Ps. 77:49

"But I said in my prosperity, 'I shall never be shaken'" (Ps 29:7 [30:6]).[1] And, "the one who says to his brother, 'empty-head' or 'fool,' will be liable to the council and to the hell of fire" (Matt 5:22); it is clear that Jesus is chastising the soul's self-conceit, [saying the above] instead of "the one who acts[2] with such arrogance against his neighbor, so as not to regard him as worthy of a trivial word."

46. In many places Scripture uses "evil"—the adjective or noun—instead of "punishment."[3] For example, "He released upon them his anger's wrath…a dispatch of wicked angels" (Ps 77[78]:49).[4] And, "I who make peace and create evils" (Is 45:7), in order to say "I who keep the peace and permit war-making." And, "increase evils upon them, O Lord" (Is 26:15)!; and, "evils descended from the Lord" (Mic 1:12);[5] and, "Sarah did evil to

46. In many places using "evil"—the adjective or noun—instead of "punishment," because of the propensity to evil of those who suffer [punishment]. For example, "He released upon them his anger's wrath…a dispatch through wicked angels" (Ps 77[78]:49). For this reason also the Lord says in the Gospels: "sufficient for the day is its evil" (Matt 6:34), as if to say "the day's work causes people a thousand troubles and sufferings."

---

[1] See Adrian., *cat. Ps.* 29:7 where this passage is glossed as follows: "I was so well-disposed with regard to my previous success."

[2] R2 supplies the article, but it is not necessary to make the participle substantival (BDF §264(6)).

[3] As is also Adrian's custom with κακία in the *Introduction*: 2; 4.1; 4.6; 4.7. Thdt., *Jonah* 3:10: Scripture "speaks of the threat of punishment as 'evil' in that it is capable of harming and distressing us."

[4] In Adrian., *cat. Ps.* 77:49 we find the following explanation of this verse: "For Scripture does not intend to say that these are evil angels that were sent…since we know from divine Scripture that never yet have such as these been commissioned by God, but rather [this is said] with a view to the disposition [to evil] of those being punished." See Thdr. Mops., *Ps.* 77:49: "He is referring to the death of the firstborn as the work of angels (see Ex. 12:22–3)…Now, he called them 'wicked' in being wicked to those destroyed by them; the divine Scripture, in fact, never calls anything naturally wicked, since nothing can be wicked of its nature…Symmachus expressed the phrase 'of wicked angels' more clearly by saying 'angels who do evil [ἀγγέλων … κακούντων]'" (mod.). Thdt., *Ps.* 77:49: "using 'wicked' not of malice of nature or of free will but of the retribution in punishment."

[5] Thdr. Mops., *Mich.* 1:12 glosses "evils" from the Lord as "the wrath of God."

RECENSION 1	RECENSION 2

κακώσουσιν αὐτό, ἀντὶ τοῦ
κακοπαθῆσαι παρασκευάσουσι·
καί, **τὴν κληρονομίαν σου**
ἐκάκωσαν· καί, **μετανοῶν ἐπὶ**
5 **ταῖς κακίαις,** ἀντὶ τοῦ ταῖς ὑπὲρ
τῶν πλημμελημάτων τιμωρίαις· καί,
οὐκ ἔστι κακία ἐν πόλεσι· καί,
ἀρκετὸν τῇ ἡμέρᾳ ἡ κακία αὐτῆς,
ἀντὶ τοῦ εἰπεῖν ὅτι ἡ ἐπ᾽ αὐτῆς
10 ἐργασία μυρίων κόπων καὶ πόνων
τοῖς ἀνθρώποις ὑπάρχει πρόξενος.

47(82[κθ′]). Ποτήριον πολλαχοῦ ἐπὶ
τιμωρίας λαμβάνει· ὡς τό, **πῦρ καὶ**
θεῖον καὶ πνεῦμα καταιγίδος ἡ μερὶς
15 **τοῦ ποτηρίου αὐτοῦ·** καί, **ἰδοὺ**
εἴληφα ἐκ τῆς χειρός σου τὸ
ποτήριον τῆς πτώσεως· καί, **τὸ**
ποτήριον τῆς ἀδελφῆς σου
πίεσαι· καὶ ὁ κύριος, **ποτήριον**
20 **μέλλω πίνειν.**

47. Τὸ ἐπὶ τιμωρίᾳ πολλαχοῦ τὸ
ποτήριον λαμβάνειν· ὡς τὸ παρὰ τῷ
Ἰεζεκιήλ, **τὸ ποτήριον τῆς ἀδελφῆς**
σου πίεσαι τὸ βαθὺ καὶ τὸ πλατύ·
ταυτῇ γοῦν καὶ ὁ κύριος, **ποτήριόν**
φησι **μέλλω πίνειν,** περὶ τοῦ οἰκείου
πάθους.

1 Gen 15:13 var.
4 Ps 93[94]:5
5 Joel 2:13
7 Amos 3:6 var.
8 Matt 6:34
15 Ps 10[11]:6 var.
17 Isa 51:22
19 Ezek 23:32
20 Matt 20:22 var.

15 Ezek 23:32
17 Matt 20:22 var.

2 παρασκευάσουσι] -σωσι L

15 σου πίεσαι] συ πίεται Z

Hagar, her handmaid" (Gen 16:6).[1] And, "they [i.e., inhabitants of the land] will do evil to it [i.e., Abram's seed]" (Gen 15:13), instead of "they will bring [it] to suffer misfortune."[2] And, "they did evil to your heritage" (Ps 93[94]:5). And, "repenting of evils" (Joel 2:13), instead of "[repenting] of the punishments because of trespasses." And, "there are no evils in the cities" (Amos 3:6).[3] And, "sufficient for the day is its evil" (Matt 6:34), instead of saying "the day's work causes people a thousand troubles and sufferings."[4]

47. In many places Scripture takes "cup" with reference to punishment. For example, "fire and brimstone and a wind of a storm are the portion of his 'cup'" (Ps 10[11]:6);[5] and, "Look, I have taken from your hand the 'cup' of destruction" (Isa 51:22);[6] and, "you will drink the 'cup' of your sister" (Ezek 23:32); and, the Lord said, "a 'cup' I am about to drink" (Matt 20:22).

47. In many places taking "cup" with reference to punishment. For example, in Ezekiel: "you will drink the 'cup' of your sister, the deep and wide one" (Ezek 23:32). Thus also the Lord says: "a 'cup' I am about to drink" (Matt 20:22), concerning his own passion.[7]

---

[1] Thdt., *qu. in Gen.* 68: Abraham "handed the servant girl over to her [i.e., Sarah] for punishment."

[2] Thdt., *qu. in Gen.* 66: "they [i.e., Hebrews] would suffer."

[3] Thdt., *Am.* 3:6: "He calls punishment 'evil,' note, by use of a general custom: we are accustomed to call diseases, chastisements, untimely deaths, famines, wars and the like 'evils,' not because they are troublesome by nature, but because they are troublesome to human beings and the source of distress and grief" (mod.).

[4] For a longer version of this paragraph that also integrates material distinctive to the corresponding material in R2, see Adrian., *cat. Ps.* 77:49.

[5] Thdr. Mops., *Ps.* 10:6: "the whole cup, filled to overflowing, will be understood to contain heavier penalties." See as well, Thdr. Mops., *Ps.* 74:9; *Abac.* 2:16.

[6] Thdt., *Is.* 51:17–18: "It calls punishment 'cup' [Ποτήριον τὴν τιμωρίαν καλεῖ]."

[7] On the association of Jesus' death with punishment, see Nest., *hom.*; Thdt., *provid.* 10.26–37.

RECENSION 1	RECENSION 2

48(83[λ´]). Τὸ ὄνομα τὸ ἐπὶ τοῦ κυρίου ἀντὶ τοῦ ἴδιον ἔχειν λέγει· ὡς τό, γνώτωσαν ὅτι ὄνομά σοι κύριος, ἵνα εἴπῃ σὺ εἶ κύριος· καί, ἰδοὺ τὸ ὄνομα κυρίου διὰ χρόνου ἔρχεται πολλοῦ, ἀντὶ ὁ κύριος.

48. Τὸ ἐπὶ τοῦ θεοῦ τὸ ὄνομα λέγειν, ἀντὶ τοῦ ὅπέρ ἐστιν· ὡς τό, γνώτωσαν ὅτι ὄνομά σοι κύριος, ἵνα εἴπῃ ὅτι σὺ εἶ κύριος· καὶ τὸ παρὰ τῷ Ἡσαΐᾳ, ἰδοὺ τὸ ὄνομα κυρίου διὰ χρόνου ἔρχεται πολλοῦ, ἵνα εἴπῃ ὁ κύριος· καὶ ὅσα τοιαῦτα παρ' ἑκάστῳ αὐτῶν εὑρεθείη.

49(84[λα´]). Τὰς τοῦ θεοῦ τιμωρίας σχηματίζει μεταφορικῶς εἰς τὸ πῦρ καὶ ξίφος καὶ βέλη· ὡς τό, τὰ βέλη σου ἠκονημένα δυνατέ.

49. Τὸ σχηματίζειν μεταφορικῶς τοῦ θεοῦ τὰς τιμωρίας εἴς τε πῦρ καὶ ξίφος καὶ βέλη καὶ ὅσα τοιαῦτα· δι' ὧν παρ' ἡμῖν τὰς τῶν φαύλων ἀναιρέσεις γίνεσθαι συμβαίνει· ὡς τὸ παρὰ τῷ Ἀββακούμ, βολίδες σου πορεύσονται εἰς φέγγος ἀστραπῆς ὅπλων σου.

50(85[λβ´]). Τὸν ἑπτὰ ἀριθμὸν ἐπὶ πλεονασμοῦ λέγει εἴτ' οὖν ἐπὶ τελείου ἀριθμοῦ· ὡς τό, ἑπτάκις τῆς ἡμέρας, ἀντὶ τοῦ πολλάκις· καί, ἀπόδος τοῖς γείτοσιν ἡμῶν

50. Τὸ τὸν ἑπτὰ ἀριθμὸν ἐπὶ πλεονασμοῦ λέγειν ἤτ' οὖν ἐπὶ τελείου ἀριθμοῦ, ἀπὸ τοῦ τὴν ἑβδόμην ἡμέραν οἱονεὶ σφραγίδα τινὰ καὶ συμπλήρωσιν τῶν λοιπῶν

4   Ps 82:19 [83:18]
6   Isa 30:27
12 Ps 44:6 [45:5]
20 Ps 118[119]:164

3   Ps 82:19 [83:18]
6   Isa 30:27
16 Hab 3:11

1 ἐπὶ] – Goessling (ex Schlüren)

9   σχηματίζειν] μετασχηματίζειν Z a. corr.
16 εἰς φέγγος–σου] καὶ τὰ λοιπά X

48. It uses "name" in connection with "Lord," instead of [simply referring to] the abiding divine nature.[1] For example, "let them know that your name is the Lord" (Ps 82:19 [83:18])!, as if to say "[let them know that] you are the Lord." And, "look, the Lord's name is coming after a long time" (Isa 30:27), instead of "the Lord."

48. Speaking of God's "name," instead of what He is. For example, "let them know that your name is the Lord" (Ps 82:19 [83:18])!, as if to say "[let them know] that you are the Lord." And in Isaiah: "look, the Lord's name is coming after a long time" (Isa 30:27), as if to say "the Lord." Examples such as these can be found in each of the biblical books.

49. It depicts God's punishments metaphorically as "fire" and "sword" and "arrows." For example, "Your arrows are sharp, O Mighty one" (Ps 44:6 [45:5]).[2]

49. Depicting God's punishments metaphorically as "fire" and "sword" and "arrows," and many similar examples; among us it is the case that the destruction of base people occurs by these devices. For example in Habakkuk: "your arrows will go forth like the brightness of the lightning of your shields" (Hab 3:11).[5]

50. It uses the number seven with reference to abundance or the perfect number.[3] For example, "'seven' times a day" (Ps 118[119]:164), instead of "often."[4] And, "return 'sevenfold' to our

50. Using the number seven with reference to abundance or the perfect number, from the fact that the seventh day has supremacy, like a kind of boundary and completion of the other days,[6]

---

[1] This translation takes the neuter adjective ἴδιον as substantival (BDF §264(2)) and as subject of the infinitive ἔχειν, which has the sense of "keeping," "maintaining," or "continuing" (s.v. ἔχω LSJ B). Note under *PGL*, s.v. ἴδιος C.2, where this term can be used as the equivalent of nature. Hence my translation of ἴδιον ἔχειν as "the abiding divine nature." (Note the different construction in R2: ὅπέρ ἐστιν, or "what He is.") Adrian is commenting on the superfluousness of the term "name" when used in conjunction with "Lord," instead of simply having "Lord" which signifies the divine essence. Note Thdr. Mops., *Ps.* 74:2: "'And we shall call upon your name'...that is, 'We shall confess you to be Lord.'" Junillus also observes that eight scriptural terms signify the divine essence, including "Lord" (*inst.* 1.13). Finally, see 17 above for the distinction between God's nature and his activity or relationships.

[2] See 27 and 38 above for the idea of expressing something metaphorically, i.e., without ὡς. Diod., *Ps.* 44:6 glosses as follows: "His meaning is, 'Direct well-aimed words, like arrows, at the hearts of the listeners, and as a result all peoples will be subjected to you as well (using a metaphor of men wounding with arrows and subjecting the wounded)." Thdr. Mops., *Ps.* 44:6 glosses as follows: "his intention being to indicate in this the severity of the punishment [τῆς ... τιμωρίας] imposed on them by God, a sharp weapon in the heart being excruciating for a warrior."

[3] Thdr. Mops., *Mich.* 5:5: "Now it is a peculiarity [ἰδίωμα] of divine Scripture sometimes to define seven as the perfect number." See also Thdr. Mops., *Zach.* 4:2–3; *Ps.* 78:12.

[4] Thdt., *Ps.* 118:164: "Some rendered 'seven times' as 'many times.'"

[5] See the similar discussion under the trope "threat" at 73.19.

[6] Compare to Adrian., *cat. Ps.* 78:12(1), where the infinitive receives a different subject and sense: "from the fact that they [i.e., the Hebrews] regard the seventh day like...."

RECENSION 1	RECENSION 2

ἑπταπλασίονα· καί, ὑπήρεισε στύλους ἑπτά.

ἡγεῖσθαι ἡμερῶν, κατὰ τὴν τοῦ νομοθέτου διήγησιν· ὡς τό, **ἑπτάκις τῆς ἡμέρας ᾔνεσά σε,** ἀντὶ τοῦ πολλάκις.

5 **51**(86[λγ']). Περὶ τοῦ θεοῦ πολλάκις διαλέγεται, ὥσπερ ἐναλλαγὴν προσώπου ποιουμένη· ὡς τό, **ἡ δικαιοσύνη σου ὡς ὄρη θεοῦ· καί, τὰ βέλη σου ἠκονημένα, δυνατέ, ἐν**
10 **καρδίᾳ τῶν ἐχθρῶν τοῦ βασιλέως,** τοῦτέστι σοῦ τοῦ δυνατοῦ βασιλέως· καί, **κατ᾽ εἰκόνα θεοῦ ἐποίησε τὸν ἄνθρωπον·** καί, **ἔβρεξεν ὁ θεὸς εἰς Σόδομα πῦρ καὶ**
15 **θεῖον παρὰ κυρίου·** καί, **δῴη αὐτῷ κύριος εὑρεῖν ἔλεος παρὰ κυρίου·** καί, **τοῦ ὁρισθέντος υἱοῦ θεοῦ ἐξ ἀναστάσεως νεκρῶν, Ἰησοῦ Χριστοῦ τοῦ κυρίου ἡμῶν.**
20

51. Τὸ περὶ τοῦ αὐτοῦ διαλεγόμενον ὥσπερ ἐναλλαγήν τινα προσώπου ποιεῖσθαι· ὡς τό, **ἡ δικαιοσύνη σου ὡς ὄρη θεοῦ,** ἀντὶ τοῦ ὡς ὄρη σου· καὶ τὸ παρὰ τῷ Μωυσεῖ, **καὶ ἐποίησεν ὁ θεὸς τὸν ἄνθρωπον, κατ᾽ εἰκόνα θεοῦ ἐποίησεν αὐτόν,** ἀντὶ τοῦ κατ᾽ εἰκόνα ἑαυτοῦ· καὶ τὸ παρὰ τῷ Ἀμὼς πρὸς τοὺς Ἰσραηλίτας ἐκ προσώπου τοῦ θεοῦ, **κατέστρεψα ὑμᾶς, καθὼς κατέστρεψεν ὁ θεὸς Σόδομα καὶ Γόμορα,** ἵνα ἑαυτὸν ἐκ δευτέρου εἴπῃ· ὅθεν καὶ παρὰ τῷ ἀποστόλῳ ἐκ τοῦ Ἑβραϊκοῦ ἰδιώματος τὴν τοιαύτην χρῆσιν εὕροι τις ἄν· ὡς τό, **δῴη αὐτῷ κύριος εὑρεῖν ἔλεος παρὰ κυρίου ἐν ἐκείνῃ τῇ ἡμέρᾳ,** περὶ τοῦ Ὀνησιφόρου.

1 Ps 78[79]:12	2 Cf. Gen 2:1–3
2 Prov 9:1	3 Ps 118[119]:164 var.
8 Ps 35:7 [36:6] var.	8 Ps 35:7 [36:6] var.
11 Ps 44:6 [45:5] var.	11 Gen 1:27
13 Gen 1:27 var.	17 Amos 4:11
15 Gen 19:24 var.	22 2 Tim 1:18 var.
16 2 Tim 1:18 var.	
19 Rom 1:4 var.	

9 post δυνατέ] λαοὶ ὑποκάτω σου πεσοῦνται + Hoeschel	13 τῷ] τοῦ XYZ
10 post ἐχθρῶν] μου + Hoeschel	15 κατέστρεψα]-στραψα X
11 σοῦ τοῦ] τοῦ σοῦ Hoeschel (ex A)	16 κατέστρεψεν]-στραψεν X

neighbors" (Ps 78[79]:12)!; and, "[Wisdom] placed 'seven' pillars under as support" (Prov 9:1).[1]

51. Scripture often speaks about God as if it is making a change of person.[2] For example, "Your righteousness is like God's mountains" (Ps 35:7 [36:6]).[3] And, "Your arrows are sharp, O Mighty one... in the heart of the king's enemies" (Ps 44:6 [45:5]), that is "in the heart of your enemies, the powerful king." And, "he made man according to the image of God" (Gen 1:27); and, "God rained fire on Sodom and brimstone from the Lord" (Gen 19:24); and, "May the Lord grant that he find mercy from the Lord" (2 Tim 1:18); and, "who was declared to be Son of God... by resurrection from the dead, Jesus Christ, our Lord" (Rom 1:4).

according to the narrative of the lawgiver (cf. Gen 2:1–3).[4] For example, "'seven' times a day I praised you" (Ps 118[119]:164), instead of "often."

51. As if making a change of person while speaking about the same person. For example, "Your righteousness is like God's mountains" (Ps 35:7 [36:6]), instead of "like your mountains." And in Moses: "and God made man, according to the image of God He made him" (Gen 1:27), instead of "according to his own image." And in Amos [the passage addressed] to the Israelites from the point of view of God:[5] "I overthrew you, just as God overthrew Sodom and Gomorra" (Amos 4:11), as if to say "I myself" the second time. Thus also one will find in the apostle such a usage derived from this Hebrew peculiarity. For example, concerning Onesiphorus, "May the Lord grant that he find mercy from the Lord on that day" (2 Tim 1:18).

[1] See Adrian., *cat. Ps.* 78:12(1) for a lengthier dossier of biblical verses that illustrate this numerological observation.

[2] See Polychr. *fr. Job* prol. 2 where the seventh reason for obscurity in Scripture is the exchange of persons, illustrated with Gen 22:12: "Now I have known [ἔγνων] that you [i.e., Abraham] fear God," instead of "now you [i.e., Abraham] have known [ἔγνως] that you fear God." See also Eus. Em., *fr. Gen.* 22:12 [Arm./cat. 1267/Proc. G.]; Diod., *fr. Gen.* 22:12 [Petit, *coisliniana Gen. no.* 204]; Chrys., *hom. in 2 Cor.* 3.6. See Mariès, *Études*, 113, 120; Devreesse, *Essai*, 65–6; Schäublin, *Untersuchungen*, 132.

[3] Thdr. Mops., *Ps.* 35:7: "he does not mean that God's righteousness is like the mountains of another god, meaning instead 'yours'; it is a Hebrew peculiarity for the one speaking about himself to make a change of person [ἐναλλαγὴν προσώπων ποιεῖσθαι]." Theodore extends his observation to the New Testament, highlighting the same verse as Adrian will cite (Rom 1:4): Paul wrote "by resurrection from the dead," "as if to say, 'By his resurrection from the dead' " (mod.).

[4] Thdr. Mops., *Mich.* 5:5: "Now it is a peculiarity [ἰδίωμα] of divine Scripture sometimes to define seven as the perfect number... For example, 'God made heaven and earth in six days and rested on the seventh' (Gen 2:2).... This is the reason the divine Scripture refers to seven as the perfect and complete number, whereas eight, as I said, is excessive" (mod.). I take σφραγίς as a "boundary" that marks an acceptable maximum, beyond which there is inappropriate excess. S.v. σφραγίζω PGL A.8.

[5] On scriptural authors composing ἐκ προσώπου, see Schäublin, *Untersuchungen*, 85–8.

RECENSION 1	RECENSION 2

52(87[λδ′]). Τὸ πρωῒ ἐπὶ ταχυτῆτος
ἐκλαμβάνει πολλάκις· ὡς τό,
βοηθήσει αὐτῇ ὁ θεὸς τὸ πρὸς πρωῒ
πρωῒ· καὶ τό, **πρωῒ πρωῒ δώσει τὸ**
5 **κρίμα αὐτοῦ**, τουτέστιν ἐκ τοῦ
παραυτίκα· καί, **ὡς ὄρθρον**,
τουτέστιν ἀθρόον.

10

53(88[λε′]). Τὴν χαρὰν ἤτοι ζωὴν φῶς
λέγει πολλάκις καὶ τὴν λύπην ἤτοι
τὸν θάνατον σκότος, ἀπὸ < τοῦ > τοὺς
15 μὲν < ἐν > εὐθυμίᾳ διάγοντας
προβλεπτικωτέρους πῶς εἶναι ἐν τοῖς
πράγμασι, τοὺς δὲ ἐν ἀθυμίᾳ
καθεστῶτας, μηδὲ τὰ ἐν ποσὶ καθορᾶν
δύνασθαι· καὶ τῶν μὲν ζώντων εἶναι
20 τὸ βλέπειν τὸ φῶς, τοὺς δὲ
ἀποτεθνηκότας ἐν σκότει διατελεῖν·

25

52. Τὸ πολλάκις ἐπὶ ταχυτῆτος τὸ
πρωῒ ἐκλαμβάνειν· ὡς τό, **βοηθήσει**
αὐτῇ ὁ θεὸς τῷ πρὸς πρωῒ πρωΐ,
ἀντὶ τοῦ ὀξεῖαν αὐτῇ καὶ ταχεῖαν
παρέξει τὴν βοήθειαν, ἀπὸ τοῦ τὸ
εὐθυβολώτατον τῆς ἡμέρας τὸ
πρωϊνὸν εἶναι· καὶ τὸ παρὰ τῷ Ὡσηέ,
διώξωμεν τοῦ γνῶναι τὸν κύριον· ὡς
ὄρθρον ἕτοιμον εὑρίσκομεν αὐτόν,
ἀντὶ τοῦ ἀθρόον, ἀπὸ τοῦ τὸν ὄρθρον
ἅπασαν ἀθρόως καταλάμπειν τὴν γῆν.

53. Τὸ τὴν χαρὰν ἤτοι τὴν ζωὴν φῶς
λέγειν πολλάκις καὶ τὴν λύπην ἤτοι
τὸν θάνατον σκότος, ἀπὸ τοῦ τοὺς
μὲν ἐν εὐθυμίᾳ διάγοντας
προβλεπτικωτέρους εἶναι πῶς ἐν
τοῖς πράγμασι, τοὺς δὲ ἐν ἀθυμίᾳ
καθεστῶτας, μήτε τὰ ἐν ποσὶ
καθορᾶν δύνασθαι· καὶ τῶν μὲν
ζώντων εἶναι τὸ βλέπειν τὸ φῶς, τῶν
δὲ ἀποτεθνηκότων τὸ ἐν σκότῳ
διατελεῖν· ὡς τό, **ὁ θεός μου φωτιεῖς**
τὸ σκότος μου, ἀντὶ τοῦ τὴν λύπην
μου εἰς χαρὰν μετασκεύασον· καὶ
ὅσα τοιαῦτα.

4   Ps 45:6 [46:5] var.
5   Zeph 3:5 var.
6   Hos 6:3

14   τοῦ] R2 Hoeschel Goessling
15   ἐν] R2 Hoeschel Goessling
21   ἀποτεθνηκότας] Goessling (ex *Schlüren*), sim.
R2, ἀποθνήσκοντας L

3   Ps 45:6 [46:5] var.
9   Hos 6:3 var.
23   Ps 17:29 [18:28]

9   εὑρίσκομεν] εὑρίσομεν YZ
21   σκότῳ] σκότει X
24   καί] Ῠ a. ras.

52. It often takes the word "morning" with reference to swiftness.[1] For example, "God will help it 'morning after morning'" (Ps 45:6 [46:5]).[2] And, "'morning after morning' he will give his judgment" (Zeph 3:5), that is "immediately."[3] And, "as 'dawn'" (Hos 6:3), that is "all at once."

53. Scripture often calls joy or life "light," and grief or death "darkness," from the fact that those who live cheerfully are in some way more farsighted in their undertakings, whereas those who are brought into depression cannot clearly perceive everyday realities; and because seeing the light belongs to the living, while those who have died remain in darkness.

52. Often taking the word "morning" with reference to swiftness. For example, "God will help it 'morning after morning'" (Ps 45:6 [46:5]), instead of "he will furnish help for it that is swift and without delay," from the fact that daybreak is the quickest part[4] of the day. And in Hosea: "We will press on to know the Lord; we will find him ready as 'dawn'" (Hos 6:3), instead of "all at once," from the fact that the dawn illuminates the whole earth all at once.

53. Often calling joy or life "light," and grief or death "darkness," from the fact that those who live cheerfully are somehow more farsighted in their undertakings, whereas those who are brought into a state of depression cannot clearly perceive everyday realities; and because seeing the light belongs to the living, while remaining in darkness [belongs to] those who have died. For example, "My God, you will light my darkness" (Ps 17:29 [18:28]), instead of "transform my grief into joy." And all such examples.

---

[1] Thdr. Mops., *Ps.* 5:4: "In the divine Scriptures we find 'in the morning' used in three ways: it is used as an indication of speed, it refers to joy, and of course to morning time."
[2] Diod., *Ps.* 45:6: "By 'in the morning' he refers to the speed and rapid support [τὸ τάχος... καὶ τὴν ὀξυτάτην ἀντίληψιν]" (Mariès, *Études*, 124). Thdr. Mops., *Ps.* 45:6: "By 'morning,' referring to the rapidity [τὸ ταχέως], since we call the first and more rapid moment of the day 'morning'" (mod.). On the double adverb, Theodore continues: "By the repetition [of the adverb] he suggested the degree of speed." So also Thdt., *Ps.* 45:6.
[3] Thdr. Mops., *Soph.* 3:5: "the phrase 'morning after morning' referring to its great rapidity [τὴν ἄγαν ταχύτητα]" (mod.).
[4] S.v. εὐθύβολος LSJ: "throwing straight," "in a direct course."

53.1. τὴν μὲν οὖν χαρὰν ἢ ζωὴν [ἢ]
φῶς· ὡς τό, **φῶς ἀνέτειλε τῷ
δικαίῳ·** καί, **ὁ θεός μου φωτιεῖς τὸ
σκότος μου,** ἀντὶ τοῦ τὴν λύπην μου
5 εἰς χαρὰν μετασκευάσαις· καὶ τό,
**ἔσται τὸ φῶς τῆς σελήνης ὡς τὸ φῶς
τοῦ ἡλίου·** καί, **φωτίζου φωτίζου
Ἱερουσαλήμ·** καί, **ἐὰν πορευθῶ ἐν
σκότει, κύριος φωτιεῖ μοι,**
10 τοῦτέστι τοὐναντίον ἐμοῦ συμφορὰν
καὶ θλίψιν ὑφορωμένου, χαρά τις καὶ
εὐωχία ἐκ παραδόξου συνήντησε·

53.2. τὴν δὲ λύπην καὶ θάνατον
σκότος· ὡς τό, **καὶ εἶπα, ἄρα σκότος
15 καταπατήσει με, καὶ τὸ νὺξ
φωτισμὸς ἐν τῇ τρυφῇ μου·** καί,
**φόβος καὶ τρόμος ἦλθεν ἐπ' ἐμὲ καὶ
ἐκάλυψέ με σκότος·** καί, **ἔθεντό με
ἐν λάκκῳ κατωτάτῳ, ἐν σκοτεινοῖς
20 καὶ ἐν σκιᾷ θανάτου.**

3 Ps 96[97]:11
4 Ps 17:29 [18:28]
7 Isa 30:26
8 Isa 60:1
9 Mic 7:8 var.
16 Ps 138[139]:11
18 Ps 54:6 [55:5]
20 Ps 87:7 [88:6]

1 ἢ] λέγει Hoeschel Goessling
5 μετασκευάσαις] -σεις Goessling (ex Pearson
Migne)
13 καὶ θάνατον] Goessling (ex Pearson Migne),
θάνατον καὶ L
15 τὸ] – Goessling

53.1. So [Scripture calls] joy or life "light": for example, "Light dawned for the righteous" (Ps 96[97]:11). And, "My God, you will light my darkness" (Ps 17:29 [18:28]), instead of "may you transform my grief into joy."[1] And, "The light of the moon will be like the light of the sun" (Isa 30:26); and, "Shine, shine, O Jerusalem" (Isa 60:1)! And, "even if I walk in darkness, the Lord will be a light for me" (Mic 7:8), that is "while I angrily eye the calamity and affliction facing me, some joy and good cheer unexpectedly happens."[2]

53.2. And [Scripture calls] grief and death "darkness": for example, "and I said, 'So then darkness will trample me, and the night will be light in my luxury'" (Ps 138[139]:11); and, "fear and trembling came upon me and darkness covered me" (Ps 54:6 [55:5]);[3] and, "they put me in the deepest pit, in dark places and in death's shadow" (Ps 87:7 [88:6]).

---

[1] Diod., *Ps.* 17:29: "By 'darkness' he refers to the tribulations, as by 'lamp' and 'light' to assistance and support."

[2] Thdr. Mops., *Mich.* 7:8: "And so, even if I have been walking in the midst of troubles like darkness, yet God's help will come to me, brighter than light."

[3] Thdr. Mops., *Ps.* 54:6: "'And darkness overwhelmed me.' This is typical of depression [Τοῦτο τῆς ἀθυμίας ἴδιον]: when anyone despairs of salvation on account of the enormity of the dangers, one is overcome by depression as though enveloped in a kind of darkness, unable to discern present realities in due fashion."

RECENSION 1	RECENSION 2

54(89[λϛ′]). Συντέλειαν τῶν στοιχείων ὁρίζεται ἐπὶ τῶν ἀμαυρουμένων καὶ καθορᾶν μὴ συγχωρουμένων· ὡς τό, ὁ ἥλιος καὶ ἡ σελήνη
5 συσκοτάσουσι, καὶ οἱ ἀστέρες οὐ δώσουσι τὸ φέγγος αὐτῶν· καὶ κύριος δώσει φωνὴν ἀπὸ προσώπου δυνάμεως αὐτοῦ, ὅτι πολλή ἐστι σφόδρα ἡ παρεμβολὴ αὐτοῦ.
10

15

20

25

54. Τὸ ἐπὶ τῶν ἀναιρουμένων ἤτοι καθορᾶν μὴ συγχωρουμένων ὥσπερ παντελῆ τινα συντέλειαν τῶν στοιχείων ὁρίζεσθαι δοκεῖν·

54.1. ἐπὶ μὲν τῶν ἀναιρουμένων· οἷον τὸ περὶ τῶν ἐθνῶν τῶν ἐπισυναχθέντων τῇ Ἱερουσαλὴμ παρὰ τῷ Ἰωήλ, ἅπερ οὖν ἄρδην ἐπὶ τῆς κοιλάδος ὁ θεὸς τοῦ Ἰωσαφὰτ κατέστρωσεν, ἦχοι ἐξήχησαν ἐν τῇ κοιλάδι τῆς δίκης, ὁ ἥλιος καὶ ἡ σελήνη συσκοτάσουσι, καὶ οἱ ἀστέρες οὐ δώσουσι τὸ φέγγος αὐτῶν· ὁ δὲ κύριος ἐκ Σιὼν ἀνακράξεται καὶ ἐξ Ἱερουσαλὴμ δώσει φωνὴν αὐτοῦ, καὶ σεισθήσεται ὁ οὐρανὸς καὶ ἡ γῆ· ὁ δὲ κύριος φείσεται τοῦ λαοῦ αὐτοῦ καὶ ἐνισχύσει τοὺς υἱοὺς Ἰσραήλ· ἐνταῦθα γὰρ οὐχὶ τὸν ἥλιον καὶ τὴν σελήνην ἢ τοὺς ἀστέρας τοῦ οἰκείου φωτὸς στερηθήσεσθαι σημαίνει, ἀλλὰ τοῖς ἀναιρουμένοις μηκέτι

---

9 Joel 2:10–11 var.

24 Joel 3:14, 15–16 var.

---

3 post συγχωρουμένων] φωτῶν + *Goessling*
(ex *Lollin Schlüren*)

12 τῇ] τῷ X
18 οἱ ἀστέρες] τὰ ἄστρα X
18 οὐ δώσουσι] δύσουσι X
19 ὁ δὲ] καὶ X
20 ἐκ Σιὼν–ἐξ Ἱερουσαλὴμ] deest X
24 καὶ σεισθήσεται–Ἰσραήλ] καὶ τὰ λοιπά X
27 στερηθήσεσθαι] -θήσεται Z
28 τοῖς ἀναιρουμένοις] in mg. ext. m. pr. YZ,
τοὺς ἀναιρουμένους XYZ

54. It decrees the destruction of the celestial elements in regard to people who are being blinded and not permitted to see clearly.[1] For example, "The sun and the moon will grow dark, and the stars will not give their brightness. And the Lord will raise his voice ahead of his force, because his army is very great" (Joel 2:10–11).

54. Seeming to decree a total cessation, as it were, of the celestial elements, in regard to people who are sentenced to death[2] or those who are not permitted to see clearly.

54.1. In regard to people who are sentenced to death: for instance, the passage in Joel about the nations gathered together at Jerusalem, whom God utterly slew in the valley of Josaphat: "Noises have rung out in the valley of judgment.... The sun and the moon will grow dark, and the stars will not give their brightness. And the Lord will cry out from Zion and will raise his voice from Jerusalem, and the heaven and the earth will be shaken. But the Lord will spare his people and strengthen the sons of Israel" (Joel 3:14, 15–16). For here it does not indicate that the sun and the moon or the stars will be robbed of their own light, but that they will no longer thereafter be able to supply this light to those sentenced to death, after they have died.[3] Such a peculiarity also

---

[1] This paragraph presents one of the more striking differences between R1 and R2. R2 reads "or" between the two participles, whereas R1 has "and." R1 presents Adrian talking about the same thing: the destruction of celestial elements points to people being blinded (s.v. ἀμαυρόω LSJ A.3) and therefore not permitted to clearly see. In R2 there is a contrast between people who are perishing (s.v. ἀμαυρόω LSJ A) and are therefore unable to see, and weather phenomena that obscure vision so that people are not allowed to clearly see. The two sets of illustrations in R2 correspond to these two categories. R1 is likely an abridgement that simplifies the text transmitted by R2.

[2] S.v. ἀναιρέω BDAG 2 (pass.).

[3] Thdr. Mops., *Joel* 3:15: "In consequence he said that there would be no light for those sentenced to death" (mod.).

RECENSION 1	RECENSION 2
	τοῦ λοιποῦ δύνασθαι τοῦτο παρέξειν μετὰ θάνατον· τοιοῦτον ἂν εἴη καὶ τὸ παρὰ τῷ μακαρίῳ Δαυίδ, **ἔπεσε πῦρ ἐπ᾽αὐτοὺς καὶ οὐκ οἶδον τὸν ἥλιον·**
	54.2. ἐπὶ τῶν καθορᾶν μὴ συγχωρουμένων· οἷον τὸ ἐπὶ τοῦ πλήθους τῆς ἀκρίδος παρὰ τῷ Ἰωήλ, **πρὸ προσώπου αὐτοῦ συγχυθήσεται ἡ γῆ καὶ σεισθήσεται ὁ οὐρανός·** ὁ **ἥλιος καὶ ἡ σελήνη συσκοτάσουσιν, καὶ τὰ ἄστρα δύσουσι τὸ φέγγος αὐτῶν· καὶ κύριος δώσει φωνὴν αὐτοῦ πρὸ προσώπου δυνάμεως αὐτοῦ, ὅτι πολλή ἐστι σφόδρα ἡ παρεμβολὴ αὐτοῦ,** ἵνα εἴπῃ ὅτι τοσαύτη δέ τις ἔσται ἡ τῆς ἀκρίδος πληθύς, ὡς τῇ παρεκστάσει συννεφείας δίκην ἀμαυροῦν δύνασθαι τὴν τοῦ φέγγους εἰς ἡμᾶς αὐτῶν χορηγίαν· ἑτέρωθι γοῦν σαφέστερον περὶ αὐτῆς λέγων· διότι φησὶ **πάρεστιν ἡ ἡμέρα κυρίου ἐγγύς, ἡμέρα σκότους καὶ γνόφου, ἡμέρα νεφέλης καὶ ὁμίχλης·** καὶ ὅσα τοιαῦτα παρ᾽ἑκάστῳ αὐτῶν εὑρεθείη.

5 Ps 57:9 [58:8] var.
17 Joel 2:10–11 var.
25 Joel 2:1–2 var.

3 ἔπεσε] ἔχεσε Χ
10 σεισθήσεται] συστήσεται ΧΥΖ
11 σελήνη] γῆ Χ
17 καὶ τὰ ἄστρα–ἡ παρεμβολὴ αὐτοῦ] καὶ τὰ λοιπά Χ
19 παρεκστάσει] παρεστάστει Χ
21 αὐτῶν] αὐτοὺς Χ
27 ἡμέρα νεφέλης–εὑρεθείη] καὶ τὰ τοιαῦτα Χ

occurs in blessed David: "Fire fell on them and they did not see the sun" (Ps 57:9 [58:8]).[1]

54.2. In regard to people who are not permitted to see clearly: for example, the passage in Joel about the locust swarm: "the earth will be disturbed before it and the heaven will be shaken; the sun and the moon will grow dark, and the stars will lose[2] their brightness. And the Lord will raise his voice ahead of his force, because his army is very great" (Joel 2:10–11), as if to say that the locust swarm will be something like this, since in a state of confusion,[3] in the manner of a clouded sky, it will be powerful enough to obscure the abundance of their [i.e., the celestial bodies'] brightness for us.[4] In another passage, speaking more clearly about the locust swarm, Scripture says: "for the day of the Lord is near, a day of darkness and gloom, a day of cloud and mist" (Joel 2:1–2).[5] Examples such as these can be found in each of the biblical books.

---

[1] Thdr. Mops., *Ps.* 57:9: "The phrase 'did not see the sun' means that they perished, they were destroyed, since it is the fate of the dead no longer to enjoy the sun's light."

[2] S.v. δύω *GELS* 2.

[3] S.v. παρέκστασις *PGL*: "spurious ecstasy." No reference to this rare term in LSJ. Note the reference in the footnote below to "confusion" (σύγχυσις) at Thdr. Mops., *Joel* 2:10.

[4] Thdr. Mops., *Joel* 2:10: "the prophet is in the habit of saying many things by way of hyperbole for greater impact on his listeners, since, no matter what the words are, they pale before the events. It is clear in this case, too, that he is not describing the elements being troubled and changed; instead, since it is typical of people caught up in troubles to adjust in many cases their ways of thought to their present state of need, so here he means, 'They will be filled with confusion when he comes on earth; it seems to those suffering such things at his hands that heaven moves and the sun, moon, and stars no longer shine, since the severity of the troubles robs the sufferers of the sense of light.'"

[5] Thdr. Mops., *Joel* 2:1–2: "the day threatened by God will be with us, capable of filling everyone with darkness and gloom so that it is impossible to see everything, once shrouded in cloud and mist."

RECENSION 1	RECENSION 2

55(90[λζ´]). Τὴν ἐπὶ τῶν ἀνθρωπίνων κακῶν συγχώρησιν τοῦ θεοῦ ὡς πρᾶξιν αὐτοῦ λέγει, ἐπειδὴ κωλῦσαι δυνάμενος τοῦτο οὐ ποιεῖ· ὡς τό, **μὴ**
5 **ἐκκλίνῃς τὴν καρδίαν μου εἰς λόγους πονηρίας**· [καί, μὴ ἐκκλίνῃς ἐν ὀργῇ ἀπὸ τοῦ δούλου σου]· καί, **ἐξέκλινας τὰς τρίβους ἡμῶν ἀπὸ τῆς ὁδοῦ σου**· καί, **ἰδοὺ ἐγὼ πλανῶ**
10 **αὐτήν**, περὶ τῆς Ἰερουσαλήμ· καί, **τί ἐπλάνησας ἡμᾶς κύριε ἀπὸ τῆς ὁδοῦ σου, ἐσκλήρυνας τὰς καρδίας ἡμῶν, τοῦ μὴ φοβεῖσθαι σε**; καί, **σκληρύνων σκληρυνῶ τὴν καρδίαν**
15 **φαραὼ καὶ τῶν θεραπόντων αὐτοῦ**· καί, **παρέδωκεν αὐτοὺς ὁ θεὸς εἰς ἀδόκιμον νοῦν**.

55. Τὸ τὴν ἐπὶ τῶν κακῶν τοῦ θεοῦ συγχώρησιν ὡς πρᾶξιν αὐτοῦ λέγειν, ἐπεὶ κωλῦσαι δυνάμενος τοῦτο οὐ ποιεῖ· οἷόν ἐστι τό, **μὴ ἐκκλίνῃς τὴν καρδίαν μου εἰς λόγους πονηρίας**, ἀντὶ τοῦ μὴ συγχωρήσῃς τοῦτο γενέσθαι· καὶ τό, **ἐξέκλινας τὰς τρίβους ἡμῶν ἀπὸ τῆς ὁδοῦ σου**· καὶ τὸ παρὰ τῷ Ὡσηὲ περὶ τῆς Ἰερουσαλήμ, **ἰδοὺ ἐγὼ πλανῶ αὐτὴν καὶ τάξω αὐτὴν ὡς ἔρημον**· ὅθεν καὶ ὁ ἀπόστολος ἐν τῇ πρὸς Ῥωμαίους, **παρέδωκεν αὐτούς** φησιν **εἰς ἀδόκιμον νοῦν ὁ θεός, ποιεῖν τὰ μὴ καθήκοντα**, καί, **παρέδωκεν αὐτοὺς εἰς πάθη ἀτιμίας, τοῦ ἀτιμάζεσθαι τὰ σώματα αὐτῶν ἐν αὐτοῖς**.

6 Ps 140[141]:4
7 Ps 26[27]:9
9 Ps 43:19 [44:18]
10 Hos 2:16[14]
13 Isa 63:17 var.
16 Ex 14:4, 5, 17 var.
17 Rom 1:28

6 Ps 140[141]:4
9 Ps 43:19 [44:18]
12 Hos 2:14 var.
15 Rom 1:28 var.
17 Rom 1:26 var.
18 Rom 1:24

7 καί–σου] – Goessling (ex Schlüren)

5 ἐκκλίνῃς] ἐκκλίνεις X
6 εἰς λόγους πονηρίας] καὶ τὰ λοιπά X
11 ὡς] εἰς X
13 ἐν τῇ] deest Z
17 τὰ] τοὺς Y a. corr. m. pr.
18 αὐτοῖς] ἑαυτοῖς Z

55. It speaks of God's consent to human evils as if it were his deed, because although he is able to prevent [these], he does not do it.[1] For example, "do not turn my heart to evil words" (Ps 140[141]:4). And, "you diverted our paths from your way" (Ps 43:19 [44:18]);[2] and speaking of Jerusalem, "Look, I will lead her astray" (Hos 2:16[14]);[3] and, "Why, O Lord, did you lead us astray from your path, hardening our hearts so that we would not fear you" (Isa 63:17)?; and, "By hardening I will harden the heart of Pharaoh and his servants" (Ex 14:4, 5, 17); and, "God gave them up to a degenerate mind" (Rom 1:28).

55. Speaking of God's consent to evils as if it were his deed, because although he is able to prevent [these], he does not do this.[4] For example: "do not turn my heart to evil words" (Ps 140[141]:4), instead of "do not allow this to happen." And, "you diverted our paths from your way" (Ps 43:19 [44:18]). And the passage about Jerusalem in Hosea: "Look, I will lead her astray and make[5] her a wilderness" (Hos 2:14). Therefore also the apostle, in his letter to the Romans, says: "God gave them up to a degenerate mind, to do things unbecoming" (Rom 1:28); and, "he gave them up to degrading passions" (Rom 1:26), "to the degrading of their bodies among themselves" (Rom 1:24).

---

[1] See 73.12 in R2 on the role of divine consent to Job's sufferings.

[2] Thdr. Mops., *Ps.* 43:19: "'You diverted' means, 'You allowed us to suffer this as well [ὅτι παθεῖν συνεχώρησας τοιαῦτα]'" (mod.).

[3] Thdr. Mops., *Os.* 2:16 glosses as follows: "I shall surrender her to captivity."

[4] Cf. 73.13 below on how the trope of σχηματισμός is designed to convey God's consent to evil in the case of Job's sufferings.

[5] S.v. τάσσω GELS 3.

RECENSION 1

56(91[λη´]). Τὸ δυνατὸν τοῦ θεοῦ διὰ τῆς πράξεως πολλάκις λέγει· ὡς τό, ὁ ἐπιβλέπων ἐπὶ τὴν γῆν, καὶ ποιῶν αὐτὴν τρέμειν· καί, ὁ ἀπειλῶν τῇ θαλάσσῃ καὶ ξηραίνων αὐτὴν καὶ πάντας τοὺς ποταμοὺς ἐξερημῶν· καί, ἔστη, καὶ ἐσαλεύθη ἡ γῆ· ἐπέβλεψε, καὶ ἐτάκη ἔθνη.

5 **57**(92[λθ´]). Πολλαχοῦ τὴν σάρκα λέγει

57.1. ἤτοι ἐπ᾽ αὐτῆς τῆς φύσεως· ὡς τό, ἔθεντο τὰς σάρκας τῶν ὁσίων σου τοῖς θηρίοις τῆς γῆς·

57.2. ἢ ἐπὶ φαυλότητος· ὡς τό, οὐ μὴ καταμείνῃ τὸ πνεῦμα μου ἐν τοῖς ἀνθρώποις τούτοις, διὰ τὸ εἶναι αὐτοὺς σάρκας·

10 **57.3.** καὶ ἐπὶ θνητότητος· ὡς τό, καὶ ἐμνήσθη ὅτι σάρξ εἰσι, πνεῦμα πορευόμενον· καί, πᾶσα σὰρξ χόρτος· καὶ ὁ ἀπόστολος, εἰ γὰρ καὶ ἐγνώκαμεν κατὰ σάρκα Χριστόν, ἵνα εἴπῃ θνητόν· καί, ἐν ταῖς ἡμέραις τῆς σαρκὸς αὐτοῦ· καί, σὰρξ καὶ αἷμα βασιλείαν θεοῦ οὐ κληρονομήσουσι· καί, ὃ δὲ νῦν ζῶ ἐν σαρκί, ἐν πίστει ζῶ·

15 **57.4.** ἐπὶ συγγενείας δέ, ὡς παρὰ τῷ Ὡσηέ, σάρξ μου ἐξ αὐτῶν· καί, ἰδοὺ ὀστά σου καὶ σάρκες σου ἡμεῖς, χθὲς καὶ τρίτην ἡμέραν· καί, ἀδελφοί μου ὑμεῖς, < ὀστά μου καὶ σάρκες μου ὑμεῖς >· καί, οὐχὶ ὀστοῦν μου καὶ σάρξ μου σύ; πρὸς τὸν Ἀμεσσά· καί, εἴ πως παραζηλώσω μου τὴν σάρκα.

20 **58**(93[μ´]). Τὸν υἱὸν ἀντὶ τοῦ ἄνθρωπος λέγει· < ὡς τό >, τί ἐστιν ἄνθρωπος, ὅτι μιμνῄσκῃ αὐτοῦ ἢ υἱὸς ἀνθρώπου, ἀντὶ τοῦ ἄνθρωπος· καί, υἱὲ ἀνθρώπου, ἀντὶ τοῦ ἄνθρωπε· < οὕτω καὶ περὶ ζῴων· > καί, σκύμνος λέοντος, ἀντὶ τοῦ

---

2 Ps 103[104]:32   3 Nah 1:4 var.   4 Hab 3:6 var.
7 Ps 78[79]:2 var.   9 Gen 6:3 var.   11 Ps 77[78]:39
11 Isa 40:6   12 2 Cor 5:16 var.   13 Heb 5:7
14 1 Cor 15:50 var.   14 Gal 2:20   15 Hos 9:12
16 2 Kgdms 5:1–2 [2 Sam 5:1–2] var.   17 2 Kgdms 19:13 [2 Sam 19:12]
18 2 Kgdms 19:14 [2 Sam 19:13]   19 Rom 11:14   21 Ps 8:5[4]
21 Ezek 2:1, *passim*; Dan 8:17   22 *Fortasse* Nah 2:12[11]

---

4 ante ἔστη] κατὰ πόδας αὐτοῦ + Hoeschel Goessling
9 τούτοις] om. Hoeschel
17 ὀστά μου–ὑμεῖς] + Schlüren
20 post υἱὸν] ἀνθρώπου + Goessling (ex Lollin Schlüren)
20 ὡς τό] + Goessling
22 οὕτω καὶ περὶ ζῴων·] vel sim.

56. Scripture often proclaims God's power through an activity. For example, "He who gazes upon the earth and causes it to tremble" (Ps 103[104]:32); and, "he who threatens the sea and dries it up and makes desolate all the rivers" (Nah 1:4); and, "he stood, and the earth shook; he gazed, and the nations melted away" (Hab 3:6).

57. It often uses the term "flesh":[1]

57.1. either of the organism itself, as in, "they placed…the 'flesh' of your saints for the beasts of the earth" (Ps 78[79]:2);

57.2. or of badness, as in "my spirit will not remain among these people…since they are 'flesh'" (Gen 6:3);[2]

57.3. and of mortality, as in, "and he remembered that they are 'flesh,' a passing breath" (Ps 77[78]:39); and, "all 'flesh' is grass" (Isa 40:6). And the apostle [writes], "for if we also knew Christ according to the 'flesh'" (2 Cor 5:16), that is "the mortal [Christ]."[3] And, "in the days of his 'flesh'" (Heb 5:7);[4] and, "'flesh' and blood will not inherit the kingdom of God" (1 Cor 15:50);[5] and, "but that which I now live in 'flesh,' I live in faith" (Gal 2:20);[6]

57.4. and of kinship, as in Hosea: "my 'flesh' from them" (Hos 9:12);[7] and, "behold, we are your bones and your 'flesh,' yesterday and on the third day" (2 Kgdms 5:1–2 [2 Sam 5:1–2]); and, "You are my brothers, you are my bones and my 'flesh'" (2 Kgdms 19:13 [2 Sam 19:12]); and [spoken] to Amessa, "are you not my bone and my 'flesh'?" (2 Kgdms 19:14 [2 Sam 19:13]); and, "in order to provoke my 'flesh' to jealousy" (Rom 11:14).

58. It speaks of "son" instead of a "man." For example, "what is man, that you are mindful of him, or the son of man?" (Ps 8:5[4]), instead of "man." And, "son of man" (Ezek 2:1, *passim*; Dan 8:17) instead of "man." So also of animals: and, "cub

---

[1] See Adrian., *cat. Ps.* 78:2 for a similar dossier of biblical passages that illustrate the variable use of σάρξ. On the ambiguous use of σάρξ in Scripture, note Thdr. Mops., *Gal.* 5:13.

[2] Diod., *fr. Gen.* 6:3–4 [Deconinck no. 20]: σάρξ is glossed as ἁμαρτία. Also see Thdr. Mops., *Gal.* 5:19–21.

[3] Thdt., *2 Cor.* 5:16: "having learned that death was destroyed by the Lord's death, we now realize no human being is mortal. I mean, even if Christ had a body that was subject to suffering, yet after the passion he made it incorruptible and immortal."

[4] Thdt., *Heb.* 5:7: "'Days of flesh' means the time of mortality, namely, when he had a mortal body."

[5] Thdt., *1 Cor.* 15:50: "By 'flesh and blood' he refers to mortal nature; it is impossible for it, mortal as it is, to attain the heavenly kingdom."

[6] Thdr. Mops., *Gal.* 2:20: "He [Paul] customarily uses 'flesh' to mean mortality." Also see Thdr. Mops., *Gal.* 3:3; 4:29. Thdt., *Gal.* 2:20: "in this mortal life I prefigure the immortal life and see it through faith."

[7] Thdr. Mops., *Os.* 9:12 glosses as follows: "admittedly, my feeling for them was formerly so great that I considered myself one of them."

RECENSION 1

λέων· καί, ὡς πρόβατον ἐπὶ σφαγὴν ἤχθη, καὶ ὡς ἀμνὸς ἐναντίον τοῦ κείροντος αὐτὸν ἄφωνος.

59(94[μα′]). Πολλαχῶς κέχρηται τῇ τοῦ πνεύματος προσηγορίᾳ ἤτοι ἐπὶ προαιρέσεως ἢ ἐπὶ χαρίσματος ἢ ἐπὶ ἀγγέλου ἢ ἐπὶ ψυχῆς ἢ ἐπὶ φωνῆς ἢ ἐπὶ
5 ἀέρος·

59.1. ἐπὶ μὲν προαιρέσεως τοῦ θεοῦ· ὡς τό, **ἐποιήσατε συνθήκας, οὐ διὰ τοῦ πνεύματός μου,** ἀντὶ προαιρέσεως· καὶ τό, **μεταβαλεῖ τὸ πνεῦμα αὐτοῦ,** ἀντὶ προαίρεσιν· τῆς δὲ ἐφ᾽ ἡμῶν· ὡς τό, **καὶ πνεῦμα εὐθὲς ἐγκαίνισον ἐν τοῖς ἐγκάτοις,** τουτέστι προαίρεσιν· καί, **οὐκ ἐπιστώθη**
10 **μετὰ τοῦ θεοῦ τὸ πνεῦμα αὐτῆς,** ἤγουν ἡ προαίρεσις· καί, **πνεύματι πορνείας ἐπλανήθησαν·** καί, **Ἐφραὶμ πονηρὸν πνεῦμα·** καί, **ὅτι μὴ εὑρεθῇ πνεῦμα ἕτερον ἐν αὐτῷ·** καί, **νῦν δεδεμένος τῷ πνεύματι πορεύομαι εἰς Ἰερουσαλήμ·** καὶ ὁ κύριος, **μακάριοι οἱ πτωχοὶ τῷ πνεύματι·**

59.2. ἐπὶ δὲ χαρίσματος· ὡς τό, **καὶ πνεύματι ἡγεμονικῷ στήριξόν με·**
15 καί, **πνεῦμα σοφίας καὶ συνέσεως, πνεῦμα βουλῆς καὶ ἰσχύος, πνεῦμα γνώσεως καὶ εὐσεβείας, πνεῦμα φόβου θεοῦ ἐμπλήσει αὐτόν·** καί, δισσῶς **ἐλθέτω τὸ πνεῦμα σου ἐπ᾽ ἐμέ·** καὶ ὁ ἀπόστολος πνεῦμα τὸ χάρισμα πολλαχοῦ φησίν· οἷον, **τὸ πνεῦμα μὴ σβέννυτε·**

59.3. ἐπὶ δὲ ἀγγέλου· ὡς τό, **καὶ ἦλθεν ἐπ᾽ ἐμὲ πνεῦμα, καὶ ἀνέλαβέ με, καὶ**
20 **ἐξῆρεν·**

2 Isa 53:7   7 Isa 30:1 var.   8 Hab 1:11 var.
9 Ps 50:12 [51:10]   10 Ps 77[78]:8   11 Hos 4:12
11 Hos 12:2[1]   12 Num 14:24 var.   13 Acts 20:22 var.
13 Matt 5:3   14 Ps 50:14 [51:12] var.   16 Isa 11:2–3 var.
17 4 Kgdms 2:9 [2 Kgs 2:9] var.   18 1 Thess 5:19   20 Ezek 2:2

7 τό] τότε Goessling

of a lion" (perhaps Nah 2:12[11]), instead of "lion."[1] And, "like a sheep he was led to slaughter, and like a lamb is silent before the one shearing it" (Isa 53:7).

59. It often makes use of the term "spirit" either with reference to will, or a gift, or an angel, or soul, or voice, or wind.

59.1. Of God's will: for example, "you made covenants, not through my 'spirit'" (Isa 30:1), instead of "[not through my] will." And, "he will alter his 'spirit'" (Hab 1:11), instead of "will."[2] And of our will: for example, "and renew an upright 'spirit' within me!" (Ps 50:12 [51:10]), that is "[renew an upright] will."[3] And, "its 'spirit' was not faithful to God" (Ps 77[78]:8), that is to say "[its] will."[4] And, "they were led astray by a 'spirit' of fornication" (Hos 4:12);[5] and, "Ephraim is an evil 'spirit'" (Hos 12:2[1]);[6] and, "since another 'spirit' was not found in him" (Num 14:24);[7] and, "now bound in my 'spirit' I am going to Jerusalem" (Acts 20:22); and the Lord [says], "blessed are the poor in 'spirit'" (Matt 5:3).

59.2. Of a gift: for example, "with a guiding 'spirit' support me" (Ps 50:14 [51:12]);[8] and, "a 'spirit' of wisdom and understanding, the 'spirit' of counsel and strength, a 'spirit' of knowledge and piety, a 'spirit' of the fear of God will fill him" (Isa 11:2–3); "let your 'spirit' come twice upon me" (4 Kgdms 2:9 [2 Kings 2:9]). And the apostle often affirms that "spirit" is gift: for example, "do not quench the 'spirit'" (1 Thess 5:19).[9]

59.3. Of an angel: for example, "and a 'spirit' came upon me, and took me up, and lifted up" (Ezek 2:2).[10]

[1] Thdr. Mops., *Nah.* 2:12: "by 'cubs' referring to the same thing, namely, the lions."
[2] Thdr. Mops., *Abac.* 1:11: "God will alter his wrath against us."
[3] Diod., *Ps.* 50:12: "by an 'upright πνεῦμα' meaning a sound free will [προαίρεσιν ἀγαθήν]." Thdr. Mops., *Ps.* 50:12: "that is, 'Fill me completely with good thoughts, an upright mind, a good will [πλήρωσον καλῶν λογισμῶν, ὀρθῆς διανοίας, ἀγαθῆς προαιρέσεως]. By πνεῦμα he refers to free will [τὴν προαίρεσιν], not only here but also elsewhere."
[4] Thdr. Mops., *Ps.* 77:8: "with πνεῦμα meaning free will [ἡ προαίρεσις]."
[5] Thdr. Mops., *Os.* 4:12: "adopting the attitude of a prostitute [πορνικῇ χρησάμενοι γνώμῃ]."
[6] Thdr. Mops., *Os.* 12:1, comments as follows: "as if to say, a depraved will, by πνεῦμα Scripture referring in many places to will [πνεῦμα γὰρ πολλαχοῦ καλεῖ τὴν προαίρεσιν]" (mod.). Then Theodore illustrates with Hos 4:12, Ps 50:12, and Num 14:24, all passages also here in the *Introduction*.
[7] See Thdr. Mops., *Ps.* 50:12.
[8] For a gloss on this verse, see Adrian., *cat. Ps.* 50:14: "as if to say, establish me [κατάστησόν με] again over the first kingdom and its rule." Similar language in Thdr. Mops., *Ps.* 50:14: "make me so strong [κατάστησον ἰσχυρόν] as not only to be freed from captivity and removed from the present servitude, but also to lead and control others. He spoke of 'a guiding spirit' in the sense of receiving from him [i.e., Holy Spirit] the power to control."
[9] Thdr. Mops., *1 Thess.* 5:19 takes "spirit" to refer here to "spiritual gifts." Thdt., *1 Thess.* 5:19–20: "'Do not extinguish the spirit.' And what does this involve? 'Do not despise prophecy.'... So he urges them not to put a stop to the charism of prophecy [τὴν προφητικὴν μὴ κωλύειν χάριν]" (mod.).
[10] Thdt., *Ezech.* 2:3 glosses "spirit" as "some divine power."

Adrian's *Introduction to the Divine Scriptures*

RECENSION 1

59.4. ἐπὶ δὲ ψυχῆς· ὡς τό, ἐξελεύσεται τὸ πνεῦμα αὐτοῦ, καὶ ἐπιστρέψει εἰς τὴν γῆν αὐτοῦ·

59.5. ἐπὶ δὲ φωνῆς· ὡς τό, τῷ λόγῳ κυρίου οἱ οὐρανοὶ ἐστερεώθησαν, καὶ τῷ πνεύματι τοῦ στόματος αὐτοῦ πᾶσα ἡ δύναμις αὐτῶν· καὶ ὁ ἀπόστολος, 5 προσεύξομαι τῷ πνεύματι, προσεύξομαι δὲ καὶ τῷ νοΐ·

59.6. ἐπὶ δὲ ἀέρος· ὡς τό, ἐν πνεύματι βιαίῳ συντρίψεις πλοῖα Θαρσεῖς· καί, ἀπέστειλας τὸ πνεῦμά σου, ἐκάλυψεν αὐτοὺς θάλασσα· καί, ἐκ τῶν τεσσάρων πνευμάτων ἐλθέτω.

60(95[μβ´]). Τὸ ἕως πολλαχοῦ οὐκ ἐπὶ χρόνου λέγει, ἀλλ᾽ ἐπὶ τοῦ αὐτοῦ 10 πράγματος· ὡς τό, **καὶ ἐν τῇ σκιᾷ τῶν πτερύγων σου ἐλπιῶ, ἕως οὗ παρέλθῃ ἡ ἀνομία·** οὐ γὰρ μετὰ τοῦτο τῆς πρὸς θεὸν ἐλπίδος ἔμελλεν ἀπαλλάττεσθαι· καί, < **κάθου ἐκ δεξιῶν μου,** > **ἕως ἂν θῶ τοὺς ἐχθρούς σου ὑποπόδιον τῶν ποδῶν σου·** καί, **ἐγώ εἰμι, ἕως ἂν καταγηράσητε·** καί, **ἐκζητήσατε τὸν κύριον ἕως τοῦ ἐλθεῖν ὑμῖν γενήματα δικαιοσύνης·** καί, 15 **οὐ προσέθετο Σαμουὴλ ἰδεῖν τὸν Σαοὺλ ἕως ἡμέρας θανάτου αὐτοῦ·** καὶ τό, **ἰδοὺ ἐγὼ μεθ᾽ ὑμῶν εἰμι πάσας τὰς ἡμέρας, ἕως τῆς συντελείας τοῦ αἰῶνος·** καί, **οὐκ ἐγίνωσκεν αὐτήν, ἕως οὗ ἔτεκε τὸν υἱὸν αὐτῆς τὸν πρωτότοκον.**

---

2 Ps 145[146]:4   4 Ps 32[33]:6   5 1 Cor 14:15
6 Ps 47:8 [48:7] var.   7 Ex 15:10   8 Ezek 37:9 var.
11 Ps 56:2 [57:1]   13 Ps 109[110]:1   13 Isa 46:4 var.
14 Hos 10:12 var.   15 1 Kgdms 15:35 [1 Sam 15:35] var.
17 Matt 28:20   18 Matt 1:25 var.

---

17 αὐτῆς] αὑτῆς Goessling

59.4. Of soul: for example, "his 'spirit' will depart, and he will return to his earth" (Ps 145[146]:4).

59.5. Of voice: for example, "the heavens were established by the word of the Lord, and all their power by the 'spirit' of his mouth" (Ps 32[33]:6); and the apostle [writes], "I will pray with my 'spirit,' I will pray also with my mind" (1 Cor 14:15).[1]

59.6. Of wind: for example, "with a violent 'spirit' you will shatter ships of Tharsis" (Ps 47:8 [48:7]);[2] and, "you sent your 'spirit'; the sea covered them" (Ex 15:10); and, "come from the four 'spirits' " (Ezek 37:9)![3]

60. Often Scripture does not use the word ἕως with regard to a period of time ("until"), but with regard to the continuation of the same activity.[4] For example, "and in the shadow of your wings I will hope, 'until' lawlessness passes by" (Ps 56:2 [57:1]), for the Psalmist was not intending to abandon hope in God after this moment.[5] And, "Sit at my right hand 'until' I make your enemies a footstool for your feet" (Ps 109[110]:1);[6] and, "I am, 'until' you grow old" (Isa 46:4); and, "seek out the Lord 'until' the offspring of righteousness come to you!" (Hos 10:12); and, "Samuel did not bring himself to see Saul 'until' the day of his death" (1 Kgdms 15:35 [1 Sam 15:35]);[7] and, "Behold, I am with you all your days, 'until' the end of the age" (Matt 28:20); and, "he did not know her 'until' she gave birth to her firstborn son" (Matt 1:25).[8]

---

[1] Thdt., *1 Cor.* 14:15: "By 'spirit' he refers to the gift, and by 'mind' to the clarity of what is said." The "gift" Theodoret has in mind is the gift of tongues mentioned in the preceding lines of Paul's letter.

[2] See Thdr. Mops., *Ps.* 47:8.

[3] Diod., *fr. Gen.* 1:2 [Deconinck no. 4]: πνεῦμα as wind (Schäublin, *Untersuchungen*, 46).

[4] Here Adrian notes that ἕως is not exclusively a temporal marker that denotes "the point of time up to which an action goes, with reference to the end of the action" ("until"—s.v. ἕως LSJ). The argument is that the ἕως clause does not always circumscribe the state or action described by the main clause by identifying a time in the future when this state or action ceases. For example, "in the shadow of your wings I will hope" does not occur "*only until* lawlessness passes by," but also *after*. Thus, when Adrian says the term ἕως is spoken with reference "to the same activity," he seems to mean that what led up to the future event also continues after it, hence my looser translation: "the continuation of the same activity." In the examples Adrian provides the term ἕως connotes something like "even after." Note esp. Isid. Pel. *ep.* 1.18: τὸ ἕως πολλάκις καὶ ἐπὶ τοῦ διηνεκῶς ἐν τῇ θείᾳ γραφῇ εὑρίσκομεν κείμενον. S.v. ἕως PGL A.1.a.

[5] Thdr. Mops., *Ps.* 56:2: "The term ἕως is not spoken definitively [ὁριστικῶς]: he did not mean, 'I hope to that point but no longer'; instead, he intends the denial of the opposite. Scripture habitually speaks this way."

[6] See the lengthy discussion of this particle in Thdt., *Ps.* 109:1.

[7] That is, after his death Samuel was not really raised by the medium to converse with Saul (1 Kgdms 28). A similar position can be found in Eust., *engast.*

[8] Adrian here refers to Mary's *post partum* virginity: Joseph refrained from sexual relations with his wife up until the time when she gave birth to her firstborn son, but also after this event. See Chrys., *hom. in Mt.* 5.5; Cass., *Ps.* 88:27.

61(96[μγ´]). Τῇ τῶν χρόνων ἐναλλαγῇ κέχρηται συνεχῶς·

61.1. μέλλοντι μὲν ἀντὶ παρεληλυθότος· ὡς τό, **λούσω καθ᾽ ἑκάστην νύκτα τὴν κλίνην μου**, ἀντὶ τοῦ ἔλουσα· καί, **ἐν ποταμῷ διελεύσονται ποδί**, ἀντὶ τοῦ διῆλθον· καί, **ὡς χελιδὼν οὕτω φωνήσω**·

5 **61.2.** καὶ παρεληλυθότι ἀντὶ μέλλοντος· ὡς τό, **ἐγὼ πρὸς τὸν θεὸν ἐκέκραξα, καὶ ὁ κύριος εἰσήκουσέ μου**, ἀντὶ τοῦ εἰσακούσεταί μου· καί, **τότε ἔσπευσαν ἡγεμόνες Ἐδώμ**·

61.3. καὶ μέλλοντι ἀντὶ ἐνεστῶτος· ὡς τό, **παροικήσουσι καὶ κατακρύψουσιν**, ἀντὶ τοῦ παροικοῦσι· καί, **φθέγξονται καὶ**
10 **λαλήσουσιν**.

62(97[μδ´]). Τὸν αἰῶνα τριχῶς λέγει ἤτοι τὸν τῆς ζωῆς ἑκάστου χρόνον ἢ τὴν τοῦ χρόνου καθόλου παρέκτασιν ἢ τὸ διηνεκές τε καὶ ἀτελεύτητον·

62.1. ἐπὶ μὲν οὖν τοῦ τῆς καθ᾽ ἕκαστον ζωῆς χρόνου· ὡς τό, **καὶ ἐκοπίασεν εἰς τὸν αἰῶνα, καὶ ζήσεται εἰς τέλος**· καί, **ἔδωκας αὐτῷ μακρότητα ἡμερῶν**
15 **εἰς αἰῶνα αἰῶνος**· καί, **εἰς τὸν αἰῶνα ἐξομολογήσομαί σοι**, < ἵνα εἴπῃ > ἄχρις ἂν ζῶ καὶ εἰμί· καί, **οὐ σαλευθήσεται εἰς τὸν αἰῶνα, ὁ κατοικῶν Ἰερουσαλήμ**· καί, **δουλεύσει σοι εἰς τὸν αἰῶνα**· καί, **οὐ μὴ νίψῃς τοὺς πόδας μου εἰς τὸν αἰῶνα**· καί, **οὐ μὴ φάγω κρέα εἰς τὸν αἰῶνα**· καί, **οὐ μὴ διψήσῃ εἰς τὸν αἰῶνα**·

---

3 Ps 6:7[6]   3 Ps 65[66]:6   4 Isa 38:14
6 Ps 54:17 [55:16] var.   7 Ex 15:15   9 Ps 55:7 [56:6]
10 Ps 93[94]:4   14 Ps 48:10 [49:8–9] var.   15 Ps 20:5 [21:4]
15 Ps 29:13 [30:12]   17 Ps 124[125]:1   17 Ex 21:6 var.
18 John 13:8 var.   19 1 Cor 8:13   19 John 4:14

61. It continually exchanges tenses.[1]

61.1. [It uses] the future instead of the past: for example, "I will drench my bed each night" (Ps 6:7[6]), instead of "I drenched."[2] And, "they will cross the river on foot" (Ps 65[66]:6), instead of "they crossed."[3] And, "like a swallow, so will I sing aloud" (Is 38:14).

61.2. And the past instead of the future: for example, "I cried to God and the Lord heard me" (Ps 54:17 [55:16]), instead of "will hear me."[4] And, "then Edom's rulers hastened" (Ex 15:15).[5]

61.3. And future instead of the present: for example, "they will be foreigners and hide" (Ps 55:7 [56:6]), instead of "they are foreigners." And, "they will utter and they will speak" (Ps 93[94]:4).

62. It uses the word αἰών in three ways, either of the length of an individual life, or of the passing of time in general, or of perpetuity and endlessness.[6]

62.1. With reference to the length of an individual life: for example, "and he toiled 'forever' and will live to the end" (Ps 48:10 [49:8–9]);[7] and, "you gave him length of days 'forever and ever'" (Ps 20:5 [21:4]).[8] And, "I will acknowledge you 'forever'" (Ps 29:13 [30:12]), as if to say "as long as I live and exist."[9] And, "the one who inhabits Jerusalem will 'never' be shaken" (Ps 124[125]:1); and, "he will serve you 'forever'" (Ex 21:6); and, "you will 'never' wash my feet" (John 13:8); and, "I will 'never' eat meat" (1 Cor 8:13); and, "you will 'never' thirst" (John 4:14).[10]

---

[1] Diod., *Ps.* 3:5: "One tense replaces another in the verses, and this is found in many places in the psalms." See esp. Thdr. Mops., *Os.* 12:9 and *Joel* 2:18 for his observations on the prevalence of tense changes in the Psalms and prophets. Discussion in Mariès, *Études*, 113; Devreesse, *Essai*, 59–60 fn. 3; Schäublin, *Untersuchungen*, 131–2.

[2] Same observation in Diod., *Ps.* 6:7; Thdr. Mops., *Ps.* 6:7.

[3] See Thdt., *Ps.* 65:6: "The tense has been changed here: he spoke of the past as future, whereas the others retained the tense, Symmachus saying, '... they crossed the river on foot [διέβησαν ποδί].'" Note that Adrian does not gloss the verse with Symmachus' verb.

[4] Thdr. Mops., *Os.* 12:9.

[5] Anonymous., fr. *Ex.* 15:15 [Petit, *chaîne* no. 460] where the gloss on this verse explains how Scripture uses the past for the future or future for the past.

[6] It seems that Adrian thinks that first two categories of αἰών/αἰώνιος are connotations that are hyperbolic, whereas the third category is the proper denotation. Hence the scare quotes around 'forever' (and related terms) for the first two categories. On the word αἰών in Scripture, see Diod., *Ps.* 89 (Mariès, *Études*, 124).

[7] Thdr. Mops., *Ps.* 48:10: "αἰών means 'period of time' [καιρός]."

[8] Thdr. Mops., *Ps.* 20:5: "He refers indiscriminately even to a brief time as an age [*Saeculum... breve tempus*]."

[9] Thdr. Mops., *Ps.* 29:13: "by αἰών referring to the span of his own life [τὸν τῆς οἰκείας ζωῆς χρόνον]."

[10] See also Diod., *Ps.* 47:9 on using αἰών to speak of limit amounts of time.

RECENSION 1

62.2. ἐπὶ δὲ τῆς τοῦ χρόνου καθόλου παρεκτάσεως· ὡς τό, **εἰσελεύσεται ἕως**
γενεᾶς πατέρων αὐτοῦ, ἕως αἰῶνος οὐκ ὄψεται φῶς, ἀντὶ τοῦ ἄχρις ἂν
ἡ παροῦσα μένῃ κατάστασις· οὐ γὰρ ἐπ᾽ ἀναιρέσει τῆς ἀναστάσεως
ἀπεράντως ἐφθέγξατο· καί, **ὄνειδος αἰώνιον ἔδωκεν αὐτοῖς·** ἐπὶ
5 τῶν ἀλλοφύλων, ἵνα εἴπῃ χρόνιον, ὥστε καὶ ὑπὸ τῶν αὖθις αἰσχίστων
μνημονεύεσθαι· καὶ τό, **εἰς μνημόσυνον αἰώνιον ἔσται δίκαιος·** καί,
Ἰσραὴλ σῴζεται ὑπὸ κυρίου σωτηρίαν αἰώνιον· καί, **οὐδὲ μὴ**
ἐντραπῶσιν ἕως τοῦ αἰῶνος· < καί, > **ἐν ὄρει Σιὼν ἀπὸ τοῦ νῦν καὶ εἰς**
τὸν αἰῶνα, ἀντὶ τοῦ ἐπὶ πολὺν χρόνον· καί, **Ἰουδαία εἰς τὸν αἰῶνα**
10 **κατοικισθήσεται·**

62.3. ἐπὶ δὲ τοῦ διηνεκοῦς τε καὶ ἀτελευτήτου· ὡς τό, **ὁ θρόνος σου, ὁ θεός,**
εἰς τὸν αἰῶνα τοῦ αἰῶνος· καί, **εἰς τὸν αἰῶνα κύριε ὁ λόγος σου διαμένει**
ἐν τῷ οὐρανῷ· καί, **κύριος εἰς τὸν αἰῶνα μένει·** καί, **ἡ βασιλεία αὐτοῦ**
βασιλεία αἰώνιος· καί ὁ κύριός φησιν, **ἑκατονταπλασίονα λήψεται ἐν τῷ**
15 **νῦν αἰῶνι, καί ἐν τῷ μέλλοντι ζωὴν αἰώνιον κληρονομήσει·** καί, **αὕτη δέ**
ἐστιν ἡ αἰώνιος ζωή· καί, **ἐγὼ ζωὴν αἰώνιον δώσω αὐτοῖς.**

63(98). Τὰ εὐκτικὰ προστακτικῶς λέγει· ὡς τό, **ἐξαλειφθήτωσαν ἐκ βίβλου**
ζώντων, < **καὶ μετὰ δικαίων μὴ γραφήτωσαν** >, ἀντὶ τοῦ ἐξαλειφθεῖεν
καὶ μὴ ἐγγραφεῖεν· καί, **μεγέθει βραχίονός σου ἀπολιθωθήτωσαν,** ἀντὶ
20 τοῦ ἀπολιθωθεῖεν· καί, **ἀναβήτω ἐκ φθορᾶς ἡ ζωή μου,** < ἀντὶ τοῦ
ἀναβαίη >.

64.1(50). Τὸ βέβαιον τῆς βασιλείας αὐτοῦ καὶ ἑδραῖον ἕτοιμον ἐκφωνεῖ· ὡς τό,
ἕτοιμος ὁ θρόνος σου ἀπὸ τότε, ἀντὶ τοῦ ἀπ᾽ ἀρχῆς ἑδραῖος ἀμετακίνητος·

---

2 Ps 48:20 [49:19]   4 Ps 77[78]:66   6 Ps 111[112]:6
7 Isa 45:17   8 Isa 45:17   9 Mic 4:7 var.   10 Joel 3:20 var.
12 Ps 44:7 [45:6]   13 Ps 118[119]:89   13 Ps 9:8[7]
14 Dan 3:100 [4:3]   15 Matt 19:29 var.   16 John 17:3
16 John 10:28 var.   18 Ps 68:29 [69:28]   19 Ex 15:16
20 Jonah 2:7[6] var.   23 Ps 92[93]:2

---

4 αὐτοῖς] Hoeschel (notae) Goessling, αὐ⁻ LA, αὐτοῦ F, αὐτῶν B, τοῖς Hoeschel
5 τῶν¹] αὐτῶν Hoeschel sed τῶν in notis
5 αἰσχίστων] cat. Ps. 77:66 A p. corr. Goessling (ex A), αἰσχίστως L, αἰσχίσων Hoeschel
6 ἐπὶ τῶν ἀλλοφύλων–μνημονεύεσθαι] susp. Goessling
8 οὐδὲ μὴ ἐντραπῶσιν] οὐ μὴ ἐντραπήσονται Hoeschel (notae)
8 καί¹] + Goessling   18 καὶ–γραφήτωσαν] + Goessling (ex Schlüren)
20 ἀναβήτω] Goessling (ex Schlüren), ἀναβαίη L
21 ἀντὶ τοῦ ἀναβαίη] + Goessling (ex Schlüren)

TRANSLATION: R1

62.2. And with reference to the passing of time in general: for example, "he will enter into the company of his ancestors, 'never' again will he see light" (Ps 48:20 [49:19]), instead of "as long as the present age abides"[1]—for the Psalmist did not make an unqualified pronouncement in order to refute the resurrection. And, "he gave them an 'eternal' insult" (Ps 77[78]:66)—with regard to foreigners, as if to say "for a long time," so that they would be remembered hereafter even by the most shameful.[2] And, "the righteous will be in 'eternal' remembrance" (Ps 111[112]:6); and, "Israel is being saved by the Lord with an 'eternal' salvation" (Isa 45:17) and, "they will not be disgraced 'forever'" (Isa 45:17). And, "on Mount Zion from now and 'forever'" (Mic 4:7), instead of "for a long time."[3] And, "Judea will be inhabited 'forever'" (Joel 3:20).

62.3. With respect to perpetuity and endlessness: for example, "Your throne, O God, is forever and ever" (Ps 44:7 [45:6]);[4] and, "Forever, O Lord, your word endures in heaven" (Ps 118[119]:89); and, "the Lord abides forever" (Ps 9:8[7]); and, "his kingdom is an eternal kingdom" (Dan 3:100 [4:3]); and the Lord says, "he will receive one hundred-fold in this age, and in the coming one will inherit eternal life" (Matt 19:29);[5] and, "this is eternal life" (John 17:3); and, "I will give them eternal life" (John 10:28).

63. It expresses things wished for in the imperative mood.[6] For example, "Let them be blotted out from the book of the living, and let them not be enrolled with the righteous!" (Ps 68:29 [69:28]), instead of "May they be blotted out and not enrolled!" And, "Let them be turned to stone by the greatness of your arm!" (Ex 15:16), instead of "May they be turned to stone!" And, "Let my life ascend from corruption!" (Jonah 2:7[6]), instead of "May it ascend."

64.1.[7] It calls the permanence and stability of his kingdom, "preparedness." For example, "Your throne is prepared from that time" (Ps 92[93]:2), instead of "[Your

---

[1] S.v. κατάστασις PGL B.6. As a technical term in Theodore's thought: catech. 1.4; 3.9; Gal. 2:15; Junil., inst. 1.11; 2.1–26. Thdr. Mops., Ps. 48:20: "he will inevitably join his ancestors... whence there is no returning or enjoying again the present life [ἀπολαῦσαι τῆς παρούσης ζωῆς]."

[2] See Adrian., cat. Ps. 77:66 for a nearly identical gloss on this verse.

[3] Thdr. Mops., Mich. 4:7: "The phrase 'from now and αἰών,' in fact, clearly means for a long time [δι' ὅλου τὸ μέχρι πολλοῦ]."

[4] Thdr. Mops., Ps. 44:7: "you reign over everyone from eternity, you will reign always, and your kingdom abides without end [καὶ εἰς ἀεὶ βασιλεύσεις, καὶ ἡ βασιλεία σου μένει διηνεκής]."

[5] Presumably Adrian thinks only the second reference to αἰών in this verse illustrates the sense of the noun he is highlighting in 62.3.

[6] Thdr. Mops., Zach. 11:4 and 13:7 on expressing the future in the imperative mood. For a dossier of related texts, see Mariès, Études, 116; Devreesse, Essai, 59–60 fn. 3.

[7] Goessling thinks 64.1–2 was added by a later scribe. However, the assertion is not self-evident (Adrians ΕΙΣΑΓΩΓΗ, 41–2). This material is certainly misplaced in the ms tradition where it occurs between 17 and 18—it does not fit into the structure of problems and solutions in that section of the Introduction. But it is difficult to assert its spuriousness since the observations in this material are in

RECENSION 1

καί, δικαιοσύνη καὶ κρίμα ἑτοιμασία τοῦ θρόνου σου· καί, ἐν τοῖς
οὐρανοῖς ἑτοιμασθήσεται ἡ ἀλήθειά σου·

64.2(51). καὶ βασιλεῦσαι λέγει τὸν θεόν, ὅταν τῶν ἐχθρῶν κρατήσας, τοὺς
ἰδίους ἐγείρει· ὡς τό, **ὁ κύριος ἐβασίλευσεν, ὀργιζέσθωσαν λαοί·** καί, < ὁ
5 **κύριος ἐβασίλευσεν,** > **ἀγαλλιάσθω ἡ γῆ.**

65(105). Ὁ μέντοι μακάριος Δαυὶδ τῇ ἐν ἀντὶ τῆς σὺν κέχρηται· ὡς τό, **καὶ
μετατίθεσθαι ὄρη ἐν καρδίαις θαλασσῶν·** καί, **ἐν ὁλοκαυτώμασιν,** ἀντὶ
σὺν ὁλοκαυτώμασιν· καί, **ἐν εἰρήνῃ ἐπὶ τὸ αὐτό·** καί, **ἐγὼ δὲ ἐν ἀκακίᾳ
μου ἐπορεύθην·** καί, **ἀνέβη ὁ θεὸς ἐν ἀλαλαγμῷ·** καί, **φωνὴ κυρίου ἐν
10 ἰσχύϊ, φωνὴ κυρίου ἐν μεγαλοπρεπείᾳ.**

Ἀρχὴ τῶν ἐπὶ τῆς συνθέσεως

(99) Ἴδια τοῦ μακαρίου Δαυὶδ εἴη ἂν ταῦτα·

66. Κατ' ἔλλειψιν· ὡς τό, **ἀλλ' ἢ ὡσεὶ χνοῦς, ὃν ἐκρίπτει ἄνεμος ἀπὸ
προσώπου τῆς γῆς** λείπει τὸ εἰσί· καὶ τό, **εἰπὼν** ἢ **λέγων** ἢ **εἶπας** ἢ
15 **λέγοντες** ἢ **λέγουσιν** ἢ τί τοιοῦτον·

---

1 Ps 96[97]:2 var.   2 Ps 88:3 [89:2]   4 Ps 98[99]:1
5 Ps 96[97]:1   7 Ps 45:3 [46:2]   7 Ps 65[66]:13   8 Ps 4:9[8]
9 Ps 25[26]:1 var.   9 Ps 46:6 [47:5]
10 Ps 28[29]:4   14 Ps 1:4 var.

---

5 Τὸ βέβαιον–ἡ γῆ] in codd. et edd. inter 17 et 18, del. *Goessling* (ex *Lollin Schlüren*)
10 Ὁ μέντοι–ἐν μεγαλοπρεπείᾳ] in codd. et edd. inter 71.5 et 72
11 Ἀρχὴ τῶν ἐπὶ τῆς συνθέσεως] titul. L, in app. cr. transp. *Goessling*
14 εἰσί] ἔσται L
15 ἢ λέγοντες] om. *Hoeschel*

throne is] stable [and] immoveable from the beginning."[1] And, "Righteousness and judgment are the preparation of your throne" (Ps 96[97]:2); and, "Your truth will be prepared in the heavens" (Ps 88:3 [89:2]).[2]

64.2. And Scripture says that God "reigns," whenever he rouses his own by conquering their enemies. For example, "The Lord reigned, let peoples be enraged" (Ps 98[99]:1)!; and, "The Lord became king! Let the earth rejoice" (Ps 96[97]:1)![3]

65. Blessed David uses the preposition "in" (ἐν) instead of "with" (σύν).[4] For example, "and the mountains are transposed in the hearts of the seas" (Ps 45:3 [46:2]).[5] And, "in burnt offerings" (Ps 65[66]:13), instead of "with burnt offerings." And, "in peace at that moment" (Ps 4:9[8]); and, "I walked in my innocence" (Ps 25[26]:1); and, "God ascended in a shout" (Ps 46:6 [47:5]); and, "the voice of the Lord in strength, the voice of the Lord in majesty" (Ps 28[29]:4).

PART III: PECULIARITIES OF SYNTAX

These are blessed David's peculiarities of syntax:[6]

66. Ellipsis: for example, the passage, "rather like dust, which a wind sweeps away from the face of the earth" (Ps 1:4) is missing "they are." And [Scripture often

keeping with Adrian's own style of commentary. Moreover, they are attested in both Diodore and Theodore. Schlüren thinks it belongs to section 2, which is where I have placed it ("Zu Adrianos," 147).

[1] Diod., *Ps.* 32:14: "By 'preparedness' Scripture refers to permanence and stability [τὸ βέβαιον καὶ τὸ ἑδραῖον], as when it says, 'Your throne ready from of old,' that is, stable and permanent [ἀντὶ τοῦ ἑδραῖος καὶ βέβαιος]" (mod.). Also Diod., *Ps.* 7:14 and Mariès, *Études*, 123.

[2] Thdr. Mops., *Ps.* 32:14, where instead of ἐξ ἑτοίμου κατοικητηρίου αὐτοῦ (LXX) Symmachus has ἀπὸ τῆς ἑδραίας κατοικίας αὐτοῦ. Also Ps. 56:8.

[3] See Thdr. Mops., *Ps.* 62:12 for "reigning" is associated with the rejoicing of people when their enemies are punished.

[4] On the exchange of prepositions, see Mariès, *Études*, 114. On the instrumental use of ἐν to which Adrian here refers: Jannaris, *Historical Greek Grammar*, §§1559–62; s.v. ἐν BDAG 5.

[5] See Thdr. Mops., *Ps.* 45:3 where the same observation is made of the preposition ἐν in this verse and Ps 65:13, another verse that Adrian cites in this paragraph.

[6] The peculiarities of syntax listed here in the third section of the treatise correspond to what many Greco-Roman authors called "figures" (σχήματα). Adrian labels them as such in 76 below, but he offers no formal definition of them, nor does he explain how they differ from the τρόποι that he lists in 73. Figures and tropes were not always clearly distinguished from one another in antiquity, and Adrian is no exception (Lausberg, *Literary Rhetoric*, §557, 601). Note, for instance, how the trope of omission (73.21) is an instance of the figure of ellipsis (66) (also see Thdr. Mops., *Ps.* 58:9). Furthermore, among the tropes there are cases of overlap: e.g., ἀπόχρησις (73.10) resurfaces in σχηματισμός (73.12). This third section of the treatise presents a catalogue of ways in which syntax is altered—i.e., where words are subtracted, added or rearranged. Note Ps.-Plu., *vit. Hom.* §15 where the modification of syntax serves as the definition of a σχῆμα: ἡ δὲ τῆς συνθέσεως [ἐκτροπὴ καλεῖται] σχῆμα. By contrast, "tropes" for Adrian are usually deviations in the standard use or meaning of words. For orientation to figures and tropes in classical and post-classical antiquity, including definitions and illustrations, see Rutherford, *History of Annotation*, 183–335; Martin, *Antike Rhetorik*, 261–315; Lausberg,

RECENSION 1

66.1. καὶ τὸ μὲν εἰπών· ὡς τό, **πρὸς κύριον ἐν τῷ θλίβεσθαί με ἐκέκραξα,** εἰπών, **κύριε ῥῦσαι τὴν ψυχήν μου** · < καί, εἰπών, > **τίς ὠφέλεια ἐν τῷ αἵματί μου;** ἐνήλλακται δὲ ὁ χρόνος· καί, **ἐκ βαθέων ἐκέκραξά σοι κύριε,** εἰπών·

5   **66.2.** τὸ δὲ λέγων· ὡς τό, **ᾄσω καὶ ψαλῶ τῷ κυρίῳ,** λέγων·

66.3. τὸ δὲ εἶπας· ὡς τό, **ὅταν λάβω καιρόν** · < εἶπας, > **ἐγὼ εὐθύτητας κρινῶ** · καί, < εἶπας, > **συνετιῶ σε καὶ συμβιβῶ σε** · οὐ γάρ ἐστιν ἐν τοῖς Ψαλμοῖς ἐναλλαγὴ προσώπου·

---

2   Ps 119:1, 2 [120:1, 2]   3   Ps 29:10 [30:9]   4   Ps 129[130]:1 var.
5   Ps 26[27]:6 var.   7   Ps 74:3 [75:2]   7   Ps 31[32]:8

---

2   ante κύριε] καί + *Goessling*
2   κύριε–μου] in codd. et edd. post κύριε, εἰπών in 66.1
2   καί, εἰπών] καί + tantum *Goessling*
4   post κύριε, εἰπών] κύριε ῥῦσαι τὴν ψυχήν μου in 66.1 supra transp.
5   post κυρίῳ, λέγων] οὐ γάρ ἐστιν ἐν τοῖς Ψαλμοῖς ἐναλλαγὴ προσώπου in 66.3 infra transp.
8   οὐ γάρ–προσώπου] in codd. et edd. post κυρίῳ, λέγων in 66.2, susp. *Goessling* (ex *Schlüren*)

omits] εἰπών ("saying"), or λέγων ("saying"), or εἶπας ("you said"), or λέγοντες ("saying"), or λέγουσιν ("they say"), or anything like this.[1]

66.1. "Saying" (εἰπών): for example, "I cried out to the Lord when I was being afflicted... *saying*, 'O Lord, rescue my soul'" (Ps 119[120]:1, 2); and, "*saying*, 'what profit is there in my blood?'" (Ps 29:10 [30:9])—the tense is exchanged;[3] and, "out of the depths I cried to you, O Lord, *saying*..." (Ps 129[130]:1).

66.2. "Saying" (λέγων): for example, "I will sing and make music to the Lord, *saying*..." (Ps 26[27]:6).

66.3. "You said" (εἶπας): for example, "when I seize an opportune moment; *you said*, 'I will judge with uprightness'" (Ps 74:3 [75:2]);[4] "*you said*, 'I will give you understanding and instruct you'" (Ps 31[32]:8). In the Psalms there is no change of speaker.[5]

Literary Rhetoric, §§552–98, 600–910; Conley, "Byzantine Teaching on Figures and Tropes," 339–45; Granatelli, "Le definizioni di figura in Quintiliano *Inst*. IX 1.10–14," 383–425. A number of Greek treatises on tropes and figures are collected in Spengel, *Rhetores Graeci*, vol. 3.

[1] Both Diodore and Theodore emphasize how prevalent the omission of saying verbs is in Scripture. Diod., *Ps*. 2:2: "The meaning is given here with an ellipse of the word 'saying,' as often happens in Scripture, as we shall proceed to demonstrate." See esp. Thdr. Mops., *Ps*. 44:2; 54:24; 58:9; 74:3; *Abd*. 1:1 for extended discussions of this tendency to imply the saying verbs without actually mentioning them. The related observation is that sometimes a saying verb *is* present in Scripture, but the intent is not to convey speech, but rather a disposition or action (*intro*. 45 and Thdr. Mops., *Ps*. 44:2) (Devreesse, *Essai*, 61–2). Also see 38 above where Adrian discusses the ellipsis of ὡς.

[2] I have transposed the words "O Lord, rescue my soul," which are misplaced in the ms tradition. They belong here and not after the citation from Ps 129:1 further below in 66.1.

[3] Thdr. Mops., *Ps*. 29:9 notes that "I will cry to you, O Lord," is an example of the future tense being used instead of the past: it means, "I cried." So also for verse 10 (which Adrian cites): it should be prefaced with "I said [ἔλεγον]." Note also that in verse 11 the Psalm reverts to the past tense. Adrian's elliptical comment gestures to this issue.

[4] Thdr. Mops., *Ps*. 74:3: "Now, there is no need for surprise that he did not say 'I shall narrate your wonders when I take the opportunity' *because you said* [ὅτι εἶπας] 'I shall deliver upright judgments,' for it is typical of him to include things said by people in the flow of the thought and not to insert the word 'stating' or 'saying' or the like."

[5] On the surface, this is an odd claim considering Adrian's discussion above in 51 of the change of persons in Scripture (including the Psalms). It is tempting to consider this sentence a corruption. However, note Theodore's lengthy discussion of the clause, "I will tell of my works to the king" (Ps 44:2), which he interprets as David speaking his prophecy to Christ. Theodore's concern is to rebut a Jewish reading that switches speakers in this verse, so that it is, instead, God speaking to David. Thdr. Mops., *Ps*. 44:2: "Now, this is our claim in response to those Christians who are of such a mind as vehemently to support the Jews' malpractice by introducing a change in person; if this were conceded, it would be easy for the Jews to distort the true sense of the psalm entirely, as is possible to see in the rest of the commentary, especially if they were to take the king in the psalm to refer to some person other than Christ. It emerges, then, that this is said not by God to David but by David of Christ... A change of persons is not at all in keeping with the true sense of the psalms ['Εναλλαγὴ δὲ προσώπων ἐστὶ μὲν κατὰ τὸ ἀληθὲς ἐν τοῖς ψαλμοῖς οὐδεμία]." A few lines later: "nowhere in the psalms does it occur in this way, that sometimes the author speaks to God and sometimes God speaks to the author [ὡς νῦν μὲν τοῦ προφήτου φθεγγομένου πρὸς τὸν θεόν, αὖθις δὲ τοῦ θεοῦ πρὸς τὸν προφήτην ἀντιφθεγγομένου]."

RECENSION 1

66.4. ἐπὶ δὲ τοῦ λέγοντες· ὡς τό, **κατὰ τοῦ κυρίου καὶ κατὰ τοῦ Χριστοῦ αὐτοῦ**, λέγοντες·

66.5. ἐπὶ δὲ τοῦ λέγουσιν· ὡς τό, † **καὶ μὴ λαλεῖτε κατὰ τοῦ θεοῦ ἀδικίαν**, ἀντὶ τοῦ λέγουσιν· οὐδαμῶς **ἀπὸ ἐρήμων ὀρέων**. †

5 **67**(100). Τῇ ταυτολογίᾳ κέχρηται πανταχοῦ· ὡς τό, **ἰδοὺ γὰρ ἐν ἀνομίαις συνελήφθην, καὶ ἐν ἁμαρτίαις ἐκίσσησέ με ἡ μήτηρ μου·** καί, **ἐγὼ ἐκοιμήθην καὶ ὕπνωσα·** καί, **γηγενεῖς καὶ υἱοὶ τῶν ἀνθρώπων·** καί, **ὁ ποιῶν τοὺς ἀγγέλους αὐτοῦ πνεύματα, καὶ τοὺς λειτουργοὺς αὐτοῦ πῦρ φλέγον·** καί, **ἐγένετό μοι κύριος εἰς καταφυγήν, καὶ ὁ θεός μου εἰς**
10 **βοηθὸν ἐλπίδος μου·** καί, **κύριος ἐλάλησε καὶ ἐκάλεσε τὴν γῆν·** καί, **φθέγξονται καὶ λαλήσουσι·** καί, **τὰ ῥήματά μου ἐνώτισαι, κύριε,** < **σύνες τῆς κραυγῆς μου·** > < **πρόσχες τῇ φωνῇ τῆς δεήσεώς μου** >· (101) τριχῶς τὸ αὐτὸ πολλάκις.

---

2 Ps 2:2   4 Ps 74:6 [75:5] var.   4 Ps 74:7 [75:6]
6 Ps 50:7 [51:5]   7 Ps 3:6[5]   7 Ps 48:3 [49:2] var.
9 Ps 103[104]:4   10 Ps 93[94]:22   10 Ps 49[50]:1
11 Ps 93[94]:4   12 Ps 5:2–3[1–2] var.

---

4 τοῦ] τούτου Goessling (ex *Schlüren*)   4 οὐδαμῶς] οὔτε Goessling
9 πῦρ φλέγον] πυρὸς φλόγα Hoeschel (ex A a. corr.)
12 σύνες τῆς κραυγῆς μου] + Goessling (ex *Schlüren*)

66.4. Concerning[1] "saying" (λέγοντες): for example, "against the Lord and his anointed, *saying...*" (Ps 2:2).[2]

66.5. Concerning "they say" (λέγουσιν): for example, † †.[3]

67. It uses tautology everywhere.[4] For example, "For, look, I was conceived in lawlessness, and my mother yearned after me in sin" (Ps 50:7 [51:5]); and, "I lay down and slept" (Ps 3:6[5]); and, "earthborn men and sons of men" (Ps 48:3 [49:2]);[5] and, "He who makes his messengers winds, and his ministers flaming fire" (Ps 103[104]:4); and, "The Lord became my refuge, and my God the helper I hoped for (Ps 93[94]:22); and, "The Lord spoke and summoned the earth" (Ps 49[50]:1);[6] and, "they will utter and talk" (Ps 93[94]:4). And, "give ear to my words, O Lord, understand my cry. Attend to the sound of my prayer" (Ps 5:2–3[1–2])—it often says the same thing three times.[7]

Theodore continues, acknowledging that speakers *do* change in the Psalms, and often when a "saying" verb is elided. However, a change of speaker in the Psalms, especially when it pertains to God, is only an "apparent change [ἡ δοκοῦσα ἐναλλαγή]." He gives two examples of God being ostensibly introduced as a speaker: Ps 31:8 and 74:3. In both cases, it is not an actual speech, but divine action that is in view (the same point, incidentally, that Adrian makes in 45 above).

Theodore's discussion points to the authenticity of this sentence in the *Introduction*. He is juxtaposing the issue of an elided saying verb—the topic here in 66.3—with the issue of the change of speaker. But Adrian's sentence in R1 is underdeveloped. It is also misplaced in the ms tradition after the quote from Ps 26:6 in 66.2 above. It seems to make more sense—especially in light of Theodore's discussion—to move the sentence down to where I have placed it, after the two examples from Ps 74 and Ps 31 where, in both cases, God is ostensibly introduced as a speaker in the midst of a Psalm. These are the very same passages that Theodore identifies as having only an apparent shift to a divine speaker.

[1] Note that the introductory lemma for this and the next sentence are different from the introductory lemmas of the preceding paragraphs.

[2] Diod., *Ps.* 2:2: "The meaning is given here with an ellipse of the word 'saying,' as often happens in Scripture, as we shall proceed to demonstrate." So also Thdr. Mops., *Ps.* 58:9; 74:3.

[3] The obelized text begins: "'do not speak injustice against God, [Ps 74:6]' instead of 'they say.'" The scriptural words are ostensibly a case of ellipsis to which the reader needs to supply instead the verb "they say" to understand the passage properly. The problem is that the words cited by Adrian are prefaced in the Psalm with "I said" (εἶπα) (74:5), so that it is difficult to see how these words illustrate the discussion of ellipsis in this section. What is also unclear is how the words "from desolate mountains" (Ps 74:7) fit into this section.

[4] On this figure, see Mariès, *Études*, 119, 120.

[5] Diod., *Ps.* 48:3: "He means the same thing."

[6] Thdr. Mops., *Ps.* 49:1: "'spoke' and 'summoned' not implying different things, but meaning, 'He spoke to summon the earth.'"

[7] Diod., *Ps.* 5:2–3: "He says the same thing three times (Τὸ αὐτὸ λέγει τρίτον); tautology is the mark of someone ardently concerned for their request, people very desirous of something often having no qualms about repeating themselves" (mod.).

RECENSION 1

68. Κατὰ ἀντιστροφήν τινα· ὡς τό, **βλέπεις** < **ὅτι** >, ἀντὶ τοῦ ὅτι βλέπεις· καί, **σὸς ὁ βραχίων**, ἀντὶ τοῦ ὁ σός· (102) καὶ διὰ μακροτέρου τὴν ἀντιστροφὴν ποιεῖται· ὡς τό, **ἐν τοῖς περιλοίποις σου ἑτοιμάσεις τὸ πρόσωπον αὐτῶν**, ἀντὶ τοῦ ἐν τοῖς περιλοίποις αὐτῶν < ἑτοιμάσεις τὸ
5 πρόσωπόν σου >· ὡς καὶ παρὰ τοῖς λυρικοῖς εὑρίσκονται τοιαῦτα.

69(103). Ὑπερβατοῖς καὶ ὑπερθέσεσι κέχρηται· ὡς τό, **ἐν τῷ ὑπερηφανεύεσθαι τὸν ἀσεβῆ ἐμπυρίζεται ὁ πτωχός, ὅτι ἐπαινεῖται ὁ ἁμαρτωλός**· παρεγκειμένου τοῦ **συλλαμβάνονται·** καί, **ὅτι ἡμέρας καὶ νυκτὸς ἐβαρύνθη ἐπ᾽ ἐμὲ ἡ χείρ σου, ἐν τῷ ἐμπαγῆναί μοι ἄκανθαν·** τὸ
10 γὰρ **ἐστράφην εἰς ταλαιπωρίαν**, τῷ ἀπὸ τοῦ κράζειν με ὅλην τὴν ἡμέραν, εἰκότως ἀποδίδοται· καὶ τό, **τὰ βέλη σου ἠκονημένα δυνατέ,** < **ἐν καρδίᾳ τῶν ἐχθρῶν τοῦ βασιλέως** >· παρεγκειμένου τοῦ **λαοί.**

---

1 Ps 9:35 [10:14]   2 Ps 88:14 [89:13]   4 Ps 20:13 [21:12]
8 Ps 9:23, 24 [10:2, 3]   9 Ps 31[32]:4 var.
11 Ps 31[32]:3   12 Ps 44:6 [45:5]

---

1 ὅτι] cf. cat. Ps. 9:35
2 τριχῶς–ὁ σός] partem integram indic. L *Hoeschel Goessling,* susp. *Goessling* et propos.: *Τριχῶς τὸ αὐτὸ πολλάκις· ὡς τό,* < *ἐπίβλεψον ἐξ οὐρανοῦ καὶ ἰδὲ καὶ ἐπίσκεψαι τὴν ἄμπελον ταύτην* (Ps 79:15 [80:14]), *ἀντὶ τοῦ ἁπλοῦ βλέψον·*> *καί, σὸς ὁ βραχίων* < *μετὰ δυναστείας κραταιωθήτω ἡ χείρ σου, ὑψωθήτω ἡ δεξιά σου* > (Ps 88:14 [89:13]), *κατὰ ἀντιστροφήν τινα, ἀντὶ τοῦ ὁ σός*
5 ἑτοιμάσεις τὸ πρόσωπόν σου] cat. Ps. 9:35 et 20:13 *Schlüren*
5 καὶ διὰ μακροτέρου–τοιαῦτα] partem integram indic. L *Hoeschel Goessling*
12 ἐν καρδίᾳ–βασιλέως] + *Goessling* (ex *Schlüren*)
12 post λαοί] ὑποκάτω σου πεσοῦνται + *Goessling* (ex *Schlüren*)

68. It says some things by inversion:[1] for example, "you see, *because*" (Ps 9:35 [10:14]), instead of "*because* you see."[2] And, "*Yours* is the arm," (Ps 88:14 [89:13]), instead of "*your* arm." It also makes a more extended inversion: for example, "in *your* remnants you will prepare *their* countenance" (Ps 20:13 [21:12]), instead of "in *their* remnants you will prepare *your* countenance." Similar examples of inversion are also found in the lyrical poets.[3]

69. It transposes or relocates clauses.[4] For example, "when the ungodly person behaves arrogantly, the poor person is inflamed...because the sinner is commended," however, the phrase "they are being caught..." is interpolated [between these two clauses] (Ps 9:23, 24 [10:2, 3]).[5] And, "because day and night your hand was heavy upon me... when a thorn was stuck in me," for [the interpolated clause] "I was turned to wretchedness" (Ps 31[32]:4) is properly referred to the [preceding] line, "from my crying all day long" (Ps 31[32]:3).[6] And, "Your arrows are sharp,

---

[1] The more common designation for inversion is ἀναστροφή (Lausberg, *Literary Rhetoric*, §§713–15). I am taking τινα as the neuter plural object of an implied verb (following the similar syntax in Adrian, *cat. Job* 1:11: πολλάκις τινὰ κατὰ ἀντίφρασιν λέγει).

[2] Similar text in Adrian., *cat. Ps.* 9:35. Thdr. Mops., *Ps.* 9:35: "The order of the words is back to front: 'You do see, because' means 'Because you see.' Now this results from translation from the Hebrew." See Mariès, *Études*, 121; Schäublin, *Untersuchungen*, 132.

[3] See Adrian., *cat. Ps.* 9:35 and 20:13 where a longer explanation is provided for the use of extended inversions in the Psalms: these seem to occur because of the metered composition (ἀπὸ τῆς ἐμμέτρου συνθέσεως) of the book. In these two catenae fragments Adrian notes that inversion is found very frequently in the non-Christian poets, especially the lyric poets. For examples, see the discussion of inversions in Homer and Simonides in Ps.-Greg., *trop.* 5. Thdr. Mops., *Ps.* 20:13 provides a very clear parallel to Adrian: "At this point there is a considerable change in the order and the words, the statement being made with transposition [*per conversionem*]; if you did not notice it, you would not be able to explain the meaning of the words. It is difficult to understand because a lengthy insertion has been made, as a result of which the thought seems to be interrupted by a lengthy gap. It has been altered from 'In their remnants you will prepare your countenance,' with the result that 'their' at the end of the verse should be joined to 'remnants,' while 'your' has to be moved down to 'countenance.' This change in words, [*conversio verborum*] in fact, often is found also in profane writers. Now, as we said, this is the sequence of the words: 'In their remnants you will prepare your countenance.'" On Theodore's references to Hebrew meter to explain syntactical oddities, see Devreesse, *Essai*, 6 fns. 2–3; Schäublin, *Untersuchungen*, 136–8.

[4] "Hyperbaton is the separation of two syntactically very closely linked words by the insertion of a (one-word or two-word) sentence part which does not directly belong at this point" (Lausberg, *Literary Rhetoric*, §716). On this figure in Theodore, see Devreesse, *Essai*, 63; Schäublin, *Untersuchungen*, 136–8.

[5] Thdr. Mops., *Ps.* 9:23–4: "The sequence of meaning is as follows: 'The poor person is inflamed by the disdainful behavior of the godless because the sinner is commended for the desires of his soul.' The statement 'They will be caught up in the schemes they have devised' occurs in the middle, being placed in the middle for the sake of meter. You see, since the body of the psalms was composed on the basis not simply of content but also of some kind of meter, frequently to preserve the meter something is inserted in the middle, as in this case, and we find other cases as well." The clause that is interpolated, Theodore continues, does not refer to what immediately precedes (the poor person who is inflamed with the arrogance of the ungodly), but rather is in reference to the ungodly.

[6] See Adrian., *cat. Ps.* 31:4(1) for a similar text. Thdr. Mops., *Ps.* 31:3–4: "The phrase 'I was reduced to distress' was inserted on account of the need of the meter, as we have often shown in many other

RECENSION 1

70(104). Κατ᾽ ἐπίτασιν τὸ αὐτὸ λέγει· ὡς τό, **παιδεύων ἐπαίδευσέ με ὁ κύριος**· καί, **ὑπομένων ὑπέμεινα τὸν κύριον**· καί, **ἢ μὴν εὐλογῶν εὐλογήσω σε.**

71.1. Τὸ ἰδοὺ κατὰ περίσσειαν πολλάκις λέγει· ὡς τό, **ἰδοὺ γὰρ ἀλήθειαν**
5 **ἠγάπησας**· < καί, > **ἰδοὺ ἡ παρθένος ἐν γαστρὶ ἕξει**·

71.2. καὶ τὸ πλὴν οὐδὲν ὅλως συμβαλλόμενον· ὡς τό, **πλὴν μάτην ταράσσεται·**

71.3. καὶ τὸ σύν· ὡς τό, **κύριος ἐξετάζει σὺν τὸν δίκαιον καὶ σὺν τὸν ἀσεβῆ**· καί, **σὺν τὸν δίκαιον καὶ σὺν τὸν ἀσεβῆ κρινεῖ ὁ θεός·**

2 Ps 117[118]:18   2 Ps 39:2 [40:1]   3 Gen 22:17
5 Ps 50:8 [51:6]   5 Isa 7:14   7 Ps 38:7 [39:6] var.
9 Ps 10[11]:5 var.   9 Eccl 3:17

2 ἢ] ἦ Hoeschel Goessling   5 καί] + Goessling

O Mighty one...in the heart of the king's enemies," however, the phrase "peoples..." is interpolated [between these two clauses] (Ps 44:6 [45:5]).[1]

70. It says the same thing for emphasis.[2] For example, "In disciplining, the Lord disciplined me" (Ps 117[118]:18); and, "Waiting, I waited on the Lord" (Ps 39:2 [40:1]);[3] and, "surely will I bless you with blessings" (Gen 22:17).[4]

71.1. Scripture often uses the word ἰδού superfluously:[5] for example, "for ἰδού you loved truth" (Ps 50:8 [51:6]); and, "ἰδού the virgin will be pregnant" (Isa 7:14).[6]

71.2. It also uses the term πλήν which contributes nothing at all: for example, "πλήν he is in turmoil for nothing" (Ps 38:7 [39:6]).[7]

71.3. Also the term σύν: for example, "The Lord examines σύν the righteous and σύν the impious" (Ps 10[11]:5); and, "God will judge σύν the righteous and σύν the impious"(Eccl 3:17).[8]

---

cases...He means, 'Since I cried out incessantly, grief and pain came upon me, and I constantly suffered the effect of exhaustion through crying out incessantly.'"

[1] Diod., Ps. 44:6: "The clause, 'peoples will fall under you' is inserted [παρέγκειται], the sequence being, 'Yours arrows, O mighty one, in the heart of the king's foes, and then peoples will fall under you.' As it is, however, as I remarked, the clause is inserted [παρέγκειται] and causes confusion." Thdr. Mops., Ps. 44:6: "The clause 'peoples will fall under you' he inserted in the middle on account of the meter, as has been pointed out by us elsewhere as well...meaning...striking the enemy with arrows, terrifying the others and subjecting them to himself in deep fear."

[2] This figure goes by several names: διπλασιασμός ("doubling"; "reduplication"); ἀναδίπλωσις ("repetition"); παλιλλογία ("recapitulation"). See Rutherford, History of Annotation, 268–70; 256–7; Lausberg, Literary Rhetoric, §§608, 612–24; Mariès, Études, 119; Devreesse, Essai, 62–3; Schäublin, Untersuchungen, 133. Emphasis (ἔμφασις, ἐπίτασις) or amplification (αὔξησις) is usually associated by Theodore with comparisons and metaphors (Schäublin, Untersuchungen, 116, 122–3).

[3] See esp. Thdr. Mops., Ps. 39:1 where this verse and Ps 117:18 are both cited, as by Adrian, to illustrate the same peculiarity of Scripture: "This is characteristic of the divine Scripture when it wishes to bring out the intensity [τὴν ἐπίτασιν] of an event. For example, when it says, 'Disciplining he disciplined [Ps 117:18], it means, 'He really and truly disciplined; likewise also, 'Waiting, I waited' [Ps 39:1] means, 'I really waited on the Lord'" (mod.). Also see Thdr. Mops., Ps. 74:2.

[4] Similar observation to this paragraph in Eus. Em., fr. Gen. 31:43 [Arm.] who calls this literary feature a "special custom of the Hebrews."

[5] The addition of one or two words too many was usually called πλεονασμός: Rutherford, History of Annotation, 255–7; Lausberg, Literary Rhetoric, §§502–3; Devreesse, Essai, 60; Schäublin, Untersuchungen, 132–3. Recall as well the observation that the scriptural style can be, conversely, concise: the phenomenon of ellipsis discussed above (66), as well as the sometimes confusing omission of ὡς (27, 38; Thdr. Mops., Ps. 76:11).

[6] On the superfluous use of ἰδού, see Thdr. Mops., Ps. 48:16; 50:7; 54:8; 58:8 ("Here, too, ἰδού has been inserted by a Hebrew peculiarity," and Theodore goes on to cite Symmachus' version, which lacks the particle).

[7] There are several comments on the insignificance of the particle πλήν by Diod., Ps. 31:6; 38:7 (where the superfluousness is attributed to the careless translation of the Hebrew), and by Thdr. Mops., Ps. 38:6 (where the particle was inserted already as a Hebrew peculiarity); 38:7; 48:16; 61:5.

[8] Note Eus. Em., fr. Gen 1:1 [Arm.] on the superfluous use σύν, illustrating with Eccl 3:17. Also see Thdr. Mops., Ps. 38:6; 48:16.

RECENSION 1

71.4. καὶ τὸ γάρ· ὡς τό, **φωνὴν ἔδωκαν αἱ νεφέλαι καὶ γὰρ τὰ βέλη σου διαπορεύονται·** < καί, > **καὶ γὰρ ἀπειθοῦντας τοῦ κατασκηνῶσαι·** καί, **ὅτι γὰρ ἀδελφός μου εἶ·**

71.5. καὶ δὴ καὶ τὴν τοῦ γε, ἣν μάλιστα παρὰ μὲν τοῖς πλείστοις αὐτῶν
5 οὐ σπανιάκις ἐστὶν εὑρεῖν, ἐξαιρέτως δὲ παρά τε τῇ τῶν Βασιλειῶν βίβλῳ καὶ τῷ Σολομῶνι.

---

2 Ps 76:18 [77:17]   2 Ps 67:19 [68:18]   3 Gen 29:15

---

2 καί¹] + *Hoeschel* Goessling
4 post γε] lac. indic. *Goessling*
4 post μάλιστα] lac. indic. *Goessling* (ex *Schlüren*)
6 καὶ δὴ καὶ–Σολομῶνι] susp. *Goessling*

71.4. Also the term γάρ: for example, "the clouds gave a sound and γάρ your arrows are passing through" (Ps 76:18 [77:17]); and, "and γάρ they were disobedient to encamp" (Ps 67:19 [68:18]); and, "because γάρ you are my brother" (Gen 29:15).[1]

71.5. And what is more, [Scripture uses] a surplus of the particle γε, which one can certainly find frequently in most of the biblical books, but particularly in the book of Kingdoms and in Solomon.[2]

---

[1] For a similar discussion of the redundant use of γάρ note Adrian., *cat. Ps.* 76:18, as well as Thdr. Mops., *Ps.* 70:22 (with reference also to Ps 67:9).
[2] See Diod., *Ps.* 38:7 on the redundancy of μέντοι γε.

RECENSION 1	RECENSION 2

72(106). Οἱ σπουδαῖοι οὖν τὰς ἀφορμὰς ἐντεῦθεν δανεισάμενοι ὁδόν τινα καὶ πύλην τῇ φιλομαθίᾳ εὑρήσουσι πρὸς τὴν τῆς ἱερᾶς
5 γραφῆς ὁδηγηθῆναι διάνοιαν.

10

72. Κωλύσειεν δ᾽ ἂν οὐδὲν καὶ τὴν ἀπὸ τῶν γενικωτάτων τρόπων σαφήνειαν πρὸς λυσιτελεστέραν τῆς τῶν θειῶν παιδευματῶν ἑρμηνείας κατάληψιν ἡμᾶς παραλαβεῖν, ὥστε καὶ τοῖς τῶν ὁμοπιστῶν ἰδιωτέροις σπουδαίοις δ᾽ ἂν οὖν ὅμως καὶ φιλομαθέσιν ὁδόν τέ τινα καὶ πύλην πρὸς τὴν τῆς ἱερᾶς γραφῆς ὑποδεῖξαι διάνοιαν.

73(107). Εἰσὶ δὲ καὶ τρόποι αὐτῆς γενικώτατοι οὗτοι· κατὰ μεταφοράν, κατὰ παραβολήν, κατὰ σύγκρισιν, κατὰ συνεκδοχήν, κατὰ ὑπόδειγμα,
15 κατὰ μετωνυμίαν, κατὰ ἀντίφρασιν, κατὰ περίφρασιν, κατὰ ἀνακεφαλαίωσιν εἴτ᾽ οὖν

73. Ἃ μὲν οὖν αὐτῆς εἴρηται κατὰ μεταφοράν· ἃ δὲ κατὰ παραβολήν· ἃ δὲ κατὰ σύγκρισιν· ἃ δὲ καθ᾽ ὑπόδειγμα· ἃ δὲ κατὰ μετωνυμίαν· ἃ δὲ κατὰ συνεκδοχήν· ἃ δὲ κατ᾽ ἀντίφρασιν· ἃ δὲ κατὰ περίφρασιν· ἃ δὲ κατὰ ἀνακεφαλαίωσιν ἤτ᾽ οὖν ἐπανάληψιν·

1 ante Οἱ] Ὁ μέντοι–ἐν μεγαλοπρεπείᾳ in 65 supra transp.
11 αὐτῆς] τῆς θείας γραφῆς K₂

1 Κωλύσειεν] + τοῦ Y. pr. m. s. l. (ex errore pro τοῦ αὐτοῦ?)
5 παραλαβεῖν] καταλαβεῖν Z

72. After acquiring resources from this treatise, diligent students will discover in their zeal for knowledge that a path and gate leads[1] [them] toward the meaning of sacred Scripture.[2]

72. Nothing should prevent us from also attaining clarity about the most common [scriptural] tropes for the purpose of a more beneficial apprehension of the literary style of the divine precepts,[5] so that we might also indicate some path and gate that leads to the meaning of sacred Scripture for those individuals of the same community of faith who are equally[6] diligent and eager for knowledge.

APPENDIX 1: A LIST OF TROPES[3]

73. The following tropes also occur very commonly in Scripture:[4] metaphor, comparison, correspondence, synecdoche, exemplar, metonymy, antiphrasis, periphrasis, summary or repetition, irregular usage, personification, representational language, allegory, hyperbole, mockery,

73. Scriptural precepts[7] are expressed with metaphor, comparison, correspondence, exemplar, metonymy, synecdoche, antiphrasis, periphrasis, summary or repetition, irregular usage, personification, representational language, allegory, hyperbole, mockery, irony,

---

[1] Reading ὁδηγέομαι, otherwise unattested in LSJ or BDAG. If ὁδηγηθῆναι is read as the passive of ὁδηγέω then the sentence could be translated as follows: "diligent students will discover in their zeal for knowledge a path or gate [and discover that they] are led to the meaning of sacred Scripture."

[2] See 75–8 below for similar metaphors where scriptural interpretation is likened to potentially perilous travel by sea or land. Like travel, interpretation properly conducted leads to its final destination, Scripture's meaning.

[3] Tryph., *trop.* offers a taxonomy of fourteen different tropes, the first such list in antiquity. Adrian's list includes twenty-two tropes, most of which are defined and illustrated. Some of these tropes are not sharply demarcated from one another (e.g., in 73.12 on σχηματισμός, the trope "irregular usage" surfaces). For a related list among Antiochene authors, see Diod., *Ps. hypoth.* 118, where ἱστορία, ἀλληγορία, θεωρία, τροπολογία, παραβολή, ἔλλειψις, and αἴνιγμα are discussed (commentary in Mariès, *Études*, 117–19). Note also Thdr. Mops., *fr. Heb.* [Petit, *coisliniana Ex.* nos. 20–1] for his discussion of παράδειγμα, ὑπόδειγμα, τύπος, μίμημα, ὁμοίωμα, σύμβολον, μήνυμα, and ὑπόμνημα. For a bibliographic orientation to tropes in classical and post-classical antiquity, see fn. 6 on p. 221 above.

[4] Adrian's introductory sentence echoes what we find in Tryph., *trop.*: τρόποι δέ εἰσιν οἱ γενικωτάτην ἐμφαίνοντες στάσιν τέσσαρες καὶ δέκα (Spengel, *Rhetores Graeci*, vol. 3, 191.14–15), and in an anonymously transmitted work also entitled *trop.*: τρόποι δέ εἰσι πλείονες, γενικώτατοι μέντοι τάξιν ἔχοντες ιε′ (ibid., 227.17–18). On γενικός, see Rutherford, *History of Annotation*, 201 fn. 4.

[5] S.v. παίδευμα LSJ II: "thing taught." For the narrower sense of "precept," see Cyr., *Lc.* 13:26: τῶν εὐαγγελικῶν . . . παιδευμάτων. Note also the reference to Scripture as a ὑποθημοσύνη ("counsel," "precept," "command") at 75 (R1).

[6] S.v. ὅμως BDAG on taking the term in the sense of ὁμῶς, as I have done.

[7] The relative Ἅ refers back to scriptural παιδεύματα.

RECENSION 1	RECENSION 2

ἐπανάληψιν, κατὰ ἀπόχρησιν, κατὰ
προσωποποιΐαν, κατὰ σχηματισμόν,
κατὰ ἀλληγορίαν, κατὰ ὑπερβολήν,
κατ᾽ ἐπιτωθασμόν, κατὰ εἰρωνείαν,
5 κατὰ σαρκασμόν, κατὰ αἴνιγμα,
κατὰ ἀπειλήν, κατὰ ἀπόφασιν, κατὰ
ἀποσιώπησιν, κατὰ παραίνεσιν·
παρεκτὸς δηλονότι τῶν ἰδιωμάτων
αὐτῆς·

10 **73.1**(108). κατὰ μὲν μεταφοράν· ὅταν
τὰ ἑτέροις ἢ κατὰ πρᾶξιν ἢ κατὰ
φύσιν ἔνοντα εἰς ἔτερα μεταφέρῃ,
οἷον εἰς ἡμᾶς τε καὶ τὸν θεόν· ὡς τό,
κύριος ποιμαίνει με· καί,
15 **ποιμαίνειν Ἰακὼβ τὸν δοῦλον**
αὐτοῦ· καί, **μὴ βόσκωσιν οἱ ποιμένες**
ἑαυτούς; καί, **διεσπάρη τὰ**
πρόβατά μου, διὰ τὸ μὴ εἶναι
ποιμένας· καί, **δεῦτε ὀπίσω μου**
20 **καὶ ποιήσω ὑμᾶς ἁλιεῖς**
ἀνθρώπων· δίκτυα γὰρ πολλάκις καὶ
ἀμφίβληστρα τὰς χειρώσεις τῆς τοῦ
θεοῦ δίκης λέγει· οἷον, **ἐκπετάσω τὸ**
δίκτυόν μου ἐπ᾽ αὐτόν· ʼκαὶ
25 κατακλυσμὸν δὲ, τὴν ἐρήμωσιν τῶν
πολεμίων ἀποφαίνει· ὡς τό, **κύριος**
τὸν κατακλυσμὸν κατοικιεῖ· καί,
ὁ προσκαλούμενος τὸ ὕδωρ τῆς
θαλάσσης, ἵνα εἴπῃ τοὺς
30 Ἀσσυρίους καὶ τὸ πλῆθος·ʼ καί,

ἃ δὲ κατὰ ἀπόχρησιν· ἃ δὲ κατὰ
προσωποποιΐαν· ἃ δὲ κατὰ
σχηματισμόν· ἃ δὲ κατ᾽ ἀλληγορίαν· ἃ
δὲ καθ᾽ ὑπερβολήν· ἃ δὲ κατὰ
ἐπιτωθασμόν· ἃ δὲ κατ᾽ εἰρωνείαν· ἃ
δὲ κατὰ σαρκασμόν· ἃ δὲ κατὰ
αἴνιγμα· ἃ δὲ κατὰ ἀπειλήν· ἃ δὲ κατὰ
ἀπόφασιν· ἃ δὲ κατὰ ἀποσιώπησιν· ἃ
δὲ κατὰ παραίνεσιν·

73.1. τὰ μὲν οὖν κατὰ μεταφοράν
ἐστιν· ὅταν τὰ ἑτέροις ἢ κατὰ πρᾶξιν
ἢ κατὰ φύσιν ἐνόντα εἰς ἔτερα
μεταφέρῃ· ὡς τό, **κύριος ποιμαίνει**
με, καί, εἰς τόπον χλόης ἐκεῖ με
κατεσκήνωσεν, καὶ τὰ ἑξῆς· καὶ ὡς
τό, **ἐξόπισθεν τῶν λοχευομένων**
ἔλαβεν αὐτὸν ποιμαίνειν Ἰακὼβ τὸν
δοῦλον αὐτοῦ· καὶ ὡς τὸ παρὰ τῷ
Ἰεζεκιήλ, **τάδε λέγει κύριος ὦ**
ποιμένες Ἰσραήλ, καὶ τὰ ἑξῆς· καὶ
μὴν ὑπὸ τοῦ κυρίου πρὸς τοὺς
ἀποστόλους, **δεῦτε ὀπίσω μου καὶ**
ποιήσω ἡμᾶς ἁλιεῖς ἀνθρώπων· καὶ
ὡς τό, **πεσοῦνται ἐν ἀμφιβλήστρῳ**
αὐτῶν οἱ ἁμαρτωλοί· καὶ ὡς τό,
ὑπερασπιστὰ ἡμῶν ἴδε ὁ θεός· καὶ
ὡς τό, **ἐν σκέπῃ τῶν πτερύγων σου**
σκεπάσεις με·

---

14 Ps 22[23]:1	15 Ps 22[23]:1, 2
16 Ps 77[78]:71 var.	18 Ps 77[78]:71 var.
17 Ezek 34:2	20 Ezek 34:2
19 Ezek 34:5	23 Matt 4:19 var.
21 Matt 4:19	25 Ps 140[141]:10 var.
24 Ezek 12:13	26 Ps 83:10 [84:9]
27 Ps 28[29]:10	28 Ps 16[17]:8
29 Amos 9:6	

---

30 καὶ κατακλυσμὸν–τὸ πλῆθος] cf. 73.13 (R1 et R2)	10 ante Τὰ] ὅπως κατὰ μεταφοράν titul. YZ
	21 μὴν] μὲν Z

irony, sarcasm, riddle, threat, verdict, omission, exhortation. These tropes clearly go along with Scripture's literary peculiarities.[1]

sarcasm, riddle, threat, verdict, omission, exhortation.

73.1. Metaphor: whenever the properties of one thing—either those in accordance with its conduct or nature—transfer over to a different thing, such as to us humans and God.[2] For example, "The Lord shepherds me" (Ps 22[23]:1); and, "to shepherd Jacob, his servant" (Ps 77[78]:71); and, "do shepherds feed themselves?" (Ezek 34:2); and, "my sheep were scattered because there were no shepherds" (Ezek 34:5). And, "Follow me, and I will make you fishers of people" (Matt 4:19), for Scripture often calls God's justice when it conquers, "nets" and "casting nets." As an example, "I will spread out my net over him" (Ezek 12:13).[3] ʰAnd it renders the devastation wrought by his enemies a "flood." For example, "The Lord will inhabit the flood" (Ps 28[29]:10).[4] And, "he who summons the water of the sea"

73.1. Metaphor: whenever the properties of one thing—either those in accordance with its conduct or nature—transfer over to a different thing. For example, "The Lord shepherds me" and "in a verdant place, there he made me encamp" (Ps 22[23]:1, 2), and what follows; and, for instance, "from behind the lambing ewes he took him to shepherd Jacob, his servant" (Ps 77[78]:1); and, for example, in Ezekiel: "This is what the Lord says, oh you shepherds of Israel" (Ezek 34:2), and what follows; and [this is said] by the Lord to his apostles: "Follow me, and I will make you fishers of people" (Matt 4:19); and for instance, "Sinners will fall into their net" (Ps 140[141]:10); and for example, "Look, O God, our protector" (Ps 83:10 [84:9]); and, for example, "in the shelter of your wings, you will shelter me" (Ps 16[17]:8).[5]

---

[1] S.v. πάρεξ *GELS* I: "besides, on a level with." A number of these tropes have already surfaced in sections one and two of the *Introduction* above: e.g., metaphor (27), comparison (38), synecdoche (17), representational language (2; 4.10), and omission (38).

[2] Metaphor for Adrian is comparison (the next trope on the list) without the particle ὡς. See 27, 38, and 44 above. On these tropes in Theodore, see Schäublin, *Untersuchungen*, 115–20.

[3] Thdt., *Ezech.* 12:13: "In every detail he [God] conveyed the fact that he would use the enemy as instruments for calling to account the king, the rulers and all their subjects for impiety."

[4] Diod., *Ps.* 28:10: "since the enemy in their vast numbers threatened to bring on the places a 'flood,' as it were."

[5] See Adrian., *cat. Ps.* 90:4 for a longer discussion of this bird metaphor.

RECENSION 1	RECENSION 2

ὑπερασπιστὰ ἡμῶν ἴδε ὁ θεός· καί,
ἐν τῇ σκέπῃ τῶν πτερύγων σου
σκεπάσεις με· καί, διεὶς τὰς
πτέρυγας αὐτοῦ ἐδέξατο αὐτούς·
5 καὶ ἐναπομένει τῷ σχηματισμῷ·

73.2(109). κατὰ δὲ παραβολήν· ὡς τό,
ἠγρύπνησα καὶ ἐγενόμην ὡς
στρουθίον· καί, ὡς πρόβατον·

73.2. τὰ δὲ κατὰ παραβολήν· ὅταν
ἡμᾶς ἀπὸ τῶν προσόντων πρὸς ἅπερ
εἰκάσειεν τῶν λοιπῶν ὁμοίως ἔχειν
παραβάλλει· οἷον ὡς τό, **ἐγενήθην**
ὡσεὶ νυκτικόραξ ἐν οἰκοπέδῳ,
ἠγρύπνησα καὶ ἐγενόμην ὡς
στρουθίον μονάζον ἐπὶ δώματος·
καὶ τὰ ὅμοια·

---

1 Ps 83:10 [84:9]
3 Ps 16[17]:8 var.
4 Deut 32:11
8 Ps 101:8 [102:7] var.
8 Isa 53:7

12 Ps 101:7–8 [102:6–7] var.

6 ante Τὰ] ὅπως κατὰ παραβολήν titul. YZ
9 οἷον] del. Z
12 ἠγρύπνησα–δώματος] in ext. mg. Y

(Amos 9:6),[1] in order to indicate the Assyrian throng.[2][3] And, "Look, O God our protector! (Ps 83:10 [84:9]); and, "in the shelter of your wings you will shelter me" (Ps 16[17]:8);[4] and, "spreading out his wings, he received them" (Deut 32:11)—Scripture provides additional examples of this image.[5]

73.2. Comparison:[6] for example, "I lay awake and became like a sparrow" (Ps 101:8 [102:7]);[7] and, "like a sheep . . . [he was led toward the slaughter]" (Isa 53:7).[8]

73.2. Comparison: whenever Scripture compares us, on the basis of our characteristics, to those characteristics which it portrays as similar in others.[9] For example, "I became like a night raven in a ruined house, I lay awake and became like a lone sparrow on a rooftop" (Ps 101:7–8 [102:6–7]). And similar passages.

---

[1] Thdr. Mops., *Am.* 9:6: "He is the one who takes the water of the sea and pours it out over the whole earth; he is now doing the very same thing in bringing upon your land the Assyrian, who in his vast numbers resembles the sea."

[2] Taking καί to form a hendiadys (s.v. καί BDAG 1.a.δ). Also note 29 above where Adrian observes hendiadys in Scripture.

[3] "And it renders the devastation . . . Assyrian throng." These lines have almost certainly been transposed from the section on allegory below (73.13), where Adrian makes the same observation about "flood" and "waters" but does not cite any scriptural verse to support his claim there, which is unusual. Note as well the parallel passage on allegory in R2 where "flood" and "waters" surface again. Since the distinction between metaphor and allegory is not crisply made, the transposed material is still intelligible here. It was likely moved because the immediately preceding lines discuss the metaphor of fishing.

[4] Thdr. Mops., *Ps.* 16:8: the Psalmist "begs the help of careful protection through a comparison with birds [*a similitudine avium*], which by enclosing the chicks in their wings not only nourish them, but also protect them from being snatched by poachers."

[5] A few observations about this sentence. First, note the blurring of tropes: the metaphor of God as a winged protector is here called σχηματισμός, a trope listed separately below. Second, my rendering of the verb ἐναπομένω is influenced by ἀπομένω (s.v. *PGL* 2: "continues"). Third, and related, this sentence might reflect an abridgement of material witnessed in the catenae. In Adrian., *cat. Ps.* 90:4 we find text not attested in R1 that discusses this ornithological metaphor: "for it is especially a feature in domestic birds, by an inborn affection, first to spread out their wings so that these stand guard over their own chicks, then to lift [them] so as to carry [them] effortlessly on their own backs."

[6] Note that R1 fails to provide a definition of this trope. This might be an instance of excessive abridgement, but note that Diodore also does not define comparison: he simply says that "comparison is easy to recognize when it is introduced by the word ὡς" (*Ps. hypoth.* 118).

[7] Thdt., *Ps.* 101:7–8: "He employs many comparisons in his wish to do justice to the calamities; through each of the birds mentioned he suggests fear and the lack of care: the 'sparrow' keeps sleep at bay with its struggles, and the 'night-raven' flees the inhabited parts of building and makes for deserted and forsaken ones."

[8] See Adrian., *cat. Ps.* 101:7–8 for a related discussion of comparison.

[9] For similar text to this paragraph, see Adrian., *cat. Ps.* 101:7–8.

73.3(110). κατὰ σύγκρισιν· οἷον τὰ
παρόντα τοῖς παλαιοῖς ἐκ τῶν
ὁμοίων ἐθέλει εἰκάζειν, τὴν τοῦ
βαπτίσματος χάριν τῇ Ἐρυθρᾷ
5 Θαλάσσῃ, καὶ τὴν τῶν θείων
μυστηρίων μετάληψιν τῇ τε τοῦ
μάννα καὶ τῷ ἐκ πέτρας ὕδατι·

10

15

73.3. τὰ δὲ κατὰ σύγκρισιν· ὅταν
τὰ πάροντα τοῖς παλαιοῖς ἐκ τῶν
ὁμοίων εἰκάζειν ἐθέλῃ· οἷον ὡς ὁ
ἀπόστολος τὴν τοῦ βαπτίσματος
χάριν τῇ τῶν Ἰσραηλιτῶν διὰ τῆς
Ἐρυθρᾶς Θαλάσσης παρόδῳ, καὶ τὴν
τῶν θειῶν μυστηρίων μετάληψιν τῇ
τε τοῦ μάννα καὶ τῷ ἐκ πέτρας ὕδατι·
παραδόξως αὐτοῖς τῷ τηνικαῦτα
παρασχεθεῖσιν ἀπολαύσει, ὥσπερ
οὖν καὶ ἡμῖν παρ᾽ ἐλπίδα πᾶσαν τὰ
παρόντα δεδώρηται· τήν τε τῆς
νῦν πολιτείας ἐλευθερίαν πρὸς τὴν
Σάρραν ἄτε δεσπότιν τῆς Ἄγαρ
τυγχάνουσαν, καὶ τὴν ὑπὸ νόμον
δουλείαν τὴν Ἄγαρ· τόν τε
Χριστὸν καὶ τὴν ἐκκλησίαν τῷ τε
Ἀδὰμ καὶ τῇ Εὕα· καὶ ὅσα
τοιαῦτα·

---

7 Cf. 1 Cor 10:1–4

8 Cf. 1 Cor 10:1–4
16 Cf. Gal 4:21–5
18 Cf. Eph 5:31–2

---

1 οἷον] ὅταν R2 Goessling (ex *Schlüren*)
3 ante τὴν] ὡς + Goessling, οἷον + *Schlüren*

1 ante Τὰ] ὅπως τὰ κατὰ σύγκρισιν titul. Z

73.3. Correspondence: for instance, it wishes to liken present realities with past events on the basis of their similarities—the grace of baptism to the Red Sea, and the partaking of the divine mysteries to the partaking of the manna and to the water from the rock (cf. 1 Cor 10:1–4).[1]

73.3. Correspondence: whenever it wishes to liken present realities with past events on the basis of their similarities. For instance the apostle [likens] the grace of baptism to the Israelites' crossing through the Red Sea, and the partaking of the divine mysteries to the partaking of the manna and to the water from the rock (cf. 1 Cor 10:1–4). These former events were unexpectedly provided at that time for the Israelites' enjoyment, just as these present realities now have also been given to us beyond all hope.[2] [Paul compares] the freedom of our current way of life with Sarah, because she was Hagar's mistress, and the slavery under the law with Hagar (cf. Gal 4:21–5).[3] And [Paul compares] Christ and the church with Adam and Eve respectively (cf. Eph 5:31–2).[4] And all such passages.

---

[1] Note 38 above where 1 Cor 10:1–4 illustrates the trope of metaphor and not correspondence, as here.

[2] See 38 above where 1 Cor 10:1–4 is an example of the trope of metaphor and not correspondence, as here. Thdt., *1 Cor.* 10:1–4: "The rock also resembled the Lord's side: streams sprang up for them unexpectedly, as he [Paul] brings out more clearly, 'They drank from a spiritual rock that followed them, remember; the rock was Christ.' Now, his meaning is that for them it was not the rock but divine grace which ensured that that rock unexpectedly gushed floods."

[3] Note 73.13 below, where amidst a discussion of the trope of allegory, Adrian says Paul misspoke in Gal 4 by using the term "allegory": in fact he was drawing a "correspondence" between events of old and new. Thdr. Mops., *Gal.* 4:24, writes similarly. He glosses Paul's reference to an "allegory" by explaining that he was actually making a comparison (*similitudo*, perhaps the translation of σύγκρισις) between events of old and present realities. Paul "was doubtless making a comparison, and no comparison can be made unless the terms of the comparison continue to exist." A little later, on this same verse: "He called allegory the comparison made by relating events that had already taken place to present circumstances" [ἀλληγορίαν ἐκάλεσεν τὴν ἐκ παραθέσεως τῶν ἤδη γεγονότων πρὸς τὰ παρόντα σύγκρισιν].

[4] See Thdr. Mops., *Eph.* 5:32 where again Paul is drawing a *similitudo* between Adam and Eve and Christ and the church.

RECENSION 1   RECENSION 2

73.4(111). κατὰ συνεκδοχήν· ὅταν
ἀπὸ μέρους τὸ ὅλον δηλοῖ· ὡς τό, **τὴν
ψυχήν μου ἐπέστρεψεν,** ἵνα εἴπῃ
ἐμέ· καί, **ἔτι δὲ καὶ ἡ σάρξ μου**
5 **κατασκηνώσει ἐπ' ἐλπίδι,** ἀντὶ
τοῦ ἐγώ· καί, **ἐκ γαστρὸς πρὸ
ἑωσφόρου ἐγέννησά σε,** ἀντὶ πρὸ
πάσης τῆς κτίσεως·

73.5(112). κατὰ ὑπόδειγμα· ὅταν τὰ
10 πρακτέα δι' ὁμοίων τινῶν
ὑποτίθεται· οἷον, **ἔγνω βοῦς τὸν
κτησάμενον·** καί, **ἡ ἀσίδα ἐν
τῷ οὐρανῷ ἔγνω τὸν καιρὸν
αὐτῆς·** καί, **ἄνθρωπός τις ἦν**
15 **οἰκοδεσπότης·** καί, **ἀνθρώπου
τινὸς πλουσίου·**

73.5. τὰ δὲ κατὰ ὑπόδειγμα· ὅταν
τὰ πρακτέα δι' ὁμοίων τινῶν
ὑποθῆται· οἷον τὸ παρὰ τῷ Ἡσαΐᾳ,
**ἔγνω βοῦς τὸν κτησάμενον καὶ ὄνος
τὴν φάτνην αὐτοῦ·** καὶ ὅσα
τοιαῦτα·

73.6(113). κατὰ μετωνυμίαν· ὅταν
ἢ ἀπὸ τῶν περιεχόντων τὰ
περιεχόμενα ἢ ἀπὸ τῶν
20 οἰκουμένων τοὺς οἰκοῦντας
μετονομάζει· καὶ ἀπὸ μὲν τῶν
περιεχόντων τὰ περιεχόμενα· ὡς
τό, **καὶ τὸ ποτήριόν σου μεθύσκον με**

73.6. τὰ δὲ κατὰ μετωνυμίαν·
ὅταν ἢ ἀπὸ τῶν περιεχόντων τὰ
περιεχόμενα ἢ τῶν οἰκουμένων τοὺς
οἰκοῦντας μετονομάζει· ὡς τό, **καὶ
τὸ ποτήριόν σου μεθύσκον με ὡσεὶ
κράτιστον·** καὶ ὡς τό,
προσκαλέσατε τὸν οὐρανὸν ἄνω καὶ

3 Ps 22[23]:3
5 Ps 15[16]:9
7 Ps 109[110]:3 var.
12 Isa 1:3
14 Jer 8:7
15 Matt 21:33 var.
16 Luke 12:16

13 Isa 1:3 var.
22 Ps 22[23]:5 var.

12 ἡ ἀσίδα] Hoeschel, ἡ ἰασίδα L, ἰασίδα
Goessling
14 ἦν] deest Hoeschel Goessling (ex A)
18 ἢ] Goessling (ex Pearson Migne), ᾗ L, ᾗ Hoeschel (ex AB)
19 ᾗ] R2, καὶ L
20 ἀπὸ τῶν οἰκούμενων τοὺς οἰκοῦντας] ἀπὸ
τῶν οἰκουμένων τὰ οἰκοῦντα Schlüren, ἀπὸ
τῶν οἰκούντων τὰ οἰκούμενα L
22 περιεχόντων] Hoeschel Goessling,
περιεχομένων L

10 δι'] δ'Z
17 ante Τὰ] ὅπως τὰ κατὰ μετωνυμίαν titul. Z
20 τῶν οἰκουμενῶν τοὺς οἰκοῦντας] τῶν
οἰκούντων τὰ οἰκούμενα YZ
21 μεθύσκον με] μεθύσκομαι YZ

73.4. Synecdoche: whenever it indicates the whole from its part.[1] For example, "he restored my soul" (Ps 22[23]:3), in order to say "[he restored] me." And, "moreover, my flesh will dwell in hope" (Ps 15[16]:9), instead of "I."[2] And, "from the womb, before the morning star I brought you forth" (Ps 109[110]:3), instead of "before all of creation."

73.5. Exemplar: whenever it prescribes what must be done through similar things.[3] For instance, "the ox knows its owner" (Isa 1:3); and, "the stork in the sky knew its time" (Jer 8:7); and, "there was a landowner..." (Matt 21:33); and, "[the land] of a certain rich man..." (Lk 12:16).

73.5. Exemplar: whenever it prescribes what must be done through similar things. For instance, in Isaiah: "the ox knows its owner and the donkey its manger" (Isa 1:3). And all such passages.

73.6. Metonymy: whenever it renames things—either contents get called by their containers, or inhabitants get called by the areas they habit.[4] Contents by their containers: for example, "and your cup that intoxicates me like strongest wine" (Ps 22[23]:5); and,

73.6. Metonymy: whenever it renames things—either contents get called by their containers, or inhabitants get called by the areas they inhabit. For example, "and your cup that intoxicates me like strongest wine" (Ps 22[23]:5); and for example, "summon[5] heaven

---

[1] See 2.15 and 17 above for additional discussion of synecdoche. See Mariès, *Études*, 119; Devreesse, *Essai*, 66; Schäublin, *Untersuchungen*, 111–12, for discussions and illustrations of this trope in Theodore.

[2] Thdr. Mops., *Ps.* 15:9: "By 'my flesh' he means 'I myself,' naming the whole from the part, the divine Scripture normally referring to the whole person by flesh and likewise by soul—by flesh in saying, 'All flesh had corrupted its way' [Gen 6:12], and by soul in saying, 'Jacob went down into Egypt with seventy-five souls' [Gen 46:27]."

[3] Diod., *Ps. hypoth.* 40: the Psalmist "takes Hezekiah as an example [Ὑπόδειγμα γὰρ λαμβάνων] to exhort all people to be merciful." Thdr. Mops., *Ps.* 41:2: "Wanting to bring out the deep longing, he employed the example [τῷ ... ὑποδείγματι] of deer, not finding among human beings an adequate example for the desperation of the longing." Other instances of this trope: Thdr. Mops., *Ps.* 58:16 (dogs); 77:13 (wine bottle); 77:65 (someone asleep); *Os.* 12:11 (turtle); *Am.* 5:19–20.

[4] On this trope in Theodore, see Schäublin, *Untersuchungen*, 113–15.

[5] The form προσκαλέσατε is attested in some mss according to the apparatus on this verse in Rahlfs, *Psalmi cum Odis*.

RECENSION 1	RECENSION 2

ὡσεὶ κράτιστον· καί, ὀλολύζετε
πλοῖα Καρχηδόνος· καί, τὸ
ποτήριον τῆς ἀδελφῆς σου
πίεσαι· ἀπὸ δὲ τῶν οἰκουμένων τοὺς
5 οἰκοῦντας· ὡς τό, προσκαλέσεται
τὸν οὐρανὸν ἄνω· καί,
Ἰερουσαλὴμ Ἰερουσαλήμ, ἡ
ἀποκτέννουσα τοὺς προφήτας·
καί, ἀγαλλιᾶσθε νῆσοι πολλαί·

τὴν γῆν τοῦ διακρῖναι τὸν λαὸν
αὐτοῦ·

10

73.4. τὰ δὲ κατὰ συνεκδοχήν· ὅταν
ἀπὸ μέρους τὸ ὅλον τῇ λέξει
συμπεριλαμβάνοιεν· ὡς τό, τὴν
ψυχήν μου ἐπέστρεψεν, ἵνα εἴπῃ
ἐμέ· καὶ τό, ἐκ γαστρὸς πρὸ
15 ἑωσφόρου ἐγέννησά σε, ἀντὶ τοῦ
πρὸ πάσης κτίσεως· καὶ ὅσα
τοιαῦτα·

73.7(114). κατὰ ἀντίφρασιν· ὅταν δι᾽
ἐναντίου τὸ ἐναντίον δηλοῖ· οἷον, εἰ
20 μὴν εἰς πρόσωπόν σε εὐλογήσει,
ἀντὶ τοῦ βλασφημήσει· καί,
εὐλόγησε θεὸν καὶ βασιλέα, ἀντὶ
τοῦ ὕβρισεν, ἐκάκωσεν· καί, ὅτι
δεδόξασται ὁ βασιλεύς· καί,
25 < ἐπικατάρατος ἄνθρωπος ὁ
εὐαγγελισάμενος τῷ πατρί μου
λέγων ὅτι ἐτέχθη σοι ἄρσεν· >

73.7. τὰ δὲ κατὰ ἀντίφρασιν· ὅταν
ἕτερον ἀνθ᾽ ἑτέρου λέγει· οἷον τὸ περὶ
τοῦ Ἰὼβ ὑπὸ τοῦ διαβόλου· οὐ μὴν
ἀλλὰ ἐξαπόστειλον τὴν χεῖρά σου
καὶ ἅψαι τῶν ὀστέων αὐτοῦ ἦ μὴν
εἰς πρόσωπόν σε εὐλογήσει, ἀντὶ
τοῦ εἰπεῖν βλασφημήσει· καὶ τὸ ἐν τῇ
τῶν Βασιλειῶν βίβλῳ περὶ τοῦ
Ναβουθαί, εὐλόγησε θεὸν καὶ
βασιλέα, ἀντὶ τοῦ ἐβλασφήμησεν,

1 Ps 22[23]:5 var.
2 Isa 23:1
4 Ezek 23:32
6 Ps 49[50]:4
8 Matt 23:37 var.; Luke 13:34 var.
9 Ps 96[97]:1 var.
20 Job 2:5
22 3 Kgdms 20:10 [1 Kgs 21:10]
24 2 Kgdms 6:20 [2 Sam 6:20] var.

2 Ps 49[50]:4 var.
13 Ps 22[23]:3
15 Ps 109[110]:3 var.
23 Job 2:5 var.
27 3 Kgdms 20:10 [1 Kgs 21:10]

5 ἀπὸ δὲ τῶν οἰκουμένων τοὺς οἰκοῦντας]
ἀπὸ δὲ τῶν οἰκουμένων τὰ οἰκοῦντα Schlüren,
ἀπὸ δὲ τῶν οἰκούντων τὰ οἰκούμενα L
27 ἐπικατάρατος–ἄρσεν,] cat. Job 1:11

10 ante Τὰ] ὅπως κατὰ συνεκδοχήν titul. Z
18 ante Τὰ] ὅπως κατὰ ἀντίφρασιν titul. Z

"wail, you ships of Carthage!" (Isa 23:1); and, "drink the cup of your sister!" (Ezek 23:32). And the inhabitants by the areas they inhabit: for example, "he will summon heaven above" (Ps 49[50]:4);[1] and, "Jerusalem, Jerusalem, who kills the prophets" (Matt 23:37; Luke 13:34); and, "let the many islands rejoice" (Ps 96[97]:1)!

above and the earth below to judge his people" (Ps 49[50]:4).

73.4. Synecdoche: whenever in a passage Scripture's authors include the whole from its part.[4] For example, "he restored my soul" (Ps 22[23]:3), in order to say "[he restored] me." And, "from the womb, before the morning star I brought you forth" (Ps 109[110]:3), instead of "before all creation." And all such passages.

73.7. Antiphrasis: whenever it signifies exactly the opposite of what is said. For example, "surely he will bless you to your face" (Job 2:5), instead of "he will blaspheme."[2] And, "he blessed God and king" (3 Kgdms 20:10 [1 Kings 21:10]), instead of "he insulted," "he did evil."[3] And, "how the king has honored himself" (2 Kgdms 6:20 [2 Sam 6:20]); and, "Cursed be the person who

73.7. Antiphrasis: whenever it mentions one, rather than the other, of two contrasting things.[5] For example, [what is said] by the devil about Job: "However, stretch out your hand and touch his bones . . .; surely he will bless you to your face" (Job 2:5), instead of saying "he will blaspheme." And in the book of Kingdoms concerning Naboth: "he blessed God and king" (3 Kgdms

---

[1] Diod., *Ps.* 49:4: God summons the "heavenly powers from one high." So too Thdr. Mops., *Ps.* 49:4: "that is, the heavenly powers."

[2] The same gloss occurs in Polychr., *fr. Job* 2:5 and Olymp., *fr. Job* 2:5: Polychronius identifies the source of this gloss as what "the Hebrew has" (ὁ Ἑβραῖος . . . ἔχει). For orientation to ὁ Ἑβραῖος, see: Marcos, *Septuagint in Context*, 161–3.

[3] Note the juxtaposition of Job 1:11 (which also reads as Job 2:5: εἰς πρόσωπόν σε εὐλογήσει) with 3 Kgdms 20:10 in Polychr., *fr. Job* 1:11 and Olymp., *fr. Job* 1:11—both authors say that Scripture speaks euphemistically (εὐφήμως) and that "blaspheming" is intended.

[4] For the significance of the verb συμπεριλαμβάνω note Theodore's discussion of synecdoche at *Zach.* 14:20: he remarks that "divine Scripture normally implies whole from part whenever it considers chasing detail superfluous." Theodore presents this trope as a form of shorthand designed to capture or include the whole by only mentioning the part.

[5] S.v. ἕτερος, -α, -ον BDAG 1.a. The definition of the trope in R1 is more satisfactory.

RECENSION 1	RECENSION 2

εὐφραινόμενος ἔστω ὁ ἄνθρωπος ἐκεῖνος·

ὕβρησε, κατηγόρησεν· ὁμοίως δὲ καὶ τὸ παρὰ τῆς Μελχὸλ πρὸς τὸν Δαυίδ, ὅτι δεδόξασται ὁ βασιλεὺς ἀποκαλυφθεὶς καὶ γυμνωθεὶς ἐνώπιον γυναικῶν, καθὼς γυμνοῦνται οἱ ὀρχούμενοι, ἀντὶ τοῦ εὐτελὴς καὶ ἀσχήμων ὦπται· καὶ ὅσα τοιαῦτα·

73.8(115). κατὰ περίφρασιν· ὅταν τοῖς δι' ὀλίγων ἐκφωνεῖσθαι δυναμένοις τὴν διὰ πλειόνων φράσιν περιτίθησιν· οἷον, **καὶ ἰδοὺ ἀλλόφυλοι καὶ Τύρος καὶ λαὸς τῶν Αἰθιόπων, οὗτοι ἐγεννήθησαν ἐκεῖ·**

73.8. τὰ δὲ κατὰ περίφρασιν· ὅταν τοῖς δι' ὀλίγων ἐκφωνεῖσθαι δυναμένοις τὴν διὰ πλειόνων φράσιν περιτιθῇ· ὡς τό, **ἀπώσατο τὸ σχήνωμα Ἰωσὴφ καὶ τὴν φυλὴν Ἐφραὶμ οὐκ ἐξελέξατο· καὶ ἐξελέξατο τὴν φυλὴν Ἰούδα·** παρὸν συντόμως εἰπεῖν προέκρινεν τῶν λοιπῶν τὴν Ἰούδα φυλήν· καὶ τό, **ἰδοὺ ἀλλόφυλοι καὶ Τύρος καὶ λαὸς τῶν Αἰθιόπων, οὗτοι ἐγεννήθησαν ἐκεῖ·** δέον ἀρκεσθῆναι μόνῳ τῷ ἰδοὺ ἀλλόφυλοι·

73.9(116). κατὰ ἀνακεφαλαίωσιν εἴτ' οὖν ἐπανάληψιν· ὅταν τὰ διὰ πλειόνων ποικίλως εἰσηγηθέντα διὰ τὴν ἀπὸ τῆς τῶν παρεκβάσεων ἀνωμαλίας δυσχέρειαν ἐν ὀλίγοις αὖθις διεξέρχεται· ὡς ὁ Μωσῆς φησίν, **αὕτη ἡ βίβλος γενέσεως**

73.9. τὰ δὲ κατὰ ἀνακεφαλαίωσιν ἤτουν ἐπανάληψιν· ὅταν τὰ διὰ πλειόνων ποικίλως εἰσηγηθέντα διὰ τὴν ἀπὸ τῆς τῶν παρεκβάσεων ἀνωμαλίας δυσχέρειαν, ἐν ὀλίγοις αὖθις διεξέρχηται, ὡσὰν τὸν σκοπὸν τῆς εἰσηγήσεως ἐπὶ τὴν οἰκείαν

2 Jer 20:15–16
14 Ps 86[87]:4 var.

6 2 Kgdms 6:20 [2 Sam 6:20] var.
15 Ps 77[78]:67–8 var.
19 Ps 86[87]:4 var.

14 ἐξελέξατο] ἐξελέξα Z

brought the good news to my father, saying 'A male child was born to you.' Let that person be glad..." (Jer 20:15–16).[1]

20:10 [1 Kgs 21:10]), instead of "he blasphemed," "he insulted," "he accused." Similarly, also [the words] by Michal to David: "how the king has honored himself, who was uncovered and naked in the view of his women, just as the dancers strip themselves naked" (2 Kgdms 6:20 [2 Sam 6:20]), instead of "he has appeared worthless and shameful." And passages such as these.[3]

73.8. Periphrasis: whenever it confers a verbose style on things that can be expressed through a few words. For example, "and look, foreigners and Tyre and a people of Ethiopians, these were born there" (Ps 86[87]:4).[2]

73.8. Periphrasis: whenever it confers a verbose style on things that can be expressed through a few words. For example, "he rejected the tent of Joseph and did not choose the tribe of Ephraim; and he chose the tribe of Judah" (Ps 77[78]:67–8)—it is possible to say concisely: "he preferred the tribe of Judah to the others."[4] And, "look, foreigners and Tyre and a people of Ethiopians, these were born there" (Ps 86[87]:4)— "look, foreigners" would be enough.

73.9. Summary or repetition: whenever it goes through again with a few words, what was narrated in various ways with many words, because of the difficulty caused by the unevenness of the digressions. For example, Moses says, "This is the book of the creation of

73.9. Summary or repetition: whenever it goes through again, with a few words, what was narrated in various ways with many words, because of the difficulty caused by the unevenness of the digressions. It does this in order to restore the aim of the narration[5] to its proper liter-

---

[1] See Adrian., *cat. Job* 1:11 for a similar, though more expansive, discussion of this trope. There Jer 20:15–16 is glossed as follows: "it says 'be glad' instead of 'be distressed.' "

[2] For references to passages being written περιφραστικῶς, see Diod., *Ps.* 16:14; 25:3; 35:12 and Mariès, *Études*, 120.

[3] See the related discussion of this trope in Adrian., *cat. Job* 1:11.

[4] Thdr. Mops., *Ps.* 77:67–8: "The terms 'tribe of Ephraim' and 'tent of Joseph' mean the same thing, Ephraim being Joseph's son."

[5] I am proposing "narration" as a definition for εἰσήγησις, taking my cue from εἰσηγέομαι, LSJ A.4: "relate, narrate, explain."

RECENSION 1	**RECENSION 2**

οὐρανοῦ τε καὶ γῆς· τοιαῦτα καὶ
ἐν ταῖς βασιλείαις καὶ ἐν τῷ
ἀποστόλῳ·

5

ἀκολουθίαν ἀνακαλέσοιτο· ὡς τό,
αὕτη ἡ βίβλος γενέσεως οὐρανοῦ τε
καὶ γῆς, ὅτε ἐγένετο, ᾗ ἡμέρᾳ
ἐποίησεν κύριος ὁ θεὸς τὸν οὐρανὸν
καὶ τὴν γῆν καὶ πᾶν χλωρὸν ἀγροῦ
πρὸ τοῦ γενέσθαι ἐπὶ τῆς γῆς,
καὶ τὰ ἐξῆς· ἐντεῦθέν τε λοιπὸν
ἀκολούθως τὰ κατ᾽ αὐτὸν
συναπετέλεσεν· καὶ ὅσα τοιαῦτα·

10 **73.10**(117). κατὰ ἀπόχρησιν· ὅταν τῇ
ἑτέρων προσηγορίᾳ καὶ ἐν ἑτέροις
καταχρᾶται· οἷον, ὡς τό, **φύλαξόν**
με κύριε ὡς κόρην ὀφθαλμοῦ·
καί, ἐν σοὶ τοὺς ἐχθροὺς ἡμῶν
15 **κερατιοῦμεν·** καί, ὁ στεγάζων ἐν
ὕδασι τὰ ὑπερῷα αὐτοῦ· καί, ὡς
ὄρθρος χυθήσεται ἐπὶ τὰ ὄρη λαὸς
πολὺς καὶ ἰσχυρός, περὶ τῆς
ἀκρίδος λέγων·

20

73.10. τὰ δὲ κατ᾽ ἀπόχρησιν· ὅταν
τῇ ἑτέρων προσηγορίᾳ καὶ ἐν ἑτέροις
εὐλόγως καταχρῶτο· ὡς τό, **φύλαξόν**
με κύριε ὡς κόρην ὀφθαλμοῦ·
ἀπεχρήσατο γὰρ ἐπὶ τῆς βλεπτικῆς
περιφερείας τῇ τῆς παιδὸς
προσηγορίᾳ εἰκότως διὰ τὸ καὶ
αὐτὴν ὑπὸ τοῖς βλεφάροις, καθάπερ
οὖν ἐκείνην ὑπὸ τοῖς οἰκείοις
κρύπτεσθαι θαλάμοις· καὶ τὸ παρὰ
τῷ Ἰωήλ, **ὡς ὄρθρος χυθήσεται ἐπὶ**
τὰ ὄρη λαὸς πολὺς καὶ ἰσχυρός, τὴν

---

1 Gen 2:4 var.
13 Ps 16[17]:8 var.
15 Ps 43:6 [44:5]
16 Ps 103[104]:3
18 Joel 2:2

6 Gen 2:4–5 var.
13 Ps 16[17]:8 var.
21 Joel 2:2

---

12 οἷον] – *Hoeschel Goessling*

10 ante Τὰ] ὅπως κατὰ ἀπόχρησιν titul. YZ

heaven and earth" (Gen 2:4).[1] Similar examples also [occur] in the Kingdoms and in the apostle.[2]

ary sequence. For example, "This is the book of the creation of heaven and earth, when it originated, on the day that the Lord God made the heaven and the earth and all greenery of the field before it came to be on the earth" (Gen 2:4–5), etc. From here, and in what follows, Moses finished the words sequentially in accordance with the aim of the passage.[4] And all such passages.

73.10. Irregular usage: whenever it uses the term for one thing in an irregular manner also for a different thing.[3] For example, "guard me, O Lord, like a pupil of an eye" (Ps 16[17]:8); and, "through you will we gore our enemies" (Ps 43:6 [44:5]); and, "He who roofs his upper stories with waters" (Ps 103[104]:3); and speaking about the locust, "like dawn, a people numerous and strong will spread out over the mountains" (Joel 2:2).

73.10. Irregular usage: whenever it uses the term for one thing in an irregular manner for a different thing, but with good reason. For example, "guard me, O Lord, like a pupil of an eye" (Ps 16[17]:8).[5] For Scripture used the term for a girl irregularly with regard to the pupil, but did so reasonably, since the pupil also is protected by the eyelids, just as a girl is protected by the inner quarters of her house.[6] And in Joel: "like dawn, a people numerous and

---

[1] Thdr. Mops. (?), *fr. Gen.* 2:4 [Petit, *chaîne* no. 190] where this verse is an ἀνακεφαλαίωσις of what precedes, written with "much conciseness" (μετὰ πολλῆς . . . τῆς συντομίας). Note also the similar, and more expansive, observation about repetitions in Scripture in Eus. Em., *fr. Gen.* 2:4 [Arm.] and *fr. Gen.* 2:6 [Proc. G.]: the Armenian version associates this feature with the establishment of clarity, whereas the Greek fragment links ἀναλήψεις with obscurity. Thdt., *qu. in Gen.* 22: "The historian has related the story of creation once again, this time in summary fashion ['Εν κεφαλαίῳ]."

[2] See Thdt., *qu. in Jud.* 1; *qu. in Jud.* 7.2.

[3] Taking ἀπόχρησις in the sense of speech that is loose, inexact or irregular (s.v. καταχρηστικῶς PGL). This trope is difficult to distinguish from others on this list, as is illustrated by Theodore's discussion of Ps 43:6, which Adrian uses to illustrate this trope: for Theodore, the trope in question is metaphor.

[4] Note two important exegetical terms in this paragraph: σκοπός ("aim" or "intent") and ἀκολουθία ("sequence"). This trope re-establishes order in a pericope: Gen 2:4–5 restates the aim of the opening chapters of Genesis that has been lost due to preceding digressions. From this point on, the narrative proceeds sequentially and in harmony with the aim.

[5] The traditional rendering of Ps 16:8 in English ("apple of the eye") distorts the imagery. The noun in question (κόρη) signifies a young woman or girl (LSJ I), but by extension, the eye's pupil (LSJ III) because of the little image that is reflected in the iris of the eye.

[6] Thdr. Mops., *Ps.* 16:8: "he does well to adduce the figure of the pupil of the eye, to which by the very quality of the work and extreme carefulness sight is marvelously communicated by the maker, with the result that it is not easily damaged from outside by any assault. For a start, you see, it is wrapped in many strong dressings; then a covering of its eyelids is spread out for its protection, as well as the placement of orbs achieved by the closeness of eyebrows and cheeks, with the result that it is fortified against any chance blow and rarely exposed to harm." On this passage, also see Schäublin, *Untersuchungen*, 150–1.

RECENSION 1	RECENSION 2

τῆς ἀκρίδος πληθύν λαὸν πολὺν
προσαγορεύσας· καὶ ὅσα τοιαῦτα·

73.11(118). κατὰ προσωποποιΐαν·
ὅταν τισὶ τῶν ἀψύχων ἐνίοτε δὲ καὶ
5 ἀνυποστάτων πρόσωπά τε καὶ
λόγους ὑποτίθεται· ἐπὶ μὲν ἀψύχων·
ὡς τό, **ἐπάρθητε πύλαι αἰώνιοι**·
καί, **οἱ οὐρανοὶ διηγοῦνται**· καί,
πορευόμενα ἐπορεύθη τὰ ξύλα·
10 ἐπὶ δὲ τῶν ἀνυποστάτων· ὡς τό,
δικαιοσύνη καὶ εἰρήνη
κατεφίλησαν· καί, **ἐκάλεσε τὴν**
δίκην ἐν πυρὶ κύριος· καί, **ἔρριψε**
τὸν λίθον εἰς τὸ στόμα τῆς
15 **ἀνομίας**· καὶ εἶπεν ἡ σοφία, **κύριος**
ἔκτισέ με, καί, **ἐγὼ ἤμην ᾗ**
προσέχαιρε καθ’ ἡμέραν· καί,
ᾠκοδόμησεν ἑαυτῇ οἶκον·

73.11. τὰ δὲ κατὰ προσωποποΐαν·
ὅτάν τισι τῶν ἀψύχων ἐνίοτε δὲ καὶ
ἀνυποστάτων πρόσωπά τε
ὑποτίθεται καὶ λόγους, οἵουσπερ
εἰκὸς ἦν τοῖς κατὰ καιρὸν
ἁρμόζει<ν> πράγμασιν· οἶον ἐπὶ μὲν
τῶν ἀψύχων· ὡς τὸ ἀπὸ τῶν πυλῶν
τοῦ ναοῦ ἀντηχούμενον μετὰ τὸ
εἰρῆσθαι πρὸς αὐτάς, **ἐπάρθητε**
πύλαι αἰώνιοι, τίς ἐστιν οὗτος ὁ
βασιλεὺς τῆς δόξης· ἐπὶ δὲ τῶν
ἀνυποστάτων· ὡς τό, **δικαιοσύνη καὶ**
εἰρήνη κατεφίλησαν· καὶ ὅσα
τοιαῦτα·

73.12(119). κατὰ σχηματισμόν· ὅταν
20 τὰ αὐτὰ σχηματοποιῇ πρὸς τὴν τῶν
πραγμάτων ὑφήγησιν· ὡς τό,
παρέστη ἡ βασίλισσα ἐκ δεξιῶν
σου· καί, **ποταμοὶ κροτήσουσι**
χειρὶ ἐπὶ τὸ αὐτό· καί, **οἱ μασθοί**

73.12. τὰ δὲ κατὰ σχηματισμόν·
ὅταν τὰ αὐτὰ σχηματοποιῇ πρὸς
τὴν τῶν πραγμάτων ὑφήγησιν· ὡς
τό, **παρέστη ἡ βασίλισσα ἐκ δεξιῶν**
σου ἐν ἱματισμῷ διαχρύσῳ
περιβεβλημένη πεποικιλμένη· καὶ

7 Ps 23[24]:7
8 Ps 18:2 [19:1]
9 Judg 9:8
12 Ps 84:11 [85:10]
13 Amos 7:4
15 Zech 5:8 var.
16 Prov 8:22
17 Prov 8:30
18 Prov 9:1
23 Ps 44:10 [45:9]
24 Ps 97[98]:8

12 Ps 23[24]:7
13 Ps 23[24]:8
15 Ps 84:11 [85:10]
24 Ps 44:10 [45:9]

3 ante Τὰ] ὅπως κατὰ προσωποποΐαν titul. Z
20 σχηματοποιῇ] σχηματοποιεῖ Z
22 παρέστη] R1, παρέστ Y, παρέστι Z

TRANSLATION: R1	TRANSLATION: R2

strong will spread out over the mountains" (Joel 2:2), designating the locus swarm as a multitude of people. And all such passages.

73.11. Personification: whenever it assigns personhood and speeches to lifeless things and sometimes even abstract concepts.[1] Concerning lifeless things: for example, "be raised up, everlasting gates!" (Ps 23[24]:7); and, "the heavens declare" (Ps 18:2 [19:1]); and, "walking along, the trees walked" (Judg 9:8). Concerning abstract concepts: for example, "righteousness and peace kissed" (Ps 84:11 [85:10]); and, "the Lord summoned for judgment by fire" (Amos 7:4); and, "he threw the stone... into the mouth of lawlessness" (Zach 5:8); and Wisdom said: "The Lord made me" (Prov 8:22) and, "I was the one in whom he delighted daily" (Prov 8:30); and, "She [i.e., Wisdom] built herself a house" (Prov 9:1).

73.11. Personification: whenever it assigns personhood and speeches to lifeless things and sometimes even abstract concepts—from time to time it was reasonable to adapt the former to the latter realities. Concerning lifeless things: for example, after addressing the gates of the temple with the words, "be raised up, everlasting gates!" (Ps 23[24]:7), the following is sung antiphonally by them: "Who is this king of glory" (Ps 23[24]:8)? Concerning abstract concepts: for example, "righteousness and peace kissed" (Ps 84:11 [85:10]). And all such passages.

73.12. Representational language:[2] whenever it depicts the circumstances in question pictorially for the purpose of instruction.[3] For example, "at your right hand stood the queen" (Ps 44:10 [45:9]);[4] and, "the rivers will clap their

73.12. Representational language: whenever it depicts the circumstances in question pictorially for the purpose of instruction. For example, "at your right hand stood the queen in gold-woven clothing, decked out in many

---

[1] On this topic, see esp. Rondeau, *Les commentaires patristiques du Psautier*, vol. 2, *Exégèse prosopologique et théologie*, 275–321.

[2] The term σχηματισμός (σχηματίζειν) surfaces several times in the treatise (2, 4.10, and 73.1). As the examples below will make clear, it is closely tied to a pictorial or imagistic representation of God or other incorporeal realities. See esp. Mariès, *Études*, 119; Schäublin, *Untersuchungen*, 140 fn. 226.

[3] S.v. ὑφήγησις PGL 1–3 and Mansfeld, *Prolegomena*, 78. Note R2, which seems to have instruction in view, as well as Olymp., *fr. Job* 1:6, who remarks that the section of Job to which Adrian refers below was written διὰ τὴν ἡμετέραν νόησιν κατὰ σχηματισμόν.

[4] Diod., *Ps.* 44:10: "In portraits ['Επὶ τῶν εἰκόνων] they picture kings seated with some women in attendance, and give as an inscription 'Kingship' or 'Righteousness' or something of the like. So by analogy with the portraits his meaning is, 'You are seated on an elevated throne, and the church will attend to you in the place of a queen.'" Thdr. Mops., *Ps.* 44:10 also sees the Psalm as a prophecy of Christ and the church and notes how its language mirrors how people "always represent in their images [ἐν ταῖς εἰκόσιν ἀεί... γράφουσι]" women standing in attendance by kings.

σου ἀνωρθώθησαν, καὶ ἡ θρίξ σου
ἀνέτειλε, σὺ δὲ ἦσθα γυμνὴ καὶ
ἀσχημονοῦσα· μασθοὺς
καταχρηστικῶς τὰ ὄρη λέγουσα ἀπὸ
5 τοῦ σχήματος, τρίχα δὲ τὴν τῆς γῆς
εὐφορίαν· κατασκευάζει δὲ καὶ ἀπὸ
πραγμάτων σχηματισμόν, ὡς ἐν τῇ
κατὰ τὸν μακάριον Ἰὼβ ὑποθέσει·
οἷον τὸ παραστῆναι τὸν διάβολον
10 ἐνώπιον τοῦ θεοῦ·

15

20

τό, ποταμοὶ κροτήσουσι χειρὶ ἐπὶ τὸ
αὐτό· καὶ τὸ παρὰ τῷ Ἰεζεκιὴλ
πρὸς τὴν Ἰερυσαλήμ, οἱ μασθοί σου
ἀνωρθώθησαν, καὶ ἡ θρίξ σου
ἀνέτειλεν, σὺ δὲ ἦσθα γυμνὴ καὶ
ἀσχημονοῦσα· μασθοὺς μὲν γὰρ
αὐτῆς καταχρηστικῶς τὰ ὄρη λέγει
ἀπὸ τοῦ σχήματος, τρίχα δὲ τὴν τῆς
γῆς εὐφορίαν· κατασκευάζει δὲ καὶ
ἀπὸ πραγμάτων ἐνίων τὸν
σχηματισμόν, ὡς ἐν τῇ κατὰ τὸν
μακάριον Ἰὼβ ὑποθέσει· οἷον τὸ
παραστῆναι μὲν τὸν διάβολον
ἐνώπιον τοῦ θεοῦ, εἶτα ἐρωτηθέντα
ὑπ᾽ αὐτοῦ, καὶ ἀποκριθέντα λάβειν
μὲν τὴν κατὰ τοῦ Ἰὼβ ἐξουσίαν,
δρᾶσαι δὲ ἐκεῖνα ἅπερ οὖν
ἀναγέγραπται· τὰ τότε συμβεβηκότα
τῷ δικαίῳ ὑπὸ τῆς τοῦ διαβόλου
δῆλον ὅτι φαυλότητος· τὸ δὲ πᾶν
ἐσχηματοποίησεν, ἵνα τὸ συμβὰν
κατὰ τὴν θείαν δείξειεν γένεσθαι
συγχώρησιν καὶ οὐ κατὰ τὴν τοῦ
δαίμονος ἐξουσίαν· καὶ ὅσα τοιαῦτα·

3 Ezek 16:7
10 Cf. Job 1:6–11

2 Ps 97[98]:8
6 Ezek 16:7
18 Cf. Job 1:6–11

12 post ὑποθέσει·] τὰ τότε-φαυλότητος in
73.12 infra transp.
17 δὲ] om. Z
20 δῆλον ὅτι] δηλονότι YZ
20 τὰ τότε-φαυλότητος] in codd. post Ἰὼβ
ὑποθέσει·
20 δὲ] om. Z

hands together" (Ps 97[98]:8).[1] And, "your breasts grew firm and your hair grew, but you were naked and disgraced" (Ezek 16:7), by an irregular usage calling the mountains "breasts" because of their shape, and the fertility of its earth "hair."[2] And it renders events pictorially, as with the historical situation[3] of blessed Job: for example, representing the devil before the presence of God (cf. Job 1:6–11).[4]

colors" (Ps 44:10 [45:9]); and, "the rivers will clap their hands together" (Ps 97[98]:8). And the passage in Ezekiel [addressed] to Jerusalem: "your breasts grew firm and your hair grew, but you were naked and disgraced" (Ezek 16:7); by an irregular usage Scripture calls the mountains of Jerusalem "breasts" because of their shape, and the fertility of its earth "hair." And it renders certain events pictorially, as with the historical situation of blessed Job: for example, representing the devil before the presence of God, then being interrogated by Him, and being chosen to seize Job's resources and to do those things which have been recorded (cf. Job 1:6–11). It is clear that, at that time, things happened to this just person by way of the devil's malice.[5] But Scripture depicted the whole matter pictorially to demonstrate that what happened transpired in accordance with divine consent and not by this demon's authority.[6] And all such passages.

---

[1] See Thdr. Mops., *Ps. hypoth.* 118 where he remarks about artists whose pictures portray rivers in human form, and how the Psalmist duplicates this artistic approach.

[2] Note how something written καταχρηστικῶς (73.10) surfaces in this discussion of pictorial imagery. Thdt., *Ezech.* 16:7: "He says everything in figurative fashion by analogy with young people [Τροπικῶς ἅπαντα ἐκ μεταφορᾶς τῶν παιδίων λέγει]."

[3] See the first note in 75 on the two basic meanings of the term ὑπόθεσις.

[4] That is, Job's actual temptations (τὰ πράγματα) are presented in an imagistic—perhaps even imaginary—way, as if these temptations were precipitated by the devil coming into the presence of God and conversing with him. Polychr. (?), *fr. Job* prol. 3: "Just as those making images are unable to present things unless they depict them in a bodily manner [ὥσπερ οἱ τὰς εἰκόνας τυποῦντες, εἰ μὴ σωματοποιήσωσιν, οὐ δύνανται παραστῆσαι τὰ πράγματα]—wishing to show the king as peaceful and victorious, they place at his side renderings of Nike and Eirene—so also the writer of this book, wishing to present the course of Job's temptations, formed an image [ὁ συγγραφεὺς ... ἀνετυπώσατο] of the devil and his conversations with God." And see Polychr., *fr. Job* 1:6 where the kind of scene chosen by the writer is identified: "For a more tangible expression of the content, the chronicler expresses what the devil intends and God concedes with the image of a drama [ὁ τοίνυν ἱστοριογράφος ἐν δράματος σχήματι τὰ κατὰ βουλὴν τοῦ διαβόλου καὶ συγχώρησιν θεοῦ τίθησι πρὸς ἐναργεστέραν σαφήνειαν τοῦ λεγομένου]." For similar reflections, see Chrys., *Job* 1:6 and Olymp., *fr. Job* 1:6–7; 1:4. Note as well Thdr. Mops., *fr. Job* (PG 66, 698 B–D) on a poet's transformation of the story of Job to reflect the pattern of pagan tragedies (Mariès, *Études*, 130; Schäublin, *Untersuchungen*, 77–83).

[5] Note that I have transposed this sentence: in the mss it occurs immediately after "the historical situation of the blessed Job." However, it seems to make more sense here.

[6] There is the tacit acknowledgement in this paragraph that some scriptural narratives contain fictions. While the devil truly afflicted Job, a scene was constructed by the biblical author in which the

RECENSION 1	RECENSION 2
73.13(120). κατὰ ἀλληγορίαν· ὅταν τὰ ἄπειρα πλήθη συνεχῶς ὕδατα λέγῃ καὶ τὴν τούτων ἔφοδον κατακλυσμόν· καὶ τό, **ἔσται ὡς τὸ** **ξύλον τὸ πεφυτευμένον**· καὶ ὁ ἀπόστολος τὴν Ἄγαρ ἀλληγορεῖ·	**73.13.** τὰ δὲ κατὰ ἀλληγορίαν· οὐχ ὥς τινες ᾠήθησαν τὸ τὴν ὑποκειμένην τῶν πραγμάτων δι᾽ ἑτέρας ἐπεισαγωγῆς παραχαράττειν διάνοιαν, ἀλλὰ τὸ ἐπὶ λέξεως μόνης ἐναλλάττειν τὴν προσηγορίαν, καθὼς καὶ ἡ τῆς ἀλληγορίας ἐτυμολογία δηλοῖ· τὸ τὰ ἑτέρως ἔχοντα τὴν ἐπωνυμίαν ἑτέρως προσαγορεύειν· οἷον τὸ τὰ ἄπειρα πλήθη συνεχῶς ὕδατα λέγειν, διὰ τὸ ταραχῶδες αὐτῶν καὶ ἠχητικόν, τὴν δὲ τούτων ἔφοδον κατακλυσμὸν εἰκότως, διὰ τὸ ἄρδην ἐξαφανίζειν τοὺς ἐφ᾽ οἷσπερ ἂν ἐπέρχοιντο τόπους· ὡς τό, **φωνὴ**

4 Cf. Ps 28[29]:3, 10
5 Ps 1:3
6 Cf. Gal 4:24

1 ante Τὰ] ὅπως κατὰ ἀλληγορία titul. Z
7 ἐτυμολογία] ἐτοιμολογία Z
15 τόπους] etiam cat. Ps. 28:3(1), om. Z

73.13. Allegory:[1] whenever it repeatedly calls the innumerable throng [of the Assyrians] "waters," and their onslaught a "flood" (cf. Ps 28[29]:3, 10).[2] And, "he will be like the tree planted..." (Ps 1:3).[3] And the apostle allegorizes Hagar (cf. Gal 4:24).[4]

73.13. Allegory: it is not as some thought, debasing the underlying meaning of events by the introduction of a different meaning, but rather exchanging a term on the verbal level alone, just as the etymology of "allegory" also makes clear: calling things that have one name by a different name.[5] For example, repeatedly calling the innumerable throng [of the Assyrians] "waters," because of their turbulent and noisy character, and suitably calling their onslaught a "flood," because they utterly destroy those places which they invade. For example, "The Lord's voice

devil was represented in a conversation with God. This imagistic scene was designed to instruct the reader that Job's afflictions, while real and suffered at the hands of the devil, were nevertheless not instigated by the devil as if he exercised sovereign authority. These afflictions only happened because God consented to them: the heavenly conversation between God and the devil was crafted by the narrator to make this point.

[1] Compare with the corresponding section in R2, which is almost certainly more authentic: there the trope is defined and a typical Antiochene critique of allegorical exegesis is offered. On the trope of allegory in Theodore, see Schäublin, *Untersuchungen*, 120–2.
[2] Note the similar material in 73.1 (metaphor). Thdr. Mops., *Ps.* 45:3–4 takes the terms "seas" and "waters" in this Psalm to refer to "the vast numbers [τὸ πλῆθος]" of enemies that besieged the southern kingdom. Here the Psalmist writes "in the figurative style [τῇ τροπολογίᾳ]." See as well, Thdr. Mops., *Ps.* 68:2 [69:1]: "By 'waters' he refers to the enemies' assaults [τὰς τῶν πολεμίων ἐφόδους] as capable of choking and destroying him." Also see Thdt., *Ps.* 68:2–3 where the text employs "various images [ταῖς διαφόροις εἰκόσιν]."
[3] Diod., *Ps.* 1:3: calls the trope here a παράδειγμα and ὑπόδειγμα. Thdr. Mops., *Ps.* 1:3 names it a "comparison" (*similitudo*—likely σύγκρισις). Thdt., *Ps.* 1:3 notes that David "compared [ἀπείκασε]" a person to trees bearing fruit.
[4] On Gal 4:24 among Antiochenes, see Diod., *proem. Ps.*; *Ps. hypoth.* 118; Thdr. Mops., *Gal.* 4:24; Thdt., *Gal.* 4:24; Junil., *inst.* 2.16.
[5] Adrian understands the trope of allegory as follows: the biblical author has a very real thing in view, but instead of calling it by its conventional name, uses a different name. Thus in the first example provided below, the psalmist has the Assyrian army in mind, yet signifies it not straightforwardly ("Assyrian army") but with allegorical language: "waters." The author has exchanged terms "on the verbal level alone." When the trope is parsed properly, it points back to the underlying meaning: "waters" signifies the Assyrian army. Adrian opens this paragraph with a critique of otherwise anonymous readers who would treat the word "waters" without regard for what it signifies. They are thereby guilty of "debasing the underlying meaning." Instead of associating "waters" with the Assyrian army, these readers link "waters" to some other reality, and are thereby guilty of a second error: the "introduction of a different meaning." There are a number of surviving Antiochene criticisms of allegorical exegesis that highlight how it undermines the underlying meaning or destroys the facticity of the events narrated in Scripture: Eust., *engast.* 21.1–22.7; Diod., *proem. Ps.*; *Ps. hypoth.* 118; Thdr. Mops., *Ps. hypoth.* 118; *Gal.* 4:24; Thdt., *Gal.* 4:24.

RECENSION 1	RECENSION 2
	κυρίου ἐπὶ τῶν ὑδάτων, ἵνα εἴπῃ
	ἤρκεσε καὶ μόνῃ τῇ φωνῇ τοὺς
	Ἀσσυρίους τροπώσασθαι· καὶ τό,
	κύριος τὸν κατακλυσμὸν
	κατοικιεῖ, ἀντὶ τοῦ τὴν τέλεον
	ἐρημωθεῖσαν ὑπ᾽ αὐτῶν γῆν αὖθις
	ἀνακτήσεταί τε καὶ κατοικεῖσθαι
	ποιήσει· τοιοῦτόν ἐστι τὸ παρὰ τῷ
	Ζαχαρίᾳ περὶ τοῦ εὐαγγελικοῦ
	κηρύγματος, **καὶ ἔσται ἐν τῇ ἡμέρᾳ**
	ἐκείνῃ ἐξελεύσεται ὕδωρ ζῶν ἐξ
	Ἱερουσαλήμ, καὶ τὸ ἥμισυ αὐτοῦ εἰς
	τὴν θάλασσαν τὴν πρώτην καὶ τὸ
	ἥμισυ αὐτοῦ εἰς τὴν θάλασσαν τὴν
	ἐσχάτην, ἐν θέρει καὶ ἔαρι ἔσται
	οὕτως· καὶ ἔσται κύριος εἰς βασιλέα
	ἐπὶ πᾶσαν τὴν γῆν, ἀντὶ τοῦ οὐκ ἔστι
	μερικῶς ἀλλ᾽ ἰσοτίμως καὶ ἐξίσης,
	ὑμῖν τε καὶ τοῖς λοιποῖς ἔθνεσιν τοῖς
	ἀνὰ πᾶσαν ὁμοῦ τὴν οἰκουμένην·
	τούτους γὰρ ἐσχάτην ἐκφωνεῖ
	θάλασσαν· ἀφθόνως παρέξει τὴν ἀπὸ
	τῆς οἰκείας ῥύμης ὠφέλειαν· πρώτην
	οὖν θάλασσαν τὴν παρακειμένην τῇ
	Παλαιστίνῃ λέγει, ἵν᾽ ἀπὸ ταύτης
	μετωνυμικῶς τοὺς ἐνοικοῦντας
	δηλώσειεν, ὥσπερ οὖν ἐσχάτην τὴν
	τὰ πέρατα κυκλοῦσαν τῆς
	οἰκουμένης, ἵνα εἴπῃ πάντα καθόλου
	τὰ ἔθνη· ἐπόμενον μέντοι τῇ
	ἀλληγορίᾳ ἐπήγαγε τὸ ἐν θέρει καὶ ἐν

1   Ps 28[29]:3
5   Ps 28[29]:10
17   Zech 14:8–9 var.

---

5   post κατοικιεῖ] καὶ κατὰ ἐξῆς Z a. corr.
10   κηρύγματος] κρύγματος Z

is over the waters" (Ps 28[29]:3), as if to say "with only his voice he was strong enough to put the Assyrians to flight." And, "the Lord will inhabit the flood" (Ps 28[29]:10), instead of "he will make inhabitable and revive again the whole earth that was laid to waste by them."[1] Such is also the case in Zechariah concerning the gospel proclamation: "And it will be on that day that living water will come forth from Jerusalem, half of it into the first sea and half of it into the last sea; even in summer and spring will it be so. And the Lord will be king over all the earth" (Zech 14:8–9), instead of "it [i.e., the gospel proclamation] will not happen partially, but equally and evenly, both for you and for the other nations throughout the whole inhabited world." For it calls the other nations the "last sea." (The gospel proclamation will provide aid ungrudgingly from its own momentum.) It calls "the first sea" the region adjacent to Palestine in order to indicate its inhabitants by this metonymous expression, just as the "last sea" encircles the boundaries of the inhabited world, so as to say "all the nations in general." Indeed, following this allegory the prophet introduced the expression "in summer

---

[1] Most of the foregoing material (from "repeatedly calling the innumerable throng") is transmitted in nearly identical form at Adrian., *cat. Ps.* 28:3(1) and *cat. Ps.* 28:10. Diod., *Ps.* 28:2: "Then he [the psalmist] gives a description by proclaiming the events themselves [αὐτὰ τὰ πράγματα], our need being to recognize it as very figurative [τροπικώτερον]." Diodore continues at *Ps.* 28:3: "By 'waters' he refers to the vast numbers of the Assyrians, his meaning therefore being, 'He routed such a vast number by his voice alone, with no need of weapons, no need of any other military equipment; instead, like a skillful general he required only his voice to get the better of the enemy.'" And Diod., *Ps.* 28:10: "Once again by 'flood' he refers to the same holy place and the city: since the enemy in their vast numbers threatened to bring on the places a 'flood,' as it were, the place that was expected to be flooded therefore offers glory to God, is occupied, and has God enthroned in it and reigning forever." Thdt., *Ps. hypoth.* 28: "referring in figurative fashion [τροπικῶς] to the multitude of the enemy as 'flood of waters.'"

RECENSION 1	RECENSION 2
	ἔαρι, καὶ διὰ τὸ ἀέναον καὶ διηνεκὲς
	τῆς θειᾶς χάριτος, ἐπειδὴ μάλιστα τῇ
	τε τοῦ θέρους ὥρᾳ καὶ τῇ τοῦ ἔαρος,
	σπάνιος ἡ τῶν ὑδάτων διὰ τὴν
	ὀλιγομυρίαν δαψίλεια· ὅπερ οὖν παρὰ
	τῷ Μιχαίᾳ σαφέστερον, ὁ **ἐκ Σιὼν**
	ἐξελεύσεται νόμος καὶ λόγος κυρίου
	ἐξ Ἰερουσαλήμ· καὶ κρινεῖ ἀναμέσον
	λαῶν πολλῶν καὶ ἐλέγξει ἔθνη
	ἰσχυρὰ ἕως εἰς μακράν· εἰδὲ τὰ κατὰ
	σύγκρισιν ὁ μακάριος ἀπόστολος
	Παῦλος τῆς τε νῦν ἐπ' ἐλευθερίᾳ
	κλήσεως πρὸς τὴν Σάρραν αὐτῷ
	διαγορευθέντα, καὶ τῆς ὑπὸ νόμον
	τότε τῶν Ἰουδαίων δουλείας πρὸς τὴν
	Ἄγαρ παιδίσκην οὖσαν τῆς Σάρρας·
	ἀλληγορίαν ἐκάλεσεν· θαυμαζέτω
	μηδεὶς τῶν οἰκείων, αὐτὸς γὰρ
	ἑαυτὸν ἰδιώτην εἶναι τῷ λόγῳ
	καθομολογεῖν οὐκ ἐπαισχύνεται·

10 Mic 4:2–3 var.
17 Cf. Gal 4:21–5
20 Cf. 2 Cor 11:6

---

6 σαφέστερον] σαφέστερα Z
16 παιδίσκην] παιδίδισκην Z

and spring" because of the ever-flowing and invariable nature of divine grace, since especially in the seasons of summer and spring the abundance of waters is scarce due to drought.[1,2] This [is said] more clearly in Micah: "The law will go forth from Zion and a word of the Lord from Jerusalem. And he will judge between many peoples and will reprove strong nations far away" (Mic 4:2–3).

The blessed apostle Paul saw[3] what was declared to him about our present calling to freedom as a *correspondence* with Sarah, and about the slavery of the Jews under the law at that time as a *correspondence* with Hagar, Sarah's handmaiden.[4] He called this an allegory (cf. Gal 4:21–5). Let none of our own[5] be astonished [by Paul's claim], for he himself was

---

[1] The term ὀλιγομυρία is not attested in LSJ or *PGL*. I am proposing "drought" (cf. πλημυρίς: "flood-tide," "flood").

[2] While Theodore does not use the term "allegory" in his commentary on Zechariah, he interprets the prophet's visions in this book in a very similar way. For example, at *Zach.* 1:8 he writes, "It is quite clear that all the things shown to the prophet were tokens of certain realities [γνωρίσματά τινων ὑπῆρχε πραγμάτων]...the prophet also sees these things by divine revelation, and each of the things shown him contained some sign or indication of a reality [ἕκαστον δὲ τῶν δεικνυμένων αὐτῷ σημεῖόν τι καὶ δήλωσιν πράγματος εἶχεν]." See also Schäublin, *Untersuchungen*, 120–1 fn. 143. As for Zech 14, however, Theodore takes this passage as a prophecy of the time of the Maccabees, where the "living water" symbolizes "an undefiled and lawful priesthood." Closer parallels to Adrian's interpretation include Didym., *Zach.* 14:8–9 (note esp. that for him much of the book is composed ἀλληγορικῶς); Thdt., *Zach.* 14:8–9. Didymus appears to have been used by Theodore: see Hill, *Old Testament in Antioch*, 33.

[3] Perhaps a reference to the "visions and revelations" of the Lord experienced by "the man I know" (2 Cor 12:1–7), which Adrian would be taking as an autobiographical reference to Paul. It is also possible that Adrian does not have this particular passage in mind, and simply thinks that Paul was privileged to receive divine revelations throughout his life. John Chrysostom writes, "Paul had so many and such continual moments of converse with God as were shared by none of the prophets or apostles" (*laud. Paul.* 5.10).

[4] Note 73.3 above where Adrian uses Gal 4:24 to illustrate the trope of correspondence.

[5] Recall the reference above at 72 to Adrian's audience: "those individuals of the same community of faith." The only other communities to which Adrian refers are "those outside" (οἱ ἔξω), likely non-Christian philosophers (2.10) and scholars of epic poems (75).

RECENSION 1	RECENSION 2

73.14(121). καθ᾽ ὑπερβολήν· ὅταν εἰς πολλὰ μείζονι κέχρηται τῷ τῆς ὑφηγήσεως μεγέθει παρὰ τὰ γινόμενα ἢ προσόντα ἢ ἐνδεχόμενα·

73.14. τὰ δὲ καθ᾽ ὑπερβολήν· ὅταν πολλῷ μείζονι χρῆται τῷ τῆς φύσεως μεγέθει παρὰ τὰ γιγνόμενα ἢ προσόντα ἢ ἐνδεχόμενα·

5 **73.14.1.** < παρὰ μὲν οὖν τὰ γινόμενα· > ὡς τό, **ἀναβαίνουσιν ἕως τῶν οὐρανῶν**· περὶ τῶν ναυτιλλομένων· καί, **πλὴν ὁ θεὸς συνθλάσει κεφαλὰς ἐχθρῶν αὐτοῦ**·
10 καί, **λούσω καθ᾽ ἑκάστην νύκτα τὴν κλίνην μου**· καί, **τὰ ὄρη ἐσκίρτησαν ὡσεὶ κριοί**· καί, **τὰ ξύλα τοῦ ἀγροῦ ἐπικροτήσει τοῖς κλάδοις**· καί, **εὐκοπώτερόν ἐστι**
15 **κάμηλον**·

73.14.1. παρὰ μὲν οὖν τὰ γιγνόμενα· ὡς τό, **ἀναβαίνουσιν ἕως τῶν οὐρανῶν καὶ καταβαίνουσιν ἕως τῶν ἀβύσσων**, περὶ τῶν ναυτιλομένων· καὶ τὸ ὑπὸ τοῦ κυρίου ἐν εὐαγγελίοις, **εὐκοπώτερόν ἐστι κάμηλον διὰ τρυπήματος βελόνης εἰσελθεῖν ἢ πλούσιον εἰς τὴν βασιλείαν τῶν οὐρανῶν**·

73.14.2. < παρὰ δὲ τὰ προσόντα· > καὶ περὶ τῆς ἀκρίδος· **ὅτι ἔθνος ἀνέβη ἐπὶ τὴν γῆν μου ἰσχυρόν, οἱ ὀδόντες αὐτοῦ ὀδόντες λέοντος**·
20 καί, **ἀπηλλοτριώθησαν οἱ ἁμαρτωλοὶ ἀπὸ μήτρας**·

73.14.2. παρὰ δὲ τὰ προσόντα· ὡς τὸ παρὰ τῷ Ἰωὴλ περὶ τῆς ἀκρίδος, **ὅτι ἔθνος ἀνέβη ἐπὶ τὴν γῆν μου ἰσχυρὸν καὶ ἀναρίθμητον, οἱ ὀδόντες αὐτοῦ ὀδόντες λέοντος, καὶ αἱ μύλαι αὐτοῦ σκύμνου**· καὶ τὸ παρὰ τῷ Ἰὼβ περὶ τοῦ θαλαττίου δράκοντος·

7 Ps 106[107]:26
9 Ps 67:22 [68:21]
11 Ps 6:7[6]
12 Ps 113[114]:4
14 Isa 55:12
15 Matt 19:24; Mark 10:25; Luke 18:25 var.
19 Joel 1:6 var.
21 Ps 57:4 [58:3]

8 Ps 106[107]:26
13 Matt 19:24 var.; Mark 10:25 var.; Luke 18:25 var.
21 Joel 1:6
22 Job 41

6 παρὰ–γινόμενα] + R2
15 post κάμηλον] διὰ τρυπήματος ῥαφίδος διελθεῖν + Goessling (ex Lollin)
16 παρὰ–προσόντα] + R2

1 ante Τὰ] ὅπως τὰ καθ᾽ὑπερβολήν titul. Z
7 τῶν οὐρανῶν] τὸν οὐρανὸν Z

not ashamed to admit that he was untrained in speech (cf. 2 Cor 11:6).[4]

73.14. Hyperbole: when it frequently uses a magnitude in its narration that is exaggerated when compared with [actual] events, attributes, or indeterminate actions.[1]

73.14. Hyperbole: whenever it uses a much greater magnitude of a thing when compared with [actual] events, attributes, or indeterminate actions.

73.14.1. Events: for example, about seafarers, "They ascend as far as the heavens" (Ps 106[107]:26); and, "but God will shatter his enemies' heads" (Ps 67:22 [68:21]); and, "I will bathe my bed every night" (Ps 6:7[6]);[2] and, "the mountains skipped like rams" (Ps 113[114]:4); and, "the trees of the field will clap with their branches" (Isa 55:12); and, "it is easier for a camel [to go through the eye of a needle]" (Matt 19:24; Mark 10:25; Luke 18:25).

73.14.1. Events: for example, about seafarers, "They ascend as far as heaven and descend as far as the depths" (Ps 106[107]:26); and the passage by the Lord in the Gospels: "it is easier for a camel to go through the eye of a needle than it is for a rich man to enter into the kingdom of the heavens" (Matt 19:24; Mark 10:25; Luke 18:25).

73.14.2. Attributes: and concerning the locust, "because a nation mighty... has arisen against my land, its teeth are the teeth of a lion" (Joel 1:6); and, "sinners were estranged from the womb" (Ps 57:4 [58:3]).[3]

73.14.2. Attributes: for example, concerning the locust in Joel: "because a nation mighty and innumerable has arisen against my land, its teeth are the teeth of a lion, and its molars those of a cub" (Joel 1:6). And the passage in Job about the sea dragon (Job 40:25–41:26[41]).

---

[1] On the prevalence of hyperbolic language in Scripture, see Diod., *Ps. hypoth.* 118; Thdr. Mops., *Joel* 2:10; *Zach.* 9:9–10; Thdt., *1 Cor.* 13:3.
[2] Thdr. Mops., *Ps.* 6:7: "Now, this is said with emphasis to suggest abundant tears of repentance, even if the expression is not precise."
[3] Thdr. Mops., *Ps.* 57:4: "The phrase 'from the womb' means, 'From the time you were formed you were estranged'—either speaking by way of hyperbole to mean 'always,' or..."
[4] A number of Antiochene authors balk at Paul's use of "allegory" in Gal 4:24: Diod., *proem. Ps.* (preferring θεωρία); Thdr. Mops., *Gal.* 4:24 (preferring σύγκρισις); Chrys., *comm. in Gal.* 4:24 (τύπος); Thdt., *Gal.* 4:21–4 (τὰ ἐν τῇ ἱστορίᾳ προτυπωθέντα); Junil., *inst.* 2.16 (*typus*).

RECENSION 1	RECENSION 2

73.14.3. < παρὰ δὲ τὰ ἐνδεχόμενα· >
καί, < σοῦ δὲ ποιοῦντος ἐλεημοσύνην
> μὴ γνώτω ἡ ἀριστερά σου τί ποιεῖ
ἡ δεξιά σου· καί, εἰ ὁ ὀφθαλμὸς ὁ
5 δεξιὸς σκανδαλίζει σε, ἔξελε
αὐτόν· καί, ἐὰν ὑμεῖς σιωπήσητε, οἱ
λίθοι κεκράξονται· καί, ἰῶτα ἓν ἢ
μία κεραία < οὐ μὴ παρέλθῃ ἀπὸ
τοῦ νόμου, ἕως ἂν πάντα γένηται >·
10 καί, < οὐ μὴ παρέλθῃ ἡ
γενεὰ αὕτη ἕως ἂν πάντα
ταῦτα γένηται· > οἱ οὐρανοὶ
καὶ ἡ γῆ παρελεύσονται <,
οἱ δὲ λόγοι μου οὐ μὴ
15 παρέλθωσιν >·

73.14.3. παρὰ δὲ τὰ ἐνδεχόμενα· ὡς
τὸ παρὰ τοῦ κυρίου εἰρημένον, < σοῦ
δὲ ποιοῦντος ἐλεημοσύνην > μὴ
γνώτω ἡ ἀριστερά σου τί ποιεῖ ἡ
δεξιά σου· καὶ ὅσα τοιαῦτα·

73.15(122). κατ' ἐπιτωθασμόν· ὅταν
ἐπὶ ταῖς τῶν ἐχθρῶν αἰσχύναις λέγῃ
< · ὡς τό, > εὖγε, εὖγε, εἶδον οἱ
ὀφθαλμοὶ ἡμῶν· καί, λάβε
20 κιθάραν, ῥέμβευσον καλῶς
κιθάρισον· καί, γὰρ πλοῖα οὐκ ἔτι
ἔρχονται ἐκ Καρχηδόνος· < καί, >
πόλις καλὴ καὶ ἐπίχαρις,
ἡγουμένη φαρμάκων· < καί, ὦ ἡ
25 ἐπιφανὴς καὶ ἀπολελυτρωμένη ἡ
πολις > ἐπὶ τῷ κυρίῳ οὐκ

73.15. τὰ δὲ κατὰ ἐπιτωθασμόν·
ὅταν ἐπὶ ταῖς τῶν ἐχθρῶν
καταθυμίαις συμφοραῖς
ἐπιγελαστικώτερον πρὸς αὐτοὺς
διαλέγηται· ὡς τό, εὖγε, εὖγε, εἶδον
οἱ ὀφθαλμοὶ ἡμῶν· καὶ τὸ ὑπὸ τῶν
Ἰουδαίων πρὸς τὸν δεσπότην,
προφήτευσον ἡμῖν, Χριστέ, τίς ἐστιν
ὁ παίσας σε; καὶ τὰ τοιαῦτα·

4 Matt 6:3
6 Matt 5:29 var.
7 Luke 19:40 var.
9 Matt 5:18
15 Matt 24:34–5 var.
19 Ps 34[35]:21 var.
21 Isa 23:16 var.
22 Isa 23:10 var.
24 Nah 3:4 var.

5 Matt 6:3
21 Ps 34[35]:21 var.
24 Matt 26:68

1 παρὰ–ἐνδεχόμενα] + R2
9 οὐ μὴ–γένηται] οὐ μὴ–νόμου + tantum
Goessling (ex Lollin Schlüren)
22 καί] + Goessling
23 πόλις] πόσις J, πόρνη Hoeschel (notae)
26 καί, ὦ ἡ ἐπιφανὴς–πόλις] καί + tantum
Goessling

16 ante Τὰ] ὅπως κατ'ἐπιτωθασμόν titul. Z

73.14.3. Indeterminate actions:[1] and, "Whenever you give alms, let not your left hand know what your right hand does" (Matt 6:3); and, "if your right eye causes you to stumble, tear it out" (Matt 5:29); and, "if you keep silent, the stones will cry out[2]" (Lk 19:40); and, "not one iota or one tittle will fall away from the law until all is accomplished" (Matt 5:18); and, "this generation will not pass away until all these things have taken place. The heavens and the earth will pass away, but my words will never pass away" (Matt 24:34–5).

73.15. Mockery: whenever it speaks of the shame of enemies. For example: "Well done! Well done! Our eyes saw!" (Ps 34[35]:21);[3] and, "take a lyre, roam… [you city, you forgotten prostitute!] … Play the lyre well" (Isa 23:16); and, "for ships no longer come from Carthage" (Isa 23:10); and, "a city beautiful and charming, a master of medicines" (Nah 3:4); and, "O the famous and redeemed city!…it did not trust in the Lord"

73.14.3. Indeterminate actions: for example, the passage spoken by the Lord, "whenever you give alms, let not your left hand know what your right hand does" (Matt 6:3). And all such passages.

73.15. Mockery: whenever it converses with enemies jeeringly concerning their depressing misfortunes. For example, "Well done! Well done! Our eyes saw" (Ps 34[35]:21)! And the passage [addressed] by the Jews to the Lord: "Prophesy to us, Christ, who is it who struck you" (Matt 26:68)? And similar passages.

---

[1] That is, hyperbolic expressions associated with future actions or events whose occurrence is not known or cannot be predicted.

[2] Reading κεκράξονται as future active indicative (s.v. κράζω GELS; BDAG) and Ps 21:3; 29:9.

[3] Diod., *Ps.* 34:21: "εὖγε, εὖγε is a cry of satisfaction, the meaning therefore being, 'All we longed to see happening to him we see, and we taunted him.'" Thdr. Mops., *Ps.* 34:21: "The term εὖγε is one of approbation; so he means, 'On seeing the tribulations befalling me, they approved and were pleased with what was happening, as though witnessing the object of their desires.' In εὖγε, εὖγε they used repetition to indicate their surpassing contentment with them." Thdt., *Ps.* 34:21: "then they unmasked their hidden hostility, loudly gloating over my calamities."

RECENSION 1	RECENSION 2

ἐπεποίθει· καί, προφήτευσον
ἡμῖν, Χριστέ, τίς ἐστιν ὁ παίσας
σε;

73.16(123). κατὰ εἰρωνείαν· ὅταν τὴν
5 εὐτέλειαν δι᾽ ἐπαίνων σκώπτῃ· ὡς
τό, **συναγάγετε αὐτῷ τοὺς ὁσίους
αὐτοῦ·** καί, **ἄμπελος
εὐκληματοῦσα Ἱερουσαλήμ·** καί,
ποῦ ἐστὶ τὸ κατοικητήριον τῶν
10 **λεόντων καὶ σκύμνος λέοντος·**
καί, **ἀσπίδες καὶ ἔγγονα ἀσπίδων**
< **πετομένων** > Αἰγυπτίοις
προσέδραμον· καὶ < περὶ τοῦ
βασιλέως Βαβυλῶνος, > **ὁ ᾅδης**
15 **κάτωθεν ἐπικράνθη συναντήσας σοι,**
< **συνηγέρθησάν σοι πάντες οἱ**
γίγαντες οἱ ἄρξαντες τῆς γῆς > καί,
< **ἐροῦσίν σοι καὶ σὺ** > **ἑάλως ὥσπερ**
< **καὶ ἡμεῖς** >, καί, **κατέβη εἰς ᾅδου**
20 **ἡ δόξα σου, ὑποκάτω σου στρώσουσι**
σῆψιν·

73.16. τὰ δὲ κατ᾽ εἰρωνείαν· ὅταν
τὴν εὐτέλειαν δι᾽ ἐπαίνων σκώπτῃ·
ὡς τὸ περὶ τῶν Ἰουδαίων,
συναγάγετε αὐτῷ τοὺς ὁσίους αὐτοῦ
τοὺς διατιθεμένους τὴν διαθήκην
αὐτοῦ ἐπὶ θυσίαις, ἀντὶ τοῦ
τουτουσί μοι τοὺς ἐν ὁσίων μὲν τάξει
μνημονευομένους, τὰ δὲ τῶν ἀσεβῶν
τοὐναντίον διαπραττομένους, οἳ ἀφ᾽
ὧν τὰς συνήθεις τῷ θεῷ τελοῦσι
θυσίας ἀφοσιοῦσθαι νομίζουσι· καὶ
ὅσα τοιαῦτα·

---

1 Zeph 3:1, 2
3 Matt 26:68
7 Ps 49[50]:5
8 Hos 10:1 var.
10 Nah 2:12[11] var.
12 Isa 30:6 var.
21 Isa 14:9, 10, 11 var.

9 Ps 49[50]:5

---

18 post ὥσπερ] καὶ ἡμεῖς + Goessling

(Zeph 3:1, 2);[1] and, "Prophesy to us, Christ, who is it who struck you" (Matt 26:68)?

73.16. Irony: whenever it scoffs at unworthiness by means of praises.[2] For example, "gather to him his holy ones" (Ps 49[50]:5);[3] and, "Jerusalem, a vine growing luxuriantly" (Hos 10:1); and, "where is the den of lions and… the lion's cub" (Nah 2:12[11])?;[4] and, "snakes and offspring of flying snakes" (Isa 30:6) ran to the Egyptians; and concerning the king of Babylon, "Hades beneath was embittered on meeting you; all the mighty ones who have ruled the earth welcomed you" and "they will say to you: 'You too were taken even as we were…,'" and "your glory descended to Hades… before you they will spread decay'" (Isa 14:9, 10, 11).

73.16. Irony: whenever it scoffs at unworthiness by means of praises. For instance, the passage about the Jews: "gather to him his holy ones who make a covenant with him by sacrifices" (Ps 49[50]:5), instead of "those mentioned by me in the rank of holy ones, but who, on the contrary, practicing acts of impiety think that they are purified from these by performing the customary sacrifices to God."[5] And all such passages.

---

[1] Note Thdr. Mops., *Soph.* 3:2 where he links this passage to Nah 3:4 (both are juxtaposed in this paragraph of the *Introduction*), as both express taunts.

[2] See Thdr. Mops., *Ps.* 51:3; Thdt., *Am.* 3:9.

[3] Diod., *Ps.* 49:5: "By 'holy ones' he refers to those considered holy for the reason of offering sacrifices, calling them not truly holy, only in those people's opinion, the result being that this name is rather a reproach to them than a commendation."

[4] Thdr. Mops., *Nah.* 2:11, comments as follows: the biblical author "proceeds to remind them of their former power… not only has the lions' dwelling gone, but even their whole pasture is gone (by 'cubs' referring to the same thing, namely, the lions). He means, 'In former times you inhabitants of Nineveh, like lions, were fearsome to everyone else, and you took from all quarters what belonged to the enemy and amassed it for yourselves, whereas now even Nineveh your dwelling is gone, and along with it everything you once possessed that was amassed for yourselves.' 'Where has the lion gone to gain entrance?' A very mocking remark [Σφόδρα διασυρτικῶς]."

[5] Most of this paragraph is found in Adrian., *cat. Ps.* 49:5. Diod., *Ps.* 49:5: "By 'holy ones' he refers to those considered holy for the reason of offering sacrifices, calling them not truly holy, only in those people's opinion, the result being that this name is rather a reproach to them than a commendation because they actually neglect virtue and give all their attention to sacrifices. Hence he added 'those who made covenant with him by sacrifice,' that is, those thinking that the covenant with God consists entirely of sacrifices and not in doing good works." Also Thdr. Mops., *Ps. hypoth.* 49: "Here blessed David emerges as directing his words in the clearest manner to the Jews, charging them, on the one hand, with neglecting lawful observances, a virtuous life, and the other commands of God, and on the other hand with attending to sacrifices and devoting themselves entirely to them, as though it were sufficient for them to discharge these while neglecting the rest."

RECENSION 1   RECENSION 2

73.17(124). κατὰ σαρκασμόν· ὅταν
διὰ τῆς ἄγαν εὐτελείας ἐπαινεῖν
ἐθέλοι· ὡς τό, **ἐγώ εἰμι σκώληξ καὶ**
οὐκ ἄνθρωπος· καί, ὀπίσω τίνος
5 **διώκεις βασιλεῦ; ὀπίσω ἑνὸς ψύλλου**
καὶ ὀπίσω κυνὸς τεθνηκότος· καὶ
ὅσα ὅμοια·

73.17. τὰ δὲ κατὰ σαρκασμόν·
ὅταν τοὐναντίον διὰ τῆς ἄγαν
εὐτελείας ἐπαινεῖν ἐθέλῃ· ὡς τό, **ἐγώ**
εἰμι σκώληξ καὶ οὐκ ἄνθρωπος·
καὶ τὰ ὑπὸ τοῦ μακαρίου Δαυὶδ πρὸς
τὸν Σαούλ, **ὀπίσω τίνος διώκεις**
βασιλεῦ; ὀπίσω ἑνὸς ψύλλου καὶ
ὀπίσω κυνὸς τεθνηκότος·

73.18(125). κατὰ αἴνιγμα· ὅταν
10 ἀσυμφώνως ὑποτίθεται
[ὑποτίθεται] τὸ διήγημα· οἷον, **τὸ**
ἀργύριον ὑμῶν ἀδόκιμον· οἱ
κάπηλοί σου μίσγουσι τὸν οἶνον
ὕδατι· καί, **εἶπον παντὶ ὀρνέῳ καὶ**
15 **πᾶσι τοῖς θηρίοις·** καί,
ἐξαποστείλατε δρέπανα ὅτι
παρέστηκεν ὁ τρυγητός· καί,
ἰδοὺ ἡ ἀξίνη πρὸς τὴν ῥίζαν τῶν
δένδρων κεῖται·
20

73.18. τὰ δὲ κατὰ αἴνιγμα· ὅταν
ἀσυμφώνως ὑποτίθεται τὸ διήγημα·
ὡς τὸ ὑπὸ τοῦ Ἰωάννου τοῦ
βαπτιστοῦ ἐν εὐαγγελίοις, **ἰδοὺ ἡ**
ἀξίνη πρὸς τὴν ῥίζαν τῶν δένδρων
κεῖται· πᾶν οὖν δένδρον μὴ ποιοῦν
καρπὸν καλὸν ἐκκόπτεται καὶ εἰς
πῦρ βάλλεται· καὶ τό, **αὐτὸς ὑμᾶς**
βαπτίσει ἐν πνεύματι ἁγίῳ καὶ πυρί·
οὗ τὸ πτύον ἐν τῇ χειρὶ αὐτοῦ, καὶ
διακαθαριεῖ τὴν ἅλωνα αὐτοῦ καὶ
συνάξει τὸν μὲν σῖτον εἰς τὴν
ἀποθήκην, καὶ τὰ ἑξῆς·

73.19(126). κατὰ ἀπειλήν· ὅταν
ἀπειλῇ διὰ τοῦ θεοῦ· ὡς τό, **ἐὰν**
μὴ ἐπιστραφῆτε, τὴν ῥομφαίαν

73.19. τὰ δὲ κατὰ ἀπειλήν· ὅταν
ἐπὶ κωλύσει τῶν ἀτόπων τὴν
τιμωρίαν προβάλληται· ὡς τό, **ἐὰν**

---

4 Ps 21:7 [22:6] var.
6 1 Kgdms 24:15 [1 Sam 24:14] var.
14 Isa 1:22
15 Ezek 39:17 var.
17 Joel 3:13 var.
19 Matt 3:10 var.; Luke 3:9 var.

4 Ps 21:7 [22:6]
8 1 Kgdms 24:15 [1 Sam 24:14] var.
16 Matt. 3:10 var.; Luke 3:9 var.
21 Matt. 3:11–12 var.; Luke 3:16–17 var.

---

11 ὑποτίθεται ὑποτίθεται] ὑποτίθεται IJK₁K₂
C et G p. corr. *Hoeschel Goessling*
14 εἶπον] εἶπον *Goessling*
17 τρυγητός] τρύγητος *Goessling*
18 πρὸς] ὑπὸ *Hoeschel*
23 ἀπειλῇ] – *Goessling* (ex *Schlüren*)
23 post θεοῦ] + τιμωρίας τοῖς κακοῖς
ἐπαγγέλλει *Schlüren*, sim. R2

1 ante Τὰ] ὅπως τὰ κατὰ σαρκασμόν titul. Z
9 ante Τὰ] ὅπως τὰ κατὰ αἴνιγμα titul. Z
22 ante Τὰ] ὅπως κατὰ ἀπειλήν titul. Z

73.17. Sarcasm: whenever it intends to praise by means of excessive unworthiness. For example, "I am a worm and not a man" (Ps 21:7 [22:6]); and, "after whom do you pursue, O king? After a single flea and a dead dog" (1 Kgdms 24:15 [1 Sam 24:14]). And all similar passages.[1]

73.18. Riddle: whenever it presents a narrative in a discordant manner.[2] For example, "your silver is worthless; your innkeepers mix the wine with water" (Isa 1:22); and, "speak[3] to every bird and to all the animals" (Ezek 39:17); and, "send forth sickles because the harvest[4] has come" (Joel 3:13); and, "look, the axe is lying at the root of the trees" (Matt 3:10; Luke 3:9).

73.19. Threat: whenever it threatens through God. For example, "if you do not turn back, he will make his sword

73.17. Sarcasm: the opposite of above, whenever Scripture wishes to praise by means of excessive unworthiness. For example, "I am a worm and not a man" (Ps 21:7 [22:6]); and the words [spoken] by blessed David to Saul: "after whom do you pursue, O king? After a single flea and a dead dog" (1 Kgdms 24:15 [1 Sam 24:14]).[5]

73.18. Riddle: whenever it presents a narrative in a discordant manner, for instance, the passage in the Gospels by John the Baptist: "look, the axe is lying at the root of the trees. Every tree therefore not producing good fruit is cut down and cast into the fire" (Matt 3:10; Luke 3:9); and, "he will baptize you with the Holy Spirit and fire. His winnowing-fork is in his hand, and he will clear his threshing-floor and will gather his wheat into the granary" (Matt 3:11–12; Luke 3:16–17), etc.

73.19. Threat: whenever it flaunts[6] a punishment for the purpose of preventing wicked deeds. For example, "if you

---

[1] See Adrian., cat. Ps. 21:7 for a similar text of this paragraph.

[2] For a discussion of αἴνιγμα in Diodore, see Mariès, Études, 128–9. A passage that is ἀσύμφωνος is one that is lacking some sort of agreement or harmony. In the Homeric scholia, for instance, the simile of a chariot within a larger passage describing a chariot race was considered an exemplary instance of correspondence (σύμφωνος) between the simile and its surrounding narrative (Nünlist, Ancient Critic at Work, 292). See Thdt., Dan. 6:16: "A pious remark, though inconsistent [ἀσύμφωνον] with the preceding." Note as well Adrian's discussion of a "fitting sense" in 77 below.

[3] Reading εἶπον with L as an imperative and not indicative verb, as is customarily the case. Goessling emended to εἰπόν to designate an imperative. S.v. εἶπον LSJ; BDF §81(1).

[4] Reading τρυγητός with L: "crop which has been (or: is to be) harvested," and not τρύγητος, as Goessling emended: "act of harvesting." S.v. τρύγητος and τρυγητός GELS.

[5] See Adrian., cat. Ps. 21:7 for a nearly identical text.   [6] S.v. προβάλλω PGL A.2.

RECENSION 1	RECENSION 2

αὐτοῦ στιλβώσει· καί, ποιήσατε
καρπὸν ἄξιον τῆς μετανοίας·
καί, ἐκεῖ ἔσται ὁ κλαυθμὸς καὶ ὁ
βρυγμὸς τῶν ὀδόντων·

5 73.20(127). κατὰ ἀπόφασιν· ὅταν
αὐτοτελῆ τὴν τῶν ἀγαθῶν καὶ
τὴν τῶν κακῶν ἐπαγωγὴν
ὁρίζεται, τήν τε αἰχμαλωσίαν καὶ
τὴν ἐπάνοδον·
10

73.21(128). κατὰ ἀποσιώπησιν· ὅταν
ἀνακαίνισιν δηλοῖ πρὸς τοῦ θεοῦ·
ὡς τό, **καὶ ἔσται Ἰερουσαλὴμ ἁγία,
καὶ ἀλλογενὴς οὐ διελεύσεται δι᾽**
15 **αὐτῆς οὐκ ἔτι,** < τὴν > δὲ
αἵρεσιν τὴν εἰ μή που
παρανομήσειαν ἀπεσιώπησε· καί,
**ἐὰν μή τις γεννηθῇ ἐξ ὕδατος καὶ
πνεύματος,** τὴν δι᾽ αἵματος
20 ἐταμιεύσατο·

μὴ ἐπιστραφῆτε, τὴν ῥομφαίαν
αὐτοῦ στιλβώσει· καὶ ἕτερα·

73.20. τὰ δὲ κατὰ ἀπόφασιν· ὅταν
αὐτοτελῆ τήν τε τῶν κακῶν καὶ τῶν
ἀγαθῶν ἐπαγωγὴν ὁρίζεται, οἱονεὶ
λόγῳ τήν τε αἰχμαλωσίαν καὶ τὴν
ἐπάνοδον τοῖς Ἰσραηλίταις· καὶ ὅσα
τοιαῦτα·

73.21. τὰ δὲ κατὰ ἀποσιώπησιν·
ὅταν ἐπί τινων ὁρίζειν μὲν δοκεῖ
κατὰ τὸ προφανές, τὸ δὲ πέρας κατά
τινα λόγον ἀπόρρητον ταμιεύεται·
οἷον φέρε εἰπεῖν ὡς ἐπὶ τῆς γῆς τῆς
ἐπαγγελείας· τὴν μὲν περιορίαν
αὐτῆς, **ἀπὸ τοῦ ποταμοῦ Αἰγύπτου
ἕως τοῦ ποταμοῦ τοῦ μεγάλου
Εὐφράτου** τοῖς ἐκ σπέρματος
Ἀβραὰμ καθυπέσχετο, τὴν δὲ
αἵρεσιν τὴν εἰ μήπω παρανομήσειαν

---

1 Ps 7:13[12]
2 Matt 3:8 var.; Luke 3:8 var.
4 Matt 8:12, *passim*
15 Joel 3:17 var.
19 John 3:5
20 Cf. 1 John 5:6–8

2 Ps 7:13[12]
19 Gen 15:18 var.

---

6 post αὐτοτελῆ] τοῦ θεοῦ + Goessling
6 τὴν] – Goessling
7 τὴν] – Goessling
12 ἀνακαίνισιν] ἀνακαίνωσιν Goessling
15 post αὐτῆς] interpun. L *Hoeschel* (ex AB)
Goessling (ex codd.)
16 τὴν δὲ αἵρεσιν] R2, διαίρεσιν L

5 ante Τὰ] ὅπως τὰ κατὰ ἀπόφασιν titul. Z
11 ante Τὰ] ὅπως τὰ κατὰ ἀποσιώπησιν
titul. Z

gleam" (Ps 7:13[12]);[1] and, "bear fruit worthy of repentance" (Matt 3:8; Luke 3:8); and, "where there will be weeping and gnashing of teeth" (Matt 8:12 *passim*).

73.20. Verdict: whenever it decrees as definitive the inception of good and evil things, [such as when it decrees] the captivity and return.[2]

73.21. Omission: whenever it signifies a renewal that proceeds from God.[3] For example, "and Jerusalem will be holy and a stranger will never pass through her again" (Joel 3:17)—it omitted discussion of their [i.e., the Jews'] possession [of Jerusalem], [which would only happen] provided that they not break the law. And, "unless someone is born from water and spirit" (John 3:5)—it left

do not turn back, he will make his sword gleam" (Ps 7:13[12]). And other passages.[5]

73.20. Verdict: whenever it decrees as definitive the inception of both evils and goods, as if by word of command the captivity and the return of the Israelites [happened].[6] And all such passages.

73.21. Omission: whenever it appears to make a determination about certain things with reference to something conspicuous, but leaves unexpressed[7] their fulfillment[8] because of some unspoken consideration.[9] Let us take the land of promise as an example: God promised its perimeter "from the river of Egypt to the river of the great Euphrates" to Abraham's seed (Gen 15:18). But God omitted discussion of

---

[1] While "threat" might not seem an obvious candidate for a trope list, note Diod., *Ps.* 7:13–14: "he refers to all shafts and swords, in a figurative manner [τροπικῶς] implying the punishment of God." Thdr. Mops., *Ps.* 7:13–14: "To present God as terrifying and threatening to sinners [*Ut terribilem peccatoribus ac minacem ostenderet Deum*], he employs terms describing our behavior, and to convey that no harmful action will escape the severity of his vengeance." Thdt., *Ps.* 7:13–14: "These are not words of punishment, note, but of threat [οὐ τιμωρίας, ἀλλ' ἀπειλῆς]." Also Thdr. Mops., *Ps.* 74:4.

[2] See Adrian., *cat. Ps.* 57:12, which presents a different text. There are a few passages where Theodore comments on the definitive verdict of God concerning the captivity or return from exile: *Os.* 2:14; *Am.* 7:7–9; 9:15; *Soph.* 1:2. In the latter text he explains why the image of a juridical verdict is used in Scripture: it was right for God "to make his disclosure by way of a sentence [ἐν ἀποφάσει] to bring out that they had made themselves responsible for this by what they had done—hence God was obliged to deliver such a sentence on them."

[3] A definition of this trope is missing in both R1 and R2. "Omission" is opposed to being explicit about something, i.e., when the scriptural author elides a word or phrase, and that what is missing is nevertheless to be understood or supplied by the reader. The term ἀποσιώπησις occurs a handful of times in Theodore, where he notes that "God" (*Ps.* 13:7; 72:7; 57:4) or a saying verb like "he says" is implied (*Ps.* 44:18; 54:24; 58:9; 74:3; *Abd.* 1:1). For a discussion of this trope, see Devreesse, *Essai*, 65; Nünlist, *Ancient Critic at Work*, 157–70.

[5] See the related discussion above at 49.   [6] See Adrian., *cat. Ps.* 57:12 for a different text.

[7] S.v. ταμιεύω PGL 3.   [8] S.v. πέρας PGL 4.

[9] In the examples that follow, Adrian draws attention to scriptural texts that appear to make a definitive promise by highlighting something conspicuous, but are actually keeping silent about conditions that must be met in order for the promise to be fulfilled. In the case of the Jews, the passage in question is silent about the requirement to keep the law as a prerequisite for possessing the promised land; for Christians, the passage is silent about Jesus' death as a condition for entering the kingdom of heaven.

RECENSION 1	RECENSION 2
	ἐκεῖνοι ἀπεσιώπησεν· οὐ μὴν ἀλλὰ καὶ ἐπὶ τῆς μελλούσης καταστάσεως· **ἐὰν μή τις**, ἔφη, **γεννηθῇ ἐξ ὕδατος καὶ πνεύματος, οὐ μὴ εἰσέλθῃ εἰς τὴν βασιλείαν τῶν οὐρανῶν**· τὴν δι᾽ αἵματος αἵρεσιν δηλονότι ταμιευσάμενος· πολλὰ δ᾽ ἂν εὕροι τις ἐπί τε τῆς παλαιᾶς καὶ τῆς νέας διαθήκης τοιαῦτα·
73.22(129). κατὰ παραίνεσιν· ὅταν πάντα ὁμοῦ τὰ τῆς θεοπνεύστου γραφῆς εἴτε διὰ λόγων εἴτε διὰ πραγμάτων, εἰς ταύτην συντελεῖν ἔοικεν εἰκότως.	**73.22.** τὰ δὲ κατὰ παραίνεσιν· πᾶς τις τῶν εὐσεβούντων ὁμολογήσειεν ὡς ἅπαντα ὁμοῦ τὰ τῆς θεοπνεύστου γραφῆς εἴτε διὰ λόγων εἴτε διὰ πραγμάτων εἰς ταύτην συντελεῖν ἔοικεν εἰκότως.
74(130). Εἴδη μέντοι τῆς θείας γραφῆς ἐστι δύο, προφητικὸν καὶ ἱστορικόν· < προφητικὸν μὲν οὖν	**74.** Εἴδη μέντοι τῆς θείας γραφῆς ἐστι δύο, τό τε προφητικὸν καὶ τὸ ἱστορικόν· προφητικὸν μὲν οὖν ἐστι

6 John 3:5 var.
7 Cf. 1 John 5:6–8

10 post ὅταν] lac. indic. *Goessling* (ex *Schlüren*)   10 ante Τὰ] ὅπως τὰ κατὰ παραίνεσιν titul. Z

unexpressed[1] the possession [of the kingdom] through Jesus' blood (cf. 1 John 5:6–8).

their possession [of it], [which would only happen] provided that they not break the law. But it is also so concerning the future age: "If someone," Jesus says, "is not born of water and spirit, he will not enter into the kingdom of heaven" (John 3:5)—clearly leaving unexpressed the possession [of this kingdom] through his blood (cf. 1 John 5:6–8). One will find many similar passages in the Old and New Testaments.

73.22. Exhortation: since taken together, all the passages of the divinely inspired Scripture, whether through words or deeds, reasonably seem to promote this end.[2]

73.22. Exhortation: anyone who is pious will agree that, taken together, all the passages of divinely inspired Scripture, whether through words or deeds, reasonably seem to promote this end.

APPENDIX 2: GENRES OF SCRIPTURE AND TEMPORAL REFERENCES OF PROPHECY

74. Now there are two kinds of divine Scripture: prophetic and narratival.[3] The[4] prophetic announces in advance

74. Now there are two kinds of divine Scripture: the prophetic and the narratival. The prophetic announces in

---

[1] S.v. ταμιεύω PGL 3.

[2] Here Adrian speaks of the σκοπός of Scripture—through its words and deeds it exhorts its readers and hearers to proper conduct. This trope is similar to ὑπόδειγμα (73.5). On the motif of παραίνεσις, see Diod., *Ps.* 90 (Mariès, *Études*, 60). On the doctrinal and moral benefit that Scripture provides its audience, see Diod., *proem. Ps.*, Thdt., *proem. Ps.*, and the discussion in Schäublin, *Untersuchungen*, 161–6. This trope is also significant because it forecasts the opening lines of 75 below where Adrian prescribes that students begin their analysis of a biblical book by first attending to its purpose or intent (διάνοια). This trope explains what that purpose is for Scripture viewed as a whole.

[3] For a similar division of Scripture into these two genres, see Chrys., *Ps.* 50:2; Thdt., *Dan.* 5:1. There is a threefold classification by Thdr. Mops., *fr. Cant.*: *species prophetica, traditio historiarum*, and *demonstrativa admonitio* (PG 66, 699A). And a fourfold classification in Junil., *inst.* 1.2: "There are four [genres—*species dictionis*]: history, prophecy, proverbs, and simple teaching."

[4] After this first sentence R1 appears excessively abridged. In the ms tradition this initial sentence is followed by the following: "Notwithstanding, each one of these [kinds of Scripture, prophetic and narratival] consists of three temporal references..."; or (taking the verb as transitive—s.v. συνίστημι LSJ A; Smyth, §1559), "Notwithstanding, Scripture constructs each one of these [kinds of Scripture, prophetic and narratival] from three temporal references..." But neither translation is desirable, since the examples that follow concern only *prophecy* having past, present, and future referents. But if the intervening material in R2 is included, the sentence in question reads more suitably: "Notwithstanding

---

RECENSION 1	RECENSION 2

RECENSION 1

ἐστι τὸ πραγμάτων τινῶν ἐσομένων
ἔκβασιν προαγορεύειν· ἱστορικὸν δὲ
τὸ τὴν τῶν πεπραγμένων
εἰσηγεῖσθαι κατάστασιν· πρὸς δὲ
5 τούτοις ἅπασιν ἰστέον ὡς τὸ τῆς
προφητείας εἶδος γνώσεως μέν ἐστι
παρεκτικὸν ἀγνοίας δὲ ἀναιρετικόν· >
ἐκ τριῶν δὲ ὅμως χρόνων ἓν
ἕκαστον αὐτῶν συνέστηκε,
10 παρῳχηκότος, ἐνεστῶτος καὶ
μέλλοντος·

74.1. παρῳχηκότος μέν· ὡς ἡ τοῦ
Μωσέως περὶ τοῦ παντὸς
συστάσεως·
15

74.2. ἐνεστῶτος δέ· ὡς ἡ τοῦ
20 μακαριωτάτου Ἐλισσαίου πρὸς τὸν
Γιεζῆ περὶ τοῦ δοθέντος αὐτῷ
χρυσίου·

RECENSION 2

τὸ πραγμάτων τινῶν ἐσομένων
ἔκβασιν προαγορεύειν· ἱστορικὸν δὲ
τὸ τὴν τῶν πεπραγμένων
εἰσηγεῖσθαι κατάστασιν· πρὸς δὲ
τούτοις ἅπασιν ἰστέον ὡς τὸ τῆς
προφητείας εἶδος γνώσεως μέν ἐστι
παρεκτικόν, ἀγνοίας δὲ ἀναιρετικόν·
ἐκ τριῶν δὲ ὅμως ἓν ἕκαστον
χρόνων συνέστηκεν· ἔκ τε
παρῳχηκότος καὶ ἐνεστῶτος καὶ
μέλλοντος·

74.1. παρῳχηκότος μέν· ὡς τὰ
Μωυσέως περὶ τῆς τοῦ παντὸς
συστάσεως, ὅπως τε καὶ ὁπηνίκα
πρὸς τουτῶν ὅλων αἰτίου τὴν
διασκευὴν ἐδέξατο· ἃ διὰ
παντελοῦς ἀγνοίας ὄντα τοῖς
ἀνθρώποις ἐγνώρισεν·

74.2. ἐνεστῶτος δέ· ὡς ἥ τε τοῦ
μακαριωτάτου Ἐλισσαίου πρὸς τὸν
Γιεζῆ περὶ τοῦ δοθέντος αὐτῷ
χρυσίου πρὸς τοῦ καθαρθέντος
λεπροῦ· καὶ ἡ τῶν ἀποστόλων
πρὸς Ἀνανίαν καὶ Σάπφειρα·

---

14 Cf. Gen 1
22 Cf. 4 Kgdms 5:1–27 [2 Kgs 5:1–27]

16 Cf. Gen 1–2
23 Cf. 4 Kgdms 5:1–27 [2 Kgs 5:1–27]
24 Cf. Acts 5:1–11

---

7 προφητικὸν–ἀναιρετικόν] + R2

9 χρόνων] χρόνον Z
15 πρὸς] πρὸ Z

TRANSLATION: R1   TRANSLATION: R2

the accomplishment of certain future events, whereas the narratival describes the circumstances of past events. In addition, one needs to know that the prophetic genre is capable of producing knowledge and destroying ignorance.[1] Notwithstanding [the aforementioned definition], each one of these aspects of prophecy consists of three temporal references: past, present, and future.[2]

advance the accomplishment of certain future events, whereas the narratival describes the circumstances of past events. In addition, one needs to know that the prophetic genre is capable of producing knowledge and destroying ignorance. Notwithstanding [the aforementioned definition], each one [of these aspects of prophecy] consists of three temporal references: past, present, and future.

74.1. Of the past: for example, the prophecy by Moses about the creation of the world (cf. Gen. 1–2).

74.1. The past: for example, the words of Moses about the creation of the world, how and when it received its arrangement from the Cause of all things (cf. Gen 1–2). Moses made these things known to people because of their complete ignorance.

74.2. Of the present: for example, the prophecy of the most blessed Elisha in regard to Gehasi, concerning the gold that was given to him (4 Kgdms 5:1–27 [2 Kgs 5:1–27]).[3]

74.2. The present: for example, the prophecy of the most blessed Elisha in regard to Gehasi, concerning the gold that was given to him from the leper [i.e., Naaman] who was cleansed (cf. 4 Kgdms 5:1–27 [2 Kgs 5:1–27]). And the prophecy of the apostles in regard to Ananias and Saphira (cf. Acts 5:1–11).

[the aforementioned definition, i.e., where prophecy is associated only with the future], each of one these aspects of prophecy [i.e., its production of knowledge and destruction of ignorance] consists of three temporal references." On the corruption of the text of R1 here, also see Bultmann, *Exegese des Theodor von Mopsuestia*, 65. This sentence makes better sense because it establishes prophecy as the subject of what is going to follow and calls into question the technical definition of prophecy as a form of Scripture referring only to the future. For similar discussions of the threefold temporal framework of prophecy (past, present, and future), see Ps.-Chrys., *synops.* (PG 56.316–17); Thdt., *proem. Ps.* 5; Junil., *inst.* 1.4; Cass., *proem. Ps.* 1. Note esp. how Diodore discusses prophecy in *proem. Ps.*: while it can relate to the past, present, and future, "strictly speaking [κυριωτέρα]" it forecasts only the future. Diodore and Adrian both seem aware of two circulating definitions of prophecy. Schäublin, *Untersuchungen*, 87–8.

[1] The distinction seems redundant (as is also suggested by 74.1 in R2). On prophecy as the revelation of the unknown, see Thdr. Mops., *Abd.* 1:1; Junil., *inst.* 1.4.

[2] Note that Junillus illustrates the past, present, and future of prophecy very similarly to Adrian. The past includes: "In the beginning God created heaven and earth" (Gen 1:1); the present: the theft by Gehasi (cf. 4 Kgdms 5:20–27); the future: "Lo, a virgin will conceive in her womb and bear a son, and his name will be called Emmanuel" (Isa 7:14)" (*inst.* 1.4).

[3] "Silver," not gold, in the biblical mss.

RECENSION 1	RECENSION 2

74.3. μέλλοντος δέ· ὡς ἡ τῶν προφητῶν τὰ περὶ τῶν Ἑβραίων καὶ τῆς Χριστοῦ παρουσίας < προήγγειλεν >, ἣν διά τε λόγων
5 καὶ ὀπτασιῶν καὶ ἔργων παρειλήφαμεν·

74.3.1. καὶ διὰ λόγων μέν· ὡς τό, ἰδοὺ ἡμέραι ἔρχονται, λέγει κύριος, καὶ διαθήσω τῷ οἴκῳ Ἰσραὴλ καὶ τῷ
10 οἴκῳ Ἰούδα διαθήκην καινήν·

15

74.3.2. δι' ὀπτασιῶν δέ· ὡς τό, καὶ ἐγένετο ἐπ' ἐμὲ χεὶρ κυρίου· καί, ἀναστήσονται οἱ νεκροί· καί,
20 ἐθεώρουν ἕως ὅτου θρόνοι ἐτέθησαν· καί, ἰδοὺ μετὰ τῶν νεφελῶν ὡς υἱὸς ἀνθρώπου ἐρχόμενος·

25

74.3. μέλλοντος δέ· ὡς ἡ τῶν λοιπῶν προφητῶν τά τε περὶ Ἑβραίων καὶ τῆς τοῦ Χριστοῦ παρουσίας προήγγειλεν, ἣν διά τε λόγων καὶ ὀπτασιῶν καὶ ἔργων παρειλήφαμεν·

74.3.1. διὰ λόγων μὲν οὖν· ὡς τό, ἰδοὺ ἡμέραι ἔρχονται, λέγει κύριος, καὶ διαθήσομαι τῷ οἴκῳ Ἰσραὴλ καὶ τῷ οἴκῳ Ἰούδα διαθήκην καινήν· καὶ ὅσα τοιαῦτα περὶ τοῦ λαοῦ τῶν Ἑβραίων· καὶ τό, ἰδοὺ ἡ παρθένος ἐν γαστρὶ λήψεται καὶ τέξεται υἱόν, καὶ καλέσουσι τὸ ὄνομα αὐτοῦ Ἐμμανουήλ· καὶ ὅσα τοιαῦτα περὶ τοῦ Χριστοῦ·

74.3.2. δι' ὀπτασιῶν δέ· ὡς τὸ παρὰ τῷ Ἰεζεκιήλ, καὶ ἐγένετο ἐπ' ἐμὲ χεὶρ κυρίου, καὶ ἐξήγαγέ με καὶ ἔθηκέ με ἐν μέσῳ τοῦ πέδου, καὶ τοῦτο ἦν μεστὸν ὀστέων ἀνθρωπίνων, καὶ τὰ ἑξῆς ἅπερ πάντα τὴν ἐλευθερίαν τοῦ Ἰσραὴλ δηλοῦσι· μνήματα μὲν τοινῦν τὰς ἐπὶ τῆς αἰχμαλωσίας αὐτῶν

---

10 Jer 38[31]:31 var.	10 Jer 38[31]:31 var.
18 Ezek 37:1	15 Isa 7:14 var.
19 1 Thess 4:16 var.	22 Ezek 37:1 var.
21 Dan 7:9	24 Ezek 37:12
23 Dan 7:13 var.	

---

2 τά] – Goessling	9 διαθήσομαι] διαβήσομαι Z
4 προήγγειλεν] + R2	23 πάντα] om. Z

74.3. Of the future: for example, the prophets' announced in advance things about the Hebrews and the coming of Christ.[1] We have received this prophecy through words and visions and deeds.[2]

74.3.1. Through words: for example, "Behold the days are coming, says the Lord, and I will set forth a new covenant with the house of Israel and the house of Judah" (Jer 38[31]:31).[3]

74.3.2. Through visions: for example, "And the hand of the Lord came upon me . . ." (Ezek 37:1); and, "the dead will rise" (1 Thess 4:16);[4] and, "I watched until the thrones were set in place" (Dan 7:9); and, "Look, as it were a son of man coming with the clouds" (Dan 7:13).[5]

74.3. The future: for example, the other prophets made announcements in advance about both the Hebrews and the coming of Christ. We have received this prophecy though words and visions and deeds.

74.3.1. Through words: for example, "Behold the days are coming, says the Lord, and I will set forth a new covenant with the house of Israel and the house of Judah" (Jer 38[31]:31), and all such passages concerning the Hebrew people. And, "Behold, the virgin will conceive in the womb and have a boy, and they will call his name 'Emmanuel' " (Isa 7:14), and all such passages concerning Christ.

74.3.2. Through visions: for example, the passage in Ezekiel: "And the hand of the Lord came upon me and He brought me out and put me in the midst of the plain, and this was full of human bones" (Ezek 37:1), and the words that follow, all of which indicate Israel's release from captivity; Ezekiel accordingly called their dwellings in the time of the captivity

---

[1] This is an important distinction between "near-range" and "far-range" prophecies—the former pertain to Hebrew prophecies about later events prior to the dispensation of the Messiah, whereas the latter reach into that dispensation. This distinction is widely operative in Antiochene circles: e.g., compare Thdr. Mops., *Ps. hypoth.* 44 where David prophesies about the post-exilic community, but in *Ps. hypoth.* 45 the prophecy is about Jesus. Note esp. the catalogue of near- and far-range prophecies in Junil., *inst.* 2.20–23. On the relationship between the prophets and Christ, see Devreesse, *Essai*, 86–93; Schäublin, *Untersuchungen*, 166–70.

[2] More commonly in the tradition "words and deeds": see Ps.-Chrys., *synops.* where he announces that prophecies of future things occur διὰ ἔργων καὶ διὰ λόγων (PG 56.316); Junil., *inst.* 2.16 on words and deeds. On prophecies διὰ λόγων καὶ διὰ ὀπτασιῶν (Cosm. Ind., *top.* 5.168).

[3] Notice how R1 does not offer the second illustration of a prophecy about Christ. The second illustration is provided in R2.

[4] Both Theodore and Theodoret refer to what Paul discloses in these lines as a "divine revelation" (*1 Thess.* 4:15). The imagistic quality of this revelation (e.g., the Lord will descend from heaven and believers will meet him in the clouds in the air) is probably what suggests this as a vision to Adrian.

[5] For the close association of "revelation" with "vision," see Thdt., *Dan.* 7:1.

RECENSION 1

RECENSION 2

κατασκηνώσεις ὠνόμασεν· καὶ τὸ
παρὰ τῷ Δανιήλ, **ἐθεώρουν ἕως οὗ
θρόνοι ἐτέθησαν, καὶ παλαιὸς
ἡμερῶν ἐκάθισε·** καὶ τὰ τοιαῦτα
περὶ τοῦ Χριστοῦ·

74.3.3. δι' ἔργων δέ· ὡς ἐπὶ τοῦ
Ἀβραάμ· **λάβε μοι δάμαλιν
τριετίζουσαν, καὶ αἶγα τριετίζουσαν,
καὶ κριὸν τριετίζοντα, καὶ τρυγόνα
καὶ περιστεράν,** καὶ τὰ ἑξῆς· καί,
**λάβε τὸν υἱόν σου τὸν ἀγαπητόν, ὃν
ἠγάπησας, τὸν Ἰσαάκ.**

74.3.3. δι' ἔργων δέ· ὡς ἐπὶ τοῦ
Ἀβραάμ, **λάβε μοι δάμαλιν
τριετίζουσαν,** καὶ τὰ ἑξῆς, τὰ
τοῖς ἐξ αὐτοῦ σαφῶς ἀπογόνοις
ἐσόμενα διὰ τῶνδε καθερμηνεύων·
καὶ τό, **λάβε τὸν υἱόν σου τὸν
ἀγαπητὸν καὶ ἀνένεγκε αὐτὸν εἰς
ὁλοκάρπωσιν·** τῆς κατὰ Χριστὸν
οἰκονομίας ἑρμηνεία τὶς ἦν τὸ
πραττόμενον ἐπὶ τοῦ Ἀβραάμ.

10 Gen 15:9
12 Gen 22:2

4 Dan 7:9 var.
8 Gen 15:9
10 Cf. Gen 15:13–16
13 Gen 22:2 var.

14 οἰκονομίας] ὑποθέσεως infra verbum
pr. m. YZ

"tombs" (Ezek 37:12). And the passage in Daniel: "I watched until the thrones were set in place and the Ancient of Days was seated" (Dan 7:9), and similar passages concerning Christ.

74.3.3. Through deeds: for example, in regard to Abraham: "Bring me a three-year-old heifer, and a three-year-old goat, and a three-year-old ram, and a turtle-dove and a dove" (Gen 15:9), and what follows; and, "take your beloved son Isaac, whom you have loved" (Gen 22:2).

74.3.3. Through deeds: for example, in regard to Abraham: "Bring me a three-year-old heifer" (Gen 15:9), and what follows, denoting[1] through these deeds the future for those who are plainly his descendants (cf. Gen 15:13–16).[2] And the passage, "take your beloved son, Isaac, and lead him into the high land" (Gen 22:2)—what was done in the case of Abraham was an expression of Christ's plan of salvation.[3]

[1] The verb καθερμηνεύω is unattested in LSJ (according to *PGL*, it is a false variant reading for καθαμαξεύω). I am taking the prefatory κατά as strengthening or intensifying the root verb (ἑρμηνεύω as "expressing" or "denoting"—s.v. ἑρμηνεία LSJ; s.v. ἑρμηνεύω PGL 2). There is a parallel between this verb and the noun ἑρμηνεία a few lines down. In both cases, a deed is considered symbolic or expressive of a future event.

[2] Thdt., *qu. in Gen.* 67: "These are obscure hints of what would happen to the race." Theodoret indicates that God ordered the sacrifice of three of the clean quadrupeds "as an indication of the three generations that would live as aliens," i.e., the future enslavement of the Hebrews in Egypt, justifying this interpretation with the words that follow the command to sacrifice: "You will know for certain that your offspring will be aliens in a land that is not theirs" (Gen 15:13).

[3] Diod., *fr. Gen.* 22:13 [Petit, *coisliniana Gen.* no. 204]: the sabek plant (signifying "forgiveness" among the Hebrews) is "indicative of the mystery of the cross" [καὶ τοῦτο δὲ τοῦ μυστηρίου τοῦ σταυροῦ δηλωτικὸν ἂν εἴη]" (lines 22–6); later, Isaac is a figure (τύπος) of Christ's passion (lines 31–3); Thdt., *qu. in Gen.* 74: "No, this was a shadow of the divine plan implemented for our benefit; for the sake of the world, the Father offered his beloved Son. Isaac was a type of the divinity, the ram of the humanity. The actual time was also of equal length: three days and three nights in both cases." Also see Eus. Em. (?), *fr. Gen.* 22:13 [Petit, *chaîne* no. 1277].
The marginal gloss ὑποθέσεως, under οἰκονομίας, suggests either of the following possible modifications of the sentence: (1) "what was done in the case of Abraham was an expression *of the theme* of Christ's plan of salvation"; or, (2) "what was done in the case of Abraham was an expression *of the particular historical situation* of Christ's plan of salvation". The latter is a distinct possibility if Adrian (or more likely a subsequent scribe) had in mind the tradition that identified the place of Isaac's near-sacrifice with the place of Christ's crucifixion. See two marginal glosses in the manuscript tradition that make this link: Diod., *fr. Gen.* 22:13 [Petit, *coisliniana Gen.* no. 204 note f].

75(131). Τούτων δὲ οὕτως ἐχόντων προσήκει προηγουμένως ταῖς τῶν ῥήσεων
ὑποθέσεσι τὴν διάνοιαν ἐφιστᾶν τοὺς μαθητεύοντας, εἶθ' οὕτως αὐτοῖς τὴν
κατὰ λέξιν ἑρμηνείαν οἰκείως ταύτην προσάγειν, ὡς ἂν διανοίας μὴ
προυπαρχούσης ἡ διὰ τῶν λόγων πλάζοιτο σύστασις· καθάπερ γὰρ ἐπὶ τῶν
5 τὰ σκάφη πηδαλιουχούντων εἰ μή που τίς αὐτοῖς ὡρισμένος τοῦ σκοποῦ

APPENDIX 3:
GUIDELINES FOR INTERPRETING SCRIPTURE

75. This being so, it is fitting that students first fix their attention on the purpose [of a scriptural book] by means of the contents of its individual passages. Then, in this manner, the book's purpose properly furnishes the word-for-word commentary to students, since the link between words would be lost if the purpose is not established in advance.[1] For just as with those who steer ships, if some defined target does not lie somewhere before them, toward which they intend to direct the

---

[1] Adrian uses a number of technical exegetical terms throughout Appendix 3. Here at the start of 75 διάνοια refers not to "meaning," but "intention" or "purpose," thereby functioning as a synonym for σκοπός, which is in keeping with the nautical analogy that immediately follows (more on this below). Adrian also employs the term ὑπόθεσις, which is not used univocally by the Antiochenes. It can often be rendered as the "subject matter" of a book—and sometimes other related glosses work well, like "topic," "theme," "summary of contents," or "outline" (s.v. LSJ II and *PGL* 2.b and c; Diod., *proem. Ps.*: "the overall ὑπόθεσις of the Psalms is twofold: moral and doctrinal"; Diod., *Ps. hypoth.* 4; Thdt., *proem. Dan.*, etc.). Other times, the term points to the "setting," "occasion," or "historical circumstances" from which a passage is written (e.g., Diod., *Ps. hypoth.* 3; Thdr. Mops., *Ps. hypoth.* 46; Thdt., *Ps. hypoth.* 50; Schäublin, *Untersuchungen*, 84, consistently glosses the noun as the "particular historical situation"). Adrian uses the noun at 73.12, twice in 75, and once in 76. It is not entirely clear how the term is to be used here in 75–6. I incline to the former sense, since it seems more natural to encourage a reader to discover a book's purpose from its "contents." Also note 73.9 in R2 where there is a close association of the aim (σκοπός) of Gen 1–2 with its content, as summarized in Gen 2:4–5. For more on this term, see Mariès, *Études*, 59–76; Devreesse, *Essai*, 69–70; Mansfeld, *Prolegomena*, 69 fn. 118; Nünlist, *Ancient Critic at Work*, 24 fn. 5.

Adrian is, then, proposing a two-step sequence for biblical interpretation: first the student attends to the book's "purpose" (διάνοια) as it is expressed through its "contents" (ὑποθέσεις) (a few lines below Adrian will speak only of attending to this content). On this basis, the "word-for-word commentary" (ἡ κατὰ λέξιν ἑρμηνεία) will become clear. While the prepositional phrase κατὰ λέξιν can be translated as "literal," this does not capture Adrian's sense. (For how the schema "literal–allegorical" misleads when applied to Antiochene exegesis, see Young, "Interpretation of Scripture," 853–5.) The phrase is better rendered as "textual" or "word for word" (s.v. λέξις *PGL* 10) because it conveys more clearly the methodological sequence Adrian is advocating: the interpreter moves from the general theme to the specific wording. This definition is also confirmed by the next clause, where Adrian speaks about the importance of capturing the "link between words [ἡ διὰ τῶν λόγων ... σύστασις]" after grasping the meaning, and a few lines later when he speaks about properly understanding the "usage of the words [τὴν τῶν λόγων χρῆσιν]" in light of the subject matter of Scripture.

There are parallels to this programmatic statement in Antiochene biblical scholarship. On the priority of determining the "purpose" (normally expressed by σκοπός and not διάνοια) before turning to the ἑρμηνεία, see Thdt., *proem. Ps.* 4: "First of all, however, we shall expose the purpose of the Psalms and then come to the commentary [πρότερον δέ γε τῶν ψαλμῶν δηλώσαντες τὸν σκοπὸν οὕτω τῆς ἑρμηνείας ἁψόμεθα]." On the priority of determining the ὑπόθεσις before turning to the ἑρμηνεία, see Thdt., *proem. Dan.*: "let us first make clear the subject of the prophecy, and then in this fashion come to the textual commentary [τὴν τῆς προφητείας ὑπόθεσιν δήλην πρότερον καταστήσωμεν, εἶθ᾽ οὕτως τῆς κατὰ λέξιν ἑρμηνείας ἁψώμεθα]" (mod.). Also see the title of Diod. *Ps.* in *Parisinus Coislinianus* 275 [Olivier, 1]; Diod., *proem. Ps.*; Thdt., *proem. Joel*; Junil., *inst.* 2.28.

προκέοιτο τόπος, εἰς ὃν ἅπασαν τὴν τῶν οἰάκων ῥοπὴν εὐθύνειν μέλλοιεν,
ἐν παντὶ τῷ πνεύματι τὴν ἑαυτῶν τέχνην διαφόρως ἐμπιστεύειν
συνελαυνόμενοι δι᾿ ὅλου φέρονται τοῦ πελάγους, ὡς ὅρμῳ τῇ ἄλῃ
προσφεύγοντες· οὕτως ἄρα καὶ ἐπὶ τῶν τῆς διδασκαλίας ἐξηγήσεων ἐξ
5 ἀνάγκης συμβήσεται, ἐπειδὰν μὴ καθυποκειμένης τινὸς πραγματείας
προβάλλοιτο· πῶς γὰρ οὐκ ἂν εἴη τῶν ἀτοπωτάτων, εἰ τὰς μὲν ῥαψῳδίας
πλάσματα καὶ οὐκ ἀληθῆ πράγματα περιεχούσας, οὐκ ἔνεστιν ἑτέρως
εἰσηγήσασθαι τοὺς ἐπιστήμονας, μὴ πρότερον τὴν ἑκάστης αὐτῶν ὑπόθεσιν
εἰς γνῶσιν ἐνεγκαμένους, ὡς ἂν πρὸς ταύτην εἰκότως καὶ μὴ πρὸς ἀνέμους
10 τὴν τῶν λόγων χρῆσιν ἐκφέροιεν, τὰ δὲ τῆς θείας ἡμῶν ὑποθημοσύνης
ἀνυποστάτοις τισὶ στοχασμοῖς ὑποβάλλοιμεν, εἰκαίας αὐτοῖς καὶ
ἀσυναρτήτους τὰς ἑρμηνείας ἐπιφέρειν οὐ δυσωπούμενοι.

76(132). Διόπερ ὃν τρόπον τοῖς εἰς ἄγνωστον πάντῃ στελλομένοις χώραν
χρή, μᾶλλον τοὺς ἐν πείρᾳ ταύτης τυγχάνοντας, πρό γε πάντων τὴν
15 ἀπάγουσαν ἀτραπὸν καταμηνύειν δι᾿ ἧς πορεύοιντο, οὕτω τε αὖ τὰ κατὰ
ταύτην αὐτοῖς γνωρίζειν σημεῖα, οἷς ἐξακολουθοῦντες μηδαμῶς τῆς εὐθείας
ἀποσφάλλοιντο· τὸν αὐτὸν ἄν τις καὶ ἐπὶ τῶν παιδεύειν ἐπαγγελλομένων
ὁρίσαιτο προηγουμένως μὲν τὴν τῶν πραγμάτων αὐτοὺς ὑπόθεσιν γνωρίμην
χρῆναι καθιστᾶν τοῖς παιδευομένοις, εἰς ἣν ἀναγκαίως ἔχοιεν τὴν τῆς
20 ἑαυτῶν διανοίας ἐπιδοῦναι ῥοπήν, εἶτα τὴν τῶν γραφικῶν ἰδιωμάτων

---

2 ἐν] om. *Hoeschel Goessling*
3 ἄλῃ] ACDGJK₁ *Hoeschel* (ex A) *Goessling* (ex codd.), ἄλῃ L, τῇ ἄλμῃ in app. cr. propos. *Goessling*
14 post χρή] lac. indic. *Goessling* et in app. cr. propos.: προηγουμένως μὲν αὐτὴν τὴν χώραν γνωρίμην καθιστᾶν
14 post μᾶλλον] δὲ + *Goessling*

whole weight of the rudders, they are driven through the whole sea, forced to entrust their expertise here and there to every wind as they search wanderingly for refuge in a harbor.[1] This is what will also certainly happen in the exegetical exercises of classroom teaching, whenever it is offered without some diligent preparatory study.[2] For how would it not be incredibly absurd, if it is impossible for scholars to interpret the epic poems which contain fictions, namely untrue events,[3] in any other way than by first learning the content of each of these poems, so as to reasonably bring forth the usage of the words in regard to their topic—and not the winds—but we were to subject the words of our divine counsel to some unfounded conjectures, not being ashamed to impose random and disconnected explanations on them?!![4]

76. Thus how necessary it is for those departing for a completely unknown land, that people who are to a greater degree acquainted with it point out, first of all, the return path by which these should travel and, moreover, make known to them the signs along this way which, if they follow these, they will certainly not be led astray of the straight path.[5] In the same way, someone—especially among those who profess to teach—should resolve that it is necessary that they first render the content, full of events, familiar to their pupils, in regard to which they might be obliged to

Finally, note the analogy that immediately follows this two-step sequence: the ship's steersman first needs to have a target in view if he is to safely bring his ship to harbor amidst stormy conditions. Adrian is punning on "target," literally "some defined place *of aim* [τις ... ὡρισμένος τοῦ σκοποῦ ... τόπος]." The term σκοπός ("aim" or "intent") was a technical exegetical term widely used to refer to authorial intent in communicating a certain message (e.g., Diod., *Ps. hypoth.* 39; Thdr. Mops., *Ps.* 39:8; Thdt., *proem. Cant.; proem. comm. in xii proph.; proem. Rom.;* Junil., *inst.* 2.28).

[1] Perhaps an allusion to Odysseus, which anticipates the reference in the next lines to epic poems: s.v. ἄλη LSJ (*Od.* 10.464). For a similar analogy between this nautical trope and scriptural interpretation, see Chrys., *de proph. obsc. hom.* 1.1.

[2] For a similar association between schooling and introductory treatises on Scripture, see the preface to Junillus, *inst.* who traces his handbook back to Paul the Persian "who was educated at the Syrian School in the city of Nisibis, where the Divine Law is taught in a disciplined manner and orderly fashion by public teachers in the same way that in a secular education grammar and rhetoric are taught in our cities."

[3] On this issue of fictions in Greek literature, especially Homer, see Nünlist, *Ancient Critic at Work*, 174–84; Kim, *Homer between History and Fiction.*

[4] For discussion and examples of *hypotheses* on a range of Greek literature, esp. the Homeric poems which Adrian likely has in view here, see Rossum-Steenbeeck, *Greek Readers' Digests?*, 53–74. Note as well that the Homeric hypotheses tended to offer summaries of the books of the poems, thus confirming the translation decision of ὑπόθεσις in 75–6. For additional discussion of the interpretation of epic (Homeric) poetry by Antiochenes, recall the two examples of allegorical exegesis of Zeus in Diod., *Ps. hypoth.* 118 and Schäublin, *Untersuchungen*, 45 fn. 9. On the wider study of myths, see Cameron, *Greek Mythography* and Fowler, *Early Greek Mythography.*

[5] A similar analogy in Thdt., *proem. Ps.* 3.

RECENSION 1

εἴδησιν, τήν τε τῶν σχημάτων διάγνωσιν καὶ τὴν τῶν τρόπων διάκρισιν· οὐχ ἥκιστα δὲ τὴν τῆς κατὰ τὴν λέξιν ἑρμηνείας σαφήνειαν, οἷα δή τινα σημεῖα τῆς ὁδοιπορίας προσυποδεικνῦναι, δι᾽ ὧν τό τε ἀσφαλὲς καὶ βέβαιον αὐτοῖς ὑπάρχοι πρὸς τὸ προκείμενον· (133) δήλου γε ὄντος, ὡς τοῖς ἵπτασθαι
5 μέν, ἀλλὰ μὴ δι᾽ ὁδοῦ βαίνειν προθεμένοις, περιττὴ καὶ ἀσύμβολος ἡ τῶν σημείων ὑπόδειξις.

77. Χρὴ δέ γε μάλιστα γενναίως ἔχεσθαι καθόλου τῆς ἀκολουθίας, ἣν καθάπερ σπαρτίον ἐκταθὲν τῆς ἐπιβουλῆς εἰς τὴν τῆς ἀκριβοῦς διανοίας περαίωσιν ἐμμελέστερον ἄν τις διακρατῶν, οὐκ ἂν ἁμάρτοι τοῦ πρέποντος.

2 post τῆς] κακίας C a. corr.   7 ante Χρὴ] non interpun. *Goessling*
8 ἐπιβουλῆς] ἐπιβολῆς *Goessling,* ὑποβολῆς *Schlüren*

supply the weight of their own understanding.[1] Then [they ought to supply] the knowledge of literary peculiarities, the distinction between figures and the differentiation of tropes[2] and, not least, the clear, word-for-word commentary[3]—just like they would point out any signs for the journey, by means of which travelers might have the sureness and steadfastness for what lies ahead.[4] It is nevertheless clear that the information provided by these signs is useless and insignificant for those who prefer to fly rather than walk along the path.

77. But it is especially necessary to cling faithfully and completely to the sequence [of words].[5] Someone who properly grasps this sequence—like the extended cord

---

[1] The subject of "they might be obliged to supply the weight of their own understanding" is not entirely clear: I am taking the whole sequence of thought to refer to teachers—they outline the contents of a biblical book, supply auxiliary knowledge from their own understanding, teach literary peculiarities, etc. But the subject might also refer to pupils: after the teacher presents the contents of a book, it is the pupils who supply the weight of their own understanding, their knowledge of literary peculiarities, etc. I prefer the former option since the paragraph is framed, beginning to end, with the image of an expert guide who assists novice travelers. After the preliminary discussion of the contents of a biblical book, then, it is the teacher who might have to supply additional knowledge: Adrian likely has in mind the instructor's ability to draw on extra-scriptural material to fill out the historical circumstances that inform the subject matter of the text (Schäublin, *Untersuchungen*, 84–94, 148–9).

Note as well how Adrian distances Christian Scripture from the Homeric epics: whereas the latter are often fictitious (75), the Christian Bible is *not* full of inventions; in fact, it is "full of events." Antiochene authors repeatedly underscore that Scripture narrates "events" (πράγματα) and "reality" (ἀλήθεια), which they contrast sharply with the epics which narrate οὐκ ἀληθῆ πράγματα. Yet recall the discussion of "representational language" in R1 and esp. R2 (73.12), where fictions in the book of Job are tacitly acknowledged. For more on the events or reality of Scripture, see Mariès, *Études*, 100; Schäublin, *Untersuchungen*, 156–7. Recall as well the critique that both Diodore and Theodore level against the allegorical exegesis of Christian Scripture, that it undermines the facticity of the events narrated in Scripture: Diod., *proem. Ps.*; *Ps. hypoth.* 118; Thdr. Mops., *Gal.* 4:24; *Ps. hypoth.* 118.

[2] Notice that Adrian is expanding on his two-step sequence for scriptural exegesis outlined above, inserting here a middle step: between attending to the subject matter of a passage and offering a word-for-word commentary, the teacher must convey a knowledge literary peculiarities, figures, and tropes—i.e., the teacher must convey the contents of the *Introduction*.

[3] I am taking this as an "attributed genitive" construction: τὴν τῆς... ἑρμηνείας σαφήνειαν is "clear commentary" and not the "clarity of commentary" (Wallace, *Greek Grammar*, 89–91).

[4] The interpreter's goal is to bring out the clarity (σαφήνεια) of the scriptural text through a detailed examination of the wording. The implication of the *Introduction* is that this clarity has been obscured by the literary peculiarities of Scripture. Thdr. Mops., *proem. Ag.*: "The blessed prophet, Haggai... to whom it falls to us now by the grace of God to bring clarity [ποιεῖσθαι τὴν σαφήνειαν]." On the problem of Scripture's obscurity (ἀσάφεια) in Diodore, see Mariès, *Études*, 126–7.

[5] Since the comments that precede and follow this point concern wording, I take ἀκολουθία here to be a reference specifically to the sequence of words. There are two other references to ἀκολουθία in the *Introduction*: at 4.10 Adrian refers to the sequence of a particular image, and at *cat. Ps.* 78:2 he mentions the "sequence of thought." The priority of this concept for regulating exegesis is well known in Antiochene circles: Eus. Em., *arb.* 8; Diod., *proem. Ps.*; Thdr. Mops., *Ps. hypoth.* 1; 9:23–4; 35:2; 37:13; Polychr., *fr. Job* prol. 2; Chrys., *Ps.* 47:3, etc. For discussion, see Bultmann, *Exegese des Theodor von Mopsuestia*, 69–74; Schäublin, *Untersuchungen*, 143–4; Hill, *Reading the Old Testament in Antioch*, 110, 111, 113–14; 116.

78. Καὶ δὴ τὴν μὲν τῶν ῥητῶν διάνοιαν ἐν σώματος τάξει θετέον, τὴν δὲ θεωρίαν ἐν σχήματος τοῦ περὶ τὸ σῶμα· τὸ μὲν γὰρ καὶ πόρρωθεν ἀθρόον ἐστὶν ἐπιδεῖξαι, τὸ δὲ διά τε μελῶν καὶ συνθέσεων ἀκριβέστερον παραστῆσαι, μηδὲν περαιτέρω φανταζομένους τοῦ σώματος.

of a snare[1]—with a view to attaining the precise meaning, cannot miss the fitting sense.[2]

78. And what is more, one ought to think of the meaning of words as the arrangement of a body, their speculative sense as the arrangement of a cloak wrapped around a body.[3] For it is possible to point out the cloak quickly, even from afar, but it is possible to describe the body more precisely by way of both its limbs and its joints, provided that people imagine nothing beyond the body.[4]

---

[1] A difficult clause: Goessling emended ἐπιβουλή to ἐπιβολή, but translated the phrase in question loosely, not clearly reflecting his emendation: "like the thread running through the entirety of the text" (*Adrians ΕΙΣΑΓΩΓΗ*, 135). I am taking ἐπιβουλή as a "snare" (s.v. ἐπιβουλεύω LSJ A.b: "lay snares for"). Note the snare cord made of σπάρτον (Xen., *cyn.* 9.13). A synonymous term, σχοινίον, is also used of a snare: καὶ σχοινία διέτειναν, παγίδας τοῖς ποσίν μου ("and they stretched cords, traps for my feet") (Ps 139:6). I thank Andrew Chronister for proposing this reading of the clause.

[2] Note three technical exegetical terms in this sentence. First, διάνοια is being used here not as "intent" or "purpose" (as in 75), but as "meaning" or "sense," the goal of exegetical inquiry (Schäublin, *Untersuchungen*, 142–3). Second, the meaning for which the exegete strives is ἀκριβής ("precise" or perhaps "undistorted"—s.vv. ἀκρίβεια, ἀκριβῶς PGL; Schäublin, *Untersuchungen*, 112). The concept surfaces again in 78 below and seems to point to the need to parse the details of the scriptural passage. Third, the exegete aims for τὸ πρέπον ("fitting sense"), a term with theological and ethical resonances. Within the framework of the *Introduction* Adrian likely has the fittingness of a de-anthropomorphized conception of God in mind (Schäublin, *Untersuchungen*, 78–9; Bonner, *Education in Ancient Rome*, 245–8).

[3] Note the ocular pun running through this paragraph: θεωρία ("seeing, viewing, beholding"), φαντάζω ("to picture" something "to oneself," "to imagine"), and σχῆμα (LSJ A.2: "appearance," "show"). There seems to be a pejorative connotation attached to θεωρία: it is distinguished from the meaning (διάνοια) of Scripture, which is what Adrian's treatise is attempting to help readers grasp; it is a sense of Scripture associated with "imagining" something beyond Scripture's "meaning"; it is likened to a σχῆμα ("cloak") though the visual pun invites readers to hear another sense of the noun (i.e., "appearance" as opposed to reality); it can be identified "quickly" whereas searching for the meaning of Scripture involves reading "precisely"; and it is a topic about which Adrian is otherwise silent in the treatise, thus leaving it quite unclear what place in his exegetical project the quest for Scripture's θεωρία might have. In an attempt to capture the negative coloration of this term, I render it "speculative sense" (s.v. θεωρία LSJ III.2.b). For other Antiochene discussions of *theoria*, see esp. Diod., *proem. Ps.* and *Ps. hypoth.* 118 and recall that Diodore wrote a treatise that no longer survives: *What is the Difference between θεωρία and ἀλληγορία?* On θεωρία in Diodore, see Mariès, *Études*, 133–44.
Finally, on the analogy between the basic meaning of Scripture and a σῶμα (body): note Eustathius' accusation that Origen did not "pay attention to the body of Scripture right-mindedly [μηδ᾽ αὐτῷ σώματι προσέχων εὐγνωμόνως]" (*engast.* 21.1). On the other hand, Theodoret can speak of the literal sense of Scripture as "bare" or "naked," though for him this expression usually has a pejorative sense that is missing in Adrian (*qu. in Ex.* 40.1).

[4] Adrian's claim about θεωρία – subordinating its discovery to the primacy of Scripture's διάνοια – is made through an analogy between Scripture and a cloaked body. The exegete's main goal is to grasp the διάνοια of Scripture, that is, to describe the body itself in close and patient detail, and not the garment that drapes it (θεωρία). Adrian specifically likens the διάνοια of Scripture to a body's "arrangement" – the term here is τάξις, a synonym for ἀκολουθία introduced in 77 above. As we saw there, the ἀκολουθία of a passage (its configuration of words) leads to its διάνοια. So too here in 78: what matters most is the very τάξις or arrangement of the body, which can only be properly described "by way of both its limbs and joints" (διά τε μελῶν καὶ συνθέσεων). What are these "limbs and joints" to which the exegete attends? Adrian's language is playfully reminiscent of the opening sentence of the *Introduction*: there he links the διάνοια of Scripture with its λέξις (individual word use) and σύνθεσις (the use of multiple words in arrangement). By analogy here in 78, then, the "limbs and joints" that are

RECENSION 1

79(134). Ἔτι μὴν κἀκεῖνο γνώριμον τοῖς οἰκείοις ἔστω, ὡς τὰ τῆς
προφητείας τὰ μὲν λογάδην εἴρηται, ὡς τὰ Ἡσαΐου καὶ Ἰερεμίου καὶ εἴ
τις ἕτερος κατ' ἐκείνους ἐγένετο, ἡ δὲ μετ' ᾠδῆς ἐν μέτρῳ, ὡς ἡ τῶν
Ψαλμῶν τοῦ μακαρίου Δαυίδ, καὶ ἡ παρὰ τῷ Μωσεῖ ἐπί τε τῆς ἐξόδου καὶ
5 τοῦ δευτερονομίου· ὅσα δὲ ἔμμετρα οὐ μετ' ᾠδῆς δὲ ῥηθέντα ἄνωθεν καὶ
παραδοθέντα, οὐκ ἄν ποτε εἴη προφητεία, οἷάπερ οὖν τὰ λοιπὰ τῶν
στιχηρῶν εἶναι συμβαίνει, ὡς τοῦ Ἰὼβ καὶ Σολομῶντος.

4 Cf. Ex 15:1–19
5 Cf. Deut 32:1–43

---

1 τὰ] – Goessling (ex *Schlüren*)
2 τὰ¹]ἡ Goessling (ex *Schlüren*)
2 λογάδην] καταλογάδην in mg. ext. A ex manu *Hoeschel* (sed λογάδην in ed. pr.)
7 post Σολομῶντος] *Τέλος σὺν θεῷ* + postscr. *Hoeschel Goessling*

APPENDIX 4: PROPHECY, PROSE, AND METER

79. Moreover, students must also be familiar with this, that some prophecies were spoken in prose:[1] for example, those by Isaiah and Jeremiah and whoever else there was among their contemporaries. But there was other prophecy [spoken] in meter and accompanied by song: for example, the prophecy in blessed David's Psalms[2] and the prophecy by Moses at the time of the exodus (cf. Ex 15:1–19) and the second giving of the law (cf. Deut 32:1–43). But as far as metrical passages originally spoken and transmitted without an accompanying song, these should never be considered prophecy, such as the rest of the passages composed in verse turn out to be, for example, those by Job and Solomon.[3]

---

crucial for describing the scriptural "body" are its individual words and their interrelationships. These words ("limbs") and their relations ("joints") make up meaning ("body").

[1] "In prose" is my rendering of λογάδην, for which there is no definition in LSJ that suits here. The adverb also occurs in Thdr. Mops., *Ps.* 9:23–4: "You see, since the body of the psalms was not composed in prose but in some kind of meter ['Επειδὴ γὰρ οὐ λογάδην εἴρηται τὰ τῶν ψαλμῶν, ἀλλὰ μέτρῳ τινί...]" (corr.). Note as well Hoeschel's proposal in the margin of A: καταλογάδην, a more common adverb for "in prose."

[2] Key statements on meter in the Psalms occur in Adrian., *cat. Ps.* 9:35 and 20:13. A more expansive discussion occurs in Thdr. Mops., *Ps.* 9:23–4. See as well, Schäublin, *Untersuchungen*, 136–8.

[3] Junillus also identifies two "modi" of divine Scripture, Hebrew meter or simple prose. The only books composed in meter are the Psalms, the story of Job, Ecclesiastes, and certain sections of other prophets (*inst.* 1.9).

Fragments of Adrian's *Introduction to the Divine Scriptures* in the Exegetical Catenae

Adrian's *Introduction* was occasionally excerpted in the exegetical catenae.[1] Jean-Baptiste-François Pitra was the first scholar to publish some of these fragments that he had discovered in a handful of catenae on the Psalms.[2] Several years thereafter, Giovanni Mercati revisited Pitra's collection of sixteen fragments and corrected paleographical errors, noted the readings of additional witnesses to these fragments, examined the authenticity of a number of passages,

---

[1] An exegetical "catena" (i.e., chain) is a form of biblical commentary that proceeds verse by verse and is made up of excerpts from earlier scholia, commentaries, homilies, or treatises on Scripture. Greek titles for the catenae included ἐξηγητικαὶ ἐκλογαί, συναγωγὴ τῶν ἐξηγητικῶν ἐκλογῶν, and συναγωγὴ ἐξηγήσεων. For the unit of biblical text in question, the catenist presented in a sequential or linked manner the materials he had extracted either directly from these diverse sources ("primary" catenae) or from other catenae ("secondary"). This procedure was repeated for the next section of biblical text. There were a handful of formats that catenists used for displaying the relationship on the page between the biblical text and their running commentary. Greek exegetical catenae began to emerge in Palestine at the beginning of the sixth century.

There are numerous interpretive difficulties associated with the catenae. Many fragments are introduced anonymously, thus challenging the reader to identify the author and work from which the fragment was excerpted. Those fragments that are attributed to authors also come with hazards for the unsuspecting reader: the same fragment will be attributed to multiple authors in a manuscript; an author's name will be abbreviated equivocally or sloppily, thereby encouraging a false attribution; reading sigla can be confused with authorial lemmas; and fragments can be attributed to authors erroneously by the catenists themselves. Even if we can be reasonably certain that a fragment is drawn from a particular text, catenists often abbreviated the work they excerpted, thereby limiting the value of the fragment for the reconstruction of a corrupt text transmitted in the direct tradition. In many cases, the catenists also corrupted the text of their source.

For excellent orientations to the Greek exegetical catenae, see Robert Devreesse, "Chaînes exégétiques grecques," *Dictionnaire de la Bible*, Supplément, vol. 1 (Paris: Letouzey et Ane, 1928), col. 1084–1233; Hans-Georg Beck, *Kirche und Theologische Literatur im Byzantinischen Reich* (Munich: Beck, 1959), 413–22; Gilles Dorival, "Des commentaires de l'Écriture aux chaînes," *Le monde grec ancien et la Bible*, ed. Claude Mondésert (Paris: Beauchesne, 1984), 360–86; Curti Carmelo and Maria Antonietta Barbàra, "Greek Exegetical Catenae," in *Patrology: The Eastern Fathers from the Council of Chalcedon (451) to John of Damascus (750)*, ed. Angelo Di Berardino, trans. Adrian Walford (Cambridge: James Clark, 2008), 605–54. For overviews of the history of research on the catenae, see Marguerite Harl, *La Chaîne Palestinienne sur le Psaume 118*, vol. 1, SC 189 (Paris: Cerf, 1972), 17–21; Ekkehard Mühlenberg, "Catena. II. Christianity," *EBR*, vol. 4 (Berlin: de Gruyter, 2009), 1061–4.

[2] J.-B.-F. Pitra, ed., *Analecta Sacra: Spicilegio Solesmensi*, vol. 2, *Patres Antenicaeni* (Tusculanis, 1884), 130–36.

and drew attention to a few previously unedited fragments.[3] In addition to these contributions and the main catalogues of the catenae,[4] I have drawn upon the more recent studies and editions to locate the fragments I print below.[5] I have collected approximately forty different fragments (the actual count varies, since some are of uncertain authenticity and a number are transmitted in multiple versions of varying length). The following dossier is not exhaustive, since many questions still remain surrounding the authorship and authenticity of the fragments in the exegetical catenae, and many catenae mss have never been systematically examined.

The fragments printed below are carried by the following mss:

Mount Athos, Μονή Βατοπεδίου, *660* (X, XI)[6]
Mount Athos, Μονή Εσφιγμένου, *73* (XIII)[7]
Mount Athos, Μονή Μεγίστης Λαύρας, *B 83* (XI–XII)[8]
Florence, Biblioteca Medicea Laurenziana, *Plutei VI.3* (XI)[9]
Jerusalem, Πατριαρχική Βιβλιοθήκη, Ἁγίου Σάββα *231* (1338)[10]
Milan, Bibliotheca Ambrosiana, *C 98 sup.* (XII)[11]

---

[3] G. Mercati, "Pro Adriano," *Revue Biblique* 11 (1914): 246–55.

[4] The catalogues of authors who appear in the exegetical catenae are: Georg Karo and Hans Lietzmann, "Catenarum graecarum catalogus," *Nachrichten von der Königl. Gesellschaft der Wissenschaften zu Göttingen*, Philologisch-historische Klasse (1902), 1–66, 299–350, 559–620; Alfred Rahlfs, *Verzeichnis der griechischen Handschriften des Alten Testaments* (Berlin: 1914), 402–10; Maurice Geerard, *CPG*, vol. 4, *Concilia. Catenae* (Turnhout: Brepols, 1980), 185–259; Maurice Geerard and Jacques Noret, *Supplementum* (Turnhout: Brepols, 1998), 485–91.

[5] Robert Devreesse, "Chaînes exégétiques grecques," *Dictionnaire de la Bible*, Supplément, vol. 1 (Paris: Letouzey et Ane, 1928), col. 1084–1233 (Adrian: col. 1134 and 1138 [where wrongly called André]); Devreesse, *Le fonds Coislin* (Paris: Imprimerie Nationale, 1945); Devreesse, *Les Anciens Commentateurs Grecs des Psaumes*, Studi e Testi 264 (Vatican City: BAV, 1970), 312–13; Marcel Richard, "Quelques Manuscrits peu connus des chaînes exégétiques et des Commentaires Grecs sur le Psautier," *Opera Minora*, vol. 3 (Turnhout: Brepols, 1977), no. 69 (mss. no. 18 and no. 36); Marie-Josèphe Rondeau, *Les commentaires patristiques du Psautier (IIIᵉ–Vᵉ siècles)*, vol. 1, *Les travaux des Pères grecs et latins sur le Psautier: Recherches et Bilan* (Rome: Pont. Institutum Studiorum Orientalium, 1982), 224; Gilles Dorival, *Les Chaînes Exégétiques Grecques sur les Psaumes: Contribution à l'Étude d'une Forme Littéraire*, 4 vols. (Louvain: Peeters, 1986–95), with vol. 5 in preparation (material relevant to Adrian generously shared with me in advance of publication by Professor Dorival); Ursula and Dieter Hagedorn, *Die Älteren Griechischen Katenen zum Buch Hiob*, vol. 1, *Einleitung, Prologe und Epiloge, Fragmenta zu Hiob 1,1–8,22* (Berlin: Walter de Gruyter, 1994), 212; Anne Debary, "La terminologie rhétoric-grammaticale dans *l'Isagogè* d'Adrien" (Mémoire de DEA, 9 October 2001, University of Paris IV-Sorbonne), 40–41.

[6] Richard, "Quelques Manuscrits," 97–101; Dorival, *Les Chaînes Exégétiques*, vol. 2, 354–8.

[7] Richard, "Quelques Manuscrits," 93–4; Dorival, *Les Chaînes Exégétiques*, vol. 4, 130–32.

[8] Richard, "Quelques Manuscrits," 96–7; Dorival, "La postérité littéraire des chaînes exégétiques grecques," *Revue des études byzantines* 43 (1985), 214–15, 226.

[9] Dorival, *Les Chaînes Exégétiques*, vol. 4, 419–20.

[10] Dorival, *Les Chaînes Exégétiques*, vol. 3, 129–30.

[11] Mercati, *Alla ricerca dei nomi degli "altri" traduttori nelle Omilie sui Salmi di S. Giovanni Crisostomo e variazioni su alcune catene del Salterio*, Studi e Testi 158 (Vatican City: BAV, 1952), 211–20; Dorival, *Les Chaînes Exégétiques*, vol. 4, 420.

Moscow, Государственный исторический музей (GIM), *Sinod. Graecus 194* (Vladimir 48) (XI)[12]

Moscow, Государственный исторический музей (GIM), *Sinod. Graecus 358* (Vladimir 47) (XI)[13]

Oxford, Bodleian Library, *Roe 4* (X–XI)[14]

Paris, Bibliothèque nationale de France, *Coislinianus 10* (X)[15]

Paris, Bibliothèque nationale de France, *Coislinianus 358* (XIII)[16]

Paris, Bibliothèque nationale de France, *Graecus 169* (XIV)[17]

Sinai, Μονὴ τῆς Ἁγίας Αἰκατερίνης, *Graecus 27* (1452)[18]

Vatican City, Bibliotheca Apostolica Vaticana, *Barberinianus Graecus 340* (X)[19]

Vatican City, Bibliotheca Apostolica Vaticana, *Ottobonianus Graecus 398* (X–XI)[20]

Vatican City, Bibliotheca Apostolica Vaticana, *Reginensis Graecus Pii II 01* (XII)[21]

Vatican City, Bibliotheca Apostolica Vaticana, *Reginensis Graecus 40* (XII)[22]

Vatican City, Bibliotheca Apostolica Vaticana, *Vaticanus Graecus 754* (X)[23]

Vatican City, Bibliotheca Apostolica Vaticana, *Vaticanus Graecus 1685* (XVI)[24]

Vatican City, Bibliotheca Apostolica Vaticana, *Vaticanus Graecus 2057* (XII)[25]

Vienna, Österreichische Nationalbibliothek, *Theologicus Graecus 297* (XI)[26]

While most of the mss identify Adrian as the source of an excerpt, Gilles Dorival discovered thirteen fragments from the *Introduction* in Paris *Gr. 169* that were introduced anonymously with the lemma ἄλλως (e.g., 43r, 115v),[27] or more commonly with no lemma at all (31r, 74r, 74v).[28] Unless otherwise

---

[12] Archimandrite Vladimir, *Description Systématique des Manuscrits de la Bibliothèque Synodale Patriarchale de Moscou*, vol. 1, Grec 1 à Grec 105, trans. Xenia Grichine, revised by M. José Johannet (Paris: 1995), 55; Dorival, *Les Chaînes Exégétiques*, vol. 4, 262.

[13] Vladimir, *Description*, 52–5; Dorival, *Les Chaînes Exégétiques*, vol. 4, 298.

[14] Dorival, *Les Chaînes Exégétiques*, vol. 4, 325–6.

[15] Devreesse, *Catalogue des manuscrits grecs*, vol. 2, *Le fonds Coislin* (Paris: Imprimerie nationale, 1945), 9; Dorival, *Les Chaînes Exégétiques*, vol. 2, 284–5.

[16] Devreesse, *Catalogue des manuscrits grecs*, vol. 2, *Le fonds Coislin* (Paris: Imprimerie nationale, 1945), 338–9; Dorival, *Les Chaînes Exégétiques*, vol. 3, 296–9.

[17] Dorival, *Les Chaînes Exégétiques*, vol. 2, 171–2.   [18] Ibid., vol. 4, 243–4, 251, 262.

[19] Ibid., vol. 3, 170–71.   [20] Ibid., vol. 4, 263–4.

[21] Hagedorn and Hagedorn, *Die Älteren Griechischen Katenen*, vol. 1, 18–19 (with lit.).

[22] Henry Stevenson, Sr., ed., *Codices Manuscripti Graeci Reginae Svecorum et Pii PP. II Bibliothecae Vaticanae* (Rome: BAV, 1888), 29–30; G. Dorival, *Les Chaînes Exégétiques*, vol. 2, 44.

[23] Devreesse, *Codices Vaticani Graeci*, vol. 3, *Codices 604–866* (Vatican City: BAV, 1950), 269–72; Dorival, *Les Chaînes Exégétiques*, vol. 2, 238–43.

[24] Dorival, *Les Chaînes Exégétiques*, vol. 4, 262–3.

[25] Membr., mm. 316 × 260, ff. 316 sec. XII (first third). Contents: (ff. 1r–301v) Catena on Pss 1:4–151:7 and on Odes (ff. 302r–316r). Type II according to Karo-Lietzmann. *CPG*, vol. 4, nr. C 15. Description courtesy of Santo Lucà.

[26] Dorival, *Les Chaînes Exégétiques*, vol. 3, 171–2.

[27] That is, "alternatively," indicating that the material that follows is from a different source than the preceding material (Dickey, *Ancient Greek Scholarship*, 108–9).

[28] Dorival, *Les Chaînes Exégétiques*, vol. 2, 381.

noted, the other mss that transmit the *Introduction* consistently supply an authorial lemma—usually referring the fragment to Adrian, though sometimes to another source. The authorial lemma for Adrian takes a variety of forms. His name is spelled out: ἀδριανοῦ (e.g., *Vat. Gr. 754*, f. 50v; *Vat. Gr. 2057*, f. 106r; *Coislin. 10*, f. 14r; *Coislin. 358*, f. 64v; *Sinod. Gr. 358*, f. 72r; *Reg. Gr. 40*, f. 28r); his name is abbreviated: ἀδρι*ͨ* (Vatopedi *660*, f. 46v) or ἀδρι (*Ottob. Gr. 398*, f. 50v). There are a few other noteable lemmas. In a derivative catena ms his name is given with a rough breathing mark: ἁδρια (Milan *C 98 sup.*, f. 37r); there is the curious reference to him as an Antiochene: ἀδριανοῦ ἀντιο*ͯ* (i.e., ἀντιοχείας) (*Coislin. 10*, f. 51r); we also find ἀνδρ*ͣ* (i.e., ἀνδριανοῦ) (*Ottob. Gr. 398*, f. 160r [twice] and *Sinod. Gr. 194*, f. 125r); and in one ms we read, ἀδριανοῦ ἐκ τοῦ περὶ τῶν ἰδιωμάτων τῆς θείας γραφῆς (*Reg. Gr. 40*, f. 13r), which is similar to the heading of R2.

The format for the presentation of each fragment is as follows: (1) I identify the verse which it glosses (LXX versification), (2) print the verse in the form of the Goettingen edition, unless Adrian cites another form in the fragment, and (3) briefly identify the section of R1 and/or R2 to which it corresponds, if it corresponds at all. Beneath this basic data I offer (4) a short discussion about how the fragment compares with these recensions. Where there are doubts about authenticity, I explain them. Then follows (5) the identification of the sources for the fragment: all known mss that transmit the fragment are listed. If the fragment has been previously edited, I list the edition, as well as the mss that its editor used to establish the text. For each fragment I indicate the mss I have inspected—in nearly every case I have examined all the mss used by previous editors, and where applicable, have inspected additional mss as well. I inspected *Plutei VI.3* and *Ottob. Gr. 398 in situ*, and the other mss on microfiche copies at the Institut de recherche et d'histoire des textes, or as digital copies sent to me from their home libraries.

I print fragments as they have been previously edited, though in a number of cases I have supplemented or corrected the work of these editors. My apparatus is negative. I note all variants in mss that editors have, or have not, consulted, though I restrict my apparatus to meaningful variants.[29] On occasion I have needed to correct paleographical errors or confusion. When I emend, and thus depart from the previously edited text, the editor's reading is always noted in the apparatus. When emending, I adopt the same principle as I have used for the recensions—even if I suspect that a better reading exists in R1 or R2, I only bring the catena fragment into conformity with the direct ms tradition if it is unintelligible (e.g., *cat. Ps. 31:4(1)*). Otherwise, I resist attempts to homogenize between the indirect and direct ms traditions. Finally, I make only minor formatting changes to the previously printed fragments, bringing them

---

[29] For the relationships between the mss that transmit the catenae on the Psalms, Dorival's aforementioned work is now fundamental.

silently into conformity with my edited text for R1 and R2 (e.g., capitalization, conventions for punctuation or quotation). For unedited fragments, I silently correct spelling, expand abbreviations, and introduce orthographic conventions already established for R1 and R2. I generally follow the accentuation of the mss, which includes accepting Byzantine peculiarities (e.g., the indefinite use of πῶς in *cat. Ps. 73:11(2)*).

1.

Ps 9:8

ἠτοίμασεν ἐν κρίσει τὸν θρόνον αὐτοῦ

R1 (11)

Comment: no corresponding material is transmitted in R2. The fragment transmits very similar text to R1.

Source: Pitra, *Analecta Sacra*, vol. 2, 130 (frg. I), using *Ottob. Gr. 398*, f. 50v. I also inspected *Sinod. Gr. 194*, f. 19v.

Τὸ τοίνυν κράτος καὶ τὴν δίκην τοῦ θεοῦ, κάθισιν αὐτοῦ καὶ θρόνον ὀνομάζει, ἀπὸ τοῦ παρ᾽ ἡμῖν τοὺς κρίνειν καὶ κολάζειν ἔχοντας ἐξουσίαν, ἐπὶ θρόνου ποιεῖσθαι τὴν ἐξέτασιν· ὡς τό, **ἐκάθισας ἐπὶ θρόνου ὁ κρίνων δικαιοσύνην.**

3 Ps 9:5[4]

---

2 ἐπὶ θρόνου] ἐπὶ θρόνον *Pitra*

2.

Ps 9:35

βλέπεις ὅτι σὺ πόνον καὶ θυμὸν κατανοεῖς

R1 (68)

Comment: no corresponding material is transmitted in R2. Fragment very similar to the text of R1, though it transmits a longer gloss on Ps 20:13 and a fuller explanation of why the figure of inversion surfaces in the Psalms. See also *cat. Ps.* 20:13 below.

Source: Pitra, *Analecta Sacra*, vol. 2, 130–1 (II), using *Vat. Gr. 754*, ff. 54r and 72r (note: Pitra conflates two separate fragments, on Ps 9:35 and Ps 20:13, into one, because of their similarity). Also inspected *Esphig. 73*, f. 40r; *Sinod. Gr. 358*, f. 64v.

Κατὰ ἀντιστροφήν· < ἀντὶ τοῦ > ὅτι βλέπεις σὺ πόνον καὶ θυμὸν κατανοεῖς· ἐνίοτε δὲ καὶ διὰ μακροτέρου τὴν ἀντιστροφὴν ποιεῖται· ὡς τό, **ἐν τοῖς περιλοίποις σου ἑτοιμάσεις τὸ πρόσωπον αὐτῶν·** ἔδει μὲν γὰρ ἀντὶ μὲν

τοῦ σοῦ κεῖσθαι τὸ αὐτῶν, ἀντὶ δὲ τοῦ αὐτῶν κεῖσθαι τὸ σοῦ, ἵνα ᾖ ἐν τοῖς
5 περιλοίποις αὐτῶν ἑτοιμάσεις τὸ πρόσωπόν σου· τοῦτο δὲ ἀπὸ τῆς ἐμμέτρου
συνθέσεως πεπονθέναι δοκεῖ, καθὼς καὶ παρὰ τοῖς ἔξω ποιηταῖς συνεχέστερόν
ἐστι τὰ τοιαῦτα εὑρεῖν καὶ μάλιστα ἐν τοῖς λυρικοῖς.

3 Ps 20:13 [21:12]

---

1 σύ] ante βλέπεις pon. Esphig.　　　3 μέν] om. *Pitra*　　　4 τοῦ²] deest Sinod., τό Esphig.
5 ἐμμέτρου] συμμέτρου Esphig.

3.

Ps 16:1 var.

εἰσάκουσον κύριε δικαιοσύνης μου

R1 (25)

Comment: no corresponding material is transmitted in R2. Fragment is
similar to the text of R1 though it offers a longer explanation of the peculiar
use of "righteousness" in Scripture.

Source: Pitra, *Analecta Sacra*, vol. 2, 131 (III), using *Vat. Gr. 754*, f. 60v and
Reg. Gr. 40, f. 28r. I also inspected *Coislin. 10*, f. 14r and *Sinod. Gr. 358*, f. 72r.

Τὸ τὴν δικαιοσύνην εἴτε ἐφ᾽ ἑαυτοῦ λέγειν, μὴ τὴν ἐκ τοῦ βίου ἀρετὴν ἑαυτῷ
μαρτυροῦντα, εἴτε δὴ καὶ ἐφ᾽ ἑτέρων ὁμοίως· ὡς τό, **εἰσάκουσον κύριε**
δικαιοσύνης μου· καὶ ὅσα τοιαῦτα· τοῦτο γὰρ ἀπανταχοῦ διὰ τῆς τοιᾶσδε
σημαίνει λέξεως, τὸν ἀδικούμενον ἐν τῷ πράγματι, περὶ οὗ ποιεῖται τὸν
5 λόγον, δικαίας τῆς παρὰ θεοῦ βοηθείας μέλλειν ἀπολαύειν διὰ τῆς κατ᾽
ἐχθρῶν τιμωρίας· καὶ τοῦτό ἐστιν ὃ δικαιοσύνην καλεῖ, εἴτε αὐτοῦ ὡς
ἀπολαύοντος δικαίως τῆς βοηθείας εἴτε τοῦ θεοῦ ὡς δικαίως παρέχοντος.

3 Ps 16[17]:1 var.

---

2 δή] deest Reg.　　　2 ὡς] deest Sinod.　　　3 δικαιοσύνης] -ην *Pitra*
3 εἰσάκουσον–τοιαῦτα] deest Reg.　　　4 σημαίνει] σημαίνεται Reg.　　　4 τόν¹] τό codd.
4 περὶ οὗ ποιεῖται] περιποιεῖσθαι Vat. Coislin. Sinod.　　　5 δικαίας] δικαίως Reg.
5 post παρά] τοῦ + Reg.　　　5 ἀπολαύειν] ἀπολαβεῖν Reg.　　　5 κατ᾽] κατὰ τῶν Reg.
7 ἀπολαύοντος] ἀπολάβοντος Reg.　　　7 δικαίως²] δικαίου *Pitra*

4.

Ps 18:4

οὐκ εἰσὶν λαλιαὶ οὐδὲ λόγοι, ὧν οὐχὶ ἀκούονται
αἱ φωναὶ αὐτῶν

–

Comment: no corresponding material is transmitted in R1 or R2, though the fragment is attributed to Adrian in the ms. It is plausibly Adrianic, since the passage is very similar to what we find in Diodore, *Ps.* 18:4.

Source: Pitra, *Analecta Sacra*, vol. 2, 131–2 (IV) and Mercati, "Pro Adriano," 254, fn. 4, both using *Reg. Gr. 40*, f. 37v.

Τοιαύταις γάρ φησι ἐνάρθροις προφητικαῖς λέξεσι κέχρηνται **οἱ οὐρανοί**, ὁποίαις καὶ ἡμεῖς οἱ ἄνθρωποι, ὥστε τοῖς πᾶσι τὰς αὐτὰς διὰ τῆς ἐκφωνήσεως γνωρίμους γίνεσθαι, βαρβάροις τε ὁμοῦ καὶ Ἕλλησι.

1 Ps 18:2 [19:1]

---

1 γάρ] om. Pitra   1 post φησι] καί + Pitra
1 ἐνάρθροις] ἐν ἄθροις Reg.   1 κέχρηνται] κέχρηται Reg.

5.

Ps 20:13

ἐν τοῖς περιλοίποις σου ἑτοιμάσεις τὸ πρόσωπον αὐτῶν

R1 (68)

Comment: no corresponding material is transmitted in R2. The fragment is very similar to the text of R1, though it offers a longer discussion of Ps 20:13 and fuller explanation of why the figure of inversion surfaces in the Psalms. See also *cat. Ps.* 9:35 above.

Source: *Vat. Gr.* 754, f. 72r; *Esphig.* 73, f. 79r; *Coislin. 10*, f. 29v.

Κατὰ ἀντιστροφήν· ἐνίοτε δὲ καὶ διὰ μακροτέρου τὴν ἀντιστροφὴν ποιεῖται· ὡς τό, **ἐν τοῖς περιλοίποις σου ἑτοιμάσεις τὸ πρόσωπον αὐτῶν**·

ἔδει γὰρ ἀντὶ μὲν τοῦ σοῦ κεῖσθαι τὸ αὐτῶν, ἀντὶ δὲ τοῦ αὐτῶν κεῖσθαι τὸ σοῦ,
ἵνα ᾖ ἐν τοῖς περιλοίποις αὐτῶν ἑτοιμάσεις τὸ πρόσωπόν σου· τοῦτο δὲ ἀπὸ
5 τῆς ἐμμέτρου συνθέσεως πεπονθέναι δοκεῖ, καθὼς καὶ παρὰ τοῖς ἔξω ποιηταῖς
συνεχέστερόν ἐστι τὰ τοιαῦτα εὑρεῖν καὶ μάλιστα ἐν τοῖς λυρικοῖς.

2 Ps 20:13 [21:12]

---

1 *Κατὰ ἀντιστροφήν*] deest Vat.   1 *μακροτέρου*] -ων Esphig.

6.

Ps 20:14

ὑψώθητι κύριε

–

Comment: no corresponding material is transmitted in R1 or R2, though the fragment is attributed to Adrian in the mss. The material approximates R1 (6) and (13). It is plausibly authentic and there is very similar language in Diodore, *Ps.* 20:13, 14.

Source: *Plutei VI.3*, f. 64r–v; Milan C 98 sup., f. 37r.

Ἀντὶ πλησίον ἡμῶν γενοῦ τῇ βοηθείᾳ ὑψηλότερος δὲ τῶν ἐναντίων ἀναδείχθητι
ὁ κατ᾽ αὐτῶν στήσας ὁ ἐκ παραδόξου τρόπου· οἷον δή τι τοῖς Ἀσσυρίοις ἐπὶ
Ἐζεκίου συνέβη ὁπηνίκα πέντε καὶ ὀγδοήκοντα πρὸς τῶν ἑκατὸν χιλιάδες
αὐτῶν ἀνηρέθησαν ἀθρόον ὑπὸ νυκτὶ μιᾷ, ὑπνὸν αὐτῶν τοῦ θανάτου τοῦ
5 δειξαμένου· καὶ γὰρ ὑπνώσαντες ἑσπέρας πρωῒ πάντες τεθνηκότες ἦσαν.

5 Cf. 4 Kgdms 19:35 [2 Kgs 19:35]

---

2 ὁ¹] τὸ codd.   2 ὁ²] deest Milan   5 πρωῒ] πρωΐας Plutei

7.

Ps 21:7 var.

ἐγώ εἰμι σκώληξ καὶ οὐκ ἄνθρωπος

R2 (73.17)

Comment: the fragment is more similar to the text transmitted in R2 than in R1.

Source: Dorival, *Les Chaînes Exégétiques*, vol. 2, 175, no. 6, using Paris *Gr. 169*, f. 31r.

Κατὰ σαρκασμὸν λέγει· κατὰ σαρκασμὸν δέ ἐστιν ὅταν τοὐναντίον διὰ τῆς ἄγαν εὐτελείας ἐπαινεῖν ἐθέλῃ τις· οἷον ὡς τό, **ἐγώ εἰμι σκώληξ καὶ οὐκ ἄνθρωπος**· καὶ τὰ ὑπὸ τοῦ μακαρίου Δαυὶδ πρὸς τὸν Σαούλ, **ὀπίσω τίνος διώκεις βασιλεῦ; ὀπίσω ἑνὸς ψύλλου καὶ ὀπίσω κυνὸς τεθνηκότος.**

3 Ps 21:7 [22:6] var.   4 1 Kgdms 24:15 [1 Sam 24:14] var.

---

1 Κατὰ σαρκασμὸν] Κατὰ σάρκας μὲν Dorival
1 κατὰ σαρκασμὸν] κατασαρκούμενος Dorival

8.

Ps 24:5

καὶ δίδαξόν με ὅτι σὺ εἶ ὁ θεὸς ὁ σωτήρ μου

R1 (20)

Comment: no corresponding material is transmitted in R2. The fragment is similar to the text of R1 but more expansive with its illustrative verse and gloss.

Source: Vatopedi *660*, f. 46v.

Τὸ δίδαξον ἀντὶ τοῦ παράσχου· ὡς τό, **δίδαξόν με τοῦ ποιεῖν τὸ θέλημά σου**· οὐ γὰρ ἀγνοοῦντες τὸν νόμον, ἀλλὰ ποιεῖν ἐν τῇ αἰχμαλωσίᾳ μὴ συγχωρούμενοι τοῦτο παρεκάλεσαν.

1 Ps 142[143]:10

9.

Ps 28:3(1)

φωνὴ κυρίου ἐπὶ τῶν ὑδάτων

R2 (73.13)

Comment: this fragment contains text nearly identical to the discussion of allegory in R2 (cf. Mercati, "Pro Adriano," 254–5).

Source: Vatopedi *660*, f. 52v. Smaller section of extract (ἤρκεσε-τροπώσασθαι) edited by Pitra, *Analecta Sacra*, vol. 2, 132 (V), using *Vat. Gr. 754*, f. 86v.

Τὸ τὰ ἄπειρα πλήθη συνεχῶς ὕδατα λέγειν, διά τε τὸ ταραχῶδες αὐτῶν καὶ ἠχητικόν, τήν τε τούτων ἔφοδον κατακλυσμὸν εἰκότως, διὰ τὸ ἄρδην ἐξαφανίζειν τοὺς ἐφ᾽ οἷσπερ ἂν ἐπέρχοιντο τόπους· ὡς τό, **φωνὴ κυρίου ἐπὶ τῶν ὑδάτων**, ἵνα εἴπῃ ἤρκεσε καὶ μόνῃ τῇ φωνῇ τοὺς Ἀσσυρίους
5 τροπώσασθαι.

4 Ps 28[29]:3

_____

3 τούς] R2, τοῖς Vatop.   3 τόπους] R2, τόποις Vatop.
4 τῇ] deest Vat.   4 τούς] τοῦ Vatop.

10.

Ps 28:3(2)

φωνὴ κυρίου ἐπὶ τῶν ὑδάτων

Spurious

Comment: no corresponding material is transmitted in R1 or R2, though each ms attributes the fragment to Adrian. It is spurious: not only is the reference to the "abyss of rational waters" suspicious, but we find a nearly identical text in Anast. S., *hex.* 3.IV.3 (*Anastasius of Sinai: Hexaemeron*, ed. Clement A. Kuehn and John D. Baggarly, S.J., Orientalia Christiana Analecta 278 [Rome: Pontificio Istituto Orientale, 2007], 68.134–7).

Source: *Coislin. 10*, f. 51r; *Coislin. 358*, f. 64v; Jerusalem *231*, f. 27 r.

Περὶ ταύτης τῆς ἀβύσσου τῶν λογικῶν ὑδάτων φησὶν Δαυίδ, **φωνὴ κυρίου ἐπὶ τῶν ὑδάτων,** ὁ **θεὸς τῆς δόξης** διὰ τοῦ εὐαγγελίου **ἐβρόντησεν, κύριος ἐπὶ ὑδάτων πολλῶν** καὶ ἀπείρων ἐθνῶν.

3 Ps 28[29]:3

11.

Ps 28:10

κύριος τὸν κατακλυσμὸν κατοικιεῖ

R2 (73.13)

Comment: this fragment is nearly identical to the text about allegory in R2 (as with *cat. Ps.* 28:3(1) above).

Sources: *Coislin. 10*, f. 52r; Jerusalem *231*, f. 27v; *Sinod. Gr. 358*, f. 102r; Vatopedi *660*, f. 54r.

Ἀντὶ τοῦ τὴν τέλεον ἐρημωθεῖσαν ὑπ'αὐτῶν γῆν αὖθις ἀνακτήσεταί τε καὶ κατοικεῖσθαι ποιήσει.

1 Ἀντὶ τοῦ] deest Coislin. Jerus. Sinod.
1 ὑπ' αὐτῶν] ὑπὸ Ἀσσυρίων Coislin. Jerus. Sinod.
1 ἀνακτήσεταί τε] R2, ἀνακτήσεταί τι Vatop., ἀνακτήσεται Coislin. Jerus. Sinod.

12.

Ps 29:7

ἐγὼ δὲ εἶπα ἐν τῇ εὐθηνίᾳ μου, οὐ μὴ σαλευθῶ εἰς τὸν αἰῶνα

R1 (45)

Comment: no corresponding section transmitted in R2. The fragment provides a gloss on Ps 29:7—the verse, but not the gloss, occurs in R1.

Source: Vatopedi *660*, f. 55r.

Ἀντὶ τοῦ οὕτω διεκείμην ἐπὶ τῆς πρόσθεν εὐπραγίας ὡς οὐδέπω ταύτης
ἐκπεσούμενος.

1 τοῦ] τὸ Vatop.

13.

Ps 30:20–21

ἧς ἔκρυψας τοῖς φοβουμένοις σε—κατακρύψεις αὐτοὺς ἐν
ἀποκρύφῳ τοῦ προσώπου σου

R1 (30)

Comment: the interpretive principle in the fragment appears in both recensions. However, the verse that is cited occurs only in R1. The fragment offers an expansion on why Scripture speaks of God guarding as "hiding" (ἀπὸ τοῦ–πειρᾶσθαι).

Source: Vatopedi *660*, f. 58r.

Τὸ κρύψαι ἐπὶ θεοῦ ἀντὶ τοῦ φυλάξαι εἴρηται· ὡς τό, **ἧς ἔκρυψας τοῖς
φοβουμένοις σε**, ἵνα εἴπῃ ἣν φυλάσσεις τοῖς φοβουμένοις σε, ἀπὸ τοῦ τὸν
ἐπιμελῶς τι φυλάξαι βουλόμενον κατακρύπτειν τοῦτο πειρᾶσθαι.

2 Ps 30:20 [31:19]

---

2 τοῦ τὸν] τούτον Vatop.

14.

Ps 31:4(1)

ἐστράφην εἰς ταλαιπωρίαν

R1 (69)

Comment: no corresponding material transmitted in R2. The fragment transmits a corrupted version of R1.

Source: Dorival, *Les Chaînes Exégétiques*, vol. 2, 178, no. 6, using Paris *Gr. 169*, f. 43r.

Μεθ' ὑπερβατόν· < τῷ > ἀπὸ τοῦ κράζειν με ὅλην τὴν ἡμέραν, < τὸ > ἐστράφην εἰς ταλαιπωρίαν < εἰκότως ἀποδίδοται >.

1 Ps 31[32]:3   2 Ps 31[32]:4

---

1 *τῷ*] R1   1 *τὸ*] R1   2 *εἰκότως ἀποδίδοται*] R1

15.

Ps 31:4(2)

ἐστράφην εἰς ταλαιπωρίαν ἐν τῷ ἐμπαγῆναι ἄκανθαν

R2 and R1 (38)

Comment: most of this fragment transmits text nearly identical to its corresponding section in R2. However, the gloss of Ps 31:4 at the beginning corresponds only to R1.

Source: Dorival, *Les Chaînes Exégétiques*, vol. 2, 178, no. 7, using Paris *Gr. 169*, f. 43r.

Τὴν παραβολὴν ἐνταῦθα ἄνευ τοῦ ὡς τέθεικεν, ἵνα εἴπῃ ὡς ἄκανθαν· διὸ καὶ ὁ θεῖος ἀπόστολος τῷδε τῷ ἰδιώματι παρακολουθήσας, ἔπινον δέ, φησί, ἐκ τῆς πνευματικῆς ἀκολουθούσης πέτρας, ἡ δὲ πέτρα ἦν ὁ Χριστός, ἵνα εἴπῃ ὅπερ ἡμῖν ἐν ἀπορίᾳ οὖσι σωτηρίας ἐκ παραδόξου Χριστὸς ἐνυπῆρξεν, τοῦτο ἐκείνοις ἀμηχανίᾳ ποτὲ τυγχάνουσιν παρὰ πᾶσαν προσδοκίαν ἡ κατὰ τὴν 5 *ἔρημον πέτρα· ἔτι τε αὐτὸς ὁ κύριος περὶ τῶν δωρεῶν τοῦ πνεύματος λέγει, ὁ πιστεύων εἰς ἐμέ, καθὼς εἶπεν ἡ γραφή, ποταμοὶ ἐκ τῆς κοιλίας αὐτοῦ ῥεύσουσιν ὕδατος ζῶντος ἁλλομένου εἰς ζωὴν αἰώνιον, ἀντὶ τοῦ ὡς ποταμοὶ ὕδατος ζῶντος.*

3 1 Cor 10:4 var.   8 John 7:38 var.

16.

Ps 41:8

ἄβυσσος ἄβυσσον ἐπικαλεῖται εἰς φωνὴν
τῶν καταρακτῶν σου

–

Comment: this fragment is transmitted in two forms. The longer version was printed by Pitra, but there is also a shorter version transmitted by a number of other mss that convey the central interpretive point found in the longer version. The shorter version is derivative of the longer (Dorival, *Les Chaînes Exégétiques*, vol. 3, 178; vol. 4, 331). Neither version of the fragment corresponds to material in R1 or R2, though two points suggest that the material is Adrianic: the interpretation of the "deep" comes close to the discussion of "waters" in the section on allegory (73.13), and there is a strong similarity between what we find in this fragment and Diodore and Theodore, *Ps.* 41:8. Several mss attribute the fragment to Adrian (*Vat. Gr. 754; Sinod. Gr. 194* and *358*). *Ottob. Gr.* does not attribute it to any author, though the immediately preceding fragment is attributed to Cyril of Alexandria; *Barber. Gr. 340, Vat. Gr. 2057,* and *Th. Gr. 297* attribute the fragment to Cyril (and it was on the authority of *Vat. Gr. 2057* that A. Mai attributed the fragment to Cyril [Mercati, "Pro Adriano," 254]).

Source: Pitra, *Analecta Sacra*, vol. 2, 132 (VI), using *Vat. Gr. 754*, f. 118r–v, *Ottob. Gr. 398*, f. 114r and *Barber. Gr. 340*, f. 128r (but printing the longer version found in *Vat. Gr.*). I also consulted *Sinod. Gr. 358*, f. 135r.

Ὅθεν καὶ τὸ τῆς πολυπληθείας ἄπειρον ἄβυσσον ἐκφωνεῖ· ὡς τό, **ἔδωκεν ἡ ἄβυσσος φωνὴν αὐτῆς, ὕψος φαντασίας αὐτῆς·** καὶ τό, **ἄβυσσος ἄβυσσον ἐπικαλεῖται εἰς φωνὴν τῶν καταρακτῶν σου,** ἀντὶ τοῦ εἰπεῖν τὴν ἀλλήλων συμμαχίαν ἐπὶ τῇ καθ᾽ ἡμῶν ἐκκαλοῦνται συνδρομῇ, διὰ τὸ τὴν σὴν
5 συγχώρησιν τῆς ἐκείνων ὁρμῆς εἶναι διέκβασιν· καταράκτας γὰρ εἰκότως τὴν τοῦ θεοῦ συγχώρησιν ὡς πρὸς τὰς ἀβύσσους ἐκάλεσεν, καθάπερ ἐπὶ τοῦ κατακλυσμοῦ τὸ τηνικαῦτα συνέβη γενέσθαι· καὶ τὸ παρὰ τῷ Ἀμῶς· **καὶ ἰδοὺ ἐκάλεσε τὴν δίκην ἐν πυρὶ κύριος, καὶ κατέφαγε τὴν ἄβυσσον τὴν πολλήν,** περὶ τῶν δέκα φυλῶν· **ἄβυσσον** γὰρ αὐτὰς ὡς ἐν συγκρίσει τῶν δύο
10 προσηγόρευσεν.

---

2 Hab 3:10   3 Ps 41:8 [42:7]   8 Amos 7:4

---

3 τὴν] τῶν Pitra   4 ἐκκαλοῦνται] ἐπικαλοῦνται Pitra   7 τῷ] τὸ Vat., τοῦ Pitra

Source: *Ottob. Gr. 398*, f. 114r; *Barber. Gr. 340*, f. 128r; *Vat. Gr. 2057*, f. 79v;
Th. Gr. 297, f. 82v; *Sinod. Gr. 194*, f. 79r; *Roe 4*, f. 163v.

Τὸ **ἄβυσσον** δηλοῖ τὸ τῆς πολυπληθείας ἄπειρον, ἀντὶ τοῦ εἰπεῖν τὴν ἀλλήλων
συμμαχίαν ἐπὶ τῇ καθ᾽ ἡμῶν ἐγκαλοῦνται συνδρομῇ, διὰ τὸ τὴν συγχώρησιν
τῆς ἐκείνων ὁρμῆς εἶναι διέκβασιν· καταράκτας γὰρ εἰκότως τὴν τοῦ θεοῦ
συγχώρησιν ὡς πρὸς τὰς ἀβύσσους ἐκάλεσεν.

1 Ps 41:8 [42:7]

---

1 *Τὸ ἄβυσσον*] *Τὸ ἄβυσσος ἄβυσσον* Ottob. Sinod., *ἄβυσσον* Vat. Barber. Th. Gr.
1 *Τὸ ἄβυσσον δηλοῖ*] deest Roe
1 *πολυπληθείας*] *πολυθείας* Vat. Barber. Th. Gr., *πολυπληνθίας* Roe
1 post *ἄπειρον*] *δηλοῖ* + Roe   2 *τῇ*] *τοῦ* Th. Gr.
2 *ἐγκαλοῦνται*] *συγκαλοῦνται* Vat. Barber. Th. Gr., *συνκ*- Roe
3 *συνδρομῇ-ἐκείνων*] deest Th. Gr.   3 *ὁρμῆς*] *συνδρομῆς* Vat. Barber. Th. Gr.
3 *διέκβασιν*] *διάβασιν* Vat. Barber. Th. Gr.
3 *καταράκτας*] *καταρράκτων* Vat. *-ρ*- Barber. Th. Gr.
4 *τῆς ἐκείνων-συγχώρησιν*] deest Roe

17.

Ps 43:24

ἐξεγέρθητι, ἵνα τί ὑπνοῖς κύριε;

R1 (8)

Comment: no corresponding material transmitted in R2. With some variation in vocabulary, the fragment is very similar to R1, but adds an explanation that is missing from R1. In both mss the fragment is assigned to Adrian.
After φροντίδα the mss use punctuation to mark a strong break. The material
that follows (ὕπνον–ζωῆς) is not assigned an author. Pitra hesitatingly attributed this subsequent material to Adrian, though Mercati demonstrated that
it is a pastiche from other patristic authors (Mercati, "Pro Adriano," 254).

Source: Pitra, *Analecta Sacra*, vol. 2, 132–3 (VII), using *Ottob. Gr. 398*,
f. 118v. I also consulted *Sinod. Gr. 194*, 82r.

Τὴν κατὰ τῶν ἐχθρῶν αὐτῶν ἀμύνης ὑπέρθεσιν τήν τε πρὸς τοὺς οἰκείους
αὐτοὺς ἐπικουρίας βραδύτητα, νυσταγμὸν καὶ ὕπνον καὶ καρηβαρίαν ἀποκαλεῖ,
ἐκ τοῦ παρ᾽ ἡμῖν τοὺς < πρὸς > ὕπνον τραπέντας οὐ μὴν δέ τινα τῶν οἰκείων
ἤτοι τῶν γνησίων ποιεῖσθαι φροντίδα.

3 *παρ᾽ ἡμῖν*] *παρείμιν* Ottob.   3 *πρὸς*] + *Pitra*

18.

Ps 49:5

συναγάγετε αὐτῷ τοὺς ὁσίους αὐτοῦ

R2 (73.16)

Comment: the fragment has text identical to R2.

Source: Vatopedi *660*, f. 79r.

Ἀντὶ τοῦ τουτουσί μοι τοὺς ἐν ὁσίων μὲν τάξει μνημονευομένους, τὰ δὲ τῶν ἀσεβῶν τοὐναντίον διαπραττομένους, οἳ ἀφ᾽ ὧν τὰς συνήθεις τῷ θεῷ τελοῦσι θυσίας ἀφοσιοῦσθαι νομίζουσι· τοῦτο κατ᾽ εἰρωνείαν.

1 τοῦ τουτουσί μοι τοὺς] R2, τουτου τοὺς ιμυτους Vatop.

19.

Ps 49:23

ἐκεῖ ὁδός, ᾗ δείξω αὐτῷ, τὸ σωτήριόν μου

R1 (24)

Comment: no corresponding material is transmitted in R2. The fragment offers a more elaborate gloss than what is found in R1.

Source: Pitra, *Analecta Sacra*, vol. 2, 133 (VIII), using *Ottob. Gr. 398*, f. 133r. I also consulted Vatopedi *660*, f. 80v; *Vat. Gr. 2057*, f. 89v; *Sinod. Gr. 194*, f. 95r.

Ἀντὶ τοῦ τοῖς ταῦτα πράττουσι καὶ θυσίαν αἰνέσεως ἀναπέμπειν ἐσπουδακόσι ὁδὸν ἐπιδείκνυμι σωτηρίας.

1 θυσίαν] θυσίαν μοι Vatop. Vat.   2 ἐσπουδακόσι] -ότι Ottob. Sinod.

20.

Ps 50:6

σοὶ μόνῳ ἥμαρτον—ὅπως ἂν δικαιωθῇς ἐν τοῖς λόγοις σου

R1 (42)

Comment: there are corresponding paragraphs in R1 and R2 that announce the same exegetical principle. Only R1 has the verse cited in this fragment, but it lacks the gloss provided below.

Source: Pitra, *Analecta Sacra*, vol. 2, 133 (IX), using *Ottob. Gr. 398*, f. 134r as the base text, but also consulting *Barber. Gr. 340*, f. 152v. In addition to these, I also consulted: *Vat. Gr. 2057*, f. 89v; *Vatopedi 660*, f. 81v; *Sinod. Gr. 194*, f. 95v–96r (microfiche illegible); *Th. Gr. 297*, f. 101r. A very similar fragment is attributed to Origen at Lavra B 83, ff. 152r–153v (ἔθος πολλάκις τὸ ἀναίτιον ὡς αἴτιον... εὐεργετούμενοι ἠγνωμόνουν). See also Mercati, "Pro Adriano," 252–3.

Τὸ τὰ ἀναίτια πολλάκις ὡς αἴτια λέγειν· ὡς τό, **σοὶ μόνῳ ἥμαρτον**· οὐ γὰρ διὰ τοῦτο ἥμαρτεν ὅπως ἂν δικαιωθῇ ὁ θεὸς ἐν τοῖς λόγοις αὐτοῦ· ἐδικαιοῦτο δὲ ὁ θεὸς εἰκότως ἀφ' ὧν ἐκεῖνοι εὐεργετούμενοι ἠγνωμόνουν.

1 Ps 50:6 [51:4]

---

1 *Τὸ*] om. Pitra   1 λέγειν] λέγει Pitra   1 αἴτια λέγειν] ἔτια λέγεις Th. Gr.
1 σοὶ] σὺ Barb. Th. Gr.   1 ὡς τό, σοὶ μόνῳ ἥμαρτον] deest Ottob. Pitra
2 ἥμαρτεν] Lavra Mercati, ἥμαρτον Vat., ἡμάρτανον Ottob. Barber. Vatop. Th. Gr. Pitra
2 ὁ] deest Vat. Barber. Th. Gr.
2 ὅπως–αὐτοῦ] ἵνα ὁ θεὸς δικαιωθῇ Ottob., ὅπως ἂν ὁ θεὸς δικαιωθῇ Pitra
3 ὁ] deest Vat.   3 ἀφ'] ἐφ Barber. Th. Gr.

21.

Ps 50:8

ἰδοὺ γὰρ ἀλήθειαν ἠγάπησας, τὰ ἄδηλα καὶ τὰ κρύφια
τῆς σοφίας σου ἐδήλωσάς μοι

R1 (26)

Comment: there is corresponding material in both recensions though the fragment is closer to R1 where Ps 50:8 is also cited. The fragment offers a lengthy gloss on the verse that is missing from R1.

Source: Pitra, *Analecta Sacra*, vol. 2, 133–4 (X), using *Ottob. Gr. 398*, f. 135r. I have also consulted: Vatopedi *660*, f. 82v; *Vat. Gr. 2057*, f. 90r; *Sinod. Gr. 194*, ff. 95v–96r [illegible microfiche]; Lavra B *83*, f. 154r–v (attributing the fragment to Origen). On this fragment, see also Mercati, "Pro Adriano," 253, fn. 1.

Καὶ τό, **ἰδοὺ γὰρ ἀλήθειαν ἠγάπησας**, ἵνα εἴπῃ διὰ μεγίστης ἡμῶν ἀληθεύων τῆς σπουδῆς τὰ περὶ ὧν ὑπέσχου καὶ δεδοκίμακας, περὶ τῆς ἀπὸ Βαβυλῶνος ἐπανόδου δηλονότι λέγων, ἅπερ αὐτοῖς μὲν **ἄδηλα, κρύφια** δὲ **τῆς** τοῦ θεοῦ **σοφίας** ὄντα διὰ τῶν προφητῶν ἐγνωρίσθαι φάσκει·
5 καὶ ὅσα τοιαῦτα.

1 Ps 50:8 [51:6]   4 Ps 50:8 [51:6]

---

1 Καὶ τό, ἰδοὺ γὰρ ἀλήθειαν ἠγάπησας] deest Vat.   1 εἴπῃ] εἴπῃς Lavra
1 post ἡμῶν] διδασκαλίας + Pitra   2 ἀληθεύων τῆς] ἀληθεύοντι Vat.
2 τῆς σπουδῆς] τῇ σπουδῇ Ottob. Pitra   2 καὶ δεδοκίμακας] deest Ottob. Pitra
2 ante περὶ] τὰ + Vat. Ottob. Pitra   3 ἀπὸ] deest Ottob. Pitra
3 δηλονότι] δῆλον ὅτι Vat. Ottob.   3 ἅπερ αὐτοῖς] ὑπ᾽ αὐτῆς Ottob. Pitra
4 ἐγνωρίσθαι] -θη Pitra

22.

Ps 50:10

ἀκουτιεῖς με ἀγαλλίασιν καὶ εὐφροσύνην

R1 (19, 19.1)

Comment: no corresponding material is transmitted in R2. The fragment has some of the corresponding language of R1, but it is a corrupted abridgement.

Source: Dorival, *Les Chaînes Exégétiques*, vol. 2, 186, no. 13, using Paris *Gr. 169*, f. 74r.

Ἀντὶ τῆς πράξεως ἤτοι τῆς ἀπολαύσεως τοῦ πράγματος λέγει † †, τουτέστι πράξεις μοι ταῦτα.

23.

Ps 50:14

καὶ πνεύματι ἡγεμονικῷ στήρισόν με

R1 (59.2)

Comment: no corresponding material transmitted in R2. The fragment is more expansive than the corresponding material in R1.

Source: Dorival, *Les Chaînes Exégétiques*, vol. 2, 187, no. 18, using Paris *Gr. 169*, f. 74v. After ἡγεμονίας (which is followed by a high stop in the ms), the following words occur: τὸ πανάγιον γὰρ λέγει πνεῦμα. This material is likely not authentic.

Ἐνταῦθα τὸ **πνεῦμα** ἐπὶ χαρίσματος κεῖται, ἵνα εἴπῃ κατάστησόν με πάλιν ἐπὶ τῆς πρώτης βασιλείας τε καὶ ἡγεμονίας.

1 Ps 50:14 [51:12]

24.

Ps 50:16

ῥῦσαί με ἐξ αἱμάτων, ὁ θεὸς ὁ θεὸς τῆς σωτηρίας μου

Spurious

Comment: this verse is not cited in R1 or R2, and there is no corresponding material in either recension. The ms attributes the fragment to three authors: αθ (Athanasius) καὶ θεοδ (Theodoret) καὶ ἀδρι (Adrian). Theodoret, *Ps.* 50:16 on this verse reads nearly the same as the fragment below: Συνεχῶς ἐν τῇ μνήμῃ περιστρέφει τὸν τοῦ Οὐρίου φόνον (PG 80, 1249B). In Ps.-Chrys., *hom. in Ps. 50* we also find: Συνεχῶς ἐπὶ τῇ μνήμῃ περιστρέφει τοῦ Οὐρίου τὸν φόνον (PG 55, 586).

Source: *Vat. Gr. 2057*, f. 92r.

Συνεχῶς ἐν τῇ μνήμῃ περιστρέφει τοῦ Οὐρίου καὶ τῶν συναποθανόντων αὐτῷ τὸν φόνον.

2 Cf. 2 Kgdms 11:6–27 [2 Sam 11:6–27]

25.

Ps 57:12

καὶ ἐρεῖ ἄνθρωπος εἰ ἄρα ἔστιν καρπὸς τῷ δικαίῳ

–

Comment: R1 and R2 discuss the trope ἀπόφασις (73.20) but there is little else similar between the recensions and this fragment. Note that this fragment is very similar to what we find in Thdr. Mops., *Ps.* 57:12 where he observes that some read this verse as posing a question (κατ᾽ ἐρώτησιν) ("is there, then, a benefit for the righteous?"), instead of making an assertion (κατ᾽ ἀπόφασιν) ("there really is a benefit for the righteous"). For a related remark in Diodore, see Mariès, *Études*, 115. The similarity of the fragment to Theodore suggests that the material could be Adrianic.

Source: *Vat. Gr. 2057*, f. 106r.

Τὸ **ἄρα** κατὰ ἀπόφασιν λέγει, ἀντὶ τοῦ ἀληθῶς ἐστὶν καρπὸς τῷ δικαίῳ.

1 Ps 57:12 [58:11]

---

1 ἄρα] ἆρα Vat.

26.

Ps 61:12

ἅπαξ ἐλάλησεν ὁ θεός

R1 (22)

Comment: this fragment is transmitted in two forms. There is no corresponding material transmitted in R2. The longer and shorter versions of the fragment both share similarities with R1, but offer more expansive glosses.

Source: Dorival, *Les Chaînes Exégétiques*, vol. 2, 192, no. 12, using Paris *Gr. 169*, f. 87r.

Τὸ **ἅπαξ** ἐπὶ τοῦ ἀμεταβλήτου κεῖται, ἀντὶ τοῦ βεβαίως ἀπεφήνατο καὶ ἀμεταθέτως· ὡς τό, **ἅπαξ ὤμοσα ἐν τῷ ἁγίῳ μου.**

1 Ps 61:12 [62:11]   2 Ps 88:36 [89:35]

Source: Dorival, *Les Chaînes Exégétiques*, vol. 2, 370, using Vatopedi *660*, f. 99r.
Dorival notes that four additional mss extend the extract found in Vatopedi
660: *Sinod. Gr. 194*, f. 114v; *Ottob. Gr. 398*, f. 147r; *Sinai Gr. 27*, ff. 215v–218r;
Vat. Gr. 1685, ff. 29v–31v (*Les Chaînes Exégétiques*, vol. 4, 275–6). Dorival
edits the extension in *Sinod. Gr.* and *Ottob. Gr.* as follows:... ἤκουσά φησι·
ἀπέφηνά μου τοῦ θεοῦ τῶν ὅλων ὅτι κρίσις ἔσται καὶ ἀντίδοσις ἀγαθῶν καὶ
κακῶν (ibid., vol. 2, 370). He notes the problematic syntax and hesitates to
assign the whole fragment to Adrian. There is no corresponding material in
either of the recensions. The mss attribute the fragment to Asterius.

Τὸ **ἅπαξ** ἐπὶ τοῦ ἀμεταβλήτου καὶ ἀντὶ τοῦ βεβαίως.

1 Ps 61:12 [62:11]

---

1 ἀμεταβλήτου] ἀμετακλήτου Vatop. Dorival

27.

Ps 67:23–4

εἶπε κύριος ἐκ Βασὰν ἐπιστρέψω—ὅπως ἂν βαφῇ
ὁ πούς σου ἐν αἵματι

R2 (42)

Comment: this fragment corresponds to material in both recensions, though
its extended explanation of Ps 67:23–4 is much closer to what we find in R2
than in R1, which glosses the verse very concisely.

Source: Pitra, *Analecta Sacra*, vol. 2, 134 (XI), using *Ottob. Gr. 398*, f. 159r.
I also consulted *Sinod. Gr. 194*, f. 124r. A large block of Pitra's fragment has
been shown to be spuriously attributed to Adrian (Κύνας–ἡ τῶν ἀποστόλων
φωνή) (Mercati, "Pro Adriano," 253; Devreesse, *Les anciens*, 312, fn. 3).

Τὸ τὰ ἀναίτια πολλάκις ὡς αἴτια λέγειν· ὡς τό, **εἶπε κύριος ἐκ Βασὰν**,
καὶ τὰ ἑξῆς· οὐ γὰρ τοὺς Ἰσραηλίτας ἐπὶ τὸ φόνον ἐργάσασθαι πολὺν
παρήγαγεν ἐκεῖθεν ὁ θεός, οὔτε τοῦτο ἦν ἐκείνου τὸ αἴτιον· ἐκ δὲ τῶν
ἐναντίων διὰ τοῦτο ἐκεῖνο ἐγένετο, ἐπειδὴ γὰρ τοὺς Ἰσραηλίτας διήγαγεν
ἀνάγκη πᾶσα τῶν ἀνθισταμένων ἱκανῶς παρακολουθήσειν.   5

1 Ps 67:23 [68:22]   5 Cf. Num 21:33–5; Deut 3:1–7

---

1 Τὸ] Ὅτι Pitra   1 λέγειν] λέγει Pitra
3 τοῦτο ἦν ἐκείνου] R2, τούτου ἦν ἐκεῖνοι Ottob. Sinod., τοῦτο ἦν ἐκεῖνο Pitra
5 τῶν ἀνθισταμένων] R2, τὸν ἀνθιστάμενον Ottob. Sinod.
5 ἱκανῶς] ἱκανὸς Ottob. Sinod.   5 παρακολουθήσειν] παρη- Pitra

28.

Ps 67:31(1)

ἡ συναγωγὴ τῶν ταύρων

R1 (27)

Comment: the fragment comes from a paragraph transmitted in both recensions, but there is only agreement with the text in R1. The fragment offers a longer gloss but is corrupt, and so I have emended it with an eye on Theodore, *Ps.* 55:7, where the same idea is expressed more lucidly: "from the fact that in herds of cattle the bulls appear as especially large [ἀπὸ γὰρ τοῦ ἐν ταῖς ἀγέλαις τῶν βοῶν τοὺς ταύρους μάλιστα μεγάλους φαίνεσθαι]."

Source: Pitra, *Analecta Sacra*, vol. 2, 134–5 (XII), using *Ottob. Gr. 398*, f. 160r. I also consulted *Sinod. Gr. 194*, f. 125r. Pitra attributes too much material to Adrian, overlooking the strong break in the mss after ταύρων. The material thereafter is spurious (cf. also Mercati, "Pro Adriano," 253).

Ἀντὶ τοῦ τῶν παμμεγεθῶν, ἀπὸ < τοῦ > τοὺς ταύρους ἐν ταῖς τῶν βοῶν ἀγέλαις < φαίνεσθαι > εἶναι τοὺς μείζονας [τῶν ταύρων].

29.

Ps 67:31(2)

διασκόρπισον ἔθνη τὰ τοὺς πολέμους θέλοντα

Spurious

Comment: spuriously attributed to Adrian. The fragment belongs to Ps.-Ath., *fr. Ps.* (PG 27, 303B) (Mercati, "Pro Adriano," 253).

Source: Pitra, *Analecta Sacra*, vol. 2, 135 (XIII), using *Ottob. Gr. 398*, f. 160r.

Τὰ νοητὰ δῆλον ὅτι· **πολέμους** δὲ τοὺς κατὰ τῶν ἁγίων.

1 Ps 67:31 [68:30]

---

1 ante Τὰ] Ἔθνη + Pitra   1 τοὺς] om. Pitra

30.

Ps 73:11(1)

ἵνα τί ἀποστρέφεις τὴν χεῖρά σου

R1 (16 and 4.7)

Comment: no corresponding paragraphs transmitted in R2. The fragment is similar to material in two different paragraphs in R1.

Source: Pitra, *Analecta Sacra*, vol. 2, 135 (XIV), using *Ottob. Gr. 398*, f. 175v. Also consulted *Sinod. Gr. 194*, f. 138v.

Ἤδει δὲ καὶ τὴν ἀναβολὴν τῆς εὐμενείας αὐτοῦ, χειρῶν ἀποστροφὴν, δι' ὧν μάλιστα τὰ σπουδαία τῶν πραγμάτων κατορθοῦσθαι πέφυκεν ἀφ' ἡμῶν· εἴη δ' ἂν ταῦτα ἀπὸ σχημάτων.

1 ἀποστροφὴν] -ῆς Ottob. Sinod.

31.

Ps 73:11(2)

ἵνα τί ἀποστρέφεις τὴν χεῖρά σου καὶ τὴν δεξιάν
σου ἐκ μέσου τοῦ κόλπου σου εἰς τέλος;

R1 (2.14)

Comment: no corresponding paragraph is transmitted in R2. This fragment offers a similar, though lengthier, gloss than what we find in R1.

Source: *Coislin 10*, f. 189v and *Vat. Gr. 754*, f. 175v. Pitra printed this fragment in *Analecta Sacra*, vol. 3, 99, using *Vat. Gr. 754, Vat. Gr. 1422, Vat. Gr. 1685*, and *Ottob. Gr. 398* (providing no foliation or apparatus)—I have not inspected the latter three mss. *Coilin* attributes the fragment to Adrian. Pitra attributed it to Origen, but he misread the marginal siglum that appeared in the above mss, confusing their abbreviation for ὡραῖον with the authorial lemma "Origen" (Mercati, "Pro Adriano," 248, fn. 1).

Ἐκ μεταφορᾶς· τὸ τοὺς παρακαλουμένους μὲν μὴ προσιεμένους δὲ τὴν παράκλησιν, πρότερον ἐπὶ τοῦ κόλπου τὰς χεῖρας ἔχοντας, ἐν τῷ ἐπιλαβέσθαι πῶς ἐθέλειν αὐτῶν τοὺς παρακαλοῦντας, ἀποστρέφειν αὐτὰς εἰς τουπίσω.

1 ante τὸ] κατὰ + Pitra   2 τοῦ κόλπου] τὸν κόλπον Pitra
2 ἔχοντας] ἔχων Pitra   2 ἐν] ἐπὶ Pitra   3 ἐθέλειν] ἐθέλει Pitra
3 αὐτῶν] αὐτὸν Vat., αὐτὸς Pitra   3 αὐτὰς] ante ἀποστρέφειν pon. Pitra
4 τουπίσω.] τὸ ὀπίσω; Pitra

32.

Ps 75:8

ἀπὸ τότε ἡ ὀργή σου

R1 (5)

Comment: no corresponding paragraph transmitted in R2. The fragment transmits the same text as we find in R1.

Source: Dorival, *Les Chaînes Exégétiques*, vol. 2, 194, no. 9, using Paris Gr. 169, f. 110v.

Τὴν πρὸς τὴν κακίαν ἐναντιότητα τῆς τοῦ θεοῦ βουλῆς, θυμὸν καὶ ὀργὴν ὀνομάζει, ἀπὸ τοῦ παρ' ἡμῖν τὴν ἀπέχθειαν πρὸς τἀναντία συμβαίνειν.

33.

Ps 76:18

καὶ γὰρ τὰ βέλη σου διαπορεύονται

R1 (71.4)

Comment: no corresponding paragraph transmitted in R2. The fragment is very similar to its corresponding section in R1 but with some expansions.

Source: Dorival, *Les Chaînes Exégétiques*, vol. 2, 195, no. 9, using Paris
Gr. 169, f. 112r.

Παρέλκει τὸ γὰρ, ἀντὶ τοῦ [σοῦ] καὶ τὰ βέλη σου διαπορεύονται· καὶ ἐν τῷ
ξζ΄, **καὶ γὰρ ἀπειθοῦντες τοῦ κατασκηνώματος**· καὶ τὸ ὑπὸ τοῦ Λάβαν
παρὰ τῷ Μωυσῇ, **ὅτι γὰρ ἀδελφός μου εἶ, οὐ δουλεύσεις μοι δωρεάν**, ἀντὶ τοῦ
ὅτι ἀδελφός μου εἶ· καὶ τὰ ὅμοια.

2 Ps 67:19 [68:18] var.   3 Gen 29:15

34.

Ps 77:49

ἐξαπέστειλεν εἰς αὐτοὺς ὀργὴν θυμοῦ αὐτοῦ, θυμὸν
καὶ ὀργὴν καὶ θλῖψιν, ἀποστολὴν δι᾽ ἀγγέλων πονηρῶν

R1 and R2 (46)

Comment: the fragment transmits distinctive material from each recension,
but is also more expansive than the corresponding material in these recensions.

Source: Dorival, *Les Chaînes Exégétiques*, vol. 2, 200–1, no. 31, using Paris
Gr. 169, f. 114r–v, and noting variant readings of *Ottob. Gr. 398*, f. 187v and
Sinod. Gr. 194 which transmit: Τὸ κακὸν–συγχωρῶν. I consulted the former
two mss.

Τὸ κακὸν ἤτοι τὴν κακίαν ἀντὶ τιμωρίας λέγει, ἀπὸ τῆς τῶν πασχόντων πρὸς
αὐτὴν διαθέσεως, ὥσπερ ἐνταῦθα· οὐ γὰρ τοὺς ἀποσταλέντας ἀγγέλους
πονηροὺς βούλεται λέγειν, ἵνα τινὰς τῶν ἀποστατῶν νομίσῃς, ἐπεὶ μήτε
πώποτε τοὺς τοιούτους ὑπὸ τοῦ θεοῦ προσταγέντας ἐπὶ τῆς θείας γραφῆς
ἐγνώκαμεν, ἀλλ᾽ ὡς πρὸς τὴν τῶν κολαζομένων ᾖ καὶ πρόσθεν ἔφην   5
διάθεσιν· < ὡς > καὶ τὸ παρὰ τῷ Ἡσαΐᾳ, **ἐγὼ κύριος ποιῶν εἰρήνην καὶ κτίζων
κακά**, ἵνα εἴπῃ ὅτι καὶ εἰρηνεύειν ἐῶν καὶ πολεμεῖσθαι συγχωρῶν· εἶτ᾽ αὖθις,
πρόσθες κακά, κύριε, πρόσθες κακὰ τοῖς ἐνδόξοις τῆς γῆς, ἀντὶ τοῦ
δαψιλέστερον αὐτοὺς τιμωρεῖ τὴν οἰκείαν αὐτοῖς ἐπιτείνων· καὶ τὸ παρὰ
τῷ Μιχαίᾳ, **ὅτι κατέβη κακὰ παρὰ κυρίου ἐπὶ πύλας Ἰερουσαλήμ**· καὶ μὴν   10
καὶ τὸ παρὰ τῷ Μωυσῇ, **ἐκάκωσεν δὲ Σαρρὰ τὴν παιδίσκην αὐτῆς**, ἀντὶ τοῦ
κάκιστα αὐτὴν αἰκισαμένη διέθηκεν· καί, **πρὸς Ἀβραὰμ γινώσκων γνώσῃ ὅτι
πάροικον ἔσται τὸ σπέρμα σου ἐν γῇ οὐκ ἰδίᾳ καὶ δουλώσουσιν αὐτὸ καὶ
κακώσουσιν ἔτη τετρακόσια**, ἀντὶ τοῦ κακῶς παρασκευάσουσι· καὶ παρὰ
τῷ Ἀμώς· **εἰ ἔστι κακία ἐν πόλει ἣν κύριος οὐκ ἐποίησε**· καὶ ὅσα τοιαῦτα·   15
διὸ καὶ ὁ κύριος ἐν τοῖς εὐαγγελίοις, **ἀρκετόν**, φησί, **τῇ ἡμέρᾳ ἡ κακία αὐτῆς**,

ἵνα εἴπῃ ὅτι ἡ αὐτῆς ἐργασία μυρίων κόπων καὶ πόνων τοῖς ἀνθρώποις ὑπάρχει πρόξενος.

7 Isa 45:6, 7   8 Isa 26:15 var.   10 Mic 1:12   11 Gen 16:6 var.
14 Gen 15:13 var.   15 Amos 3:6 var.   16 Matt 6:34

---

1 ante Τὸ] Τὸ πολλαχοῦ Ottob.
2 ὥσπερ ἐνταῦθα] ὡς τό, ἐξαπέστειλεν εἰς αὐτοὺς Ottob.   3 μήτε] μὴ Ottob.
4 τοῦ] deest Ottob.   5 κολαζομένων] κολαζόντων Ottob.
5 ἦ-ἔφην] deest Ottob.   9 ἐπιτείνων] ἐπίτεινον Paris
11 Σαρρὰ] Σαρρὰ γὰρ Paris

35.

Ps 77:66

ὄνειδος αἰώνιον ἔδωκεν αὐτοῖς

R1 (62.2)

Comment: no corresponding material is transmitted in R2. The fragment is nearly identical to the text of R1.

Source: Dorival, *Les Chaînes Exégétiques*, vol. 2, 201, no. 35, using Paris Gr. 169, f. 115r.

Περὶ τῶν ἀλλοφύλων, ἵνα εἴπῃ χρόνιον, ὥστε καὶ ὑπὸ τῶν αὖθις αἰσχίστων μνημονεύεσθαι.

36.

Ps 78:2

ἔθεντο-τὰς σάρκας τῶν ὁσίων σου τοῖς θηρίοις τῆς γῆς

R1 (57-57.4)

Comment: no corresponding material transmitted in R2. The fragment is similar to the corresponding material in R1, though it both expands upon and abridges this recension.

Dorival, *Les Chaînes Exégétiques*, vol. 2, 203, no. 4, using Paris *Gr. 169*, f. 115v–116r.

Πολλαχοῦ τὴν σάρκα ἤτοι ἐπ᾽ αὐτῆς τῆς φύσεως λέγει ἢ ἐπὶ φαυλοτάτου βίου ἢ ἐπὶ θνητότητος· ὡς καὶ ἐν τῷ οζ΄ Ψαλμῷ, **καὶ ἐμνήσθη ὅτι σάρξ εἰσιν, πνεῦμα πορευόμενον καὶ οὐκ ἐπίστρεφον·** καὶ τὸ παρὰ τῷ Ἡσαΐα, **πᾶσα σὰρξ χόρτος·** ἐντεῦθεν καὶ ὁ ἀπόστολος, **εἰ γὰρ ἐγνώκαμεν,** φησί, **Χριστὸν κατὰ σάρκα,** ἵνα εἴπῃ θνητόν, **ἀλλὰ νῦν οὐκ ἐπιγινώσκομεν,** καὶ τὸ **σὰρξ καὶ** 5 **αἷμα βασιλείαν θεοῦ οὐ κληρονομήσει·** καὶ μέντοι καὶ περὶ αὐτήν, ὅ δὲ νῦν ζῶ ἐν σαρκί, ἐν πίστει ζῶ τῇ τοῦ υἱοῦ τοῦ θεοῦ· ἢ καὶ ἐπὶ συγγενείας· ὡς παρὰ τῷ Ὠσηέ, **σάρξ μου ἐξ αὐτῶν·** καὶ τὸ ἐν τῇ τῶν Βασιλειῶν βίβλῳ, **καὶ παραγίνονται πᾶσαι αἱ φυλαὶ Ἰσραὴλ εἰς Χεβρὼν καὶ εἶπον αὐτῷ, ἰδοὺ ὀστᾶ σου καὶ σάρκες σου ἡμεῖς, χθὲς καὶ τρίτην ὄντος Σαοὺλ βασιλέως ἐφ᾽ ἡμῖν σὺ ἦσθα ὁ ἐξάγων** 10 **καὶ εἰσάγων τὸν Ἰσραήλ·** καὶ ἑτέρωθι δὲ τῆς αὐτῆς βίβλου, **καὶ ὁ βασιλεὺς Δαυὶδ ἀπέστειλεν πρὸς Σαδὼκ καὶ πρὸς Ἀβιάθαρ τοὺς ἱερεῖς λέγων, λαλήσατε πρὸς τοὺς πρεσβυτέρους Ἰούδα λέγοντες, ἵνα τί γίνεσθε ἔσχατοι τοῦ ἐπιστρέψαι πρὸς τὸν βασιλέα εἰς τὸν οἶκον αὐτοῦ; καὶ ὁ λόγος παντὸς Ἰσραὴλ ἦλθεν πρὸς τὸν βασιλέα εἰς τὸν οἶκον αὐτοῦ· ἀδελφοί μου ὑμεῖς ἐσται, ὀστᾶ μου· καὶ σάρξ** 15 **μου σύ;** καὶ νῦν τάδε ποιῆσαί μοι ὁ θεὸς καὶ τάδε προσθείη, εἰ μὴ ἄρχων δυνάμεως ἔσῃ ἐνώπιόν μου πάσας τὰς ἡμέρας ἀντὶ τοῦ Ἰωάβ· καὶ ὁ ἀπόστολός φησι, **εἴ πως παραζηλώσω μου τὴν σάρκα καὶ σώσω τινὰς ἐξ αὐτῶν·** καὶ ὅσα πρὸς τὴν τῆς κατὰ χώραν διανοίας ἀκολουθίαν ἁρμόζει παρ᾽ ἑκάστῳ αὐτῶν.

3 Ps 77[78]:39   4 Isa 40:6   5 2 Cor 5:16 var.   6 1 Cor 15:50 var.
7 Gal 2:20   8 Hos 9:12   11 2 Kgdms 5:1–2 [2 Sam 5:1–2] var.
17 2 Kgdms 19:12–13, 14 [2 Sam 19:11–12, 13] var.
18 Rom 11:14

3 ὅτι σάρξ–οὐκ] praeterit *Dorival*   3 τὸ] τῷ *Dorival*   10 ἡμεῖς] ὑμεῖς Paris
11 εἰς Χεβρὼν–ὁ ἐξάγων καὶ] praeterit *Dorival*   11 καὶ²] om. *Dorival*
17 ἀπέστειλεν πρὸς Σαδὼκ–πάσας τὰς] praeterit *Dorival*
18 παραζηλώσω–σώσω] praeterit *Dorival*

37.

Ps 78:12(1)

ἀπόδος τοῖς γείτοσιν ἡμῶν ἑπταπλασίονα
εἰς τὸν κόλπον αὐτῶν

R1 (32 and 50) and R2 (50)

Comment: the longer version of this fragment transmits distinctive material in R1 and R2, and the fragment is also substantially lengthier than the corresponding material transmitted in either recension.

Source: Dorival, *Les Chaînes Exégétiques*, vol. 2, 203–4, no. 5, using Paris *Gr. 169*, f. 116r.

Τὸν ἑπτὰ ἀριθμὸν ἐπὶ πλεονασμὸν λέγει ἤγουν ἐπὶ πλείου ἀριθμοῦ, ἀπὸ τοῦ τὴν ἑβδομὴν ἡμέραν οἱονεὶ σφραγίδα τινὰ καὶ συμπλήρωσιν τῶν λοιπῶν αὐτοὺς ἡμερῶν ἡγεῖσθαι, κατὰ τὴν τοῦ νομοθέτου διήγησιν· ὡς τό, **ἑπτάκις τῆς ἡμέρας ἤνεσά σε**, ἀντὶ τοῦ πολλάκις· καὶ τό, **ἀπόδος τοῖς γείτοσιν ἡμῶν**
5 **ἑπταπλασίονα**· καὶ τό, **πᾶς ὁ ἀποκτείνας Καὶν παρὰ τῷ Μωσεῖ ἑπτὰ ἐκδικούμενα παραλύσει**, ἀντὶ τοῦ πολυπλασίονα τὴν τιμωρίαν ἐκτίσει· καὶ τὸ παρὰ τῷ Μιχαίᾳ περὶ τοῦ Ἀσσυρίου, **καὶ ἐπεγερθήσονται ἐπ' αὐτὸν ἑπτὰ ποιμένες καὶ ὀκτὼ δήγματα**, ἀντὶ τοῦ πολλοί· καὶ τό, **ὅτι στεῖρα ἔτεκεν ἑπτὰ καὶ ἡ πολλὴ ἐν τέκνοις ἠσθένησε**, ἀντὶ τοῦ πολλούς· ἐπάγει γοῦν, **καὶ**
10 **ἡ πολλὴ ἐν τέκνοις ἠσθένησε**· καὶ τό, **ἡ σοφία ᾠκοδόμησε ἑαυτῇ οἶκον καὶ ὑπήρεισε στύλους ἑπτά**, ἵνα εἴπῃ πολλούς· καὶ τό, **δὸς μερίδα τοῖς ἑπτὰ καὶ γε τοῖς ὀκτώ**, ἀντὶ τοῦ ὑπερβάλλοντι κέχρησο τῷ ἐλέῳ· ταύτῃ γοῦν καὶ ὁ κύριος περὶ τοῦ ἀκαθάρτου πνεύματος· εὐρηκός, φησί, τὸν τόπον αὐτοῦ, **σχολάζοντα καὶ σεσαρωμένον πορεύεται καὶ παραλαμβάνει ἑπτὰ ἕτερα**
15 **πνεύματα πονηρότατα ἑαυτοῦ**· ὡσαύτως καὶ Πέτρος, **ποσάκις ἐὰν ἁμαρτήσῃ εἰς ἐμὲ ὁ ἀδελφός μου ἀφήσω αὐτῷ; ἕως ἑπτά; καὶ ὁ κύριός φησι· οὐχί, ἀλλ' ἕως ἑβδομηκοντάκις ἑπτά.**

3 Cf. Gen 2:1–3   4 Ps 118[119]:164 var.   5 Ps 78[79]:12   6 Gen 4:15
8 Mic 5:5   9 1 Kgdms 2:5 [1 Sam 2:5]   10 1 Kgdms 2:5 [1 Sam 2:5]   11 Prov 9:1
12 Eccl 11:2   15 Matt 12:44–5 var.; Luke 11:25–6 var.   17 Matt 18:21–2 var.

---

3 αὐτοὺς] αὐτῶν Paris *Dorival*   7 Ἀσσυρίου] Ἀσσουρίου *Dorival*   8 τοῦ] τὸ Paris

Comment: Pitra printed a much shorter version of the above fragment. The fragment is similar to the text of R2, but its biblical verse is only found in R1 (32 and 50), while the explanation of this verse agrees only with R1 (32).

Source: Pitra, *Analecta Sacra*, vol. 2, 135 (XV), using *Ottob. Gr. 398*, f. 192r. I also consulted *Sinod. Gr. 194*, f. 152v. In addition, this fragment is transmitted by *Vat. Gr. 1685*, ff. 85v–87v and Sinai *Gr. 27*, ff. 283v–286v (Dorival, *Les Chaînes Exégétiques*, vol. 4, 282–4).

Τὸ τὸν ἑπτὰ ἀριθμὸν ἐπὶ πλεονασμοῦ λέγειν εἴτ' οὖν ἐπὶ τελείου ἀριθμοῦ, ἀπὸ τοῦ τῶν ἑπτὰ ἡμερῶν οἱονεὶ σφραγίδά τινα καὶ συμπλήρωσιν τῶν λοιπῶν αὐτοὺς ἡγεῖσθαι ἡμερῶν, κατὰ τὴν < τοῦ > νομοθέτου διήγησιν· ὡς τό, **ἑπταπλασίονα εἰς τὸν κόλπον αὐτῶν**, ἀντὶ τοῦ καὶ ἀχώριστον αὐτοῖς
5 παράσχου τὴν πολυπλασίονά σου τιμωρίαν.

3 Cf. Gen 2:1–3   4 Ps 78[79]:12

---

1 λέγειν] λέγει Pitra   1 εἴτ' οὖν] εἴτουν Pitra   3 τοῦ] + Pitra
4 ἑπταπλασίονα] ἑπταπλασίνα Ottob., ἑπταπλάσια Pitra
4 ἀχώριστον] R1 (32), ἀχάριστον Ottob. Sinod., ἀχώρητον Pitra
5 πολυπλασίονά] -πλησ- Pitra

38.

Ps 78:12(2)

ἀπόδος τοῖς γείτοσιν ἡμῶν ἑπταπλασίονα
εἰς τὸν κόλπον αὐτῶν

R1 and R2 (32)

Comment: there is corresponding text in both recensions to this fragment and it transmits material unique to each.

Source: Dorival, *Les Chaînes Exégétiques*, vol. 2, 204, no. 6, using Paris *Gr. 169*, f. 116r.

Τὸν κόλπον πολλαχοῦ καὶ ἐπὶ τοῦ ἀχωρίστου λέγει, ἀπὸ τοῦ συνῆφθαι τὸν κόλπον τοῦ οὗπερ ἐστίν· ὡς τό, **ἀπόδος τοῖς γείτοσιν ἡμῶν ἑπταπλασίονα εἰς τὸν κόλπον αὐτῶν,** ἀντὶ τοῦ ἀχώριστον αὐτοῖς παράσχου τὴν πολυπλασίονά σου τιμωρίαν.

3 Ps 78[79]:12

2 οὗπερ ἐστίν·] οὗ προῆλθεν (?) *Dorival*

39.

Ps 90:4

ἐν τοῖς μεταφρένοις αὐτοῦ ἐπισκιάσει σοι,
καὶ ὑπὸ τὰς πτέρυγας αὐτοῦ ἐλπιεῖς

—

Comment: this fragment illustrates the trope of metaphor. However, the verse glossed does not occur in the discussions of this trope in R1 or R2 (73.1). Yet two related verses ("in the shelter of your wings you will shelter me" (Ps 16[17]:8); and, "spreading out his wings, he received them" (Deut 32:11)) surface in the discussion of metaphor in R1 and the first of these also occurs in the discussion of metaphor in R2. The comment below is also close to what we find Thdr. Mops., *Ps.* 16:8. It is plausibly authentic.

Source: Pitra, *Analecta Sacra*, vol. 2, 136 (XVI), using *Ottob. Gr. 398*, f. 212v. Also consulted *Sinod. Gr. 194*, f. 171r.

Ἴδιον γὰρ μάλιστα τοῖς ἐν οἰκιδίοις ὄρνισιν ὑπὸ φιλοστοργίας ἐμφύτου, πρότερον ἐφαπλοῦν τὰς πτέρυγας ὥστε κατὰ τὰ ἑαυτῶν νεοττὰ καταστῆσαι ταύτας, εἶτα ἀναλαβεῖν εἰς ἐπὶ τῶν οἰκείων ἀνεπαχθῶς φέρειν μεταφρένων· τοῦτο δὲ κατὰ μεταφοράν.

2 τὰ ἑαυτῶν νεοττὰ] τῶν αὐτῶν νεοττῶν Pitra   3 ἀναλαβεῖν] ἀνέλαβεν Ottob.
3 εἰς] om. Pitra   3 ἀνεπαχθῶς] ἀνεπάχθαι Pitra

40.

Ps 101:7–8 var.

ἐγενήθην ὡσεὶ νυκτικόραξ ἐν οἰκοπέδῳ,
ἠγρύπνησα καὶ ἐγενόμην ὡς στρουθίον

R1 and R2 (73.2)

Comment: the fragment transmits distinctive elements of the corresponding material in R1 and R2.

Source: Dorival, *Les Chaînes Exégétiques*, vol. 2, 209, no. 6, using *Paris Gr. 169*, f. 138r.

Κατὰ παραβολὴν λέγει· παραβολὴ δέ ἐστιν ὅταν ἡμᾶς ἀπὸ τῶν προσόντων πρὸς ἅπερ εἰκάσειεν τῶν λοιπῶν ὁμοίως ἔχειν παραβάλλῃ τις· ὡς τό, **ἠγρύπνησα καὶ ἐγενόμην ὡς στρουθίον**· καὶ τό, **ἐγενήθην ὡσεὶ νυκτικόραξ**· καὶ τὸ παρὰ τῷ Ἡσαΐᾳ, **ὡς πρόβατον ἐπὶ σφαγὴν ἤχθη καὶ ὡς ἀμνὸς ἐναντίον**.

3 Ps 101:8 [102:7] var.   3 Ps 101:7 [102:6]   4 Isa 53:7

2 ὁμοίως] ὁμοίως ὁμοίως Paris   3 νυκτικόραξ] νυκτικόραραξ Paris

41.

Job 1:11 var.

ἦ μὴν εἰς πρόσωπόν σε εὐλογήσει

R1 and R2 (73.7)

Comment: the fragment transmits distinctive elements of the corresponding material in R1 and R2.

Source: Hagedorn and Hagedorn, *Katenen zum Buch Hiob*, 212, using *Reg. Gr. Pii II 01*, f. 13r–v. Also see Mercati, "Pro Adriano," 251.

Ὅτι πολλάκις τινὰ κατὰ ἀντίφρασιν λέγει, ἕτερον ἀνθ᾽ ἑτέρου τιθεῖσα· ὡς
ἐνταῦθα τό, **ἦ μὴν εἰς πρόσωπόν σε εὐλογήσει**, ἀντὶ τοῦ βλασφημήσει· καὶ
ἐν τῇ β᾽ τῶν Βασιλειῶν περὶ τοῦ Ναβουθαί, **ηὐλόγησε θεὸν καὶ βασιλέα**,
ἀντὶ τοῦ ἐβλασφήμησεν, ὕβρισεν· καὶ τὸ περὶ τῆς Μελχῶ πρὸς τὸν Δαυίδ,
ὅτι δεδόξασται ὁ βασιλεὺς ἀποκαλυφθεὶς καὶ γυμνωθεὶς ἐνώπιον γυναικὸς   5
καθὼς ἀπογυμνοῦνται οἱ ὀρχούμενοι, ἀντὶ τοῦ εὐτελὴς καὶ ἀσχήμων ὦπται·
καὶ τὸ ὑπὸ τοῦ Ἰερεμίου, **ἐπικατάρατος ἄνθρωπος ὁ εὐαγγελισάμενος τῷ**
πατρί μου λέγων ὅτι ἐτέχθη σοι ἄρσεν· εὐφραινόμενος ἔστω ὁ ἄνθρωπος
ἐκεῖνος ὡς αἱ πόλεις, ἃς κατέστρεψεν ὁ κύριος καὶ οὐ μετεμελήθη· τὸ γὰρ
εὐφραινόμενος, ἀντὶ τοῦ ταλαιπωρούμενος εἶπεν.   10

2 Job 1:11 var.   3 3 Kgdms 20:10 [1 Kgs 21:10]
6 2 Kgdms 6:20 [2 Sam 6:20] var.   9 Jer 20:15–16 var.

---

3 post Βασιλειῶν] τὸ + *Mercati*   5 ὅτι] τί *Hagedorn Hagedorn*
5 δεδόξασται] δεδόξαστι *Reg.*
6 εὐτελὴς] R2 *Mercati Hagedorn Hagedorn,* εὐτελοὺς *Reg.*

Bibliography

I. PREVIOUS EDITIONS, REPRINTS, AND TRANSLATIONS OF ADRIAN'S *INTRODUCTION*

Debary, Anne. "La terminologie rhetoric-grammaticale dans *l'Isagogè* d'Adrien." Mémoire de DEA, October 9, 2001. University of Paris IV-Sorbonne.

Goessling, Friedrich. *Adrians ΕΙΣΑΓΩΓΗ ΕΙΣ ΤΑΣ ΘΕΙΑΣ ΓΡΑΦΑΣ aus neu aufgefundenen Handschriften.* Berlin: Reuther, 1887.

Hoeschel, David. *Adriani Isagoge, Sacrarum Literarum et antiquissimorum graecorum in Prophetas fragmenta.* Augsburg: Typis Ioannis Praetorii, 1602 (text: 1–27; notes: 88–9).

Lollin, Aloysius. *Aloysii Lollini patritii veneti Bellunensium antistitis, Episcopalium curarum characteres.* Ed. Donatus Bernardius. Belluno: Castilionis, 1630 (text: 257–73).

Pearson, John, ed. *Critici Sacri, sive Doctissimorum Virorum in SS. Biblia Annotationes et Tractatus.* Vol. 8, *Tractatuum Biblicorum.* London: Jacobus Flescher, 1660 (text: 9–23; notes: 47–50).

PG 98, 1274–312.

Schlüren, Karl Friedrich. "Zu Adrianos: Vorarbeiten." *Jahrbücher für Protestantische Theologie* 13 (1887): 136–59.

II. ANCIENT SOURCES CITED

Augustinus Hipponensis, *locutionum in Heptateuchum libri septem*

Fraipont, J., and Donatien De Bruyne, eds. *Sancti Aurelii Augustini Quaestionum in Heptateuchum libri VII; Locutionum in Heptateuchum, libri VII; De octo quaestionibus ex veteri testament.* CCSL 33. Turnout: Brepols, 1958.

Augustinus Hipponensis, *retractationum libri II*

Bogan, Mary Inez, trans. *Saint Augustine: The Retractations.* FOTC 60. Washington, D.C.: Catholic University of America Press, 1968.

Mutzenbecher, A., ed. *Augustinus: Retractationum libri II.* CCSL 57. Turnhout: Brepols, 1984.

Cassiodorus Senator, *expositio in Ps.*

Adriaen, Marc, ed. *Magni Aurelii Cassiodori. Expositio Psalmorum: I–LXX.* CCSL 97. Turnhout: Brepols, 1958. *Expositio Psalmorum: LXXI–CL.* CCSL 98. Turnhout: Brepols, 1958.

Walsh, Patrick Gerard, trans. *Cassiodorus: Explanation of the Psalms.* ACW 51–3. New York: Paulist Press, 1990, 1991, 1991.

Cassiodorus Senator, *institutiones*

Halporn, James W., trans., and Mark Vessey, intro. *Cassiodorus:* Institutions of Divine and Secular Learning *and* On the Soul. TTH. Liverpool: Liverpool University Press, 2004.

Mynors, R. A. B., ed. *Cassiodori Senatoris Institutiones*. Oxford: Oxford University Press, 1937.

Chrysostomus, Joannes, *commentarium in Gal.*

NPNF, 1st series, vol. 13, 1–48.
PG 61, 611–82.

Chrysostomus, Joannes, *de laudibus Pauli*

Piédagnel, Auguste, ed. *Jean Chrysostome: Panégyriques de S. Paul*. SC 300. Paris: Cerf, 1982.

Mitchell, Margaret M. *The Heavenly Trumpet: John Chrysostom and the Art of Pauline Interpretation*. Louisville: Westminster John Knox, 2002: 440–87.

Cosmas Indicopleustes, *topographia christiana*

Wolska-Conus, Wanda, ed. *Cosmas Indicopleustes: Topographie Chrétienne*. SC 141, 159, 197. Paris: Cerf, 1968, 1970, 1973.

Winstedt, Eric Otto, trans. *The Christian Topography of Cosmas Indicopleustes*. Cambridge: Cambridge University Press, 1909.

Cyrillus Alexandrinus, *fragmenta commentarii in Lc.*

PG 72, 476–949.

Demetrius, *de elocutione*

Roberts, W. Rhys, ed. and trans. *Demetrius on Style: The Greek Text of Demetrius* De Elocutione *Edited after the Paris Manuscript with Introduction, Translation, Facsimilies, etc.* Cambridge: Cambridge University Press, 1902.

Didymus Alexandrinus, *commentarius in Zach.*

Doutreleau, Louis, ed. *Didyme L'Aveugle: Sur Zacharie*. SC 83, 84, 85. Paris: Cerf, 1962.
Hill, Robert C., trans. *Didymus the Blind: Commentary on Zechariah*. FC 111. Washington, D.C.: Catholic University of America Press, 2006.

Diodorus Tarsensis, *fragmenta in Gen.*

Deconinck, Joseph. *Essai sur la chaîne de l'Octateuque, avec une edition des commentaires de Diodore de Tarse*. Paris: Librairie Ancienne Honoré Champion, 1912.
Petit, Françoise, ed. *Catenae graecae in Genesim et in Exodum*. Vol. 2, *Collectio coisliniana: In Genesim*. CCSG 15. Turnhout: Brepols, 1986.

Diodorus Tarsensis, *fragmenta in Pss.*

Olivier, Jean-Marie, ed. *Diodori Tarsensis Commentarii in Psalmos*. Vol. 1, *Commentarii in Psalmos I–L*. CCSG 6. Turnhout: Brepols, 1980.
Hill, Robert C., trans. *Diodore of Tarsus: Commentary on Psalms 1–51*. WGRW. Atlanta: Society of Biblical Literature, 2005.

Diodorus Tarsensis, *Ps. hypoth. 118*

Mariès, Louis, ed. "Extraits du Commentaire de Diodore de Tarse sur les Psaumes." *RSR* 19 (1919): 90–101.

Dionysius Halicarnassensis, *epistula ad Ammaeum* 2 et *de Thucydide*

Usher, Stephen, trans. *Dionysius of Halicarnassus: The Critical Essays*. 2 vols. LCL 465, 466. Cambridge, Mass.: Harvard University Press, 1974–85.

Eusebius Emesenus, *fragmenta armenia in Gen., fragmenta ex catenarum in Gen., fragmenta ex Procopii in Gen.*

Petit, Françoise, Lucas Van Rompay, and Jos J. S. Weitenberg, trans. *Eusèbe d'Émèse: Commentaire de la Genèse. Texte arménien de l'édition de Venise (1980). Fragments grecs et syriaques*. TEG 15. Leuven: Peeters, 2011.

Eustathius Antiochenus, *de engastrimytho contra Origenem*

Declerck, José H., ed. *Eustathii Antiocheni Opera*. CCSG 51. Turnhout: Brepols, 2002.
Greer, Rowan A., and Margaret M. Mitchell, trans. *The "Belly-Myther" of Endor: Interpretations of 1 Kingdoms 28 in the Early Church*. WGRW 16. Atlanta: Society of Biblical Literature, 2006.

Georgius Monachus, *chronicon*

De Boor, Carl, ed. *Georgii Chronicon*. Stuttgart: Teubner, 1978.

Isidorus Pelusiota, *epistularum libri quinque*

PG 78, 177–1646.
Evieux, Pierre, ed. *Isidore de Péluse: Lettres*. SC 422, 454. Paris: Cerf, 1997, 2000.

Junillus Africanus, *instituta regularia divinae legis*

Kihn, Heinrich, ed. *Theodor von Mopsuestia und Junilius Africanus als Exegeten. Nebst einer kritischen Textausgabe von des letzteren Instituta regularia divinae legis*. Freiburg: Herder, 1880.
Maas, Michael. *Exegesis and Empire in the Early Byzantine Mediterranean: Junillus Africanus and the Instituta Regularia Divinae Legis*. Studien und Texte zu Antike und Christentum 17. Tübingen: Mohr Siebeck, 2003.

Nemesius Emesenus, *de natura hominis*

Morani, Moreno, ed. *Nemesii Emeseni de natura hominis*. Leipzig: Teubner, 1987.
Sharples, R. W., and Philip J. van der Eijk, trans. *Nemesius: On the Nature of Man*. TTH 49. Liverpool: Liverpool University Press, 2008.

Nilus Ancyranus, *epistularum libri quattuor*

PG 79, 81–582.

Olympiodorus Alexandrinus, *fragmenta ex commentariis in Job*

Hagedorn, Ursula, and Dieter Hagedorn, eds. *Olympiodor, Diakon von Alexandria: Kommentar zu Hiob*. PTS 24. Berlin: Walter de Gruyter, 1984.

Photius Constantinopolitanus, *bibliothecae codices*

Henry, René. *Photius: Bibliothèque*. Vol. 1. Paris: Les Belles Lettres, 1959.
Wilson, Nigel G., trans. *Photius: The Bibliotheca: A Selection*. London: Duckworth, 1994.

Polychronius Apameensis, *fragmenta in Job*

Hagedorn, Ursula, and Dieter Hagedorn, eds. *Die Älteren Griechischen Katenen zum Buch Hiob*. Vol. 1, *Einleitung, Prologe und Epiloge, Fragmenta zu Hiob 1,1–8,22*. PTS 40. Berlin: Walter de Gruyter, 1994. Vol. 2, *Fragmenta zu Hiob 9,1–22,30*. PTS 48. Berlin: Walter de Gruyter, 1997. Vol. 3, *Fragmenta zu Hiob 23,1–42,17*. PTS 53. Berlin: Walter de Gruyter, 2000. Vol. 4, *Register, Nachträge und Anhänge*. PTS 59. Berlin: Walter de Gruyter, 2004.

Pseudo-Chrysostomus, *synopsis sacrae scripturae*

PG 56, 313–86.

Pseudo-Plutarchus, *vita Homeri*

Kindstrand, Jan Fredrik, ed. *[Plutarchi]: De Homero*. Leipzig: Teubner, 1990.
Keaney, J. J., and Robert Lamberton, eds. and trans. *[Plutarch]: Essay on the Life and Poetry of Homer*. Atlanta: Scholars Press, 1996.

Quintilianus, *institutio oratoria*

Russell, Donald A., trans. *Quintilian: The Orator's Education*. 5 vols. LCL 124–7, 494. Cambridge, Mass.: Harvard University Press, 2002.

Suida

Adler, Ada, ed. *Suidae Lexicon*. 5 vols. Stuttgart: Teubner, 1928–38.

Theodorus Mopsuestenus, *fragmenta in Gen.*

Devreesse, Robert. *Essai sur Théodore de Mopsueste*. ST 141. Vatican City: BAV, 1948.
Petit, Françoise, ed. *La chaîne sur la Genèse: édition intégrale*. Vol. 1, *Chapitres 1 à 3*. TEG 1. Leuven: Peeters, 1992.

Theodorus Mopsuestenus, *fragmenta commentarii in Pss.*

Devreesse, Robert, ed. *Le commentaire de Théodore de Mopsueste sur les psaumes (I–LXXX)*. ST 93. Vatican City: BAV, 1939.
Hill, Robert C. *Theodore of Mopsuestia: Commentary on Psalms 1–81*. WGRW 5. Atlanta: Society of Biblical Literature, 2006.

Theodorus Mopsuestenus, *Ps. hypoth. 118*

Van Rompay, Lucas, ed. *Théodore de Mopsueste: Fragments syriaques du Commentaire des Psaumes (Psaume 118 et Psaumes 138–148)*. CSCO 435. Leuven: Peeters, 1982.
Thome, Felix, trans. *Historia contra Mythos: Die Schriftauslegung Diodors von Tarsus und Theodor von Mopsuestia im Widerstreit zu Kaiser Julians und Salustius' allegorischem Mythenverständnis*. Bonn: Borengässer, 2004.

Theodorus Mopsuestenus, *fragmenta in Cant.*

PG 66, 699–700.

Theodorus Mopsuestenus, *commentarii in xii prophetas*

Sprenger, Hans Norbert, ed. *Theodori Mopsuesteni commentarius in xii prophetas: Einleitung und Ausgabe*. Biblica et Patristica 1. Wiesbaden: Otto Harrassowitz, 1977.
Hill, Robert C., trans. *Theodore of Mopsuestia: Commentary on the Twelve Prophets*. FC 108. Washington, D.C.: Catholic University of America Press, 2004.

Theodorus Mopsuestenus, *fragmenta syriaca in Jo.*

Vosté, Jacques-Marie, ed. *Theodori Mopsuesteni commentarius in evangelium Iohannis apostoli*. CSCO 115–16. Leuven: Peeters, 1940.
Conti, Marco, trans., Joel C. Elowsky, ed. *Theodore of Mopsuestia: Commentary on the Gospel of John*. ACT. Downers Grove, Il.: InterVarsity Press, 2010.

Theodorus Mopsuestenus, *commentarii in Pauli epistulas*

Swete, Henry B., ed. *Theodori episcopi Mopsuesteni in epistolas b. Pauli commentarii*. 2 vols. Cambridge: Cambridge University Press, 1880–2.
Greer, Rowan A., trans. *Theodore of Mopsuestia: Commentary on the Minor Pauline Epistles*. WGRW 26. Atlanta: Society of Biblical Literature, 2010.

Theodorus Mopsuestenus, *fragmenta in Heb.*

Petit, Françoise, ed. *La Chaîne sur l'Exode: Édition Intégrale. II: Collectio Coisliniana. III: Fonds Caténique Ancien (Exode 1,1–15,21)*. TEG 10. Leuven: Peeters, 2000.

Theodoretus Cyrrhensis, *quaestiones in Octateuchem*

Petruccione, John F., ed., and Robert C. Hill, trans. *Theodoret of Cyrus: The Questions on the Octateuch*. Vol. 1, *On Genesis and Exodus*. Vol. 2, *On Leviticus, Numbers, Deuteronomy, Joshua, Judges and Ruth*. LEC 1–2. Washington, D.C.: Catholic University of America Press, 2007.

Theodoretus Cyrrhensis, *commentarii in Pss.*

PG 80, 857–1998.
Hill, Robert C., trans. *Theodoret of Cyrus. Commentary on the Psalms, 1–72*. FC 101. Washington, D.C.: Catholic University of America Press, 2000. *Commentary on the Psalms, 73–150*. FC 102. Washington, D.C.: Catholic University of America Press, 2001.

Theodoretus Cyrrhensis, *commentarius in Cant.*

PG 81, 28–213.
Hill, Robert C., trans. *Theodoret of Cyrus: Commentary on the Song of Songs*. Early Christian Studies 2. Brisbane: Australian Catholic University, 2001.

Theodoretus Cyrrhensis, *commentarii in xii prophetas*

PG 81, 1546–1988.
Hill, Robert C., trans. *Theodoret of Cyrus: Commentaries on the Prophets*. Vol. 3, *Commentary on the Twelve Prophets*. Brookline, Mass.: Holy Cross Orthodox Press, 2006.

Theodoretus Cyrrhensis, *commentarius in Is.*

Guinot, Jean-Noël, ed. *Théodoret de Cyr: Commentaire sur Isaïe*. 3 vols. SC 276, 295, 315. Paris: Cerf, 1980, 1982, 1984.

Theodoretus Cyrrhensis, *commentarius in Ezech.*

PG 81, 808–1256.
Hill, Robert C., trans. *Theodoret of Cyrus: Commentaries on the Prophets*. Vol. 2, *Commentary on the Prophet Ezekiel*. Brookline, Mass.: Holy Cross Orthodox Press, 2006.

Theodoretus Cyrrhensis, *commentarius in Dan.*

PG 81, 1256–546.
Hill, Robert C., trans. *Theodoret of Cyrus: Commentary on Daniel*. WGRW 7. Atlanta: Society of Biblical Literature, 2006.

Theodoretus Cyrrhensis, *interpretationes in Pauli epistulas*

PG 82, 31–878.
Hill, Robert C., trans. *Theodoret of Cyrus: Commentary on the Letters of St. Paul*. Vols. 1–2. Brookline, Mass.: Holy Cross Orthodox Press, 2001.

Tryphon, *de tropis*

Spengel, Leonard, ed. *Rhetores Graeci*, Vol. 3. Leipzig: Teubner, 1856.

Cetera

Scripturae

Rahlfs, Alfred, ed. *Psalmi cum Odis*. 2nd ed. Göttingen: Vandenhoeck & Ruprecht, 1967.
Rahlfs, Alfred, ed. *Septuagint: Id est Vetus Testamentum graece iuxta LXX interpretes*. Stuttgart: Deutsche Bibelgesellschaft, 1979.
Aland, Barbara, Kurt Johannes Karavidopoulos, Carlo M. Martini, and Bruce M. Metzger, eds. *Novum Testamentum Graece*. 28th ed. Stuttgart: Deutsche Bibelgesellschaft, 2012.

Catenae in Gen.

Petit, Françoise, ed. *Catenae graecae in Genesim et in Exodum*. Vol. 2, *Collectio coisliniana: In Genesim*. CCSG 15. Turnhout: Brepols, 1986.
Petit, Françoise, ed. *La chaîne sur la Genèse: édition intégrale*. Vol. 1, *Chapitres 1 à 3*. TEG 1. Leuven: Peeters, 1992. Vol. 2, *Chapitres 4 à 11*. TEG 2. Leuven: Peeters, 1993. Vol. 3, *Chapitres 12 à 28*. TEG 3. Leuven: Peeters, 1995. Vol. 4, *Chapitres 29 à 50*. TEG 4. Leuven: Peeters, 1996.

Catenae in Ex.

Petit, Françoise, ed. *La chaîne sur l'Exode: édition intégrale. II: Collectio Coisliniana. III: Fonds caténique ancien (Exode 1,1–15,21)*. TEG 10. Leuven: Peeters, 2000.
Petit, Françoise, ed. *La chaîne sur l'Exode. IV: Fonds caténique ancien (Exode 15,22–40,32)*. TEG 11. Leuven: Peeters, 2001.

Catenae in Pss.

Dorival, Gilles, ed. *Les Chaînes Exégétiques Grecques sur les Psaumes: Contribution à l'Étude d'une Forme Littéraire*, 4 vols. Leuven: Peeters, 1986–95.

Etymologicum

Sturz, Friedrich Wilhelm, ed. *Etymologicum Graecae Linguae Gudianum*. Leipzig: Weigel, 1818.

III. LITERATURE

Adriani, Maurilio. "La Badia Fiorentina, appunti storico-religiosi." In *La Badia Fiorentina*. Ed. Ernesto Sestan, Maurilio Adriani, and Alessandro Guidotti. Florence: Cassa di Risparmio di Firenze, 1982, 13–46.

Alpago-Novello, Luigi. "La vita e le opera di Luigi Lollino, vescovo di Belluno (1596–1625)." *Archivio Veneto* 14 (1933): 15–116; 15 (1934): 199–304.

Altemps, Giovanni Angelo. *Catalogue des livres et des manuscrits composant la bibliothèque des Ducs d'Altemps*. Rome: Rossi, 1908.

"Antiquité Chrétienne Grecque et Bible." In *Dictionnaire Encyclopédique de la Bible*. 3rd ed. Turnhout: Brepols, 2002, 70–83 (unsigned).

Antoniou, Perséphone. "Notes sur le colophon du Parisinus Gr. 1477." *Scriptorium* 43 (1989): 101–6.

Antonopoulou, Theodora, ed. *Leonis VI Sapientis Imperatoris Byzantini: Homiliae*. CCSG 63. Turnhout: Brepols, 2008.

Asper, Markus. *Griechische Wissenschaftstexte: Formen, Funktionen, Differenzierungsgeschichten*. Stuttgart: Franz Steiner, 2007.

Asper, Markus. "Katalog." *HWRh* 4 (1998): 915–22.

Asper, Markus. "Zu Struktur und Funktion eisagogischer Texte." In *Gattungen wissenschaftlicher Literatur in der Antike*. Ed. Wolfgang Kullmann, Jochen Althoff, and Markus Asper. Tübingen: Gunter Narr, 1998, 309–40.

Assemani, Giuseppe Simone. *Bibliotheca Orientalis Clementino-Vaticana*. Vol. 3, part 1, *De Scriptoribus Syris*. Rome: Typis Sacrae Congregationis de Propaganda Fide, 1725.

Backus, Irena, and Benoît Gain. "Cardinal Guglielmo Sirleto (1514–1585), sa Bibliothèque et ses Traductions de Saint Basile." *Mélanges de L'Ecole francaise de Rome, Moyen-Age, Temps modernes* 98 (1986): 889–955.

Baldi, Davide. "Il catalogo dei codici greci della Biblioteca Riccardiana." In *La descrizione dei manoscritti: esperienze a confronto*. Ed. Edoardo Crisci, Marilena Maniaci, and Pasquale Orsini. Cassino: Università degli Studi di Cassino—Dipartimento di Filologia e Storia, 2010, 139–75.

Baldi, Davide. "Il *Codex Florentinus* del Digesto e il 'Fondo Pandette' della Biblioteca Laurenziana (con un'appendice di documenti inediti)." *Segno e Testo* 8 (2010): 99–186.

Baldi, Davide. "Sulla Storia di alcuni Codici Italogreci della Biblioteca Laurenziana." *Nea Rhome* 4 (2007): 357–81.

Bardenhewer, Otto. *Geschichte der altchristlichen Literatur*. Vol. 4. Freiburg: Herder, 1912.

Bardenhewer, Otto. *Polychronius, Bruder Theodors von Mopseustia und Bischof von Apamea: Ein Beitrag zur Geschichte der Exegese*. Freiburg: Herder, 1879.

Bardy, Gustave. "La Littérature Patristique des '*Quaestiones et Responsiones*' sur l'Écriture Sainte." *RB* 41 (1932): 210–36, 341–69, 515–37; 42 (1933): 14–30, 211–29, 328–52.

Bate, Herbert Newell. "Some Technical Terms of Greek Exegesis." *JTS* 24 (1922): 59–66.

Battifol, Pierre. "Dr. Friedrich Goessling: L'Isagoge d'Hadrien." *Bulletin Critique de littérature d'histoire et de théologie* 10 (1889): 1–2.

Battifol, Pierre. "Les manuscrits grecs de Lollino évêque de Bellune: Recherches pour server à l'histoire de la Vaticane." *Mélanges d'archéologie et d'histoire École Française de Rome* 9 (1889): 28–48.

Battifol, Pierre. *La Vaticane de Paul III à Paul V d'après des documents nouveaux*. Paris: Ernest Leroux, 1890.

Beck, Hans-Georg. *Kirche und Theologische Literatur im Byzantinischen Reich*. Munich: Beck, 1959.

Behr, John. *The Case against Diodore and Theodore: Texts and Their Contexts*. Oxford: Oxford University Press, 2011.

Beyer, K. *Semitische Syntax im Neuen Testament*. Göttingen: Vandenhoeck & Ruprecht, 1962.

Blum, Rudolf. *La Biblioteca della Badia Fiorentina e I Codici Di Antonio Corbinelli*. ST 155. Vatican City: BAV, 1951.

Bollig, Johannes, and Paulus de Lagarde. *Iohannis Euchaitorum Metropolitae quae in codice Vaticano graeco 676 supersunt*. Göttingen: Aedibus Dieterichianis, 1882.

Bonner, Stanley F. *Education in Ancient Rome: From the Elder Cato to the Younger Pliny*. London: Methuen, 1977.

Bruns, Peter. "Polychronius von Apamea—Der Exeget und Theologe." *StPatr* 37 (2001): 404–12.

Busto Saiz, José Ramón. *La traducción de Símaco en el libro de los Salmos*. Madrid: Consejo Superior de Investigaciones Científicas, 1985.

Bultmann, Rudolf. *Die Exegese des Theodor von Mopsuestia*. Ed. Helmut Feld and Karl H. Schelkle. Stuttgart: W. Kohlhammer, 1984.

Cameron, Alan. "The Authenticity of the Letters of St Nilus of Ancyra." *Greek, Roman and Byzantine Studies* 17 (1976): 181–96.

Cameron, Alan. *Greek Mythography in the Roman World*. Oxford: Oxford University Press, 2004.

Canart, Paul. "Alivse Lollino et ses amis grecs." *Studi Veniziani* 12 (1970): 553–87.

Canart, Paul. *Catalogue des Manuscrits grecs de L'Archivio di San Pietro*. ST 246. Vatican City: BAV, 1966.

Canart, Paul. *Codices Vaticani Graeci*. Vol. 7, *Codices 1745–1962*. Part 1, *Codicum Enarrationes*. Vatican City: BAV, 1970.

Canart, Paul. "Les manuscrits copiés par Emmanuel Provataris (1546–1570 environ): Essai d'étude codicologique." In *Mélanges Eugène Tisserant*. Vol. 6, *Bibliothèque Vaticane: premiere partie*. ST 236. Vatican City: BAV, 1964, 173–287.

Canart, Paul. "Reliures et Codicologie: Les Manuscrits grecs de la Famille Barbaro." In *Calames et Cahiers: Mélanges de codicologie et de paléographie offerts à Léon Gilissen*. Ed. Jacques Lemaire and Émile van Balberghe. Brussels: Centre D'Étude des Manuscrits, 1985, 13–25.

Canart, Paul. *Les Vaticani Graeci 1487–1962: Notes et Documents pour l'Histoire d'un fonds de manuscrits de la Bibliothèque Vaticane*. ST 248. Vatican City: BAV, 1979.

Caner, Daniel. *History and Hagiography from the Late Antique Sinai*. TTH. Liverpool: Liverpool University Press, 2009.

Caner, Daniel. *Wandering, Begging Monks: Spiritual Authority and the Promotion of Monasticism in Late Antiquity*. Berkeley: University of California Press, 2002.

Ceillier, Remy. *Histoire générale des auteurs sacrés et ecclésiastiques*. New ed. Vol. 11. Paris: Louis Vivès, 1862.

Chabot, Jean Baptist, ed. *Synodicon Orientale, ou, Recueil de synodes nestoriens*. Paris: Imprimerie Nationale, 1902.

Clark, Elizabeth A. *Reading Renunciation: Asceticism and Scripture in Early Christianity*. Princeton: Princeton University Press, 1999.

Collett, Barry. *Italian Benedictine Scholars and the Reformation: The Congregation of Santa Giustina of Padua*. Oxford: Oxford University Press, 1986.

Conley, Thomas. "Byzantine Teaching on Figures and Tropes: An Introduction." *Rhetorica: A Journal of the History of Rhetoric* 4 (1986): 335–74.

Courcelle, Pierre. *Late Latin Writers and Their Greek Sources.* Trans. H. E. Wedeck. Cambridge, Mass.: Harvard University Press, 1969.

Credner, Karl A. *Einleitung in das Neue Testament.* Halle: Weisenhauses, 1836.

Cribiore, Raffaella. *Gymnastics of the Mind: Greek Education in Hellenistic and Roman Egypt.* 2nd ed. Princeton: Princeton University Press, 2005.

Cribiore, Raffaella. *The School of Libanius in Late Antique Antioch.* Princeton: Princeton University Press, 2007.

Curti, Carmelo, and Maria Antonietta Barbara. "Greek Exegetical Catenae." In *Patrology: The Eastern Fathers from the Council of Chalcedon (451) to John of Damascus († 750).* Ed. Angelo Di Berardino. Trans. Adrian Walford. Cambridge: James Clarke, 2006, 605–54.

Daley, Brian E. "Finding the Right Key: The Aims and Strategies of Early Christian Interpretation of the Psalms." In *Psalms in Community: Jewish and Christian Textual, Liturgical, and Artistic Traditions.* Ed. Harold W. Attridge and Margot E. Fassler. Atlanta: Society of Biblical Literature, 2003, 189–205.

de' Cavalieri, Franchi. *Catalogus Codicum Hagiographicorum Graecorum Bibliothecae Vaticanae.* Brussels: Apud Editores, 1899.

de Durand, Georges-Matthieu. *Marc le Moine: Traités II.* SC 455. Paris: Cerf, 2000.

de Furia, Franciscus. *Supplementum Alterum ad Catalogum Codicum Graecorum, Latinorum, Italicorum etc. Bibliothecae Mediceae Laurentianae.* Vol. 1, tome B. Florence: Biblioteca Mediceo-Laurenziana, 1846.

de Montfoucon, Bernardo. *Diarium Italicum. Sive monumentorum veterum, bibliothecarum, musaeorum, &c. Notitiae singulares in itinerario Italico collectae. Additis schematibus ac figuris.* Paris: J. Anisson, 1702.

Denzler, Georg. *Kardinal Guglielmo Sirleto (1514–1585): Leben und Werke. Ein Beitrag zur Nachtridentinischen Reform.* Munich: Max Hueber, 1964.

Devreesse, Robert. *Catalogue des manuscrits grecs.* Vol. 2, *Le fonds Coislin.* Paris: Imprimerie Nationale, 1945.

Devreesse, Robert. "Chaines Exégétique Grecques." *DBS.* Vol. 1. Paris: Letouzey et Ané, 1928, col. 1084–1233.

Devreesse, Robert. *Codices Vaticani Graeci.* Vol. 3, *Codices 604–866.* Vatican City: BAV, 1950.

Devreesse, Robert. *Essai sur Théodore de Mopsueste.* Vatican City: BAV, 1948.

Devreesse, Robert. *Le Fonds Grecs de la Bibliothèque Vaticane des Origines a Paul V.* ST 244. Vatican City: BAV, 1965.

Devreesse, Robert. *Les Ancien Commentateurs Grecs des Psaumes.* ST 264. Vatican City: BAV, 1970.

Devreesse, Robert. "Les manuscrits grecs de Cervini." *Scriptorium* 22 (1968): 250–70.

Devreesse, Robert. "Pour l'Histoire des Manuscrits du Fonds Vatican Grec." *Collectanea Vaticana in Honorem Anselmi M. Card. Albareda A Bibliotheca Apostolica Edita.* ST 219. Vatican City: BAV, 1962, 315–36.

Dickey, Eleanor. *Ancient Greek Scholarship: A Guide to Finding, Reading, and Understanding Scholia, Commentaries, Lexica, and Grammatical Treatises, from Their Beginnings to the Byzantine Period.* Oxford: Oxford University Press, 2007.

Dorez, Léon. "Recherches et documents sur la bibliothèque du Cardinal Sirleto." *Mélanges d'archéologie et d'histoire* 11 (1891): 457–91.

Dorival, Gilles. *Les Chaînes Exégétiques Grecques sur les Psaumes: Contribution à l'Étude d'une Forme Littéraire*. 4 vols. Leuven: Peeters, 1986–95.

Dorival, Gilles. "Des commentaires de l'Écriture aux chaînes." In *Le monde grec ancien et la Bible*. Ed. Claude Mondésert. Paris: Beauchesne, 1984, 360–86.

Dorival, Gilles. "La postérité littéraire des chaînes exégétiques grecques." *Revue des études byzantines* 43 (1985): 209–26.

Dörrie, Heinrich, and Hermann Dörries. "Erotapokriseis." *RAC* 6 (1966): 342–70.

Dreyer, O. "Lyseis." *KP* 3.16–17 (1968/69): 832–3.

Ehrhard, Albert. *Überlieferung und Bestand der Hagiographischen und Homiletischen Literatur der Griechischen Kirche von den Anfängen bis zum Ende des 16. Jahrhunderts*. Vol. 3.2.1/2. Berlin: Akademie Verlag, 1952.

Ernesti, J. C. G. *Lexicon Technologiae Graecorum Rhetoricae*. Leipzig: Fritsch, 1795.

Ettlinger, Gerard H., and Jacques Noret, eds. *Pseudo-Gregorii Agrigentini seu Pseudo-Gregorii Nysseni: Commentarius in Ecclesiasten*. CCSG 56. Brepols: Turnhout, 2007.

Fabricius, Johann Albert. *Bibliotheca Graeca*. Vol. 9. Rev. ed. Hamburg: Bohm, 1804.

Faesch, Remigius Sebastian. *Das Museum Faesch: Eine Basler Kunst- und Raritätensammlung aus dem 17. Jahrhundert*. Basel: Merian, 2005.

Fatouros, Georgios. "Zu den Briefen des Hl. Neilos von Ankyra." In *L'épistolographie et la poésie épigrammatique: projects actuels et questions de méthodologie*. Ed. Wolfram Hörandner and Michael Grünbart. Paris: Centre d'études byzantines, néo-helléniques et sud-est européennes, 2003, 21–30.

Feron, Ernest, and Fabiano Battaglini. *Codices Manuscripti Graeci Ottoboniani Bibliothecae Vaticanae*. Rome: Vatican, 1893.

Festugière, André-Jean. *Antioche païenne et chrétienne: Libanius, Chrysostome et les moines de Syrie*. Paris: Boccard, 1959.

Festugière, André-Jean. *La révélation d'Hermès Trismégiste*. Vol. 2, *Le Dieu cosmique*. Paris: Gabalda, 1949.

Formisano, Marco. *Tecnica e scrittura: Le letterature tecnico-scientifiche nello spazio letterario tardolatino*. Rome: Carocci, 2001.

Fowler, Robert L. *Early Greek Mythography*. Vol. 1, *Text and Introduction*. Oxford: Oxford University Press, 2001. Vol. 2, *Commentary*. Oxford: Oxford University Press, 2013.

Fuhrmann, Manfred. *Das Systematische Lehrbuch: Ein Beitrag zur Geschichte der Wissenschaften in der Antike*. Göttingen: Vandenhoeck & Ruprecht, 1960.

Fuhrmann, Manfred. *Die Antike Rhetorik: Eine Einführung*. Munich: Artemis, 1984.

Gambero, Luigi. *Mary and the Fathers of the Church: The Blessed Virgin Mary in Patristic Thought*. San Francisco: Ignatius Press, 1999.

Gamble, Harry Y. *Books and Readers in the Early Church: A History of Early Christian Texts*. New Haven: Yale University Press, 1995.

Gamillscheg, Ernst, Dieter Harlfinger, and Herbert Hunger, eds. *Repertorium der Griechischen Kopisten 800–1600*. Vienna: Verlag der Österreichischen Akademie der Wissenschaften, 1981–.

Giannelli, Cyrus. *Codices Vaticani Graeci*. Vol. 5, *Codices 1485–1683*. Vatican City: BAV, 1960.

Görgemanns, Herwig. "Isagoge." *DNP* 5 (1998): 1111–14.

Granatelli, Rossella. "Le definizioni di figura in Quintiliano *Inst.* IX 1.10–14 e il loro rapporto con la grammatica e le *controversiae figuratae*." *Rhetorica: A Journal of the History of Rhetoric* 12 (1994): 383–425.

Grant Robert M., and David Tracy. *A Short History of the Interpretation of the Bible.* Rev. ed. Philadelphia: Fortress Press, 1984.

Greer, Rowan. *Theodore of Mopsuestia: Exegete and Theologian.* London: Faith Press, 1961.

Gribomont, Jean. "La tradition manuscrite de saint Nil: I. La correspondence." *Studia Monastica* 11 (1969): 231–67.

Gröbli, Fredy. "Basler Büchersammler III: Remigius Faesch (1595–1667)." *Librarium* 20 (1977): 42–9.

Grube, G. M. A. *A Greek Critic: Demetrius on Style.* Toronto: University of Toronto Press, 1961.

Gudeman, A. "Λύσεις." *PW* 13.2 (1927): col. 2511–29.

Guinot, Jean-Noël. "Les sources de l'exégèse de Théodoret de Cyr." *StPatr* 25 (1993): 72–94.

Guinot, Jean-Noël. *L'Exégèse de Théodoret de Cyr.* Paris: Beauchesne, 1995.

Guinot, Jean-Noël. "L'*In Psalmos* de Théodoret: une relecture critique du commentaire de Diodore de Tarse." In *Le Psautier chez les Pères.* Strasbourg: Centre d'Analyes et de Documentation Patristiques, 1994, 97–134.

Hadot, Ilsetraut. "Les introductions aux commentaires exégétiques chez les auteurs Néoplatoniciens et les auteurs Chrétiens." In *Les règles de l'interprétation.* Ed. M. Tardieu. Paris: Cerf, 1987, 99–122.

Hägg, Tomas. *Photios als Vermittler antiker Literatur: Untersuchungen zur Technik des Referierens und Exzerpierens in der Bibliotheke.* Uppsala: Almquist och Wiksell, 1975.

Haidacher, Sebastian. "Chrysostomus-Fragmente in der Briefsammlung des hl. Nilus." In Χρυσοστομικά: *Studi e ricerche intorno a S. Giovanni Crisostomo.* Vol. 1. Rome: Pustet, 1908, 226–34.

Hajdú, Kerstin. "Johann Jakob Fugger und seine Bibliothek." In *Kulturkosmos der Renaissance: Die Gründung der Bayerischen Staatsbibliothek. Katalog zur Ausstellung zum 450-jährigen Jubiläum.* Wiesbaden: Harrassowitz, 2008, 125–7.

Hajdú, Kerstin. *Katalog der griechischen Handschriften der Bayerischen Staatsbibliothek München.* Band 10, 1, *Die Sammlung griechischer Handschriften in der Münchener Hofbibliothek bis zum Jahr 1803. Ein Bestandsgeschichte der Codices graeci Monacenses 1–323 mit Signaturenkonkordanzen und Beschreibung des Stephanus-Katalogs (Cbm Cat. 48).* Wiesbaden: Harrassowitz, 2002.

Hamman, Adalbert. "Les Principaux Collaborateurs des Deux Patrologies de Migne." In *Migne et le Renouveau des Études Patristiques: Acts du Colloque de Saint-Flour, 7–8 juillet 1975.* Ed. A. Mandouze and J. Fouilheron. Paris: Beauchesne, 1985, 179–91.

Hänel, Gustav Friedrich. *Catalogi Librorum Manuscriptorum, qui in Bibliothecis Galliae, Helvetiae, Belgii, Britanniae maioris, Hispaniae, Lusitaniae asservantur.* Leipzig: J. C. Hinrichs, 1830.

Hardt, Ignatio. *Catalogus codicum manuscriptorum Graecorum Bibliothecae Regiae Bavaricae.* Vol. 2, *Cod. graec. 106–233.* Munich: Seidel, 1806.

Hardt, Ignatio. *Catalogus codicum manuscriptorum Graecorum Bibliothecae Regiae Bavaricae.* Vol. 5, *Cod. graec. 473–574[–583].* Munich: Seidel, 1812.

Harl, Marguerite. *La Chaîne Palestinienne sur le Psaume 118.* Vol. 1. SC 189. Paris: Cerf, 1972.

Harl, Marguerite. "Origène et les interprétations patristiques grecques de 'l'obscurité' biblique." *VC* 36 (1982): 334–71.

Heath, Malcolm. "Codifications of Rhetoric." In *The Cambridge Companion to Ancient Rhetoric.* Ed. Erik Gunderson. Cambridge: Cambridge University Press, 2009, 59–73.

Heine, Ronald E. "The Introduction to Origen's *Commentary on John* Compared with the Introductions to the Ancient Philosophical Commentaries on Aristotle." In *Origeniana Sexta.* Ed. Gilles Dorival and Alain Le Boulluec. Leuven: Leuven University Press, 1995, 3–12.

Heussi, Karl. *Untersuchungen zu Nilus dem Asketen.* Leipzig: J. C. Hinrichs, 1917.

Hidal, Sten. "Exegesis of the Old Testament in the Antiochene School with Its Prevalent Literal and Historical Method." In *Hebrew Bible/Old Testament: The History of Its Interpretation.* Vol. 1, *From the Beginnings to the Middle Ages (Until 1300). Part 1: Antiquity.* Ed. M. Sæbø. Göttingen: Vandenhoeck & Ruprecht, 1996, 543–68.

Hill, Robert C. *Reading the Old Testament in Antioch.* Leiden: Brill, 2005.

Horváth, Eva. *Friedrich Lindenbruch, Späthumanist und Hanscriftensammler des 17. Jahrhunderts: Ein Beitrag zur Hamburger Bibliotheks- und Gelehrtergeschichte.* Diss. Dr. Phil. Hamburg, 1988.

Hunger, Herbert. *Die hochsprachliche profane Literatur der Byzantiner.* Vol. 1. Munich: Beck, 1978.

Jaeger, Werner. *Nemesios von Emesa: Quellenforschungen zum Neuplatonismus und seinen Anfängen bei Poseidonios.* Berlin: Weidmann, 1914.

Jannaris, Antonius N. *An historical Greek Grammar chiefly of the Attic dialect as written and spoken from classical antiquity down to the present time, founded upon the ancient texts, inscriptions, papyri and present popular Greek.* London: Macmillan, 1897.

Jeffreys, Elizabeth. "Rhetoric." In *The Oxford Handbook of Byzantine Studies.* Ed. Elizabeth Jeffreys with John Haldon and Robin Cormack. Oxford: Oxford University Press, 2008, 827–37.

Jellicoe, Sidney. *The Septuagint and Modern Study.* Oxford: Clarendon, 1968.

Johnson, Aaron P. "Eusebius the Educator: The Context of the *General Elementary Introduction.*" In *Reconsidering Eusebius: Collected Papers on Literary, Historical and Theological Issues.* Ed. Sabrina Inowlocki and Claudio Zamagni. Leiden: Brill, 2011, 99–118.

Kamesar, Adam. *Jerome, Greek Scholarship, and the Hebrew Bible: A Study of the Quaestiones Hebraicae in Genesim.* Oxford: Oxford University Press, 1993.

Kannengiesser, Charles. *Handbook of Patristic Exegesis: The Bible in Ancient Christianity.* Vol. 2. Leiden: Brill, 2004.

Karo, Georg, and Hans Lietzmann. "Catenarum graecarum catalogus." *Nachrichten von der Königl. Gesellschaft der Wissenschaften zu Göttingen,* Philologisch-historische Klasse (1902): 1–66, 299–350, 559–620.

Kaster, Robert A. *Guardians of Language: The Grammarian and Society in Late Antiquity.* Berkeley: University of California Press, 1988.

Kennedy, George A. *The Art of Persuasion in Greece*. Princeton: Princeton University Press, 1963.

Kennedy, George A. *The Art of Rhetoric in the Roman World, 300 BC–AD 300*. Princeton: Princeton University Press, 1972.

Kennedy, George A. *The Cambridge History of Literary Criticism*. Vol. 1, *Classical Criticism*. Cambridge: Cambridge University Press, 1989.

Kennedy, George A. *Greek Rhetoric under Christian Emperors*. Princeton: Princeton University Press, 1983.

Kennedy, George A. "Historical Survey of Rhetoric." In *Handbook of Classical Rhetoric in the Hellenistic Period 330 BC–AD 400*. Ed. Stanley E. Porter. Leiden: Brill, 1997, 3–41.

Kertsch, Manfred. "Gregor von Nazianz und Johannes Chrysostomus bei Nilus dem Asketen." *Gräzer Beiträge* 18 (1992): 149–53.

Kihn, H. *Theodor von Mopsuestia und Junilius Africanus*. Freiburg: Herder, 1880.

Kim, Lawrence. *Homer between History and Fiction in Imperial Greek Literature*. Cambridge: Cambridge University Press, 2010.

Kotter, Bonifatius. *Die Überlieferung der Pege Gnoseos des hl. Johannes von Damaskos*. Ettal: Buch-Kunstverlag, 1959.

Kustas, George L. *Studies in Byzantine Rhetoric*. Thessaloniki: Patriarchal Institute for Patristic Studies, 1973.

Laistner, M. L. W. "Antiochene Exegesis in Western Europe during the Middle Ages." *HTR* 40 (1947): 19–35.

Lamberton, Robert. *Homer the Theologian: Neoplatonist Allegorical Reading and the Growth of the Epic Tradition*. Berkeley: University of California Press, 1986.

Lambros, Spyridon P. *Catalogue of the Greek Manuscripts on Mount Athos*. Vol. 2. Cambridge: Cambridge University Press, 1900.

Lausberg, Heinrich. *Handbook of Literary Rhetoric: Foundation for Literary Study*. Ed. David E. Orton and R. Dean Anderson. Trans. Matthew T. Bliss, Annemiek Jansen, and David E. Orton. Leiden: Brill, 1998.

Leader, Anne. *The Badia of Florence: Art and Observance in a Renaissance Monastery*. Bloomington: Indiana University Press, 2012.

Leconte, René. "L'asceterium de Diodore." In *Melanges bibliques redigés en l'honneur de André Robert*. Ed. J. Trinquet. Paris: Bloud & Gay, 1957, 531–7.

Lehrs, Karl. *De Aristarchi studiis Homericis*. 3rd ed. Leipzig: Hirzelium, 1882.

Lenk, Leonard. "David Höschel." *Neue Deutsche Biographie*. Vol. 9, *Hess–Hüttig*. Berlin: Duncker & Humblot, 1972, 368–9.

Léonas, Alexis. "Patristic Evidence of Understanding the Difficulties in the LXX: Hadrian's Philological Remarks in Isagoge." In *Tenth Congress of the International Organization of Septuagint and Cognate Studies*. Ed. Bernard A. Taylor. Atlanta: Society of Biblical Literature, 2001, 393–414.

Léonas, Alexis. *Recherches sur la langage de la Septante*. Göttingen: Vandenhoeck & Ruprecht, 2005.

Lucà, Santo. "Rossano, il Patir e lo stile rossanese. Note per uno studio codicologico-paleografico e storico-culturale." *Rivista di Studi Bizantini e Neoellenici* 22–3 (1985–6): 93–170.

Lucà, Santo. "Scrittura e produzione libraria a Rossano tra la fine del sec. XI e l'inizio del sec. XII." In *Paleografia e Codicologia greca*. Ed. D. Harlfinger and G. Prato. Alessandria: Edizioni dell'Orso, 1991, 117–30.

Mansfeld, Jaap. *Prolegomena: Questions to be Settled before the Study of an Author or a Text*. Leiden: Brill, 1994.

Marcos, Natalio Fernández. *The Septuagint in Context: Introduction to the Greek Versions of the Bible*. Trans. Wilfred G. E. Watson. Leiden: Brill, 2000.

Marcos, Natalio Fernández. "Theodoret's Philological Remarks on the Language of the Septuagint." In *Jerusalem, Alexandria, Rome: Studies in Ancient Cultural Interaction in Honour of A. Hilhorst*. Ed. E. G. Martínez and G. P. Luttikheizen. Leiden: Brill, 2003, 107–18.

Mariès, Louis. *Études préliminaires a l'édition de Diodore de Tarse sur les Psaumes, la tradition manuscrite*. Paris: Belles Lettres, 1933.

Martens, Peter W. "Adrian's *Introduction to the Divine Scriptures* and Greco-Roman Rhetorical Theory on Style." *Journal of Religion* 93 (2013): 197–217.

Martin, Josef. *Antike Rhetorik: Technik und Methode*. Munich: Beck, 1974.

Martini, Emidio. *Catalogo di Manoscritti Greci Esistenti Nelle Biblioteche Italiane*. Vol. 2, *Catalogus Codicum Graecorum qui in Bibliotheca Vallicellana Romae Adservantur*. Milan: Ulrico Hoepli, 1902.

Maurice, Lisa. *The Teacher in Ancient Rome: The Magister and His World*. Lanham: Lexington Books, 2013.

McLeod, Frederic. *Theodore of Mopsuestia*. The Early Church Fathers. London: Routledge, 2009.

Meijering, Roos. *Literary and Rhetorical Theories in Greek Scholia*. Groningen: Forsten, 1987.

Mercati, Giovanni. *Alla ricerca dei nomi degli "altri" traduttori nelle Omilie sui Salmi di S. Giovanni Crisostomo e variazioni su alcune catene del Salterio*. ST 158. Vatican City: BAV, 1952.

Mercati, Giovanni. *Codici latini Pico Grimani Pio e di altra biblioteca ignota del secolo XVI, esistenti nell'Ottoboniana e I codici greci Pio di Modena*. ST 75. Vatican City: BAV, 1938.

Mercati, Giovanni. *Per la storia dei manoscritti greci di Genova, di varie badie Basiliane d'Italia e di Patmo*. ST 68. Vatican City: BAV, 1935.

Mercati, Giovanni. "Pro Adriano." *RB* 11 (1914): 246–55.

Mondrain, Brigitte. "Copistes et collectionneurs de manuscrits grecs au milieu du XVIe siècle: le cas de Johann Jakob Fugger d'Augsbourg." *Byzantinische Zeitschrift* 84/5 (1991–2): 354–90.

Moreschini, Claudio, and Enrico Norelli. *Early Christian Greek and Latin Literature: A Literary History*. Vol. 2. Trans. Matthew J. O'Connell. Peabody, Mass.: Hendrickson, 2005.

Morgan, Teresa. *Literate Education in the Hellenistic and Roman Worlds*. Cambridge: Cambridge University Press, 1998.

Moule, C. F. D. *An Idiom Book of New Testament Greek*. 2nd ed. Cambridge: Cambridge University Press, 1963.

Moulton, James H., and Wilbert F. Howard. "Appendix: Semitisms in the New Testament." In *A Grammar of New Testament Greek*. Vol. 2, *Accidence and Word-Formation*. Edinburgh: T. & T. Clark, 1963, 411–86.

Mühlenberg, Ekkehard. "Catena. II. Christianity." In *EBR*. Vol. 4. Berlin: Walter de Gruyter, 2009, 1061–4.

Neuschäfer, Bernhard. *Origenes als Philologe*. 2 vols. Basel: Friedrich Reinhardt, 1987.

Nünlist, René. *The Ancient Critic at Work: Terms and Concepts of Literary Criticism in Greek Scholia*. Cambridge: Cambridge University Press, 2009.

O'Donnell, James J. *Cassiodorus*. Berkeley: University of California Press, 1979.

Omont, Henri Auguste. *Catalogue des Manuscrits Grecs des Bibliothèques de Suisse*. Leipzig: Otto Harrassowitz, 1886.

Opitz, Hans-Georg. *Untersuchungen zur Überlieferung der Schriften des Athanasius*. Berlin: Walter de Gruyter, 1935.

Palau, Annaclara Cataldi. "Il copista Ioannes Mauromates." In *I manoscritti greci tra riflessione e dibattito. Atti del V colloquio Internazionale di Paleografia Greca (Cremona 4–10 ott. 1998)*. Vol. 1. Ed. Giancarlo Prato. Florence: Gonnelli, 2000, 335–99.

Papadoyannakis, Yannis. "Instruction by Question and Answer: The Case of Late Antique and Byzantine *Erotapokriseis*." In *Greek Literature in Late Antiquity: Dynamism, Didacticism, Classicism*. Ed. Scott Fitzgerald Johnson. Aldershot: Ashgate, 2006, 91–105.

Patillon, Michel, ed. *Pseudo-Aelius Aristide: Arts Rhétoriques*. Vol. 1, *Le Discours Politique*. Vol. 2, *Le Discourse Simple*. Paris: Les Belles Lettres, 2002.

Pellegrin, Elisabeth, et al. *Les manuscrits classiques latins de la Bibliothèque Vaticane*. Vol. 1, *Fonds Archivio San Pietra à Ottoboni*. Paris: Éditions du Centre national de la recherche scientifique, 1975.

Pernot, Laurent. *Rhetoric in Antiquity*. Trans. W. E. Higgins. Washington, D.C.: Catholic University of America Press, 2005.

Perrone, Lorenzo. "Perspectives sur Origène et la littérature patristique des *Quaestiones et Responsiones*." In *Origeniana Sexta: Origène et la Bible: Actes du Colloquium Origenianum Sextum, Chantilly, 30 Aug.–3. Sept. 1993*. Ed. Gilles Dorival and Alain le Boulluec. Leuven: Leuven University Press, 1995, 151–64.

Perrone, Lorenzo. "Sulla preistoria delle *quaestiones* nella letteratura patristica: Presupposti e sviluppi del genere letterario fino al IV sec." *AnnSE* 8 (1991): 485–505.

Pfeiffer, Rudolf. *History of Classical Scholarship from the Beginnings to the End of the Hellenistic Age*. Oxford: Clarendon, 1968.

Pitra, Jean-Baptiste-François, ed. *Analecta Sacra: Spicilegio Solesmensi*. Vol. 2, *Patres Antenicaeni*. Tusculanis, 1884, 130–6.

Pohlenz, Max. "Τὸ πρέπον. Ein Beitrag zur Geschichte des griechischen Geistes." In *Kleine Schriften*. Vol. 1. Ed. Heinrich Dörrie. Hildesheim: Olms, 1965, 100–39.

Pradel, Marina Molin. *Katalog der griechischen Handschriften der Bayerischen Staatsbibliothek München*. Vol. 2, *Codices graeci Monacenses 56–109*. Wiesbaden: Harrassowitz, 2013.

Pradel, Marina Molin. *Katalog der griechischen Handschriften der Staats- und Universitätsbibliothek Hamburg*. Wiesbaden: Ludwig Reichert, 2002.

Pradel, Marina Molin. "Note su alcuni manoscritti greci della Staats- und Universitätsbibliothek di Amburgo." *Codices manuscripti* 34/35 (2001): 15–27.

Philomen Probert. *A New Short Guide to the Accentuation of Ancient Greek*. Bristol: Bristol Classical Press, 2003.

Rahlfs, Alfred. *Verzeichnis der griechischen Handschriften des Alten Testaments*. Berlin: Weidmann, 1914.

Reinsch, Diether Roderich, ed. *Michaelis Pselli Chronographia*. Vol. 2, *Textkritischer Kommentar und Indices*. Berlin: Walter de Gruyter, 2014.

Richard, Marcel. "Floriléges Grecs." *Dictionnaire de Spiritualité*. Vol. 5. Paris: Beauchesne, 1962, col. 475–512.

Richard, Marcel. "Quelques Manuscrits peu connus des chaines exégétiques et des Commentaires Grecs sur le Psautier." *Opera Minora*. Vol. 3. Turnhout: Brepols, 1977.

Roberts, Michael. *Biblical Epic and Rhetorical Paraphrase in Late Antiquity*. Liverpool: Francis Cairns, 1985.

Rollo, Antonio. "Sulle trace di Antonio Cobinelli." *Studi medievali e umanistici* 2 (2004): 25–95.

Rondeau, Marie-Josèphe. *Les commentaires patristiques du Psautier (IIIe–Ve siècles)*. Vol. 1, *Les travaux des Pères grecs et latins sur le Psautier: Recherches et Bilan*. Vol. 2, *Exégèse prosopologique et théologie*. Rome: Pont. Institutum Studiorum Orientalium, 1982, 1985.

Rossum-Steenbeeck, Monique van. *Greek Readers' Digests? Studies on a Selection of Subliterary Papyri*. Leiden: Brill, 1998.

Rostagno, Enrico, and Nicolas Festa. "Indice dei Codici Greci Laurenziani non compresi Nel Catalogo del Bandini," Vol. 1, "Conventi soppressi." *Studi italiani di filologia classica* 1 (1893): 131–96. Published as supplement in Angelo Maria Bandini, *Catalogus Codicum Manuscriptorum Bibliothecae Mediceae Laurentianae*, Vol. 3. Reprint: Leipzig: Zentral-Antiquariat der DDR, 1961.

Rowe, Galen O. "Style." In *Handbook of Classical Rhetoric in the Hellenistic Period, 330 B.C.–A.D. 400*. Ed. Stanley E. Porter. Leiden: Brill, 1997, 121–57.

Russell, Donald A. *Criticism in Antiquity*. 2nd ed. London: Bristol Classical Press, 1995.

Russell, Donald A. "Greek Criticism of the Empire." In *Cambridge History of Literary Criticism*. Vol. 1, *Classical Criticism*. Ed. George A. Kennedy. Cambridge: Cambridge University Press, 1989, 297–329.

Russell, Donald A. *"Longinus" on the Sublime*. Oxford: Clarendon, 1964.

Russell, Donald A., and David Konstan. *Heraclitus: Homeric Problems*. WGRW 14. Atlanta: Society of Biblical Literature, 2005.

Russo, Francesco. "La Biblioteca del Card. Sirleto." In *Il Card. Guglielmo Sirleto (1514–1585): Atti del Convegno di Studio nel IV Centenario della morte*. Ed. Leonardo Calabretta and Gregorio Sinatora. Cantanzaro-Squillace: Istituto di Scienze Religiose, 1989, 219–99.

Rutherford, William G. *A Chapter in the History of Annotation being Scholia Aristophanica, III*. London: Macmillan, 1905.

Schäfer, K. "Eisagoge." *RAC* 4 (1959): 862–904.

Schamp, Jacques. *Photios, historien des letters: La Bibliothèque et ses notices biographiques*. Paris: Les Belles Lettres, 1987.

Schäublin, Christoph. "Die Antiochenische Exegese des Alten Testaments." In *L'Ancien Testament dans L'Église*. Chambésy: Éditions du Centre Orhtodoxe du Patriarcat Oecuménique, 1988, 115–28.

Schäublin, Christoph. *Untersuchungen zur Methode und Herkunft der Antiochenischen Exegese*. Cologne: Peter Hanstein, 1974.

Schäublin, Christoph. "Zur paganen Prägung der christlichen Exegese." In *Christliche Exegese zwischen Nicaea und Chalcedon*. Ed. J. van Oort and Ulrich Wickert. Kampen: Kok Pharos, 1992, 148–73.

Schlüren, Karl Friedrich. "Zu Adrianos." *Jahrbücher für Protestantische Theologie* 13 (1887): 136–59.

Snyder, Gregory H. *Teachers and Texts in the Ancient World: Philosophers, Jews, and Christians*. London: Routledge, 2000.

Souter, Alexander. "Cassiodorus's Copy of Eucherius's *Instructiones*." *JTS* 14 (1912): 69–72.

Stevenson, Henry Sr., ed. *Codices Manuscripti Graeci Reginae Svecorum et Pii PP. II Bibliothecae Vaticanae*. Rome: BAV, 1888.

Swete, H. B., and Henry St. John Thackeray. *An Introduction to the Old Testament in Greek: With an Appendix Containing the Letter of Aristeas*. Cambridge: Cambridge University Press, 1902.

Ter Haar Romeny, R. B. *A Syrian in Greek Dress: The Use of Greek, Hebrew, and Syriac Biblical Texts in Eusebius of Emesa's Commentary on Genesis*. Leuven: Peeters, 1997.

Thackery, Henry St. John. "The Semitic Element in LXX Greek." In *A Grammar of the Old Testament in Greek, according to the Septuagint*. Vol. 1, *Introduction, Orthography and Accidence*. Cambridge: Cambridge University Press, 1909, 25–54.

Tiftixoglu, Victor, with Kerstin Hajdú and Gerhard Duursma. *Katalog der griechischen Handschriften der Bayerischen Staatsbibliothek München*. Vol. 1, *Codices graeci Monacenses 1–55*. Wiesbaden: Harrassowitz, 2014.

Treadgold, Warren T. *The Nature of the Bibliotheca of Photius*. Washington, D.C.: Dumbarton Oaks, 1980.

Usener, Hermann. "Ein altes Lehrgebäude der Philologie." *SBAW* 4 (1892): 582–648.

Uthemann, Karl-Heinz. *Anastasii Sinaitae: Viae Dux*. CCSG 8. Turnhout: Brepols, 1981.

Vailhé, Siméon. "10. Adrien," *DHGE*. Vol. 1. Paris: Letouzey et Ané, 1912.

Viciano, A. "Das formale Verfahren der antiochenischen Schriftauslegung: Ein Forschungsüberblick." In *Stimuli: Exegese und ihre Hermeneutik in Antike und Christentum: Festschrift für Ernst Dassmann*. *Jahrbuch für Antike und Christentum* 28 (1996): 370–405.

Viciano, A. "Ὁ σκοπός τῆς ἀληθείας. Théodoret de Cyr et ses principes herméneutiques dans le prologue du Commentaire de Cantique des Cantiques." In *Letture cristianae dei Libri Sapienziali. XX incontro di studiosi dell'antichità cristiana*. Rome: Institutum Patristicum "Augustinianum," 1992, 419–35.

Vitelli, Girolamo, and Cesare Paoli. *Collezione Fiorentina di Facsimili Paleografici Greci e Latini*. Vol. 1. Florence: Successori le Monnier, 1884.

Vladimir, Archimandrite. *Description Systématique des Manuscrits de la Bibliothèque Synodale Patriarchale de Moscou*. Vol. 1, *Grec 1 à Grec 105*. Trans. Xenia Grichine, rev. M. José Johannet. Paris: n.p., 1995.

Voelz, James W. "The Language of the New Testament." *ANRW* 2.25.2: 893–977.

Vogel, Marie, and Viktor Gardthausen. *Die Griechischen Schreiber des Mittelalters und der Renaissance*. Leipzig: O. Harrassowitz, 1909.

Volgers, Annelie, and Claudio Zamagni, eds. *Erotapokriseis: Early Christian Question-and-Answer Literature in Context*. Leuven: Peeters, 2004.

Volkmann, Richard. *Die Rhetorik der Griechen und Römer in systematischer Übersicht dargestellt*. 2nd ed. Leipzig: Teubner, 1885.

Vosté, J.-M. "La chronologie de l'activité littéraire de Théodore." *RB* 34 (1925): 70–2.

Wallace, Daniel B. *Greek Grammar Beyond Basics: An Exegetical Syntax of the New Testament with Scripture, Subject, and Greek Word Indexes*. Grand Rapids: Zondervan, 1996.

Wallace-Hadrill, D. S. *Christian Antioch: A Study of Early Christian Thought*. Cambridge: Cambridge University Press, 1982.

Walters, Peter. *The Text of the Septuagint: Its Corruptions and their Emendation*. Cambridge: Cambridge University Press, 1973.

Weber, Dorothea. "Locutiones." In *Augustinus-Lexikon*. Ed. Cornelius Mayer et al. Vol. 3.7/8. Basel: Schwabe, 2010, 1048–54.

West, Martin L. *Textual Criticism and Editorial Technique Applicable to Greek and Latin Texts*. Stuttgart: Teubner, 1973.

Wilson, Nigel G., and Leighton D. Reynolds. *Scribes and Scholars: A Guide to the Transmission of Greek and Latin Literature*. 3rd ed. Oxford: Clarendon, 1991.

Wolf, Peter. *Vom Schulwesen der Spätantike: Studien zu Libanius*. Baden-Baden: Kunst und Wissenschaft, 1952.

Wooten, Cecil W. "Appendix I: Hermogenes and Ancient Critical Theories on Oratory." In *Hermogenes' On Types of Style*. Trans. Cecil W. Wooten. Chapel Hill: University of North Carolina Press, 1987, 131–7.

Young, Frances M. *Biblical Exegesis and the Formation of Christian Culture*. Cambridge: Cambridge University Press, 1997.

Young, Frances M. "The Fourth-Century Reaction against Allegory." *StPatr* 30 (1997): 120–5.

Young, Frances M. "Interpretation of Scripture." In *Oxford Handbook of Early Christian Studies*. Ed. Susan Ashbrook Harvey and David G. Hunter. Oxford: Oxford University Press, 2010.

Young, Frances M. "The Rhetorical Schools and Their Influence on Patristic Exegesis." In *The Making of Orthodoxy: Essays in Honour of Henry Chadwick*. Ed. Rowan Williams. Cambridge: Cambridge University Press, 1989, 182–99.

Ziegenaus, A. "Jungfräulichkeit, II.1.b: Die Jungfräulichkeit in und nach der Geburt." In *Marienlexikon*. Vol. 3. Ed. Remigius Bäumber and Leo Scheffczyk. Erzabtei St. Ottilien: EOS Verlag, 1991, 465–81.

Zobel, Hans-Jürgen, and Werner Georg Kümmel. "Einleitungswissenschaft." *TRE* 9 (1982): 460–82.

Index of Scripture

Scripture	R1	R2	Catenae
	Old Testament		
Gen			
1–2	74.1	74.1	
1:3–25	12		
1:27	51	51	
2:1–3		50	37
2:4–5		73.9	
2:4	73.9		
2:7, 21–2	12		
2:7	2.10		
3:8	2.4, 4.9		
3:9	2.5		
4:15			37
6:3	57.2		
6:6	2.5		
8:21	2.2		
11:7	39		
15:9	74.3.3	74.3.3	
15:13–16		74.3.3	
15:13	46		34
15:18		73.21	
16:6	46		34
18:21	7		
19:24	51		
22:1	2.5, 7		
22:2	74.3.3	74.3.3	
22:12	2.5, 7		
22:16	44		
22:17	70		
27:36	39		
29:15	71.4		33
49:6	43	43	
49:9	38	38	
49:17	38		
Ex			
4:22	2.8		
9:16	42		
14:4, 5, 17	55		
15:1–19	79		
15:10	59.6		
15:15	61.2		
15:16	63		
21:6	62.1		

Scripture	R1	R2	Catenae
Num			
14:24	59.1		
21:33–5		42	
Deut			
3:1–7		42	
32:1–43	79		
32:11	73.1		
32:40	2.14		
Judg			
9:8	73.11		
1 Kgdms			
2:5			37
15:35	60		
24:15	73.17	73.17	7
2 Kgdms			
5:1–2	57.4		36
6:20	73.7	73.7	41
19:12–13, 14			36
19:13	57.4		
19:14	57.4		
3 Kgdms			
20:10	73.7	73.7	41
4 Kgdms			
2:9	59.2		
5:1–27	74.2	74.2	
19:35			6
Ps			
1:1	43		
1:3	73.13		
1:4	66		
2:2	66.4		
3:5	2.2		
3:6	67		
4:4	2.2		
4:7	4.6		
4:9	31, 65		
5:2–3	67		

Scripture	R1	R2	Catenae	Scripture	R1	R2	Catenae
6:2	2.3			29:10	66.1		
6:7	61.1, 73.14.1			29:13	62.1		
7:7	2.4			30:20	30		13
7:13	73.19	73.19		30:20–1			13
8:5	58			30:21	30	30	
9:5	2.9, 11		1	30:23	2.13		
9:8	62.3		1	31:3	69		14
9:22	2.11, 13			31:4	38, 69		14, 15
9:23, 24	69			31:8	66.3		
9:35	68		2	32:5	26		
10:4	2.1			32:6	59.5		
10:5	71.3			32:13	2.2		
10:6	47			33:16	2.1, 4.1		
10:7	26	26		33:17	2.1, 4.6		
13:1	45			33:19	13		
15:9	17, 73.4			34:13	32	32	
15:11	19.3			34:21	73.15	73.15	
16:1	25		3	35:7	51	51	
16:8	73.1, 73.10	73.1, 73.10		35:13	24		
				36:28	26		
16:14	30	30		36:34	41		
17:10	2.11, 4.9			38:7	71.2		
17:10, 14, 15	4.10			38:8	41		
17:11	2.2			39:2	70	41	
17:29	53.1	53		39:3	38		
18:2	73.11		4	39:12	34		
18:4			4	40:5	17		
20:5	62.1			41:8			16
20:13	68		2, 5	43:6	73.10		
20:14			6	43:19	55	55	
21:7	73.17	73.17	7	43:24	2.6, 8		17
22:1	73.1			43:25	7		
22:1, 2		73.1		43:27	6		
22:3	73.4	73.4		44:4	2.12		
22:5	73.6	73.6		44:6	49, 51, 69		
23:7	73.11	73.11		44:7	11, 62.3		
23:8		73.11		44:10	73.12	73.12	
24:5	20		8	45:3	65		
25:1	65			45:6	52	52	
25:4	43			46:6	65		
25:6	35	36		46:9	11		
26:5	30			47:8	59.6		
26:6	66.2			48:3	67		
26:9	2.13, 55			48:6	39		
26:14	41			48:10	62.1		
27:1	36			48:20	62.2		
28:3	73.13	73.13	9, 10	49:1	67		
28:4	65			49:4	73.6	73.6	
28:10	73.1, 73.13	73.13	11	49:5	73.16	73.16	18
29:7	45		12	49:13	2.2		
29:8	2.13			49:23	24		19

Scripture	R1	R2	Catenae	Scripture	R1	R2	Catenae
50:6	42		20	77:49	46	46	34
50:7	67			77:65	2.6		
50:8	26, 71.1		21	77:66	62.2		35
50:10	19.1		22	77:67–8		73.8	
50:12	59.1			77:71	73.1	73.1	
50:13	2.13			78:2	57.1		36
50:14	59.2		23	78:6	5		
50:16			24	78:12	32, 50		37, 38
52:2	45			79:2	2.9, 11		
54:6	53.2			80:6	39		
54:17	61.2			82:5	45		
55:3–4	27	27		82:13	45		
55:7	29, 39, 61.3	29		82:14	28	28	
56:2	60			82:19	48	48	
56:5	4.10			83:10	73.1	73.1	
56:12	2.11			84:11	34, 73.11	34, 73.11	
57:4	73.14.2			86:2	2.7		
57:9		54.1		86:4	73.8	73.8	
57:11	35	35		87:7	53.2		
57:12			25	87:15	2.13, 15		
59:8	21			88:3	64.1		
60:8	34			88:4	44	44	
61:12	22		26	88:9, 15	34		
63:6	45	45		88:14	68		
64:7	2.12			88:27, 28	2.8		
65:6	61.1			88:36	22		26
65:7	4.1			88:51	32		
65:12	38			90:4			39
65:13	65			92:1	2.12, 14		
67:2	2.4			92:2	64.1		
67:14	31	31		93:4	61.3, 67		
67:19	2.11, 71.4		33	93:5	46		
67:22	73.14.1			93:22	67		
67:23			27	96:1	2.9, 64.2, 73.6		
67:23–4		42	27	96:2	64.1		
67:24	39, 42	39		96:11	53.1		
67:31	27		28, 29	97:8	73.12	73.12	
67:34	27			98:1	64.2		
68:21	41			101:7			40
68:29	63			101:7–8		73.2	40
72:1	28	28		101:8	73.2		40
73:3	2.1, 4.7			103:2	2.12, 14		
73:8	45			103:3	2.10, 73.10		
73:11	2.14, 16, 32		30, 31	103:4	38, 67		
74:3	66.3			103:8	38		
74:6	66.5			103:32	2.2, 56		
74:7	66.5			105:5	19.2		
75:8	5		32	106:26	73.14.1	73.14.1	
76:18	71.4		33	109:1	60		
77:8	59.1			109:3	73.4	73.4	
77:39	57.3		36	111:6	62.2		

Scripture	R1	R2	Catenae	Scripture	R1	R2	Catenae
113:4	73.14.1			2:21	2.8, 10		
115:2	33	33		4:6	2.5		
117:16	2.1			4:12	59.1		
117:18	70			6:3	52	52	
117:25–6	23			6:9	40		
117:26	23			9:12	2.15, 17, 57.4		36
118:1	40	40		10:1	73.16		
118:11	30	30		10:12	60		
118:72	2.1			12:2	59.1		
118:89	62.3						
118:164	50	50	37	**Amos**			
119:1, 2	66.1			3:6	46		34
120:4	2.6, 8			4:11		51	
124:1	62.1			7:4	73.11		16
125:1	28			8:7	44		
129:1	66.1			9:6	2.10, 73.1		
131:7	2.1						
131:11	44			**Mic**			
138:11	53.2			1:3	2.11		
140:4	55	55		1:12	46		34
140:10	2.10, 12	73.1		4:2–3		73.13	
142:10			8	4:7	62.2		
143:4		36		5:5			37
143:7	4.7			6:5	42		
144:18	2.11			7:8	53.1		
145:4	59.4						
148:1	37	37		**Joel**			
				1:6	73.14.2	73.14.2	
Prov				1:19	38		
3:18	38			2:1–2		54.2	
8:22	73.11			2:2	73.10	73.10	
8:30	73.11			2:10–11	54	54.2	
9:1	50, 73.11		37	2:13	46		
26:9	38			2:18	9		
				3:13	73.18		
Eccl				3:14, 15–16		54.1	
3:17	71.3			3:17	73.21		
11:2			37	3:20	62.2		
Job				**Jonah**			
1:6–11	73.12	73.12		2:7	63		
1:11			41				
2:5	2.2, 73.7	73.7		**Nah**			
19:21	2.2			1:4	56		
40:25–41:26		73.14.2		2:2	2.10		
				2:12	58, 73.16		
Hos				3:4	73.15		
2:4	2.8						
2:8	2.10, 12			**Hab**			
2:14		55		1:11	59.1		
2:16	55			3:6	56		

Scripture	R1	R2	Catenae	Scripture	R1	R2	Catenae
3:10			16	49:16	2.10, 12		
3:11		49		50:4	39	39	
				51:22	47		
Zeph				53:7	58, 73.2		40
1:12	2.5, 7			54:11	38		
3:1, 2	73.15			55:12	73.14.1		
3:5	52			59:9	41		
3:8	2.4, 41			60:1	53.1		
				63:1	2.12		
Hag				63:3	2.3		
1:5	40			63:17	40, 55		
Zech				**Jer**			
3:9	2.2			3:8	2.8, 10		
5:8	73.11			4:18	40		
8:2	2.7			5:8	38		
14:8–9		73.13		8:7	73.5		
				14:8	41	41	
Mal				15:16–17		43	
1:2–3	2.7			15:17	43		
1:6	45			20:15–16	73.7		41
				38:9	2.8		
Isa				38:31	74.3.1	74.3.1	
1:3	73.5	73.5					
1:14	2.15, 17			**Ezek**			
1:20	2.1			2:1	58		
1:22	73.18			2:2	59.3		
5:2	2.10			12:13	2.10, 12, 73.1		
7:14	71.1	74.3.1		16:7	73.12	73.12	
11:1	38			23:32	47, 73.6	47	
11:2–3	59.2			34:2	73.1	73.1	
11:6	38			34:5	73.1		
14:9, 10, 11	73.16			37:1	74.3.2	74.3.2	
14:13	45			37:9	59.6		
19:1	2.11			37:12		74.3.2	
23:1	73.6			39:17	73.18		
23:10	73.15						
23:16	73.15			**Dan**			
26:15	46		34	3:100	62.3		
30:1	59.1			7:9	74.3.2	74.3.2	
30:6	73.16			7:13	74.3.2		
30:26	53.1			8:17	58		
30:27	48	48					
38:14	61.1				New Testament		
40:6	57.3		36	**Matt**			
45:6, 7			34	1:25	60		
45:7	46			3:8	73.19		
45:17	62.2			3:10	73.18	73.18	
45:23	2.1			3:11–12		73.18	
46:4	60			4:19	73.1	73.1	
47:10	45	45		5:3	59.1		

Scripture	R1	R2	Catenae	Scripture	R1	R2	Catenae
5:18	73.14.3			22:4	40		
5:22	45	45		24:14	40		
5:29	73.14.3						
6:3	73.14.3	73.14.3		**Rom**			
6:34	46	46	34	1:4	51		
8:12	73.19			1:24		55	
12:44–5			37	1:26		55	
18:21–2			37	1:28	55	55	
19:24	73.14.1	73.14.1		3:19	42		
19:29	62.3			5:20	42		
20:22	47	47		9:17	42		
21:33	73.5			11:14	57.4		36
23:37	73.6						
24:34–5	73.14.3			**1 Cor**			
26:68	73.15	73.15		8:13	62.1		
27:24	35	35		10:1–4	73.3	73.3	
28:20	60			10:4	38	38	15
				14:15	59.5		
Mark				15:50	57.3		36
10:25	73.14.1	73.14.1					
13:30–1	73.14.3			**2 Cor**			
				5:16	57.3		36
Luke				11:6		73.13	
3:8	73.19						
3:9	73.18	73.18		**Gal**			
3:16–17		73.18		2:20	57.3		36
11:25–6			37	4:21–5		73.3,	
12:16	73.5					73.13	
13:34	73.6			4:24	73.13		
18:25	73.14.1	73.14.1		5:17	42		
19:40	73.14.3						
21:32–3	73.14.3			**Eph**			
				4:30	2.5		
John				5:31–2		73.3	
1:14	28	28					
1:18	32	32		**Phil**			
3:5	73.21	73.21		3:20		37	
4:14	62.1	38					
4:32	2.2			**1 Thess**			
4:34	2.2			4:16	74.3.2		
7:38	38	38	15	5:19	59.2		
9:39	42	42					
10:28	62.3			**2 Tim**			
13:8	62.1			1:18	51	51	
17:3	62.3						
				Heb			
Acts				5:7	57.3		
5:1–11		74.2					
9:2	40			**1 John**			
19:23		40		5:6–8	73.21	73.21	
20:22	59.1						